# THE COMPLETE WISE HOME HANDYMAN'S GUIDE

# THE COMPLETE WISE HOME HANDYMAN'S GUIDE

EDITED BY

## HUBBARD COBB

THOMAS Y. CROWELL COMPANY
New York / Established 1834

Also published under the title
*The Complete Home Handyman's Guide*

Copyright © 1973 by William H. Wise & Company, Inc.
Previous editions copyright © 1948, 1949, 1962 by William
H. Wise & Company, Inc.

DESIGNED BY ABIGAIL MOSELEY

Manufactured in the United States of America

ISBN 0-690-20726-3

1  2  3  4  5  6  7  8  9  10


*Library of Congress Cataloging in Publication Data*

Cobb, Hubbard H, date, ed.

The complete Wise home handyman's guide.
1. Dwellings—Maintenance and repair. 2. Dwellings—Remodeling. I. Title.
TH4816.C59   1973
         643'.7        72-7566
ISBN 0-690-20726-3

# CONTENTS

# 1

# BASIC TOOLS

This chapter contains advice on the selection of a useful tool kit because tools —the right kind of tools—are essential for making most home repairs. You will also find that hand tools rather than the more glamorous power tools are what you'll need for most repair jobs about the house.

A word of caution when buying tools: buy only top-quality, name-brand tools. Do not purchase so-called bargains. The difference in price between top quality and poor quality is slight, and a good tool will repay you many times over for its slightly higher cost. Not even an expert can do good work with poor-quality tools. We have a theory that one of the reasons why many women have so much trouble doing simple repair jobs about the house is that, because of their sex, they are sold "five and dime" tools that are little better than toys. Most tools, such as hammers, saws, and planes, come in a variety of sizes, and women should select the same quality but a somewhat smaller size than would be suitable for a man.

No two people can agree on what makes a good basic tool kit. Some tool manufacturers do sell a packaged "home repair tool kit," and some of these are excellent. Here are the tools that we have found to be most useful in making repairs and improvements around the house:

Claw hammer

Crosscut saw

Block plane

Nail set

Putty knife

8″ adjustable wrench

½″ wood chisel

Hand drill, push-pull drill, or portable electric drill

Assorted screwdrivers

Slip joint pliers

Combination square

With this basic tool kit, along with some of the obvious materials such as nails, screws, sandpaper, and adhesives, you can probably do about 90% of the repair jobs about the house. In any event, start out with this basic kit and add to it as more specialized tools are required.

While hand tools appear simple, there is quite a bit to know in their selection and their proper use.

## Hammer

The claw hammer is the backbone of any tool kit. There are two basic types, the curved claw hammer and the straight

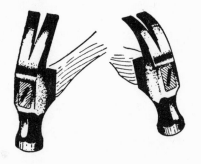

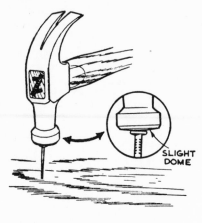

SLIGHT
DOME

claw hammer. Select the curved claw hammer because this has a better balance, and get one with a face slightly domed rather than flat. The domed face is less likely to bend the nail if not struck squarely, and it also allows a nail to be driven flush without marring the surface.

Hammers are sold in many weights, from 5 to 20 ounces. Choose the weight that feels most comfortable as you heft, that is, test the weight, and try a few swings with it. Keep in mind that a hammer that is too light requires too much muscular effort, while one too heavy will tire you unnecessarily.

The knack of driving a nail straight is to have the face of the hammer head at the same angle as the head of the nail. By doing this you will avoid the natural tendency to strike the nail head unevenly. Use sharp taps rather than heavy blows. This will give you more control over the hammer, and you will hit the nail squarely. Also, a nail driven hard breaks the fibers of the wood and loses some of its holding power. Lighter blows tend to bend the fibers aside and downward, so that when pulling strain on the nail occurs these fibers are pulled upward also, exerting considerable grip on the nail.

If the nail bends, or you wish to remove a nail, pull it out by putting a piece of scrap wood under the claw of the hammer to prevent marring the surface and exerting undue strain on the neck of the handle. The nail pulls easier, too.

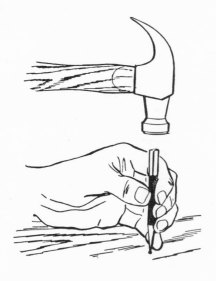

with metal or any other material that may dull them. When they do become dull, have the saw sharpened. Your local hardware store or lumber yard can do this for you or tell you where you can have it done.

When sawing wood that is green and contains a lot of sap or resin, wipe the blade off occasionally with turpentine or mineral spirits. This will make it cut easier. When sawing asbestos board, wet the blade with water but wipe dry when you have finished.

Sawing a straight line can be accomplished by observing a few simple rules. First, the line to be cut should be marked, using a square or rule, so that it will be straight. Do not trust your eye alone as a

**Nail Set.** This is a hardened-steel tool that is used to drive the heads of nails below the wood surface without marring the surface with the head of the hammer.

## Saws

**Handsaws.** There are two kinds of handsaws: the crosscut, used for cutting across the grain of the wood, and the ripsaw, for cutting with the grain. You'll have more use for the crosscut saw, which is suitable for plywood, hardboard, particleboard, and so forth, than you will for the ripsaw unless you plan to do a lot of carpentry.

The size of a saw is determined by the length of the blade; the most popular sizes are 24″ and 26″. The coarseness or fineness of the cut is determined by the number of teeth, or points, per inch. A coarse saw is good for rough wood and for green wood, but you'll get a much more accurate and smooth cut using a fine saw. A 7- or 8-point tool is good for crosscutting; 5½ or 6 points for a ripsaw.

A saw is a cutting tool, and if the teeth become dull it won't function properly. Protect the sharpness of the teeth by not allowing them to come into contact

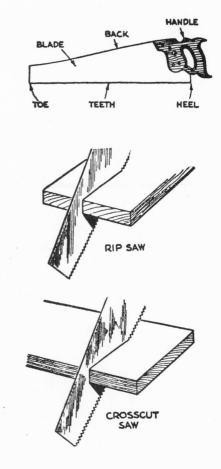

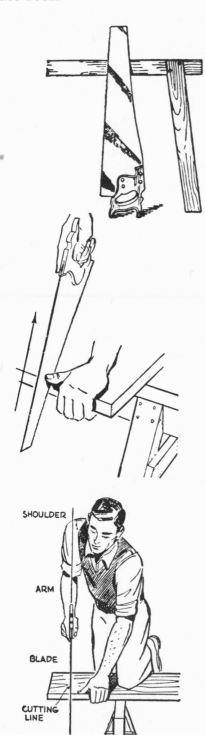

guide when sawing. By marking two or more sides of the wood before starting, you provide additional assurance that the cut will be right.

Grip the handle of the saw with thumb overlapping the middle finger, the forefinger extended along the side of the handle. Do not squeeze too hard. All you want to do is hold and guide the saw, not force it—let the saw do the work. Start with an upward cut, and use the thumb of your free hand along the side of the blade as a guide.

When ripping along a scribed line, cut on the waste side of the line; do not try to cut through the middle of it. Having started the cut, use long, easy strokes the length of the blade.

When using a crosscut saw, have the blade at about a 45-degree angle to the work and keep shoulder, arm, and hand roughly in line with the blade and cutting line. On nearing the end of a cut, always

SHOULDER

ARM

BLADE

CUTTING
LINE

support the waste piece by reaching over the saw blade with your free hand and holding the piece, to prevent it from splintering the underside of the cut. If it's a long waste piece, support it adequately with a sawhorse. Never twist off waste with the saw blade.

In ripping, the saw should be held at a 60-degree angle to the work. As you rip, the board will have a tendency to close the kerf, or slit, at the starting point, so insert a narrow wedge of wood or anything that will keep the kerf open. If you should happen to wander from the straight line, a twist of the blade will get you back on; if you are not sawing squarely, bend the blade sidewise to get square again.

**Compass Saws.** This tool is designed for cutting curved shapes, circular openings, and disks, and for starting a saw cut from a hole bored in the wood or wherever else the handsaw cannot start a cut.

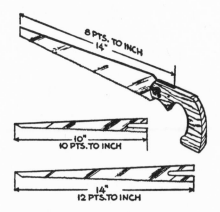

Compass saws are available with an assortment of blades, which makes them a handy tool for a lot of small sawing jobs. By inserting the correct blade they can be used for crosscutting, ripping, or circular work. They are, however, suitable only for small jobs and are not really a substitute for a good handsaw

**Back Saw.** This saw is designed for fine joinery and cabinet work. It has a heavy, reinforced back that stiffens the blade, which is of a heavier gauge and with finer

teeth than found in a handsaw. Back saws are good to use if you have a lot of fine work to do, such as making picture frames, building cabinets, or cutting interior molding.

When using a back saw, start the cut with a short *backward* stroke, elevating the handle a trifle; then, as you saw, gradually lower the handle so that the blade is

parallel to the surface. Saw with light, level strokes, using the same grip as for the handsaw. Long grooves, dadoes, and rabbets can easily be cut by clamping a wooden straightedge to the surface as a guide for the saw, with another strip clamped to the saw blade for a depth gauge. Without a gauge, watch the depth at both ends of the cut, the natural tendency being to cut deeper with the butt end of the saw.

The miter box is the companion to the back saw. This device is used to crosscut narrow lumber and molding squarely, or diagonally at a 45-degree angle. You can buy a wooden or metal miter box or make one yourself easily from 3 pieces of hardwood. The pieces should be 1″ × 4″ (¾″ × 3½″ dressed) and about 18″ long.

**Coping Saw.** The coping saw is used

for fine work and for cutting curves in thin wood and other materials. The blade is held in the frame under tension and can be turned in the frame so that cuts may be made at different angles. The blade can be removed when it becomes dull or broken. Keep a supply of extra blades in the tool kit because these thin blades are easily broken.

## Planes

Planes are basically smoothing tools, and come in many types and sizes, each designed for its particular job.

Basically, a plane is nothing more than a sharp chisel fixed securely in a metal frame equipped with adjusting devices. There are two basic types of smoothing plane; the bench and the block.

The bench plane is used for smoothing the face and side edges of lumber with the grain; the block plane is designed for smoothing end grain, that is, the end of the board. If you don't plan to do much carpentry but rather just minor repair work about the house, just get the block plane, as this is adequate for all variety of small jobs.

**Bench Plane.** Bench planes come in many different lengths as well as widths. A good size for most work about the house is one 8″ to 10″ long with a blade of about 2″.

Before trying out a bench plane, first acquaint yourself with its construction and adjustments. Everything except the frame (bottom) of any type of plane is demountable, requiring only a screwdriver to disassemble if necessary. Bench planes have a front hand knob and a handle at the back; a plane iron (cutter); and a plane cap iron, its sharp edge held tightly against the cutter and slightly back of its edge. The cap acts as a shaving deflector and prevents the wood from splitting ahead of the cutter. Assembled, the irons become a double plane iron, secured by a cap screw. This assembly is held in place by a lever cap which fits over the irons and secures the assembly to a frog by means of the lever cap screw. The frog in turn is so securely fastened with screws to

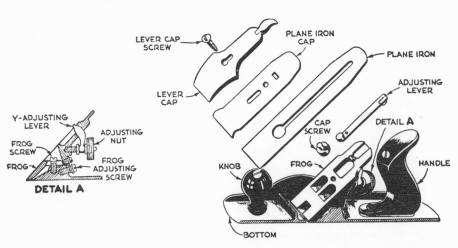

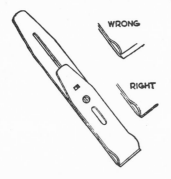

the "toe" and "heel" supports of the bottom of the plane that it is rigid and free from vibration.

To regulate the "mouth" (the slot where the iron's cutting edge projects from the bottom) of the plane, remove the lever cap and irons, loosen the two screws which secure the frog, and turn the center adjusting nut as required. Then tighten the frog screws and replace the irons and lever cap. Double plane irons are adjustable for depth of cut and are controlled by a finger adjusting screw which raises or lowers the cutter. The iron's cutting edge can also be aligned squarely with the bottom by a lateral adjusting lever which is part of the frog. For hardwood, set the cap iron just back of the cutter edge—farther back for softwood (about the thickness of a dime).

Always make certain that the cutter corners are evenly placed in the mouth, that is, that one corner does not project more than the other; otherwise you will ruin the piece you are planing. To check alignment of the blade, turn the bottom up, toe facing you, and sight along the length of the plane. Let the edge of the iron, which you adjust with the adjusting screw, protrude a hairbreadth. If the iron edge is out of alignment, adjust this with the adjusting lever.

**Using a Plane.** Using a plane is not difficult. The bench plane is always pushed with the grain, that is, in the "uphill" direction of the fibers. If the plane bucks, you are planing in the wrong direction, or the cutter is out too far. When a board has grain running in opposite directions, change the plane's direction with the grain.

With the board to be planed firmly secured either in a bench vise or on the bench or other surface, face the direction of planing, with the left foot out a trifle (right foot if you are left-handed). Hold the knob with the left hand and the handle with the right (reversed if you're left-handed), and press down on the knob as you start the stroke. Then gradually ease up on the knob pressure and apply it to the handle at the end of your stroke, leaning forward with your body as you push the plane. End the stroke with your weight carried easily on the left (or right) foot. Never let the plane drop at the end of the stroke, as this would round the edge of the board, and never drag the plane backward on the surface; lift it clear for the next forward stroke.

When squaring an edge, always keep the plane bottom at a right angle to the vertical face of the board, no matter how much bevel or center peak the edge may

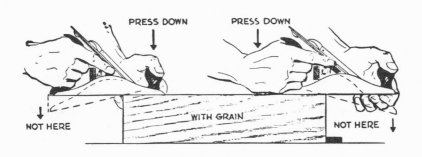

have. Plane the high part of the edge in this manner until the edge is square. To do this easily, hold the knob with the crotch of the thumb, your fingers supporting the bottom of the plane. Test for squareness frequently with a square.

When planing the end of a board, never carry your stroke to the edge; this invariably splinters off the corner. To avoid this, either bevel the corner (if it is waste to be removed) or plane from both directions to the center. You can also tightly clamp a scrap piece of lumber to the board end in a vise, the face of the scrap piece flush with the surface to be planed. However, good general practice calls for planing away from each edge.

**Block Plane.** The block plane is a very handy tool. Designed for planing board ends, it can also be used for many other jobs where a short plane works better than a long one. It is sold in a number of sizes from about $3\frac{1}{2}''$ to $7''$ long, with cutters $1''$ to about $1\frac{3}{4}''$ wide. It is a single-iron plane and is most often adjustable, which permits the mouth to be quickly opened or closed for coarse or fine work. It is also fully adjustable for depth of cut and alignment of cutter but, unlike the bench plane, it is designed for use with one hand. Block planes come in "regular" and "low angle," the latter having a cutter bevel of about 12 degrees, making it easier to plane across the grain of hardwoods. Both types consist of a bottom, iron, lever cap, lever cap screw, and adjusting screw, and some have a knuckle-joint lever cap which snaps into position and holds the cutter firmly. The plane is equipped with a finger rest at its toe, and the lever cap is designed to fit the palm of your hand. If you intend getting a block plane, the 6", 1⅝"-cutter "regular" is excellent for all-round block planing.

To adjust the plane iron for thickness of shaving (depth of cut), sight along the plane bottom and turn the adjusting screw right or left; to adjust the iron laterally, loosen the lever cap screw, sight along the bottom, press the plane iron to the right or left, and tighten the cap screw. The technique for using a block plane is the same as that for the bench plane.

## Wood-Boring Tools

If you have a portable electric drill, it can be used for all manner of jobs not only in wood but for metal and masonry as well. It can do the same jobs as a hand drill, a push-pull drill, or a brace and bit in a matter of seconds and with very little effort on your part. You may discover, however, that for a lot of small jobs it's easier to make holes with hand tools than to go to the bother of plugging in an electric drill. Hand boring tools are also required when you work outside the house where there is no convenient electric outlet.

**Brad Awl.** This is the easiest and least expensive wood-boring tool. It is a thin piece of steel pointed at one end and with a handle on the other. It is very handy for making a hole in softwood to start a nail or screw. While it has been around for centuries, it still has many uses today.

BRAD AWL

**Hand Drill.** A hand drill is powered by a handwheel geared to the drive shaft (frame), to which is attached a chuck for twist drills. The tool is steadied by the left hand on either of the 2 rigid handles while the right hand turns the crank handle attached to the gear wheel. To insert a twist drill, open the chuck only slightly more than the diameter of the drill. With the drill centered, tighten the chuck by pushing forward on the crank handle while holding the chuck shell tight with the left hand.

You can make depth gauges for use with the hand drill, as follows. Cut a small block of wood to a thickness equal to the difference between the drill length and the depth you intend to bore; bore through it with the twist drill you intend to use and slip the block up on the drill

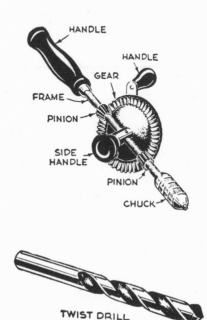

HANDLE

HANDLE

GEAR

FRAME

PINION

SIDE
HANDLE

PINION

CHUCK

TWIST DRILL

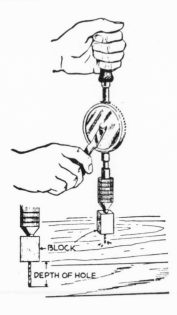

BLOCK

DEPTH OF HOLE

which at the end of its stroke returns by spring action to its original position, the drill point boring with both motions. This is a handy little tool for drilling numerous small holes. It is not suitable for use on metal or masonry.

**Brace.** The modern brace is engineered to do a number of jobs other than bore in wood. When buying a brace, get one with a ratchet. An 8″- or 10″-sweep (diameter of swing) ratchet brace is good for all-round work. The ratchet attachment transforms the brace into an improved screwdriving tool for large screws that would require considerable hand power to drive, and for jobs where a number of screws are to be driven.

The ratchet works three ways: driving to the right, inoperative to the left; center neutral, operative right and left; extracting to the left, inoperative to the right. A good brace has a chuck (jaw assembly to hold bit shanks) which will

so that it rests against the chuck, leaving exposed only that part of the drill to be used. An easier method is to wrap a thin, small rubber band three or four turns around the drill at the proper depth on the drill.

The hand drill will take twist drills up to ⅜″ in diameter; they are for use on metal as well as wood.

**Push-Pull Drill.** The automatic push-pull drill can be used on wood and plaster. It comes with a set of 8 drill points, of diameters from $\frac{1}{16}$″ to $\frac{11}{64}$″, housed in the handle of the tool when bought.

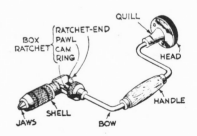

QUILL

RATCHET-END
PAWL
CAM
RING

BOX
RATCHET

HEAD

HANDLE

JAWS

SHELL

BOW

firmly grip all tapered-hank bits and also small and medium-size straight-shank drills. A ratchet brace in the medium-price class is fine. The ratchet brace is comprised of jaws enclosed in a shell, adjustable ratchet, bow, handle, quill, and head (either bronze bearing or ball bearing).

Two hands are usually required to operate a brace, but when boring horizontally you can rest the head of the brace against your stomach or chest if necessary. To insert a bit, turn the shell to the left until the jaws are wide open; be careful to center the shank of the bit within them. Turn the shell to the right tightly. Set the ratchet to "neutral" when boring, coun-

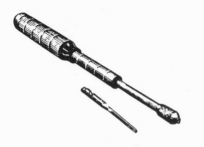

These drill points are short—limited to about 1¼″-depth holes—and are designed to bore with a continuous reciprocal motion. In practice, you push the drill,

tersinking, reaming, or starting a screw. To bore vertically, hold the brace and bit perpendicular to the surface, left hand cupped over the head.

There are a number of ways to bore straight: by sighting frequently; by comparing the bit to some nearby straight object; by setting a square near the bit; and by clamping, when feasible, a square piece of wood along the bit.

When using an auger bit to bore through a board, never bore all the way through from one direction. This splinters the edges of the hole as the bit emerges. Bore until the point just shows; then, with the hole as a guide, finish boring from the other side. When using an expansive bit, clamp a piece of waste wood against the piece to be bored and bore all the way through. This also applies to boring with twist bits and drills in wood. To bore horizontally, hold the brace cupped in the left hand against your stomach when possible, with the thumb and forefinger around the quill. Use a brace and bit for holes larger than $\frac{1}{4}''$, a hand drill for holes $\frac{1}{4}''$ and smaller.

Frequently you will want to bore one or a series of holes of certain depth only partially through a piece of wood, either with an auger bit or a Forstner bit. To do this accurately, a depth gauge is necessary. You can buy such a gauge, or you can easily make one from a block of wood. For the auger bit, bore a hole with the bit you intend to use in a short length of $\frac{3}{4}'' \times 2''$ wood. Cut this off with your back saw or crosscut saw so that you have a block $2'' \times 2''$ with the hole centered. Then saw the block in half across the center of the hole. To use, clamp the halves of the block on the bit with a small C-clamp, leaving enough of the drill to equal the depth of the hole to be bored. For the Forstner bit, bore a hole the diameter of the straight shank, and proceed as with the auger bit gauge. Make a gauge for each of your bits against the time when you will need them, and mark each pair with the size of bit to be used.

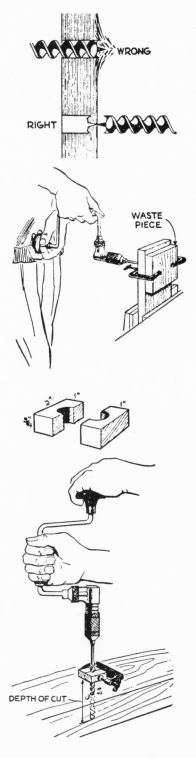

**Auger Bit.** Auger bits come in sizes from ¼″ to 1″, graduated in 16th inches. The size is stamped on the bit as the numerator of the fraction: "8," for example, stands for 8⁄16″, or a ½″ diameter of the hole bored.

**Forstner Bit.** These have no feed screw like the auger bit. They are used to bore wood part way when the screw of the auger bit would come through the wood: for end grain boring, thin wood, or near an end where the auger bit might split the wood. The sizes are marked as for the auger bit.

**Expansive Bit.** These are used in a brace to make holes larger than 1″ diameter. They come in two sizes: for holes from ½″ to 1½″, and for holes from ⅞″ to 3″.

**Countersink Bit.** This is used to ream a conical hole of shallow depth in an existing hole bored for a flathead screw, so that it may be driven flush with or below the surface. Hand-operated countersinks for wood and metal are usually called rose

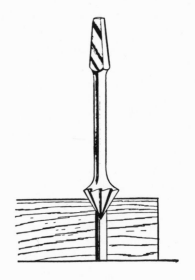

type. They have courses of cutting edges tapering to a point of the same angle as that of the head of a flathead wood screw. Flathead screws should always be driven either flush or a bit below the surface (when the heads are to be covered with putty or plastic wood).

**Reamer Bit.** This has a longer taper than the countersink and is used to taper existing holes for tight fits of tapered handles and such.

**Screwdriver Bit.** This is nothing more than a short screwdriver blade with a tapered shank to fit the brace. There is a variety of sizes. The ease with which the brace and screwdriver bit will drive heavy screws through any kind of wood makes it worthwhile getting a selection of these bits. They are also excellent for removing screws that have "frozen" in the wood and can't be started with an ordinary screwdriver.

## Chisel

The chisel is probably the third-ranking essential tool in woodworking. Without it most woodworking tasks having to do with joining would be almost impossible. Wherever wood is joined to wood, other than the common butt joint; where hinges and other devices are to be recessed, or locks mortised; where stopped dadoes and rabbets and other problems are to be solved, the chisel must be used. Woodworking chisels are basically of two types: the carpenter's-cabinetmaker's chisel, and the wood-carver's chisel, the latter having an almost endless variety of shapes, each for a special purpose. Carpenter's chisels can be roughly divided into three categories; butt, pocket, and firmer, with blades 3¼", 4½", and 6" long, respectively. The butt chisel comes in blade widths from ⅛" to 2", and the pocket and firmer blades range from ¼" to 2"; all are sized in 8ths to 1", 4ths to 2". The butt chisel is easier to control because it's short, while the longer chisels can be used with less angle because of their blade lengths.

Most carpenter's chisels have a socket in which the handle of hardwood, capped by leather washers, fits. There are also heavy-duty chisels with shanks and plastic handles of one piece in the butt and pocket sizes. Top-quality chisels have a beveled cutting edge and beveled sides, the blade ground the same width throughout and tempered its entire length so that successive grinding, sharpening, and honing will always produce the same width of cut.

There are a number of ways of holding a chisel, depending on what you intend doing with it. When using the chisel, the hands are oftener employed to drive it than is the mallet, which is usually used to drive the chisel blade across grain; when cutting a mortise which has been previously bored out with an auger bit; when roughing out where a large amount of material has to be removed; and with hardwood. Using a mallet to drive a chisel

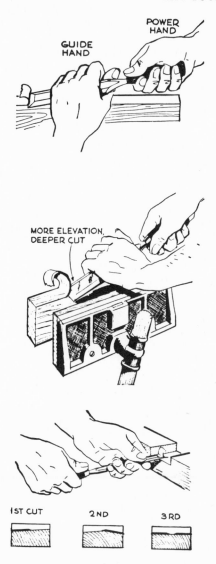

GUIDE HAND — POWER HAND

MORE ELEVATION, DEEPER CUT

1ST CUT    2ND    3RD

edge with the grain quite frequently splits the wood due to the force of the blows.

The left hand guides the chisel edge by pressing firmly on the blade and the wood being worked. The right hand supplies the power. Use a slicing cut whenever possible, rather than a straight pushing stroke. The former makes it easier and imparts to the edge a knifelike action resulting in a cleaner cut. To cut horizontally with the grain, hold the chisel slightly to one side and push away from you, bevel down for roughing cuts, bevel up for paring cuts. With the bevel up, hold the chisel as parallel as possible to the surface, pressing down with all the fingers of the left hand—the more elevation, the deeper the cut—and cut with the grain as in planing; otherwise you will split the wood.

To cut horizontally across the grain, guide the chisel edge with the thumb on top and the first two fingers under the blade, pressed together. This acts as a brake to the edge, permitting delicate cuts to be made. To prevent splintering the corners, cut toward the center each way, removing the middle portion last. When chiseling any wide surface, cut with the bevel down so that the handle clears the surface and the blade does not dig in as you push it forward.

If you are rounding a corner, use short, slanting cuts across the edge and tangent to the curve guide line. When using the chisel vertically across grain, the bevel should face out, the edge cutting across the grain in a slicing motion. Corners cut vertically on boards should be started from the edge of the board. When you are cleaning the corners of a tenon, dado, or rabbet, grasp the chisel near the cutting edge with the handle tilted to one side so that you are working with the corner of the blade. Draw the blade toward

you, holding the work with your left hand. To cut concave corners, the bevel should be against the surface; as you press down on the chisel, pull the handle slightly toward you, producing a sweeping curve cut. Again, always cut with the grain from the edge toward the end.

Practice these basic cuts on a piece of scrap wood, and in no time you will have the knack of handling a chisel for every type of problem. Just remember that it is better to take numerous small cuts rather than a couple of large ones, if you are doing a precision job. Also bear in mind that the chisel is in many respects a knife, and sometimes does the work of a plane where a plane cannot reach. As with all cutting tools, the edge must be razor-sharp; if it is kept in this condition, the pleasure of seeing it respond to your slightest touch will be ample reward for the time taken in sharpening.

**Gouges.** Gouges are chisels also, but with rounded cutting edges which make a concave cut. They are known as firmer and paring gouges, and range in blade width from $\frac{1}{8}''$ to $2''$. Firmer gouges have the bevel on the inside or outside face, and with tang or socket shank; a paring

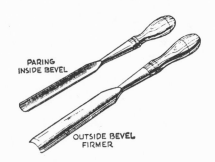

PARING
INSIDE BEVEL

OUTSIDE BEVEL
FIRMER

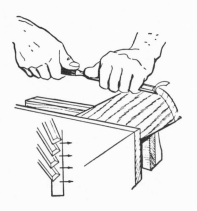

gouge has its bevel on the inside face and is furnished with a tang handle, straight or offset. Both types come in flat, medium, and regular sweeps, with parallel sides, allowing them to be ground, sharpened, and honed for a considerable distance back from the original length. Although, strictly speaking, not wood-carvers' tools, they can be classified as such, being used for irregular grooving and where a groove width is small and cannot be handled in any other manner. They are usually manipulated with the hands. A few of these, such as the ⅛″, ¼″, and ½″ widths, are handy to have when needed for cabinet-making and repair jobs, but they are not essential for average home carpentry.

When storing edged tools, or even laying them down, never let their cutting edges contact metal or other hard objects which, more likely than not, will nick or at best dull the sharp edges. A moment's carelessness may cost you hours of needless grinding, sharpening, and honing.

## Screwdrivers

The screwdriver is certainly a well-known tool and it hardly seems necessary to mention its purpose, but the truth is that an amazing number of users are unaware of its proper application. They may have been misled by the claims of manufacturers who, in their enthusiasm over their fine products, state that their handles are virtually breakproof; that their steel defies bending stresses, and on and on. Yet no manufacturer would dream of suggesting that his screwdriver be used as a substitute for a crowbar, a cold chisel, a nail extractor, or a can opener! Nevertheless, a surprising number of owners of screwdrivers employ them for everything but driving screws—with the result that when needed for their original purpose, their tips are so badly chewed up that that is about all they will do to the wood surface and screw head.

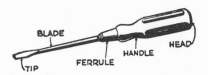

A good screwdriver is a well-engineered tool. It is forged from special-anal-

ysis alloy steel best suited for driving screws, with a slightly tapered tip, in most sizes, ground flat and true. Handles are of various compositions and woods. Regardless of how tough these handles may be, do not hit them with a hammer. A good screwdriver is not particularly cheap, so why ruin it unnecessarily?

Look at your collection of screwdrivers and examine their tips. If they have rounded corners, or twisted or damaged edges, they will do more damage to the wood surface or/and screw slot than they are worth. Take your mill file and file the faces of the tip edges *square* and *true*—and keep them that way. Then use each screwdriver only for the size of screw slot it fits properly.

**Using a Screwdriver.** When using a screwdriver, choose the longest one convenient for the work. More power can be applied to a long blade than to a short one, with less chance of the tip slipping

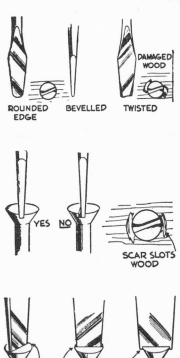

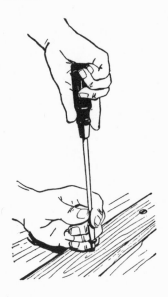

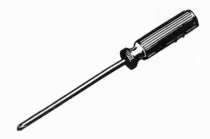

ratchets built into the ferrule, doing away with grip changing. Some of these types have interchangeable tips, housed in the handle. Then there is the spiral ratchet

out. Grasp the handle firmly in the palm of the right hand, the thumb and forefinger holding it near the ferrule. With the left hand, steady the tip and keep it pressing in the slot while renewing your grip on the handle. Keep the screwdriver vertical (or horizontal) with the screw—slanting it will result in the tip slipping out and marring both slot and work.

The following table shows what width of tip to use for a particular size of slotted wood screw.

| Screw Size | Blade-Tip Width |
|---|---|
| 0 | $\frac{1}{8}''$, $\frac{9}{64}''$ |
| 1 | $\frac{9}{64}''$ |
| 2 | $\frac{5}{32}''$ |
| 3, 4 | $\frac{3}{16}''$ |
| 5 | $\frac{7}{32}''$ |
| 6, 7 | $\frac{1}{4}''$ |
| 8, 9, 10, 11 | $\frac{5}{16}''$ |
| 11, 12, 14 | $\frac{3}{8}''$ |
| 14, 16, 20 | $\frac{7}{16}''$ |
| 20, 24 | $\frac{1}{2}''$ |

There is also a patented screw head which is recessed and partially cross-slotted, known as the Phillips screw; it requires a screwdriver tip designed to fit the recess. Screwdrivers are also made with

screwdriver with removable tips, ideal for production work where innumerable screws must be driven quickly. This driver works like the automatic push-pull drill in principle, the main differences being the cross-spiral driving shaft and the ratchet, which permits positive motion 3 ways. The driver comes in medium-, heavy-, and light-duty design. It can also be used as a drill, with the same drill points as used in the push-pull drill.

## Measuring Tools

**Rule.** A good, accurate rule is essential for precision measurements of wood and for other work around the house. We suggest you have two rules: a 6' folding (zig-

zag) rule with a 6'' sliding extension built into one end; and an 8' or 10' flexible steel pull-push rule. Get the type of pull-

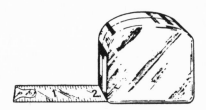

**Carpenter's Level.** This is used to establish true verticals and horizontals. You'll have use for it not only in carpen-

push rule with a locking device, so that after a measurement has been made the rule can be locked in the exact position. Buy the best-quality rules you can afford. The cheap ones often not only 'are inaccurate but also break easily.

**Combination Square.** This is a handy tool that can be used for a variety of purposes. It is good for marking a right-angle or 45-degree-angle cut and for measuring small work. It also contains a level, which can be used to determine if a surface is

try but also for such jobs as laying out forms for a terrace. A 24″ level is good for most jobs around the house.

## Putty Knife

This is one of the most essential tools in your kit as far as repair work is concerned. It is used for applying the putty around window glass but also is handy for

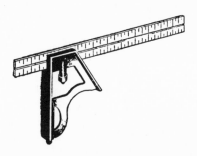

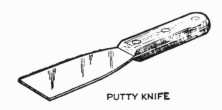

PUTTY KNIFE

perfectly vertical or horizontal. Apply a light coating of oil to the blade of this square so that it won't rust and make it hard to read the graduations.

If you plan to do any large jobs such as cutting sheets of plywood or hardboard or doing rough framing, a steel framing square will come in handy. These measure 24″ × 16″.

scraping loose paint, repairing cracks in plaster walls and ceilings, applying plastic fillers to holes in wood and other materials, and a lot of other odd jobs. Putty knives come in a wide range of sizes, but we've found that one with a 2″-wide blade is good for most work about the house.

## Pliers

Slip joint (adjustable) pliers are another essential item for a repair kit. One

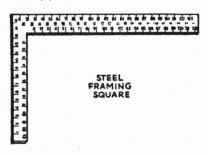

STEEL
FRAMING
SQUARE

ADJUSTABLE PLIERS

excellent type has parallel jaws with a locking action so that they can be used as an adjustable wrench as well as pliers.

## Wrenches

An 8″ adjustable wrench will be needed to do minor plumbing repair jobs such as fixing a leaky faucet. A pipe (stillson) wrench is essential only if you plan

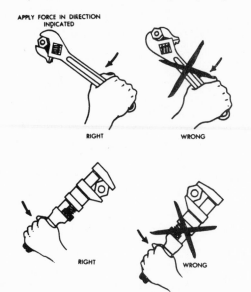

APPLY FORCE IN DIRECTION INDICATED

RIGHT          WRONG

RIGHT          WRONG

NUT IS AT FRONT OF JAWS AND PULLING FORCE IS APPLIED TO WRONG SIDE OF HANDLE

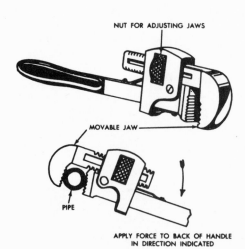

NUT FOR ADJUSTING JAWS

MOVABLE JAW

PIPE

APPLY FORCE TO BACK OF HANDLE IN DIRECTION INDICATED

to do extensive plumbing work using galvanized iron pipe. You may need it at times for other repair jobs, but rather than buy one we suggest that you rent one.

## Other Useful Tools

**Clamps.** These are used to hold pieces together, especially when gluing. If you do much furniture repair work, you'll have use for them. The C-clamp is good for a lot of jobs and comes in a variety of sizes. The hand screw clamp is also worth having.

**Files and Rasps.** These are cutting tools used to shape and sharpen metal and to shape wood. Rasps are used on wood, files on metal. You may want to purchase these from time to time as the need arises.

**Hacksaw.** This tool is used for cutting metal, plastic, and other materials too dense for a handsaw. One type consists of a frame in which the blade is fastened so that it can be removed when it becomes dull. A handy hacksaw for home use is the one with a pistol grip.

**Utility Knife.** This knife is used for cutting wood, stripping insulation off electric wiring, and so forth.

## Power Tools

There are any number of power tools available. Some are more specialized than others. How many and which ones to buy depend not only on your budget but on the amount of specialized work you plan to do. If you plan to do a lot of cabinet work, investing in an electric saw of one type or another might be wise. If, on the other hand, you require specialized tools for only a short period, it's better to rent them than to purchase them outright.

**Portable Electric Drill.** This is the one power tool so useful that it belongs in almost every home tool kit. You can get the small ¼″ drills for under $10, but we recommend the larger 3/8" drill. And it's worth buying the type with reverse action, variable speed, and shockproof casing. This tool can be used safely for any manner of drilling job—wood, metal, masonry—and does a faster job than the smaller 1/4" drills. The variable speed and reverse action make it handy for inserting or removing wood screws and bolts without the need for a special screwdriver attachment.

**Twist Drills.** These are inserted in the drill tool for making holes in wood, metal, plastic, or other materials. The smallest is 1/16" diameter. For a 1/4" electric drill the maximum size is 1/4"; for a 3/8" drill the maximum is 3/8". You can get twist drills suitable for both wood and metal, or ones that are suitable only for wood. It's wise to buy a set of drills rather than pick them up one at a time.

**Wood Bits.** These are used for drilling larger holes than with a twist drill and should be used only in wood. They range from 3/8" diameter to 1 1/4" diameter.

**Masonry Carbide Drills.** These are used for drilling in all forms of masonry, such as concrete, brick, or stone. Sizes are from 3/16" to 1/2".

**Screwdriver Attachment.** This is used on an ordinary power drill, either 1/4" or 3/8", so that it can be used to insert or remove screws. The attachment gears down the speed of the drill and has a clutch that stops the movement when the screw is in place. It is often sold in a kit which contains the speed reducer and clutch element along with the various sizes and types of screwdriver bits required.

**Hole-Saw Attachments.** These are either set or adjustable, and can be used to cut holes up to 2 1/2" diameter in wood, plywood, or hardboard.

**Circular Saw Attachment.** This has a 5 1/2" blade and can be used for cutting through 1"-thick boards, plywood, and the like.

**Buffer-Sander-Polisher.** This is a handy attachment for rough sanding as well as fine buffing and polishing.

**Water Pump Attachment.** This can be used to remove water from small pools, fixed containers, and so forth. It will pump about 200 gallons an hour.

**Wood Screw Pilot Bits.** These are used to drill pilot holes as well as countersinks for wood screws. They do three drilling operations in one.

It seems that almost every year someone comes up with another attachment for the portable electric drill which makes it more and more useful around the house.

It does not require any special skills to use an electric drill. The main requirement is to hold it steady when in operation, for if you move it you may break the twist drill. Also, don't try to speed up the drilling process by putting too much pressure on the drill, because if the speed is reduced the motor may burn out. Do not operate the drill under heavy loads such as can occur when drilling into masonry, or for a long period when it can become overheated. When the drill begins to feel warm in your hand, pull out the bit, stop the drill, and let it cool down before beginning to drill again.

**Portable Circular Saw.** This is a worthwhile tool to buy if you are doing any sort of extensive rough construction, such as putting up a garage or remodeling. A good size for home use is the 7" type with a 1 3/4-hp motor.

Saws of this type have a depth adjustment, and the blade can be set at any desired angle up to 45 degrees to make angle cuts. To speed up cutting 2" × 4" and 2" × 6" stock, you can't beat them. They are also very handy for cutting large sheets of plywood, hardboard, and the like. Combination blades are available that can be used for crosscutting or ripping; but when fine work is required, it's better to use either a crosscut or a rip blade, depending on the work involved. There are also carbide-tipped blades used for cutting through asbestos-cement board, and even special blades for masonry.

You can get an attachment that can convert a portable circular saw into a table saw, but it will not turn out the precision work that a good-quality bench or radial saw can.

In spite of the fact that a good-quality portable saw has a blade guard on it that automatically swings up to cover the blade except when it is cutting, tools of this type must be handled with care, for they can be dangerous. It is important that the wood or other material is securely set in place so that it can't move when being cut. If you push the saw too fast, there is danger of the blade jamming and kicking the saw back toward you. Don't wear loose clothing when using this tool, and keep the work area clean. Adjust the depth gauge for each piece of work so that the blade will just cut through the piece rather than extend much beyond the bottom.

**Saber Saw.** This saw cuts stock up to 1″ thick and can be used for straight as well as curved cuts. It can also start a hole in the middle of a piece of work or wall panel. The saber saw comes with a wide selection of blades suitable for different kinds of work and materials. Unless you are doing a lot of rough construction, this tool can be used in place of a portable circular saw for cutting boards, plywood, hardboard, and similar materials used around the house.

When using the saber saw on work that is not fixed in place, be sure that the work is securely supported; for if it is not, the vibration of the saw when in operation will make it difficult to perform an accurate cut.

**Fixed Saws.** There are two types of fixed saws available to the homeowner. One is the radial arm saw, the other the tilting arbor bench saw. They both come in a range of sizes, and there is a great deal of optional equipment available. Both these saws can do a variety of jobs besides cutting wood. Of the two, the radial arm is the more versatile, as it can be used for shaping, drilling, cutting dadoes, routing, or sanding.

These saws are good if you enjoy woodworking as a hobby or if you are doing extensive remodeling that involves fine work such as cabinets, built-ins, and the like. Good-quality units can cost several hundred dollars with all the attachments. To get the most out of one of these tools, though, you should read and study material that covers its proper use.

**Electric Sanders.** There are three basic types of sanders: rotary, belt, and finishing. The rotary sander and belt sander are intended for rough work such as removing accumulations of paint or taking a heavy surface thickness off a piece of wood. They are handy for stripping exterior paint from porch floors, siding, and so on, and for use on the hulls of boats. They should not be used on furniture or for fine work because they do not leave a smooth surface and also because they cut so quickly that they may go right through a thin veneer.

For furniture and other fine work, the finishing sander is the only kind to use. This is a slow-cutting sander, for smoothing rather than removal of surface material.

# 2

# MATERIALS
# AND SUPPLIES

It takes the right materials and supplies as well as proper tools to keep a house in repair and to make improvements when required. You will find that new products that can make a job easier are constantly coming on the market. The wise homeowner will take the time to visit a good local hardware store, lumber yard, or building supply house from time to time to see what's new in the way of specialized products. It will also benefit you if, when you have a particular repair or improvement problem, you ask your dealer what he suggests. He probably knows about most available materials and can often save you both time and money.

## FASTENERS

### Nails

Whoever first thought of the nail as a fastener for wood was a genius, because his idea has stood the test of more than 3,000 years. Mention in the Bible of David's use of nails is probably the first official recording of man's recourse to this ingenious metal device. Today there are more than 1,000 varieties and sizes of nails, both old and new forms developed for specific purposes. There are even certain types of lath nails that are sterilized by considerate manufacturers so that you can hold a mouthful while lathing without running the risk of infection. (Using the mouth as a receptacle for nails is not recommended, since the stomach has not as yet learned to digest them.)

Nail sizes are designated in terms of "penny" (d), a term which originated in England long ago. Its original meaning is debated, some holding that it meant so many English pennies per 100 nails; others maintaining it signified that 1,000 nails weighed a certain number of pounds ("pun"—"penny"); and still others, that the English measure of 1,000 nails to the "pennyweight" is the answer. Incidentally, the hand-forged nail of antiquity (now machine-cut) with its tapered 4-corner shank, still holds better than the modern "wire" nail because it tends to cut rather than spread the wood fibers, as does the smooth, round wire nail.

**Kinds of Nails.** Nails are made of steel, aluminum, copper, and brass. Always use rust-resistant aluminum, galvanized iron, or copper nails for any work that is exposed to the weather or to moisture. This would include outdoor furniture and the exterior of the house, as well as boats.

The illustration gives you some idea of the variety of head, shank, and point design of the modern nail. But unless you have a particular project (as roofing or lathing) requiring a particular nail, you need not be too upset by the bewildering variety. Four types will about take care of most woodworking problems around the home: common, box, finishing, and casing. A mention, however, of the qualities of special-type nails is in order.

A nail, whatever its type, should be at least 3 times longer than the thickness of the piece into which it is driven. A "regular" diamond point (the most common form of 4-cornered point on nails) works fine in all but hardwood—which it is liable to split unless a lead hole of slightly smaller diameter than the nail is bored. A

"blunt" diamond point is best for hardwood, such as flooring—or use a steel-cut flooring nail. The "long" diamond point is a "speed" nail to drive. Smooth, round-tapered points are best for nailing fabrics, as the point spreads rather than cuts the fibers. Chisel points are usually found on "spikes" for hardwood. Lengths of wire spikes start at 10d and run to 12", their thickness being greater than for wire nails of comparative lengths. They are used for heavy timbers, girders, and the like. The table shows sizes and approximate number per pound of the most commonly used nails.

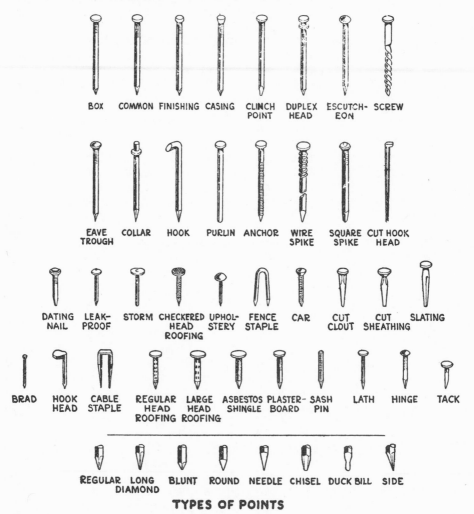

BOX   COMMON   FINISHING   CASING   CLINCH POINT   DUPLEX HEAD   ESCUTCH-EON   SCREW

EAVE TROUGH   COLLAR   HOOK   PURLIN   ANCHOR   WIRE SPIKE   SQUARE SPIKE   CUT HOOK HEAD

DATING NAIL   LEAK-PROOF   STORM   CHECKERED HEAD ROOFING   UPHOL-STERY   FENCE STAPLE   CAR   CUT CLOUT   CUT SHEATHING   SLATING

BRAD   HOOK HEAD   CABLE STAPLE   REGULAR HEAD ROOFING   LARGE HEAD ROOFING   ASBESTOS SHINGLE   PLASTER-BOARD   SASH PIN   LATH   HINGE   TACK

REGULAR   LONG DIAMOND   BLUNT   ROUND   NEEDLE   CHISEL   DUCK BILL   SIDE

**TYPES OF POINTS**

**WIRE NAILS**

| | | Common | | Finishing | | Casing and Box | | Spikes | |
|---|---|---|---|---|---|---|---|---|---|
| Size | Length (In.) | Gauge | No. per lb. | Gauge | No. per lb. | Gauge | No. per lb. | Gauge | No. per lb. |
| 2d | 1 | 15 | 876 | 16½ | 1,351 | 15½ | 1,010 | | |
| 3d | 1¼ | 14 | 568 | 15½ | 807 | 14½ | 635 | | |
| 4d | 1½ | 12½ | 316 | 15 | 584 | 14 | 473 | | |
| 5d | 1¾ | 12½ | 271 | 15 | 500 | 14 | 406 | | |
| 6d | 2 | 11½ | 174 | 13 | 309 | 12½ | 236 | | |
| 7d | 2¼ | 11½ | 161 | 13 | 238 | 12½ | 210 | | |
| 8d | 2½ | 10¼ | 106 | 12½ | 189 | 11½ | 108 | | |
| 10d | 3 | 9 | 69 | 11½ | 121 | 10½ | 94 | 6 | 41 |
| 12d | 3¼ | 9 | 63 | 11½ | 113 | 10½ | 87 | 6 | 38 |
| 16d | 3½ | 8 | 49 | 11 | 90 | 10 | 71 | 5 | 30 |
| 20d | 4 | 6 | 31 | 10 | 62 | 9 | 52 | 4 | 23 |
| 30d | 4½ | 5 | 24 | | | 9 | 46 | 3 | 17 |
| 40d | 5 | 4 | 18 | | | 8 | 35 | 2 | 13 |
| 50d | 5½ | 3 | 14 | | | | | 1 | 10 |
| 60d | 6 | 2 | 11 | | | | | 1 | 9 |
| | 7 | | | | | | | 5/16 | 7 |
| | 8 | | | | | | | ⅜ | 4 |
| | 9 | | | | | | | ⅜ | 3½ |
| | 10 | | | | | | | ⅜ | 3 |
| | 12 | | | | | | | ⅜ | 2½ |

Common flathead nails of larger sizes are used chiefly in home-construction framing, although they are being replaced these days by box nails, which are slightly thinner and can be driven in more easily. Finishing nails are used when the nail head is to be set and covered. Casing nails are frequently used for "blind" nailing of flooring, their tapered heads fitting snugly into the base of the tongue of the board—a good squeak preventer. There is an expanding, self-clinching nail designed for use where asbestos or shingle siding is applied over fiberboard outdoor sheathing, doing away with the necessity of nailing furring strips (wooden nailing strips) on the sheathing first—ordinary nails will not hold in fiberboard sheathing alone.

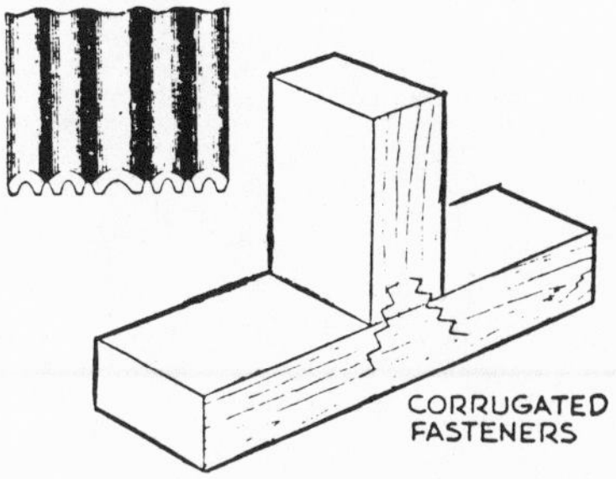


**Corrugated Fastener.** The corrugated fastener is a special kind of nail, being a piece of corrugated steel, in width ¼″, ⅜″, ½″, or ⅝″, with one end chisel-edge-pointed. Two of these fasteners are driven between two joints, straddling them. It holds joints together well enough but allows some lateral motion. Corrugated fasteners are used chiefly for repairing furniture when the parts cannot be readily taken apart to reglue, and for reinforcing weakened joints. It is not the best method of securing joints.

**Clinching.** For added holding power where the nail point does not show, nails longer than the thickness of the wood are frequently used, and the ends bent over on the blind side of the wood. This is called "clinching." The common practice is simply to hammer the nail over flat with the surface; but a workmanlike and perfect clinch is made by laying another,

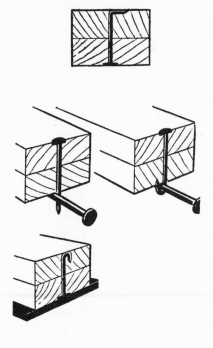

it. Then drive a finishing nail in the opening, set it below the underside of the shaving, and apply glue to the underside. Clamp until the glue has dried, and smooth with abrasive paper.

**Toenailing.** Toenailing is employed when the pieces to be nailed cannot be joined by straight nailing, as when nailing the feet of studding and laying finished flooring. Toenailing exerts considerable drawing power to the part nailed and is frequently used for such purposes as pulling siding into position. As a rule, toenailing is done from both sides and frequently on all sides of the piece.

First, place the piece on the line marked for its position, then drive the nail almost in. The piece will have moved somewhat from the line. Then toenail the opposite side all the way in, which forces the piece back on line again. Finish driving the first nail and toenail the remaining sides, if desirable.

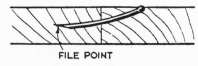

FILE POINT

larger nail against the point and hammering the point over it, forming a staple which is then driven flush into the wood. When clinching, use a metal plate between the head and work surface; otherwise the head will be driven out.

Where two pieces of hardwood are to be nailed edge to edge, but not to another surface, the trick is to file one side of the nail point to a chisel edge. The nail will then, on entering, bend in the direction of the flat side of the point. There are nails manufactured this way for curve nailing.

Blind nailing is not recommended, since it is a tricky technique dependent on the type of wood being nailed—which, if brittle, works even less well. There is always a slight depression left after the nail has been driven, which must be filled.

Use a razor-sharp ¼"-wide chisel to lift a shaving, being careful not to break

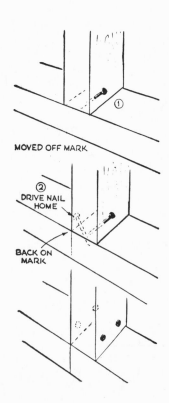

① MOVED OFF MARK

② DRIVE NAIL HOME

BACK ON MARK

**Extracting.** Extracting nails successfully depends on the condition of the hammer claw. More often than not a good claw will extract even a headless nail, if the claw edge is twisted against the shank of the nail when pulling. When removing nails from framed wood, as, for example, boxlike assemblies, drive the joint apart slightly, placing a piece of wood between the hammer head and surface to prevent marring and splitting. Then tap the joint back again, using a piece of wood to pry against. This usually leaves the nail heads protruding far enough to insert the claw, under which you should place a piece of cardboard—or anything thin.

When the nail is sufficiently drawn out, use a block of wood under the claw. Where this method cannot be employed, chisel away the wood around the nail head sufficiently to grip it with a pair of end cutters. Then use the claw.

When removing finishing nails from old lumber you wish to salvage, pull the nails through from the back if you do not want to disturb the filling and paint on the face side.

## Screws

The wood screw is a decided improvement over the nail, as it will draw pieces of wood tightly together and, properly driven, will not loosen its grip. It also has the advantage of being removable when necessary without damage to the wood. For solid, permanent framing of wood members or other materials to wood, as in cabinets, tables, and bookshelves, the screw should be used in preference to the nail. In many instances the added time required to prepare wood surfaces for screwing repays in quality results.

Wood screws are made of steel, bright-finished; zinc, cadmium- and chrome-plated; blued steel; stainless steel; aluminum; and brass. They come slotted in flat-head, oval-head, and round-head design. There is also the Phillips screw,

partially cross-slotted and recessed, with the same types of heads, requiring a special Phillips screwdriver. The flat-head is measured from head edge to point; oval-head from bevel edge to point; round-head from shoulder to point.

**Sheet-Metal Screws.** These are self-tapping and are used to join relatively thin pieces of metal or other dense material They are used primarily on such items as furnace ducts, kitchen appliances, TVs, radios, and automobiles.

**Lag Screws.** Lag screws are much heavier and longer than slot-headed wood screws and have coarser threads and bolt heads, either square or hexagon-shaped. The square-head lag screw is most common and has a gimlet point. These screws are used to fasten timbers when spikes are not strong enough and ordinary wood screws would be too short and light for the job. A wrench is necessary to drive a bolt-head lag screw.

**Driving a Screw.** First bore a hole, of the diameter of the body of the screw, through the wood to be held by the screw, and a smaller lead hole in the piece anchoring the screw. The smaller hole should have a diameter less than that of the threads, and a depth $\frac{1}{2}$ to $\frac{2}{3}$ the length of the threaded part anchored. The diameter of this hole depends on the

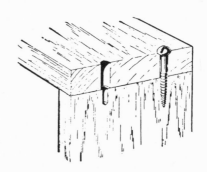

wood. Hardwoods like maple and oak require a larger hole than softwoods, but no exact information is possible, as the texture of wood varies. In end grain the hole should be smaller than in straight grain. Holes for screws are bored for the sake of accuracy of placement, ease of driving, and prevention of splitting. In hardwood, a screw can easily be twisted off in attempting to drive it without lead holes. Remember it is the thread of a screw which holds, not the unthreaded portion.

Flat-head and oval-head screws are countersunk flush with the surface or below the surface, or the body hole is counterbored for the screw head to seat considerably below the surface. Counterboring means boring a hole larger than the diameter of the screw head, just large enough to permit the widest part of the screwdriver blade to turn. This is done so

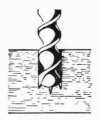

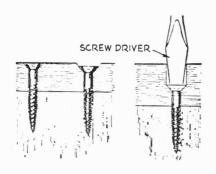

SCREW DRIVER

that the screw slides into the wood for a given distance. Counterboring is usually done when a thick piece of wood is framed to another piece and, for practical purposes, the screw is only as long as, or shorter than, the thick piece.

If you intend counterboring with an auger bit, first bore the larger hole and then the body hole; otherwise the feed screw of the bit has nothing to take hold of. Where counterboring must be done on a surface which shows, good practice is to fit a wood plug, of the kind of wood being bored and of shallow depth, glued in the

hole flush with the surface. The plug initially should protrude slightly beyond the surface. When the glue has thoroughly dried, chisel off the projection flush with the surface. Round-head screws are not countersunk, but are often counterbored. They are used when fastening metal too thin to receive a flat-head screw flush, to wood; also as pivots for wood-to-wood or metal-to-wood fastening.

When flat-head screws are to be hidden, they should be countersunk slightly deeper than flush, just enough for the covering material to take hold. Plastic wood is the usual covering for screw heads in wood and, as it is primarily an adhesive, it holds well. It shrinks, however, which requires the building of a slight mound above the wood surface which, when dry, is sanded flush.

Water-mix wood putty is another excellent filler for countersunk screws and set nails, and wherever a depression or damaged corner needs filling. It comes in powder form, to which you add enough water to make a stiff paste. Dampen the wood first, then apply the putty with a spatula or putty knife and let it dry about 15 to 20 minutes. It can then be sanded smooth, filed, or carved, and has a finer texture than plastic wood. It will readily take any finish—stain, varnish, or paint. Most paint stores carry it.

Use the chart given here to guide you in selecting the right size of screw for your particular project. The approximate diameters shown can be used to select the size of drill that will allow a loose fit for the screw.

## SCREW SIZES AND CORRESPONDING LENGTHS
(Flat-Head, Oval-Head, Round-Head)

| Nominal Size | #0 | #1 | #2 | #3 | #4 | #5 | #6 | #7 | #8 | #9 | #10 | #12 | #14 | #16 | #18 | #20 | #24 |
|---|---|---|---|---|---|---|---|---|---|---|---|---|---|---|---|---|---|
| Approx. Dia. (In.) | 1/16 | 5/64 | 3/32 | 3/32 | 7/64 | 1/8 | 9/64 | 5/32 | 11/64 | 11/64 | 3/16 | 7/32 | 15/64 | 9/32 | 19/64 | 21/64 | 3/8 |
| **Length (In.)** | | | | | | | | | | | | | | | | | |
| 1/4 | X | X | X | X | X | | | | | | | | | | | | |
| 3/8 | X | X | X | X | X | X | X | X | X | X | | | | | | | |
| 1/2 | | X | X | X | X | X | X | X | X | X | X | X | | | | | |
| 5/8 | | X | X | X | X | X | X | X | X | X | X | X | | | | | |
| 3/4 | | | X | X | X | X | X | X | X | X | X | X | X | X | | | |
| 7/8 | | | X | X | X | X | X | X | X | X | X | X | X | | | | |
| 1 | | | | X | X | X | X | X | X | X | X | X | X | X | X | X | |
| 1 1/4 | | | | | X | X | X | X | X | X | X | X | X | X | X | X | X |
| 1 1/2 | | | | | X | X | X | X | X | X | X | X | X | X | X | X | X |
| 1 3/4 | | | | | | X | X | X | X | X | X | X | X | X | X | X | X |
| 2 | | | | | | X | X | X | X | X | X | X | X | X | X | X | X |
| 2 1/4 | | | | | | | X | X | X | X | X | X | X | X | X | X | X |
| 2 1/2 | | | | | | | X | X | X | X | X | X | X | X | X | X | X |
| 2 3/4 | | | | | | | | X | X | X | X | X | X | X | X | X | X |
| 3 | | | | | | | | X | X | X | X | X | X | X | X | X | X |
| 3 1/2 | | | | | | | | | X | X | X | X | X | X | X | X | X |
| 4 | | | | | | | | | X | X | X | X | X | X | X | X | X |
| 4 1/2 | | | | | | | | | | | | X | X | X | X | X | X |
| 5 | | | | | | | | | | | | X | X | X | X | X | X |
| 6 | | | | | | | | | | | | | X | X | X | X | X |

## Glues and Adhesives

These terms can be used more or less interchangeably; glue is the older of the two and generally refers to an adhesive used in woodworking. Today the common term is "adhesives," and a wide range of them are available not only for wood but for almost every other material you will find in the house or apartment. Some are all-purpose and can be used on a variety of materials; others have a more limited use. Before you buy and use any of them, read the printed matter on the container to be sure that it is suitable for your purpose.

Modern chemistry has made tremendous strides in developing synthetic adhesives far superior to the animal and vegetable glues of yesterday. Those glues are still available and are extremely strong, but they have the disadvantages of being highly moisture-absorbent, reacting unfavorably to temperature changes and fungi, and often requiring special preparation of material, as well as speed in application, to secure a strong joint. They are still used, however, in repairing antique furniture because, unlike some of the modern adhesives, they can be softened with water; thus, if the need ever arises to undo a joint so that other repairs can be made, it can be taken apart without damage to the wood.

**Resorcinol Resin Glue.** Resorcinol resin glue is perhaps the most amazing of all the modern synthetic glues. It comes in two units: one a dark-wine-colored, syrupy liquid, the other a light-colored powder which is the catalyst—the chemical agent which, when added to the liquid, transforms it into one of the strongest glues yet devised for wood. Once set—and the higher the temperature the quicker it will set—nothing affects its adhesive power. It is absolutely waterproof, not affected by

27

temperature changes or fungi, and can be used on loose or tight joints. It has but one disadvantage, when applied to light-colored woods—it stains. However, if the excess is *immediately* wiped off with *cold* water, staining can be avoided to a large extent. If you want a wood joint to outlast the wood itself (boats have been built without any other fastening device!), use resorcinol resin glue. The directions on the container are very easy to follow.

**Urea Resin Glue.** Urea resin glue comes in powdered form, and cold water should be added in whatever quantity is needed for the immediate job. It is highly water-resistant and stainfree, but requires tight clamping of a close-fitting wood joint. It is an extremely strong glue for veneering, making inlaid designs, and all-round woodworking.

**Casein Glue.** Casein glue also comes in powdered form and is mixed with cold water. This glue will secure loose or tight-fitting joints of wood—including oily woods—is stainfree, but is not highly water-resistant. It is very strong and is popular around home workshops.

**Rubber-Base Glue.** Rubber-base glue, which comes in a creamy paste, will glue metal to wood, metal to metal, glass to metal, glass to wood, cloth to cloth, cloth to wood, and end-grain wood to wood. It will hold practically anything, but is not as strong on wood to wood as other glues formulated for wood.

**Thermoplastic Cement.** Thermoplastic cement (polyvinyl) is a quick-drying liquid with strong adhesive powers. It is fine for veneer work, furniture repair, toys, and odd jobs around the house. It makes an inconspicuous joint, which will separate when considerable heat is applied.

**Cellulose Cement.** Cellulose cement is a clear, syrupy adhesive which dries very quickly—too quickly for large areas. It makes a strong joint and will adhere to almost anything. It is usually sold in tube form and is excellent for household mending jobs, toys, and model projects.

**Contact Cement.** This is a type of adhesive that requires no clamping. It was originally developed for bonding plastic laminate (Formica) to a wood base, but it can also be used for many other jobs about the house where it is impractical to use clamps. It can be used on wood, leather, metal, and tile. A coat of the adhesive is spread on each of the surfaces to be joined and is allowed to set for several minutes, depending on the manufacturer's instructions. Then the pieces are placed together; they will immediately grip so that they cannot be pulled apart. This makes working with contact cement tricky, because you have to be right the first time—you can't easily slide the pieces about once they are in contact with each other. One coat is sufficient on dense materials, but two coats may be required on a porous material.

**Epoxy Adhesives.** These are the strongest of all adhesives; they will make a joint so secure that you will break the pieces before you can break the joint. Epoxy adhesives come in two separate elements, each in its container. These are mixed in equal parts for use. The adhesives are available in clear form as well as in colors. Drying time will differ according to brand. You can use epoxy adhesives for almost every kind of repair job about the house—fixing a leak in a water pipe, fastening a fixture to a bathroom wall, repairing china so that it can withstand washing even in an automatic dishwasher.

There are also special epoxy adhesives that resemble liquid steel and aluminum, which are excellent for repairing large holes in gutters, drainpipes, and tanks.

## Clamps

All glued joints, whatever the glue, should be and, with some glues, must be clamped until the glue has dried. A variety of clamps exist for this, although they may have other functions as well. Three kinds of clamps are C-clamps, hand screws, and bar clamps; all are actuated by a threaded screw or screws capable of tremendous pressure. Whatever type of clamp you use on a glued joint, apply only enough pressure to hold the joint tightly, and no more.

C-clamps are made of metal and come in many sizes. They are limited in the thickness of material that they will clamp, but are used more often than other types.

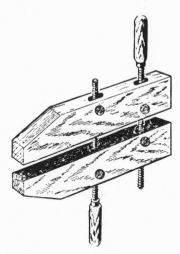

Hand-screw clamps are perhaps the oldest form of gluing clamp, having been in use since wood has been used for furniture. The hand-screw clamp has hardwood jaws actuated by 2 screws from opposite directions, and is fully adjustable for any type of gluing job within the limits of the length of the screws; the jaws can be offset, tapered, or set parallel.

The bar clamp consists of 2 metal jaws, one of which has a screw or is actuated by a screw, while the other jaw is fixed at the end of the bar. It is used to hold glued joints of wide dimensions, such as a table top made up of individual boards.

The most popular clamp of this type has for its bar a ¾″-threaded standard pipe which you buy separately—as short or long as you please. This assembly costs about half the price of the type which comes as a unit and is limited as to length —about 3′ to 6′. There is, however, a short bar clamp which is inexpensive and will clamp up to 6″ of material. This clamp weighs less than a C-clamp of the same capacity and is quicker-acting, hav-

ing tooth edges on the bar for fast adjustment of one jaw. A few C-clamps and short bar clamps should be part of the equipment of every home workshop; the longer variety of bar clamp is necessary only if you plan to do wide jobs of gluing.

## Miscellaneous Fasteners

All sorts of metal fasteners are used to frame and strengthen two or more pieces of wood; or to hold temporarily one piece against another, such as catches of various kinds; or to articulate wood, such as a wide variety of hinges.

Permanent strengthening fasteners are basically of five kinds: flat corner plates, mending plates, T-plates, inside corner irons, and steel brackets. All but the steel brackets are recessed flush with the surface (for a workmanlike job), or attached to the surface with screws. All have predrilled countersunk holes for flathead wood screws to seat flush.

cabinets and shelves. Quite frequently wood joints and corners, although well glued and screwed, are not strong enough and require this additional method of reinforcing—where it will not show.

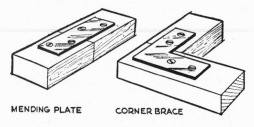

MENDING PLATE          CORNER BRACE

Flat corner plates (corner braces) are L-shaped for butt, lapped, or mitered corners, and are made in a variety of leg lengths, thicknesses, and widths.

Mending plates are flat, straight pieces of various lengths for strengthening running butt or lapped joints.

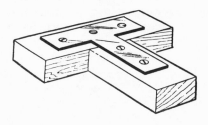

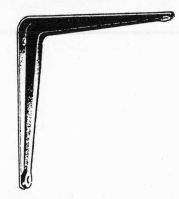

Steel brackets with reinforcing webs are used to support shelving under unusually heavy loads, and come in a number of leg lengths. The pressed-steel type has no cross-piece to hamper storage.

Adjustable steel shelf brackets for bookshelves and the like are short brack-

T-plates are flat, T-shaped pieces of various leg lengths for strengthening T-shaped joints.

Inside corner irons are narrow-width angle irons of various leg lengths used to reinforce pieces of wood at right angles to each other, on their inside faces, as for

ets which fit in sockets in steel straps runing the height of the shelves or cabinet. Four brackets are required for each shelf.

**Catches.** Catches are basically of six types: hook-and-eye, sliding bolt, bayonet-type friction, friction, snap, and bullet.

SNAP CATCH

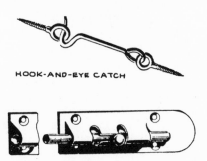

HOOK-AND-EYE CATCH

SLIDING BOLT CATCH

CUPBOARD TURN

The hook-and-eye or the sliding bolt depending on its size, can be used for any door from cabinet to barn. Friction-type catches are used to hold cabinet doors by friction alone, requiring only a pull on the door to open it. The bullet catch is a friction type which is used chiefly on furniture doors, being practically invisible. It requires that a hole be bored, the diameter of the barrel, into the jamb of the door. The "bullet," actuated by a coil spring, projects slightly beyond the jamb and engages a strike recessed in the edge of the door.

Bayonet-type friction catches hold better than the bullet type and are quite frequently used on doors of larger cabinets, light wardrobes, and kitchen cabinets. A snap catch is generally used to hold one door of a 2-door cabinet, and re-

quires finger pressure to release it. The other door is usually secured by a cupboard turn, which snaps shut when closed but requires finger turning to open.

There are also hidden types of catches which are quite involved in their construction. They operate by pressing, or sharply striking, the door at their location, causing the catch to release. These secret catches operate only for those in the know, the door having no visible means of being opened. One disadvantage to these trick catches is that if they should decide not to work, you open the door with a wrecking tool!

**Hinges.** There are many hinges made for a variety of purposes, but basically they fall into three types, whatever their form: strap hinge, butt hinge, and knife hinge. Originally hinges were of the strap variety only, masterpieces of the blacksmith's art. They were forged into intricately designed scrolls, serving the purpose of swinging the door while being beautifully ornamental and reinforcing the wood. Cathedral and palace doors of Europe have beautiful examples of the medieval strap hinge at its finest. Today ornamental hinges are rarely used except when simulating period furniture and architectural styles. Among the period strap hinges most frequently used are the 18th-

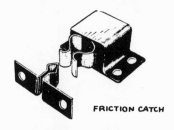

FRICTION CATCH

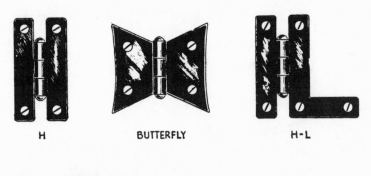

H         BUTTERFLY         H-L

BUTT STRAP

century American H-binge, butterfly, H-L-hinge, and ornamental butt-strap.

The butt hinge is probably used more often than any other type, being employed on doors ranging in size from large doors between rooms to small cabinet doors. There are two types of butt hinge: swaged and nonswaged, with the pin loose, tight, or half-tight. The swaged hinge permits the leaves to almost touch when closed; the nonswaged type produces a space between the leaves equal to the diameter of the knuckles. Loose and half-tight pins permit the door to be removed without removing the hinge—not possible with the tight-pin type. Cabinet and smaller doors are usually swung on tight-pin hinges, as they are seldom if ever removed. Narrow cabinet butt hinges are made to fit the lesser thicknesses of cabinet doors.

The width of a butt hinge is measured with the leaves open, including the knuckle; its length is the length of the leaves. There are a number of ways to attach a butt hinge: recessed flush; recessed deeper than flush by an amount half the thickness of the leaves; attached without recessing; or with only one leaf recessed.

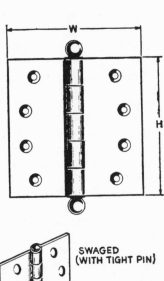

SWAGED
(WITH TIGHT PIN)

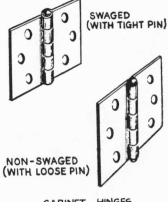

NON-SWAGED
(WITH LOOSE PIN)

CABINET HINGES

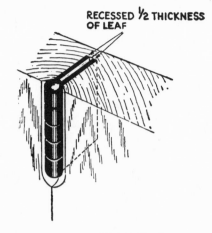

RECESSED ½ THICKNESS OF LEAF

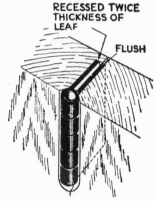

RECESSED TWICE THICKNESS OF LEAF

FLUSH

with unequal-width leaves, and chest hinges with one leaf offset.

When a door must fit with no possibility of sagging, there is the continuous, or piano, hinge, which comes in long

lengths and in sizes for anything from a cigarette case to a 10′ door. This type can be cut to the length needed.

A hinge leaf that shows should be recessed flush for a neat appearance, unless it's ornamental in design. Recessing deeper than flush by half the thickness of the leaves is done where a hinged edge must fit tightly and squarely against the other piece to support it, as in the case of a folding table leg on a wall drop-leaf table when the leaf is down. This can also be accomplished by recessing one leaf twice the thickness, but setting the other leaf flush.

With either method, notches the length of the knuckle and clearing it in depth must be cut in the hinged pieces.

Cabinet hinges are also made in semi-concealed and in full-surface design for flush and overlapping doors. These hinges have leaves of unequal width, one of which is offset. There are also table hinges

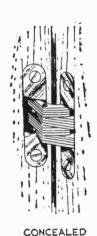

CONCEALED

Then there's the invisible cabinet hinge, which is of the knife type. This hinge must be recessed or mortised flush with the edge of the door and jamb, and operates by a series of pivoted flat metal plates. Minimum thickness of doors for the several sizes are: $\frac{9}{16}''$, $\frac{5}{8}''$, and $\frac{3}{4}''$. There is also a knife cabinet hinge used extensively on radio and TV cabinets,

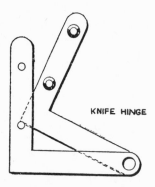

KNIFE HINGE

which is made of 2 flat metal strips offset and pivoted, with a stop to prevent the doors from swinging back too far. Unlike other hinges, this one is recessed flush at the top and bottom edges of the door.

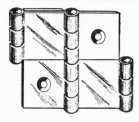

Screens for rooms are usually equipped with double-acting butt hinges which permit the screen sections to be swung right or left, or folded flat. And the kitchen swinging door has double-acting butt hinges with built-in springs to return the door to normal position.

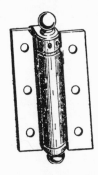

A comparatively new, light butt hinge has appeared on the market which

requires no mortising. One leaf is cut out in such a manner that the other leaf fits into it when the door is closed.

Strap hinges are used mostly on frame buildings where doors are heavier.

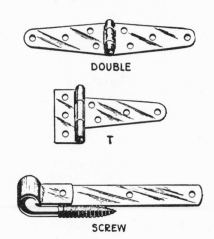

DOUBLE

T

SCREW

They are made in 3 types: double strap, T-strap, and screw strap. The screw strap has a long leaf, looped at the end, which fits over an L-shaped lag screw with a shoulder to support the strap.

## LUMBER

Wood has a complex cellular structure with characteristics as varied as the number and kinds of trees. Wood can, however, be classified as soft or hard, and as seasoned or unseasoned.

Lumber must be seasoned to be of any practical use in construction. This means it must be partially dried out to prevent excessive shrinkage, checking, and splitting. There was a time when all lumber was seasoned naturally, requiring at least a year, each piece being turned every few days. The result was a superior product with considerable elasticity not equaled by today's kiln-drying. Kiln-drying is an oven-heat process which cuts down the seasoning time to days instead of years. The result is satisfactory enough for all practical purposes, although it leaves the wood somewhat brittle because of this overly rapid drying process. You cannot bend a piece of kiln-dried lumber the way you can a naturally seasoned piece.

## Softwoods

Some of the most commonly used native softwoods are:

**Basswood.** Light, straight-grained, and of fine texture. It is easy to work, suitable for both turning and carving, and is used mostly for picture frames, molding, furniture, and toys.

**Cedar.** Light, fine-textured, with a beautiful grain. Works easily and takes a fine finish. It is used for moth-proof chests and closets, toys, furniture, shingles, exterior trim, sheathing, and siding.

**Cypress.** Easy to work and has a rich, reddish-brown color. It is highly weather-resistant, and is used for interior and exterior trim, inside and outside flooring, shingles, sheathing, and siding.

**Fir.** Stiff, strong, and even-textured. It has an orange-brown color and is used mostly for porch flooring, framing, roof boards, subflooring, and sheathing.

**Poplar.** Light and very soft. It is easy to work but is not too durable or suitable for rough handling. Used for interior trim, shelving, and laths.

**Gum.** Heavy, strong, and fine textured. It is usually cross-grained, and twists and warps easily when exposed to weather. It is used extensively for cheaper furniture and interior trim.

**Redwood.** Light and fairly strong, and takes a fine finish. It is very durable and is used for cabinet work, exterior trim, porch flooring, shelving, shingles, and siding.

**White Pine.** Very light and soft, and varies greatly in quality. It is very easy to work and is used for cabinets, interior trim, paneling, laths, sash, shelving, siding, and sheathing.

**Yellow Pine.** Varies considerably. It is light, medium hard, with a smooth but pronounced grain; works easily and is quite durable. It is used mostly for porch flooring, framing, interior trim, roof boards, and subflooring.

**White Spruce.** Light, stiff, and fairly strong; can be used for the same purposes as white pine.

## Hardwoods

The most commonly used hardwoods are:

**Maple.** Heavy, strong, and very hard. It has a fine texture, with wavy grain. It is fine for carving, turning, and scroll work. It takes a beautiful finish and is widely used for furniture, finished flooring, and occasionally shelving.

**Oak.** Very heavy, hard, strong, and durable. It has a strong tendency to check (grain opening at board ends). It is used for furniture, carving, exterior and interior trim, finished flooring, shelving, steps, and deluxe house framing.

**Birch.** Heavy, tough, close-grained, and very durable. It is frequently stained to imitate black walnut and mahogany, and is used extensively for furniture. Other uses are interior trim and shelving.

**Walnut.** Hard, heavy, and strong, with a smooth grain which works well and takes a fine polish. It is used largely for fine furniture and cabinet work; also for interior trim and occasionally shelving.

**Mahogany.** Light to dark reddish-brown, and fine-grained. It works easily with or against the grain, and takes one of the finest finishes. It is used for fine furniture and boats.

The suggested uses mentioned for both softwoods and hardwoods are for first choice only; many of them are often used for other projects. Almost every species of wood grows in a number of varieties. For example, pine has a number of relatives: northern white, western white,

## MEASUREMENTS FOR STANDARD SIZES OF YARD LUMBER
(Each standard width obtainable in all standard thicknesses)

| Product | Nominal Thickness (In.) | Nominal Width (In.) | Actual Thickness (In.) | Actual Width (In.) |
|---|---|---|---|---|
| Finish | — | 3 | $5/16$ | $2\frac{5}{8}$ |
| | — | 4 | $7/16$ | $3\frac{1}{2}$ |
| | — | 5 | $9/16$ | $4\frac{1}{2}$ |
| | — | 6 | $11/16$ | $5\frac{1}{2}$ |
| | 1 | 7 | $25/32$ | $6\frac{1}{2}$ |
| | $1\frac{1}{4}$ | 8 | $1\frac{1}{16}$ | $7\frac{1}{4}$ |
| | $1\frac{1}{2}$ | 9 | $1\frac{5}{16}$ | $8\frac{1}{4}$ |
| | $1\frac{3}{4}$ | 10 | $1\frac{7}{16}$ | $9\frac{1}{4}$ |
| | 2 | 11 | $1\frac{5}{8}$ | $10\frac{1}{4}$ |
| | $2\frac{1}{2}$ | 12 | $2\frac{1}{8}$ | $11\frac{1}{4}$ |
| | 3 | | $2\frac{5}{8}$ | |
| Common boards and strips | 1 | 3 | $25/32$ | $2\frac{5}{8}$ |
| | $1\frac{1}{4}$ | 4 | $1\frac{1}{16}$ | $3\frac{5}{8}$ |
| | $1\frac{1}{2}$ | 5 | $1\frac{5}{16}$ | $4\frac{5}{8}$ |
| | — | 6 | — | $5\frac{5}{8}$ |
| | — | 7 | — | $6\frac{5}{8}$ |
| | — | 8 | — | $7\frac{1}{2}$ |
| | — | 9 | — | $8\frac{1}{2}$ |
| | — | 10 | — | $9\frac{1}{2}$ |
| | — | 11 | — | $10\frac{1}{2}$ |
| | — | 12 | — | $11\frac{1}{2}$ |
| Dimension | 2 | 2 | $1\frac{5}{8}$ | $1\frac{5}{8}$ |
| | $2\frac{1}{2}$ | 4 | $2\frac{1}{8}$ | $3\frac{5}{8}$ |
| | 3 | 6 | $2\frac{5}{8}$ | $5\frac{5}{8}$ |
| | 4 | 8 | $3\frac{5}{8}$ | $7\frac{1}{2}$ |
| | 5 | 10 | $4\frac{5}{8}$ | $9\frac{1}{2}$ |

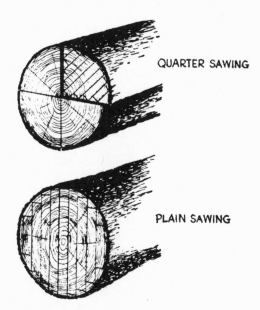

QUARTER SAWING

PLAIN SAWING

sugar, ponderosa, and southern yellow, each having its own characteristics. A fine softwood for all-round purposes in the home is western white pine, in its several grades.

## Sawing Logs

Logs are sawed into lumber by either plain sawing or quarter sawing, the latter method being used on some hardwoods, chiefly oak, to produce a distinctive grain which identifies this type of sawing. Quarter-sawed is superior to plain-sawed lumber, but quite expensive, as it is a wasteful method resulting in relatively narrow widths. The log is first cut into quarters and then sawed into boards by different methods of arrangement. At one

## MEASUREMENTS FOR STANDARD SIZES OF MACHINED LUMBER
(Each standard width obtainable in all standard thicknesses)

| Product | Nominal Thickness (In.) | Nominal Width (In.) | Actual Thickness (In.) | Actual Face Width (In.) |
|---|---|---|---|---|
| Bevel siding | | 4 | $7/16 \times 3/16$ | $3\frac{1}{2}$ |
| | | 5 | $5/8 \times 3/16$ | $4\frac{1}{2}$ |
| | | 6 | | $5\frac{1}{2}$ |
| Wide bevel siding | | 8 | $7/16 \times 3/16$ | $7\frac{1}{4}$ |
| | | 10 | $9/16 \times 3/16$ | $9\frac{1}{4}$ |
| | | 12 | $11/16 \times 3/16$ | $11\frac{1}{4}$ |
| Rustic and drop siding (shiplapped) | | 4 | $9/16$ | $3\frac{1}{8}$ |
| | | 5 | $3/4$ | $4\frac{1}{8}$ |
| | | 6 | | $5\frac{1}{16}$ |
| | | 8 | | $6\frac{7}{8}$ |
| Rustic and drop siding (D & M) | | 4 | $9/16$ | $3\frac{1}{4}$ |
| | | 5 | $3/4$ | $4\frac{1}{4}$ |
| | | 6 | | $5\frac{3}{16}$ |
| | | 8 | | 7 |
| Flooring (D & M) | | 2 | $5/16$ | $1\frac{1}{2}$ |
| | | 3 | $7/16$ | $2\frac{3}{8}$ |
| | | 4 | $9/16$ | $3\frac{1}{4}$ |
| | 1 | 5 | $25/32$ | $4\frac{1}{4}$ |
| | $1\frac{1}{4}$ | 6 | $1\frac{1}{16}$ | $5\frac{3}{16}$ |
| | $1\frac{1}{2}$ | | $1\frac{5}{16}$ | |
| Ceiling (D & M and shiplapped) | | 3 | $5/16$ | $2\frac{3}{8}$ |
| | | 4 | $7/16$ | $3\frac{1}{4}$ |
| | | 5 | $9/16$ | $4\frac{1}{4}$ |
| | | 6 | $11/16$ | $5\frac{3}{16}$ |
| Partition (D & M and shiplapped) | | 3 | $3/4$ | $2\frac{3}{8}$ |
| | | 4 | | $3\frac{1}{4}$ |
| | | 5 | | $4\frac{1}{4}$ |
| | | 6 | | $5\frac{3}{16}$ |
| Other (D & M) | 1 | 4 | $25/32$ | $3\frac{1}{4}$ |
| | $1\frac{1}{4}$ | 6 | $1\frac{1}{16}$ | $5\frac{1}{4}$ |
| | $1\frac{1}{2}$ | 8 | $1\frac{5}{16}$ | $7\frac{1}{4}$ |
| | | 10 | | $9\frac{1}{4}$ |
| | | 12 | | $11\frac{1}{4}$ |

Note: In all tongued-and-grooved flooring, and tongued-and-grooved and shiplapped ceiling, of $5/16$", $7/16$", and $9/16$" thickness, the tongue (lap) is $3/16$" wide, with face widths $3/16$" wider than listed.

In other machined material $11/16$", $3/4$", 1", and $1\frac{1}{2}$" thick, the tongue is $1/4$" wide in tongued-and-grooved lumber, and the lap $3/8$" wide in shiplapped lumber; and face widths are $1/4$" and $3/8$" wider, respectively, than listed.

time quarter sawing was extensively used for fine furniture and finished flooring.

Plain sawing produces lumber of two types of grain, flat and edge, depending on what portion of the annular rings (yearly growth rings) is sawed. There are also the heartwood (center rings--and the best) and the sapwood (outer rings). The best grade of shingle, for instance, is edge-grain-sawed; it has little or no warping tendency. It also costs more, since fewer pieces can be sawed out of a log. Flooring of hard and semihard woods comes in both flat grain and edge grain.

## Grades of Lumber

After the log has been sawed into planks, it is graded for imperfections in the wood. The best grade is called select, by the lumber industry, and in turn is divided into four qualifications: A, B, C, and D. "A-select" is by no means flawless, but is practically so. (No piece of lumber can be termed absolutely flawless.) The four select grades are top-quality lumber, the C and D grades having only minor imperfections which finishing usually covers.

Lumber further graded from this point is termed common, and is qualified by number: 1 through 5. Common grades 1, 2, and 3 are used for rough carpentry, such as house framing, which includes roof boarding and sheathing. Grades 4 and 5 can also be used, but there is considerable waste in cutting out bad imperfections. These terms may be confusing at first, but when ordering lumber from a yard, the language of the lumber industry must be used if you wish to be understood.

## Machining Lumber

Lumber as it comes from the mill saw is extremely rough and unusable for most woodworking projects. The mill, therefore, machines it—planes it smooth on one or more sides and edges. This planing is designated by the abbreviations S1S, S2S, S1E, S2E, and S4S. S1S means, for example, "Surfaced 1 Side"; S1E, "Surfaced 1 Edge;" S4S, "Surfaced 4 Sides." For lumber you plan to use around the home, get either A-select S4S, or No. 1 common S4S.

Sawed green lumber is denoted in even, half, or quarter inches (nominal size). However, when kiln-dried and surfaced smooth, its size is considerably less than the nominal dimensions. A nominal $2'' \times 4''$ stud actually measures $1\frac{5}{8}'' \times 3\frac{1}{2}''$, although it is called a $2'' \times 4''$—and so on.

## Board Foot

A board foot is defined as a piece of lumber 1″ or less thick, 12″ wide, 12″ long—a square foot. All lumber except moldings, splines, and screening strips is sold by the "foot" (board foot—square foot) on the basis of it being 1″ or less thick, nominal size. If no thickness is mentioned, it is assumed to be 1″ or less. A $1'' \times 12'' \times 12''$, a $2'' \times 6'' \times 12''$, and a $3'' \times 4'' \times 12''$, are all one foot, board measure, or one square foot. Again, rather confusing, but necessary to understand when ordering from a lumber yard. One final example: a $2'' \times 4'' \times 12''$ length of studding would be sold as 8 *board feet:*

$$2'' \times 4'' = 8'' = \frac{2}{3}' \times 12' = 8'$$

Moldings, screening strips, and splines are sold by the linear foot. Softwood lumber is sold in lengths of 2′ multiples (actual size). Hardwood usually comes in random lengths. You can usually save money by ordering "shorts," which most lumber yards have in odd lengths. The following are other terms used in the lumber industry:

Yard lumber: Less than 6″ thick

Structural timbers: 6″ or more thick and wide

Strips: Less than 2″ thick and less than 8″ wide

Boards: Less than 2″ thick, but 8″ or more wide

Dimension lumber: At least 2″ but less than 7″ thick—any width

Planks: At least 2″ but less than 4″ thick, 8″ or more wide

Scantlings: At least 4″ but less than 6″ thick, less than 8″ wide

Heavy joists: At least 4″ but less than 6″ thick. 8″ or more wide

## Moldings

Moldings are used to soften and ornament square edges and right-angle joints, to hide joints, and to add depth to flat faces. There are eight basic traditional forms, borrowed from Greek and Roman

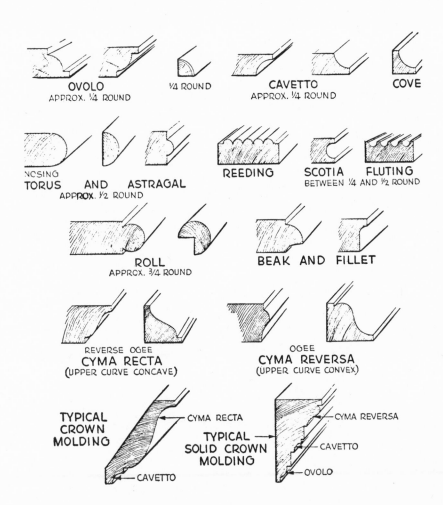

OVOLO
APPROX. ¼ ROUND

¼ ROUND

CAVETTO
APPROX. ¼ ROUND

COVE

NOSING
TORUS AND ASTRAGAL
APPROX. ½ ROUND

REEDING

SCOTIA FLUTING
BETWEEN ¼ AND ½ ROUND

ROLL
APPROX. ¾ ROUND

BEAK AND FILLET

REVERSE OGEE
CYMA RECTA
(UPPER CURVE CONCAVE)

OGEE
CYMA REVERSA
(UPPER CURVE CONVEX)

TYPICAL
CROWN
MOLDING

CYMA RECTA

CAVETTO

TYPICAL
SOLID CROWN
MOLDING

CYMA REVERSA

CAVETTO

OVOLO

classic architecture: ovolo; cavetto; torus and astragal; scotia; roll; beak and fillet; cyma recta; and cyma reversa. These forms, used singly and combined, produce an endless variety of molding forms for architectural embellishment and picture frames.

Modern designers use molding sparingly and of simple form, or none at all. The choice of molding depends on what type of home you have and what your personal taste may be.

For architectural purposes, lumber yards stock traditional and combined traditional molding forms, in both softwoods and hardwoods. They are stocked in many sizes and for every conceivable purpose. Space permits mention of only three of the most commonly used forms: quarter round, half round, and cove. Lumber yards also stock rounds which are not moldings. They are used when stock dowel lengths (36″) are not long enough, and for curtain and clothes poles, and usually are made from North Carolina pine and redwood (softwoods) or ash (hardwood). Diameters run from ½″ to 2¾″ in softwood, and from ⅞″ to 1¾″ in hardwood. Moldings are fastened either with finishing nails, set and covered, or flat-head wood screws, countersunk and covered.

## NUMBER OF BOARD FEET FOR VARIOUS LUMBER PIECES

| Nominal Size (in.) | Length (in.) | | | | | | | |
|---|---|---|---|---|---|---|---|---|
| | 10 | 12 | 14 | 16 | 18 | 20 | 22 | 24 |
| 1 × 2 | 1⅔ | 2 | 2⅓ | 2⅔ | 3 | 3⅓ | 3⅔ | 4 |
| 1 × 3 | 2½ | 3 | 3½ | 4 | 4½ | 5 | 5½ | 6 |
| 1 × 4 | 3⅓ | 4 | 4⅔ | 5⅓ | 6 | 6⅔ | 7⅓ | 8 |
| 1 × 5 | 4⅙ | 5 | 5⅚ | 6⅔ | 7½ | 8⅓ | 9⅙ | 10 |
| 1 × 6 | 5 | 6 | 7 | 8 | 9 | 10 | 11 | 12 |
| 1 × 7 | 5⅚ | 7 | 8⅙ | 9⅓ | 10½ | 11⅔ | 12⅚ | 14 |
| 1 × 8 | 6⅔ | 8 | 9⅓ | 10⅔ | 12 | 13⅓ | 14⅔ | 16 |
| 1 × 10 | 8⅓ | 10 | 11⅔ | 13⅓ | 15 | 16⅔ | 18⅓ | 20 |
| 1 × 12 | 10 | 12 | 14 | 16 | 18 | 20 | 22 | 24 |
| 1¼ × 4 | 4⅙ | 5 | 5⅚ | 6⅔ | 7½ | 8⅓ | 9⅙ | 10 |
| 1¼ × 6 | 6¼ | 7½ | 8¾ | 10 | 11¼ | 12½ | 13¾ | 15 |
| 1¼ × 8 | 8⅓ | 10 | 11⅔ | 13⅓ | 15 | 16⅔ | 18⅓ | 20 |
| 1¼ × 10 | 10⁵⁄₁₂ | 12½ | 14⁷⁄₁₂ | 16⅔ | 18¾ | 20⅚ | 22¹¹⁄₁₂ | 25 |
| 1¼ × 12 | 12½ | 15 | 17½ | 20 | 22½ | 25 | 27½ | 30 |
| 1½ × 4 | 5 | 6 | 7 | 8 | 9 | 10 | 11 | 12 |
| 1½ × 6 | 7½ | 9 | 10½ | 12 | 13½ | 15 | 16½ | 18 |
| 1½ × 8 | 10 | 12 | 14 | 16 | 18 | 20 | 22 | 24 |
| 1½ × 10 | 12½ | 15 | 17½ | 20 | 22½ | 25 | 27½ | 30 |
| 1½ × 12 | 15 | 18 | 21 | 24 | 27 | 30 | 33 | 36 |
| 2 × 4 | 6⅔ | 8 | 9⅓ | 10⅔ | 12 | 13⅓ | 14⅔ | 16 |
| 2 × 6 | 10 | 12 | 14 | 16 | 18 | 20 | 22 | 24 |
| 2 × 8 | 13⅓ | 16 | 18⅔ | 21⅓ | 24 | 26⅔ | 29⅓ | 32 |
| 2 × 10 | 16⅔ | 20 | 23⅓ | 26⅔ | 30 | 33⅓ | 36⅔ | 40 |
| 2 × 12 | 20 | 24 | 28 | 32 | 36 | 40 | 44 | 48 |
| 3 × 6 | 15 | 18 | 21 | 24 | 27 | 30 | 33 | 36 |
| 3 × 8 | 20 | 24 | 28 | 32 | 36 | 40 | 44 | 48 |
| 3 × 10 | 25 | 30 | 35 | 40 | 45 | 50 | 55 | 60 |
| 3 × 12 | 30 | 36 | 42 | 48 | 54 | 60 | 66 | 72 |
| 4 × 4 | 13⅓ | 16 | 18⅔ | 21⅓ | 24 | 26⅔ | 29⅓ | 32 |
| 4 × 6 | 20 | 24 | 28 | 32 | 36 | 40 | 44 | 48 |
| 4 × 8 | 26⅔ | 32 | 37⅓ | 42⅔ | 48 | 53⅓ | 58⅔ | 64 |
| 4 × 10 | 33⅓ | 40 | 46⅔ | 53⅓ | 60 | 66⅔ | 73⅓ | 80 |
| 4 × 12 | 40 | 48 | 56 | 64 | 72 | 80 | 88 | 96 |

## Plywood

Natural lumber is temperamental. It reacts unfavorably to temperature and moisture changes; and the wider and thinner the board, the greater its tendency to twist and warp. Wide-dimensional lumber is also difficult to obtain and costly because a wide board must come from a large tree, and fewer pieces are obtainable from that tree. Moreover, the grain pattern of natural lumber is limited. Thus, although natural lumber is absolutely essential to every type of wood construction, it has inherent disadvantages in its thinner and wider sizes.

To overcome these disadvantages, plywood as we know it today was developed. The idea stems from the ancient practice of veneering a wood surface to achieve patterned grain effects—the early Egyptians have left us some beautiful examples of veneered cabinet work. Modern manufacturing techniques are a vast improvement over these early efforts, for we now build houses out of plywood.

Plywood is natural wood in thin sheets and strips glued with plastic resins under heat and tremendous pressure, in such a manner that the grain of each layer runs at right angles to that of the next layer. On a weight-for-weight basis, plywood is stronger than steel; its great strength is due to its cross-grain construction, which distributes strain in two directions and eliminates splitting.

**Grain Effects.** Beautiful and unusual grain effects are possible with plywood because of the methods used in cutting the top veneer, which is basically of three types: rotary-cut, flat-sliced, and quarter-sliced.

Rotary cutting means peeling the log on giant lathes, similar to peeling the skin of a potato. This produces the "wild grain" usually seen in fir plywood because

ROTARY CUTTING

the peeling process follows the annual rings of the log. It has the advantage of producing exceptional widths. Flat slicing is done with the log first cut in half. Each half is then sliced by a razor-sharp blade, similar to slicing a potato for potato

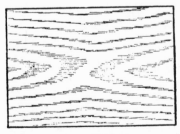

FLAT SLICING

chips. Flat-sliced veneer has a striped grain effect at the edges, changing to a larger, wild grain toward the center. Walnut is often cut in this manner.

Quarter slicing, an expensive method, is done similarly to flat slicing, but the log is quartered before slicing. This technique

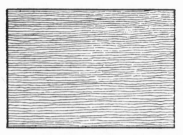

QUARTER SLICING

produces grain in straight stripes running the length of the veneer, due to cutting approximately at right angles to the annular rings. Quarter slicing is used for almost all the finer imported and for some domestic woods where a definite striped effect is wanted. Mahogany and vertical-grain cedar are examples.

**Grades.** There are two types of plywood veneer, softwood and hardwood; and basically two grades, interior grade and exterior grade. Interior grade is highly moisture-resistant, but not waterproof, and should not be used where unusually damp conditions exist. Exterior grade is bonded with phenolformaldehyde resin and is absolutely waterproof, making it excellent for exterior use where exposed to the weather, and for boat-building.

Softwood and hardwood veneer is also graded primarily as "Sound 1 Side" and "Sound 2 Side." As a rule, the first of these is fine for all practical purposes where only one face will show or is required to be flawless. In furniture-making, however, where two surfaces are exposed to view, sound veneer of the same species is obviously required on both surfaces—and is proportionately higher in cost.

**Striated Surface.** In recent years special patented treatments of plywood surfaces have been developed, capable of being combined in numerous ways for decorative effects. One such surface is striated, with a parallel striping, in re-

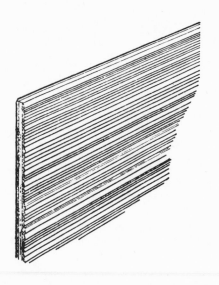

lief, the length of the panel. Used vertically, horizontally, or combined with mitered or butt joints in squares and other forms, it is quite "modern" and attractive for both interior and exterior use. The striations are mechanically produced, resulting in irregular-width beading which, in fir plywood—most often used—visually destroys the wild grain characteristic of rotary slicing.

**Laminated and Lumber Core.** Hardwood plywood veneer in the ¾″ thickness

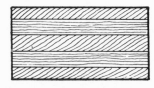

LAMINATED CORE

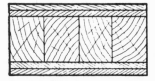

LUMBER CORE

is obtainable in two special forms known as laminated core and lumber core. The lumber core is usually fabricated, from solid basswood or poplar, of strips edge-glued, resulting in edges which do not require facing and hold screws, dowels, and splines very well. Facing plywood edges, laminated or lumber core, is a matter of personal taste—to disguise the fact that plywood has been used. These edges, if well sanded and filled with water-mix wood putty when necessary, are rather decorative.

The use of lumber core is being gradually discarded due to scarcity of material. It will probably be supplanted eventually by particleboard, a new, superior wood product of resin-bonded compressed wood chips, which is now obtainable in ⅜″ and ¾″ thicknesses for paneling, furniture, doors, and other structural purposes. It has no grain, but the glass-smooth surface of light tan or redwood color is beautifully mottled, producing something new in furniture and paneling surface patterns.

**Uses.** Plywood is used extensively for furniture, interior cabinets, counters, paneling, shelving, subflooring, and structural girders. For exterior work it is used for sheathing, roofing, finished-wall treatments, and outdoor furniture. In fact, many contemporary architectural designers specify that the entire home, excluding structural members such as sills, studs, joists, and rafters, be built of interior- and exterior-grade plywood.

## Particleboard

Also called chipboard, this is made of wood chips mixed with an adhesive and then put through a press to produce a dense composition board. Particleboard is extremely stable and will not warp readily; it is therefore superior to plywood for sliding doors, cabinet doors, counter tops, and other jobs where it is important to have complete stability. It can be worked with wood tools and comes in a standard 4′ × 8′ sheet ¾″ thick.

## Hardboard

This is a dense composition board made of wood fibers. It can be worked with wood tools and takes paint well. The standard sheet is 4′ × 8′ and comes in either ⅜″ or ¼″ thickness. It can be used for hundreds of jobs around the house. It is excellent as an underlayment for resilient and carpet flooring, for exterior siding, wall paneling, furniture backing, and so forth.

## Perforated Hardboard

This is the same as ordinary hardboard except that holes are drilled through it. It makes an ideal storage wall, as there are a variety of hangers made to accommodate all manner of items, from bookshelves to lawn mowers.

## Gypsum Wallboard

This is also called plasterboard, Sheet Rock (a trade name), and dry wall. It consists of a core of gypsum plaster covered with kraft paper. It has become the accepted surface material for interior walls and ceilings and has pretty much replaced plaster except in commercial construction. Installation is not difficult for the amateur (see chapter 13, page 313). The 4′ × 8′ sheets go up very fast with a minimum of mess, and when the joints are properly covered it is difficult to tell wallboard from a wall made of plaster. Sheets come in ⅜″ and ½″ thicknesses.

## Asbestos Boards

These are 4′ × 8′ sheets made of asbestos fibers and cement. The boards are both fire- and moisture-resistant and are excellent for both interior and exterior work where these particular qualities are important. The board can be cut with a saw; the work goes faster if you keep the blade moist with water. Holes for nails and screws should be predrilled.

The woods listed in the accompanying table come in a variety of plywood cuts and grain patterns. The usual panel size is 48″ × 96″, but some woods are also available (though not stocked everywhere) in variant sizes.

### PLYWOOD VENEERS AND THICKNESSES[a]

| Product | Thickness (in.) | | | | | | | | Striated | |
|---|---|---|---|---|---|---|---|---|---|---|
| | ⅛ | ¼ | 5/16 | ⅜ | ½ | ⅝ | ¾ | 13/16 | 7/16 | ⅜ |
| **Softwoods:** | | | | | | | | | | |
| Douglas fir | | I-E | I | I-E | I-E | I-E | I-E | | I | E |
| California pine | | I | | I | I | I | I | I | | |
| Idaho knotty pine | | I | | | | | I | | | |
| Sitka spruce | | I | | I | I | I | I | I | | |
| Cedar | | I | | | | | | | | |
| **Hardwoods:** | | | | | | | | | | |
| Maple | | I | | I | | | I-E | | | |
| Oak | I | I | | I | I | | I-E | | | |
| Walnut | I | I | | I | I | | I-E | | | |
| Birch | I | I | | I | I | | I-E | | | |
| Southern gum | I | I | | I | I | | I | I | | |
| American elm | | I | | | | | | | | |
| Philippine mahogany | | I | | I | | | I | I | | |
| African mahogany | I | I | | I | I | | I-E | | | |
| Korina | I | I | | I | | | I-E | | | |
| Primavera | I | I | | | | | I-E | | | |

[a] I = Interior grade.
E = Exterior grade.

# 3

# SIMPLE CARPENTRY

## WOOD JOINTS

There are many methods of joining two or more pieces of wood. Some joints are easy to make; others require considerable craftsmanship. All, however, require care when laying them out. The marking gauge, try (or combination) square, T-bevel, and a sharp knife for marking, are necessary for accurate layout.

The simplest method of joining two pieces of wood is the plain lap. You simply lay one piece over the other and screw or nail, or glue (or both). This joint is as strong as the fasteners used. It is one of the most common framing methods in house construction.

The butt joint is another often used method, particularly in house framing. As a joint for only two pieces of wood it is the weakest of all, being simply the end of one piece butted against the face of another. Since the end is, for joining purposes, the weakest part of a piece of wood, the joint can be no stronger than the characteristics of the end grain. Nails in end grain pull out easily, and few glues hold well because it soaks up the glue. Screws

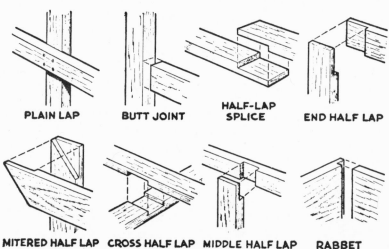

PLAIN LAP          BUTT JOINT          HALF-LAP SPLICE          END HALF LAP

MITERED HALF LAP   CROSS HALF LAP   MIDDLE HALF LAP   RABBET hold best, if large and long enough. A combination of glue and screws makes the butt joint strong enough for most purposes where pulling strain is not excessive. In house framing, butt joints are usually toenailed, strengthening the joint. For cabinet work, butt joints are usually reinforced with glued corner blocks, if the joints are hidden.

A half-lap splice is used to make one length from two pieces of wood when the faces must be flush. It is a stronger joint than that made by laying one piece over the other, as the shoulders, if they fit properly, act somewhat as a lock, preventing any pivoting tendency. The laps should be long enough to have adequate bearing surfaces.

An end half lap is used for window, screen door, and other frames. It is a strong corner joint if properly fitted, preventing any pivoting or slipping tendencies. It does, however, expose end grain at both corners.

A half-lap splice or an end half lap is easily made by gauging the work with a marking gauge and sawing out the laps, preferably with a back saw. Be sure to saw on the waste side of the line; otherwise the laps will be oversize by the thickness of the saw.

The mitered half lap, used on corners to hide one end-grain face, makes a neat 45-degree-angle joint for a flat-surface face. It is used for frames of various kinds, excluding picture frames, but is not quite as strong as the half lap, lacking the same amount of joining surface. To make a mitered half lap, gauge the work and first saw the miter on one piece to a depth of half the thickness. Then saw out the lap to the miter cut. The other piece can be made as a straight lap and then mitered, using your miter box.

Cross half-lap joints are used for joining two crossed pieces to obtain flush faces. Each piece is notched, or dadoed, to half its thickness. This joint adds strength to the pieces, locking them together. For the cross half lap, saw to a depth of half

the thickness of the stock and remove the wood between the cuts with a chisel.

The middle half lap is used to join bracing members between frames, forming a strong T-joint. To make a middle half lap, saw out the end lap on one piece, and chisel out the middle lap on the other piece as for a cross half lap.

A rabbet is made by cutting out one piece to receive flush the edge of the other. It is used a lot for drawers, cabinets, and the like, concealing one end-grain edge and preventing a twisting tendency of the joint. The backs of most cabinets are joined this way, with the end grain facing the rear.

**Dadoes.** The dado is a groove, either across or lengthwise with the grain, usually to receive the butt end of another piece. This joint provides a supporting ledge for the fitting piece and, in best practice, is used for shelves and the like, where downward pressure is exerted. A

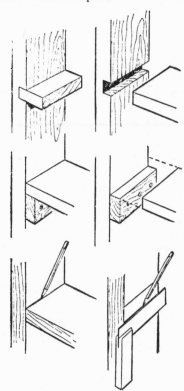

dado requires only glue for fastening and therefore has great utility where fasteners cannot be used. The only alternative for shelves between uprights is to butt-join them against the uprights and use supporting pieces framed under the shelves and against the uprights; this method is more frequently used than dadoing.

A dado is made by sawing its sides to the depth required and then removing the waste with a chisel or—much more easily —with a combination plane, or router. Use the piece to be fitted in the dado as a marking guide and then square the lines with a square before making a cut.

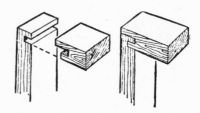

An end dado locks the two pieces, a decided improvement over the rabbet; but here again, for ordinary purposes it is hardly worthwhile going to all the trouble to make this joint by hand.

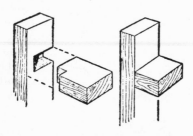

A stopped dado extends to only one edge of the piece. This requires the fitting piece to be notched out to butt against the receiving piece. When making a stopped dado, first remove a portion of the stopped end with a chisel before sawing the sides with a back saw. The dado is, of course, marked out before any cutting is done.

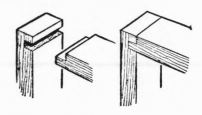

The dado-and-rabbet joint works as well as the end dado and is not difficult to make, requiring only a groove in one piece and a rabbet in the other. Like the end dado, it is much stronger than a plain rabbeted joint.

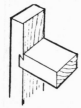

DOVETAILED DADO

The dovetailed dado adds additional strength to the common dado. It is a difficult joint to make with hand tools, and for all practical purposes the common dado is quite adequate.

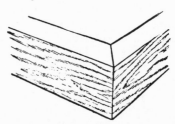

**Miter Joints.** A miter joint is a 45-degree-angle joint which hides end grain on both pieces. It is the only joint possible for picture frames and moldings of all kinds where molding contours continue around corners. The edges of fine furniture also, are always mitered. It is a very weak joint, however, without some reinforcing adjunct, as only edge-grain surfaces are in contact. For long miter joints, gluing strips are usually used, if they can be hidden.

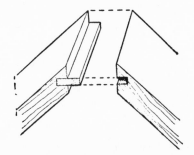

THROUGH
SINGLE
DOVETAIL

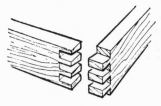

THROUGH MULTIPLE DOVETAIL

This joint requires accurate cutting, as the slightest variation in angle between the joined pieces results in a poor joint or an off-square corner. Mitered pieces are frequently splined—the miter edges grooved to receive a narrow strip, or spline. Another method is to use a "feather," which is similar to a spline but wider and thinner, the grooves usually only the thickness of the saw kerf. Where mitered pieces are framed against other material, as in moldings and the like, these reinforcements are not necessary.

The through multiple dovetail joint is a series of single dovetails of small dimensions. With modern glues and other methods of fastening, this joint is hardly worth the effort, save in the satisfaction of accomplishing a craftsmanlike job on a corner joint.

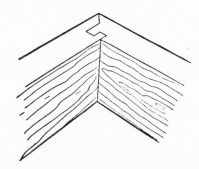

HALF-BLIND DOVETAIL

The lock miter joint requires no reinforcing, but obviously it is not worth attempting on long edges with hand tools.

## Dovetail Joints

A through single dovetail joint is the easiest of dovetail joints to make. It is a locked joint (in one direction), but as 7 joints show on the combined faces there is not much reason for making it, unless extreme pulling stresses occur against the locked side.

A half-blind dovetail is used for drawer fronts in fine cabinet work. Since the drawer front receives most of the strain against the contents of the drawer when pulled out, this dovetail is of sound value. It requires extreme care in laying out and cutting, as the meshing pieces must fit accurately. It is not a "must," however, as a rabbeted drawer front, *glued and screwed,* will work as well and can be accomplished with no particular woodworking skill.

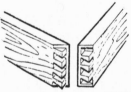

BLIND DOVETAIL

The blind dovetail is an extremely tricky job of woodworking, as the dove-tailing is hidden by the mitered shoulders of the joint. It is used in the finest cabinet work where the craftsman really wishes to show his skill.

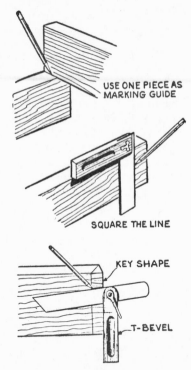

USE ONE PIECE AS MARKING GUIDE

SQUARE THE LINE

KEY SHAPE

T-BEVEL

When making dovetail joints, use one of the pieces as a marking guide for the depth of the pins and sockets, and square the line with a square. The key-shaped pins and corresponding sockets are best laid out with a T-bevel, which is set for the desired socket angle and then turned over to mark the opposite angle for the key shape. The sockets and pins are sawed with a back saw, and the bottoms of the sockets cut with a chisel.

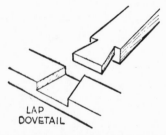

LAP DOVETAIL

A lap dovetail is a locked middle half lap of top-quality craftsmanship. It is as easy to make as the latter, mostly with the saw, and requires very little extra time to lay out.

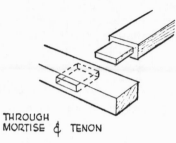

THROUGH MORTISE & TENON

The through mortise and tenon is a superior T-joint, possible only with stock thick enough to make a strong joint. The mortise is a square or rectangular hole which receives a shouldered tongue, or tenon. It is frequently pinned with a wooden peg. This joint was the most commonly used method of framing 18th-century houses and barns—which, after 200 or more years, are still as sound in the joints as when originally framed!

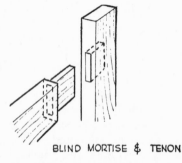

BLIND MORTISE & TENON

The blind mortise and tenon is the same as the above, but with the mortise and tenon extending only part way into the wood. When assembled it looks like an ordinary butt joint.

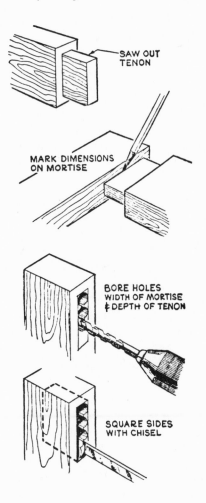

SAW OUT TENON

MARK DIMENSIONS ON MORTISE

BORE HOLES WIDTH OF MORTISE & DEPTH OF TENON

SQUARE SIDES WITH CHISEL

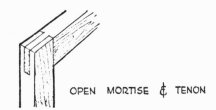

OPEN MORTISE & TENON

joint is assembled and the pin driven in, it will draw the shoulder of the tenon tightly against the receiving piece.

An open mortise and tenon is another type of corner joint, with greater locking power than the end half lap. It is also used for splicing instead of the half-lap splice. Well-made frames of various kinds, other than picture frames, are joined in this way. Use a saw and chisel to make it.

## Dowel Joint

The dowel point transforms a weak joint into a strong one. Dowels come in stock diameters from $\frac{1}{8}''$ to $1''$, all $36''$ long, and usually made of hardwood.

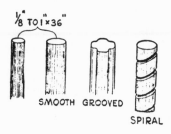

$\frac{1}{8}$" TO 1"×36"

SMOOTH    GROOVED

SPIRAL

To make a mortise-and-tenon joint, first saw out the tenon. Then use it to mark the dimensions of the mortise. Bore a series of holes the width of the mortise and, using a depth gauge, to the depth of the tenon, and square the sides with a chisel. If you plan to pin the tenon, first bore the hole for the pin through the mortise. Insert the tenon and mark the location of the hole on it. Remove the tenon and bore the hole *just off center* and toward the shoulder. Then, when the

Lumber yards and many hardware stores stock dowels in the more popular smaller sizes. Some stores also stock short lengths of spiral dowels made especially for gluing. The reason for the spiral is so that glue can fill in the grooves for better adhesion. A dowel which is to be glued should *not* fit the hole tightly; otherwise when the pieces are joined the glue is squeezed out. A sliding fit is best. If the dowel is not spiraled when purchased, cut

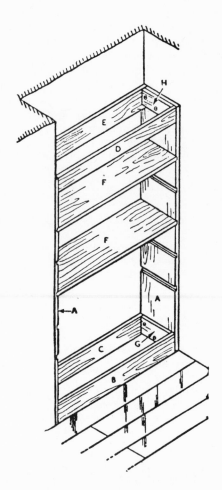

spirals in it with the corner of a file, by holding the file at an oblique angle and turning the dowel as you file. Shallow grooves are sufficient. A dowel should be slightly shorter than the depth of the hole.

There are other, more complicated wood joints, all stemming from the basic ones described. Most of them require the skill of a master craftsman or the use of power tools. Modern glues, being stronger than wood itself, together with screws have to a great extent replaced most of the intricate wood joints of the cabinet-maker's art—at least where the amateur craftsman is concerned. It is, however, a matter of pride and joy forever to make a perfect dovetail joint, and for this reason well worth trying. If you have ever had the opportunity of examining a drawer of a cabinet made by an 18th-century crafts-man, you will agree that the almost paper-thin pins of his dovetail joints are a lasting tribute to his incredible skill with saw and chisel.

## SINGLE-TIER BOOKSHELVES

A simple tier of bookshelves can be built into a wall recess. The tier shown in the accompanying illustration is about 6½' high. Shelves in a bookcase should be deep enough for medium-sized books—7" or more. (The shelves in the illustration are 13½" deep. The recess is assumed to be 4' wide and 13½" deep.) Bring the top of the structure a few inches below the line of the picture molding. This will avoid the difficult problem of lining up the cornice with the picture molding, which seldom looks well.

### Preliminary Work

Remove the baseboard in the recess. Cut a piece of ¾" × 1" stock so that it will fit easily into the recess from wall to wall near the floor. Test the width of the recess with this rod at, say, 3' and 6' above the floor. This will disclose whether or not the walls are reasonably free from bulges. The sides of the shelving will have to be vertical when fixed but must be close against the wall (at the sides of the recess). If the wall bulges a little at about the 3' height, insert some packing or wedges at top and bottom in order to bring the woodwork vertical and to give a firm backing. Likewise, if the wall is hollow or concave at a midway point, but is satisfactory at higher and lower levels, insert packing between the woodwork and wall at the concave position. This packing should consist of pieces of thin plywood, or layers split from plywood, cut down to give a firm backing at the required place.

Make a gauge rod by cutting a piece of stock about 7' long and squaring the ends. Sweep out the floor of the recess, test the floor with a spirit level, and if necessary nail down a thin strip of wood at one side to bring the two sides level. Test for level also from front to back and make any similar adjustment which may be necessary. These preliminary details may seem tedious, but no satisfactory work can be done if we ignore them. Next, mark on the gauge rod the distance from the top edge of the molding to the floor line. Note that this line is the *leveled* line at which the foot of the bookshelf upright stands, and it denotes, in fact, the lower edge of the bookshelf sides.

Mark the positions of the shelves, indicating the top side of each shelf. Mark off the position of the top edge of the bookshelf sides at 6½'—if that is the height selected. All these lines should be squared across the front face of the gauge rod and carried around one adjoining face. We will use the rod to mark the lumber.

## Lumber

One-inch tongued-and-grooved boards are as good material as any for the sides and shelves (for a shelf length up to 4'). If the wood for the shelves is too thin, they will sag in the course of time. The boards also must be wide enough to fill

the depth of the recess when the tongues are fitted into the grooves and the tongue on the outermost board has been sawed off. Remember that tongued-and-grooved boards of nominal 6" width will be only about 5½" when fitted, as the tongue is cut out of the 6" width; in other words, 2 such boards when fitted together will have a total width of only 11". You may find it convenient to have the lumber yard saw a board for each side, in order to get the desired final width.

In assembling the bookshelf sides, put the grooved edge of one board at the back, and the tongues on all the boards will face the front. If a board has to be sawed to obtain the proper width, it will have a plain edge at the front. If a board of ordinary width can be used, the tongue must be sawed off or taken off with a jack plane—perhaps the easiest method for a novice. The same considerations apply when making up the shelves.

## Assembling the Sides

Saw the boards for the sides to length. Put one set together and stand it in the recess, close against the wall. Have an assistant hold it while testing for vertical position, and note where any packing may be required. This gives an opportunity to see whether or not the front edge comes in line with the front of the recess. If the edges protrude slightly when the sides are in place, remove the surplus material with a plane. It may be advisable to make the width of the sides a fraction less than the depth of the recess from front to back.

On referring to the illustration, it will be seen that C is fitted between the sides at the rear, and that a similar board B parallels it at the front. Note also the similar members D and E at the top. Between B and C and between D and E, short pieces of wood G and H should be fixed to the sides by screws after the side boards are assembled and glued. Besides serving as a stop for attaching the members B,C and D,E, these short strips hold the side boards in place. The sides A should be notched out at the back edge to fit around the members C and E, which extend from one side wall of the recess to the other. The members B and D fit between the sides A and are nailed to the front end of the short strips G and H.

Clean the sides A for assembly. Have some good wood glue ready, and a pair of adjustable wood clamps. Glue the tongues and grooves and put the boards together with a sliding movement to squeeze out any surplus glue. Lay the side assembly on a level surface and apply clamps near top and bottom to pull the joints together. If the clamps tend to open the joint midway, ease one clamp slightly and move it along a few inches. Tack strips of wood across the side at two places to secure the boards temporarily. Put on the battens G and H (previously prepared, with screw holes bored and countersunk), then screw on firmly. Lay the assembled side on a level floor in a warm room to dry and set. Assemble the other side in the same manner.

## Assembling the Shelves

Assemble the shelf boards, putting them together with glue and clamps. If you lack sufficient clamps, use those you have to hold the boards until you can attach short strips of wood to hold them together, as suggested above. The net length of the shelf must be decided, of course. Whatever the distance between the inner faces of the sides when standing in place in the recess, add ½″ for the depth of 2 grooves (each ¼″ deep); this will give the extreme length of the shelves. It is safer to make the shelves about 2″ longer and then saw them to actual length when the sides have been fixed to the recess walls. These 2″ extra allow for final cuts at each end.

**Grooves for Shelves.** When the sides have set hard, lay them down on edge, face to face, and hold them together with a pair of clamps. If a bench is available, fix the 2 sides in the vise and support the farther ends with a stool or bench.

Place the gauge rod on top and transfer the markings for the top faces of the shelves. Make these marks on the front edge of the side assemblies and mark both at the same time. Take off the clamps and square the marks across the inner faces of the sides. Remember that the marks indicate the location of the top face of the shelf. Measure the exact thickness of the shelf boards. If they vary, and they may, take the thickness for each shelf separately and mark them 1, 2, 3, and so on, so that you may fit them in their proper grooves. Mark these thicknesses on the side boards by squaring lines across the front edge and inner face, *below* the shelf lines previously drawn. The distance between each pair of lines on the side boards should equal thickness of shelf.

Set a marking gauge to a bare ¼″ and scribe this distance on the edges of the side boards, front and back, where the parallel lines have been penciled. Use a fine-pointed, hard pencil for marking or, better, a fine scriber. Use a fine-toothed back or tenon saw to outline the grooves. Saw down the ¼″ depth lines on the edges, then across the face of the boards. Take out the waste wood with a sharp paring chisel of suitable width. Be careful not to make the grooves too deep. At the back of the side boards cut out notches to receive the boards C and E.

**Installing the Shelves.** Put the board C in place at the back of the recess; stand the two sides in place, fitted over C. With someone holding the sides, fit the top board E in place and mark its position on the back wall. Ease the notches if necessary. Mark the position of E by a pencil line on the wall at top and bottom edges. Bore 2 holes through E, about 6″ from each end. To secure E to a plaster wall, you will have to use rawl plugs. Mark through the holes the points for drilling. If an assistant holds the sides in place while all this is done, so much the better.

Take down the sides, drill holes in the wall, and insert the plugs and screws. Use No. 12 iron screws, flathead, about 1¾″ long. Fix boards E and C, secured to the wall in the same way.

Try the sides in place again. If correct, remove the right-hand one and bore it for 3 screws, one midway, the others about 6″ from floor and top line. Be sure they are clear of the grooves. Mark the wall for rawl plugs; drill; secure the side to the wall. Fasten the other side in the same manner. Fix B and D in place, secured to G and H. Board B will be about 1″ lower than the top of the molding attached later to the sides. The depth of the board D will depend on that of the molding used as a cornice. This cornice should be far enough above D to permit a dust board made of plywood, seated on top of D, E, and A, to fit behind the cornice and be flush with the top of the cornice.

Put in the shelves one by one. They should fit tight enough for a gentle tap with a wood mallet to drive them into position. Try a shelf in its groove; ease the ends with a smoothing plane (or a block plane if available), should this be necessary. Hold a smooth piece of wood against the front edge of the shelf and tap against this with a mallet.

Cut the bottom shelf to fit snugly in place and screw it to the top edges of B, C, and G. This shelf should be flush with the front edges of the side boards. Screw on the trim, fix the cornice and dust board in place, sand your work with 2 grades of sandpaper used in succession, and you are ready for staining and varnishing.

You can achieve a handsome, finished appearance by facing the edges of the side pieces and the shelves with strips of oak, walnut, or mahogany, about 1¼″ deep, and by using the same wood for trim and cornice. Groove the strips of hardwood so that they fit over the tongue of the lumber used in the construction of the bookshelf.

After the shelving has been completed, fix a strip of molding to align with the baseboard and chamfer the ends of this molding to match the pattern used for the front face. The baseboard and molding are now aligned, but they are marked off from each other by the slight molding of the abutting ends. Details such as these are large factors in the appearance of the work.

## SHORT BOOKSHELVES

The illustration shows a set of shelves 3′ high, 23″ wide, and 6½″ deep. The principles here used can be applied to larger constructions, but the span should not exceed 3′ between the sides, and the wood in such case should not be less than 1″ thick for the actual shelves. In the fittings illustrated, the outer members are from 1″ board, while the shelves are ¾″ thick. Cut out the sides, 1″ less in height than the

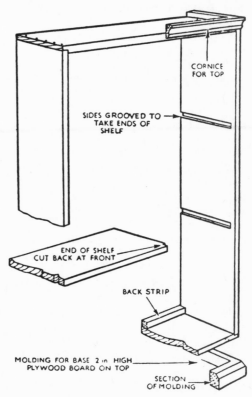

CORNICE FOR TOP

SIDES GROOVED TO TAKE ENDS OF SHELF

END OF SHELF CUT BACK AT FRONT

BACK STRIP

MOLDING FOR BASE 2 in HIGH PLYWOOD BOARD ON TOP

SECTION OF MOLDING

total overall height; but cut the top and bottom boards to full width.

Use a marking gauge to scribe the line for the rabbet at each end of both top and bottom boards, a little less than $\frac{1}{2}''$ deep and extending back from the end to the width of the side boards. Saw across with a tenon saw to the proper depth and remove the waste wood by chisel or saw it out with a fine saw, cutting entirely in the waste wood. Smooth off the rabbet with a rabbet plane, if one is at hand, or use a broad chisel, and finish with coarse sandpaper wrapped around a block of wood.

Cut and fit all rabbet joints, and carefully square off the ends of the side boards. Do not fix together yet. Cut the 2 shelves to length, allowing for the depth of the housings, or dadoes, into which the shelf ends fit. Cut out these dadoes, of a size to receive the thickness of the shelf boards. It will be seen that the dado ends are about $\frac{3}{4}''$ from the front of the bookcase, so that no groove will show from the front.

Make 2 saw cuts for each groove, working from the back of the side boards and going down as far as the saw will allow; then finish the work with a chisel of the proper width, first deepening the saw cuts at the front end, where the saw has not cut to full depth. Use the chisel to separate the waste into small portions by midway cuts from the face of the board and also to chisel out the waste and gradually form the groove. Avoid making the dado too wide for the board; it is better to have the dado a little tight and to pare off the end of the board that will go into the dado. Fit each board to its intended dado; they are sure to vary slightly, and when once fitted should be marked.

Having made sure the shelves will fit, and can be driven in from the back with light blows of a mallet, we can assemble the outside 4 members and nail them, through the top and bottom, into the ends of the vertical pieces. Bore holes with a fine brad awl a little smaller than the nails. Two-inch finishing nails are suita-

ble, the heads being invisible after a slight punch with a nail set. Next, tap in the shelves, inserting them from the back. Any defect in fit will force out the sides, so work carefully and pare the shelf if necessary. A little glue can be used on the ends if desired, though nails put in from the side boards will hold them quite firmly.

Screw down at the bottom of the bookcase a strip of wood; on this, and on the top edge of the base molding, nail a board cut from plywood. This comes flush at front and back. The base molding is a piece $1'' \times 2''$, planed to a bevel at the top edge and mitered. It is nailed to the front and sides. The board at the back must align with the top of the base molding, and the latter, for about half of its thickness, must be square at the top, to provide a seating for the plywood. When nailing the latter, use veneer pins, having bored holes first.

Finish the top of the bookcase with a piece of molding to form a cornice; miter and pin it to the sides and to the edge of the top member of the frame. Cut a sheet of plywood to cover the entire back of the bookcase and attach with veneer pins.

The piece may then be sanded, stained to match the other furniture in the room, and given a finish of either shellac or varnish.

## 2-TIER BOOKCASE

Each tier of this bookcase can be built in such a way that it can be dismantled and reerected, and each can stand free in a recess—not secured to the wall. In the illustration, the depth of the recess has again been taken as $13\frac{1}{2}''$. The bottom shelf is $13\frac{1}{2}''$ deep; the top shelf is $8\frac{1}{4}''$ deep.

The preliminary work and the shelving are much the same as for the bookshelves previously described, but the sides are spaced in from the recess walls by the blocking pieces E. These pieces, plus the

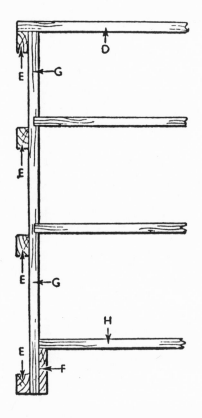

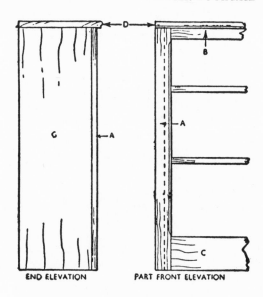

END ELEVATION          PART FRONT ELEVATION

thickness of the side boards G, equal the width of the hardwood facing on the sides A. Screw the blocking pieces E to the outside of G, but otherwise follow the procedure previously outlined for assembling and shelving. Screw bottom boards F to the bottom of the uprights of the lower tier to support the bottom shelf H. This shelf is situated behind, and level with the top of, the facing piece C. The facing C should be tenoned into A, or halved enough to make a sound and neat joint.

After you have glued and assembled the sides of the lower tier and attached the blocking pieces E, stand the sides in the recess and screw down the top board D. Screw the bottom shelf H to boards F. This lower tier should fit easily into the recess and is not normally secured to the walls; but should it be necessary, you can insert backboards at the top and at the floor line—as C and E in the single-tier

shelves (see page 50)—and attach them to the wall by means of rawl plugs.

**Top Tier.** Prepare the top tier. Backboards (not shown) may be needed at the bottom and at the top; fit these in the same manner as C and E on page 50. Insert the shelves after the top tier has been placed in position on top of the board D of the lower tier. The entire assembly should stand firmly, but if necessary you can screw 2 brass mirror plates to the backboards and to the wall with rawl plugs. This will not be necessary, however, if the bookcase stands tightly in the recess.

**Hardwood Facing.** Use hardwood facing pieces on the front edges A of the sides; face the rest of the front framing in hardwood to match. The front of D should also be of hardwood.

Join the rail B and trim C (shown above) in some simple manner for neatness. You can do this by forming tenons, or projecting tongues made by cutting away the wood, and inserting the tenons into mortises cut from the rails; you may also join them by short halved joints, at the corners. Screw the trim to the sides G with fine screws (No. 6), countersink, and plug

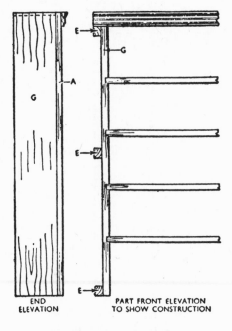

END
ELEVATION

PART FRONT ELEVATION
TO SHOW CONSTRUCTION

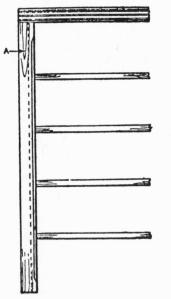

the holes with similar plastic wood stained to match the rest. To further improve the appearance of the bookcase, face the edges of the shelves with hardwood strips to show the same grain as the front framework.

Fix a simple cornice at the top of the upper tier, with a rail behind it—like B on page 55. Screw on a dust board. Dusting will be easier if the top of the dust board is made flush with the top edge of the cornice, fitting behind the latter. When the bookcase is fully erected, you may want to put a small molding around the feet of the top tier. Use quarter-round molding about 3/8″ across the flat face for this; miter or bevel it to fit and secure it to D with veneer pins.

**Variations.** The bookcases as illustrated, are each of moderate height, but the number of shelves and the height may be varied to suit individual requirements. Where the depth of the recess is great, it will be found more practicable not to carry the shelves back to the full depth. To eliminate an unsightly gap behind the bookcase, secure a thin sheet of plywood to it. You can carry the topmost shelf to the full depth of the recess, but if the top of the bookcase extends beyond the rest, it will be necessary to secure a light wooden batten to each of the side walls of the recess.

# VALANCE

The use of the valance in window treatment should be confined to those windows which are greater in height than in width. The wide, short window which one meets in some houses is much better treated simply with curtains and without valances.

The designing, making, and fitting of window valances form one of the most interesting and useful jobs the handyman can undertake to improve the appearance of a room.

A valance may be of either fabric or wood, the latter being most useful in effecting the more formal and simple designs.

The making of a wooden valance is very simple. It is a 3-sided box of 3/4″ plywood, and the formal pattern is made on the facing piece. Hardwood, such as oak, walnut, or mahogany, should be used

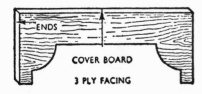

ENDS

COVER BOARD

3 PLY FACING

for the job and then stained and polished, or it may be constructed of softwood and painted to match the other woodwork in the room.

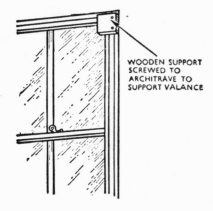

WOODEN SUPPORT SCREWED TO ARCHITRAVE TO SUPPORT VALANCE

The valance should be deep enough to enclose the hanging device from which the curtains are suspended, say 3" or 4", and it may be conveniently fixed to metal brackets fixed to the architrave, or frame of the window, or to wooden supports screwed to the edge of the frame. A very heavy valance may cause too much strain on the window molding, and an alternative method is to fix it to the wall by means of rawl plugs.

Strictly formal designs are most suitable for use with tall, narrow windows and with French casement doors.

An even simpler form of wooden valance may be made by the use of deep section molding, which may be purchased and cut to length with miter joints to suit the angles and length required. This method of constructing a valance is particularly suited to a bay window, being both effective and unobtrusive in appearance. This type of valance is, of course, very

suitable in many cases for use with the ordinary double hung window.

A valance made of fabric to match the curtains and permit less formality in design may be used in a variety of ways. Care should be taken, though, to avoid any suggestion of Victorian fussiness caused through overelaboration. Whatever fabric is used, it will be necessary to provide a lining or backing. Buckram made especially for this purpose is the most suitable and may be bought in widths up to a yard. Buckram linings are essential for heavy fabrics, such as velvets. For lighter materials such as silks or cottons, heavy calico sheeting is good enough. The covering fabric is stitched to the lining after the shape has been cut out of both. In the case of buckram, hand stitching is to be preferred as it is beyond the capabilities of the ordinary sewing machine. The edges of the valance may be finished with a narrow braid.

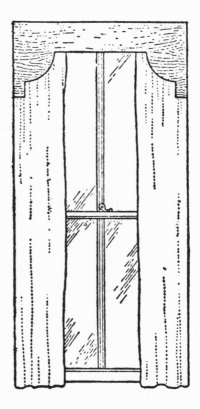

In order to ensure symmetry of design at both ends of the valance, it is advisable to cut a pattern out of stiff paper or cardboard and use the same pattern at both ends.

A point to remember is that a calico lining may be washed with the fabric cover attached, but a buckram lining will have to be detached for washing as the buckram is stiffened with a glue solution. On the whole, it is better to make a valance from washable material, so that it may be renovated whenever necessary. When installing such a valance always be sure it can be removed without damage to the valance material.

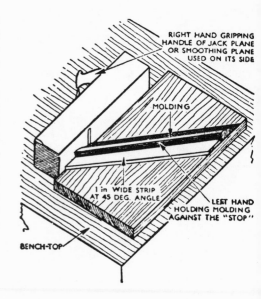

RIGHT HAND GRIPPING HANDLE OF JACK PLANE OR SMOOTHING PLANE USED ON ITS SIDE

MOLDING

1 in WIDE STRIP AT 45 DEG. ANGLE

LEFT HAND HOLDING MOLDING AGAINST THE "STOP"

BENCH-TOP

## PICTURE FRAME

In estimating the length of molding required for making a wooden picture frame, the basis is the length and width of the picture plus the mount (if the picture is to be mounted). The length and width of the mount must agree with the distance between the limits of the rabbet (the recess at the back of the molding) as measured from side to side and from top to bottom. But allowance has to be made for the width of the molding, and also for a certain amount of wastage in cutting the 8 miters.

Each piece of the frame is cut, with a tenon saw, at an angle of 45 degrees. In marking for the cuts remember that each of the 8 miters must slope inward to the rabbet; the first attempt at making a frame can easily be marred by going wrong, in this respect, with just one miter.

For accurate cutting, a miter block or a miter box is desirable (see page 74). If a miter box is used, the molding to be cut is placed on the bottom of the box and pressed there and against the back while the saw is worked between the corresponding guide lines and through the molding. Mark off the exact length for each side of the frame and carry the pencil marks vertically up the outer side of the molding in order to permit the molded face to be turned uppermost and at the same time give visible location for the saw cut. Sawing from the face downward avoids the chipping of the molded surface which is apt to result if the wood is cut through from the back to the face of the molding. Having cut the first miter, turn the molding and be sure that the next miter to be cut will agree with the joint angle to be made.

An alternative method, dispensing with the miter box or block, is to mark the lines directly on the molding with a 45-degree square, or with a bevel gauge set at that angle, and do the cutting with the molding in the bench vise, the jaws of the latter gripping the rabbet and the outside edge. But this is practicable only when the molding is plain-faced and flat; also, it tends to be inaccurate.

When the 4 lengths have been cut they should be placed together, flat on the bench, to form the frame. Any inaccuracy in cutting will then be apparent, after testing with a square, and can be remedied with a jack plane or smoothing plane used in conjunction with a shooting board. This, at its simplest, takes the form of a

¾"-thick baseboard to which is nailed or screwed an inch-wide strip of wood ½" thick, this forming an angle of 45 degrees with the perfectly straight edge of the baseboard. The outer edge, against which the jack plane or smoothing plane, used on its side, will run, ensures each miter being trued and smoothed at the same time. Pressure of the left hand, which holds the molding against the inch-wide strip, keeps the shooting board steady on the bench.

After the 8 miters have been given this final attention, the frame is ready for gluing. Place newspaper below the corners to prevent sticking to the bench. There are several methods of clamping the frame while the glue is setting, one being to run a stout cord or string around the frame, with corner blocks to prevent the molding

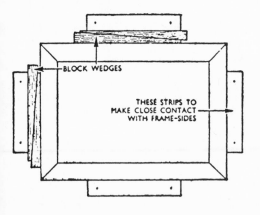

from injury. After the tightly pulled string has been tied, wedges can be used to increase the tension, but care must be exercised that the sides are not forced out of square. Another method is to butt strips of wood as tightly as possible to each of the four sides of the frame, screwing the strips to the bench, looseness being corrected by the use of folding wedges.

If the latter method is adopted, further securing of the miters (when the glue has set) by nails or screws is simplified.

Before the fine screws or thin nails are driven home, holes should be bored at the corners with a brad awl. If the string method of tension is adopted, and it is thought desirable to strengthen the joint after the glue has set, the nailing or screwing will require caution, to prevent both splitting and weakening of the joints.

The nails or screws should be sunk well into the wood, ample depressions being made for the head at the same time the holes are bored. These depressions are later leveled up with plastic wood which is stained to match the wood. An alternative method is to fill them with pieces of waste wood from the frame; these are cut and glued into the holes.

Surplus glue should be cleaned from the jointed frame, and the wood should be rubbed with fine sandpaper, though use of this will be possible only on the back if the front is heavily molded. Then the glass, picture mounting, and backing can go into position, though oil paintings are generally left unglazed. If there is any difficulty with surplus glue on the face and sides of the frame, this can be removed with a wad of cloth dipped in hot water.

The glass should be thoroughly cleaned, particularly on the inner surface. It should be cut to an easy fit for the rabbet, though not too loose, and it should not be fingered on the inside while the picture is being placed on top of it. The mounting (if any) and picture having been put in place, a backing of thin plywood or very stiff cardboard is introduced and secured with glazing brads or other fine nails.

These are driven horizontally into the sides of the rabbet, while the frame is flat on its face. It is advisable to make certain that the bench or table has no loose nails or other small items on its surface to scratch or indent the molding, and a flatiron on edge, or block of wood, should be pressed against the outside edge of the frame (the edge that is being dealt with) as a support during the hammering. The backing must not be pressed down too tightly or the glass may crack, but the brads must be sufficiently low in the rabbet to hold the back securely in the frame.

Do not drive the brads into the rabbet more than half their length. For a neat finish, and to exclude dust, a sheet of brown paper, in area a shade less on all sides than the overall dimensions of the frame, may then be pasted or glued over the back. When this has dried, any surplus due to the paper's stretching during the pasting should be cut away. Small screw eyes (preferably the kind with loose rings) may now be inserted in line with each other in the back of the molding, to take the cord—or, if the frame is heavy, flexible picture wire will be found more satisfactory.

**Hanging.** The screw eyes may be about one third of the distance from the top of the frame, though this depends on the angle at which the picture is required to incline from the wall. If the inclination is to be slight, the rings will be inserted higher up. If the molding is thin, the eyes should be screwed in cautiously, to prevent the screw points from penetrating the front surface of the frame.

Generally speaking, the pictures on one wall should have the same inclination, and there should be some symmetry as to height. The most convenient method of hanging is from picture molding, but patented fasteners or rawl plugs can also be used.

# SHELVES

The essentials for strong shelving are (a) boards stiff enough not to sag noticeably over the span required; and (b) good support at the ends and at intermediate points, according to the span. It is assumed, for example, that several shelves are needed in the kitchen for pots and pans. The walls are usually of plaster on laths, or wallboard, so that one end of the

shelves can be fixed to the wall, with brackets for the other.

**Saucepan Shelf.** Inch-thick board is suitable, 2 pieces of 6″ tongued-and-grooved board being used to make up a width of slightly less than a foot. For the outer end of each shelf a steel bracket, about 12″ × 10″, will be needed. A common length for shelves in such a position —flanking the sink, say—is about 39″; the bracket will be set in about 6″ from the outer end of the shelf.

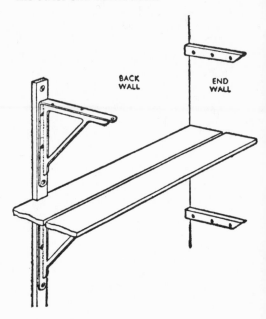

BACK WALL

END WALL

Begin by measuring on the wall the position of the bottom face of the shelf or shelves. It is a good plan to measure from the floor to the lowest shelf, then to lay off the distance above, from the first line. Remember that the top of the shelf will come about 1″ higher than the line.

On the end wall we shall need a bearer for each shelf, cut from 1″ × 2″ stock, neatly planed and cut back to a slope at the outer end. Prepare these bearers first, and bore holes for the screws. Use rawl plugs or toggle bolts to fix them to the wall. If the wall is constructed out of wallboard, the bearers should be nailed only at points where there is studding in back of the wallboard. Countersink the holes in the bearers, so that the screws go in flush. If the bearer is to be nailed to the studding this will not be necessary, as the nail heads may be punched in to provide a flat surface. Square off pencil lines on the wall to show the line for the top of the bearer (bottom face of the shelf). Hold the lowest bearer in position, with a spirit level on top, and verify the level. Use a fine awl to mark, through the screw holes, the location of the plugs. Drill the wall for the latter, fit the appropriate size of plug, and screw on the bearer.

Fix the bearers for the remaining shelves. Now put in place the upright to which the steel brackets are screwed. This upright may be made from the same timber as used for the bearers. Cut it to length and chamfer the two front edges. Bore holes for the screws as before. Get someone to hold the upright in position while testing it for vertical. A plumb bob and line will give the true upright, but it may be had approximately by measurement from the end wall, though the wall may not be dead true. Mark the back wall through the upright for rawl plugs, drill the holes, and secure the board.

Cut the inch-thick board to length; plane off the tongue, and let the groove on the other side go against the wall. The shelf can be strengthened by screwing a ledge (made from 1″ × 2″ board) underneath across the boards, midway in the length. Do this before fixing the shelf. The shelf, at the open end, should be rounded, planed, and sandpapered.

The back edge of the shelf should be notched to fit around the vertical board, close to the back wall. After fitting—but before nailing—the lowest shelf, it can be used as a guide for marking those above it, after attaching the ledge. In any case, where several shelves are installed, do not fasten the lowest, or fix brackets, until the preparatory work above has been completed. If large saucepans are to be accommodated, remember that they often have a

loop handle opposite the long handle; when turned upside down, the loop will prevent the vessel from lying flat unless there is an open space at the far side of the shelf. In such cases, do not place the boards close to the wall.

When ready to fix the brackets, lay a shelf in place on the end-wall bearer and adjust the height of the other end until a level placed on top shows the shelf to be horizontal. Mark the position on the upright (for the underside of the shelf). Place the bracket so that its top arm is level with the line and bore for a screw through one of the holes in the vertical arm of the bracket; insert the screw, adjust the bracket for perpendicular, and put in the next screw. Lay the shelf in place and test with a level; if correct, insert remaining screws in the upright. Only short screws are needed to hold the shelf to the bracket. No. 8, ⅜″ long, will do. Two oval brads will hold the other end of the shelf to the bearer on the wall.

## Shelves in a Recess

Two types of recessed shelves are described. The first is used when the recess has a baseboard and picture rail which for some reason cannot be cut.

Fix two vertical strips at each side of the recess, on the flanking walls. (Only one side wall is shown in the diagram on page 62.) Cut the uprights (1″ × 2″ or 1″ × 3″ stock) at the bottom to fit close to the baseboard and bevel them for that purpose. At the top make a longer bevel to bring them over the picture rail; if this is a thick rail, the uprights can be fitted only part way over the molding. The essential requirements are that the uprights shall come close to the wall and fit tightly to baseboard and picture rail.

Nail the uprights at top and bottom, after plugging them at two intermediate points to the wall. Next, cut and fit cross bearers where the shelves are to be. The sketch shows these screwed flush to the

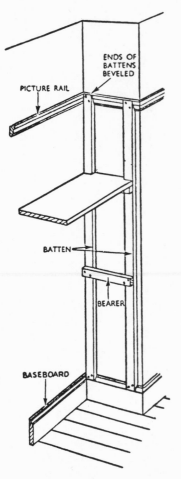

used when the baseboard and rail can be removed. Remove them, and fit the uprights straight through to the floor and up to the height required. When the uprights have been fixed solidly, screw on cross pieces as before, to support the shelves. Where the baseboard and picture rail were taken down, glue short end pieces and nail them to make a miter joint with the flanking lengths of baseboard and picture rail.

It has been assumed that the full depth of the recess has been taken up by shelving. If this is not the case, suitable pieces of baseboard and rail will have to be fitted in, to make a neat finish.

## FORMAL TABLE

A formal table—for the hall or to hold the radio—can be constructed in oak, walnut, or mahogany. The top, consisting of 2 or possibly 3 boards glued together, is 24″ long, 15½″ wide, and ¾″ thick. The edges may be left square or may be scalloped with a coping saw. The 4 legs are 27″ long and 1¾″ square. If these can be turned on the lathe, the appearance of the table is improved; or turned legs may be purchased.

The top rails are secured to the legs by mortise-and-tenon joints; the long sides measure 17½″ from leg to leg, the short

verticals and of the same thickness, but a better way is to use 2″ bearers and notch them around the verticals, so that they also fit close to the walls and give double the bearing surface for the shelf ends. When cutting the shelves, cut them long enough to fit tightly against the uprights. Do not attempt to make the projecting narrower portions fit close to the wall. The shelves, wedged tightly to the uprights, will hold everything firm and solid. Put in the lowest shelf first and work upward; tilt the shelves to insert them, then gently tap with a mallet, or a hammer on a block of wood. Undue force will loosen the assembly.

The second method of construction is

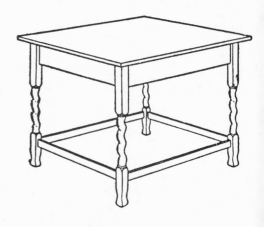

sides 10″; the wood is 3″ wide and ¾″ thick. The tenons are ½″ long and ⅜″ thick.

The bottom rails are 1¾″ wide and 3″ thick, and the joining is done with dowels, ¼″ in diameter and 1″ long. These rails are positioned 4″ up from the bottom of the legs; their lengths correspond, of course, with those of the top rails. Joints of top and bottom rails should be completed and the frame given a trial assembly. Any slight correction indicated can then be made before the frame is finally glued together. One dowel per rail is sufficient, and it should be situated centrally.

When the glue has dried, any which has been squeezed out should be removed carefully with the chisel, and the frame tested for level. If it does not stand perfectly level, a shaving can be removed from the bottom of any faulty leg. Alternatively, if one leg is just a trifle short, a piece of wood of the necessary thickness can be glued to the lower end, and shaped so this addition is not noticeable, being next to the floor.

The top is then secured with glue and screws, the latter being inserted at an angle from the inner face of each of the 2 long pieces of rail so that they bite into the underside of the table top. Four screws are needed, each 2″ in from the end of the long rails. First, glue the top to the frame, taking care that the top is placed centrally. When the glue is dry, the positions of the 4 screws should be marked, ¾″ down from the top edges of the long rails, and a trial hole at each position should be bored with a brad awl or small twist drill.

The angle at which the holes are bored will determine the length of the screw, from 1″ to possibly 1½″. It is sufficient if the screw passes about ¼″ into the underside of the table top. When the holes have been made, a larger drill completes the boring and the screws are driven all the way in. The heads should be countersunk so that there is no projection on the inner face of the rail.

## FLUSH DOOR

It is presumed that a room door fitted with a mortise lock is to be the subject of the operations. First of all, examine the door to make sure it hangs correctly and is not warped. It is impossible to make a success of a door that has bent or warped out of line.

In order to avoid complications, endeavor to work so that hinges need not be shifted. This means, if both faces of the door are to be covered flush, that the plywood cover on the inside face (the side where the knuckles of the hinges are) will have to be beveled back and cut around the knuckles. The plywood, of course, adds to the thickness of the door, but if the edge mentioned is beveled, the fact that the door projects inward here will hardly be noticed. At the locking side, the

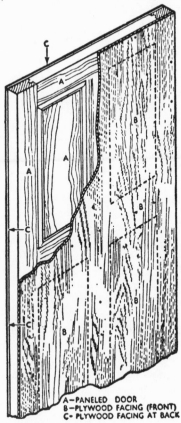

A—PANELED DOOR
B—PLYWOOD FACING (FRONT)
C- PLYWOOD FACING AT BACK

door stop can be adjusted so that the face of the door, after covering, comes flush with the door casing. The door stops will have to be taken down and replaced to suit the added thickness of the door on the outer side (opposite to the knuckle face).

The lock will not be altered, and the striking plate also should stay as before. Obviously, any defects should be noted and remedied before fitting the flush covering or in the process of that work.

Furthermore, the door hardware will have to be taken off, and it is probable that a longer shaft for the doorknobs will be needed to allow for the extra thickness of the altered door.

Take off the doorknobs first, unscrewing the setscrew in one knob and then drawing the other knob and the shaft out. The escutcheon plates should be removed and marked in accordance with the side of the door to which each belongs. Next, unscrew the hinge from the doorjamb, not from the door itself. If the hinge plates are held together by means of a removable pin, it will not be necessary to remove the hinge; merely take out the pin. If any molding around the door panels stands out from the general level of the door face, this must be taken off or planed away and sandpapered down level. If the door is painted or varnished, take a cabinet scraper and scrape off the finish all around the door framing, that is, the stiles and rails or upright members. The object is to leave a clean surface to which glue will properly adhere. If the door is merely stained, rubbing with coarse sandpaper at the places mentioned will suffice. Remember that furniture polish, grease, or oil will repel glue and must be removed before gluing is begun.

**Plywood.** Choose 2 sheets of plywood having a pleasant grain and reasonably matching, for the faces of the door. Cut to size, a piece for each face of the door. Mark the pieces for the respective sides and for top and bottom. The plywood may be left a little wide and long, and

planed down after fixing. It should be cut with a fine-toothed saw while resting solidly on 2 sawhorses or benches. This is a job where some assistance will be required. The saw will leave a burr on the underside, so cut from the top or best side, to leave the burr on the side that will not show.

**Flush Facing.** The method recommended is to perform the main fixing by means of fine screws (No. 4, ⅝″ long), and to use 1″ veneer pins where the board shows any tendency to belly out. Hot or cold water wood glue is to be applied to the underside of the board where it will come against the cleaned parts of the frame, and these parts also are to be spread with glue. The worker will need as many small clamps or handscrews as he can provide—up to 8 or 12. Go around the edges of the plywood, about 1″ in from the outer edge, and bore holes with a drill to take the shanks of the screws. These holes should be placed about a foot apart. Countersink the holes somewhat deeply, but leave enough wood for the screw heads to bite on. After the screws have been inserted, the holes are filled with plastic wood, which on drying is sanded level and stained to match the plywood. Plastic wood will not adhere in very shallow holes, so countersink as deeply as is safe. Screws are to be inserted wherever there are crossbars or intermediate rails or uprights in the old door. There is not time to do all this once we have laid the plywood in place on the glued surface.

Use sandpaper to smooth off any burr left by drilling on the underside of the plywood; try the plywood in place, while the door is resting ready for the job. Then apply glue to the door frame, fairly liberally; lay the plywood in place and test it at the edges for correct position. Tap four 1″ veneer pins partly through at the corners, to prevent movement of the sheet of plywood; these pins will have to be pulled out later. Now, working from the middle part of the door, bore holes one by one into the door frame for the screws, going in through the holes already made in the plywood. Insert the screws and turn them until they are securely set (avoid overtightening). Work from the center toward the edges of the door, to sides, top, and bottom. If these operations proceed satisfactorily, insert the screws in the holes bored along the edges.

Now is the time to use the clamps, inserting slips of waste plywood between the jaws of the clamp and the faces of the door. Take out the temporary pins first inserted. Watch carefully to see that the plywood does not bulge or belly out between the screwed fixings. By taking out a screw here and there, such a defect can be at once remedied. Speed is as important as cautious and accurate assembly, if disappointment is to be avoided. Perhaps here and there a veneer pin can be driven in so as to take down any swelling, but if the door face is level there should not be much trouble. Go over the screws to ensure that they are fully set; then the door, with clamps on, should be placed approximately upright against the wall in a warm room, with the faced side showing. It will thus rest on the uncovered edge, and there will be no end pressure on the plywood edge at the bottom.

Face the second side of the door after the glue has set hard. But before the second side is put on, mark and bore the holes for the doorknobs and keyhole. These are marked with a fine brad awl from the uncovered side of the door, where the existing holes will serve as guide. The knob shaft hole is merely a round one of ample diameter; after marking its center with a fine brad awl from the uncovered side, bore through the exposed outer face of the plywood sheet with a brace and bit; this will avoid splitting the plywood.

Similarly, mark 2 holes to show where the bit has to go in at top and bottom of the keyhole; bore these holes through the exposed face of the plywood panel, as before.

A keyhole saw can be used to connect the 2 holes and form a slot to allow the doorkey to enter. Do not drill and saw out the second piece of plywood until it is finally fixed.

The final job is to glue on and fix the second sheet of plywood. Lay the door on some clean paper to protect the face already covered. Proceed with the attachment of the second sheet of plywood as with the first. Allow this side to rest until the glue has set hard, and then clean off the edges of the plywood sheet all round, using a block plane and a chisel, and finish with sandpaper. Mark and bore the holes for the shaft and key. If the door was painted, the edges will have to be cleaned and stained to match the plywood. The edges of the plywood will have to be stained also; but be careful not to use more stain than is necessary to give them the proper color.

When all the rest of the work has been done, the door hardware can be replaced. As mentioned earlier, the shaft, if short in the first place, may need replacement by a longer one, which can be bought at most hardware stores. Usually, however, there is ample length as fitted.

**Door Stops.** Take off the stops carefully if they have to be used again. Pry them away with a thin chisel; the nails may come out easily, or the stop may pull away over the heads of the nails, leaving the nails to be pulled out with pincers. In some cases the edge of the stops may require planing down to reduce the width, though usually there is plenty of room in the casing to allow the stop to set farther back, and it is merely a question of readjustment in a suitable position to accommodate the extra thickness of the door. Knock out the nails, and use new finishing nails to fix the stops again.

But before putting the stops back we must rehang the door, so as to see where they should go. When the door has been hung again, cut slips of cardboard about as thick as a penny, and, with the door fastened by its latch, place one of the long stops against the door face with 2 pieces of cardboard inserted, one about 6″ from the floor and the other at the same distance from the top. The idea is to allow a little clearance between the door and the inner face of the door stop. After the latter has been secured, there will be the thickness of the cardboard between it and the door face. Tack the stop in place temporarily with two nails driven in only part way. Attach the top stop similarly, and the remaining long side. If all is correct, and the door shuts satisfactorily without too much play, proceed to nail the stops tightly. The nails are driven in, the heads punched below the wood surface, and the holes filled with putty or plastic wood.

Since so much trouble has been taken to remodel the door itself, it is worthwhile, when the other decorative finish is in keeping, to fix new door stops made of wood to match the plywood face on the door.

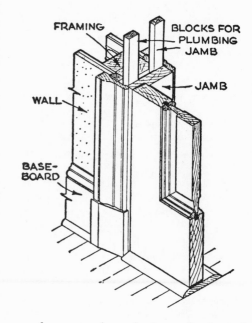

## BUILDING A DOORWAY

In an effort to make a house more comfortable and efficient, the home mechanic is often faced with the task of putting a doorway through an inside wall. This is a sizable undertaking and calls for much planning and measuring before the real work begins. On the other hand, the home carpenter possessing average skill with saw and hammer can do the job and do it well, provided he takes his time and utilizes all his skill.

The first point to settle is the exact location of the doorway in the wall. After you have selected the approximate position for the doorway, try to visualize the door in place and see how this fits in with the rest of the room. It may be that a door in the spot you first had in mind would spoil the appearance of the room, or not be as conveniently located as at another position. Give this matter of location plenty of time and thought, because once

you have cut through the wall, the only alternative, besides going ahead with the project, is to try to patch up the damage.

Try to locate one side of the doorway to take advantage of the vertical wall studding. This will make the job easier and also save lumber. You can usually locate the position of the studding by tapping on the wall surface. If the wall is made of wallboard instead of plaster, then the studding can be located by the nail heads in the wallboard.

Once you have the studding located, you can set about measuring for the opening in the wall. To find out how wide the opening should be, measure the width of the door and the thickness of the two jambs, or casing, which go on each side of the door frame. You must also allow $1/8″$ between each side of the door and the jambs for clearance, and $1/2″$ between the jambs and the studding or rough door frame. The purpose of this $1/2″$ clearance is to allow you to plumb the jamb with blocks of wood or wood wedges. The final consideration for the width of the opening is the frame. This should be made of $2 \times 4s$. If it has been possible to use one of the lengths of wall studding in the door frame, then you will have to add only the widths of three 2 × 4s to get the final measurement for the width of the opening.

As for the height, you first measure the height of the door and add to this the thickness of the threshold (if one is to be used), plus the thickness of the top casing and the thickness of a head 2 × 4, which is nailed horizontally between the vertical studding. Leave 1/2″ clearance between the head 2 × 4 and the top casing so that you will be able to bring the casing up level.

At this point you may decide that it would be a great deal easier to purchase a door complete with casing, and these can be had at most lumber yards. They naturally are more expensive than just a door with the necessary boards for the casing, because all the work of cutting and fitting the casing has been done at the lumber mill.

When the width and height of the opening for the doorway have been determined, the next job is to mark out the area on the wall. Use both a level and plumb line to get these lines true, or the door will neither fit nor hang correctly.

Now begins the job of cutting through the wall. If the wall is made of wallboard, there is not much of a problem as this material is easily cut with a handsaw. Cut out one side of the wall first and remove the wallboard. In almost every case it will be necessary to pull some nails holding the board to the studding. If these nails are pulled out carefully you will have sections of wallboard that can be used for some other job, but if you try to rip the wallboard off, you will ruin it for any other possible use. With the wallboard out of the way, the studding and back side of the opposite wall will be exposed. Mark out the doorway on this side; cut and remove the wallboard. Now all that is left in the opening will be some studding, and this can be removed by cutting at the top and then pulling out the nails holding it at the bottom. Studding is

usually nailed at the bottom to a piece of 2 × 4 resting on the floor. This is called the shoe, and a section of it will have to be cut out to the same width as the doorway. The usual method of framing a door is to have the inner pieces of framing on each side of the door nailed at the bottom onto the shoe. The shoe is then cut off flush, and the outer pieces of framing are nailed directly to the floor and sideways to the shoe.

Plaster walls present more of a problem so far as the cutting out is concerned. One way of doing this job is to cut through the plaster with a cold chisel and then cut through the laths with a saw. Be as careful as possible when you cut the plaster, because if large chunks are broken off, the edges will not be covered by the door trim and you will be in for an extensive patching job. Another point to watch for is to be certain that all the plaster has been cut before you begin sawing. If you try to saw through plaster, the saw will become dulled. Once the plaster has been cut along the marked lines, a compass saw can be inserted, and this will quickly and efficiently cut through the wood laths.

The job of cutting and removing plaster will naturally make a considerable mess, so it is a good plan before starting to cover the surrounding floor with newspapers or, better still, a large sheet of canvas.

Once the plaster and laths have been removed, the studding can be taken out.

The next job is to frame the doorway. If you were lucky enough to arrange the location of the doorway in such a manner that the wall studding forms one or even both sides of the door, this job will not be too difficult, because the additional framing can be spiked to the wall studding. If such an arrangement is impossible, then additional plaster must be removed so that the door framing can be nailed securely at the ceiling.

Take the necessary time to get the door frame as plumb as possible, as this will save you time and work when you put in the jambs. When the vertical frame is up and nailed at top and bottom, place a horizontal stud between the sides to frame the top of the doorway. Check this with a level and toenail it to the vertical pieces.

When the frame is finished, the opening is ready for the jambs. These must be plumb or else the door will never open and close properly. Use wood wedges or blocks placed between the jamb and the frame to hold the jambs plumb in the frame.

## STORM PORCH

Two of the greatest sources of heat loss in a house are the front and back doors, which are opened innumerable times each day to let in a blast of icy wind and let out a lot of warm air. One way to combat this difficulty is to build a storm porch around one of the doors and use the remaining door as little as possible. The storm porch will act more or less as an intermediary between the warm interior of the house and the cold outside. Not only will a well-built storm porch help to keep the house comfortable, but if it is built large enough it also will provide a place for members of the household to remove their heavy overshoes, leave their umbrellas, and so forth, and thus save the house from being tracked up with snow and water.

As to the question of size, the porch should be at least large enough for the house door to be closed by the person on the porch with sufficient room to turn comfortably to open the porch door. In the long run, it is best to build a porch large enough to accommodate several persons.

The porch can be as decorative as you can make it. Some householders have the porch made out of the same material as that used for the house. Thus, the porch might have white clapboard siding to match the outside walls of the house, and a roof of shingles the same as the main roof. This is purely a question of taste, but it should be remembered that a storm porch is up for only a few months of the year and no great harm is done by letting it look like what it is—a temporary structure.

The average home mechanic would want a porch that he could take down and put up by himself, and for this purpose he will find that asbestos board, plywood, or a composition wood is best suited for the sides of the porch. These materials come in large sheets, are light in weight, and can be sawed and nailed. They can be

purchased in sheets of such size that one sheet alone will serve as an entire side of the porch.

If there is an open porch or large stoop at the front doorway, this can be used as the floor of the storm porch and a base upon which to attach the sides. If there is not sufficient space, or no stoop or porch at all, the floor should be made as a separate unit. Another question that must be decided in advance is whether or not the storm porch is to have a separate roof. If there is a roofed porch at the front of the house and the roof is less than 8′ from the floor, this can serve as the roof of the storm porch. Should the house porch roof be over 8′ high, it is better to build a separate one for the storm porch.

Once you have a base or floor for the porch and have decided what size it is to be, make up your 3 wall sections accordingly. The frames for these units can be made of 2 × 2 stock, although a smaller size can be used in some cases. The opening for the door of the porch should be framed with 2 × 4 lumber as these frames will have to carry the entire weight of the door. You will find it easier to set all the sections up first and then hang the door when the porch is completed.

The best method of fastening the sections of the porch together is by the use of hooks and screw eyes, using at least 2, and better still 3, sets for each joint. The porch in turn is fastened to the side of the house by the same method. If the house siding is made of wood, you will have no difficulty in attaching the screw eyes; but if the walls are made of brick, stone, or stucco, you will have to use rawl plugs or some type of expansion bolt.

Mark on the floor or porch base the exact location of each side. Place the section upright on this mark and brace it while you attach it to the floor with wood screws. Put the two side sections up first and attach these to the walls of the house. When these are secure, the door or front section can go up and will be supported by the two side pieces.

If a roof is required, it can be of the same material as that used for the sides. Cut the section for the roof so that it overhangs at the front and at the sides. The frame for the roof should be fixed in such a way that it will fit snugly around the inside of the opening made by the three other sections. In this way it will be possible to attach the roof to the sides with hooks and screw eyes.

When the porch is to be equipped with a separate roof, the tops of the two side sections should be cut at an angle so that the roof has pitch.

# PROTECTING YOUR TOOL INVESTMENT

It cannot be said too often that tools are no better than the condition in which they are kept. Assuming that you have invested a considerable amount of hard-earned money in a collection of top-quality tools, it is only good judgment to proect your investment by adequately and safely storing your tools. In this way you not only insure their long life but also when you need a particular one, will know precisely where it is.

## Portable Tool Boxes

A portable tool box is a handy device for transporting tools whenever and wherever you need them. If your available storage space is limited, the portable tool box can also take the place of a permanent cabinet. The portable boxes suggested are intended for this purpose: they can be stored in a minimum of space and will protect your tools. Several of them will be needed to reduce size and carrying weight. An additional smaller portable box with removable compartment trays is fine for keeping nails, screws, bolts, and other small hardware.

The dimensions of the boxes depend

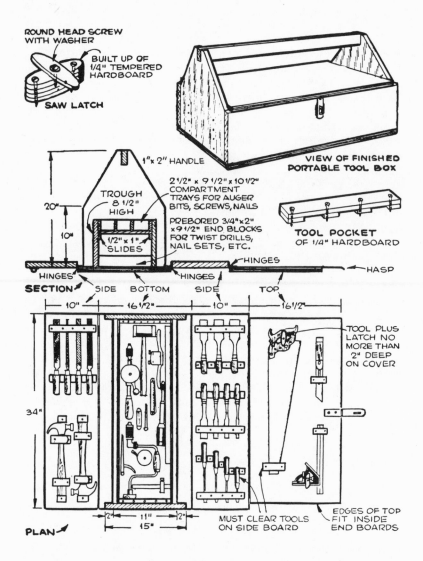

ROUND HEAD SCREW WITH WASHER

BUILT UP OF 1/4" TEMPERED HARDBOARD

SAW LATCH

VIEW OF FINISHED PORTABLE TOOL BOX

1"x 2" HANDLE

2 1/2" x 9 1/2" x 10 1/2" COMPARTMENT TRAYS FOR AUGER BITS, SCREWS, NAILS

TROUGH 8 1/2" HIGH

20"

10"

PREBORED 3/4"x2" x 9 1/2" END BLOCKS FOR TWIST DRILLS, NAIL SETS, ETC.

1/2" x 1" SLIDES

TOOL POCKET OF 1/4" HARDBOARD

HINGES

HINGES

HINGES

HASP

SECTION

SIDE

BOTTOM

SIDE

TOP

10"

16 1/2"

10"

16 1/2"

34"

TOOL PLUS LATCH NO MORE THAN 2" DEEP ON COVER

2"

11"

2"

15"

PLAN

MUST CLEAR TOOLS ON SIDE BOARD

EDGES OF TOP FIT INSIDE END BOARDS

on the equipment you have. As overall sizes of tools vary, the dimensions shown in the illustrations are only suggestions, based on housing 26" handsaws and other tools of average size. Before beginning construction, measure the overall dimensions of your tools so they will fit in a minimum of space. To keep the weight down as much as practical, 3/4" Idaho white or sugar pine is good and easily workable for the ends, sides, and handles; 7/16" stock for the partitions and trays;

and 1/2" fir plywood for the top and bottom pieces, because of their width. For the pockets and latches which secure the various tools, use 1/4" tempered hardboard (a dense, highly compressed fiberboard) or fir plywood. Use flathead wood screws to frame the various members of the box; countersink them either flush or slightly deeper than flush, and cover the heads with either water-mix wood putty or plastic wood, sandpapered smooth.

First cut out all the pieces; then arrange your tools and mark the location of latches and pockets. These should be raised just enough for a snug fit of the tools. Secure them with flathead screws through both face and separating strips. Latches should be pivoted on roundhead wood screws with a thin washer between head and latch.

Hinge the sides and top with 3 narrow 1½″-long cabinet butt hinges with tight pins, each piece hinged in the center and at both ends. Frame the bottom to the end pieces, and the partitions to the bottom and end pieces. In box No. 1, also attach with screws the prebored blocks for twist drills and for nail set and countersink shanks.

Attach the hinges to the bottom piece. The handles fit tightly into slots on the end pieces and are anchored with 2 flathead screws driven in the edges of each end piece. With the top and sides closed,

locate the screw hooks and eyes, one at each end for each piece.

Removable trays for box No. 2 are butt-joined to all surfaces. They are glued (if you wish) and nailed with 2d finishing nails, set and covered. You can fit each compartment either separately crosswise or with the strips half-lapped lengthwise and crosswise.

## Tool Cabinet

So far as storage space is concerned, a tool cabinet is more desirable than a tool box. Moreover, as it is a fixed storage space, its weight is not a matter of concern as with the portable box. If you are so situated that a small workshop is not practical, you can still enjoy the knowledge that your tools are well taken care of and easily accessible by making a tool cabinet

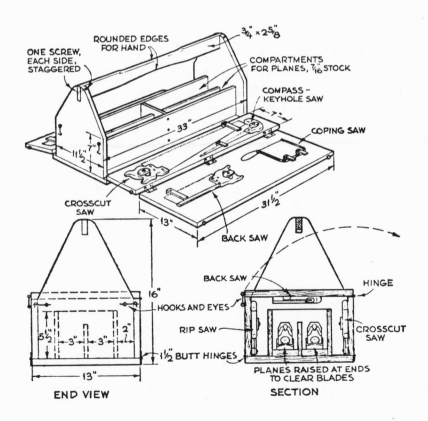

END VIEW                    SECTION

which you can attach to the inside of a closet door. If you have space for a workshop, the same cabinet can be mounted over your workbench.

Since this project is not intended to be a showpiece, there is no need to make mitered, rabbeted, or dadoed joints—with one exception: the drawer fronts should be rabbeted. Stock lumber is used except

for the back, which, because of its width, is ½″ fir plywood. All other cabinet material, except the ¾″ hardwood-dowel pulls, is ¾″ and ½″ Idaho white or sugar pine. Pockets and latches are ¼″ tempered hardboard or fir plywood.

The center partition for the drawers will have to be planed ¼″ (the stock size being 6½″) and the drawer components

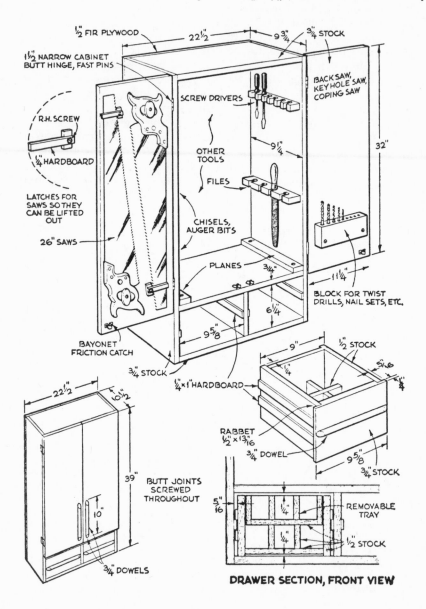

DRAWER SECTION, FRONT VIEW

ripped to size. Use either resorcinol resin, urea resin, or casein glue on all joints before screwing them with flathead wood screws. Since the screws are driven immediately after applying the glue, clamps are not necessary. Glue is not absolutely essential, but as there are a number of end-grain joints and considerable weight stresses, a stronger, more permanent job will result by using glue. Countersink all screws on the outside of the cabinet slightly deeper than flush and cover the heads with water-mix wood putty or plastic wood.

The dimensions are based on 26″ handsaws and other tools of average overall size. Even though you are not completely stocked with every tool the cabinet will accommodate, it would be wise, while you are at it, to make it large enough for future expansion of your tool collection. The cabinet is equipped with two drawers with removable trays for screws, nails, and other small hardware.

After cutting the various pieces to size, arrange your collection of tools similarly to the order suggested in the drawings, keeping in mind future additions. An easy way to establish the locations after experimenting with arrangements, is to trace the outline of the tool with a pencil directly on the wood surface. Since tools vary in thickness, each one will have to be custom-fitted for its pocket or latch which should receive the tool snugly. Attach all pockets with flathead screws, countersunk flush, through the face and separating strips, and all pivoting latches with roundhead wood screws with washers under the heads.

Make twist drill holders out of ¾″ stock, boring each receptacle with the drill it is supposed to contain. Do this also with the auger bit holders, which in this case are bored for the diameters of the tapered shanks. It is a good idea to use gummed labels marked with the drill sizes for quick selection. Nail sets, countersinks and tools of similar type can be stored in the same manner. Attach these various

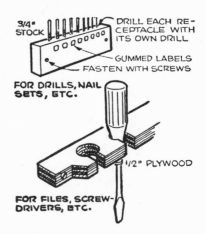

holders with flathead screws, one at each end of each holder being sufficient. File, screwdriver, and chisel holders can be made from ½″ fir plywood bored with holes of smaller diameter than the handles, slotted to pass the tangs, blades, and sockets. Lumber stock for these is apt to split unless hardwood is used.

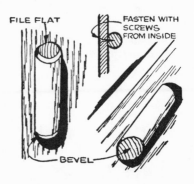

Drawer and door pulls are made from ¾″ hardwood dowels. To make these, file the contacting surface of the dowel slightly flat, bevel the ends and then the edges of the ends, and attach with flathead screws from the inside of the door or drawer front, countersinking the screw heads flush. Two screws for each pull are sufficient.

**Framing.** To frame the cabinet, mark the center of the butting edge of each interior member by means of a line on the outer face, as most of the screws are driven from the outer face of the cabinet. Also mark off, evenly spaced, the locations of the screws along the line, and bore lead holes for them. Fit the joining piece; insert a screw at each end and tap it lightly with a hammer to locate the smaller lead hole in the joining edge. Bore these smaller holes; again assemble the members and drive the two screws part way in, just enough to hold the pieces. Then continue boring the small lead holes for the remaining screws. Bore all screw holes in this manner. Then join the cabinet pieces, starting with the back, by framing each member with glue applied to the edge, then screwing it—one piece at a time. Wipe off all excess glue immediately with a clean cloth wrung out in cold water. Attach the doors with 1½"-long, narrow cabinet butt hinges with tight pins, recessing the leaves flush. Fit bayonet-type friction catches, one for each door.

It is best to make the drawers after the cabinet is assembled, so that any slight inaccuracy can be allowed for. Make the trays from ½" stock nailed with 2d finishing nails, set and filled. The easiest way to make the compartments is to cross-lap and glue them, framing the ends against the

drawer sides with glue and 2d finishing nails. Make the drawer slides and guides from ¼" tempered hardboard, and attach with small flathead screws countersunk flush.

When the cabinet is finished, sandpaper all surfaces smooth, *slightly* rounding all sharp corners. The cabinet should be either stained, given a few coats of clear lacquer, painted, or enameled.

## Miter Block and Box

In order to cut wood or other material at an angle, a miter block or a miter box is desirable. Either can be purchased, but the box is more accurate because of its paired guide lines. Manufactured miter boxes that can be set to cut at any angle are available. However, as the angle most used is one of 45 degrees, the handyman will find the less expensive single-cut box or block satisfactory for most of his needs, if not for all of them.

Construction of either presents no great difficulty. For the block, 2 pieces of

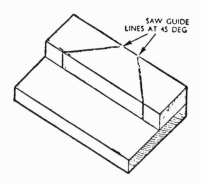

wood are used. The bottom piece should be about 6" wide and the top or back piece 3" wide. Both should be of ¾" stock and 18" long. These are screwed or glued together and the saw guides (miter lines) marked out as shown. They are then cut through to the top side of the bottom piece with a backsaw. The utmost care should be taken to ensure the cuts being absolutely vertical.

The miter box offers the advantage of paired guide lines which hold the saw securely in place so that it cannot deviate from the correct angle. Three pieces of

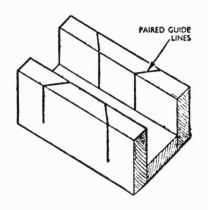

PAIRED GUIDE LINES

wood are required to construct it, the inside measurement of the box being about 4″ from front to back, and the depth about 3″. Use ¾″ stock about 18″ in length. The pieces should be screwed or glued together. Before cutting the guides it is important to mark guide lines on both faces, as well as on the top of the side pieces—because the accuracy of the marking and cutting will govern the trueness of the mitering done with the box.

The molding, or other material to be mitered, is placed on the bottom of the block or box and pressed there against the back while the saw is worked between the corresponding guides until the desired cut is made.

If no combination try square is available, the 45-degree angle can be determined easily by the following method. Lay an ordinary carpenter's square across the top of the 2 uprights of the box and mark them. Now measure the distance between the outside edges of the uprights and, starting at the marks you made, measure the same distance along the outside edges of the tops of the uprights. Mark these points

and again lay the carpenter's square across the tops of the uprights and mark each one. Where these 4 marks you have made intersect the outside edges of the uprights, you have the 4 corners of a square. A straightedge laid diagonally across this square from 2 opposite corners provides an angle of 45 degrees. Mark these lines and continue the lines down on the inside surfaces of the sides or uprights of the box, making sure that these latter lines are absolutely vertical. Then make your cuts as previously described.

## Workbench

If you have a bit of space which you can allocate to the "maintenance and building department" of your home, by all means do so. Lacking a cellar, perhaps your garage or attic will allow space that will hold a small workbench with a few feet in front of it. A workbench is an invaluable piece of furniture for woodworking and home projects of all kinds. True, you can build almost anything without the aid of a workbench, but that is doing it the hard way, particularly if you are working on small projects which require a vise to hold them. The smaller the project, the more necessary the workbench.

The ideal workbench is the traditional one with a maple top 2″ or more thick; the narrow maple boards are face-glued and bolted together, similar to a maple chopping block. This is a very expensive and difficult job of work, requiring unusual bolt lengths, perfect joining, and much clamping.

Another method of making the top for a workbench is to use maple boards glued edgewise and glued and screwed to a supplementary top of board lumber. This, too, is expensive and, as the maple is tougher than the foundation on which it is framed, any warping tendencies of the maple will warp the entire assembly beyond repair. This method also requires fine joining of perfect edges, with the

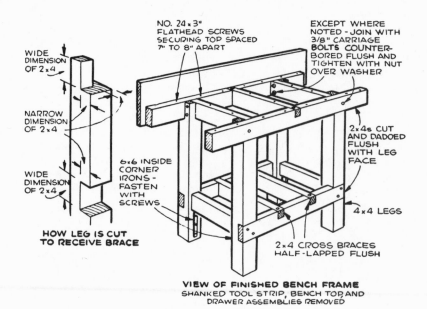

WIDE DIMENSION OF 2x4

NARROW DIMENSION OF 2x4

WIDE DIMENSION OF 2x4

6x6 INSIDE CORNER IRONS - FASTEN WITH SCREWS

HOW LEG IS CUT TO RECEIVE BRACE

NO. 24 x 3" FLATHEAD SCREWS SECURING TOP SPACED 7" TO 8" APART

EXCEPT WHERE NOTED - JOIN WITH 3/8" CARRIAGE BOLTS COUNTER-BORED FLUSH AND TIGHTEN WITH NUT OVER WASHER

2x4s CUT AND DADOED FLUSH WITH LEG FACE

4x4 LEGS

2x4 CROSS BRACES HALF-LAPPED FLUSH

VIEW OF FINISHED BENCH FRAME
SHANKED TOOL STRIP, BENCH TOP AND DRAWER ASSEMBLIES REMOVED

DRAWER STOP NO. 16 x 1 1/2" ROUND HEAD SCREW WITH HEAD CUT OFF - SET IN TOP OF GUIDE

24"

SHANKED TOOL STRIP

60"

3/4" x 24" x 60" FIR PLYWOOD TOP

10"

DRAWER 20 3/4" LONG

2x4 BRACES

6x6 INSIDE CORNER IRONS

APPROX. 34"

DRAWER FRONTS

2x4 CROSS BRACES

2x4 x 36" FRONT AND BACK BRACES

7"

36"

2x4 x 56" FRONT AND BACK

4x4 LEGS

END VIEW

FRONT VIEW

added difficulty of producing a flat, smooth surface for the top.

The important factors in a workbench are weight and solidity, and a tough top which will take a beating. The workbench suggested here is tough and sturdy, but with a ¾" fir plywood top instead of maple. Plywood, thickness for thickness, is considerably heavier than comparable lumber due to its structure

and, if framed properly, will not warp, bend, or vibrate. Moreover, fir plywood is uncommonly tough and offers the advantage of a single smooth piece for the top without any joining problems.

Most workbenches have a trough at the back for odds and ends, but experience shows that this is nothing but a catchall for wood shavings, chips, sawdust, and dirt. It is also an invitation to park small tools where they should not be. The trough is eliminated here primarily for these reasons, and also because it would complicate construction of the top unnecessarily. Provision is made for keeping lengths ot lumber on the bottom braces, adequately taking care of the average lumber storage problem around the home. The bench is equipped with two drawers having removable compartmented trays for screws, nails, and small hardware. The average height of a bench is about 34", but if you are short or quite tall, it should be changed to about 6" below your waistline.

Here is your opportunity to show your skill with middle half laps and dadoes (see page 45), which are not hard to make, requiring only careful layout and a bit of sawing and chiseling. Remember: always saw on the waste side of the marked line for tight joining.

**Legs and Framing.** The legs and framing for the bench are Douglas fir lumber: 4" × 4" (3⅝" × 3⅝") for the legs, and 2" × 4" (1⅝" × 3½" or 3⅝") for the bracing and top supports. The tops of the legs are cut back to receive the 2 × 4s flush. The bottom front and back braces are dadoed flush, while the center cross braces are half-lapped flush. The bottom end braces are butt-joined with 6" × 6" inside corner irons. All framing except the corner irons is done with carriage bolts,

counterbored for flush-fitting heads and tightened with nuts over washers. This results in a rigid frame which can be disassembled either completely or with the ends left intact. The top, too, a ¾" panel of fir plywood, is removable, being secured to the frames with screws counterbored and driven from the underside of the frames. From time to time bolt nuts will have to be tightened; if the demountable feature of the workbench is of no importance, apply resorcinol resin glue to all joints before bolting, and nothing will loosen them.

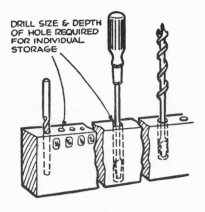

DRILL SIZE & DEPTH OF HOLE REQUIRED FOR INDIVIDUAL STORAGE

Screwed to the backboard of the top is a strip ¾" × 2⅝" × 60" for twist drills, countersinks, nail sets, and any other shanked small tools. Bore holes in this strip, using the size of twist drill it is to receive—and making holes of the correct diameters for other tools such as screwdrivers and auger bits. Use gummed labels marked with the size of each drill for easy selection of the size you want.

To support the two drawers, screw ¾" plywood to the cross braces. For the drawer guides and slides, maple or oak is best, screwed to the braces and drawer sides. Drawer stock can be ¾" white pine or plywood, but the drawer bottoms should be ¼" tempered hardboard for added strength. The drawer sides, front, back, and bottom are butt-joined to each other and framed with screws through

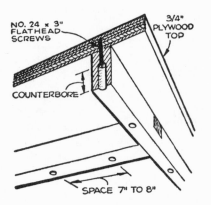

NO. 24 × 3" FLATHEAD SCREWS

¾" PLYWOOD TOP

COUNTERBORE

SPACE 7" TO 8"

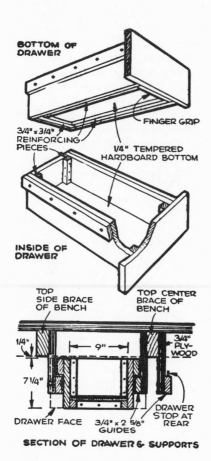

**Woodworking Vise.** A woodworking vise is an essential adjunct to the bench. This can be purchased and attached to the bench with screws; or you can save a considerable amount of money by buying a bench screw—which provides the motivating power of a vise—and making your own. Two pieces of ¾″ fir plywood screwed together make an efficient and strong jaw; and all that remains to be done is to bore a hole, slightly larger than the screw diameter, with an expansive bit, through both jaws and the $2 \times 4$ extension and then attach the screw assembly.

You can also make a bench stop for the vise out of a ¾″ hardwood dowel, glued. Bench stops hold short lengths of lumber for planing, sanding, and the like; two of them are required—one on the vise

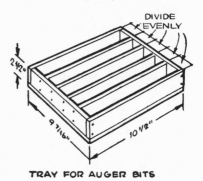

TRAY FOR AUGER BITS

¾″ × ¾″ corner reinforcing pieces and ¾″ × ¾″ pieces for the bottom. Make drawer stops by driving a No. 16 × 1½″ flathead wood screw into each drawer guide 1⅞″ from its end, letting the head project about ⅜″. Then cut off the head with a hacksaw or other metal-cutting saw. The drawer fronts require no pulls as they project below the bottom for finger grips.

Make sliding trays, about half the depth of the drawer, out of ½″ lumber stock for the sides, ends, and compartments, and ¼″ hardboard for the bottoms. Cross-lap the compartments with glue and frame the trays with glue and 2d finishing nails.

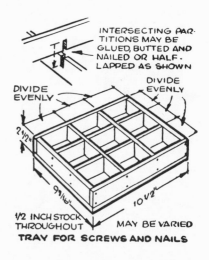

TRAY FOR SCREWS AND NAILS

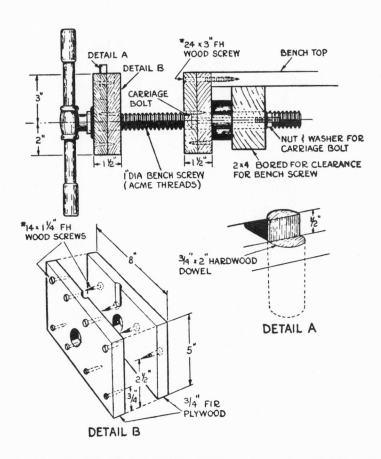

DETAIL A

DETAIL B

3"

2"

←1½"→

←1½"→

#24 x 3" FH WOOD SCREW

BENCH TOP

CARRIAGE BOLT

NUT & WASHER FOR CARRIAGE BOLT

1" DIA BENCH SCREW (ACME THREADS)

2x4 BORED FOR CLEARANCE FOR BENCH SCREW

#14 x 1¼" FH WOOD SCREWS

8"

¾" x 2" HARDWOOD DOWEL

5"

2½"

¾"

¾" FIR PLYWOOD

DETAIL A

DETAIL B

and the other let into the bench top. Holes are bored at intervals through the bench top to accommodate various lengths of lumber. The commercial bench stops are adjustable for height (thickness of lumber) but are designed for thicker bench tops. You can easily make these described here, which will work as well. Since your homemade ones are not adjustable, make three, using ¾", ½", and ¼" material, glued with resorcinol resin glue to ¾" hardwood dowels. The holes in the bench to receive these stops should be just large enough for a snug, sliding fit. You can use a bit of the same diameter as the dowel, and then carefully enlarge the hole slightly with coarse sandpaper wrapped around a dowel of smaller diameter.

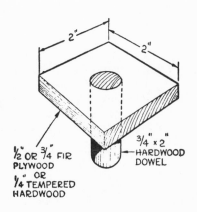

2"

2"

½" OR ¾" FIR PLYWOOD
¼" OR ¼ TEMPERED HARDWOOD

¾" x 2" HARDWOOD DOWEL

A well-equipped woodworking bench has two vises, one at the left front and one at the opposite end, its jaws facing the length of the bench. This vise (when there are two) is used in conjunction with bench stops to accommodate long pieces of lumber. You can make the two vises with two bench screws for less than half the cost of one complete commercial vise of good quality.

**Bench Hook.** There is one other valuable addition to your workbench equipment which comes in handy for all sorts of woodworking jobs, such as chiseling out dadoes, sawing dadoes, and the like. This is the bench hook, which is simply a piece of lumber with a stop screwed to the bottom at one end and a stop screwed to the top at the other end. Make several of these from $\frac{3}{4}'' \times 5\frac{1}{2}'' \times 10''$ stock, with

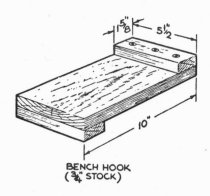

BENCH HOOK
($\frac{3}{4}''$ STOCK)

stops of $\frac{3}{4}'' \times 1\frac{5}{8}''$ stock. In use, the bottom stop butts against the front edge of the bench top, and the lumber to be worked butts against the top stop. Use two bench hooks for long pieces of lumber.

## Sawhorse

Sawhorses are the age-old portable workbenches of the carpenter, and up to the present day no better substitute has been invented for cross-cutting and rip-

ping lumber of any length. They are also invaluable for cutting plywood panels, which at best are awkward to saw. Carpenters on a construction job will often make a miter box and nail it to the top of a sawhorse, ready for any mitering job that presents itself. At least two sawhorses are needed; for large panels of thin plywood, a third is a good idea to support the middle.

Use $2 \times 4$s for the legs and crosspiece, and $\frac{3}{4}''$ fir plywood or $\frac{3}{4}''$ lumber stock for the end braces (gussets). Douglas fir is a good tough wood to use. There are two ways of positioning the cross piece: edge up or face up. The face gives more surface on which to work and is preferred by some craftsmen. It offers less bevel surface for the legs, but as they are end-braced this disadvantage is offset. However, edge up is the commonest method of framing; and if you want a wider work surface, you can nail a 6'' board on the $2 \times 4$.

The height of a sawhorse depends on the user's height, and usually ranges from 18'' to about 24''. It should be low enough for comfortable sawing when the knee is used to hold down the piece—20'' is about average. Length is optional, but 36'' is a good overall dimension. Spread of legs is important, so that the horse does not rock—18'' between the outer edges of the legs at the bottom is about right. For a horse with a spread of 18'', and 20'' high, the angle of the bevel of the legs is 22 degrees. You can mark this off with your T-bevel, adjusted with the use of a protractor; or, if you have a protractor head on your combination square, use the square. The easiest way to make the bevel is to saw it. Use flathead wood screws to assemble the horse, for rigid framing.

If you do not have space to store sawhorses, you can buy metal frames into which the 2 × 4s are clamped without the use of screws. These demountable frames do not make as sturdy a sawhorse as a homemade one, but they are adequate, with the added advantage that they can be disassembled and stored in a small space.

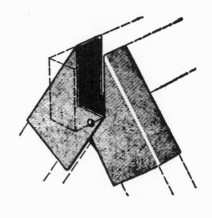

# 4

# FURNITURE

## UPHOLSTERED FURNITURE

Renovating the upholstery of chairs, sofas, and settees is a task which can be undertaken very satisfactorily by the home mechanic. It should be noted, however, that this chapter does not deal with extensive repairs to the frame and upholstery, which are best left to a skilled craftsman.

**Equipment.** A hammer, screwdriver or old chisel, pincers, an upholsterer's needle, and an appliance for stretching the new webbing tightly are all the tools required. The necessary materials are burlap and spring, if replacement is necessary, webbing, a ball of good twine, and a package of ½″ tacks. If a regular upholsterer's needle cannot be procured, a packing needle will do. Buy the very best qual-

PACKING NEEDLE

ity webbing you can, because the success of the work will largely depend upon its strength and durability. The twine should be real upholsterer's twine, and its life is lengthened if it is drawn across a lump of beeswax before use. The beeswax not only

protects the twine from deterioration but also discourages rust where the knots secure the spring.

For purposes of instruction, it is assumed that the article to be repaired is an ordinary settee, but the method of repair is applicable as well to easy chairs and other upholstered furniture.

**Repairs.** The first operation is the removal of the canvas or burlap cover on the underside. Turn the settee upside down, supporting the center of the seat on a chair. Pull out the tacks holding the burlap in place, and remove it completely. If it is still strong and undamaged, lay it aside to be used again; but if it is faulty, measure it carefully for replacement.

To remove tacks from burlap and webbing, hold an old screwdriver or old chisel against the head of the tack and give it one or two sharp blows with the hammer. Be careful to sweep up all the tacks later, as they are dangerous to the worker when kneeling at the settee during later stages of the work.

The webbing, with the springs attached, is now exposed. Unless only one or two springs are to be repaired or replaced, it is advisable to replace all of the webbing. Release the tacks holding the webbing to the frame of the settee and cut loose the twine securing the springs. Take careful note of the method used by the

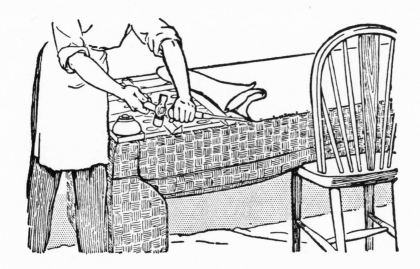

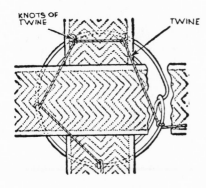

KNOTS OF TWINE       TWINE

upholsterer to tie the springs in place. A typical method is illustrated here.

Next, turn the settee back to its normal position, release the top cover along the front of the settee, and turn it back, complete with the stuffing. It will be necessary, of course, to first remove the covered studs, brass head nails, or other ornamental fixing, together with any binding employed. Lay aside specimens of all these for use when selecting replacement patterns.

The released springs should now be examined for wear and distortion. Take an old spring to the upholsterer's supply house when ordering new ones. It may be necessary to buy a size of spring different

from the original to allow for the results of long compression of the remaining springs.

At this stage, it is best to examine the joints of the frame for any looseness or weakness. Ordinarily, the joints may be repaired with glue and screws. A point to remember here is that when regluing any joint, the old glue must first be completely removed or the result will be unsatisfactory.

When the frame is secure, cut a strip of new burlap or canvas about 5" or 6" wide and as long as the front of the frame. Double back about 1" of this and attach it firmly to the top member of the front frame with tacks. Tack loosely a length of twine close to the tacked edge of the strip of canvas, to act both as a guide and as a support to the stuffing for the rolled edge (of the canvas). Take the old stuffing, if you are going to reuse it, and beat it with a stick to loosen it and give an even texture; then form it into a roll by tucking it around the twine fastened at the edge. Turn back the canvas strip over the rolled stuffing and firmly fix it to the top member of the front frame.

Turn the settee bottom up to facilitate putting in new springs. Remember, also, to strengthen the old springs where necessary. The new springs should be secured exactly on the site of the old ones which they replace. Note that in all good work the springs are not only strongly secured to the canvas underside of the top cover but are also tied to each other to prevent any chance of slipping. Examine all springs which are to remain and fasten firmly wherever necessary.

The new webbing may now be fixed in place. Double back 1" to 2" of the webbing, and secure it by 3 or 4 tacks to the site of the old cross strip. Attach the webbing first with 2 tacks through a single thickness, cut off about 2" beyond the width of the settee, and turn back and fasten the overhang with 2 or 3 more tacks.

Continue this process until all the cross strips are in place. Fix in place the lengthwise strips. Note that they are threaded alternately over and under the cross strips.

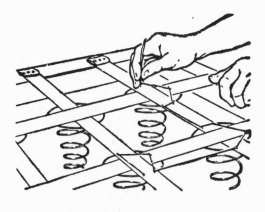

Stitch the springs into position at the intersections of the webbing. During this stitching, the string is joined in one continuous length from spring to spring throughout.

Place the settee on its legs for the next stage—the replacement of the cover over the boxed frame. First, stretch the canvas lining down and secure it to the frame. Arrange the stuffing carefully and spread it evenly over the rolled edge.

Draw down the top cover and fix it in position tightly. The edge of the cover is hidden by binding, depending upon the kind of cover used.

Use ornamental nails to secure the edge of the cover. When the canvas or burlap is fastened over the springs and webbing on the underside, the work is complete.

When repairing the springs in upholstered chairs, stitch them as shown in the illustration. You will usually find that an odd number of springs, most often 5 or 7, have been used originally. If you need extra furniture, it is worthwhile to buy the pieces secondhand and spend a few leisure hours putting them into good repair.

# WOOD FURNITURE UPKEEP

Heat, dampness, and too much bright sunshine can be harmful to a piece of good wood furniture. If the piece is near a radiator or register, the heat will dry out the wood and cause glued joints to fail. Dampness can be equally harmful for it can damage the finish as well as soften certain types of glues. When a finish is exposed to the rays of the sun for too long a period, it will break down and require replacing. So never put a good piece of furniture where it can get too hot, and don't place it near a window unless you draw the curtains during the bright part of the day.

About all the care that a good piece requires is waxing or polishing. Many experts feel that wax is superior to polish but this is usually because wax is rubbed down until it is hard and bright whereas the tendency with polish is just to slap it on and not polish it hard enough, so that it remains sticky and catches dust and dirt. In any event, don't fall for the line that polish will nourish the wood; it can't because there is a finish over the wood.

The main thing to do is to rub the wax or polish with a clean lintless cloth until you get a hard coating.

**Cleaning.** A piece of furniture which has become grimed cannot be expected to respond to ordinary polishing or waxing. It should first be cleaned. This can be done with turpentine or a mineral spirit. If you wish, warm soapy water will do, but you should apply only the foam to the piece and not the water. Use a lintless cloth to rub the foam over the surfaces, then wipe dry with a clean cloth. Once the piece is clean, wax or polish.

**Water and Heat Stains.** White rings and white discolorations on the finish of a piece of furniture caused by hot dishes placed on it, or by water that has been allowed to remain on it for any length of time, can be removed in one of several ways. Often you can get rid of the discoloration by wiping the area lightly with a cloth dampened in denatured alcohol, turpentine, mineral spirits, or a lacquer thinner. First test this method on an inconspicuous area of the finish to make sure that the solvent does not harm it. If this treatment does not work, use powdered rottenstone and linseed or camphorated oil. Put the powdered rottenstone into a saucer, dampen a piece of felt with the oil, and dip it into the rottenstone. Polish over the mark, lightly rubbing in the direction of the wood grain. Wipe the surface clean with your finger or a cloth frequently to see the results. Polish just enough to remove the stain and after wiping the area clean, apply a coat of wax.

**Scratches.** The method of dealing with scratches depends on their depth. Light scratches can often be concealed by waxing. Use a wax that is pigmented so that it has about the same color as the wood. Scratches in mahogany can often be touched up by brushing a little iodine into them. An old-time remedy for scratches in walnut is to rub the meat of a walnut over them. Shoe polish is also effective for scratches, and paint and hardware stores ·sell special touch-up crayons for furniture;

these come in a variety of colors to match the more common wood finishes.

The best way to deal with a deep scratch is with something called "stick shellac," available in a variety of colors at better hardware and paint stores. This is applied somewhat like old-fashioned sealing wax. Heat the blade of a thin flexible knife over a flame that does not produce soot, or with a soldering iron, and then melt some of the shellac on the stick. Apply it to the scratch and let it come a bit above the wood surface. When it is hard, shave it down level with a razor blade held flat against the surface. Polish the patch with powdered rottenstone and linseed oil.

**Cigarette Burns.** These can sometimes be polished out with powdered rottenstone and linseed oil. If the burn is deep, however, more extensive treatment is needed. Remove the charred finish and wood by scraping with a knife. Then smooth the area with fine steel wool. Fill in the area with stick shellac as explained above.

**Dents.** A simple way to remove these is to wipe away the wax or polish with turpentine or a mineral solvent. Put a piece of damp felt over the dent and put a metal bottle cap or metal washer over the felt in the exact spot of the dent. Now take a hot iron and hold it over the cap or washer. The heat from the iron will be transmitted to the cap or washer and through the damp felt, and the steam formed will swell the wood fibers in the dent and make them expand to their original shape. For a very deep dent it may be necessary to remove the finish and prick the wood with a large needle and then steam.

**Loose and Blistered Veneer.** Much of the furniture in the home is made of veneered wood, that is, solid but inexpensive stock that has been covered with a thin slice of wood (veneer) selected for the beauty of its grain and coloring. The thin layer of wood serving as the veneer is attached to the solid base wood with glue.

Sometimes, due to heat or cold, dryness or moisture, the glue will fail to hold, causing the veneer to crack around the edges, or form blisters on the surface of the wood.

When the veneer becomes loose along the edges of a piece, it should be repaired at once, for aside from the chance of moisture getting into the opening to loosen up more glue, the slightest knock may chip off, split, or otherwise damage the thin veneer.

The first step in regluing the veneer is to slip the thin blade of a knife between the veneer and the base wood and scrape out as much of the old glue as possible along with any dirt or dust that may have collected there. The glue that remains can be roughened a little with a knife or a strip of sandpaper so that it will make a good bond with the new glue. Now a thin coat of glue should be spread under the veneer and worked as far back into the opening as possible. A thin knife blade will do for this job. After the glue has been spread on, press the veneer down gently and use a weight or clamps to hold it down until the glue is dry. Protect the finish from being damaged by the clamp or weight by covering it with a heavy cloth, a piece of cardboard, or a piece of wood. If the veneer is brittle, and there is a chance of its splitting or breaking as it is forced back into place, steam it with the steam from a steam iron to make it pliable.

For a blister, use a thin, very sharp knife to split the blister, cutting in the direction of the wood grain. Use a knife with a very thin and flexible blade to reach under the veneer and scrape away as much of the old glue as possible and then apply fresh glue with the same tool. Press down the veneer and remove any glue that oozes out of the split.

**Sticking Drawers.** Most drawers stick because the wood used for the sides has swollen due to damp atmosphere. Drawers on inexpensive pieces often don't have any finish and the bare wood quickly absorbs moisture out of the air. You can help prevent sticking drawers if you coat all unfinished wood with shellac. This will seal the wood against moisture, and as it is such a thin coating, it will not cause the drawers to stick as would a thick coat of paint or varnish.

Another remedy for sticking drawers is to lubricate the edges of the side pieces. This can be done with soap or a wax candle, but a silicone lubricant available at hardware stores is far superior. If this fails to make the drawer work easily, sand down the edges of the side pieces. Do not take off too much, for interior heating during the winter dries out the wood and causes it to shrink and then the drawer will be too loose.

Sometimes a sticking drawer is due to a loose bottom. The bottom of an inexpensive drawer is generally made out of a thin piece of plywood or hardboard, and if it comes loose or bulges from too much weight, it will prevent the drawer from moving easily. This difficulty can be overcome by securing the bottom in place with a few small brads.

Often a drawer can't be pulled out all the way to make the necessary repairs. If the trouble is due to dampness and swelling of the wood, put a lighted lamp bulb in the drawer and allow it to remain long enough to dry out the wood. When the wood is dry, the drawer can usually be pulled out and the sides either sanded down or coated with a lubricant.

**Loose Joints.** Probably the most common repair job on furniture is gluing joints that have worked loose over a period of time. Excessive heat and moisture will weaken certain kinds of glue to the point where they will not hold the joints properly, and this is another reason to keep furniture well away from radiators, registers, and other sources of heat.

Never use nails in making repairs on furniture, and even screws and metal mending plates should be avoided whenever possible. Glue is the accepted and best thing to use on furniture repairs and, if properly used, will provide all the strength usually required.

When it is necessary to reglue a loose joint, first try to remove the piece if this can be done without damage to it or having to take solid joints apart. Remove all traces of the old glue from both surfaces by scraping with a knife.

If you use fine sandpaper to remove the glue, be careful not to take off any of the wood along with the glue because this will prevent your being able to ever achieve a tight joint. When both surfaces are clean, put a thin coat of glue on each. It is not necessary to use more than a very light coat of glue, as too much will weaken rather than strengthen the joint. For most furniture repairs, a white glue is adequate. Fit the two glued surfaces together and apply pressure to the joint until the glue is hard. This pressure can be applied with adjustable clamps, but if these are not available, wrap several layers of string around the joint and insert a piece of wood under the string. Twist the wood several times so that the string is pulled tightly over the joint. It is a good idea to put a piece of cloth under the string to prevent damage to the finish on the furniture. On joints where it is impossible to use either string or clamps, the necessary amount of pressure can be achieved by placing bricks or books on the joint.

It is very often found, when regluing chair rungs, that the rung has shrunk or the hole has become enlarged so that the rung fits loosely in it. Do not expect such a joint to hold after it has been glued, because glue cannot possibly function unless the two pieces of wood fit snugly together.

WOOD
WEDGE

The only remedy is to make the end of the rung larger so that it will fit tightly in the hole. There are several ways of doing this. The best is to make a thin cut across the diameter of the rung with a fine saw. This cut should be about ½" deep, and should be located in the center of the rung. After the cut has been made, drive a small wedge of hardwood into it so that the sides of the rung are spread slightly. The wedge should be very thin, and great care must be taken when driving it in not to split the wood. Now apply the glue and force the rung into the hole.

Another way of making the rung fit tightly is to give the end a coat of glue and wrap silk thread around it until you have built up the surface to fit tightly in the hole. Apply another coat of glue over the thread and then force the rung into place. Another remedy, if the joint is not too loose, is to mix a little fine sawdust with the glue. This gives the glue more body and it will often hold better.

It is always best to take a joint apart for gluing, but this isn't always possible. What you can do here is to inject glue into the joint with a little glue injector, available at most good hardware stores. This device is somewhat similar in design to a hypodermic needle and with it you can inject glue into any joint where there is enough space to allow the point to enter. You can also drill a small hole through the wood to allow the glue to be injected into the right place.

Chair legs and rungs cannot be expected always to remain firm, and if any looseness in the joint is neglected, the strain is likely to be thrown on the piece as a whole, necessitating major repairs.

**Reinforcing Joints.** Loose joints of legs on tables and chairs, like many other joints, can be reinforced with hardwood blocks which are secured in place with glue and screws. The blocks usually have a triangular shape designed to fit snugly into the joint. Surfaces that are to be glued should be sanded to make them perfectly smooth and ensure a tight fit.

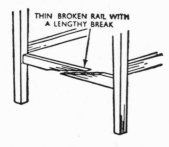

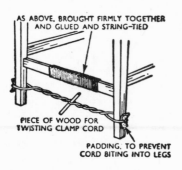

niture, first remove as much of the old finish as you can. By doing this you make it easier to find screws or nails that hold the joints together. With most of the old finish out of the way, you can go to work on the portions of the piece you want to eliminate. Joints which are held together with glue can be opened by steaming or soaking the glue with water. Screws and nails holding two pieces of wood together are sometimes hard to find because the heads have been sunk below the surface of the wood, and the holes then filled with putty or even wood plugs. Where a nail is set below the surface, the two pieces of wood should be pried apart gently so that the wood will not be split.

One type of fastening that is very hard to find is the blind dowel. Here a hole is drilled part way through each of the two pieces of wood that are to be joined. A length of dowel is glued and set

Breaks in chair rails, rungs, and so forth, can be repaired rather easily if the break is parallel to the grain. Coat the surfaces with wood glue and hold them together with string and a clamp cord.

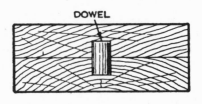

## REMODELING FURNITURE

In practically every attic or basement you can find pieces of furniture which are in good condition but which are never used because of their design. This heavy, over-elaborate furniture that was made half a century or so ago does not fit in with modern home decorating. Much of it, however, is well constructed and made of good materials. It is often possible to remodel furniture of this sort, strip off much of the machine carving, and give it a light finish, with the result that it may be used in good taste. Often, the basic design is good; altering the shape of legs or decoration will do much.

When dismantling a piece of old fur-

in one of the holes; glue is applied to the portion of the dowel above the surface, and the second piece of wood is set down so that the dowel goes into the hole drilled for it. The dowel, naturally, cannot be seen, and the two pieces of wood cannot be taken apart unless the glue is softened with steam or water.

Any of the machine carving which cannot be removed in sections can be dealt with by planing or with a chisel.

When you have removed all the woodwork necessary, check the rest of the joints to see if any need regluing. Attend to these and then give the entire piece a good sanding to remove the remainder of the finish and to smooth out areas that may have been damaged during dismantling.

# REFINISHING FURNITURE

To obtain the best results, all finishing operations should be done in a room free from dust. If dust is present, it is almost sure to stick on the freshly applied finish, usually spoiling the work.

Workshops are usually not suitable for finishing because of the amount of sawdust present. This is especially true where power saws and sanders have been used. Basements, too, are usually dusty. The best course is to select a room in the house which is not only free from dust but also has good natural light and good ventilation and where the temperature is about 70°F. This is important in order to get the best results. Furniture and the floor of the room should be protected with a drop cloth or two.

Separate as many parts of the piece as possible before finishing, and treat each as a separate unit. This, you will find, is easier and actually quicker than trying to finish the entire unit as a whole. Also, it will eliminate the possibility that doors and drawers will stick due to hardened paint or varnish in the seams or around the edges. On very fine work, it will be wise to remove the hardware.

Small articles, such as chairs, should be placed on a table for finishing. A nail

-TACKS-

or tack driven into the end of each leg will raise the piece high enough to allow you to get at the underparts with ease. As a rule, it is better to do the small and hard-to-get-at portions first. Leave the large areas until the end. By doing the inconspicuous portions first you also have an opportunity of seeing if the finish is going to come out as you desire.

There are many different kinds of finishes you can use on old and new furniture. Which one to select depends on how much time and effort you want to put into the project, the kind of wood you are dealing with, and the condition of the old finish.

**Enamel.** This is the easiest type of finish to apply and is almost foolproof. It can be used on both new work and old work. To apply it on an unpainted piece of furniture, first sand the wood lightly to make it absolutely smooth, dust it clean, and then apply a coat of enamel undercoater. If the finish is to be a color other than white, the undercoater can be tinted either by mixing some colors in oil into it or by adding a little of the colored enamel you plan to use as the finish coat. Allow the undercoater to dry at least 24 hours and then give the surface a sanding with No. 2/0 sandpaper. Remove all traces of dust with a clean cloth dampened in mineral spirits or turpentine.

The surface is now ready for the enamel. Enamel is best applied with a special chisel-tip enamel brush. Enamel, unlike paint, is flowed onto the surface and the action of the enamel removes the brush marks so that the surface dries completely smooth. Once the finish has been

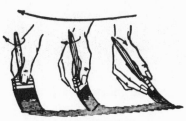

SHORT, LIGHT STROKES

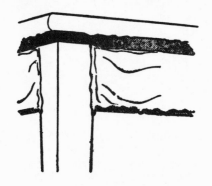

applied, do not go back over it for additional brushings as this may leave marks which won't flow out. Be careful of accumulations of enamel around the edges. These must be removed at once before they are dry.

In most cases, one coat of enamel will be sufficient. If it is not, allow it to dry thoroughly, give it a light sanding and dusting, and then apply a second coat.

If the piece of furniture has been previously finished with shellac, varnish, or enamel, and the old finish is in good condition, new enamel can be applied directly over the old. But if the old finish has deep scratches or spots where the old finish has chipped away, these will naturally show up after the enamel has been applied. Assuming that the old finish is in good condition, wipe it clean with mineral spirits or turpentine and then sand lightly. It is essential that you do this; if you apply enamel over a very smooth surface, it will not make a good bond and may chip off rather easily. After sanding, dust.

Although the finish coat of enamel may be applied right over the old finish, you will get a better job if you first apply a coat of enamel undercoater. This provides the best base for the enamel and also ensures an excellent bond between the enamel and the old finish.

If the old finish on a piece of furniture is in poor condition—peeling, cracking, rough, and so on—strip it off down to the wood and then treat the surface as you would for a new piece of furniture. The best way to remove the old finish is with a paste-type remover (see chapter 6, page 138).

**Glazing (Antiquing).** This is a method of finishing that is very popular today. It is used to produce "period" pieces with interesting shades. Glazing liquids can be purchased in various shades at paint and hardware stores. It is also possible to buy complete glazing kits which contain everything you need for the job.

To produce this finish, the wood is first given a coat of enamel or, sometimes, paint. The exact shade of glaze to use should depend on the color used for the base coat. If the base coat is light, then a rather light glaze will be sufficient to produce the desired amount of shading. As darker base colors are used, darker glazes must also be used to produce the right amount of contrast.

The glaze is applied over the entire surface with a brush. Before it has a chance to harden, it is wiped off with a piece of clean cheesecloth. The wiping should begin in the center of the surface and should be done with a circular motion. The amount of glaze left on the surface depends on the amount of pressure used in wiping.

More and more glaze is allowed to remain as the wiping gets closer to the edges of the surface. The final effect should be a gradual blending, with little or no glaze at the center and with a greater and greater intensity of glaze as the edges are approached. If the glaze appears to be too heavy in some places, or if it becomes too stiff for easy wiping, dampen the cloth with a little turpentine or mineral spirits.

Interesting effects can be achieved by using your finger or a brush instead of a cloth. For large surfaces it is best to add a little linseed oil to the glaze to slow up the drying so that the work can be accomplished unhurriedly.

Getting the proper technique with glaze will require a little practice. Your first attempt may not be entirely satisfactory. If so, it is a simple matter to remove all the glaze with some turpentine or mineral spirits and start again.

**Varnish.** Varnish, if properly applied, will produce a very fine finish for wood furniture. Use a top-quality varnish designed for furniture and apply it with a good varnish brush.

Varnish is a clear type of finish, so it cannot be used over paint—the paint must first be removed. Sand the wood until it is perfectly smooth. If you wish to darken the wood, apply a coat of oil stain. Allow the stain to dry for 24 hours and then rub down the surfaces with fine steel wool. If you are working with open-grain woods such as oak or mahogany, a filler should be applied. Use a filler of the same color or tone as the stain. When the filler is dry, steel-wool the surface and dust. The final step in making the surface ready for the varnish is to give it a coat of white shellac. Use a 3-pound cut and be sure that the shellac is fresh. Sand with steel wool after the shellac is dry.

Varnishing should not be done during wet weather or when the humidity is very high. For best results, select a warm, dry day and be sure that the room in which you work is not damp. Varnish applied in a damp basement will not dry properly. The temperature of the air has a good deal to do with how well varnish dries out. For best results, the temperature should be between 70 and 80°F. This means that during the winter months, varnish must be applied indoors in a heated room. If the varnish container has been stored in a cold room, place it in a pan containing warm water until the varnish has reached a good working temperature.

The application of varnish by brush is divided into three operations. The first step is called "cutting in." In this operation the brush is dipped about one third the length of the bristles into the container. The varnish is then applied to the surface with smooth strokes. The next step is "cross-brushing," that is, the brush is drawn across the wood grain. Start from

VARNISH

either side and work the brush halfway across. The final step is "tipping off." Here the brush is drawn with the wood grain so that the tips of the bristles just touch the surface. Excess varnish around the edges of the piece or in the molding should be removed immediately, before it

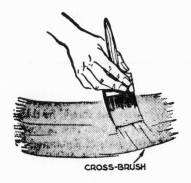

CROSS-BRUSH

has set. Make a careful inspection of the piece to be sure that there are no areas which have been missed.

Give the first coat of varnish about 24 hours to dry, and then give it a light sanding with fine steel wool to cut the gloss. Dust the surface and apply the second coat. The number of coats required is a matter of personal taste. Two coats will produce a very adequate finish for most jobs.

**Shellac.** This also makes a good natural finish, but it is not as resistant to heat or water as varnish and therefore is not suitable for dining-room tables and other surfaces where liquids or heat may get to the shellac. The wood should be sanded smooth, and stained if desired. Use a 3-pound cut of either white or orange shellac, depending on whether you want a light or dark finish.

Take the same precautions when applying shellac as outlined above for varnish. Shellac sets and dries rather rapidly, so you must work fairly fast to get it on properly. On the other hand, since it dries rapidly, there is less chance of its picking up dust.

After the first coat of shellac is hard and dry, rub it down with fine steel wool, dust, and then apply the second coat. Two or three coats should be enough.

**French Polishing.** This is one of the oldest methods of finishing fine furniture. White shellac should be thinned down to a 1-pound cut. This is done by adding 2 quarts of denatured alcohol to each quart of shellac, assuming the shellac is originally a standard 4-pound cut. The shellac is applied to the surface with a piece of soft, lintless cloth rolled into a ball. The cloth is dipped into the shellac and then rubbed over the wood in straight strokes. Use very light pressure. Allow the surface to dry and then sand lightly with No. 6/0 sandpaper. Dust and then apply a second coat of shellac in the same way as the first. Additional coats are applied until a light glow begins to appear on the finish. At this stage, add several drops of boiled linseed oil to the shellac and apply this mixture to the surface with the cloth, using a circular motion. Add additional drops of oil to each coat until the deep finish you want has been satisfactorily obtained.

**Dip-and-Rub Finish.** This is another type of shellac finish. It is somewhat easier and faster to apply than with the French polishing method. Fill one saucer with pure turpentine and another saucer with white shellac from a 4-pound cut. Roll a piece of lintless cloth into a pad and dip it first into the turpentine and then into the shellac. Rub the pad over the surface with a circular motion. Apply 4 or 5 coats in the same fashion. When the final coat is dry, rub the surface down with a cloth dipped in linseed oil.

**Stencils.** Many pieces of furniture, both modern and period, can be improved considerably by stenciling designs on them in contrasting colors. Ready-made stencils are available at paint and art supply stores, but it is a simple matter to make your own. Draw the design and then transfer it to stencil paper. The design is then cut out with a very sharp knife or a razor blade. The cuts must be very sharp or the final transfer will have rough edges. After the stencil has been cut out, it should be coated with shellac or lacquer to stiffen the paper. The stencil is then placed on the work and held securely with masking tape. If you are going to use a spray gun, mask a sufficiently large area around the stencil to protect it from the spray.

Paint can be applied either with a spray gun or with a stencil brush. A spray gun will produce better results than applying the paint by hand, but care must be taken not to allow the paint to become too thick. And don't hold the gun in such a fashion that some of the paint gets under the edges of the stencil and spoils the design.

If the paint is to be applied with a brush, then a special stencil brush should be used. Ordinary paint is too thin for good stenciling. Colors in oil are far superior. As they come from the tube too thick for application with the stencil brush, they must be thinned down to the proper consistency with turpentine.

After the paint is dry and the stencil has been removed, the design can be protected against wear with a thin coat of clear varnish.

**Wax.** This is a relatively easy technique to use and one that will provide a long-wearing finish. The wood should be sanded smooth, stained if desired, filled, and then given 2 coats of thin shellac or one coat of varnish or lacquer. After the final coat is dry, sand lightly with steel wool and then apply a rather heavy, but even, coat of good paste wax.

Allow the wax to dry for about one hour and then rub with a piece of felt, in the direction of the wood grain. Allow the wax to dry for a day or so and then apply a second coat somewhat more lightly than the first. Several additional coats should be applied in the same manner, allowing a day for drying between each 2 coats. The success of this finish depends on the quality of the wax used and the thoroughness with which the rubbing is done.

**Linseed Oil.** This finish produces excellent results, especially on walnut. The final finish is extremely resistant to heat and scratches. When wear begins to show in certain areas, it is a simple matter to patch them up with additional coats of oil. Several methods are used in producing this finish. A simple method is to mix two thirds boiled linseed oil to one third turpentine. This solution may be tinted with a stain, but it should be remembered that the linseed oil alone will darken the wood somewhat, and this usually gives enough color.

Warm the linseed oil solution in a double boiler. Don't place it over an open flame, as the solution is a highly inflammable one. The oil mixture is applied to the wood with a brush or clean cloth and rubbed into the surface. Put on a heavy coat.

Allow the oil to remain on the wood for several hours and then wipe off the excess with a clean cloth. The piece should then be rubbed down with a piece of felt wrapped around a block of wood. Allow the oil to dry for several days, and then apply a second coat of linseed oil in the same manner. This process is repeated until the wood will no longer absorb oil.

Additional rubbings at frequent intervals over a period of many weeks will improve the appearance of the finish. Rubbing several times a year will maintain it.

Another method of applying this finish calls for the application of linseed oil without the turpentine. The oil is applied with a cloth or brush and then rubbed into the wood by hand until the wood will no longer absorb oil. Frequent hard rubbings by hand over a period of months are necessary to produce the final effect. But many people consider it well worth the trouble.

An oil finish is often used on knotty-pine paneling and on other pine articles where a natural finish is desired. The mixture used here is one that consists of 1 part linseed oil to 2 parts turpentine.

**Limed Oak.** This type of finish is used extensively on modern furniture. The wood must first be bleached with a commercial bleaching agent. After this, the wood may be tinted with stain or left as it is. Seal it with a wash coat of water-white lacquer and then fill with a white filler (made by adding zinc white to natural filler). The top coat of the finish must be water-white lacquer.

**Pickled Pine.** This finish can be used on a wide variety of woods. Dark woods must first be bleached to a light color. In the case of pine, a gray stain is applied to the wood. This is followed by a thin wash coat of white shellac. A light filler is then applied, or a light wiping stain. Finally a thin coat of white shellac is applied.

**Honey Tone.** This finish is particularly effective on light-colored woods like maple and birch. If dark woods are to be used, they must first be bleached. A toner of one part white lacquer and four parts clear lacquer is applied directly to the wood. This produces a thin and transparent coating. Several applications of the toner are made. The final coating consists of 2 coats of water-white lacquer.

**Heather Mahogany.** In this case the effect desired is created by using a white filler in the wood. Remove the excess filler by wiping across the grain and then apply a top coat of water-white lacquer.

**Blonde Finishes.** A wide variety of finishes fall under the general classification of "blonde finishes." The blonde effect can be obtained with light-colored woods by the application of a tinted coat of flat varnish or of a blonde sealer. Either will produce a blonde effect without covering the wood grain. The top coat must produce a transparent covering. In the case of dark woods, it is necessary to bleach them to a lighter shade.

# OUTDOOR FURNITURE

Because it is often exposed to a variety of weather conditions, outdoor furniture requires more care and maintenance than indoor furniture.

**Wood Furniture.** In making any repairs, use rustproof nails, screws, and other hardware. Brass is excellent but expensive. Aluminum is good, as is hot-dipped galvanized hardware such as screws, nails, and hinges. Never use ordinary steel nails, screws, or other hardware items because they rust.

If outdoor wood furniture is to be painted, use a good-quality trim and shutter enamel or one designed for outdoor furniture. Don't use ordinary house paint since this is not as elastic as enamel and may chalk off on clothing.

Many pieces of outdoor wood furniture are not painted but left natural. Unfinished wood is easily stained by liquids and foods and absorbs dirt. It is wise to give the wood a coat of a clear exterior wood sealer. This will protect the wood from the weather and also prevent it from absorbing stains. Wood pieces, as well as other kinds of outdoor furniture, are often left outside the year around, but it is better for the furniture if it can be put under cover during the winter months.

**Aluminum Furniture.** After it has been exposed to the weather for a time, the metal will become discolored due to oxidation of the aluminum. It can be made bright again by first wiping it with a metal conditioner containing phosphoric acid. These conditioners are sold under various trade names at paint and hardware stores. After cleaning the metal, polish it with fine steel wool until it is bright. Wipe it down with a paint thinner and then coat it with a clear nonyellowing acrylic lacquer. This will keep the metal bright.

The fabric webbing for most aluminum furniture is made of fiberglass. When it begins to fail it can be replaced. Replacement kits containing sufficient webbing for a chair or chaise are sold at garden, hardware, and furniture stores and come with directions on how the webbing should be applied.

**Iron Furniture.** This requires the most upkeep because if the metal is not coated with paint, rust will appear. You can assume that iron furniture will need some work on it at least once a year. The most practical time to do this is in the spring, or in the fall before the furniture is put away.

# 5

# MASONRY

By masonry we refer to those constructions in and around the house that are made of poured concrete, masonry block (concrete or cinder), brick, and stone. There are relatively few houses where you won't find masonry in one form or another, such as foundation walls, piers, fireplace and chimney, garage floors, walks, drives, and so forth. From time to time some of these will require repairs. Masonry also lends itself to do-it-yourself projects. It is not expensive, and with a little experience it is possible for the amateur to build a variety of items, such as an outdoor fireplace, brick wall, concrete-block retaining wall, or garden pool.

Portland cement is the basic ingredient for all forms of masonry. When mixed with water it undergoes a chemical change that transforms it into a paste adhesive that will bond the materials mixed with it —sand or sand and gravel—into a strong mass. Portland cement is sold by the bag and each bag contains 1 cubic foot. The bags are moisture-resistant, but they should not be left out in the rain, and when they are opened they must be stored in a dry place. If the cement becomes damp before use, it will be ruined.

Sand is another essential element of masonry. It is mixed with cement to produce mortar to lay up bricks and block. When gravel is added to the sand and cement in the right proportions, it produces concrete. Sand should be clean and free of dirt, clay, and vegetable matter. Sand from ocean beaches, unless washed with fresh water, is not very satisfactory because it contains so much salt. You can buy sand either by the bag or by the cubic yard at lumber yards and masonry supply houses. Gravel is also available from these same sources and is sold by the cubic yard. It may be obtained in sizes from $1/2''$ to $2''$, depending on the job.

When working on a thin wall or floor, the size of the gravel should not be more than one third the thickness of the wall or floor. The gravel should be clean and as free of any impurities as the sand.

## CONCRETE

This is a mixture of cement, sand, gravel, and water. It is used for floors, walks, driveways, and poured concrete walls. Dry-mixed concrete is available at hardware and building supply stores. All you need to do is add water as directed on the package and mix either in a metal wheelbarrow or on a wood or concrete floor. This product is good for small jobs, but it is expensive compared with other kinds of concrete and therefore seldom used when a good deal of concrete is required. For very large jobs you can get ready-mixed concrete that is delivered ready to pour from a truck. This is a good method when you need several cubic yards of concrete for a big job, such as a poured concrete floor or driveway or a reinforced retaining wall. The cost will be around $20 a cubic yard and usually a minimum charge is involved. You can also rent a power concrete mixer for around $15 a day from tool rental stores; this is a good way to get a lot of concrete at low cost.

If you mix the concrete yourself, either in a power mixer or by hand, watch the proportions. The proportions of cement, sand, gravel, and water used depend on the nature of work to be done and the condition of the sand and gravel. These two materials are seldom completely free of moisture, and this must be taken into account when adding water. The amount of moisture in the sand and gravel (aggregate) will vary from a damp condition to very wet. The water required for very wet aggregate is considerably less than that required for damp aggregate.

The strength of concrete depends upon the union of the water and cement to form a paste which, when hard, will bind the particles of sand and gravel together. Accordingly, it is very important that the proper proportions of water and cement be maintained. The accompanying table gives recommended quantities of water for various jobs. Make up a trial batch of concrete, using this table as a guide. If the mixture is too stiff to work, use less sand and gravel in the next batch. If the mixture is too wet, add more sand and gravel. Do not change the amount of water, as this will affect the bonding properties of the mixture. In other words, keep the ratio of cement to water as set down in the table, and control the workability of the mixture through the use of more or less aggregate. Always make up a trial mixture of concrete, and get it right, before mixing a large batch for the job.

Concrete that has been properly mixed can be poured into a form with ease and packed down until it forms a dense mass. The concrete should be plastic enough to prevent the pebbles or gravel from falling out when the mixture is handled. There should be no space between the elements of the coarse aggregate. The stiffness of the mixtures varies with the job, so that the mixture used for a garage floor can be stiffer than that used for small forms.

Mixing the various ingredients should be done with care. To make certain that the right amount of each material is used, have a pail marked in quarts and gallons for measuring the water and a bottomless box for the sand and coarse aggregate. The box should be built to hold exactly one cubic foot.

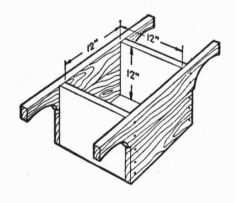

If you are mixing the concrete in a metal wheelbarrow or on a floor or platform, measure out the quantity of sand and then measure out the cement and spread it over the sand. These two materials should be mixed until they form a mass with a uniform color. There should be no streaks—an indication that the work has not been done thoroughly. After the sand and cement have been mixed, measure out the coarse aggregate or gravel and spread it over the mixture. Continue mixing until the pebbles or gravel are well distributed throughout the sand and cement. Measure out the correct amount

**RECOMMENDED CONCRETE MIXTURES FOR VARIOUS KINDS OF CONSTRUCTION**

| Kind of Work | U.S. Gallons of Water to Add to Each 1-Sack Batch | | | Trial Mixture for First Batch (1 cu. yd.) | | | Maximum Aggregate Size (in.) |
|---|---|---|---|---|---|---|---|
| | Damp sand and pebbles | Wet sand and pebbles | Very wet sand and pebbles | Cement (sacks) | Sand (cu. ft.) | Pebbles (cu. ft.) | |
| Foundation walls which need not be watertight, mass concrete for footings, retaining walls, garden walls | 6¼ | Average sand 5½ | 4¾ | 1 | 2¾ | 4 | 1½ |
| Watertight basement walls, walls above ground, lawn rollers, hot-beds, cold frames, well curbs and platforms, cisterns, septic tanks, watertight floors, sidewalks, step-pingstone and flagstone walks, driveways, play courts, outdoor fireplace base and walls, refuse burners, ash receptacles, porch floors, basement floors, garden and lawn pools, steps, corner posts, gate posts, piers, columns | 5½ | Average sand 5 | 4¼ | 1 | 2¼ | 3 | 1½ |
| Fence posts, grape arbor posts, mailbox posts, flower boxes and pots, benches, birdbaths, sundials, pedestals and other garden furniture, work of very thin section | 4½ | Average sand 4 | 3¾ | 1 | 1¾ | 2 | ¾ |

of water and pour it into a depression formed in the middle of the pile of dry concrete. Start mixing again and continue until there is no question that all the materials have been combined and the water distributed throughout the mixture.

A hoe and a long-handled shovel are the only tools you need to mix concrete by hand. If you are using a power mixer, add the elements in the same order as for hand mixing.

**Pouring Concrete.** The best practice is to pour the concrete quickly, and in no event later than 45 minutes after mixing. Before doing so, all debris should be removed from the forms.

Concrete is deposited in level layers, usually not more than 6″ deep. As it is placed, it is tamped and spaded just enough to settle it thoroughly and produce a dense mass. Working the concrete next to the forms ensures an even, dense surface.

At the end of a day's run, or where the work has to stop long enough for the concrete to begin to harden, the top surface is roughened just before it hardens so as to remove laitance, or scum, and provide a good bonding surface for the next layer of concrete. Just before resuming concreting, the roughened surface is cleaned and then brushed with cement-water paste of a thick, creamy consistency. This paste is applied in a thick brush coating just a few feet ahead of the concreting operation so that it does not have a chance to dry.

**Finishing Concrete.** A smooth finish is produced with a steel trowel, care being taken to prevent too early or excessive troweling. This care is required because troweling too soon or too much is likely to result in surfaces that will dust or will develop numerous fine cracks called hair checks. These can be avoided by proper finishing to produce surfaces that will be dense and smooth, and will prove durable in service.

The best practice is to allow the concrete to stand until it is quite stiff but is still workable. Then the steel trowel compacts the concrete and produces a dense surface. When the mixture is quite stiff, cement and fine particles are not drawn to the surface under the action of the trowel. Consequently such finishes are free from objectionable dusting and hair checking.

The concrete is struck off carefully just after it is placed in the forms. This removes all humps and hollows, leaving a true, even surface for the final troweling operation.

**Use of Wood Float.** For sidewalks, driveways, and some floors, an even yet gritty, nonslippery surface often is desired. When a finish of this type is required, final finishing is done with a wood float instead of a steel trowel. Final finishing is delayed until the surface has become quite stiff. The finish produced with a wood float is commonly described as a "sidewalk" finish.

**Curing Concrete.** Concrete hardens because of a chemical reaction between portland cement and water. This process continues as long as temperatures are favorable and moisture is present to hydrate the cement.

The gain in strength of concrete during the first week is approximately as great as that during the succeeding 3 months. Once concrete has become thoroughly dry, there is no further gain. For this reason, it is especially important to protect concrete from drying or chilling immediately after it is placed if you want it to achieve the maximum strength, watertightness, and general durability.

The best temperatures for curing concrete are from 70° to 80°F. At higher temperatures, hardening takes place too rapidly. As the temperature is lowered below 70°F, the rate of hardening decreases. No strength gain whatever can be expected while concrete is frozen. Freezing within the first 24 hours is almost certain to result in permanent injury to the concrete.

Wet burlap, canvas, sand, or straw coverings are often used to protect newly placed concrete. The covering is placed as soon as it can be done without marring the surface, care being taken to keep the covering continuously wet by sprinkling. When a cover is not used, wetting the concrete is begun soon after finishing.

**Concrete Forms.** Concrete weighs about 125 pounds per cubic foot, and the forms used for it must be solidly built if they are to stand this strain.

Green lumber is good to use for forms because it will not absorb moisture from the concrete and, consequently, is not liable to warp. If well-seasoned lumber is used, it is wise to cover it with

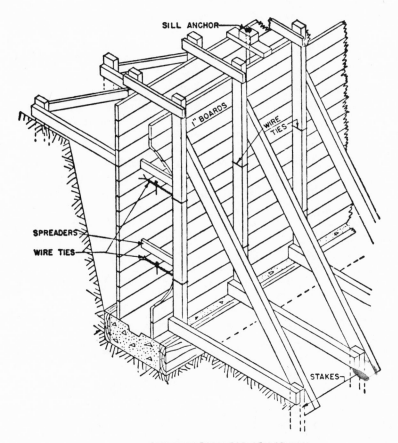

SILL ANCHOR

1" BOARDS

WIRE TIES

SPREADERS

WIRE TIES

STAKES

CONCRETE FORM FOR CELLAR WALL

waterproof building paper or plastic so that it won't absorb moisture. Exterior plywood is good for forms and so is tongued-and-grooved lumber. A 2″ × 4″ stock is suitable for the frame of the form.

Plan the form so that very little cutting of the wood is necessary. In this way you will be able to use the same wood for many jobs. Construct the forms so that they can be taken apart easily and without damage to the wood or concrete. Use the double-head concrete-form nails, as these can be pulled out easily.

After the concrete has been poured, leave the forms in place until you are certain that it is hard. Do not make the mistake of ruining a good concrete job by ripping off the forms too soon.

## Mortar

Mortar is the bonding agent used for building with brick, masonry block, and stone. It is also used for repairing cracks and holes in masonry surfaces such as walks, driveways, foundation walls, and stucco surfaces.

The chief ingredients of ordinary mortar are portland cement, sand, and clean water—and sometimes hydrated lime if the mortar is to be used for brick. If lime is used, it replaces that much cement. The proportions most generally advocated are 1 part portland cement to 3 parts sand, with enough water to make the mixture pliable. That ratio forms the strongest mortar and should be used wherever masonry is to be exposed to weather, fire, water, vibration, or load. However, such mortar sets quickly and is therefore more difficult to use.

"Ten-percent lime" is the name of another mortar formula. In this, the 3 parts sand are added to 1 part consisting of 90% cement and 10% lime. This mixture is easier to use than the one described above.

Mortar sets rather quickly, so don't mix more than you can use in 30 minutes. If, after that amount of time, some of the mortar has not been used up, throw it away and mix a fresh batch.

**Mixing Mortar.** It will prove helpful to build a mixing box as near as practicable to the site of your bricklaying operations, as the less distance you have to carry the mortar the better. Use planks 1″ or 2″ thick to form a box about 8′ long, 4′ wide, and with sides 8″ or 10″ high. The end pieces should slant out at an angle of about 45 degrees. Nail the floor of the box to crosspieces under it. Then nail the sides to the diagonal end pieces, and finally toenail the sides to the floor of the box.

Similarly, a large metal wheelbarrow can be used as a mixing box. Use a pail or small box for measuring your ingredients. Put the sand in first, 3 pails full. Then, if you are using the 3-and-1 mix, add a pail full of cement.

If you are using the 1:1:6 mix, add ½ pail of cement to the 3 of sand, mix it in well with a shovel or hoe, and finally add ½ pail of hydrated lime, mixing in well.

Add water slowly and mix it in well with hoe or shovel. When the mixture is stiff, add a little more water and stir some more. When the mortar becomes smooth and plastic and falls from the shovel or hoe as a soft mass, it is ready to use. It should not be watery. If you get too much water in it by mistake, add more sand and cement within the proportions you are following.

**Ready-Mixed Mortar.** This is available at hardware stores and lumber yards. It is sold by the bag, and these come in various sizes. Ready-mixed mortar requires only the addition of water for use. While it is more expensive than mortar you would mix yourself, it is very convenient and is most suitable for small jobs and repair work.

Considerably more expensive than the ready-mixed mortar made of portland cement and sand, are the newer vinyl or plastic mortars and patching cements. These products may cost as much as $2 for a 15-pound bag, but they do have certain advantages over other types, especially for repair work. These materials produce a far stronger patch than you could make with portland-cement mortar, and they can be applied in very thin coats, which makes them ideal for smoothing out rough or worn spots on concrete floors, walks, and steps. Some of them are mixed with water for use; some come supplied with a special solvent which is added just prior to use. Because of their high cost, these newer mortars are seldom used for extensive jobs such as building a wall or outdoor fireplace of brick, masonry block, or stone.

**Planning Brickwork.** Before any mortar is mixed and spread, you should lay out the whole first course of brick the full length of the job to see if you come out with an even number of bricks. Allow about ½″ between bricks. Then increase or decrease the space between each 2 bricks to make the bricks come out even. That is usually possible only on distances of 8′ or more. On shorter walls you may have to use a partial brick. Cutting bricks can be done with the cold chisel and hammer.

The following table gives the probable number of bricks needed to build 100 square feet of wall, that is, a wall 10′ long and 10′ high:

| Thickness of joint | 8″ wall | 12″ wall | 16″ wall |
|---|---|---|---|
| ⅜″ | 1,310 | 1,965 | 2,620 |
| ½″ | 1,232 | 1,848 | 2,465 |
| ⅝″ | 1,161 | 1,742 | 2,322 |

# BRICKLAYING

Soak bricks in a pail of water before laying them. If this is not done, the dry brick will absorb so much water from the mortar that it will dry out too soon and not bond well. Then the mortar will crumble away after it dries, and you will have cracks in your wall.

**Kinds of Bricks.** There are many kinds of brick, but the most common types are common brick, face brick, and firebrick.

Common brick is the usual red type which can be purchased at the lumber yard in practically any town or city. Its size is always 8″ long, 3¾″ wide, and 2½″ thick.

Face brick is generally the same size as common brick but comes in other sizes as well. It is made more carefully and generally of better materials, comes in a variety of colors and finishes, and is often made to order. Face brick is sometimes called enameled or glazed brick.

Firebrick is specially made for use in fireplaces, ovens, and chimneys, where flame or high temperature is generally present. It is made of a particular kind of clay that resists intense heat without crumbling. Dried differently than other brick, it is repressed after partially dry and then fired again. Firebrick is generally 9″ long, 4½″ wide, and 2½″ thick.

Brick is produced in a variety of colors, some of which may harmonize in certain locations better than others. Also in recent years brick has been painted with cement or oil paint. However, painting brick walls does not usually add to the durability or weather resistance of the structure.

**Courses.** Each row of bricks is called a course. There are two main types: (a) the "stretcher" course wherein bricks are laid flat, end to end, and (b) the "header" course wherein bricks are laid flat and side by side.

Bricks laid in a header course naturally form a wall 8″ thick, as the bricks are 8″ long. The 8″ width is generally

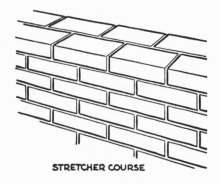

STRETCHER COURSE

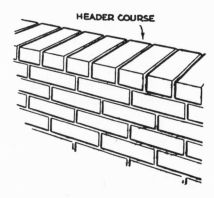

HEADER COURSE

considered to be the minimum thickness for any independent brick wall. Two stretcher courses laid side by side, with mortar between them, also form a wall 8″ thick.

In both stretcher and header courses, bricks are laid on their 3¾″ × 8″ surfaces. When laid on their sides (the 2¼″ × 8″ surfaces) they are said to be laid "on face," or in a "rowlock course."

**Bond.** A brick wall is made by laying several courses, one above another, and the arrangement of the courses is called the bond. Actually, it is the pattern of the wall.

The commonest arrangement is "common bond." You will notice that there are 5 stretcher courses topped by a header course. If the wall is built higher, 5 more stretcher courses will be followed by another header course. This process continues to the top of the wall. As the width of

**101**

COMMON BOND

FLEMISH BOND

the bricks on the stretcher course is only 3¾″, a second stretcher course has to be laid beside the first, with mortar between, to make the total width 8″. The header course will then tie in these 2 courses and prevent the wall from coming apart in the middle.

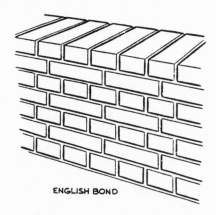

ENGLISH BOND

Another type of bond is "English bond." In this bond, courses of headers and stretchers alternate. A header course is laid first, and then 2 stretcher courses side by side on top of it. Then comes another header course, and so on. In laying 2 stretcher courses alongside each other, be sure to stagger all vertical joints.

A third type of bond is "Flemish bond," in which each course is a combination of headers and stretchers. With each

successive course the headers center on the stretchers in the course below.

**Bricklaying Tools.** Professional bricklayers use a wide variety of tools to speed up the work of laying bricks. As far as the home handyman is concerned, he can readily get along with a trowel, spirit

TROWEL

HAMMER

COLD CHISEL

RAKER

LEVEL

level, heavy hammer, raker, and cold chisel. The level should be about 2′ long, and of the type that can be used to check both vertical and horizontal lines.

Another way to help ensure that your brick wall is straight is to make and use a straightedge. Take a seasoned piece of lumber 10′ to 12′ long, 6″ wide, and 1″ to 2″ thick. Finish one edge so that it is perfectly straight and true. The ends of the other edge can be beveled down from the 6″ width to about 1″ to decrease the weight and make it easier to handle. Use this straightedge to check that the sides of your wall are straight and that the top of each course of brick is horizontal.

**Joints.** There are numerous ways to finish the outsides of the mortar joints between bricks so that they will look attractive. The commonest method is the flush

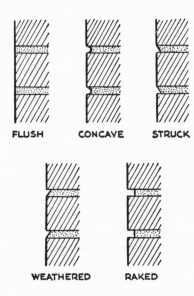

FLUSH     CONCAVE     STRUCK

WEATHERED     RAKED

joint; but this does not wear too well on exterior brick surfaces, as water drains down, dampens the mortar, and eventually wears some of it away. The concave joint is one that is easily made with a raker having a beveled edge. The mortar should be permitted to set for a few minutes before this joint is made. The struck joint and the weathered joint are made by using the point of the trowel. The raked joint is probably the most difficult to make, and amateur bricklayers would do well to avoid it.

## Laying Brick

Lay the end bricks first. Spread mortar with your trowel on the foundation to form what is called the bed joint and place the brick on it. Press the brick down so that it is ½″ from the foundation. Scrape up excess mortar.

After both end bricks of a course are laid, stretch a taut line from one end to the other to aid you in setting the rest of the bricks in an exact straight line. Your eye is not exact enough, and it is essential to have the foundation course exactly straight.

Expert bricklayers pick up enough mortar on a trowel to form a bed joint for 4 or 5 bricks, but the novice will do well to place just enough mortar for one brick at a time. Place some mortar against the

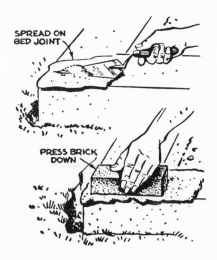

SPREAD ON BED JOINT

PRESS BRICK DOWN

head of the brick already laid and also on the head of the next brick to be laid so that each head joint (between the ends of 2 bricks) will be solidly filled. Surplus mortar squeezed out of joints should be picked up with the trowel and placed on the bed for the next brick.

Try to avoid picking up a brick after it has been laid in position; if a brick is moved, once the mortar has begun to set, the bond will not be perfect, and slight cracks may result that will allow water to get into the wall.

**Closure Brick.** When you come to the last brick (called the closure brick) to be laid in a course, be sure to place mortar

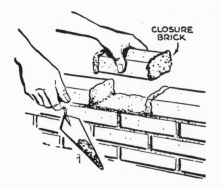

on the ends of both bricks already in place, and on both ends of the closure brick.

If you come to the end of a course of brick and find you have misjudged and left too much or too little space for the last brick, do not go back and try to tap several bricks closer or farther apart. Remove all the bricks you need to shift and all the mortar holding them, and re-lay them with fresh mortar.

When removing excess mortar squeezed out when a brick is laid, lift the trowel upward rather than sideways. Also, lift up slightly in the direction of bricks already laid rather than away from laid bricks. Failure to do this may result in small cracks in either the head or bed joints.

Speed and accuracy are important in laying brick. You must get bricks in place before the mortar sets, and you must lay them straight and fill the joints completely. After each course is laid, raise your guide line another brick's thickness. Check with your straightedge frequently to make sure bricks are laid level.

After every 3 or 4 rows, before the mortar hardens, tool the joints with the raker. This presses the mortar tight against the brick.

**Wall Variations.** Of course if you are building a wall 4″ wide (the approximate width of one brick) and it goes in a straight line, each successive course will start with a half-brick so that the head joints will be staggered. There might be cases where a low 4″-thick wall would suffice, but in most cases a brick wall needs to be thicker than that.

An 8″ wall is 2 bricks wide in stretcher courses. In common bond every sixth course should be a header course. In English bond every other course is a header. The combination of header and stretcher courses gives a much more solid wall, more than twice as strong as 4″ walls.

A 12″ wall can be a combination of stetcher and header courses, with 3 rows of stretchers in some courses. Such a wall is more than three times as solid as a 4″ wall.

If a number of bricks become broken, a 12″ wall is ideal for using them. When

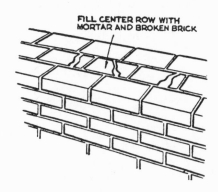

laying the 3 rows of stretcher courses, lay the 2 outside rows with full brick and mortar, and fill the center with mortar and broken pieces of brick.

An ordinary wall such as we have been considering should be topped with a ½″ layer of concrete to help prevent water from settling in the joints and working down.

**Corners.** Most brickwork turns corners, and corners provide a means for staggering joints without using half bricks.

There is nothing very complicated about a simple corner in common bond. Some of the more complicated patterns have fancy corners, but the novice will be wise not to attempt them.

## MASONRY BLOCK

This provides a most workable material for one-man construction projects such as walls and small buildings. The nominally 8″ × 8″ × 16″ blocks are easily available

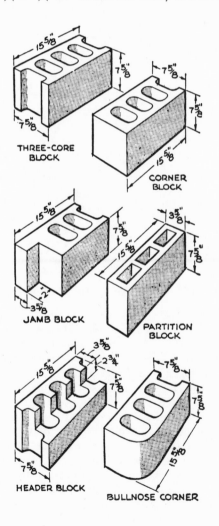

THREE-CORE BLOCK

CORNER BLOCK

JAMB BLOCK

PARTITION BLOCK

HEADER BLOCK

BULLNOSE CORNER

and can be competently handled by the amateur after a short time. Corner blocks with one square end and half-blocks which facilitate building are also available.

Concrete blocks are made of portland cement, sand, and gravel. Cinder blocks have cinders instead of the gravel. Although lacking the great strength of concrete blocks, cinder blocks are nevertheless very durable and have greater sound-absorption qualities which make them good for basement and house walls. They are also lighter in weight than the concrete blocks and therefore easier to handle.

**Footings.** Every masonry-block wall must have a firm base to support it. Local weather conditions will determine the type of footing and foundation. The footing should be set below the frostline and should be twice the width of the wall that

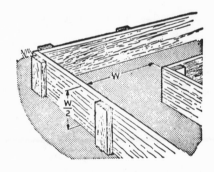

it is to support. The depth should be about half the width. In other words, an adequate footing for a masonry-block wall one block thick (8″) would be 16″ wide and 8″ deep.

The footing should be of poured concrete and it should be square and straight.

**Concrete-Block Construction.** Store concrete blocks in a dry place until they are installed. Check the footing for the foundation to make sure that it is straight, and stretch chalk lines to serve as building guides.

A suitable mix for concrete-block mortar can be made from 1 part cement

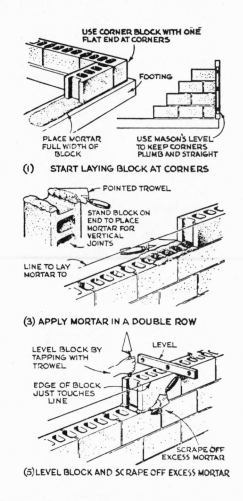

USE CORNER BLOCK WITH ONE FLAT END AT CORNERS

FOOTING

PLACE MORTAR FULL WIDTH OF BLOCK

USE MASON'S LEVEL TO KEEP CORNERS PLUMB AND STRAIGHT

(1) START LAYING BLOCK AT CORNERS

STRETCH LINE BETWEEN CORNERS TO LAY BLOCK TO

1"x2 WITH SAW MARKS 8" APART HELPS TO SPACE COURSES AT CORNERS

MORTAR JOINTS ARE 3/8 THICK

BLOCKS SHOULD BE DRY WHEN LAID IN WALL

(2) BUILD WALL BETWEEN CORNERS

POINTED TROWEL

STAND BLOCK ON END TO PLACE MORTAR FOR VERTICAL JOINTS

LINE TO LAY MORTAR TO

(3) APPLY MORTAR IN A DOUBLE ROW

BLOCK IS PICKED UP AND SHOVED FIRMLY AGAINST BLOCK PREVIOUSLY LAID

BED JOINT

(4) SET BLOCK FIRMLY IN PLACE

LEVEL BLOCK BY TAPPING WITH TROWEL

LEVEL

EDGE OF BLOCK JUST TOUCHES LINE

SCRAPE OFF EXCESS MORTAR

(5) LEVEL BLOCK AND SCRAPE OFF EXCESS MORTAR

SHAPED WOOD BLOCK

HALF-ROUND BAR

SHAPING TOOLS ARE RUN ALONG JOINTS TO COMPACT MORTAR ON FACE OF EXPOSED WALL

(6) TOOL THE JOINTS TO COMPRESS MORTAR

to 2 parts sand. Add enough water to this mixture to produce a workable plastic mass. Do not make more mortar than you can use in 30 minutes. The normal mortar joint, horizontal or vertical, is about 3/8".

For the first course of block, place mortar the full width of the block wall. For subsequent courses, place the mortar in a double row on the block already laid. This method of placing mortar is called face shell bedding.

Butter one end of the block with mortar and shove it firmly against the unit previously placed. Level and plumb the block and scrape off the excess mortar squeezed out between the joints.

After the mortar has become quite stiff, run a pointing tool along the mortar joints. This compacts the mortar and helps make tight, strong joints. To give vertical joints the same texture as that of the concrete or cinder blocks, they should be rubbed with a piece of carpet, cork, or some other rough material.

When building retaining walls, it is usually wise to reinforce the wall with steel reinforcing rod. Vertical lengths of the rod can be set into the concrete footing when it is poured; the rods should be long enough to extend into the top blocks of the wall. Horizontal reinforcing is done with metal grids available for this purpose, which are set along each course and embedded in the mortar.

## CURBS

Curbs are frequently used in connection with the various types of paving. They may be of either two-course or one-course construction, but the tendency is toward one-course work, that is, the same mixture throughout: $1:2\frac{1}{2}:3\frac{1}{2}$ (cement, sand, gravel).

The plain curb is usually built so that it is 18″ to 24″ deep, 8″ to 10″ thick at the bottom, and 6″ to 8″ thick at the top. The illustration shows how the forms

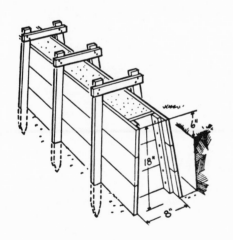

should be constructed and braced. Note that an 18″ curb has 6″ of it above ground and 12″ below. If the curb is deeper, only part of the added depth should be above ground. With a curb 24″ deep, only 7″ or 8″ should be above ground.

Forms for alternate sections 5′ or 6′ long can be built and the concrete poured. When the concrete in these sec-

tions has set and has become self-sustaining, the forms can be removed and set up for the intervening sections, and the latter poured.

For a combined curb and butter, sections should be built no more than 10′ in length, and expansion joints should be

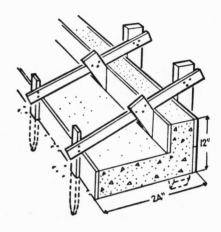

provided every 25′. Generally a gutter is formed at the intersection of a curb with the street paving, and care should be taken to pitch the gutter toward outlets or drains.

Plain curbs of reinforced concrete may be precast in sections 4′ to 8′ long. These are usually 4″ to 8″ thick and 18″ to 24″ high. The reinforcement may consist of longitudinally laid rods $\frac{1}{4}$″ in diameter, spaced 6″ apart. A piece of heavy woven-wire fencing 1″ shorter in length and height than the curb section makes a satisfactory reinforcement. The wire should not be less than No. 10 gauge.

## DRIVEWAYS

There are two types of concrete driveways that you can build. One is the ribbon type, which consists of 2 concrete ribbons 2′ wide with a space of 2′ 10″ between them. This is the less expensive type to build, but even with curbs on the outer edges of the ribbons, there is always the chance of a driver running off the ribbons and messing up the adjacent ground.

The slab type of concrete driveway is much better, as there is less danger of driving off it.

## Ribbon-Type Driveway

It is very important when building this type of driveway that the subbase be compact and solid. If it is not, your drive will crack very easily. If the subsoil is well drained, you do not need any special base; but if it is clayey, you should use a base of gravel or cinders 6″ thick under the slab. The slab itself should be 5″ thick—unless heavy trucks are going to go over it, in which case it should be 6″ thick.

The first step in making the driveway is to lay out the forms. Either 2″ × 6″ or 2″ × 8″ lumber can be used for the job. The pieces are set on edge, and stakes are driven in along the outside to hold them in place. Spacers the width of the ribbon should be placed between the 2 side forms to hold them the correct distance apart. They should be placed every 6′. A ribbon without curbs should be 2′ wide; but if you plan to include a curb, increase the size to 2½′ for each ribbon. If there are curves in the driveway, the forms for these can be made of plywood.

You will need an expansion joint in the driveway every 40′ or so. You should also have one where the driveway joins

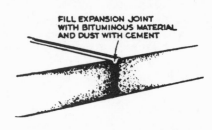

FILL EXPANSION JOINT WITH BITUMINOUS MATERIAL AND DUST WITH CEMENT

the apron of the garage or any other concrete or masonry work. If expansion joints are not used, there is danger of the concrete's cracking. An expansion joint can be made by placing a strip of asphalt felt between 2 sections before the fresh concrete is poured, or by leaving a space and filling it later with a bituminous compound.

**Pouring the Concrete.** Refer to the table on page 97 for the correct mixture to use for this job. The entire ribbon is not poured in one operation. Alternate 6′ sections are poured and then, when the concrete is sufficiently hard, the spacers

ROUND CORNERS WITH EDGING TOOL TO PREVENT CHIPPING

are removed and the remaining sections poured. This allows for a slight expansion joint between each two 6′ sections. The corners of the sections should be rounded with an edging tool to prevent chipping.

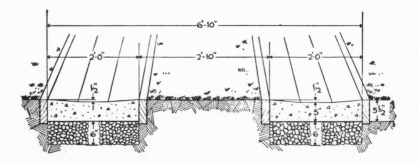

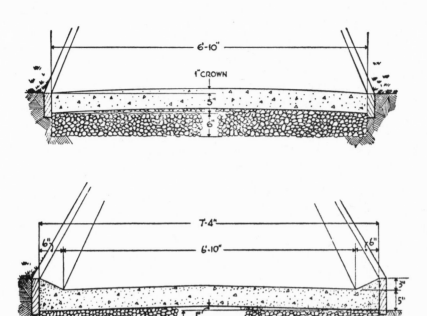

## Slab-Type Driveway

Drives of this sort without curbs should be 6' 10" wide. If curbs are to be installed, increase the overall width of the drive to 7' 4". This allows for 2 curbs 6" thick on each side.

The precautions taken in preparing the subbase and using a fill in clayey soils apply to this type of drive as well as to the ribbon drive. The slab type of drive should be 6" thick if it is to handle heavy trucks. To allow for proper drainage, it is best to have the top of the concrete slab about 2" above the finished grade. The driveway should also be given a slight crown so that water will drain off. A board with a hollowed-out edge is used to make the crown. This board is placed with its ends on top of the form boards and is then worked along a section of fresh concrete, molding it to the slight crown desired.

The forms for a slab driveway, along with the expansion joints, the mixture, and the method of pouring, are just the same as those used for the ribbon type.

When you are working over the surface with a wood float, make certain not to remove the crown.

## OUTDOOR FIREPLACE

Nearly anyone can build a satisfactory outdoor fireplace, and the only difference between one built by an expert and one made by a beginner will be in the appearance.

A fireplace can be built of bricks, stone, or poured concrete. Bricks are probably the most popular of these materials because they come in a standard size, are light in weight, easy to work with, and inexpensive. In fact, for an outdoor fireplace, even used bricks (secured from a demolished building) may prove entirely satisfactory.

Stones are excellent—provided there

is an ample supply nearby. A rather large supply of stones is required to finish a fireplace, so be sure that you will not run out of stones before the work is completed. Since stones are of irregular size, many will require splitting before they can be used. You will need a sledgehammer for that.

Poured concrete makes a good fireplace but requires wood forms. These must be carefully made and the concrete especially well mixed, poured, and cured, so as to withstand the extremes of heat when the fireplace is used.

## Outdoor Brick Fireplace

### Materials Required

#### Fireplace Foundation

14 cubic feet cinder or gravel fill
2¾ bags cement
⅖ cubic yard gravel, or 14 cubic feet ready-mixed concrete
⅕ cubic yard sand

#### Fireplace

5 bags cement
4 bags hydrated lime
1 cubic yard sand, or 25 cubic feet ready-mixed mortar
1,700 common bricks
200 firebricks
3 pounds fireclay (add 25% portland cement)
2 angle irons $3'' \times 4'' \times \frac{1}{4}'' \times 54''$
1 mantel $2'' \times 10'' \times 12'$

#### Cabinets

8 pieces $2'' \times 8'' \times 34''$
8 pieces $2'' \times 4'' \times 49''$
2 pieces $2'' \times 4'' \times 42''$
8 pieces $2'' \times 4'' \times 35\frac{1}{2}''$
2 pieces $2'' \times 4'' \times 34''$
4 pieces $2'' \times 4'' \times 33\frac{3}{4}''$
4 pieces $2'' \times 4'' \times 22\frac{3}{4}''$
18 pieces $1'' \times 8'' \times 49''$
2 pieces $1'' \times 3'' \times 38''$
4 pieces $1'' \times 3'' \times 30''$
8 carriage bolts and nuts $\frac{1}{4}'' \times 6''$
4 butt hinges $3''$
2 barrel bolts $4''$
2 strap irons $\frac{1}{16}'' \times 1''$

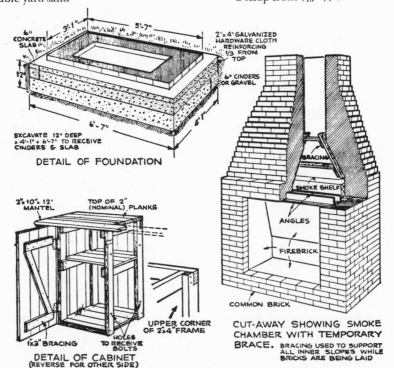

DETAIL OF FOUNDATION

DETAIL OF CABINET
(REVERSE FOR OTHER SIDE)

CUT-AWAY SHOWING SMOKE CHAMBER WITH TEMPORARY BRACE. BRACING USED TO SUPPORT ALL INNER SLOPES WHILE BRICKS ARE BEING LAID

**Building the Fireplace.** Lay out the first course of bricks as shown in the foundation detail of the illustration. Fill the cavity in the center with gravel and mortar, and then lay one more course. Lay firebricks along the bottom of the fireplace opening, bringing them flush with the third course of bricks along the front of the opening. Extend the 2 side walls and back wall 12″ up from the bottom of the opening, lining them with firebrick.

At 12″ from the base, the firebrick of the back wall begins to slope forward, while the side walls and common-brick portion of the back wall continue upward in a straight line. The inside surface of the back wall slopes forward and upward until it is 4′ from the fireplace foundation; it is also 11″ out from the common bricks of the back wall, forming a throat 8″ × 3′ 6″. The space between the firebricks and the common bricks can be filled with small stones and mortar. You can save time and trouble by making a rough wood pattern or form for the firebricks to follow.

Bring the side walls up 2′ 10″ from the bottom of the fireplace opening and then install the 2 angle irons between these walls to support the front breast of the fireplace. The back of the fireplace should be carried up so that the 11″-wide smoke shelf can be formed. Make this shelf just as flat as you can.

The rest of the masonry is all common brick; no more firebrick will be required. At the point where the angle irons are installed, the side walls of the fireplace start coming together, so that 18″ above the smoke shelf, the side walls are 15″ apart. This makes a flue opening 11″ × 15″. Smooth the side walls with mortar.

Three courses of bricks are built up on the front of the fireplace supported by the angle irons. After the third course, a 4″ recess is formed in the front to carry a 10″ mantel.

The brickwork for the chimney should extend 9′ 4″ above the fireplace foundation. The bricks at the top of the chimney should be capped with mortar, and the mortar sloped so that water will drain off the masonry. Allow the masonry a week to harden before removing the wood forms from the inside, and then give it another week before building a fire.

**Building Cabinets.** The cabinets on each side of the fireplace are 3′ 1″ deep and 2′ 10″ wide. Their height, without the top covering of 2″ planks, should be 4′ 1″ from the fireplace foundation. These cabinets are fastened to the fireplace ma-

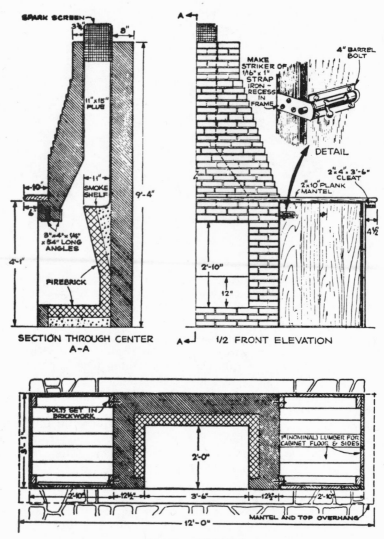

SECTION THROUGH CENTER
A-A

1/2 FRONT ELEVATION

DETAIL

PLAN - SECTION

sonry with bolts set into the mortar joints during the construction of the fireplace.

The cabinets are made with a framework of 2 × 4s covered with 1″ and 2″ boards. Don't install the top covering of boards until the cabinets are in place and the fireplace mantel has been fastened in position. The mantel extends out along the edge of each cabinet and forms the first board of the top. After this is in place, the remaining boards can be installed.

As the cabinets will be exposed to the weather, noncorrosive hardware, such as brass, should be used for bolt, striker, and hinges. The cabinets can be covered with several coats of spar varnish or linseed oil thinned with turpentine. Either finish will preserve the wood from decay, though the best practice is to use a decay-resistant wood.

## GARDEN POOL

A garden pool will greatly enhance the attractiveness of a garden. Fish may be kept in it or not. Build it of watertight concrete which is reinforced so that it will not crack from the pressure of the water or the soil around it. The illustration gives cross-sectional views of two types of pools. Once the essentials discussed have been incorporated into a pool, any number of variations can be made to suit your particular inclinations.

In selecting a site for the pool, keep in mind that it will have to be drained from time to time; regardless of whether or not you keep fish in it, the water will need to be changed. Therefore it might be well to have it situated near the house rather than at the far end of your property. The best and easiest way of draining the pool is to put down a drainpipe at the bottom and run it to some point lower than the lowest portion of the pool. If no drainpipe is installed, the pool will have to be emptied by hand; and although this is not difficult with small pools, it requires a considerable amount of work to drain larger pools in this fashion.

Dig out the necessary amount of earth and set the drainpipe in place. The opening should be at the lowest point in the pool. A very effective way of combining an overflow pipe with a drainpipe is to attach a coupling to the drainpipe so that the coupling is almost covered by the concrete bottom of the pool. Screw a length of pipe into the coupling, and this pipe will act as an overflow. When draining the pool, unscrew the overflow pipe, and the water will flow out through the coupling.

If the soil is solid, only inside forms will be required; if it is loose, both out-

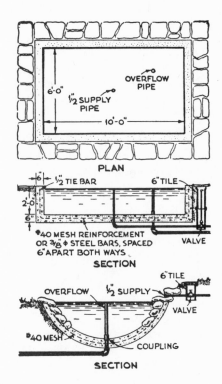

side and inside forms will be needed. To reinforce the concrete, use 40-pound mesh wire, placed in the middle of the 6″ thick concrete. The faces of the forms should be covered with oil so that they can be removed easily.

Mix the concrete in proportions of 1:2¼:3; take great pains that the proportions are exactly right. To prevent seams in the concrete, do all the pouring in a continuous operation. Shovel in about 8″ of concrete and spade it so that it becomes a well-packed mass. Then shovel in another batch, and continue until the entire pool has been completed. Keep the fresh concrete moist and covered for a week or 10 days until it has set. Do not try to remove the forms for several days.

Small pools of course can be filled with a garden hose, but a ½″ water line connected to the house plumbing system is more convenient. The illustration shows two methods of providing such a line. The inlet line should be fitted with a valve so that the flow of water can be easily controlled from a point near the pool.

The alkali that is present in new concrete will kill fish. It is possible to check the amount of alkali in the water with pink litmus paper, obtainable at a drugstore. If the paper turns blue when placed in the water, it is not safe for fish. Change the water at weekly intervals until pink litmus paper remains pink. Then fish can be placed in the pool.

## SIDEWALKS

Sidewalks made of properly proportioned concrete fulfill all the essentials of any good footway. They withstand the ravages of traffic and time, are attractive and easy to sweep or shovel.

Many communities have set regulations regarding the construction of public sidewalks. These regulations must be followed.

Use should determine the width of any walk not specifically dictated by law. A main pathway from the street to the house entrance should be wide; 4' to 5' is usually a good width. Those on the side or rear of the house may vary from 1½' to 3'.

A ½" expansion joint will have to be included for every 50' of sidewalk constructed. This can be made by inserting a board ½" thick between adjacent sections. The board should be removed when the concrete is sufficiently hard to permit its removal without damaging the edges. The joint between sections may be filled with a bituminous material dusted with cement.

If you wish to build the walk in consecutive sequence, place strips of tarred felt against the divider boards. These strips, which should extend across the entire walk for its full depth, remain permanently in position, assuring a definite joint between sections. Concrete is placed

on both sides of the divider board. When the board is removed, the pressure of the concrete from both sides holds the tarred felt vertical.

The proper mixture of concrete to use will be found in the table on page 97. Familiarize yourself with the instructions for proportioning, placing, and curing, on pages 96 to 99.

The concrete, when of the right plasticity, can easily be leveled off by a strikeboard resting on the edges of the side forms. Pass the strikeboard across the forms in a sawlike motion. Several hours later the concrete should be finished with a wood float to produce an even, gritty surface, and all edges should be rounded with a cement finisher's edging tool.

If the soil is not well drained naturally, a subbase of well-compacted, clean coarse gravel, or clean cinders, must be provided. A good subbase should be about 6" thick. It should be rolled or tapped firm and should be wetted before the concrete is poured.

If the sidewalk is to be used only as a walk, 4" of concrete should be sufficient thickness; but if a heavy vehicle—such as a truck delivering coal—is likely to be driven over it, the thickness should be 6".

Side forms can be made of 2 × 4s or 2 × 6s, and they can be held in place by stakes. The top edges of the forms will later serve as guides in leveling off the concrete. Always build walks about 2" above grade so that they will be well

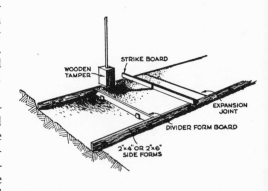

drained. In building a 6"-thick walk, therefore, the area that is to be concreted will have to be excavated to a depth of 4" plus the thickness of the fill. The walk should be sloped toward one side for drainage; a pitch of from $\frac{1}{4}$" to $\frac{1}{2}$" is satisfactory.

Walks are best built in one-course construction. This means that the full thickness of concrete is poured at one time, using the same mixture throughout.

## Expansion Joints

To allow for the expansion and contraction of cement, walks should be divided at 4' to 6' intervals, with partition strips placed at right angles to the side form. Every other section should first be concreted. After these have hardened enough to be self-sustaining, the cross strips are removed and the remaining slabs placed.

# 6

# PAINTING
# AND WALLPAPERING

Paints and various finishes are used for decorative purposes and to protect a surface so that it won't be harmed or discolored by absorbing moisture, dirt, or stains. When we speak of "paint," we are talking about a coating that contains enough pigments to hide the surface to which it is applied. This would include outside house paints, wall paints, and the various types of enamels. When we speak of "finishes," we mean coatings that contain few pigments and are more or less transparent, so that they do not conceal the grain, color, or texture of the material to which they are applied. In this group you will find such coatings as shellac, varnish, sealer, and clear lacquer. Unless we are talking about a specific finish, however, most of us lump everything under the general heading of "paint."

You will find literally hundreds of different kinds of paints and finishes. Many of them are designed for a particular material, situation, or condition. Some paints are designed for wood, some for metal, some for masonry, and some for fabrics. Some outside house paints are designed for use in damp, humid climates; some for use where the air contains excessive industrial fumes; and some for areas where the air has much dirt and soot in it, so that the paint must be self-cleaning. Some paints are good for all inside walls,

and some are better than others for bathroom and kitchen walls. Certain kinds of floor paint do well on inside masonry floors, and some can be used for outside concrete slabs as well. By and large, you are better off if you use a paint or finish designed for the particular material and situation on hand than to take a chance with a so-called "all-purpose" paint.

About the best way to make sure that you are getting the right paint or finish for a job is to have a good paint dealer. Today in most communities you can find a good paint store or a hardware store with a good paint department. Look for a shop that carries several brands of paints and finishes and can mix custom colors for you. Also look for a shop that has a good line of painting equipment, including rollers, brushes, sandpaper, thinners, and a variety of accessories that can save you time and effort on many jobs. Toss a few questions at the clerk to see if he will take the time and has the knowledge to give you the answers. Once you find a good paint store and a good dealer, rely on his opinion when you have a problem or when ordering paint. You must, of course, give him some essential information before he can recommend a particular type for the job in question. He's got to know the kind of material you are going to paint—wood, masonry, metal, and so forth. He also must know the condition of the material—has it been previously painted or finished, and if so with what? You should also tell him if the surface is exposed to the weather or to wear, as in the case of a floor or deck, and also the area to be covered.

## TYPES OF PAINT

Although there are many different paints, most of them fall into four general classifications: latex, alkyd, oil-base, and catalytic.

**Latex Paints.** This is by far the most popular paint available today. There are latex paints designed for the outside of the house, for interior walls, for masonry walls and floors, for woodwork, and even as primers for metal. Latex paints are almost perfect for the homeowner because they are so simple to use. They dry very quickly—sometimes in an hour or so. This means that you can give a room several coats of paint in a single day and have it ready to use that evening. Latex paints are practically odorless and don't have the strong smell associated with oil-base paints that have been thinned with turpentine. They can be applied over a damp surface, and if they are applied over a latex primer they will help to reduce the chances of the blistering and peeling that often occurs when oil-base paint is applied to outside walls. Equipment used to apply latex paint can be cleaned by washing in water.

**Alkyd Paints.** Next to latex paints, these are the most commonly used paints today. They contain a resin called alkyd and produce a very tough paint film. They are used extensively in paints for outside woodwork such as windows and shutters and in interior wall paints and enamels. They are very washable and therefore better for the walls and woodwork in baths and kitchens than the latex paints. They have a slight odor and should be thinned with an odorless thin-

ner rather than turpentine, to keep it to a minimum.

**Oil-Base Paints.** These were once very popular for both interior and exterior work, but today they have been more or less replaced by latex paints—particularly for interior work. They are used, however, under certain conditions, especially when repainting a house where the old paint is chalking or in poor condition, because they adhere better than the latex paints. They have a strong odor compared with the latex or alkyd paints.

Linseed-oil emulsions are somewhat similar to the oil-base house paints, except that they are thinned with water rather than turpentine or mineral spirits.

**Catalytic Coatings.** These are very new, and differ from other paints in that they become hard through a chemical action rather than through the evaporation of the solvents in the paint. They are very tough and durable, and can be used for swimming pools, outside concrete slabs, bathroom fixtures, and other items to which ordinary paints and finishes would not adhere.

Paints are also classified according to the location where they are to be used or according to the material to be painted.

**Exterior Paints.** These are designed for outside work. They are formulated to resist damage from moisture and to adjust to changes in temperature. In this group are the house paints used for the main body of the house; trim and shutter enamels, used for outside woodwork and other jobs such as fences; and so forth. Always use an exterior paint on any surface exposed to the weather.

**Interior Paints.** These are paints designed for use inside the house—for walls, ceilings, woodwork, furniture, and so on. They are not designed to stand up when exposed to the weather and therefore should never be used outdoors.

**Masonry Paints.** Most masonry contains a certain amount of alkali, which is harmful to certain paints. Masonry paints are designed so that they will not be harmed by the alkali, and you will be wise never to use anything for masonry other than a paint recommended by the manufacturer for this purpose.

**Floor Paints.** These are specially designed to take hard wear. Some are intended for interior and exterior or wood floors, and some for interior and exterior concrete floors.

**Special Paints.** Among these are paints for children's toys and furniture which will not be harmful if the piece is chewed on by a small child; marine paints, for use on all types of boats and marine equipment; and metal paints, for interior and exterior metal objects.

## Paint Thinners

Many paints and finishes don't require any thinning and can be used just as they come from the container. But most manufacturers will specify that if the paint does not go on easily, it can be thinned. Thinning is often the general rule when applying a paint or finish with spray equipment. It is essential to use the correct thinner as recommended by the manufacturer.

Latex and other water-base paints can be thinned with clear water. Never use a solvent thinner such as mineral spirits or turpentine for these paints.

Alkyd and oil-base paints are thinned with mineral spirits or turpentine. Of the two, mineral spirits has the least odor.

Shellac is thinned with denatured alcohol, varnish with mineral spirits, and lacquer with a lacquer thinner.

Use the same type of thinner for cleaning painting equipment, such as brushes and rollers, as you use for thinning the paint.

## Primers

The primer is the first coat, and in a way it's the most important one because the primer's job is to make a bond between the surface and the subsequent coats of paint or finish. Sometimes the prime coat is just the same paint as that to be used for the finish coat, thinned down somewhat so that it will be absorbed by the surface; but often it must be a special primer to ensure a good job.

In connection with this, more and more paint manufacturers are recommending that you follow a "painting system," which means that the primer must be compatible with the finish coats. Usually the manufacturer will specify on the label the type of primer that should be used. You should follow these recommendations. In fact, you will be wise to use a primer made by the manufacturer of the finish coat, as this will ensure good adhesion between the primer and finish coats.

Generally speaking, primers are always required on new work such as interior walls or house siding. Recommended types of primers will be included later in this chapter in discussing the various areas of the house to be painted.

## Enamel

This is an opaque finish which differs somewhat from ordinary paint in that it is designed to produce a very smooth, hard coating. There are exterior and interior enamels. Exterior enamels are designed to withstand the weather and are used on outside woodwork. Interior enamels don't hold dirt easily and can be washed without dulling the surface. They are used for interior woodwork, furniture, and walls, especially in the bathroom and kitchen. Enamels come in gloss, semigloss, and eggshell. (See page 89.)

## Varnish

This is a clear finish used on floors, woodwork, and furniture. There are three basic types of varnish: interior varnish, used inside the house; exterior, or spar, varnish used for outdoor work and on boats; and floor varnish, to be used on wood floors. (See page 91.)

## Shellac

This is another type of clear finish. It consists of natural resins reduced in denatured alcohol. The resins come from a small insect, *Tachardia lacca*. Shellac is a

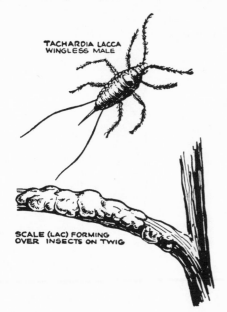

TACHARDIA LACCA
WINGLESS MALE

SCALE (LAC) FORMING
OVER INSECTS ON TWIG

very fast-drying finish and is used on furniture and floors, and as a primer. There are two types of shellac: orange and white. (See page 92.)

## Lacquer

This is another fast-drying finish and is available in clear or white as well as in colors. Lacquer is best applied with a spray gun or spray can, but there is a special "brushing lacquer" that can be applied by brush. It produces a smooth, glasslike surface. You have to be careful never to use lacquer over paint or varnish, as it will act like a paint remover and soften up the old finish. Lacquer is sometimes used on floors, but its primary use in the home is for furniture and small articles.

**Mixing, Storing, and Handling Paint.** Some paints and finishes require that they be mixed before use; some do not. Read the label carefully before you mix, because mixing some paints and finishes will produce air bubbles in the paint that will give you a rough effect after the paint is hard.

For paints that do require mixing, it is best to have the paint dealer shake the can in a special paint mixer. But this is adequate only if you plan to use the paint almost immediately. If you don't, you'll have to mix by hand to blend in the solid matter that settles to the bottom of the container. To do this, have a clean container on hand; open the paint can and pour about half the liquid into the clean container; now, with a wood paddle, stir the remaining liquid in the original container until it becomes a smooth paste; then begin to add to it the liquid from the second container, stirring as you add. When the original container is full, pour it back into the second container. Repeat this a few times, and the paint will be ready for use. It may be necessary to stir the paint from time to time as it is being used, if you find the pigments are settling to the bottom of the container.

When you have finished with the paint for the day or whatever, be sure to seal it tightly. If you don't and you are using an oil paint, a skin will form on the surface, and this will have to be removed before you begin again. As it is often impossible to get the skin off in one piece, you may have to strain the paint through a piece of cheesecloth or an old nylon stocking to remove traces of the skin. It's a good idea to save glass containers with tight-fitting lids and pour paint into these. The less air there is in the container, the less chance there is of the skin forming.

Oil paints should be stored in a spot where there is no chance of their feeding a fire, and latex and water-thinned paints should not be stored where they might freeze.

## PAINTING EQUIPMENT AND SUPPLIES

Most paints and finishes can be applied with a brush, roller, or spray gun. On large jobs such as walls, using the paint roller is the fastest way to do the job, but you will still have to use a brush for areas that can't be reached by the roller. Spray equipment is fine on big jobs if you have good-quality equipment, but it's not much use on small jobs because the time spent in setting up the equipment and then cleaning it after you have finished is more than it would take to do the job with a brush or roller.

### Paintbrushes

These are the oldest and still the most essential tools for the application of paint and other finishes. Brushes work on the simple principle of adhesion. When a brush is dipped into paint, the paint adheres to the surface of the bristles. When the loaded brush is placed in contact with the surface being painted, which has greater adhesion for the paint, the paint flows off the bristles and coats that surface. The greater the amount of bristle surface, the greater the amount of paint the brush will hold.

The quality of brush you buy depends entirely upon yourself. If you don't intend to take the time to clean and store it properly after use, buy the least expensive brush that is adequate for the job. There are also disposable brushes, which cost considerably less than ordinary brushes and are designed for the occasional painter. But if you will take the

LARGE BRUSH HAS SQUARE EDGE

NATURAL BEND OF BRISTLES TOWARD TIP CENTER

BRISTLES NAILED IN FERRULE IN RUBBER SETTING

HANDLE NAILED IN FERRULE

METAL FERRULE

SECTION THROUGH BRUSH

FLAG END

HORSE HAIR

BRISTLE

BRISTLE TAPERS FROM BUTT TO FLAG END - IS OVAL. HORSE HAIR HAS NO TAPER - IS ROUND - HAS NO FLAG

time to care for a brush, a good-quality one can be a good investment and will last for many years.

A brush should be dipped in the paint to only half the length of the bristles. If you dip it further than this, paint will get into the heel of the bristles and will be difficult to clean out; also, the brush will tend to drip paint. Remove excess paint from the bristles by tapping them against the side of the container. This is better for the brush than pulling the bristles across the rim of the container to remove the excess paint. When painting wood, apply the paint in the direction of the wood grain. Apply the paint to any surface with short strokes of the brush, and after the surface has been coated, smooth out the paint with long strokes.

**Care of Brushes.** All new brushes shed a few bristles; it is nothing to be alarmed about. Before you begin to paint, bring out any loose bristles by spinning the brush between the palms of your hands, bristles down. When the loose bristles are seen extending beyond the others, pick them off.

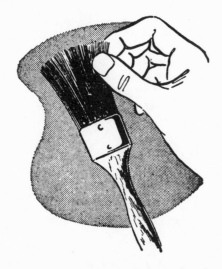

Some painters soak new brushes in linseed oil for a day or two, and then rinse them in turpentine or mineral spirits before using them.

Any brush that is used with latex paint, water-thinned paint, glue, or paste should be washed thoroughly with a household detergent and water and rinsed as soon as the work is completed. Then the water should be shaken out and the bristles combed out straight with an ordinary hair comb. To dry the brush, hang it up by a string around the handle. Water remaining in any bristles harms the brush.

Brushes that have been used with shellac should be thoroughly rinsed twice in denatured alcohol. Shape the brush between your fingers, and lay it on a flat surface to dry. If you intend to use the brush in shellac on the following day, do not wash it in water; it might not be entirely dry the next day and that would cause your shellac to bloom.

Paint and varnish brushes which are going to be used the next day should be thoroughly rinsed in turpentine, mineral spirits, or benzine. Be particularly careful to get the paint out of the heel of the brush. (The heel is the section of the brush where the bristles disappear under the metal ferrule.) Use a comb for this. While it is still wet, lay the brush on a piece of aluminum foil or kraft freezer paper, and fold the foil or paper in the same way as the wrappings in which the brush came; this will keep the brush moist overnight.

If you have finished a paint job and will have no more use for the brush for some time, you must clean it more thoroughly. Rinse it out in turpentine, mineral spirits, or benzine. Comb out the paint. Rinse again. Then wash it thoroughly in detergent and water. When its original black color has returned, rinse it in clear water. Then comb out the bristles again. Hang the brush up by a piece of string attached to the handle and let it dry. When dry, wrap it in a piece of paper so as to preserve its shape.

Many containers are on the market for overnight storage of brushes which are in constant use. Some of these containers must be filled with a vaporizing solvent; the brushes are hung in the vapor, and a tight-fitting top prevents excessive evaporation of the solvent. These devices are re-

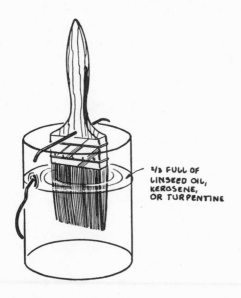

2/3 FULL OF
LINSEED OIL,
KEROSENE,
OR TURPENTINE

latively expensive. Another method of storing a brush is to remove the heavy paint from the bristles and then suspend the bristles in a solvent such as turpentine. Drill a hole in the handle just above the ferrule, pass a piece of stiff wire through the hole, and suspend the brush in the container with the ends of the bristles just above the bottom of the can.

One thing you have to watch for here is the evaporation of the solvent. Turpentine, for example, will evaporate at the rate of about ½″ overnight. Using kerosine rather than turpentine, mineral spirits, or benzine is good because, aside from the fact that it is less flammable, it does not evaporate as quickly as the other solvents. Sealing the top of the container with aluminum foil will help reduce evaporation.

## Paint Rollers

Most amateurs prefer paint rollers to paintbrushes because they get the paint on in a hurry—especially on large surfaces such as walls, ceilings, and house sidings. Rollers are available in a wide range of sizes and shapes—many designed for par-

ticular jobs such as room corners, window sashes, fences, and even barbed wire.

Rollers are made of several different materials. Which type to use depends on the paint or finish that is to be applied. For oil-base paints, lamb's-wool rollers are good, but they should not be used with latex and other water-thinned paints. Mohair rollers and those of synthetic fibers can be used with most paints, but you should check with your dealer when you make the purchase.

The length of the nap will vary with the roller. For smooth surfaces, a roller with a short nap is best. For concrete, stucco, and rough plaster, use a roller with a ¾″ nap; for rough masonry, one with a 1¼″ nap is the most suitable.

Before you begin work with the roller, apply the finish with a brush or special applicator to all surfaces that can't be reached with the roller, If you are painting a room, for example, you will have to paint the corners and a strip along the ceiling and floor as these areas cannot be reached with the standard 7″- to 9″-long roller. The roller tray should be filled to about two thirds of its depth with paint. Set the roller into the paint and work it back and forth over the corrugated section of the tray to remove excess paint and to distribute the paint evenly over the entire surface of the roller. The roller should not drip paint when removed from the tray. The first stroke with the roller should be an upward one; this will keep paint from dripping off it. A good painting pattern is to work the roller so that a large "W" is formed first, and then the sections between the painted areas can be filled in. Do not try to work the roller too fast or it will spin and make a mess of things. This is important to watch for at the end of a stroke.

The better-quality rollers are designed so that an extension can be fastened to the handle; this will enable you to paint an entire wall or ceiling without having to work from a stepladder.

When you have finished with the

roller, run it over some old newspapers to remove as much of the paint from the nap as possible. If the roller has been used with latex or water-thinned paints, wash it under a faucet until it is free of paint. Dry it by working it over newspapers. If the roller has been used with an oil-base paint, place it in a large container of solvent such as mineral spirits and then shake it until it is clean.

You can save yourself the chore of having to clean the roller tray if before you fill with paint you line it with heavy-duty aluminum foil. When the job is finished, you just remove the foil and throw it away, and the tray is ready for use again.

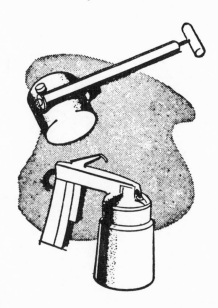

## Spray Painting

Modern mechanical developments inevitably led to the invention of the spray gun, a device which speeds up the application of paints, enamels, varnishes, stains, and other materials. The spray gun works with air under pressure directing a stream of paint through a spray head. The spray head breaks up the stream into small particles and aims them toward the surface to be painted. The gun also makes possible the application of fast-drying lacquer and synthetic gums. Unfortunately, its speed is not entirely a blessing, since it has introduced the hazards of fumes and flammable vapors. For this reason its use on a large scale is generally limited to factories where hoods and ventilating systems can be installed. Fumes are the mass of particles of the pigment which do not stay on the sprayed surface. They float in air and, if poisonous—like white lead—can be harmful to the operator. The vapors are the volatile thinners. All thinner vapors, with the exception of water, are highly inflammable in concentration and must be directed away from the work area.

Spray guns are available in several models. They vary from the simple hand-pump type used for whitewashing cellars to complicated automatic types used in assembly-line production work.

**Household Spray Gun.** Small motor- or magnet-driven types are manufactured for household use. They are good if their use is limited to occasional pieces of furniture and hobby work. They will not lay in a large area with evenness or the speed of a professional model. However, the cost is only about one twentieth that of a complete professional outfit. You must show care in cleaning the apparatus if you expect favorable results. Follow the directions for maintenance, and note carefully recommendations for the types of paints to use. These machines do not build up the pressure nor the volume of air necessary to handle the heavier paints, especially the new synthetics; but they are useful, within limits.

**Compressor Spray Gun.** All professional machines are basically composed of two parts—gun and composer. The compressor is generally electrically driven and pumps air into a storage tank. The more expensive types have automatic controls which cut out the pump when the pressure falls below or rises above set limits.

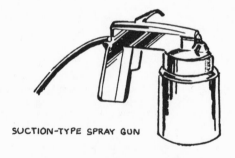

SUCTION-TYPE SPRAY GUN

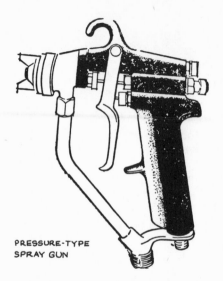

PRESSURE-TYPE
SPRAY GUN

The less expensive ones generally have a safety blow-by valve. When pressure in the tank exceeds the setting, air is released until the danger is passed.

In the interest of safety, or to avoid the cost of a burned-out pump motor, have one or both of these controls on your compressor.

The air under pressure is led through a regulator which drops the pressure from 100 or more pounds to the working pressure of between 20 and 70 pounds. The amount of working pressure depends upon the type of paint and the type of gun you are using.

Heavier paints, like the synthetics, require heavier pressures to spray effectively.

When buying a compressor, an important factor to consider is "cubic feet of air per minute." No compressor having a capacity of less than 4 to 5 cubic feet should be considered. Better yet, contemplate getting one which delivers 8, 10, or 12 cubic feet per minute. Too much air will seldom spoil work, but to run out of air in the middle of a big panel can be more frustrating than losing a big fish. Better to buy a big compressor and a small gun than the reverse.

The principal differences in guns lie in the spray heads and the method of supplying the paint flow to the spray head. Paint is directed to the spray head by either suction or pressure. Almost all small types of guns have cups attachable to the gun. By suction they draw the paint up and into the nozzle. However, a pressure-cup type is recommended if you intend to use synthetic paints. Large commercial types have paint tanks of 2- to 5-gallon capacity which stand on the floor. Air under pressure is fed to the tank, thus forcing paint up through a rubber hose to the gun.

**Spray Heads.** The spray heads are either internal- or external-mix types. Of the two the internal-mix type is less popular. It mixes air and paint inside the spray head. The vaporized paint and air are blown out through a slot. Some slots are

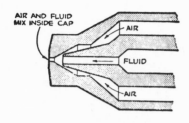

made to handle a certain kind or consistency of paint or finish. If you change the paint material for which the slot was designed, you may lose the spray pattern.

The external-mix spray head with its multiple jets thoroughly atomizes the paint. Also, it fans out the paint spray into a wide and evenly distributed pattern. This spray pattern is very important in obtaining even, wide coats of paint.

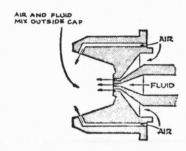

Each sweep of the gun, held 6″ to 10″ from the surface, should deposit an even band of paint 6″ to 12″ wide. The thickness of paint should not be heavier in the center. It should not thin or feather out until it reaches the last inch of each end of the pattern. With this good pattern, one need overlap only an inch on each stroke of the gun to get a perfect job.

**Size.** If you intend to use several paint materials, get a gun with a removable head and several nozzles. These come in a variety of sizes, form A to G. They are made in sizes to accommodate different kinds of paint materials. Nozzles E, FF, FX, and F are the most commonly used

sizes. The larger nozzles, A to D, are used for extremely heavy paints.

Before you buy expensive equipment, investigate the market thoroughly. Manufacturers will cooperate in supplying you with complete information.

**Paint.** The best paints and finishes for spraying are those made especially for this purpose. Many painters who are dismayed by brush marks in their work, think spraying is the answer to the problem. Unfortunately this is not necessarily so. Ordinary paints or enamels when sprayed have a tendency to run or sag, since they are not fast-drying. In addition, spraying vertically is not very successful with the average gun; you must turn each piece on its side to do the top. If you consider the annoyance and danger of fumes and vapors, the extra handling of each piece, and the preparation and clean-up, you will find that sometimes you have not saved so much after all. However, if you use recommended materials, especially on production work, you will save time and get a better job.

**Spraying.** Load the cup with properly thinned material. Test the air pressure and clear the nozzle by pulling the trigger part way in. Practice on a piece of old board to check the adjustment and operation of the gun. There is no set rule for the pressure, because it varies with the nozzle, paint, and surface to be covered.

Hold the gun perpendicular to the surface to be sprayed and 6″ to 10″ away from it. Move the gun beyond the edge of the surface to be painted. Now you are ready for the first stroke. Pull the trigger all the way back. As the spray begins, move steadily across the surface to be sprayed, always holding the gun perpendicular to it and taking care to maintain the distance of 6″ to 10″. No exact directions can be given for the speed of the stroke. This will vary with the material used. Use a free arm motion, and release the trigger before the end of the stroke; this is known as feather-cutting. Stop an inch or so short of outside corners.

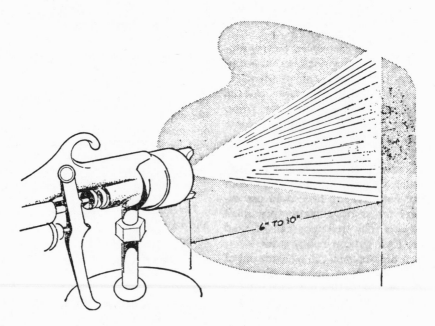

To paint the corners, turn the gun on its side or turn the cap to the horizontal position. In this way you will cover both sides of the corner at once and avoid overspraying and consequent sagging.

If the paint sags or runs, you are spraying too slowly. If it looks dull and does not cover properly, you are moving too fast. A little experience will guide you. The trick is to put on the thickest coat which does not sag or run.

The fan pattern of the spray may be heavy on one side. This is probably caused by dried material in the vents that clog up one side of the air passage. Thinner should be used to dissolve the dried material. Sometimes the material can be reamed out, but this should always be done with something soft like a straw or matchstick so as to avoid damaging the openings. It may also be necessary to remove the air nozzle and clean it, but first check to see that it is tight. Some defects in spray patterns are merely the result of a loose nozzle.

Incorrect pressure may be indicated by a spray pattern that is more or less divided in the middle or by one that is either heavy in the middle or has a salt-and-pepper appearance. You may also get a divided pattern when the pressure is correct because you are trying to get too wide a spray with thin material. In this case the answer is, of course, to reduce the width of the spray. "Blushing" and "blooming," excessive offspray, and fogging of adjacent areas are also the result of faulty control of air pressure.

**Defects.** The chief defects that may occur in the gun itself are spitting, air leakage, and paint leakage. Spitting is the interruption of an even flow of mixed paint and air by alternate discharges of the paint and the air. To locate the causes of the interruption, check for the following. (1) The packing around the needle valve has dried out. Place two drops of oil on the packing; in extreme cases, replace the packing. (2) The material nozzle is loose or its seat is dirty. Clean with thinner and reinstall tightly. (3) Nuts on the siphon cup or material hose are loose. Tighten or replace the nuts. (4) Water and lubricating oil have accumulated in the gun. Remove the oil and water. This possibility should be checked frequently;

water can accumulate in the gun by condensation.

Air leakage may result from improper seating of the air valve or from wear or damage in some part of the air-valve assembly. You may be able to correct the condition by tightening, by cleaning, or by lubricating. If there is some damage or excessive wear, the affected parts must be replaced.

Paint leakage usually indicates something wrong with the fluid needle. Check to see if it is damaged or dirty, or improperly seated. If none of these is the cause, check the packing nuts to see if they are too tight.

There are other troubles you may run into, like "orange-peeling," splattering, streaking, and fogging. These are described in the literature obtainable from manufacturers. No gun manufacturer wants you to blame his equipment for the trouble.

When spraying indoors, have the room ventilated but without drafts. When spraying outdoors, you must choose a time when there is no wind at all, unless you aren't going to be bothered by flying spray.

**Masking.** It is impossible to spray to a sharp line the way you can paint to one with a brush. In order to achieve this, you must cover the areas not to be painted with paper. To make the paper stay in place, a tape with an adhesive back is used. Simple masking is usually done with wrapping paper or other heavy paper. Cut pieces of wrapping paper to almost cover the area to be masked out, leaving a thin strip of space at the edges to be covered by the outer half of the tape. Lay the paper in place. Stick the tape partly on the surface and partly on the paper. Spray-paint the remainder. When the paint is dry, remove tape and paper.

Stencils can also be used for masking. But unless made with an adhesive back, the spray paint tends to blow or creep under their edges, producing a sloppy job. (See chapter 4, page 92.)

Liquids which can be painted on and later stripped off like a sheet of gelatin are available. They are particularly good for working with glass.

It is always advisable to cover the head, especially the hair, when spraying. A simple respirator mask is often advisable too.

## Dipping

One of the commonest factory processes of painting small objects is dipping. The process is simplicity itself. A tank of paint is prepared and the objects are dipped into the paint. They are hung over the tank for a few minutes to allow excess paint to drip off. They are then generally put immediately in a drying room or a paint-baking oven. The process does not lend itself to household use except for painting many very small objects. The technique can be used for toys, gifts, or hobby work.

A dipping tank can be made out of an old paint can or some other container

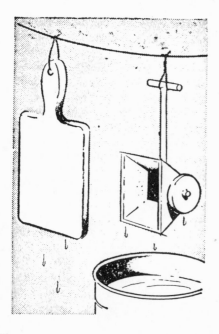

that is the proper size for the objects you have in mind. The closer the size of the tank is to the size of the objects, the less paint you will need; but allow some room to spare so that you can work freely and will be able to put in enough paint for all the objects you are going to dip in one session. Otherwise, you may find that by the time you get to the last object, you have already used so much paint that what remains will not cover it.

Do not have the paint too thick, and be sure that it is of an even consistency.

Objects can be dipped most conveniently by means of a simple wire hook. They need be immersed only long enough to be sure that the paint has reached every part of the surface. They do not need to be swizzled around. A practical method of work for the home is to make a wire hook for each object and a shallow trough with an open end that feeds back into the tank. Thus, when the object has been dipped, it may be hung over the trough to allow the excess paint to drip off. When the paint has ceased dripping, the objects may be left hanging or they may be placed on wax paper to dry. If placed on other materials, the wet paint or enamel will make them stick. Drying may be hastened by placing the objects near the furnace if it is not too hot or by directing a gently turning fan at them.

Dipping can also be used for larger objects, such as fence posts and pickets, by building a trough of sufficient size and filling it with paint. This is usually too expensive a method for painting, but it is often used for staining shingles and for soaking wood in preservatives.

## Aerosol Spray Paints and Finishes

These are handy for a variety of purposes. Although they are relatively expensive and are not too suitable for large projects, you may find that for many jobs they won't cost more than what you would pay for the paint plus a brush or roller. For some subjects, such as wicker furniture, they are the most practical method of application. Almost every type of paint or finish is now available in these containers. There are also spray kits you can purchase, so that you can spray custom-mixed paints.

Before using an aerosol spray container, be sure to read the directions on the container and then follow them. Some finishes require that the container be shaken to ensure that the paint will be ejected evenly. There is usually a metal ball inside the container; when the container is shaken, the ball rolls about to help mix the paint.

When spraying, keep the nozzle 8″ to 12″ from the surface. Move the nozzle in a straight line because if you swing it in an arc you'll get an uneven job.

## Knives

**Broad Knife.** This is a short, blunt-edged spatula which is used for spackling, patch-plastering, scraping off lumps, and so many other odd jobs that it would be impossible to list all of them. A 3½″ or

4″ flexible knife is good for all ordinary spackling or plaster-patching. Buy one made of the finest grade of steel you can find; you will be repaid many times over for the small additional cost.

**Putty Knife.** This is a 1″ version of the broad knife. It may have either a flexible or a stiff blade. A 1″ stiff blade is best for all window puttying, and a 1″ flexible knife is good for nail holes and for spackling small imperfections. It is recommended that you buy one of each; but if you want only one, select the flexible kind. Get the best steel you can find; cheap knives break easily.

## Paint Pots and Cans

The containers can be the cans in which the paint is bought. However, you will do well to have another pot into which to pour some of the paint for working—it is difficult to load a brush properly from a full pot. When you empty a gallon can of paint, trim off the lip with one of those can openers which leaves the top edge smooth. The lip interferes with proper loading of the brush. Pots with handles are more easily lifted and set than those without. If you have a little paint left over at the end of a job, put it in a smaller can and clean up the big can for use on the next job. The leftover paint will keep better in the smaller can anyway —less skin will form.

Cardboard paint pots are available and are useful when you do occasional painting. However, you will have to get one of the metal holders for them too.

Paint pots are probably a painter's

greatest source of annoyance. They are always dirty. Keeping pots clean is a chore that should be done when the brushes are rinsed out. You can use the dirty turpentine or benzine to rinse out the pots, and then they will be in good shape for use on the following day. This consistent rinsing is by far the simplest and best way to keep your paint pots in good working order.

If, however, your paint pots should become encrusted with paint, you can remove it with a solution of lye in water. Invert the pot in the solution (using any container that is large enough), and allow it to soak for a day or two.

## Ladders, Planks, and Scaffolding

**Stepladders.** A 6' stepladder is adequate for most work around a house. For painting the interior of the average house, 5' stepladders are high enough. These ladders will be easier to keep clean if you varnish or shellac them, but this is by no means necessary.

Stepladders taller than 6' are available, but you may feel safer if you use trestles instead.

Good stepladders are made of Norway pine, Douglas fir, or spruce. The steps should have metal braces, and there should be a sturdy spreader between the front and back sections. For safety, the ratio for the spread between these sections should be 5½" for each foot of height. A folding platform, for holding a pot of paint, is a useful accessory. (Always remove the pot of paint before moving the ladder.)

**Trestles.** These are similar to stepladders, but they have rungs instead of steps.

They are intended to support planks rather than the worker directly. A variation is an extension center ladder. With such a ladder, it is possible to place a plank as far as 10' above the ground or the floor. The trestles may be shellacked or varnished to keep them clean.

**Straight Ladders.** A 12' or 14' straight ladder will be adequate for exterior work on a single-story house. The sides, or rails, should be made of sound, knotfree spruce or fir. The rungs should be of sound hick-

ory or ash, and should be mortised into the rails.

**Extension Ladders.** Exterior work above the first floor will require the use of an extension ladder, which is an adapta-

tion of the straight ladder. A rope and pulley permit one 12′ straight ladder to be slid up over another one, making an extended length of 20′. Clamps are attached to the rails. These ladders can usually be rented. If you purchase your own, you can shellac or varnish it.

An extension ladder should be *set at a distance from the wall equal to one-fourth of its height.*

Extension ladders up to 40′ in two sections and 50′ in three sections are available. The longer they are, the heavier and more awkward to handle they become. A 32′ ladder is adequate for most two-story houses. If you are going to work at any considerable height, you might well consider renting scaffolding.

When judging the length of ladders you need, remember that you will lose a little height because the foot of the ladder must be set away from the wall. For example, a 20′ ladder set 5′ from a wall reaches to approximately 19′.

**Planks.** You can buy or rent extension planks to use with trestles or ladders, but you will probably find it simpler and more economical to make your own planks for painting around the house. Twelve feet is a convenient length, though in your particular case you may find that a shorter length will serve all your purposes. The planks should be 2″ thick. As for the width of the plank, the safety code recommends 20″. A plank of this size is heavy, expensive, and not always available, and most persons get along with something less. A 12″ width will do, but it is better to use two 2 × 6s or 2 × 8s held together with two or three battens. Whatever you decide on, you should have a width to stand on that is at least equal to the length of your foot.

To make the planks, buy fir or spruce that is free of cracks and checks, and with as few knots as possible. Sandpaper the corners to protect your fingers against splinters. For maximum safety, the planks should be dressed on all four sides and coated with boiled linseed oil. Most persons don't bother to do this, but it does allow you to spot any cracks that may eventually appear in the wood. This practice will also, of course, help keep the planks clean and reduce the splinter hazard.

**Extension Planks.** An extension plank is comprised of a series of wooden strips which can be doubled over one another or opened out. Extension planks are safer than plain planks because they are wider, usually 18″ to 20″. They are also far more convenient than plain planks; they can be collapsed to a length of 6′ or 8′, thus permitting easier transportation. However, they are also far more expensive. Coat them with oil, as paint would gum the slides.

**Scaffolding.** For safety's sake, don't attempt to erect your own 2″ × 4″ scaffolding unless you have had building experience. You can have a scaffold for either interior or exterior use built by a competent carpenter. The principal objection to this is that you must purchase the lumber, and when you have finished with it, it has only second-hand value.

It is best to rent sectional-unit scaf-

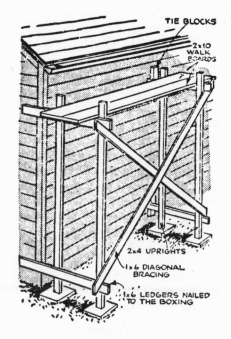

folding. This is erected and dismantled by the company from which you rent it. It is flexible and safe, being approved by even the strictest state safety codes.

**Swing Stages.** These platforms are sup-

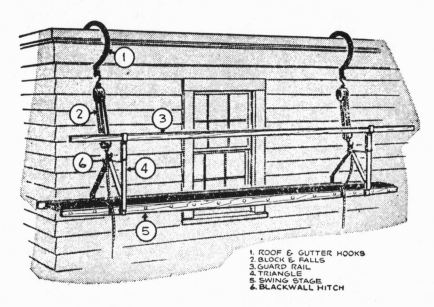

1. ROOF & GUTTER HOOKS
2. BLOCK & FALLS
3. GUARD RAIL
4. TRIANGLE
5. SWING STAGE
6. BLACKWALL HITCH

ported by ropes which are attached to hooks on the roof. If you are not familiar with them, don't try to rig one. It is better to rent one from one of the many companies handling them and to let the company men rig it for you. Swing stages look very simple, but an improperly made Blackwall hitch can cause one end of the scaffold to fall. And if the scaffold is not raised or lowered evenly, an improperly secured stirrup iron can come loose and let it drop.

Once rigged, swing stages are simple to handle if you carefully follow the rigger's instructions for raising and lowering.

**Ladder Stages.** There are several devices which can be attached to a pair of straight ladders to support a platform between them. If the ladders are properly set (a distance away from the wall equal to one-quarter of their height), and if the devices are securely attached to the ladders, the stages are relatively safe. Your

paint dealer can provide you with literature and information on ladder stages. The most common types consist of iron braces that are set over the rungs of the ladders.

## Spackle

This is a compound used for filling small holes in plaster, wallboard, and wood, and for smoothing small rough areas before painting. One type of Spackle comes in powder form and is mixed with water to a thick paste for application. The more convenient type for small jobs is the ready-mixed Spackle, which can be used directly out of the container. Spackle can be applied with a putty knife or with the finger. For work outside use exterior Spackle, which will not be harmed by moisture. Spackle dries rather quickly. Once it is dry, sand it with medium sandpaper to get a smooth surface and then prime.

## Putty

Putty is the right material for filling holes or cracks in wood. It is a simple mixture of whiting, white lead, and linseed oil. Buying it is much easier than mixing it, and there is less danger of your getting the white lead on your hands and perhaps into your mouth. (White lead is enough of a hazard to have provoked many ordinances controlling its use.) If you find that the putty is too hard in the can, simply knife in a little linseed oil; if it is too soft, knife in a little whiting. Knifing-in is best done on a board. You can do it and not get a single speck on

your hands. Putty will stick only to a prepared surface. Make sure there is some paint or oil on any surface you are going to use it on. One of the commonest failures of putty—falling out of windows—is due to its application on raw wood when the glass was set.

## Glazing Compounds

These are usually latex compositions and are used for setting window glass in frames, but they can also be used to fill cracks and holes before painting. They are somewhat easier to use than putty and have less tendency to dry out and crack with age.

## Sandpaper

Once all the holes are filled in and the rough surfaces smoothed over, you will have to use sandpaper to complete the smoothing operation. Sandpaper is made in many grades, from very rough to very smooth; and, for painters' use, in two types, flint and garnet. Wood finishers use a third type known as wet-or-dry. The roughest grade is #3 and the finest #9/0. The best grades for ordinary painting are: #2, for tearing the nibs off lumpy areas; #0, for ordinary purposes; and #2/0, for finer work. The flint paper is the cheaper but does not keep its cutting ability as long as the garnet. This is not too important if you are working on paint, as the paint will clog the paper rapidly anyway.

Proper sanding is done with the paper wrapped around a block, but for simply taking the nibs off paint you can do as well by folding a whole sheet into one-quarter of its original size, refolding to expose a new side when it clogs. Frequent slapping of the paper on your hand or a board will shake out a lot of the accumulated paint dust and give you more use of a sheet.

The simplest type of block to use for wrapping sandpaper is a short piece of a 2 × 4. This is perfectly satisfactory for all ordinary jobs. A cork block—which you can make yourself—5″ long, 3″ wide, and 1½″ thick, is ideal. It does not have the hard corners of a piece of wood and so will not accidentally gouge the surface you are sanding. Also, many manufactured devices for holding sandpaper are available at paint and hardware stores. The advantage of these is that they have mechanical means of holding the sandpaper tight and firm.

## Steel Wool

Steel wool, which is actually steel shavings, is also a very useful material for smoothing operations. It, too, comes in a variety of grades. The coarsest is #3 and the finest in common use is #3/0. It is particularly useful on curved surfaces where a piece of sandpaper would rub all the paint off the projecting edges. Again, use the coarser grades for the roughest surfaces and the fine for real smoothing. The common household steel wool used for cleaning pots and pans is #1 or #0.

The finest grade, #3/0, is particularly useful in wood finishing. Simply dip a handful of the steel wool into some liquid or paste wax and rub the shellacked or varnished surface. Four or five strokes over the same area, in the direction of the grain, will smooth the surface and deposit enough wax to enable you to polish the wood to a fine luster when the wax has had several hours to dry.

## Protective Covers

**Paper.** When interior painting is being done, floors, fixtures, and pieces of furniture too heavy to move out of the room need protection from paint drippings. In connection with exterior painting, the shrubbery may need protection, though most persons don't bother with this.

Fixtures should be loosened and moved away from the wall if possible, and then covered with cloth or heavy paper. Small pieces of furniture should be moved out of the room and the rest gathered in one convenient spot, if they can be moved. These large pieces of furniture and the floors should be covered with paper or cloth. Most people use newspapers. Five or six sheets will give enough protection unless a quantity of paint or water is spilled directly on them. If you have trouble with breezes, a few pieces of tape will hold the paper in place.

On new, unfinished floors, you may find it worthwhile to tape down building paper while finishing the ceiling and walls.

For the furniture, you may find it easier to use heavy wrapping paper, taped in place, rather than newspapers. This method also works particularly well around sinks, tubs, and so on. An old sheet or old bedspread will often be enough for a simple job, particularly outdoors where paper can be readily blown away.

**Dropcloth.** Professional painters use dropcloths to catch any paint drippings. A new development in this line is plastic and crepe paper dropcloths. They come in a 9′ × 12′ size and are tough and resistant to paint and water. They cost a few dollars and can be folded up and stored after any paint on them has dried.

Dropcloths of duck are frequently used by professionals, as you have undoubtedly noticed. They are too expensive an investment to be worthwhile for painting around the house. They also come in 9′ × 12′ size. And they need laundering every once in a while.

## Miscellaneous Materials

**Masking Tape.** Masking tape is a most satisfactory material for protecting stationary fixtures, such as sinks, where they meet the surface that is to be painted. It is also a good solution to the problem of painting a window sash; to determine how many rolls of tape you will need for these, simply measure the distance around a single pane of glass and multiply this by the number of windows.

As you gain experience, you will find it easier and faster to paint sashes freehand without masking tape. What paint accidentally gets on the glass can be removed, after it dries, with a razor blade.

Masking tape is also a great help in achieving straight edges when painting borders, stripes, and so on. It is put along the edge to be protected and removed as soon as you have finished painting.

**Strainer or Cheesecloth.** If you are going to mix or tint your own paints, you will need either cheesecloth or a fine wire strainer. Cheesecloth will do a more thorough job, but it cannot be used for more than a day or two before the paint begins to harden in it. The best cheesecloth for this purpose has about a 30-by-40 thread count. The finer the thread count, the slower the paint will pass through but the better the straining. Allow about one yard for each room. You can prolong its usefulness by leaving it in water.

A wire strainer is simple to use and is easily kept clean. The best strainers have 18 to 24 wires to the inch and measure about 6″ in diameter. These are considerably finer than the average kitchen strainer.

Ready-made paints should not need straining. But if they get lumpy, you will have to strain them to avoid streaking. In this case, an old piece of (clean) wire screen may be enough to do the trick.

**Rags.** You will need a number of paint rags. You can, if you wish, provide a can with a hinged top for storing them; but by far the safest procedure for avoiding spontaneous combustion is simply to spread or hang the rags so that the heat of oxidation will be dissipated into the air.

For the sake of safety, remove all oily rags from the building each night.

**Sponges.** Sponges are good for general washing and cleaning up. The new cellulose sponges are very good; they are stronger than the natural type and much cheaper.

**Hand Cream or Gloves.** The painter who wishes to minimize the problem of cleaning his hands after work should use gloves or a hand cream. A good hand cream can be removed with water and will take all of the accumulated paint away with it. Even though hand creams work very well, most persons don't bother to use them.

**Stirring Paddles.** Pieces of wood 16" or 18" long. 2" wide, and ¼" thick are very useful for stirring paint. Many paint stores give them to you free when you buy paint. There is nothing elaborate about them—any stick that is clean enough, strong enough, and long enough will do.

**Leftover Paint.** Leftover paint should not present a serious problem if you have carefully estimated how much of each kind you need. However, it is not unusual to find that some does accumulate. A simple method of storing it is to pour all light colors in one pot and all dark colors in another. These mixtures can be used for painting bins in the cellar, floors, fence posts, or anything else that requires protection more than a decorative color. If this paint should dry to a very dull finish, its protective qualities can be considerably improved by the addition of about one pint of raw linseed oil or reinforcing oil to each gallon.

You must, however, keep separate the paints with different bases. The general rule is to keep oil-base paints and rubber-base paints apart. Water-base paints should be thrown out, as they will not keep anyway.

## ESTIMATING

While you are cleaning, smoothing, patching, or otherwise preparing to paint,

you can be assembling the necessary information to estimate the amount of paint you will need. Round number methods will work satisfactorily.

Most paints cover about 400 square feet to the gallon. Primers may go a little further, and finish coats not quite so far.

### Finding the Area

To find the number of gallons you will need, you must first, of course, find out the number of square feet to be covered. To find the quantity of paint needed for a ceiling, simply multiply its length by its width in feet and divide the product by 400. To find the quantity for the walls of a room, if the opposing walls are parallel, measure the length of two adjacent walls; double this figure; multiply it by the height of the room; subtract the areas of any doors and large windows; and divide by 400. If the walls are irregular, you will have to measure their length all the way around the room; then multiply by the height of the room and continue as before. The procedure for woodwork is much the same. Find the areas of the windows, doors, paneling, and so on (and don't forget there are two sides to a closet door). Be generous in your measurements here; woodwork usually includes moldings, which take up more paint than a flat surface. When you have the total area of woodwork to be painted, divide by 400.

### Number of Gallons

Always get your measurements in square feet. When you have divided by 400, you will know the number of gallons needed for *one coat*. Multiply this figure by the number of coats you are going to put on, and you will know the amount of paint that you will need.

### A Typical Example

As a typical example, take a bedroom 10′ × 14′ × 8′ with two windows, two doors, and one closet. The perimeter of the room is 48′ and the height 8′. The total wall area is therefore 384 square feet. The area of each window is 16½ square feet; the total for the two windows, 33 square feet. The total area of the two doors is 42 square feet. The total area to subtract from the wall area is 75 square feet. This leaves 309 square feet. Divide this figure by 400—and we know that the walls will take ¾ gallon of paint per coat.

The area of the ceiling equals 140 square feet. This means you will need ⅓ gallon per coat. The woodwork is composed of two windows totaling 33 square feet and three sides of doors, each of which is 21 square feet; the total of all these is 96 square feet. If you allow one foot in height for the baseboard (which is probably 8″ or less), you will have 48 square feet to add to the 96—and a total woodwork area of 144. This means ⅓ gallon of paint per coat.

Assuming that you are doing a two-coat job and that you will use the same wall flat paint for the ceiling and walls, you will need for them a total of 2 gallons 1 quart (1½ gallons for the walls, ⅔ gallon for the ceiling). The best practice is to do the woodwork with one of the interior semiglosses, and you will need ⅔ gallon for that. Buying a half-gallon and a quart is only slightly less expensive than buying a whole gallon, so you will proba-bly do as well to buy the full gallon of semigloss.

By doing this estimating beforehand, you can buy the right amount of paint, and have only a little left over for any touching up that may eventually become necessary.

## PAINT REMOVAL

There are several ways to go about remov-ing old paint and other finishes such as varnish and enamel. Which method to use depends somewhat on the amount of paint to be removed and what sort of work is involved.

### Heat

This is one of the least expensive ways to remove paint and is about the best choice when a large area of paint is involved, as on exterior siding or the hull of a boat. You can either use a flame, to generate enough heat to melt the paint, from a gasoline or propane blowtorch, or use an electric paint remover. One type of electric remover has a coil which becomes sufficiently hot to melt the paint; the other uses a special type of lamp bulb. The electric units are the safer because there is no open flame; but they can, if left in one place long enough, generate enough heat to set the paint on fire. So if you use the heat method of removing paint, observe simple precautions. Because there is a chance of charring the wood with any form of heat, don't use this method on furniture or woodwork that is to be given a natural or transparent finish. If the wood is to be painted, a slight amount of discoloration because of charring won't be any problem—but it will show up under a natural finish.

When you use heat to remove paint, you do not, or should not, actually burn the paint off. The heat should be applied just long enough to melt the paint, which then should be immediately removed, while it is still soft, with a broad-blade putty knife. It will take a bit of practice before you know at just what moment the paint is ready to be removed. Usually it will start to bubble and blister; this is the time it's ready to be stripped off.

Never use a flame-type remover on clapboard house siding, for if the flame gets under a section of the siding it can start a fire inside the wall.

### Chemical Removers

These are far safer than heat, but more expensive. There are two basic types of chemical removers, the liquid type and the paste type. The liquid type is good for horizontal surfaces and for removing paint from intricate moldings and so forth. The paste type is good for vertical as well as horizontal surfaces because it will hold in place.

For home use it is best to use a remover that is nonflammable and nontoxic. Many removers are highly flammable, and the fumes they give off can be extremely dangerous. This type of remover may be fine if you use it outdoors, but don't take a chance using it indoors. Select a remover that is as safe to use as possible.

Any substance strong enough to remove paint can be harmful if it gets on your skin or in your eyes. When working with a remover it's best to wear old clothes and rubber gloves. If any of the remover should get on your skin or in your eyes, flush it out at once with water. Many of the removers on the market today are the water-rinse type; these are better for home use than the older ones that required rinsing with a solvent.

**Using a Paste-Type Remover.** Pour some of the remover into a clean container. Use an old brush to apply—one without paint in the bristles or on the handle, as the remover will soften such paint and it may stain the wood on which you are working. In the case of furniture or wood that is to be given a natural finish, use an inexpensive brush with a handle of unpainted wood.

A paste remover should be applied in a thick coating. Do not brush out the coating; if you do, you will reduce the effectiveness of the remover. Put it on with one full stroke and don't go back over it with the brush. Let the remover remain on the paint for 15 or 20 minutes and then test the paint with a putty knife to see if it comes off easily. If it does not, let the remover work a little longer. The softened paint can be removed with the putty knife or a wad of coarse steel wool. Have a pail of water with some household detergent in it for rinsing off the steel

wool when it becomes loaded with soft paint.

If several coats of paint are involved, you will probably have to remove them one coat at a time. After one coat has been removed, apply more remover and repeat the applications until the wood is free of paint. When the paint has all been removed, rinse the surface clean with water and then allow it to dry.

**Using a Liquid-Type Remover.** The difference in using a liquid rather than a paste remover is that you apply fresh remover as soon as the first coating begins to evaporate. You have to keep the remover fresh so that it will work properly.

## Scraping

This can be an effective way to remove old paint, especially if it is peeling or blistering. Several types of paint scrapers are available. One of the best types has an interchangeable head that can be set for fine or coarse work. Many experts in refinishing furniture prefer to use a cabinet-type scraper for removing paint and varnish from fine pieces because, properly used, such a scraper will not harm the wood.

## Sanding

Using an electric rotary or belt sander is an effective way to remove heavy accumulations of paint where you are not concerned about possible damage to the wood surface. They are handy to use on the hulls of boats and for bad spots on house siding. Don't use them for fine work or on furniture, as it is too easy to take off some of the wood along with the paint. A sander is used, of course, to remove the old finish from a wood floor and smooth the wood before applying a new finish.

Both sandpaper and steel wool are handy for removing thin coats of paint.

first blister the paint; when the blisters break, the paint will begin to peel. The solution to this problem is to find and correct the cause of the dampness in the siding. (See chapter 7, p. 187.) In the case of house siding, blistering and peeling can also be reduced and often eliminated if a latex paint is applied. This type of paint will "breathe," allowing the moisture in back to flow out without damage to the paint. However, you can't apply the latex directly over the old paint; you must strip off all the old paint and apply a special latex primer first.

## PAINT FAILURE

Paint on a surface can fail for a variety of reasons. Most of the problems you'll run into will occur with painted surfaces outdoors, but you will also encounter a few problems inside the house.

**Peeling and Blistering.** These conditions frequently occur on outside walls; the main cause is moisture in back of the paint. If the wood siding becomes damp, for one reason or another, the heat of the sun will draw the moisture out and it will

Peeling (without blisters) will also occur if the surface over which the paint was applied was dirty, greasy, or too smooth, or if a poor quality of paint was used. Peeling often occurs on kitchen cabinets and woodwork; the cause here is usually grease.

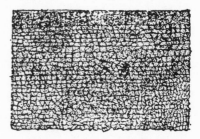

**Checking.** These hairline cracks on the surface of the paint indicate that the first coat was too soft to support the finish coat. As the cracks are only in the finish coat, they can be sanded and a new coat

applied. Or you can fill them in by applying a thin coat of Spackle—use the exterior type and, when hard, smooth it out with a light sanding.

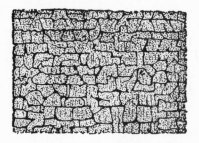

**Alligatoring.** This is somewhat similar to checking except that the cracks in the paint extend down to the wood. It may be that the final coat was applied before the previous coats were hard; or perhaps the paint film is no longer elastic enough to endure the expansion and contraction of the wood. The best thing is to remove the old paint and start off fresh.

**Nondrying Paint.** If paint is still soft to the touch after a decent interval after application, it can be that the surface was greasy or that the paint was of poor quality. Also it can be that the wrong kind of thinner was used. Most paints dry through evaporation of the solvents in them, so that when the weather is very humid, it may take the paint much longer to dry hard than in dry weather.

## ENAMELING

Enamel produces a very smooth, durable, and hard coating. It is used for interior and exterior wood trim, kitchen cabinets, furniture, garden and lawn equipment, and also for floors. There are many different types of enamel; you should be careful to select one that is specified for the job you want to do. An enamel suitable for interior woodwork would not, for exam-

ple, be suitable for a floor; some enamels are suitable for masonry, some not.

Enamel can be applied with a roller as well as a brush, but you will get better results using a brush. It should be a special enamel brush, which has a chisel tip.

For the best results with enamel, always apply it over an enamel undercoater —a special primer designed for use under enamel. Although an ordinary primer of flat paint can be used, it will not produce as smooth a final job as you will get if you first use the enamel undercoater. After the undercoater has been applied and is dry, it should be lightly sanded and the surface dusted thoroughly, as any speck of dust will spoil the smooth enamel finish.

Apply enamel with a full brush— fuller than you would use with ordinary paint. Flow the enamel onto the surface —do not brush any more than is necessary to get proper coverage and smooth out the enamel. Do not be concerned about the brush marks on the fresh enamel. Enamel is designed to flow out after it has been applied, and the brush marks will disappear. You must, however, pick up any runs or sags that may occur around the edges of the work immediately; if you try to brush these out after the enamel has set, you will mar the finish.

If another coat is required, wait until the enamel is perfectly dry, sand lightly, dust, and then apply the next coat.

## VARNISHING

Varnish is somewhat like enamel except that it does not contain pigments and is therefore more or less clear. Varnish is used primarily for interior woodwork, furniture, and floors. Spar, or exterior, varnish can be used for outside work, but as it does not contain pigments it fails more quickly when exposed to the sun than paint or enamel. When this happens, the varnish must be removed before a fresh coat can be applied. For this reason, varnish is not recommended for outside work except for special uses, as on boats.

There are as many different types of varnish as there are enamels, so be sure to use the right one for the job at hand.

Varnish is not an easy finish to apply successfully. It is moderately slow-drying, which means that it will remain soft for a good length of time. If there is dust or dirt in the air around, specks will spoil the finish. Varnish should not be applied when the temperature in the area is much below 70 degrees, and you should avoid varnishing when the humidity is very high.

Never stir varnish before using it because this will create air bubbles which will spoil the finish. The best tool for varnish is a good-quality varnish brush. Never use a brush for varnishing that has been used with paint; as no matter how clean the bristles may appear, chances are there is a small amount of paint in the heel of the brush. The varnish will dissolve the paint and become discolored.

Flow the varnish over the surface working with the grain of the wood, and then brush lightly across the grain. Pick up runs and sags at once—and do not go back over the surface after the varnish has begun to set.

# STAINING

Stains are used primarily on wood. They can change the color of the wood or bring out its natural beauty without hiding the grain or the texture.

Stains must always be applied directly to bare wood. If the wood has previously been painted, it cannot be stained unless the paint is removed. A stain as a rule does not provide any protective coating, so a coat of varnish, shellac, or clear lacquer must go on over it to provide a protective finish.

Stains can be used to darken the wood, but not to lighten the color.

If you want to make a wood lighter in color, it must be bleached (see page 142). Stains are available in wood tones as well as colors. Before you stain an entire piece, make a test on an inconspicuous part to see what the result is going to be. Once you have stained a piece, the only way you can remove the stain is by sanding or using a remover. And remember that you can always get a deeper or darker effect by applying a second coat of stain, but there is no way to lighten the work if you find it too dark.

**Oil Stains.** These are the most common and are very easy to use. They are available in a wide range of colors as well as clear natural wood tones. The pigmented exterior type used on outside work is one of the few stains that does not require any protective coating. The ordinary oil stains suitable for interior use will require a coat of shellac or varnish.

Oil stains are applied with a brush or lintless cloths. Apply the stain to the surface, let it soak in for a few minutes, and then wipe off the excess with a clean cloth. If a second coat is required, it can be applied immediately. Let the stain dry for 48 hours or so before applying the finish.

**Water Stains.** These are more difficult to work with than oil stains. Unlike the oil stains, which can be used right out of the container, water stains come as a powder, which must be dissolved in warm water just before use. The stain penetrates very deeply into the wood and dries very fast, so that there is no room for error. If you work too slowly or if you don't get a very even application, the results may be disappointing. Once the stain has been applied, the wood must dry for at least 12 hours. After this it must be sanded very lightly to smooth down the wood grain that has been raised by the water.

**Non-Grain-Raising Stains.** These are much the same as the water stains except that a solvent is used instead of water to dissolve the powder. Hence sanding is not required after the wood is dry.

# BLEACHING

Bleaches are used to lighten the natural color of the wood and also to remove stains that do not respond to sanding. Whatever bleaching agent is used, it must be applied directly to the bare wood. It cannot work if there is a coat of paint, varnish, shellac, or other finish on the wood. It may take several applications of the bleach to get the result you want.

Many types of wood bleaches are available. One that gives excellent results is a household liquid laundry bleach such as Clorox. Another good bleach can be made by mixing ½ cup of oxalic acid crystals, available at drug and some paint stores, with 1 quart of hot water. Apply this solution while hot and allow it to remain until it is dry and crystals have formed on the wood surface. Brush away the crystals and repeat the process if necessary. After the final application has been made and is dry, neutralize the wood by wiping it with a solution of 1 part household ammonia in 10 parts water. When the wood is dry, sand it smooth.

You may prefer to use a commercial wood bleach, available at hardware and paint stores. These usually come in two containers; they are very satisfactory.

Regardless of the type of bleaching agent you use, protect your hands by wearing rubber gloves, and wear old clothes so that if the liquid gets on them it won't matter. And be very careful to keep the bleach off any surrounding areas such as floors and walls.

# FILLERS

Many open-pored woods, such as oak, ash, chestnut, mahogany, and walnut, are treated with a filler before being given a finish of varnish. The purpose of this is to fill the pores flush with the surface of the wood. The filler can be the same color as, or lighter or darker than, the stained wood. The most commonly used form of filler is made of silica, raw linseed oil, turpentine, and drier. It is obtainable in a natural shade (almost white), or tinted with a variety of colors to match most stains.

The application of a filler is relatively simple. Most labels carry specific instructions as to the amounts of turpentine to add for various woods. The larger the pores in the wood, the less thinning of the filler, is a good general rule. With blonde finishes the filler may be applied to the raw wood after bleaching. On stained wood, it is best applied after the stain. Use a color to match the stain.

To tint a filler, it is the common practice to buy natural filler and add any of the common colors ground in oil. This way you can match your stain color more closely.

Stir the filler well, and continue to stir it as you apply it; the filler settles rapidly and will not fill the pores unless it is of an even consistency. Brush the filler on, using a partly worn brush with stiff bristles. Brush with the grain and then across it to force the paste into every pore. Finish with a light stroke along the grain. After the filler has dried for the time indicated on the label, (generally 15 to 30 minutes), it is ready for wiping. You can check when it is ready by the appearance of light or dull areas.

The wiping operation is generally done with excelsior or burlap. Start by going across the grain. This will remove most of the excess filler but will leave the surface streaked. Complete the wiping by going with the grain. Be careful not to use too much pressure on these strokes or you will pull the moist filler out of the pores. Allow 24 hours for drying.

# PAINTING MASONRY

Until recently painting masonry has always been a problem because the alkali in portland cement, which is used for all forms of masonry—brick, concrete block, stucco, poured concrete, and even asbestos siding shingles—is harmful to ordinary oil paints. It is especially harmful when the masonry is new or when the alkali is brought to the surface of a wall by dampness. Today, however, there are several kinds of paint that make it possible to cover even fresh masonry with success.

**Latex Masonry Paints.** These are without doubt the best paints to use on most masonry around the house, with the exception of cinder block. The reason for this exception is that the cinders in the block often contain iron, and the water of the latex paint will cause the iron particles to rust and discolor the paint. Otherwise, latex paints can be used for both interior and exterior work. Many of the latex paints suitable for wood are also good for masonry, but you should always read the specifications on the container to make sure.

Latex paint should be applied to a damp rather than a dry masonry surface. Spray the surface down with a garden hose just before you start painting, and spray further as required so that you are always painting over a damp surface. A roller with a long nap is the easiest tool for painting a large masonry surface, but it can be done with a brush.

If you are applying a latex paint over old paint, it is best to use a special primer first. This is absolutely essential if the old paint is chalking.

Latex masonry paints are also available in floor enamels, suitable for both inside and outside.

**Rubber-Base Masonry Paints.** These are solvent-thinned paints. They are somewhat more expensive than the latex paints but are especially good for concrete floors, swimming pools, walks, and the like, where a finish is required that is highly resistant to water penetration and to abrasion. They are not very resistant to grease and oil and therefore should not be used on garage floors. They are suitable for use on cinder block.

**Catalytic Coatings.** These are the epoxy type of paints, which are very durable and highly resistant to wear and abrasion. They are the most expensive type of masonry paint available and the most difficult to apply.

**Other Masonry Paints.** A low-cost finish for basement walls is portland cement paint, which comes in powder form and is mixed with water before application. When properly applied, it becomes an integral part of the masonry, and will not peel or chip or be harmed by moisture in the wall. It is not suitable for floors. Stucco and masonry paints are a type of oil paint designed to be more resistant to the akali in masonry than ordinary paints. They are suitable for old masonry surfaces if you are certain that the masonry is perfectly dry and will always remain so.

## Preparing Masonry Surfaces

Regardless of what type of paint you use, the surface to be painted must first be made suitable. Use a wire brush to remove any loose dirt or other matter from the surface. If there are cracks or if mortar between brick or block is missing, these conditions should be repaired. (See chapter 11, page 265.)

**Concrete Floors.** Do not attempt to paint a concrete floor that is constantly damp, because no paint can hold under this condition. Also do not try to paint a new concrete floor until it has had several months to cure.

If the floor has been previously painted and the paint is not in good condition, suitable as a base for a fresh coat, it should be removed. This can be done by covering it with a solution of 1 pound of lye in 5 pints of water. This is a strong solution, so be careful how you handle it. Wear old clothes, rubber gloves, and goggles and brush the solution over the floor with a long-handled brush. Let the solution remain until the paint becomes soft and then scrape it off with a hoe. Several applications may be required to get off the old paint.

With either a new or an old floor, there is a better chance that the paint will make a good bond if the concrete is etched to open up the pores. This is done with 20% solution of muriatic acid. Take the same care in handling this solution as you would with lye. Let the acid remain on the surface until bubbling stops, then rinse thoroughly with fresh water and allow to dry before painting.

**Masonry Sealers.** These are transparent coatings applied to many masonry surfaces to prevent them from absorbing dirt and stains, or where painting is not desirable or practical. The sealers are most suitable for brick or flagstone walks and terraces and other surfaces where you want a protective coating that will not hide the natural color of the masonry.

# PAINTING METAL

Paint is used to protect metal surfaces in and around the house—as in the case of iron and steel, which rust unless painted—and for decorative purposes. There is no particular problem in painting metal if you first prepare the surface and then use the correct type of paint.

## Aluminum

Aluminum objects inside the house can be painted with a good interior paint—either a flat paint or an enamel—but they do not require painting except for decorative reasons. Aluminum that is exposed to the weather will in time develop a gray discoloration which is not harmful but is unsightly. This discoloration makes a good base for paint, however. Just wipe the surface clean with a cloth and mineral spirits. If the gray film is badly pitted, smooth it with sandpaper or steel wool.

If the aluminum is new and the film of discoloration has not formed, the surface should be treated so that it will make a good bond with the paint. The best thing to use for this is a prepared metal conditioner that you can get at a paint or hardware store. If you are unable to get this, wipe the metal down with mineral spirits.

Aluminum needs a prime coat; any good-quality primer designed for either wood or metal can be used. After this is dry apply a finish coat.

## Copper

Like aluminum, copper seldom requires painting to protect it. Copper objects on the outside of the house, such as gutters, flashing, and lamp fixtures, are often painted because if the copper is left bare, water washing over the metal will stain the adjoining painted surfaces.

If you wish to paint copper, do not remove the tarnish from it, as this helps to make a good bond with the paint. But remove any green discoloration with steel wool and then apply a metal primer, followed by an exterior trim paint. If you wish to leave the copper its natural color but to protect it and the adjoining painted surfaces, clean the metal with a metal polish, and then wipe it with a solvent, and then coat it with a clear exterior lacquer.

## Iron and Steel

Any object made of these metals which is exposed to moisture—even moist air, as might be the case in a basement—must be painted to protect it from rust. If the piece has not been previously painted, wipe it with a rag wet with mineral spirits to remove any traces of grease and dirt. If there are any rust spots, remove them with sandpaper or steel wool. After this, coat the metal with a metal primer, and then with one or two coats of paint.

If the piece is badly rusted, all the rust must be removed. A scraper is good for this job if the scales are heavy. You may find a stiff wire brush helpful, but you should complete the job with sandpaper, steel wool, or emery cloth. Once you have the metal as bright and free from rust as you can get it, coat it with a metal conditioner containing phosphoric acid. This product will get the rust out of areas you can't reach with steel wool or sandpaper, and also will provide a good bond between the primer and the metal. After this treatment, apply the primer and then two coats of paint.

If the piece has been previously painted and the old paint is in perfect condition, wipe it clean and apply a fresh coat. But if some of the old paint has cracked, it should be removed along with any rust and then treated as suggested above.

**Galvanized Steel.** This is steel with a thin protective coating of zinc; as long as the zinc holds up, the metal under it won't rust. In time, however, the zinc coating is worn or scratched away, and then the metal will rust unless protected by paint.

Galvanized steel that has not been exposed to the weather does not take paint very well, and the best policy with new objects is to let them weather for a period of time. However, some special paints are made for galvanized steel which the manufacturers claim can be used at once, without waiting for this weathering process.

The key in painting galvanized steel is to use the right metal primer; it should be one containing a high percentage of zinc dust. And be sure that the finish paint you use is compatible with the primer.

As with ordinary iron and steel, if there are any rust spots on the galvanized steel they should be removed before priming.

## PAINTING A ROOM

The first step in getting a room ready for painting is to move as much of the furniture out of it as you can. Pieces that are too heavy or large to move into other areas can be set in the middle of the room in a group and covered with a dropcloth. Take pictures and mirrors from the walls. Remove all electric switch and outlet plug plates because even if you plan to paint them, they should not be painted while in place. Loosen canopy-type or bracket-type wall and ceiling fixtures so that they hang free from the wall or ceiling, and cover them with paper held in place with masking tape. If you are painting a kitchen or bathroom, protect nonremovable plumbing and fixtures with heavy paper. It will make the job go easier if you can move such fixtures as refrigerators, freezers, and ranges away from the walls so that you can easily reach behind them to paint. If you have radiators but don't need heat, it pays to take the time to disconnect and remove them now.

Unless you are planning on refinishing the floor, it must be protected from paint. A dropcloth is good, but a better solution is to cover the entire floor with building paper held in place with masking tape. If you do this, there will be no chance of paint getting on the floor even if you pick up some on the soles of your shoes, which often happens unless you are a very tidy painter.

**Cleaning.** Nearly all surfaces should be washed before painting except in the case of new work, where it's usually not necessary. But it should be done when re-

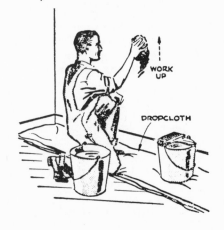

WORK UP

DROPCLOTH

painting a room, especially the kitchen and bathroom because their surfaces become covered with grease carried by the moist air. A good cleaning will remove not only dust, which can streak paint, but also grease that can keep it from sticking properly. Give the walls and ceiling a good vacuuming to remove loose dust and then wash them with a household detergent and water, or a commercial wall cleaner available at paint and hardware stores. Some of these cleaners do not require rinsing. Wash from the bottom of a wall up so that the washing solution will not streak the paint.

**Removing Calcimine.** In many older homes you may find that the ceiling was painted with calcimine; this should be removed before you apply fresh paint because it does not make a good base for anything—even more calcimine. You can find out if the old finish is calcimine easily enough—just go over it with a damp sponge. If the finish comes off on the sponge, it's calcimine, and you should go to work with warm water, washing soda, and the sponge and get it all off.

**Wallpaper.** There are two schools of thought about painting over old wallpaper. One says "don't"; the other says "do." Well, there is no doubt that the safest policy is to remove the old wallpaper before you paint. If you do this, there will be no chance that the paint will act as a solvent on the dyes of the paper and cause them to discolor the paint. There will also be no chance that the paint will soften the paste holding the paper in place so that it begins to come loose. And once you have painted over wallpaper, if the time ever comes when you want to take it off, it's going to be a more difficult job than before it was painted.

But most people prefer to take the chance and paint over the paper. If this is the route you want to go, be sure that the paper is securely attached to the wall and that there are no large loose areas or big blisters. Test the paint on the paper to see how it reacts to the dyes; give it several days or even a week to act because sometimes it takes a while for any reaction to occur. If the paint and the dyes seem to get along, you can begin to get the paper ready for the paint. Repaste any loose edges. If there are some blisters, split them with a razor, work paste in back of the paper, and then press it back against the wall. If there are spots where the paper is missing, smooth these out with Spackle.

Any unevenness in the paper is going to show through the paint. Some paper is applied using lap joints, which will stand out like sore thumbs through the paint unless you take the time to sand them down. Sometimes it takes as much time to get the old paper ready for paint as it would to get rid of it completely.

The best way to remove wallpaper is with a wallpaper steamer, which you can rent for a few dollars a day from paint, hardware, and tool rental stores. A steamer does a good job with a minimum of mess; your dealer will instruct you in how to operate the type he handles. The other method is to use warm water and a liquid wallpaper remover, available at paint and hardware stores. These liquids are designed to allow the water to cut through the paper and reach the paste very quickly. They cost only a dollar or so.

Taking off wallpaper is a messy job, especially if you are using the liquid remover, so cover the floor adjoining the wall. Have a large container handy to put the paper in as it comes off the wall.

A good way to apply the remover is with a hand spray gun. Soak an area and then use a broad putty knife to help in pulling the paper off the wall. If it doesn't come off easily, apply more liquid. Be careful not to damage the plaster with your knife, because when it is wet it becomes slightly soft. Remove the paper in vertical sections, getting the wall as clear of it as you can. After the wall is dry, you can go over it with sandpaper and smooth out any rough spots or areas where bits of the paper are still clinging.

If the paper has been previously painted, you will first have to sand the paint so that the steam or liquid can reach the paper. Coarse sandpaper is adequate for this job. You don't have to remove all the paint—just scratch it enough to let the water through.

**Patching, Spackling, and Sanding.** Any flaws in walls, ceilings, or woodwork should be repaired before painting. Cracks and holes in plaster can be repaired as suggested in chapter 10 (page 245). Small holes and hairline cracks can be filled with Spackle and sanded smooth when it is dry. If the paint on any of the interior woodwork is peeling or cracked, it should be removed and any rough spots sanded smooth. Pay particular attention to windows, since the paint on them is often in poor condition because of exposure to the weather. It may be necessary to remove a considerable amount of the old paint. Any holes in woodwork should be filled with Spackle. If the woodwork has not been previously painted, wait until it has been primed and then spackle over nails, screws, and so on.

**Selection of Paint.** The best paint to use on walls and ceilings is a latex, which dries so quickly that you can give a room a couple of coats of paint in a few hours and have it ready for use that evening. If the room has been previously painted and you are going to use the same color, one coat of paint is usually sufficient; but if it's new work or you are going to change colors, two coats will be required. The two areas in the house where latex is not necessarily the ideal paint are the bathroom and the kitchen. Although latex dries very quickly, it requires several weeks to cure enough to be washable; therefore, in the bath and kitchen, where moisture and the need for washing are present, an alkyd paint or oil paint may be a better choice.

The general rule is to use a flat wall paint in all rooms but the bathroom and kitchen, where a semigloss enamel is advisable.

## Schedule of Work

In painting an entire room, do the ceilings first, then the walls. Next comes the woodwork; start at the highest point and work down so that you do the baseboards last. If the floor is to be painted or refinished, this should be done when all the rest of the work has been completed.

**Ceilings.** These can be painted with a roller with an extension handle, or with an ordinary roller or a brush—in which case you will have to work from a ladder or, better yet, two stepladders or trestles with an extension plank between them.

You can rent this equipment at paint and tool rental stores; it will save you a good deal of time not having to move a single stepladder around at frequent intervals. If you are using a brush on the ceiling, don't try to work with one too full of paint, as it will drip down the handle; use as dry a brush as you can. Take advantage of the natural light, or artificial light if necessary, so that you will get good coverage.

**Walls.** It is best to begin from the window wall and work back into the room, so that the reflection from the wet paint will reveal any spots that have not been properly coated. Obviously, it is best to begin at a natural break in the wall, such as a corner.

As you paint from ceiling to floor, adapt the width of the stretch to the type of paint and to your convenience. When

working with an oil paint and a brush, if the paint is very fast-setting, take narrower stretches to avoid dry laps.

**Trim.** The main concern here is to keep the trim paint off the walls. Special applicators are available at paint stores that will be helpful, or you can use one of those little metal guards designed to keep paint from places where it doesn't belong. But the best tool to use is a small good-quality trim or sash brush, along with care and patience on your part. It's best

not to apply masking tape over freshly painted surfaces, even if the paint appears dry, since it may not have cured. In that case, when you remove the masking tape the paint will come off with it in spots.

## SPECIAL PAINTING PROBLEMS

Certain objects and surfaces inside the house require special paints or special attention.

**Ceramic Wall Tile.** If this is to be painted, use an epoxy paint, which is the only type that will hold on such a smooth surface and also withstand the moisture around a recessed bathtub. Before painting, the wall must be thoroughly washed with a detergent and water. After this, scrub it with a thin paste of powdered pumice stone and water. Rinse thoroughly and then apply the epoxy according to the manufacturer's directions.

**Kitchen Cabinets.** Enamel is the most satisfactory finish to use on these. The cabinets should be thoroughly washed with water and a detergent to remove all traces of grease; then, when the surfaces are dry, they should be rubbed down with steel wool or medium sandpaper. This is necessary to cut the high gloss on the finish so that the new enamel will make a good bond. If you fail to do this, there is a good chance that even a light tap will cause the enamel to chip off.

**Radiators.** These should not be painted with a metallic paint such as bronze or aluminum, which reduces the heat output. The best paint is a flat wall or radiator enamel. If the units have been coated with a metallic paint, it need not be removed; just apply the new paint right over it. The best color to use is the same one as on the wall in back of the radiator—this makes the radiator less conspicuous. The simplest way to paint radiators is with a spray gun or spray can, but a thin, long-handled brush is adequate.

**Plumbing Fixtures.** Bathtubs, wash-basins, and sinks can be painted with an epoxy paint in the same manner as suggested above for ceramic tile.

# PAINTING A HOUSE

The success of this operation depends on using first-grade paint and giving careful attention to the preparation of the surface. Under average conditions, a good-quality paint job should last 5 or 6 years.

The best time of year to paint a house, in most sections of the country, is late spring or early fall. Most house paints should not be applied when the temperature is below 40 degrees. On the other hand, if they are applied in very hot weather, they may dry too rapidly. If you must paint outside in the hot summer months, do it early in the morning before the temperature gets too high.

Oil-base house paints should never be applied over a damp surface—even one damp from morning dew—or if there is a possibility of rain in the next 24 hours. Latex house paint can be applied over a damp surface; and as it dries in an hour or so, you can use it when there is a forecast of rain in the near future. On the other hand, if there is rain before the latex paint has had a chance to dry, it will be washed right off the surface.

For most jobs, latex house paint is the easiest for the amateur, and gives excellent results. It is not, however, so satisfactory if the old paint is badly chalking or so worn that the wood under it is exposed. In these cases, a latex primer should first be applied, followed by the latex exterior paint. As this requires two coats of paint, time and money can be saved if an oil-base house paint is used instead; often one coat will do the job.

For shutters, windows, trim, and so on, use either an alkyd exterior trim and shutter enamel, or a latex exterior trim enamel.

## Preparing the Surfaces

It's a wise idea to wash the house down before painting. This gets rid of dirt and grime that not only might streak the paint but also might prevent it from making a good bond with the old paint. If the house is near the seashore, it's essential that you wash the house no more than 24 hours before painting.

Inspect the siding carefully and re-nail any loose shingles or clapboards with rust-resistant aluminum nails. If any rusty nailheads are exposed, remove the rust with sandpaper and put a dab of paint on the nailhead. Drive the nailheads below the surface of the wood and fill in over them with putty or exterior Spackle.

Remove rust from any iron or steel objects attached to the house and prime them with a metal primer.

Window shutters, window screens, and storm windows should be taken down so that the areas around them can be painted. You'll also find it easier to paint these items if they can be placed on a workbench or table, rather than trying to paint them when they are in place.

Check all painted surfaces for flaws in the old paint. Areas where the paint has blistered or peeled should be scraped down to the bare wood and given a coat of primer. Rough spots can be sanded smooth or filled in with exterior Spackle.

If there are any open seams between the siding and the window and door frames, fill these with caulking compound before you start painting. Also fill any other seams you may find, as where the siding joins an outside chimney.

A ladder is perfectly adequate for a one-story house, but if you have a two-story house you may find that it's worth the money to rent some scaffolding. This will make it much easier to prepare the surface as well as to paint it.

Before you begin painting, use drop-cloths to protect foundation plants, shrubs, concrete walks, and other areas that you don't want to have splattered with paint. No matter how careful you may be, some paint is almost sure to drip from the surface; often it will be picked up by a breeze and carried some distance.

## Application

Paint can be applied with either a brush or a roller. If you are working from a ladder, it will pay you to get a hook so that the paint container can be hung from the ladder, or, if you are using a roller, a special clamp so that the roller tray can be attached to the ladder.

The general rule in painting a house is to do the siding first. Start at the highest point and work down. After the siding is done and is dry, go back and do the trim around windows and doors.

In painting siding, the paint should be applied across in a strip 2′ to 4′ wide, depending on whether you are working from a ladder or scaffold. You don't want to paint a strip much wider than 4′—because if you do, by the time you start on the next strip the edge of the fresh paint will be dry, and you may get lap marks. This isn't a problem with latex paints, but it is with oil-base paints.

After the siding has been painted, do the trim. Tie old rags to the top of the ladder so that it won't scar the freshly painted siding. Use a small trim-and-sash brush, and be as careful as you can not to splash any of the trim paint on the siding if you are using a different color from the siding.

**Exterior Straining.** Many home today have shingles, clapboard, or plywood siding which is stained rather than painted. Applying a fresh coat of stain is not difficult, as it goes on faster than paint, and about the only surface preparation necessary is a thorough dusting or washing beforehand.

**Porch Floors.** Use an exterior floor or deck enamel on these. Ordinary house and trim paints will not stand up under the wear.

**Canvas Decks.** These should also be painted with a good-quality deck enamel. If the old paint is in poor condition, take it off with a paint remover. Do as little work with the scraper as possible, because it is easy to tear the material.

If a section is worn, patch it. Cut out the worn material, and coat the exposed wood with white-lead paste. Cut a new piece of canvas to fit the area, allowing an extra 2″ on all sides. Coat the underside with white-lead paste, set the patch in position, and secure it with copper tacks. Wipe away the excess white lead from the edges and then paint with deck enamel.

**Roofs.** Wood shingle roofs should not be painted, but they can be stained with a wood shingle stain. Asphalt roofs can be coated with a special roofing compound available in several colors. It is often used to give the roof a few additional years of use. Tin roofs can be coated with a similar compound.

(For information on painting asbestos cement, stucco siding, or concrete block, see page 142.)

## FINISHING A FLOOR
### Kinds of Floors

About a dozen woods are regularly used for interior flooring in homes. There are two principal types, hardwood and softwood.

Those in the first category include mahogany, oak, chestnut, cherry, walnut, maple, beech, and birch. These are also identified as "broad-leaved type, porous group." The complexity of the fiber structure is the distinguishing characteristic of these woods. The hardwoods wear more uniformly than softwoods, are less likely to sliver, take a better finish, and are generally better-looking. Most often used in flooring for homes are oak and maple, with beech and birch ranking next. Each piece of wood usually bears the trademark of the association under whose rules it was graded.

The softwoods regularly manufactured into flooring are southern pine, Douglas fir, western hemlock, western larch, western red cedar, redwood, and southern cypress. Somewhat less expensive than hardwoods, they are entirely satisfactory for flooring in the less-frequented areas of a home such as bedrooms and closets, and can be used instead of plywood for floors to be covered with composition flooring. As with the hardwoods, each piece of softwood flooring is usually stamped to show the trademark of the association under whose rules it was graded, the grade name, and the name or mill identification number of the manufacturer.

**Grain.** Both hardwoods and softwoods are regularly manufactured in flat-grain and vertical-grain stock.

Flat-grain lumber is sawn, plank after plank, from one side of the log to the

other. Other terms for flat-grain are slash-grain, "bastard" grain, plain-sawed, and tangential cut.

Vertical-grain lumber is that in which the wide surfaces have been sawn in a

plane approximately at right angles to the annual rings of growth. It is also known as edge-grain, rift-grain, comb-grain, and quarter-sawn.

The vertical-grain is generally considered to have better wearing qualities in both hard and softwoods and has a more pleasing, uniform figure.

Whether the flooring be hardwood or softwood, interior or exterior, the homeowner's problem is to apply a finish that will stand the ravages of time and active living. No one type of finish is better in every respect than any other. The secret of good floors lies in thorough understanding of the nature and limitations of the particular kind of finish chosen. No less important are care and maintenance after the job is done.

**Composition Floors.** Among the various materials included under the heading of "composition" flooring are linoleum, asphalt tile, cork, rubber tile, and mastics. Cement floors are used for basements, garages, and porches.

## Types of Finishes

Where the owner's chief requirement is a long-lasting finish, varnish and shellac are likely to prove most satisfactory. The durability of coatings can be improved and preserved by keeping them properly waxed. Fresh wax every 4 to 6 months is a general maintenance procedure. The time interval will naturally vary according to the amount of wear on the floor.

The following discussion of finishes is intended only to identify the various types and their customary use, some of their advantages and disadvantages, and details of preparation and application.

**Varnish.** Although tending to show scratches, this finish has a durable, glossy appearance which is highly resistant to spots and stains. The application is simple; use a 3″ or 4″ brush and flow on a good even coat. Some skill is needed, however, to patch worn spots without leaving lines of demarcation between old and new varnish. Varnish will give satisfactory results if properly waxed and otherwise maintained. It is available in quick 4-hour- or regular 24-hour-drying types.

**151**

**Shellac.** Its quick-drying qualities and ease of application make this a widely used floor finish. It has only moderate resistance to water and other types of stains, and will spot if liquid is allowed to dry on it. Among other qualities, it has a high gloss, is transparent, and does not darken with age as quickly as varnish does. As in the case of varnish, durability of the finish is increased by waxing.

**Floor Sealer.** For floors subject to heavy traffic, floor sealer produces excellent results on oak, maple, beech, birch, and edge-grain pine and fir. It is a finish which shows wear less than varnish or shellac, but soils more easily. The process requires application of wood filler, sealer, and wax.

**Lacquer.** This finish has about the same durability as varnish. It provides a glossy appearance, and worn spots may be retouched with good results. Lines of demarcation are not visible because the new lacquer dissolves the old application rather than forming an additional layer. It is extremely difficult to apply, however, because of its quick-drying properties. It has less depth of finish than varnish and is somewhat more expensive.

**Wax.** Important in finishing and maintaining wood, composition, and cement flooring is wax. Not only does it give a shine, but it also forms a protective film that prevents dirt from penetrating the pores of wood floors. When it becomes dirty, new applications of wax can be made easily. It comes in paste or liquid form, requiring rubbing to polish. Self-polishing types are also available.

**Paint.** This finish is more suitable than any other coating for exterior floors of both wood and cement. Though painting interior wood floors is sometimes done, it is not recommended because paint wears more rapidly than other finishes. Also, it hides the natural beauty of woods. Basement floors are satisfactorily painted, helping to preserve the material and keep the dust down.

**Stains.** If you want to change the natural color of the wood, colored oil stains are an answer. They are used to give a darker color to a natural wood. Popular types are oil, penetrating oil, and water stains.

## Preparation of Floors

Preliminary to floor finishing or refinishing, surfaces should be checked for loose boards, slivers, unfilled cracks, loose joints, stains, and other defects. The flooring should then be scraped or sanded. Stains and burns should be sanded out. In brief, the surface should be smooth, free from marks or gaps in the wood, and ready for the succeeding steps of finishing.

Previously finished floors may be mopped or scrubbed with warm water and a mild soap. Wash worn spots with a detergent soap and water. Some discolorations can be removed with a mild bleach (see page 142). Your floor must be free of all traces of oil, grease, and wax or the finish will not adhere properly. It must also be perfectly dry.

**Sanding.** You'll need a sanding machine. They can be rented by the day from most builder's supply houses or paint stores, complete with instructions. You'll also need a small edger for scraping near the baseboards and inside closets.

Surface dirt should be swept up before using the sander. On softwood floors move the sander with the grain at all times. Start with a coarse sandpaper, then use a paper of medium coarseness. Finish with a paper of fine grade in the last scraping operation. Carefully sweep up the dust each time; if possible, use a vacuum cleaner. Hardwood floors are sanded the same way except that the rough scraping is done either across the grain or at an angle of 45 degrees to it. (Finish sanding is always done with the grain.)

The floor should not be walked on after the last scraping until the stain, filler, or first coat of finish has been applied and has dried thoroughly. For such walking as is unavoidable, wear heavy socks over—or without—shoes. It is important that at least the first coat of the finish, no matter which method is used, be applied the same day as the final buffing in order to prevent moisture in the air from raising the grain of the newly sanded floor.

**Cracks.** Cracks in wood floors should be filled before sanding, finishing, or refinishing. Slivers or wedges of wood can be cut to fill large cracks. Glue them in firmly and fill any recesses remaining with wood paste or wood putty. Finally, sand or plane smooth the repairs you have made—unless, of course, you are planning to sand the entire floor. (Smaller cracks can be filled with the wood paste or wood putty alone.)

Use slivers and paste or putty of approximately the same color as the surrounding wood, if possible. The sliver should preferably be of the same kind of wood as the floor, but you can stain it if you can't make a match otherwise. Wood paste and putty are usually available in a variety of colors, but if you can't get what you want, match the shade by mixing a little color into the material.

**Replacing Damaged Sections.** Patching badly battered sections of flooring becomes necessary when other repair techniques fail. It means lifting up old flooring and inserting new sections of wood.

Boards which have become warped or worn are replaced by cutting through their width approximately 2″ on either side of the damaged area with a compass saw or floor saw, taking care not to cut into the subfloor. Then split the board down the center of the damaged area with a chisel and pull out the two pieces. Next, measure a new piece of flooring, saw it to length, and cut off the bottom edge of the groove. Set the new piece of board in place and nail it into the subfloor. Tap the nails slightly below the surface with a nail set, fill the hollow with wood filler, and sand the surface smooth.

If your flooring is not tongue-and-groove (single flooring), the problem of replacing floor sections is somewhat simplified.

Drill a hole right through the floor on either side of the worn board, large enough for you to insert the point of a keyhole saw. Cut the plank so that it is flush with the joists at either end. Nail some 2″ × 3″ wooden cleats to the sides of the joists to support the new board.

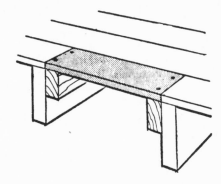

Measure and cut the new piece of flooring and nail it to the cleats. With a nail set, countersink the nails, fill with wood filler, and sand the surface smooth.

**Creaky Floors.** Some creaking floors are caused by the omission of subflooring. Others have inadequate joist support, or are improperly nailed.

For floor boards that have lifted slightly from the joists or the subflooring, better first try tapping them down. Lay a piece of old burlap or carpeting over the bulge. Place a block of wood over this, and tap with a wooden mallet or the flat back of a hatchet, taking care to hit the wood block and not the floor. If this doesn't bring results, try driving 10d nails in the areas of the loose boards. Sink the nails just below the surface, fill with wood filler, and sand the surface smooth.

Another method of stopping creaking floors is possible if you can get at the joists. Tap a slim wedge under the joist near the offending area of flooring. Do not overdo this or you will raise the floor boards at the wedged point and create the worse problem of an uneven floor. In the event that you can't drive in a wedge, nail a wooden cleat to the joist at the point where the creaking occurs, so that it supports the flooring.

## Applying the Finish

**Wood Filler.** The purpose of wood filler is to fill the surface pores of large pored woods, preventing the top coating of finish from sinking into the pores. A flat surface is thereby ensured. Filler is generally used with the hardwoods rather than the softwoods.

For a natural or light-colored floor, use colorless wood filler; of course, colored wood fillers are used for a dark-stained floor. You apply the wood filler *after staining*, if you are using stain, but always *before all other* finishing materials. It should dry in 24 hours.

Thin the filler with turpentine or mineral spirits to the consistency of thick cream. Using a short-bristle brush, brush it freely across the grain and then with the grain, rubbing it well into the pores. Don't try to cover too large an area at one time. When the surface appears dull, indicating that the volatile portion has evaporated, wipe off the excess with burlap or a wad of excelsior, or use a floor-buffing machine. The wiping operation is important; it is done first across the grain and then lightly along the grain.

**Varnish.** In using varnishes, select the type made especially for floors—all-purpose varnishes will not dry hard enough. Instructions for the application of varnish vary from product to product; in any case, follow the directions of the manufacturer. As a rule, three coats are required when varnish is used on bare wood; two coats where a wood filler has been used; and one where a coat of shellac has been applied. Make very sure that each previous coat is thoroughly dry before applying a new coat. The application of varnish is best at 70 degrees; below 60 degrees it will

not flow to an even surface. After the last coat has dried, apply wax and polish the surface. (See page 91 for refinishing.)

**Shellac.** This finishing material is often used as an undercoating for varnish; it makes a good bond between raw wood and the varnish. A type of shellac is also satisfactory as a final interior coater and is somewhat cheaper than most standard varnishes.

The shellac should always be fresh; shellac that has stood long in metal containers may have salts of iron that discolor oak and other woods containing tannin. It should be applied with a wide brush, and the strokes should be long, even ones. Take care to join the laps smoothly. The first coat on bare wood requires 2 to 4 hours to dry. It should then be rubbed lightly with steel wool or sandpaper, after which the floor should be swept clean. A second coat should be allowed to dry 2 or 3 hours and then should be gone over with steel wool and swept again, before the third and last coat is laid on. Three coats are generally required for hardwood floors; for softwood floors, two coats will usually be satisfactory. After applying the last coat of shellac, don't use your floor until the next morning, if possible. If you must use the room, wait at least 3 hours.

An application of wax should be made to maintain the appearance and preserve the finish. Wait at least 8 hours after the last coat has been put on before applying the wax. Avoid using water-emulsion waxes manufactured for linoleums and composition floors, as the water may cause the shellac to "bloom"—become milky in appearance. (See page 92 for refinishing.)

Some shellacs need thinning to conform with a consistency needed for a particular job. The correct thinner for reducing shellac is 190-proof denatured alcohol. Never use antifreeze alcohol or methanol, as they usually contain water.

Recently, colored shellacs, known as French lacquers, have become available to the consumer. Looking like enamel, they have all the sealing and surface qualities

## QUANTITIES FOR REDUCING SHELLAC

| Shellac | Alcohol Added |
|---|---|
| 5-lb cut to 3 lb | 3½ pints to 1 gal shellac |
| 5-lb cut to 2 lb | 1 gal to 1 gal shellac |
| 5-lb cut to 1 lb | 2⅔ gals to 1 gal shellac |
| 4-lb cut to 3 lb | 1 qt to 1 gal shellac |
| 4-lb cut to 2 lb | ¾ gal to 1 gal shellac |
| 4-lb cut to 1 lb | 2⅛ gals to 1 gal shellac |

of regular shellac. They come in white and black, and can be tinted by mixing in dry pigments dissolved in denatured alcohol. Extremely difficult to apply, they must be put on with great skill and under ideal conditions or they won't flow to a smooth finish. They are not recommended for use by the amateur.

**Floor Sealer.** This finish is good for floors that get heavy traffic. The process requires the application of wood filler, sealer, and wax. (For application of filler, see page 154.)

Floor sealer is essentially a thinned spar varnish. Its application requires no special skill. Apply the sealer with a paintbrush, a lamb's-wool applicator, a mop, or a squeegee—as much as the floor will absorb. Depending on the type of grain, some boards will absorb more sealer than others. After the first coat has been applied, spread out the surplus sealer with an applicator or cloth to areas which will absorb it, and then wipe off any excess before it becomes tacky. Before the first coat dries, burnish the surface with steel wool. Allow it to dry overnight. Apply the second coat in the same way, but do not use more sealer than the floor will absorb. Repeat the burnishing operation with a power-driven steel-wool burnishing machine and allow the floor to dry overnight. Lastly, apply wax.

**Lacquer.** The difficulty for the beginner in applying lacquer is a factor limiting its use: it dries so quickly that it takes quite some experience to apply it well. It is not recommended for the amateur. If used, particular attention should be given to the instructions of the manu-

facturer. It has about the same finishing properties as varnish.

**Wax.** Almost all finishing operations require wax to intensify the beauty of the floor and to preserve the finish. Two types are paste, or liquid, waxes; and water-emulsion waxes, commonly called nonrubbing or "self-polishing" waxes, which are widely used on cement, linoleum, rubber tile, cork, asphalt tile, mastic, and other floorings. Follow the directions of the manufacturer for applying a particular product.

Wax on varnished floors tends to make them slippery unless it is kept thin. To ensure a nonslippery surface, allow the wax to dry from 30 minutes to an hour before polishing. Be careful in using water-emulsion waxes, since the water base frequently causes a raising of the grain of the wood, which in turn results in a rough surface. Apply a good-quality paste wax over the final shellac, varnish, or floor sealer finish, and polish, either by hand or with a buffing machine.

To apply paste wax, put a thin coat on the floor, using a cloth applicator or machine. For an applicator cloth, fold cheesecloth into a thick pad and place the wax between the folds; pressure on the pad forces wax to the rubbing surface and ensures an even coating. Let the wax set for 15 to 30 minutes, then polish the surface with a polishing machine or by rubbing with soft cloths on a weighted floorbrush.

You can easily make a floor-polishing brush by attaching an old broom handle to a piece of plank about 8" wide and 12" long. Use a strap hinge so that the handle can swing up and down as you push the polisher back and forth. Cover the bottom with 5 or 6 thicknesses of burlap or other strong cloth, and wire or otherwise secure a couple of bricks onto the top side of the plank. This added weight will speed up the polishing.

**Paint.** Although paint is not generally suitable for indoor floors, it is better than any other coating for exterior wood floors.

It is more durable than varnish or sealer and usually affords greater protection against weathering.

Make certain that wood floors are free of moisture before painting. Wood floors in contact with the earth are usually damp; adequate provisions for damp-proofing should be made. This means separating the wood from the earth by metal, cement, or air.

You must also consider the weather. Choose a day when the humidity is low and the temperature is pleasant. Paint dries very slowly at low temperatures, so do not paint when the level is expected to fall below 40 degrees.

Remove dust and dirt, and smooth rough or uneven spots. Fill all nail holes, open joints, and cracks with putty after the surface has been primed. One of the softwoods is generally used for exterior flooring; if so, filler will not be needed. If a large-pored hardwood has been used, you should apply filler.

If a floor is to be repainted, and the paint has worn away but is generally in good condition, showing no blisters or flaking, spot-prime the worn areas and apply one coat of paint over the entire floor. For severe paint failures, such as blistering, flaking, alligatoring, and cracking, strip the old coating from the wood surface, using paint or varnish remover. Determine whether or not construction defects are responsible for the failure and if so, correct them. Prepare and paint the surface in the same way as for a new surface.

## Touching Up a Good Floor

Restoring a floor in fair condition is simple. Hardwood floors with some finish will stand a good washing with one of the detergent washing powders and water; apply with a mop. Scrub the stubborn spots with number 2/0 steel wool. Rinse with clean water, and mop up excess water. If you do the washing carefully, using a minimum of water and not allowing it to stay on the surface, the amount of absorption will not harm the wood.

**Discoloration.** Check the areas of greatest travel for wear and discoloration. The discoloration can generally be removed with one or two applications of an oxalic acid bleach. Place ½ pound of oxalic acid crystals in a quart of warm water and mix thoroughly. Spread some of the solution over the discolored areas. Wear rubber gloves or make a small mop by tying a rag to the end of a stick—the oxalic acid is very poisonous. When the bleach has dried, you will find a frostlike layer on the wood. Remove this with a moist rag. If the area has been bleached enough, it is ready for touch-up staining. If not, apply the bleach again.

Purchase a small quantity of penetrating oil stain similar in color to the floor, and touch up the bleached area. Blend out the edges with a dry brush to eliminate the dark line of the stain. Apply one coat of shellac or varnish to the stained area. When dry, shellac or varnish the whole floor. Always work toward the door through which you are going to leave the room.

This treatment of washing, bleaching, touching up, and finishing will work equally well for an unstained finished floor; simply omit the staining operation.

**Filling Cracks.** If the joints of the flooring are open as a result of shrinkage, you can fill them successfully by using one of the prepared crack fillers. Select the color which most closely matches the finished floor. After the first coat of shellac or varnish, push this paste into the open cracks with your broad knife. Wipe off the excess with a turpentine rag before it has a chance to dry too hard.

**Scraping.** If the floor is softwood, the finish poor, or the boards warped, it is best to scrape (see page 138).

**Finishing.** Proceed with the finishing by staining, by staining and filling, by filling alone, or simply by shellacking the raw wood. (For repainting cement floors, see page 142).

## Refinishing an Old Floor

Where a floor has become badly discolored and worn by neglect or improper maintenance, the most practical procedure, and often the only one that will restore it, is to have the old finish removed and the floor reconditioned by power sanding. Where the floor has been reasonably well maintained but the finish has become dingy with age, refinishing without power sanding may be practicable. The method of removal depends upon the kind of finish used originally.

**Floors Originally Finished with Varnish.** Old, discolored varnish is usually removed most easily by power sanding. If desired, it can be done with liquid varnish remover. Alkaline solutions in water and removers sold in powder form to be dissolved in water should not be used. The directions for using liquid remover should be followed carefully. Since some of the old, discolored varnish remains imbedded in the wood, complete restoration of the natural wood should not be expected. Traffic channels where the old varnish has long been worn through and dirt has been ground into the wood should be cleaned by sanding.

**Floors Originally Finished with Shellac.** Old shellac-and-wax finishes that have merely become soiled by dirt in the wax coating may be cleaned by going over the floor with steel wool saturated with clean turpentine. Any white spots in the shellac caused by contact with water may be taken out by rubbing them lightly with a soft cloth moistened with denatured alcohol—but the alcohol must be used with care to avoid cutting the shellac coating.

On floors where the dirt is ground into the shellac itself, or white spots penetrate through the coating, more drastic treatment is necessary. First, wash the floor with a neutral or mildly alkaline soap solution followed by clear water, using as little water as possible in each operation. Then scour the floor with No. 3 steel wool and denatured alcohol. If the floor boards are level and are not warped or cupped, the scouring can be done to advantage with a floor-polishing machine fitted with a wire brush to which a pad of the No. 3 steel wool is attached. After the scouring, the floor should be rinsed with a minimum amount of clean water, mopped up to prevent blooming, and allowed to dry thoroughly before refinishing with shellac or other finish.

**Floors Originally Finished with Oil.** Clean the surface with water and detergent and apply a new coating of oil. Make necessary repairs and smooth rough spots if the floor is in poor condition. To remove oil, wet about 10 square feet of floor with a mop and warm water, and sprinkle the area liberally with a mixture of one part soap powder and three parts trisodium phosphate. Scrub the floor with a stiff brush, using only as much water as needed to form an emulsion and float the oil to the surface. As the oil is loosened and comes to the top, remove it with a squeegee and mop. Rinse the area with clean water and mop it dry. Treat the other sections in the same way. When the entire floor has been cleaned, let the surface dry 24 hours, then sand with a machine and finish as desired.

## Floor Maintenance

To reduce the need for frequent refinishing of floors, you must be familiar with the principles of floor cleaning and maintenance. You should clean floors with wet or damp cloths or mops only often enough to meet sanitary requirements, because repeated wetting and drying softens varnish coatings, thus causing more rapid wear. Strong alkaline soap also softens wood and raises the grain, causing splintering.

**Wood Floors.** Dust unwaxed varnished and shellacked wood floors with a soft brush or dry mop. Rub the floor with an oiled mop or a cloth slightly moistened with turpentine, floor oil, kerosine, or furniture polish. In general, avoid using water, but if surfaces are badly soiled, wipe them with a mop or cloth dampened with warm, slightly soapy water, and then with a cloth moistened with clear water. Wipe the surface dry at once and polish it with an oiled mop or cloth. Apply wax to worn surfaces.

**Oiled and Painted Floors.** Use a soft brush to sweep these and then rub them with an oiled mop or cloth. They may be occasionally washed with slightly soapy water and rinsed with a wet cloth or mop, then wiped dry and polished with an oiled cloth or mop. Floors may usually be reoiled or repainted without sanding.

**Waxed Floors.** Clean these with a soft brush or mop. Do not use oil, since oil softens wax. To remove a dirt-and-wax film which darkens the surface, use a cloth dampened with warm soapy water. Although gasoline and turpentine are more satisfactory than water, these liquids are flammable and care must be taken.

Water dulls and whitens many waxes. If water-cleaning has already whitened a wax floor, restore luster and color by rubbing with a woolen cloth or a weighted brush, applying a little wax if needed.

Daily sweeping with an untreated dust mop is one point of good maintenance. If you should spill water on the floor, wipe it up promptly with a dry cloth.

### Finishing While Painting

The dust created by sanding is so fine that it penetrates the dust bag of the machine and settles on all the exposed surfaces in the room. If the floors are to be finished and the room painted at the same time, it is best to complete the floors, except for the final coat of finish, before doing any painting.

After applying the first coat of finish and allowing it to dry, cover the floor with paper. When you have completed the painting, remove the paper, remove any paint spots on the floor with a turpentine-soaked rag, and proceed with the finishing.

**PRECAUTION:** Gasoline, turpentine, volatile mineral spirits, acetone, and many other volatile organic solvents are highly flammable. Care should be taken when using these solvents or preparations containing them. Have good ventilation and avoid open flames and smoking in the rooms or other spaces where they are used. Pilot lights should be turned off. Oily and greasy rags should be kept in closed metal containers or spread like washed clothes to dry; otherwise they are likely to cause spontaneous combustion.

## WALLPAPERING

Wallpaper is one of the simplest and most attractive room decorations. By looking at one of the sample books available in any paint supply store, you will be able to plan the color harmony and the decorative effect of the finished room. Almost without exception, the manufacturers of wallpaper have staffs of color consultants for the development of the colors and designs found in their papers. Many of the designs are reproductions of those developed during famous periods of decoration. These designs maintain their popularity on the basis of good taste and experience. Modern artists often contribute to the development of new wallpaper designs to go with modern interior decorating.

Wallpaper has a sound historical background as a form of decoration. The Chinese were the first to use it—more than two thousand years ago. Traders with the East brought back rolls of it; soon it was manufactured in Europe. Early in the history of our own country, its manufacture became one of our industries. In many museums you will find examples of actual Colonial papers. By carefully removing them from the walls of old houses it was possible to restore them in reconstructed rooms in the museums.

## Types of Wallpaper

Wallpaper is available in a wide variety of types—many more than there is room to describe here. But we can list the broad classifications and some of their characteristics. The simplest wallpapers are merely a good grade of uncoated paper stock upon which a water-color paint has been applied. If a decorative design is wanted, this is printed on top of the water-color paint. The obvious disadvantage of this type of paper is its sensitivity to water. However, it is the least expensive of all.

Manufacturers have also developed washable papers. These are made with casein water paints. As casein glue dries, it becomes insoluble in water. Emulsion binders and even oil paints are used, too. The development of very special types of the latter has been necessary, as most oil paints would become too hard and would crack. These papers are waterproof and reasonably washable. To further improve the washability of the wall covering, some manufacturers use a light grade of cloth instead of paper. The added strength of the fabric makes washing a safer procedure.

**Embossed Papers.** Paper stocks are also embossed. This type of paper is not enjoying the popularity it once had, but as texture becomes more and more important in our modern decoration of large flat walls, it may return to general favor. The colors and designs are usually of the water-color type, though some of these papers are advertised as being washable.

**Border Papers.** Border papers are available in almost all types. They come in narrow widths, intended for use as bordering.

**Metallic Papers.** Metallic papers are very popular. There are two types: one is coated with a metallic pigment such as aluminum, the other with a metallic foil. The first type presents no unusual problems to the paperhanger. The second, however, has probably made aspirin addicts of many would-be decorators. When the paper backing is pasted, it expands a bit, while the metallic foil facing does not. This causes the wallpaper to curl in from the edges, making it difficult to hang properly. In addition, when the backing curls over, the paste frequently soils the fragile metallic facing. It is possible to minimize the problem by using one of the adhesives with a low moisture content; but for the amateur it is better to avoid this type of paper.

**Wood Papers.** Real wood papers are available to the home decorator. The Japanese have supplied the market with a wall covering of wood sliced so thin that it can be handled like paper. Needless to say, it is fragile, but when waxed it makes an attractive wall covering. An American manufacturer has solved the problem of using real wood by mounting thin slices on fabric backing. This is strong and satisfactory but requires special techniques for hanging. If you choose this type, the manufacturer will be glad to supply you with all the necessary information. The method was developed with the assistance of master paperhangers and works very well.

**Scenic Papers.** For impressive decoration jobs there are the "scenics." These are the royalty of wallpapers. They are sold in sets and by the strip. Frequently they are hand-painted or hand-blocked, and almost always they make attractive wall coverings. If you plan hanging this type, it is suggested that you get experience with paperhanging first. Actually the scenics are no harder to hang than ordinary papers, but the higher cost should make one think twice before trying the job without previous experience.

**Ready-Pasted Papers.** The latest development in the field of wallpapers is the ready-pasted type. The manufacturer applies a paste to the back side of the paper and lets it dry before rolling. Full instructions for the wetting and hanging of these papers are included in each package; follow them carefully and your job will turn out satisfactorily. The greatest danger is blistering; but thorough preparation of the surface and careful smoothing will eliminate this.

## Measuring Wallpaper

No matter how wide or long the paper, the standard American roll contains 36 square feet. The measure of 36 square feet is known as a "single roll"—though wallpaper rarely comes in single rolls. Generally, it is packaged in double or triple rolls.

Wallpapers are made in various widths, the narrowest being 18" and the widest, 48". The most frequently used widths are 18" and 30". A convenient length for the narrower papers is the double roll. An 18" paper would then be 48' in length. In the average room, this would provide 6 strips for hanging, each 8' long. The wider 30" paper is usually sold in the triple roll. It is approximately 43' long, providing 5 strips for the average room. The horizontal measure provided by either of these two sizes of rolls is about 12'. You will cover the same area of wall surface with either.

If all ceilings were of equal height, the problem of packaging wallpaper would be easy. Though the paper is bought in rolls, it must be hung in strips of the appropriate length. Measure from the baseboard to the ceiling or picture molding; this will give you the approximate length of each strip. For straight patterns or lining paper, 3" to 6" additional length at the top and bottom is enough allowance for waste. But for drop patterns (see page 163), you may have to allow as much as an extra 2' or more, depending on the pattern size.

By dividing the proper length of each strip into the known length of the roll of paper, you will be able to determine the number of strips in each double or triple roll. When you have determined the number necessary to cover the walls, you can easily figure the number of rolls to buy.

**Estimating.** The easiest way to estimate wallpaper needs is to make a small sketch of the floor plan of the room. Measure the width of each wall and mark it on the sketch. Divide this by the width of the paper, and you will know the number of strips you need. In doing this, subtract the area of any large openings, such as archways, but include doors and windows. The pieces which would cover these areas will come in handy at the tops and bottoms of the windows, over doors, and for other small spaces. When you know the length of each strip and the number of strips, then you know the number of rolls to buy. It is wise to buy several more rolls than you need, to allow for errors in cutting or pasting. (Any good paint store will be willing to take back clean and uncut full rolls of paper.)

The trade practice in estimating quantities of wallpaper is to take the wall area and add 10 to 20% to allow for waste in cutting. However, you can use it as a quick check on your own estimate.

## Tools

You should have the tools listed below to do a good paperhanging job. If you use the ready-pasted wallpaper or have your paper trimmed at the store, you can eliminate the special table and straightedges. Sets of tools are available from the larger mail-order houses as well as from your local paint store.

Table (top: 3 white pine boards 6' × 12" × ⅜"; legs: 2 folding trestles or other adequate support)
Straightedge, 6' long, true, can have brass edge
Paperhanger's knife

Scissors, preferably 12″ blades

Paste brush, 7″ or 8″ (similar to calcimine brush)

Seam roller, either 1″ or 1½″

Smoother (make sure it has plenty of bristle)

Plumb bob, line, and blue chalk

Rule, 2′ folding type

Tear stick, short straightedge, 2½″ × 3″ × ⅜″ (make it yourself)

You will also need ladders, planks, pails, a sponge, clean rags, and a small

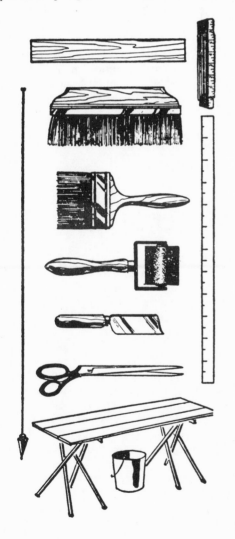

piece of #0 emery cloth. The sponge and rags are used to clean up the paste you get on the woodwork. One of the pails is for paste and the other for cleaning water. The emery cloth is to keep your paperhanger's knife sharp. Newspapers or a dropcloth will come in handy for protecting the finish on the floor.

## Preparation of Walls

**Light Fixtures.** All switch plates and lighting fixtures should be removed before taking any other steps in preparing the walls for paper. Remove the correct fuses and cut the wires if necessary; they can always be easily reconnected by using the simple twist type of connector. Any other fixtures which will interfere with applying a full strip of paper should also be removed from the walls. After you gain some experience you may be able to avoid some of these preparatory jobs, but it is wise to do them until you are well able to judge how to cut the paper to accommodate obstacles.

**Plaster Walls.** New plaster walls should be first treated to neutralize the active alkali in the plaster. To do this, mix a solution of 2 pounds of zinc sulfate crystals in a gallon of water. These crystals are available at paint and hardware stores. When this solution is dry, brush off the crystals.

Then size the plaster so that the paste will adhere properly to the surface. Size is simply a thin glue mixture. You can make your own, but this is not recommended, as glues vary greatly in strength. Considering the small cost involved, it is better to buy one of the standard brands and follow the directions on the package. Apply the size generously to the plaster surface and let it dry. Avoid any holidays (untouched spots) by working from a window toward the darker part of the room. You can then constantly check the surface just covered by its wet shine.

**Wallboard.** Wallboard presents no

difficulties. Joints have to be filled and covered with tape, and all nail holes have to be filled. Do not use a glue size on gypsum wallboard, but instead a varnish size. This will make it possible to remove the wallpaper at some future date without damage to the kraft-paper covering of the wallboard.

For hard wallboard, after the preliminaries described in the paragraph above, apply a coat of size as directed for plaster. If the manufacturer of the wallboard recommends some particular size, you will do well to follow his advice.

For soft wallboard, after taking care of the joints and nail holes, apply one coat of glue size.

**Painted Walls.** Previously painted walls should be cleaned by washing if necessary. If the paint is one of the glossy types—real enamel or one of the enamel-like paints—you should use washing soda or a similar strong solvent to cut the hard surface of the paint; the glue size will usually "crawl" on a smooth, shiny surface. Steel wool is also useful for this. Now cut out all plaster cracks and patch them. Small checks or dents can generally be spackled smooth.

You are now ready to apply the size. Add about 4 ounces of household vinegar to each gallon of size to lessen the possibility of crawling; the vinegar will aid the size to penetrate the paint. If the manufacturer of the size you have bought recommends the addition of something else or states that it is not necessary to add anything, follow his instructions. Spread the size generously and make sure that every part of the wall has received its fair share.

**Plywood Walls.** Plywood can be successfully papered if you follow the instructions issued by its manufacturers. They suggest covering the surface with a paper felting material before hanging the wallpaper. This is recommended because the paste used for the wallpaper would raise the grain so much that it would show through. The felting is hung with a special adhesive, and should be done only after all the joints have been filled and taped over.

**Papered Walls.** Previously papered walls can be successfully repapered either over the old paper or—better—after its removal. It is considered reasonably safe practice to place up to 3 layers of paper on a sound wall. More than this will almost certainly pull the underlayers loose, and your work will be wasted.

In papering over old paper, make sure that there are no loose patches. If you find any, scrape them off and sandpaper down the edges until they are smooth with the surrounding wall. Carefully check all the joints, scrape any loose ones, and sandpaper all of them. If the paper is one of the shiny-surface varieties or has been coated with shellac or one of the preparations for making it washable, remove it—the paste will not stick.

## Preparing the Paper

**Lining Paper.** Before proceeding to the actual hanging of wallpaper, it would be well to consider the use of lining paper. This is a plain uncoated type of paper applied to the walls to provide a better surface upon which to hang the wallpaper. It is inexpensive, costing less than the cheapest wallpaper, and is simple to hang. If you are going to run into any trouble with adhesion, it will show up in the lining paper application and can be remedied. For a butt-jointed job, follow the instructions on page 168.

**Wallpaper Patterns.** Before describing methods of cutting wallpaper into strips before pasting it for hanging, let us consider the two chief types of paper patterns.

With a straight pattern, if you find part of a design, such as a flower, at the left side of the paper, you will find the other half on the right-hand side directly opposite. This is the easiest type of wallpaper to cut into strips and hang, as each

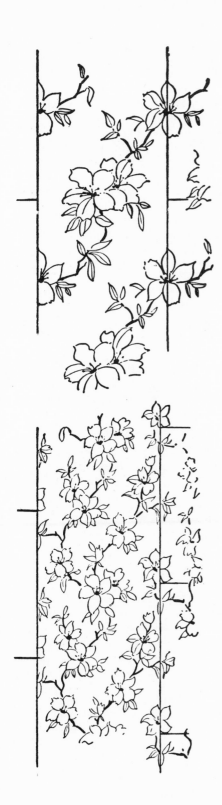

strip is exactly the same as the one next to it.

When the matching part of the design is at a different level on the other side of the paper, it is known as a drop pattern. This type gives greater freedom in decoration and reduces the effect of repetition at the same level around the room. The repetition is not eliminated, but it is lessened by the wider spacing between the repeats; the pattern becomes saw-toothed rather than horizontal. This type of pattern slightly complicates the hanging of the paper, but not greatly. If you cut your strips continuously from one roll of paper, there will be considerable waste. But if your use two rolls, and cut all the odd-numbered strips from the first roll and all the even-numbered strips from the second roll, the waste will be minimized.

**Cutting.** Measuring from baseboard to picture molding or ceiling will give you the actual dimension for placing patterns, but this is too exact for paperhanging. It is customary to allow at least 3″ extra at the top of each strip and the same amount at the bottom. If you are hanging lining paper, simply unroll a strip to the actual measurement and add 6″. Lay the strip on the table. Placing the tear stick in position, grasp the roll in the right hand. Lifting up and away from the tear stick,

tear the paper. Match the two torn ends and use the piece you have just torn off to measure out another one. Repeat the tearing operation. When you have torn the correct number of strips, you are ready for pasting.

If the paper is a decorated one, you will have to decide what part of the design you prefer at the top edge. Hold the end of an unrolled sheet at the top of the wall and study the design for effect. (You will generally get ample assistance from members of the family in this, so prepare yourself for some lengthy discussion before a decision is reached.) If the paper is of the drop-pattern type, you had better hold up two strips, properly matched, so that all the possibilities can be explored.

When a decision has been reached, mark the first roll about 3″ above the picture molding or the ceiling line; this will be your guide for cutting all the strips. Lay the roll on the table and measure out the first strip, including the extra 3″ at the top and bottom. Place the tear stick at the measured length and tear off the first strip.

Place the roll at the other end of the table and unroll enough to match the pattern on the first strip at its top end. Then unroll the roll to the tear stick, place the tear stick on the second strip, and tear to the same length as the first strip. Continue the operation until you have enough to go around the room.

When using a drop pattern, you will have to be more careful in the matching of the design so that your strips are all long enough. By planning your work and knowing how many strips you are going to need to go around the room, you will be able to do the cutting of the drop-pattern strips with ease. Place a roll of the paper on the table and measure out the length of the first strip, not forgetting the necessary extra top and bottom for trimming. Simply continue to tear strips to this length until you have a number equal to half the total required strips. Then carefully match the design on the second strip

to that on the first, unroll to the proper length, and tear; again continue until you have torn the remaining half of the total number of strips. You are now ready for the pasting operation.

**Pasting.** For best results in hanging paper, use a prepared paste. Homemade mixtures may prove to be satisfactory, but don't chance using them—only winter wheat should be used in the mixture, and it is quite difficult for the average grocer to know whether or not his flour is of the winter variety. The paste is such a small part of the cost of the job that it hardly pays to save on it. Simply follow the directions on the label.

Turn the pile of paper over and place it at the back of the table. Pull the top sheet to the front and let the edge extend about 1/4″ over the front. Spread the paste evenly, but generously, over the paper for the full length. Then pick up one end of the pasted strip and fold it nearly to the other end (this is the long fold). Gently smooth the pasted sides together and carefully match the outside edges.

Pull the strip back across the table so

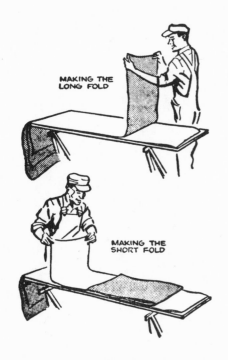

MAKING THE
LONG FOLD

MAKING THE
SHORT FOLD

that the overhanging end is now on the table. Then paste the remaining dry back of the paper. Fold this in toward the center (this is the short fold), lapping over the already pasted section about 1″ or 2″. Again carefully match the sides of the paper. Fold this pasted strip once more and set it aside to let the paste soak into the paper.

Draw the next strip to the front of the table and repeat the pasting operations as for the first strip. Set this one aside, and continue the pasting for the remaining strips.

If the paper is a drop pattern, make two piles of the pasted strips so that you can alternate them in hanging.

The pasted paper, when folded over on itself, will keep fresh and usable for 2 or 3 hours or even longer, except in the case of lining paper and the very thinnest stock.

**Trimming.** Trimming is necessary, since the manufacturer always makes paper with a selvage—a narrow border on either side that ensures a straight edge to

the design. If you have carefully folded the strips so that the edges match, the operation is simple. The marks to which you trim are printed on the edge of the paper. Your paper will all have been folded so that the design is on the outside; the printed trim marks are then plainly visible. Fold the paper end for end until it is slightly less than the length of the straightedge. Lay the straightedge on the paper so that only the selvage to be cut projects beyond it. Hold the straightedge down with one hand and cut off the selvage by running your paperhanger's knife along the side of the straightedge.

Spin the paper around so that the other selvage is now on the working side of the table, and repeat the cutting operation. This strip is now ready for hanging. Repeat with the other strips, and you can proceed with the hanging.

It is possible to buy store-trimmed paper. Some stores have one of the patented trimming tables and will gladly do the trimming for you. Remember, though, that you cannot return trimmed paper which you have not used. However, if you are certain of the quantity of paper to be used, the trimmed paper will reduce the number of operations in putting up your wallpaper. The ready-pasted types of papers are trimmed by the manufacturer.

## Hanging the Paper

The hanging of the paper should always proceed from a plumb line so that the design will be straight up and down. Chalk your plumb line and hang it at a distance of about 17½″ or a little less

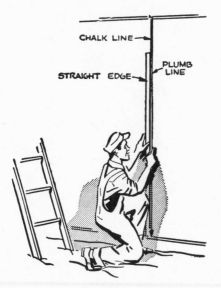

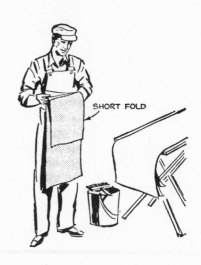

from a window or door trim. A string with an ordinary weight will serve as a plumb. When the bob has stopped swinging, gently draw back the string and let it go. You will find a neat chalk line on the wall. This is the correct distance for the regular 18″ papers. If the paper is wider, map the line at a distance of at least ½″ less than the width of the paper. It is generally best to strike the line on the right-hand side of the door or window, and proceed with the hanging in that direction.

**First Strip.** Lift this and hold it so that the short folded-in end can readily be placed at the top of the wall. Mount the ladder and gently strip apart the folded-in end. Place this at the top of the wall so that the extra 3″ extend above the picture molding or against the ceiling, and so that the left-hand edge is on the chalk line. Gently press several feet of the strip of paper in place, being careful always to have the left-hand edge on the chalk line. You can support the rest of the strip with your foot while you are pasting. Using your smoother, brush the rest of the opened strip in place without forcing or stretching it.

Now, dismount from the ladder and reach behind the loosely hanging part of

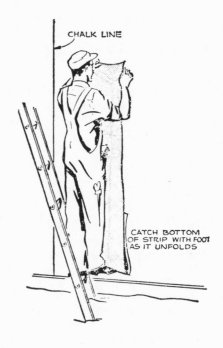

166

SIGHT DOWN EDGE OF STRIP TO SEE WHEN ON LINE

CREASE

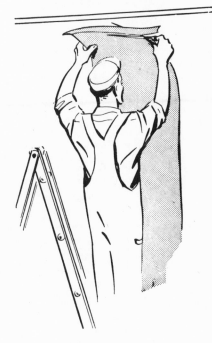

PULL OUT FROM WALL ABOUT ONE FOOT AND CUT ALONG CREASE

the strip. Carefully separate the fold in the bottom section of the strip by grasping the end and gently pulling downward. When the paper is completely open, continue pressing the left-hand edge to the chalk line. When the left-hand edge is in place, smooth the rest of the strip to the wall.

Do not stretch or pull the paper in any of these steps, or the right-hand edge will not hang straight. If it is necessary to adjust the paper, pull a goodly length loose from the wall and smooth it into the correct position. The wet paste will withstand several of these removals and replacings, though it is not recommended that it be done often. If the paste should show signs of drying, place the strip back on the table and repaste.

The top and bottom must now be trimmed. Remount the ladder and run the point of your scissors against the paper along the joint of the picture molding or the ceiling. This will mark the surface of the paper. Now pull the paper loose from the wall for a distance of about 1'. Using your scissors, cut along the line and smooth the paper back in place. Do the same at the bottom of the strip. The first strip is now hung.

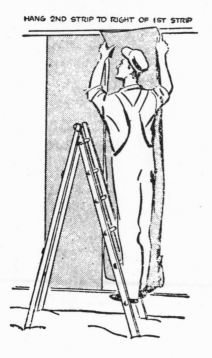

HANG 2ND STRIP TO RIGHT OF 1ST STRIP

**Butt Joints.** In a butt joint, both sides of the seam lie flat on the wall. The paper must be trimmed on both sides. The first strip is hung as instructed above; then you are ready for the joining of the second. Holding the second strip over your arm, mount the ladder, loosen the top pasted section, and place it next to the right-hand edge of the first strip. Match the pattern, and make sure that the excess extends up above the picture molding or the ceiling joint. Join the right-hand edge of the paper on the wall and the left-hand edge of the new piece by gently pressing the new one in place. Again, do not stretch or pull the paper into place, or the right-hand edge won't lie true. If necessary, pull the paper loose from the wall and reapply. Continue down the wall by loosening the folded paper and placing it against the right-hand edge of the previously hung paper. Mark the top with your scissors, cut, and replace. When you have done the same on the bottom of the strip, gently run your seam roller down the joint and flatten the seam.

**Cutting Around Obstacles.** Special procedures are necessary for hanging around doors, windows, and the like. Experienced paperhangers can measure their way around an opening, coming back to fill in later. This is not recommended for the amateur. It is for him better to hang a strip which partly covers the opening, and cut as necessary. If possible, get someone to help you when you do this operation.

Drape a strip over your arm and mount the ladder. Loosen the top part and butt or lap the joint, always allowing for the excess at the top and always matching the pattern. Let your helper hold the rest of the strip while you find the place to cut across it by outlining it with your scissors. Cut and press down the upper section of the paper.

Now continue the joint by loosening the bottom section of the strip and placing it against the previously hung strip. If the opening is a window, you can rule in across the bottom of the trim and cut to

**Second Strip.** Hang the second strip to the right of the first, and so on around the room. You have your choice of hanging by the butt method or the lap method.

**Lap Joints.** In using the lap method, mount the ladder with the second strip over your arm and loosen the pasted top. Press the paper in place with the design matching and the trimmed edge overlapping the previously hung strip to the selvage trimming mark. This should leave you with the extra 3" or 4" at the top. Continue down the wall as for the first strip and smooth into place. Roll the seam gently with the seam roller to prevent the paper from curling. If you press too hard, you may make the paper shiny and also squeeze some of the paste from underneath onto the surface, where it will be difficult to remove. Mark the top of the paper and cut with your scissors to the proper length. Press it back into place and repeat the operation on the bottom. Continue, strip after strip, around the room.

fit. Smooth the bottom section into place. Now you can trim off the excess down the side of the window trim. Use your paperhanger's knife, running it down in the angle of the trim and wall. There are knife rollers for this purpose, and they are the best tool to use. But if you are careful and do not pull the paper, you can do a satisfactory job with a knife. You can help prevent rough cuts by placing a thin ruler or straightedge on the wall next to the trim and pressing on it while you do the cutting.

If the opening is wider than the next strip, simply cut the strip to a length slightly in excess of the distance from picture molding to top of trim.

You may find it wise to strike a new plumb line when you have located the place for the first seam to the right of the opening, because the short distance from the picture molding or ceiling to the top of the opening will not give you a true line to the baseboard. Take the right-hand edge of the strip that will partly cover the opening and hang it to the line, and you can proceed safely along the wall.

**Fitting for Wide Openings.** Wide openings, such as archways, can be pieced out on the top with parts of full-length strips cut for the purpose. Simply make sure that you match the pattern with each succeeding strip, and you will have no trouble. When you have determined where the first following full-length strip will start, strike a plumb line and hang the strip to this line at its right-hand edge. Continue along the wall until you come to the corner.

**Papering Corners.** Seams should never appear in corners of the room. It is customary to have the paper go around the corner for at least 2″ to 4″. It is best to assume that the corner is not square. To make sure that the seams on the new wall will all be plumb, you should strike a chalk line at the right-hand edge of the strip hung around the corner.

You can place your straightedge on the wall and carefully cut the edge of the paper to a true line. The matching may suffer slightly in this operation, but that is not as bad as having the whole wall out of square. You will barely notice the small mismatch in the corner.

**Removing Excess Paste.** The small amount of paste which inevitably gets on the trim and moldings should be removed with the sponge as you go along. Dip the sponge in the pail of clean water, wring it out, and gently wipe the surfaces on which the paste has accumulated. If the paste has not dried, it will come off readily without shining the painted surface.

## Special Problems

**Papering Over Wallpaper.** Hanging paper over a previously papered surface requires only that the old and new seams do not coincide. Strike a plumb line for the first strip so that the new seam does not fall on the present one. Continue around the room, being careful not to locate the corner seams on top of those already there. Doing this avoids a double pull in shrinkage, which might open the under seam and make a difficult job of re-pasting.

**Border Designs.** Borders come in two types: narrow and cutout. Narrow borders are printed parallel to one another on an 18″-wide paper. They must be cut to width after being torn to appropriate lengths—usually about 8′. Paste the back side of the paper, fold the pasted side in, and cut into proper widths with the straightedge and the paperhanger's knife. The hanging is simply a matter of placing the border where you want it.

Cutout borders are perforated on the bottom edge of the design and are printed parallel on an 18″-wide roll. They are cut to width the same as narrow borders; then they are pasted. Finally, when the paste has softened the paper, the border can be separated along the perforations by gently pulling on the side. The hanging is the same as for narrow borders. The corners are mitered.

**Papering Panels.** Panels to be hung with wallpaper should be carefully measured and their centers located. Strike a plumb line down the center of the panel, and hang the paper either way from this line to the outside molding of the panel. The top and bottom should be trimmed exactly as you would if hanging the full length of the wall.

**Papering Ceilings.** Ceilings can be hung with wallpaper, though this can be troublesome for the amateur. The problem of supporting the paper until enough of it is fastened up to perform the smoothing operation is usually the stumbling block. Probably the best way is to fold the pasted paper into a short enough length to carry over one arm; with your free hand you can smooth the short piece which hangs free from the ceiling. You will have to work to a line previously marked on the ceiling to make sure that the seam is straight. It is best to start near a window wall and work away from it.

**Horizontal Wallpapering.** Paper can also be hung horizontally. Some interior decorators have used the striped papers to good effect in this manner. Mark on the wall a line that is parallel to the ceiling or picture molding and is lower by the width of the paper. Hang to this line. Striking a line parallel to the floor is not as good as striking one parallel to the ceiling; it is generally better to have any irregularity at the base line rather than near the ceiling, where it would be more obvious.

**Two Patterns in One Room.** Do not be afraid to use one paper on one wall and another on an adjoining wall. It is popular to have patterned paper flanked by a plain paper.

This is a good device to indicate the divisions of a room. For instance, the dining end of a living-dining room or the sitting end of a large bedroom can have a contrasting paper design. Use your imagination freely.

**Matching Shades.** Your principal

problem in paperhanging will be the shading of the paper's color. The manufacturers try to match each run of paper as faithfully as possible, but you may find that the shade of several rolls will vary slightly. You can either return the paper to the store or use the two different shades on different walls. Make the usual joint in one of the less conspicuous corners, and you will scarcely notice the variation in the shading. But the next time you buy paper, look at the mill-run numbers on the edges of the rolls and make sure they are all the same. Then you can be sure that the paper was all made with exactly the same color.

## Fabric Wall Coverings

In addition to wallpapers, there are fabrics which can serve as wall coverings. It was a custom years back to cover walls to be painted with muslin, either plain or specially prepared. The muslin was hung like wallpaper and provided a pleasant texture to the painted surfaces. It also hid the inevitable cracks which appear in plaster walls. Unbleached muslin is available in any width up to 108"; but the narrower widths, up to 36", are recommended, as they are easier to handle. Prepared canvas, as the prepared types are called, generally comes in a 48" width and has a filling, which makes it easy to paste and handle. Butt the joints as you would for a paper-hanging job.

## Patching and Repairing

**Blisters.** Blisters, a common failure in paperhanging, can be repaired in one of two ways. The simplest is to cut the blister in two lines at right angles to one another. Gently fold back the paper and apply just enough paste to the back side to wet it. With a bunched large, clean rag, gently push the paper back into place and hold it there for 5 or 10 minutes until the paste has set. Do not let the paste have a chance to soak into the back side of the paper before pushing it back on the wall, as it will swell and create an overlap.

The second method is to put a little paste into a hypodermic needle, insert the tip into the blister, and squeeze in some paste. Better to squeeze in too little than too much—too much and the blister will never lie flat again.

**Seams.** Seams which have opened should be repasted with a very small brush and gently held in place until the paste has set. Be careful to avoid excess paste, as you may smear the wallpaper in wiping it off.

**Bruises.** Bruises not only damage wallpaper but also the plaster underneath. Repair the plaster first. Remove the damaged paper to a point just beyond the bruise. Clean out the loose plaster, and patch. When this plaster is dry, apply a little glue size, just as you would for a new wall. While this is drying, rough-tear a piece of the same wallpaper as that on the wall to a size slightly larger than the patch. Carefully apply paste to the back of this piece and stick the paper patch in place. The feather edge of the rough-torn piece will almost blend into the rest of the paper if you have been careful of the amount of paste.

**Stains.** Grease stains can rarely be completely removed from most wallpapers. But they can be so reduced that they will be hardly noticeable. Make a paste of carbon tetrachloride and fuller's earth. Get the fuller's earth at a large paint supply store or a drugstore; carbon tetrachloride is the common dry-cleaning fluid. Apply this paste to the stained area and, when dry, dust it off. Apply a second and even a third coat to remove stubborn spots.

Absorbent types of wallpaper cleaners are available and will clean loose airborne dirt from wallpaper. But if not kneaded and rolled over the surface of the paper properly, such a substance will streak it. Very fresh bread used to be the standard

**171**

paper-cleaner; it is almost as effective as the rubberlike absorbent cleaners common today.

The dark streaks generally found over exposed radiators are caused by the circulation of warm air, which carries dust with it. This dust becomes so well imbedded in the wallpaper that it will not yield to the absorbent types of cleaners; you can remove some of it, but you are unlikely to get it all out. Water streaks can rarely be removed. Generally it is better to repaper the soiled areas. If the existing paper is in good condition, you can usually paper right over it. If it is loose, remove all of the strip and rehang.

# 7

# HEATING AND COOLING

Four basic types of central heating systems are used in houses: circulating hot water, forced warm air, electric, and steam. Circulating hot water and forced warm air are found in every kind of house in every part of the country. Electric heat is found primarily in newer houses and in those areas where there is a favorable electric rate. Steam is found only in older homes along the Atlantic coast and in apartment buildings. But regardless of the kind of heating system you have, its efficiency as well as economy of operation is going to depend on how well the house is protected against heat loss and on the proper operation and maintenance of the heating equipment.

HEAT PENETRATES

## REDUCING HEAT LOSS

The first step in reducing heat loss to a minimum is to make certain that the house is well insulated. Most houses today have some degree of insulation, but it is usually inadequate. The only exception to this rule is where a house was designed and constructed to be heated by electric heat. In this instance, the insulation is usually adequate, but in older houses it seldom is. There should be a layer of insulation 6″ deep at the top of the house—ei-

HEAT ESCAPES

ther in the attic floor or along the attic ceiling. If the insulation has been applied between the attic or attic crawl-space floor joists and is exposed, it's a simple matter to add more insulation to bring it to the desired depth. Use the loose fill insulation that comes in a bag and spread it over the old insulation to bring the total depth to 6″.

Insulating the walls of an existing house or adding more insulation is not a do-it-yourself project because it requires special equipment. Firms that specialize in this work blow insulation into the wall cavity. If the house has no insulation, this is worth the price. If there is some insulation already, you probably won't save enough fuel to justify the expense.

The underside of floors over unheated areas such as garages, crawl space, or even basements should also be insulated. This is done with standard roll insulation which can be fastened to the floor joists. The vapor-barrier side of the insulation should face up against the flooring.

In the average house there may be critical areas where insulation is often omitted. One of these is on the underside of the eaves near the walls of the house. Another is along the sill where the woodwork of the house joins the foundation wall. Fill the seam between wood and masonry with caulking compound and then tuck strips of insulation between the floor joists to seal off these areas.

**Windows and Doors.** Next to the walls and roof of the house, the greatest amount of heat loss occurs through windows. Glass is a good conductor of heat and ordinary window glass allows vast amounts of heat to escape. The best solution to this problem is to install storm windows. These should be tight fitting and the joint between the frame of the storm sash and the window frame should be sealed with caulking compound so that no cold air from the outside can enter the space between the storm sash and the regular window. If you cannot afford standard storm windows, you can make an effective one

using heavy-duty clear plastic sold at hardware stores and lumberyards. Staple the plastic along the outside frame of the window and then cover the edge with strips of wood lath to make a tight seal. Be sure to use the heavy-duty type of plastic, because the thin material often sold for storm windows can be easily ripped by a strong wind. Plastic is also good to use on large picture windows which cannot ordinarily be covered with a storm sash except at great expense.

Even with storm windows it will pay you to weatherstrip the regular window to prevent air inside the house from getting into the space between the two windows. The effectiveness of a storm window depends to a great extent on there being no movement of air between the two windows.

Outside doors also allow considerable cold air to enter the house and warm air to escape. The door should be weatherstripped and a storm door should be installed. If you wish, an ordinary screen door can be converted into a storm door by covering the screening with heavy-duty plastic just as you would for a storm window.

**Caulking.** In even the best-constructed house there are bound to be open joints on the outside that allow warm air to flow out and cold drafts to enter. These can be closed with caulking compound or caulking tape. Points that usually require caulking are the seams where the house siding joins window and door frames, where cornice joins the top of the walls, and where the foundation wall joins the woodwork of the house. Also caulk around outside light fixtures and other items such as the vent on exhaust fans where a hole has been made into the wall of the house.

**Attic Insulation.** The roof is the most exposed part of the house. It is subject to strong cold winds in winter and to direct rays of sun in summer. If an attic is uninsulated, a great deal of heat may be lost through the roof during winter months.

One evidence of this is very rapid melting of snow on the roof. In the summer, an attic that is hotter than other parts of the house also indicates poor insulation.

If the attic is not being used for living quarters and it is unnecessary to keep the temperature in that space at a comfortable level, insulation in the form of batts, blankets, or loose-fill material should be laid between the floor joists of the attic, on top of the ceiling below. If the attic is not floored, lay boards across the floor joists so that you can walk on them while you are laying the insulation. When the attic is being occupied and you wish to keep the temperature there comfortable throughout the year, apply insulation to the underside of the roof between the rafters, and to the end walls. If there is a metal or asphaltic roofing, which offers resistance to escaping water vapor, place a good vapor barrier on the underside of the rafters.

Roof insulation should be installed so that there is a space of 2″ to 3″ between it and the undersides of the roof boards. Sufficient ventilation of this space should also be provided. This can be done by leaving small openings or cracks at the eaves, or by installing louvers in the end walls which communicate with the triangular space between the roof and a false ceiling over the attic. Vapor barriers and ventilation between insulation and roof will prevent condensation of moisture in winter which could wet and damage the roof structure and cause dampness below.

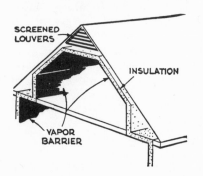

SCREENED LOUVERS

INSULATION

VAPOR BARRIER

If the attic is to be completely equipped for occupancy, the enclosing walls and ceiling should be insulated and vapor barriers installed. Then a finish surface material may be applied.

Other ways to guard against heat loss are: not to run a kitchen or bathroom exhaust fan anymore than is necessary; to equip outside doors with door closers so that they will shut tight on their own; and to teach the members of the family not to open and close outside doors anymore than is absolutely essential.

A good deal of heat can be lost if members of the family open their windows at night. If they do this, be sure that the radiator or register in their rooms is turned off when the window is opened. If certain rooms in the house are not required, it will pay to turn the heat off in them and close the door.

It has been found that if the house has the right amount of moisture vapor in the air, you can be comfortable at a lower temperature than when the air is dry. Most experts believe that a humidity of around 40 percent is an optimum level for most people and if this is maintained, you can be comfortable at a lower temperature than otherwise (see page 182).

Fireplace dampers should be closed when there is no fire; if they are not, a good deal of heat will escape through the chimney. If there is no damper, often the case in older houses, cut a sheet of plywood or hardboard to fit over the fireplace opening and secure it in place with masking tape.

If radiators are painted with aluminum, bronze, or some other metallic paint, their heat output is reduced. It is not necessary to remove the metallic paint to restore the unit to its normal efficiency. Just apply a coat of flat wall or wall enamel paint over the metallic paint. A metallic paint can reduce the output of a radiator by as much as 20%.

Keep radiators and baseboard units clean, as a coating of dust will act as insulation and reduce output. With a warm-air furnace, the filters should be replaced or cleaned when they become soiled. You can tell when a filter needs cleaning or replacing by holding it up to the light: if you can't see through it, it's time to clean or replace it.

Do not waste heat in areas of the house where heat is not required, such as the basement and attic. If there are water pipes in these areas, provide just enough heat to prevent the lines from freezing, or install heating cables on the pipes.

On bright days, open draperies and window shades to take full advantage of the heat from the sun, but as soon as the sun goes down, pull the draperies and shades to help reduce heat loss.

## Thermostat

The location of the thermostat and the way it is used can have an influence not only on comfort, but also on the cost of heating. The thermostat should be on an inside wall—never on an outside wall. It should be in a room where it will not be exposed to drafts from the outside or to heat from such sources as a nearby radiator, register, fireplace, or even a candle or an electric light. All of these can cause the thermostat to function improperly, so that the house becomes too hot or too cool.

Thermostats are not difficult to move. They usually run on a low voltage and use bell wire. It's a simple matter to turn off the burner or the power, move the thermostat to a new location, and replace the wiring.

Many thermostats do not operate properly because they are old and worn. If the thermostat is over 7 years old, the chances are that the efficiency of the system can be improved by installing a new one.

Don't change the thermostat setting any more than is necessary. It is best if you keep it at one setting throughout the day. You can, however, save a good deal of

fuel over the year if you reduce the setting at night by about 5 degrees from the normal daytime setting. But don't set it much more than 5 degrees lower; if you do, the house will become chilled during the night and you'll spend all the fuel you saved making it comfortable again. It is also best if you can keep the thermostat setting no higher than 70 degrees. There is about a 3% increase in fuel consumption for each degree over 70 degrees. If some members of the family find that 70 degrees is a little too cool, they might consider wearing heavier clothes when indoors. Also, when the outdoor temperature is very low—10 degrees above zero or lower—you may find that the 70-degree setting will not be enough to keep the house comfortable. This comes about because when the outside temperature is very low, heat is drained out of the house so rapidly that even when the air temperature in the room is 70 degrees, it is not enough to keep you comfortable.

# HEATING SYSTEMS

You will find it much easier to maintain a heating system if you understand how it operates and also where trouble is likely to occur.

## Circulating Hot Water System

In this system the water is heated in a boiler that is fired by gas or oil. The heated water is then pumped through pipes to the radiators, convectors, or baseboard units throughout the house. The temperature of the water is around 180 degrees when it leaves the boiler. In many systems there will be an expansion tank near the boiler.

With this system, all elements—boiler, pipes, radiators, and so forth—must be completely filled with water. If there are air pockets, the heated water

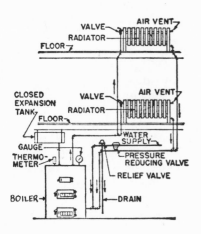

water in the system. This gauge has two needles, one black and the other generally red. The red needle is set at the proper water level for the system. The black needle indicates the true water level and varies with the water-level change. When the red needle is over the black, the system is properly filled with water.

Difficulties in hot-water heating can usually be attributed to air in the lines, radiators, baseboard units, convectors, and the like. On each radiator, baseboard unit, and so forth, there will be a little air valve, and when this is opened it allows the air to escape. At the beginning of the heating season, each of these valves should be opened to remove any air in the system. Start with the highest unit in the system. Some valves require a special wrench to open them; you can get it at most hardware and heating stores. Other valves can be opened with a screwdriver or adjustable wrench. Hold a container under the valve when it is opened and keep the valve open until water starts flowing out of the valve. Then close it and go to the next unit in the system. If there is an automatic feed to the boiler through a pressure-reducing valve, water will be added as the air is drained off. If there is a hand feed, open the valve so that water will flow into the system as the air is removed. When all the air valves have been opened and the various units are free from air, close the feed-line valve.

can't enter and, therefore, there will be less heat. In a modern system, water is automatically added to the boiler when required by a pressure-reducing valve. In older systems, the valve on the water feed line to the boiler must be opened by hand when more water is required for the system. On most boilers, you'll find an altitude gauge that shows the level of the

Water contains a certain amount of air and when it is heated, the air is released. This means that it may be necessary to bleed the system from time to time during the heating season. When a particular radiator fails to heat properly, chances are that it contains air and should be bled, as previously explained.

Radiators, convectors, and baseboard units should be cleaned from time to time, and this can be done easily with a wand attachment to the vacuum cleaner.

The other primary cause of trouble in this system can be that the shutoff valve to a particular radiator is not open, or

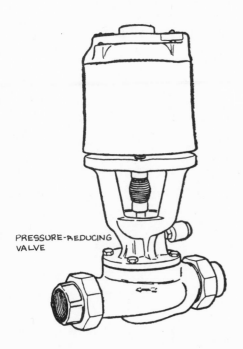

PRESSURE-REDUCING VALVE

only partially open, and this reduces the flow of water not only to that radiator, but also, in some systems, to several units in different parts of the house.

## Forced Warm Air System

Here you have a furnace in which air is heated by either an oil- or gas-fired burner. There is a fan or blower which forces the heated air through ducts to registers set in floors or walls throughout the house. There are also cold-air return registers and ducts to allow the cool air to be brought back to the furnace where it is filtered, reheated, and then forced through the ducts again. This is basically a simple system, but it can require more maintenance and adjustments than a circulating hot-water system if it is to operate efficiently and provide comfortable heat.

The filters must be cleaned or replaced when they are dirty. If they are not, the output of the system will be reduced considerably.

Unless the system is properly balanced, some rooms or areas of the house will get too much heat and others will not get enough heat. Balancing the system is done by the proper adjustment of the dampers in the ducts. The dampers are set rather close to the furnace. It is best to have them adjusted by a qualified serviceman for forced warm air systems who has special equipment to measure the velocity of the air flowing out of the registers, but the adjustment can be made by the homeowner through a trial-and-error approach. Have someone hold their hands over a particular register while you move the damper on that particular duct open or closed, depending on what is required. Eventually, you can get the system in pretty good balance.

Another problem with this system is that when the blower goes on there is first a rush of cold air out of a register followed by a rush of hot air—both being uncomfortable. This can be corrected by having the blower adjusted so that it runs constantly or at rather frequent intervals. The burner can also be adjusted to operate for short periods but at frequent intervals. These adjustments will produce a continuous flow of warm air rather than bursts of cold air followed by hot air.

Forced warm air systems are sometimes quite noisy. Often the noise is due to a worn blower belt or to the fact that the moving parts of the blower need a bit of oil. Often, however, the trouble is due to vibrations in the furnace being carried throughout the house by the metal ducts. This difficulty can be overcome by inserting a canvas or fiber-glass sleeve in each of the ducts close to the furnace to break the metal-to-metal connection.

## Steam System

Here the water in the boiler is heated until steam forms and it is the steam that flows through the pipes to heat the radiators. There are two basic kinds of steam systems, the one-pipe system and the two-pipe system. In the one-pipe system, the same pipe brings the steam to the radiators and returns the water to the boiler.

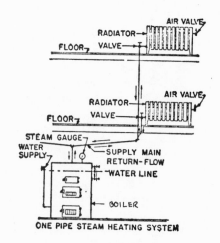

ONE PIPE STEAM HEATING SYSTEM

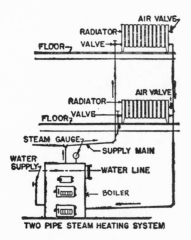

TWO PIPE STEAM HEATING SYSTEM

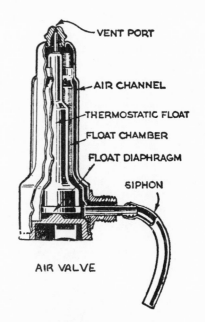

AIR VALVE

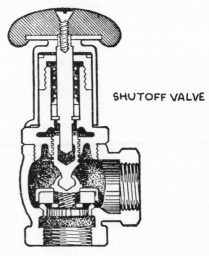

SHUTOFF VALVE

In the two-pipe system, one pipe brings steam to the radiators, and the other pipe carries the water back to the boiler. The two-pipe system is considerably more expensive to install and is not very often found in the home. The one-pipe system gives adequate service in most cases.

Each radiator in a steam system is equipped with an air valve, and this allows the air in the system to be driven out by the pressure of the steam coming through the pipes. This valve is so designed that when steam comes in contact with the inner mechanism, the valve closes and prevents any steam from escaping from the radiator.

If one radiator in a steam system fails to heat, it is probably because the air valve is clogged with dirt or grease. You can usually clean the valve by removing it from the radiator and soaking it for a time in white gasoline. Swish it around in the gasoline, let it dry, and then replace it.

If some radiators near the boiler get hot while others some distance away do not, it means that the system is out of balance. This can be corrected by installing adjustable air valves on the radiators. These can be set so that the air in the radiators near the boiler flows out more slowly than the air in radiators some dis-

tance from the boiler. This allows these radiators to get their share of the steam. Adjustable air valves cost around $4.00 and are well worth it.

Radiators will not heat properly and will often pound when steam is coming up if the shutoff valve is only partially open. It should be either all the way open or closed.

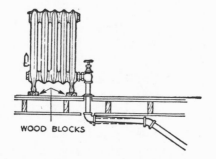

WOOD BLOCKS

Pounding will also occur in the system if water is trapped in the pipe near the radiator. This can usually be corrected by putting small blocks of wood under the legs of the radiator. This will usually change the pitch of the pipe just enough to allow the water to flow back to the boiler.

Dirty boiler water can also make the system noisy. There are boiler cleaning compounds which can be added to the water that will help eliminate this problem.

In a steam system there is usually a glass water gauge that shows the water level in the boiler. If there is no indication on the glass gauge as to the correct level that the boiler water should be, keep the level about halfway up the gauge. It is wise to have a low-water cutoff installed on a steam boiler to turn off the burner should the water level in the boiler be-

come too low. This is not so essential in the case of a hot-water system, as there should not be any decided drop in the water level of the system during the heating season; but with steam there will be a constant loss of water, so that water must be added to the boiler at rather frequent intervals.

## Electric System

In this system heat is provided by resistant wiring, usually in the form of baseboard units, but sometimes as coils set into the walls and ceilings of the room or by individual heaters set into the walls. This type of system requires a minimum amount of maintenance. Baseboard or wall units should be vacuumed occasionally to remove any dust or dirt that may collect on them.

## Oil Burner

An oil burner may be used in either a warm-air, circulating hot-water, or steam system. Burners should be checked and adjusted at least once a year, and the best time is just before the heating season begins. It should be done by a qualified oil-burner serviceman. Many fuel oil delivery companies provide this type of service, and it is well worth the price. It will include cleaning and adjusting the burner, and checking the efficiency of the operation. A properly adjusted oil burner should not smoke except perhaps for a minute or so when it first goes on and the firebox is cold, so that combustion of the oil is not complete. If it does smoke after this period, it is not properly adjusted and you are wasting fuel as well as allowing the air around you to be fouled by the oily smoke.

The modern oil burner is relatively trouble-free, but now and then it will fail to operate. The first thing to check is whether or not the thermostat is set high enough to demand heat. It may also be that a speck of dust has got inside the thermostat, so that electric contact is not made. Move the thermostat back and forth a few times. This may do the trick. Also be sure that there is oil in the oil storage tank. All oil burners have an emergency cutoff switch, which is usually located by the door of the utility room or by the basement stairs. Often someone will turn this switch off by mistake, thinking it an ordinary electric switch (in spite of the fact that it has a red faceplate on it). The next point to check is the fuse to the oil-burner circuit, as a temporary overload may have blown the fuse or the circuit breaker may have kicked off. Another point to check is the red reset button found on the motors of many oil burners. If there was a temporary overload, this button will have popped out. If the condition is not serious, the button can be pushed back and the motor will then start up.

A major cause for an oil burner not running is that dirt or soot has gotten into the stack switch. This switch is in a little metal box fastened into the metal stovepipe that runs from the furnace or boiler to the chimney. It is a safety device, designed to cut off the oil burner if the oil fails to ignite after a certain interval of time. There is a little metal lever or button on this switch, and if you flick it or push it, the burner will begin to operate.

## Gas Burner

As a gas burner has a minimum number of moving parts as compared with an oil burner, it seldom requires service or acts up. Obviously, if you should ever smell gas, you should close the gas shutoff valve, call the gas company, and leave the house. If the burner should fail to operate, it may mean that the pilot light has gone out. This can occur if the light was subject to a sudden draft or if a speck of dust or soot closed the tiny opening.

Directions for lighting the pilot light are usually given for each particular unit. Usually there is a plate on the side of the furnace or boiler with instructions. If the pilot light fails to light after you have tried to relight it according to these instructions, call your local gas company.

## End-of-Season Care

When the heating system is shut down at the end of the cold weather, several things should be done to ensure against damage during the off-season. First, don't drain the water out of the boiler. Leave the water in and add water, if necessary, so that the system is full. This will reduce rusting of the boiler and pipes during the summer months. Oil storage tanks should also be filled at the end of the season to reduce rusting and to prevent condensation inside the tank which will produce water that will form a sludge at the bottom of the tank. It is also wise to run an oil burner for an hour or so during the summer months.

## Leaky Shutoff Valves

The shutoff valves of radiators will sometimes leak a little. Repair this as soon as possible, or the water will damage the flooring around the radiator.

Sometimes a valve will leak because the packing nut is not tight. It can be turned down with a wrench. If this fails to correct the leak or prevents the handle of the valve from turning easily, then the valve should be repacked.

On a hot-water radiator, turn off the boiler and drain enough water out of the system to bring the level below that of the radiator you are working on. You can draw water out of the system by opening either the drain valve on the boiler or the valve at the lowest point of the system near the boiler. To see if the water is low enough, loosen the packing nut around the valve. If water starts to drip, the water level is too high. In a steam system, just turn off the burner—it is not necessary to drain any water out of the system.

Packing used for these valves can be purchased at most hardware stores. With the packing nut unscrewed from the valve body, pack the compound in the nut around the valve stem. After the valve has been packed, screw down the packing nut and check to see whether or not the valve can be turned on and off with ease. If it can't, loosen the nut slightly.

### Humidity

This term is used to indicate the amount of moisture vapor present in the air. It is most important to maintain proper humidity during the heating season for a number of reasons. First, with proper humidity, it is possible to feel comfortable at a lower temperature indoors than when the air is too dry. If the air is too dry, the nasal passages dry out, making one feel uncomfortable and also making one more susceptible to colds and other respiratory ailments. And last, but not least, dry air is very hard on furniture.

Most experts agree that the ideal humidity indoors in winter is around 40%. This is measured on a special instrument called a "hygrometer," which you can buy for less than $10.00.

The reason that we have a problem with indoor humidity in the winter is that moisture vapor flows from hot to cool air, and as the inside temperature is higher than that outside, there is a constant flow of water vapor from inside the house to the outside. And the higher the indoor temperature, the more water vapor will escape. Steam radiators are the worst offenders, because when they are hot, they are very hot—sometimes as much as 200 degrees. Hot-water radiators are better, as they do not become this hot.

Most modern forced warm air systems have a type of humidifier which adds water to the air as it passes through the furnace. Often, however, these humidifiers are not connected or they have become clogged and fail to work. If you have a forced warm air system and are troubled with dry air in the house, check the humidifier to see if it is operating. If it is not, you can have a serviceman connect it or attempt to do it yourself.

You can also buy humidifiers—portable or fixed. These units start at around $75.00 and have a fan that pulls in the air, adds water to it, and passes it though a filter that removes dust and dirt.

There are are also special pans which you can fasten to radiators. These are filled with water and help keep the air moist. One of the nicest ways to maintain proper humidity is with indoor plants, which give off vast amounts of moisture. Keeping a kettle boiling on the range will help somewhat, and so will filling a bathtub with hot water and allowing it to stand for as much time as possible.

## COOLING THE HOUSE

There are many ways to make a house cooler in hot weather short of installing air conditioning. And even when certain rooms or the entire house is cooled by air-conditioning equipment, these suggestions will improve the efficiency of the system and also reduce operating costs.

Many of the steps to keep a house cool in hot weather are exactly the same as those used to keep down heat loss in cold weather. For example, insulating the underside of the roof or attic floor will keep a house very much cooler in hot weather. In fact, in warm climates insulation is just as important for keeping cool as it is in cold weather for keeping warm. And it is absolutely essential if the house is to be air-conditioned, because without it even the best equipment will not be satisfactory. It is best if there is 6" of insulation on the underside of the roof or under the floor.

Cracks around doors and windows should be sealed with caulking compound because they allow the cool air inside the house to escape and warm air to enter. If the house is air-conditioned, there is some value to be gained by leaving storm windows in place throughout the year.

**Window Shades.** A great deal of heat enters the house through the window glass. One way to reduce this is to use window shades and the best kind are the heavy room-darkening shades which have considerable value in reflecting heat away from the room. Shades on the east side of the house should be pulled down early in the morning to keep out the sun. When this area of the house gets in the shade, these can be raised and those on the west side of the house pulled down.

Special thermal shades are also available and are excellent because they allow light and air to enter a room, but will keep out a good deal of the sun's heat.

Awnings are another good way to protect windows from the sun. They can be of canvas or metal, and it is best if they do not have side panels because these allow air to become trapped under the awning where it is heated by the sun and the heat is reflected into the house.

Picture windows and sliding glass doors can be a problem, as they are difficult to equip with awnings. It is important to remember, too, that units of this type made of insulating glass will not keep out the heat from the sun. The insulating glass is effective in cutting down heat loss in the winter, but the rays of the sun can penetrate the glass and warm the room. The only type of glass that will reduce heat gain in summer is the rather expensive heat-absorbing glass, or glass that has been coated with a heat-absorbing plastic. A less expensive approach is to use louvered blinds on sliding glass doors, or room-darkening shades which can be raised easily to allow the doors to be used.

The inside of a house can be kept cooler in hot weather if certain things are done to the outside. For example, a dark or black roof absorbs heat, whereas a light-colored or white roof reflects it away from the house. It would probably not be economically practical to reroof just for this reason, but the point is worth remembering when and if new roofing is required. The same thing holds true of the paint used on the outside of the house. Dark paint absorbs heat and makes the house warmer, and white paint reflects the heat away.

Grass and green ground cover around the house absorb heat and keep it away from the house, but concrete, unless it is painted blue or green, will reflect heat into the house. Blacktop will absorb a lot of heat and store it up, so that the area around the blacktop will be warmer than other portions of the grounds. If you have a considerable blacktop around your house, it's worth taking the time in later afternoon to hose it down so that it is cooled and won't give off heat for hours after the sun has gone down.

**Attic and Window Exhaust Fans.** If these are the proper size and are used correctly, they are an inexpensive way to make a house considerably cooler during the day and night. The size and number of fans required depend on the climate, where the house is located, and its size. The capacity of a fan is measured according to the cubic feet of air (in volume) that it will circulate per minute. This is known as CFM (cubic feet per minute). In warm climates, you will need a fan or fans with a capacity to change the cubic volume of air in the room or house every minute. In colder areas, a change in every 2 or 3 minutes is adequate. You can figure out the number of cubic feet in a room by multiplying the length by the width by the height measured in feet. If you want to find the total cubic feet for the house, measure each room and then add the figures together.

Attic fans are relatively large, and one is often sufficient to cool an average-size house. It can be installed in the attic ceiling or at one end of the attic or attic crawl-space, assuming that there is a sufficient-size opening into the house proper. Window units are not as large, and several may be required to handle a house. They should be securely fastened to the window, and there should be side panels so that there are no openings between the fan unit and the window frame.

The best type of fans to buy are those with a thermostat or timer on them so that they can be set to operate at the times required. In the early morning, for example, the fan should not operate. Close windows and pull shades because at this time the house is usually cooler than the outside air. If you were to run the fan, you'd simply remove all that nice cool air and bring in the warm outside air. During the course of the late morning and early afternoon, the fan should be run for very short periods to remove some of the heated air that is beginning to build up inside the house. Open windows on the shady side of the house, but keep the ones on the hot west side closed.

In late afternoon when the sun is down, the air close to the ground will be cooler than the upper air. Open lower windows and let the fan pull in the cool ground air.

At night, before retiring, close all windows except those in the bedrooms. Close doors to all rooms except bedrooms, but leave the bedroom doors open. The fan will pull cool air across the bedrooms and make them comfortable. If the fan is equipped with a thermostat or timer, it can be set to turn itself off after everyone is asleep and the house is comfortably cool. If not, turn it off the very first thing in the morning.

**Room Air Conditioners.** These can be installed in windows or in the walls and do an excellent job. Before you buy one, however, there are several things you should check on. First, the capacity of the electric wiring. Most of these units are designed to operate on a 20-amp circuit and

this is not always available in many houses, especially the older ones. There are also units that can operate on a standard 15-amp circuit, assuming that the circuit is actually delivering 15 amps to the outlet where the unit is to be plugged in. If you have any doubt as to the adequacy of the wiring in your house, it would be worth paying an electrician to check out the circuits to see if they can handle an air-conditioning unit. For unless the unit gets the amount of electric power required, it will never run efficiently and may require constant repairs.

The capacity of these units is measured by the number of BTU's (British Thermal Units) of cooling they produce. Your dealer can tell you what size you will require, but before he can do this with any degree of intelligence, he must know certain facts about the room. He needs to know the total volume (cubic feet) —height times length times width, measured in feet. He should know the number of windows and doors in the room and also how the room is to be used. For example, it will take a larger unit to keep a living room comfortably cool than a bedroom of the same size because there is more activity in a living room; more people use it, and people generate heat.

When one of these units is installed in a window, it is important that there be no open joints between the unit and the window frame. All joints should be sealed with caulking compound or masking tape and it is wise to apply weather stripping to the window, especially if it's an old window and the sash fits loosely in the frame.

The primary reasons for trouble with window air conditioners are low voltage and dirty filters. If you live in an area where the air contains much soot and dirt, the filters may have to be changed every few months during the seasons the conditioners are in use. Trouble also occurs when a unit is asked to cool more space than it was designed for. If there is a single unit in a house, it can't be expected to keep the entire house cool. The doors to the room where it is located should be kept shut when the unit is in operation.

# CONDENSATION

When there is a temperature change in the air the humidity or water vapor in the air is also affected. If the temperature rises, the humidity increases; if the temperature drops, the humidity drops accordingly. Now, if a mass of warm air in a room comes in contact with a colder object, for example, the effect at the point where the contact is made will be to cause the warm air to throw off some of its humidity or water vapor. Condensation takes place and liquid or droplets of water are formed. This is exactly what happens when the warm air in the basement during the summer comes in contact with cold pipes or walls and causes dripping, puddles, or water stains.

Another example of condensation is seen in windowpanes which become "cloudy" or "sweaty" when the weather is

cold outside and warm indoors. It is especially important today because many of the newer homes with thermal insulation, weather stripping, and storm windows are built so "tight" that mosture in the warm air inside has no way of joining the cold air outdoors. The result is that it then condenses on cooler, interior surfaces. You then find paint peeling and wood deteriorating. Water deposits drip on floors and other surfaces, causing dampness and discoloration. Older homes, especially frame houses, are often more porous, on the other hand, and thus enable the warm, humid air inside to mix more freely with the outside air. This would appear to be critical of the newer dwellings which are built to conserve heat through greater insulation, but such is not the case. Condensation can be controlled in all homes.

## Causes of Condensation

Extensive use of appliances which give off water vapor, such as washing machines and various cooking appliances, causes condensation. It also occurs in

many of the newer homes today where low-cost designs make for small rooms and low ceilings. The amount of space in which the air can circulate is important. Water vapor in a small area will condense more rapidly. Plants, animals, and people also contribute to the amount of water vapor in a home. So does vapor from showers, baths, and indoor clothes-drying.

Many homes today which are being built without basements create problems due, again, to condensation. In this type of home an enclosed crawl-space takes the place of the standard cellar. This area beneath the first floor often gets damp and, if there is no ventilation, the water vapor finds its way up into walls, attics, and living areas and condenses.

Exterior paint can be badly damaged by condensation. Free water or ice that collects behind the siding may run over the surface of the siding when it condenses. It will frequently absorb extractives from the wood and cause stains. If it soaks the siding it may cause the paint to blister and peel. Where moist conditions are present for a considerable length of time, decay may occur.

Generally, the outside walls "breathe" enough to take off the moisture that does form. A masonry wall, for example, is quite porous and the water vapor that it collects will be thrown back out if it is blocked on the inside by a vapor barrier. In the case of wood sheathing and siding, as noted above, water vapor is often collected and condensation results. It is often advisable to construct small vents just under the cornice and above the footing. These should be protected from the weather by moldings.

**Snow and Ice Dams.** Leakage of water into buildings is sometimes caused by ice dams and is often mistaken for condensation. Snow and ice dams are usually found after heavy snowfalls. If the temperature is a little below freezing, the heat from indoors will melt the ice and snow along the roof surface. Then the water creeps down over the surface, and when it reaches the overhang of the roof, freezes and builds up a ledge of solid ice. The rest of the ice and snow which is melting then has no place to go because of the barrier set up by the ice ledge. Consequently it backs under and between the shingles and enters the building.

To prevent such leakage, the eaves must be protected. A single course of heavy roofing felt should be placed over the eaves. Extend it upward and well above the inside line of the wall. This will prevent ice and snow dams from forming in the eaves. Sheet metal can also be used as a lining material. Though this condition is often referred to as condensation, it is essentially a matter of drainage and insulation.

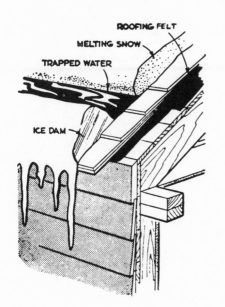

## Tests for Water Conditions

A water condition in the house is due to one of three things: seepage, leakage, or condensation. Unless the condition is obviously due to condensation, it will be useful to apply one of the following tests:

1. Take a small pocket mirror, or thin sheet of bright metal or glass, and glue or cement it to the portion of the floor or wall that frequently becomes damp, using the smallest amount of adhesive that will give firm contact. Leave it in place for a few hours so that it may assume the temperature of the floor or wall. Then examine the surface of the mirror or other object. If no droplets of water have formed on its surface, but the area continues to be damp, the cause of the difficulty is not condensation. If droplets do appear, however, condensation has occurred. It may not, however, be the only cause of dampness in the surrounding areas.

2. Place a thermometer in contact with the damp portion of the floor or wall and cover it with several layers of woolen cloth or blanket so that the temperature of the thermometer will approximate that of the area being tested. By means of wet- and dry-bulb thermometers and psychrometric tables (available from the Superintendent of Documents, Government Printing Office, Washington, D.C. 20025), determine the temperature of the dew point of the air in the basement. If the temperature of the surface is lower than the dew point of the air, condensation contributes to the dampness.

3. Make a plaster of paris ring about 3″ in diameter and attach it to the surface to be tested. Before the plaster sets, place the closed end of an ordinary drinking glass tightly on the surface of the plaster so that no air reaches the surface under the glass. The ring should be at least 1″ thick so that the glass is at least 1″ away from the surface to be tested. After 24 hours have elapsed, examine the surfaces. If the one surrounding the plaster is damp

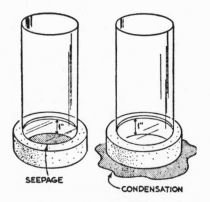

SEEPAGE          CONDENSATION

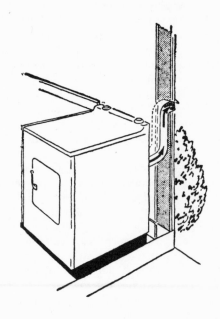

but the surface under the glass is dry, the dampness is caused by condensation. If moisture appears under the glass, water seepage is indicated.

4. Select a spot on a basement wall which is wet and chip off about one square inch of the surface with a chisel and hammer. Examine the color of the exposed surface and the wall where the piece has been chipped away. If water has been seeping through the wall, this exposed surface will be dark and damp. If the presence of water was due, however, to condensation, the exposed surface will be light in color, dry, and dusty in appearance.

## Corrective Measures

If we could remove the causes of condensation, we might have a simple solution to the problem. Unfortunately it is not so easy as that. We cannot do without our many appliances and other comforts, and there is no reason why we should. It is more practical to contrive to maintain even temperatures and reduce marked differences at points where warm air strikes cold surfaces. Ventilation, therefore, and some form of vapor barrier or insulation, are the principal methods employed to control condensation.

Wherever possible, appliances which give off large quantities of water vapor,

such as automatic clothes-dryers, should be equipped with some means of ventilation which can carry the vapor directly outdoors. Gas-operated hot-water heaters and stoves often give off hydrogen which combines with the oxygen in the air to form water vapor and increases the humidity in the house. Care should be taken to keep vents working properly and, where vents or flues are absent, they should be installed.

## Crawl-Space

In recent years there has been a tendency to cut costs by omitting basements in home construction. Instead, such dwellings usually have what is known as a crawl-space. This is an enclosed area between the ground and the first floor. It may be only a foot or two, or it may be several feet high. The crawl-space must, however, be suitable for the installation and maintenance of mechanical lines and equipment when they are placed below the first floor. Walls enclosing the area are usually made of masonry, wood siding, asbestos cement board, metal sheets, or other similar materials supported on light framing.

Soil around the crawl-space must be graded away from the building to prevent water from entering into the area and wetting the inside earth. In addition, drains in the crawl-space wall are recommended—especially if the floor is below the outside grade. When this has been

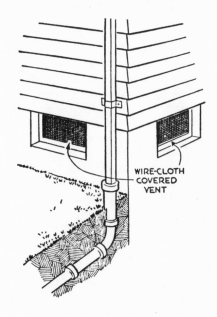

WIRE-CLOTH
COVERED
VENT

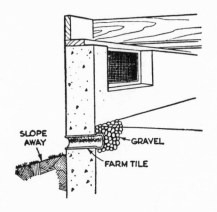

SLOPE
AWAY

GRAVEL

FARM TILE

properly attended to and moisture and dampness are still a serious problem in the living quarters above, condensation caused by excessive moisture in the crawl-space is generally at fault.

**Control by Ventilation.** Where there is no other means of controlling condensation, at least 4 ventilating openings should be installed. Place one near each corner of the building. Figure the total net amount of crawl-space ventilation required on the basis of 2 square feet of ventilating space per 100 linear feet of building perimeter, plus $\frac{1}{3}\%$ of the crawl-space ground area. Openings should be placed as high up as possible in the walls of the crawl-space. If this ventilation is the only means of controlling condensation, keep the vents open throughout the year. Also make sure the floors over the crawl-space are properly insulated. Plumbing pipes should also be insulated.

**Control by Ground Insulation.** In many northern areas where it is not practical to allow a completely free sweep of cold air below a dwelling floor, another method can be used. In this instance, condensation is reduced by stopping the moisture from the ground from entering the air in the crawl-space. The ground is covered with a vapor-resistant durable material, like a good waterproof concrete slab, heavy roll roofing, or plastic sheeting. The

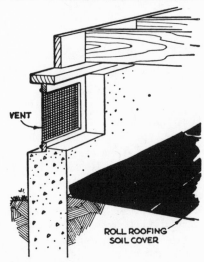

VENT

ROLL ROOFING
SOIL COVER

roll roofing, either mineral-surfaced or plain, should be laid over a rough graded surface. At least 2" lapped joints must be allowed, but generally they do not require any cementing material. The roll roofing should weigh at least 55 pounds per 100 square feet. Some ventilation should also be provided, but it need be only 10% of that required when ventilation is the only method used. Even if the soil is not completely smooth, the roofing material will become soft and will conform to the contour of the soil within a short time. If there is a chance that water might get inside the foundation wall, be sure the soil surface below the building is kept above the outside grade. A soil cover will be especially valuable where the soil has high capillarity and the water table is continually near the surface.

Condensation control may also be obtained by spreading a 4" layer of gravel over the soil in the crawl-space. The gravel should be small in diameter so that there will not be too much space between pieces, but should not be less than $\frac{1}{8}$" in diameter.

## Ventilating the Attic

In order to work effectively as a means of controlling condensation in the attic, the amount of ventilation must be adequate and should be properly located and operated continuously. For a gable, or modified hip roof, louver-type ventilators are recommended. Place them as high up as possible, since warm air moves upward and out of the building. Use a mesh size which is not too small, but which will keep out insects. Extremely fine wire cloth should be avoided because it restricts the movement of air and is easily clogged by dust and lint. In flat-roof structures, vents should be installed below the eaves, communicating with the space above the thermal insulation between the roof joists. Make certain that airways above the insulation are clear from one side of the build-

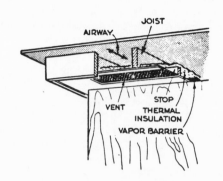

ing to the other. Install vents as near the outside of the cornice as possible to minimize the amount of snow driven through the ventilators by the wind. A vapor barrier should also be used on the warm side of the ceiling.

## Vapor Barriers

Condensation on walls, floors, ceilings, and roofs may be remedied most effectively by means of a vapor barrier, used alone, or combined with ventilation. The barrier blocks the passage of water vapor. It is usually placed on the interior side of the insulation, thus preventing the cold, outside air from coming in contact with the warm inside surfaces where it might condense. Effective vapor barriers are: building papers that are saturated and coated with a high-gloss asphalt; laminated or duplex uncreped kraft papers having an undamaged layer of asphalt between them and spread to a thickness of 60 pounds per ream; metal foils without folds or creases that have been mounted on materials such as paper- and composition-board lath; sufficient coats of lead and oil paint, rubber-base paint, asphalt, and certain types of aluminum paint which result in a smooth unbroken, glossy finish on the surface to which they are applied; and certain specialty wall coverings of thin material having special vapor-resistant coatings. The latter are often used in bathrooms and kitchens where the surface must be cleaned often.

Two coats of aluminum paint applied under the decorative wall or ceiling finish will prove helpful as a vapor barrier when it is not practical to install sheet materials. Such coatings may be aluminum, asphalt, or oil paints, as well as some enamels. First remove the wallpaper, and then thoroughly clean and patch the plaster.

Before applying aluminum paint, give the plaster one coat of plaster primer or sealer; then apply 2 coats of aluminum paint. This will reduce penetration of vapor into the wall, and the surface can then be covered with wallpaper or other interior finish. Asphalt should not be used on exposed walls, but if enough coats are applied to the back of plywood or similar inside finishes to give them a glossy surface, it will prove satisfactory as a barrier also. Oil paints, semigloss wall enamels, or gloss wall enamels may be used on plastered walls, provided the walls have been primed with 2 coats of wall primer.

In new construction, vapor barriers may be installed on the inner face of wall studs, or the bottom of top-floor ceiling joists, before the inside finish is applied. Barriers will be most effective if they are fitted to form a continuous, unbroken membrane and are installed on the warm, or room, side of the insulation, which is usually behind the lath and plaster or other finish material.

Place sheet-form vapor barriers in the attic above existing top-floor ceilings and cut them so that they will fit between the joists. Then lay them on top of the ceiling. Loose-fill, batt, or blanket-type insulation may then be placed between the joists on top of the vapor barrier. Some batt or blanket-type insulation has a vapor barrier attached to it, in which case no additional barrier is necessary. Lay this type of insulation between the joists on the ceiling with the vapor-barrier side down.

In an unfinished attic, install batt or blanket-type insulation between the ex-

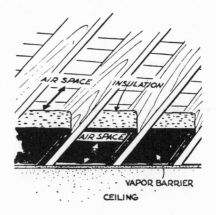

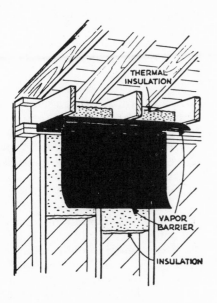

posed roof rafters. Tack it to the side of the rafters so as to leave one air space between the top of the insulation and bottom of the roof boards, and another air space between the bottom of the insulation and the bottom of the rafters. If the insulation has a vapor barrier attached to it, install it with the vapor-barrier side down. If it does not have the vapor bar-

**191**

rier, apply sheet-form vapor barrier material to the bottom edge of the rafters. When this has been done, apply ceiling finish.

If loose-fill insulation is used between the rafters of an unfinished attic, tack sheet-form barrier material to the lower edge of the rafters and apply ceiling finish before the insulation is blown in. If loose-fill insulation is to be blown between the rafters in a finished attic and no vapor barrier exists, paint the warm side or face the ceiling with at least two coats of aluminum paint before wallpaper or other decorative finish is applied.

Whenever insulation is placed between roof rafters, it is necessary to provide space between the bottom of the roof boards and the top of the insulating material. The space will serve as a good insulator if properly ventilated with outdoor air.

Vapor barriers should be well fitted around electric switch and outlet boxes to prevent water vapor from getting through to the wall. Staple the paper to the wood structure and lay it over the outlet box. In this position it can be broken or cut by striking it above the edge of the box with a hammer. This will crush or break the paper. It can also be cut along the edge of the box with a sharp knife. Then push the barrier over the edge of the box. Be especially careful not to tear it. The flow of water vapor through the box itself cannot be completely eliminated. However, no more openings should be made by the electrician than are absolutely necessary. Blanket insulation with a vapor barrier attached to it should be cut diagonally over the box. Remove most of the fiber between the covers and tuck the corners down at the sides of the box.

## Condensation on Pipes

Cold-water pipes in the basement can be prevented from causing condensation in hot, humid weather if they are covered.

A cylindrical-shaped, split pipe covering of wood insulating felt with a canvas jacket is one type of insulation which may be used for this purpose. It comes in 3' lengths of various thicknesses and is made for standard pipe sizes.

Pipes should be in good condition and clean. Loosen the canvas lap on the pipe covering and brush along the edge with paste to refasten the lap. Encase the pipe with a section of covering placed with the open side up, and with the end which has no canvas-joint overlap placed tightly against the fitting and pressed closely together. Paste the lap securely over the longitudinal joint. Apply the second section in the same manner and push it tightly against the first. Then seal the joint between the two sections by pasting the overlap attached to the first section over the joint. Continue covering the pipe in this way until the next fitting is reached. When a short section is needed, cut the covering with a sharp knife or handsaw.

To the first coat of asbestos cement on the fittings, apply a ½" second coat, or one of the same thickness as the pipe covering. This coat should be troweled smooth and beveled down to meet the surface of the pipe covering. The asbestos cement on the fittings is then protected by a canvas jacket, which should be the same weight as that used on the pipe covering. It should be pasted down smoothly and a vapor-resistant covering applied to the surface to prevent water vapor from reaching the surface of the metal pipe.

To improve the appearance, apply two coats of spar-varnish aluminum paint to the canvas jacket, followed by one or two coats of paint in any desired color. Aluminum foil, such as is sold for kitchen use, may be wrapped around the jacket instead of using aluminum paint. It is wise to use a paint which contains a fungicide to prevent mildew if the basement is inclined to be damp. If appearance is not an important consideration, the canvas jacket may be wrapped and sealed with alumi-

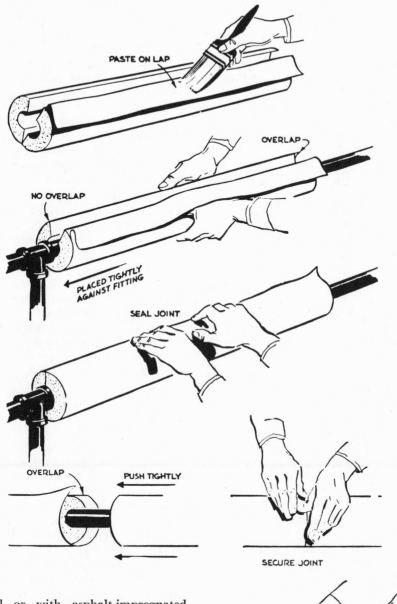

num foil or with asphalt-impregnated paper, or it may be painted with an unbroken coating of asphalt.

Tape-form insulating coverings, also available, may be wrapped spirally around cold-water pipes to a thickness of about ¼″; and thick paints mixed with insulating materials may be applied to pipes in a coating of about ¼″ thickness.

## Insulating Cold Walls

Cold walls will often "sweat" or show damp spots when warm water vapor in the room strikes them. This is caused by condensation and can be a serious source of trouble. The walls should be treated and made warmer by applying furring strips. These are nailed over the old plaster. New lath and plaster, insulating board, or insulating material and wallboard are then applied. Remove the trim before applying the new surface. When the wall is finished, insert pieces of wood behind the trim before it is replaced to bring it forward to form a suitable offset. You can also leave the old trim in place and apply new trim on top of it after plastering.

**Brick Walls.** Brick walls which have been furred on the inside may be satisfactory without further insulation unless the climate is severe. If more insulation is desired, however, the inside finish should be removed and blanket or other type of insulation placed between the furring strips.

Lath, composed of either gypsum board or fiberboard with or without aluminum foil on the back, may be used as a plaster base. Where a foil-backed board is used, a reflective air space is formed which has 2 or 3 times the insulating value of an ordinary air space, or about that of $\frac{2}{3}''$ of blanket insulation. Different types of wallboard, with or without metal foil on the back, may be used instead of lath and plaster.

**Storm Windows.** During the winter, windowpanes often become frosty. When the frost melts it runs down the pane, spills onto the sill and floor, and can cause considerable damage. If this condition cannot be corrected by reducing the amount of water vapor in the house, the installation of storm windows will help keep the cold air away from the panes and the possibility of condensation will be reduced. Unless the storm windows are also needed to help retain heat in the house, they do not have to be put on all window openings. They should be provided only for the windows on the side of the house facing prevailing winds.

**Basement Walls.** Detection of condensation in the basement is more important than in any other part of the house. Basement walls are frequently subjected to contact with outside water and often to water under hydrostatic pressure. The appearance of water on the surface of the basement wall will naturally raise the suspicion that water is penetrating from the outside to the inside. If this is the case, the wall will probably need to be waterproofed. If, on the other hand, the presence of a wet surface on the inside is due to condensation of warm humid air on a cold foundation wall, this cannot be cured with waterproofing. Instead, the condensation must be corrected, if possible, with better ventilation, air conditioning, or some other means of raising the temperature of the wall. This has been known to have been accomplished by simply shifting the position of a hot-water heater to a more advantageous position.

## Bathroom Floors

During summer months, when humidity is high, water frequently drips on bathroom floors as a result of condensation on the outside surfaces of the toilet tank or bowl. It may also occur at other times of the year when someone takes a hot bath, or especially a hot shower. The hot water fills the air with water vapor at a room temperature which is considerably greater than that of the fixtures. When the hot vapor given off by the shower or bath strikes the cooler surfaces around the toilet tank or bowl, it condenses. This may not be troublesome on ceramic tile floors, but on wooden floors it can readily cause decay.

If it is possible to raise the temperature of the water entering the tank, by as much as 15 to 20 degrees, this may prevent condensation or reduce it enough to render it harmless. This can be accomplished by putting the tank on a separate system from the remainder of the water supply. The water is then preheated to about room temperature either in a heater in the basement, or by coils placed outdoors or in the attic during the summer. A simple electric heater placed in the tank, controlled by a thermostat, is another possibility. They do not come readymade, but an electric heater like those used to heat tropical fish bowls would serve the purpose. Shallow pans can be bought, however, which may be slipped under the tank to catch water dripping down after condensation. They have a small drain which leads into the toilet bowl.

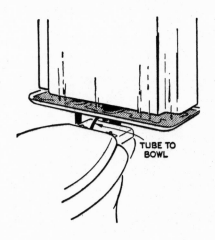

TUBE TO
BOWL

# 8

# PLUMBING

Every adult member of the household should be familiar with the plumbing system so as to deal with any emergency that may arise as well as make minor repairs when required.

There is nothing very complicated about the house plumbing system. There is the fresh water system that supplies hot and cold water to the various fixtures. There is the drainage system that carries the liquid waste out of the house. The fresh water system is under pressure; the drainage system depends on gravity to carry the liquid from fixtures to the sewer line. In spite of a few minor differences, all modern house plumbing systems are about the same. If you understand one,

you can easily understand another. It is wise, however, when you buy a house, to have the builder or the seller check you out, as this will save you time and effort. In an existing house, sometime when the plumber is there, ask him to run through the particular system with you if there are any aspects of it that you don't completely understand.

## FRESH WATER SYSTEM

Fresh water is brought into the house from a city street main or from a well. Regardless of the source of the water, there is

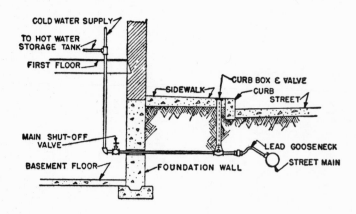

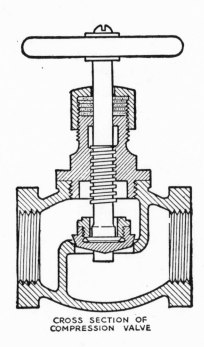

CROSS SECTION OF
COMPRESSION VALVE

they control. In a modern plumbing system, there will also be shutoff valves under each fixture, such as washbasin, sink, and toilet, so that water to them can be shut off when required. As shutoff valves get little use, they often become hard to operate. It's a good idea to close and open them every six months or so just to keep them working freely.

In a modern plumbing system the pipes for the fresh water supply—both hot and cold—are made of copper tubing. In a few systems the cold waterlines will be of plastic and the hot of copper. In older homes you may find brass pipe or even galvanized iron. Galvanized iron can be a problem because the inside of the pipe will rust, which can cause leaks, or the rust can accumulate to such a degree that the flow of water inside the pipe is reduced to a trickle. In this event the only thing to do is to replace the pipe.

Hot water for the system is furnished either by an independent hot water heater that runs on electricity, gas, or oil, or by a coil inside the house boiler, if the house is heated by circulating hot water or steam.

usually a main shutoff valve close to the point when the main supply line enters the house. If this is turned off, all water supply to fixtures and pipes around the house will be cut off. There are usually other shutoff valves throughout the system so that when repairs are needed water to a particular area can be shut off without affecting other fixtures. It's a good idea to tag each of these shutoff valves so that anyone will know immediately what areas

## DRAINAGE SYSTEM

This consists of the drainpipes attached to the various fixtures that are connected to the main sewer line which carries all liquid waste out of the house. As we mentioned before, unlike the fresh water system, which is under pressure, the waste system is a gravity system and there is no pressure in the lines; therefore you won't find any shutoff valves in this system. One or more of the house drainage lines extends through the house and up through the roof. This is necessary to prevent a partial vacuum from forming which might interfere with the free flow of water through the drainage system, and also to allow sewer gas to flow outside rather than back up and escape through fixture drains.

KITCHEN
FAUCETS

## Clogged Drains

These are probably the most common household plumbing headache. They usually occur because things were allowed to go down the drain that shouldn't have. The kitchen sink is one of the worst offenders, and the cause is usually grease. Try to keep grease from going down the kitchen drain. If some does, turn on the hot water and let it run down the drain for a minute or so to flush the grease out of the lines before it has a chance to harden. But almost any semisolid matter, as well as solid matter, can clog up a line —coffee grounds, large particles of food, and so forth. The only time it's safe to allow grease and food particles to go down a sink drain is when there is a garbage disposer unit in the drain which will handle them.

Most drain stoppages occur in the trap. This is that curved section of pipe that fits directly under most fixtures. The

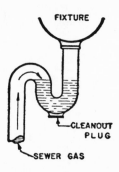

FIXTURE

CLEANOUT PLUG

SEWER GAS

purpose of the trap is to prevent sewer gas from coming up through the fixture drain. The trap is so designed that it is full of water, which is replaced each time water goes down the drain.

Most fixture drains can be cleared with something called a "plumber's friend" or plunger, and every household should have one. You can get them at any hardware store. The way to use this tool is to partially fill the fixture so that the drain opening is covered with water and

PLUMBER'S FRIEND

then place the rubber cup of the plunger over the drain opening. Work the handle up and down, and the resulting alternating compression and suction will generally dislodge any object caught in the drain.

If you don't have any luck with the plumber's friend, it is often possible to clear the obstruction by removing the clean-out plug at the bottom of the trap, or by removing the trap entirely by unscrewing the two large nuts that hold it in place. Put a large pan under the trap before you try either of these methods so that you'll catch the water that will flow out of the trap. If you find nothing inside the trap, stick a piece of wire up into the pipes and perhaps you can snag whatever is causing the trouble.

Fixture drains can also be cleaned by the use of chemicals, but these are not too effective when there is a complete stoppage. They are good to use, however, to keep a drain clear and as a remedy when it begins to drain slowly. If used frequently on the kitchen drain, they'll prevent a stoppage caused by grease or food particles. Of course they will not do much good when the obstruction is caused by some dense matter such as a spoon or rag that has somehow gotten down the drain and become stuck fast in the pipe.

## Clogged Toilet Trap

In a toilet, the trap is built into the toilet bowl. When a toilet gets clogged, your first attempt at clearing it should be made with a plumber's friend. The usual reason for the trouble is that a wad of

auger in place, while the second person rotates the handle. The idea is that the point of the auger will either break up the obstruction so that it will flow away, or will engage it so that it will be pulled out of the trap when the auger is removed. These augers, by the way, are also good for clearing stopped-up lines when the stoppage occurs some distance from a fixture trap.

paper, a cloth, or some other bulky object has gotten stuck in the trap; and if given a good push from the pressure of a plumber's friend, it will be moved into the larger sewer pipe connected to the toilet bowl and be on its way through the line. If this should fail, try a spring steel auger. You can usually rent one of these from a hardware or tool rental store. This tool really takes two people to operate it properly. One inserts the point of the auger in the toilet trap and holds the

## Sewage Problems

Sometimes a fixture won't drain properly and the cause is not in the fixture but at some other point in the draining system. Drains will back up and overflow if there is a stoppage in the main household line, in the underground line from house to sewer main or septic tank, or in the septic tank itself.

**Stopped-up Sewer Line.** The usual cause for a stopped-up sewer line—the one that runs underground from house to sewer main or septic tank—is tree roots. If there are any nearby trees and if there is a leak in the line, which often occurs, the tree roots will enter the line in search of moisture and rapidly grow until they clog the line. One remedy worth trying is to dissolve two pounds of copper sulfate crystals in water and pour down the fixture

SPRING STEEL AUGER

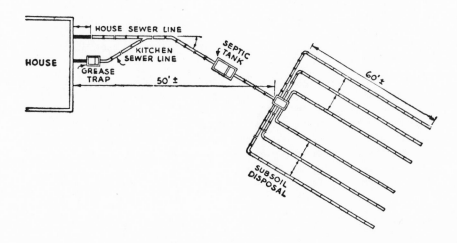

drain nearest the main sewer line. It will take at least overnight for this treatment to produce results, assuming that it does. What most homeowners do in this situation is to call in a firm with specialized equipment that can be inserted in the line and will cut out the roots. Once the line is clear, the copper sulfate treatment every few weeks may keep it clear. There are, of course, types of sewer lines that are root-proof; these are not expensive, but the cost of installing them, unless you dig the trench yourself, can be high.

The sewer line for an older home is sometimes made of clay tile. Now and then, if a heavy truck runs over the ground above them, one of these will break apart and produce a stoppage. The only remedy here is to replace the broken section of tile pipe.

**Septic Tank.** Where there is no city sewer line, liquid waste from the house flows into a septic tank or cesspool. Of the two, the septic tank is far superior and the only one that is allowed in most communities today. It consists of an underground concrete tank, set some distance from the house, into which the liquid waste flows. The tank is so constructed that the waste is held in one compartment for a period of time until solid matter is reduced by the action of bacteria into a liquid—almost all of it, that is. The liquid then flows into a second compartment of the tank and eventually into a disposal field where it is absorbed by the soil. If it has been properly installed and maintained, a septic system is a safe and hygienic means of disposing of household waste.

The first thing you should find out is the location of the septic tank. Ask the builder, previous owner, or your plumber to point out the location and mark it so that even if there is heavy snow on the ground, you can find it if the need arises.

A septic tank should be inspected once a year and cleaned out if necessary. Although most of the solid waste that enters it is made into a liquid, some of it remains as a sludge at the bottom of the

tank. If the depth of the sludge becomes too great, the action of the tank will cease and, what can be worse, the sludge will get into the disposal field, clog up the pipes, and require an extensive repair operation. As a general rule, the sludge should be removed when it is about halfway up from the bottom of the tank. The inspection and cleaning of septic tanks should be left to professionals; there are such firms in about every community, listed in the yellow pages under "Septic Tanks."

A septic tank will not be harmed by a normal amount of household detergents flowing into it. You should not, however, connect lines from the house roof gutters into it because this will flood it; for the same reason, you should not use it to dispose of water from a swimming pool. The normal amount of household drain cleaners won't harm a septic tank. If you decide to install a kitchen-sink garbage grinder, consult a septic tank firm to see if your present tank will handle this additional load. A septic tank can handle the discharge from an automatic dishwasher and washing machine, but a garbage disposer unit will throw a large volume of waste into it, which can flood the tank if it is not large enough.

**Cesspool.** You find these only in rural areas, as they are often unsanitary and can pollute water sources as well as the soil around them. A cesspool is just a large hole in the ground, lined with stone or block laid without mortar, and having a cover. Raw sewage from the house flows into it and then is absorbed by the surrounding soil. If the soil becomes saturated with moisture, as often happens during a rainy season, the cesspool overflows.

Another reason for a cesspool to overflow is that grease from the kitchen sink has filled the voids around the block or stone as well as the surrounding soil so that water can't escape from the cesspool. This problem can be eliminated by installing a grease trap between the kitchen sink drain and the cesspool. When a cess-

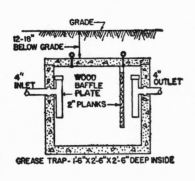

GREASE TRAP-1'-6"X 2'-6"X 2'-6" DEEP INSIDE

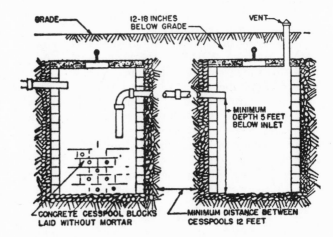

CONCRETE CESSPOOL BLOCKS LAID WITHOUT MORTAR

MINIMUM DISTANCE BETWEEN CESSPOOLS 12 FEET

pool begins to act up, there are only two things to do: one is to dig a second cesspool and connect them; the other is to replace the cesspool with a septic system, which is by far the best approach.

## HOT WATER PROBLEMS

One of the most common complaints about a hot water system is that there isn't enough hot water. In the case of an independent hot water heater—electric, gas, or oil—the trouble is that the hot water storage tank is too small. What you can do here is to either get a larger unit or add a second one to the system. The latter approach is very sound if you have a large, rambling house. Modern hot water heaters are very compact, and the electric types can be located almost anywhere in the house—in a closet, under the stairs, or even in the bathroom.

. If water is heated by a coil in the boiler, inadequate hot water is often a problem because there is no storage tank. Adding a storage tank will help matters.

**Dirty Hot Water.** This can occur if the water is heated in an independent hot water heater. All water contains a certain amount of foreign matter, and when this

is heated the water often takes on a rusty color. The foreign matter collects as a sediment in the bottom of the hot water heater, but if allowed to accumulate, it will be drawn into the pipes and flow out of the faucets. When this condition occurs, don't use any hot water at all for several hours. This will give the sediment a chance to settle to the bottom of the hot water tank. At the end of this time, open the drain faucet at the base of the tank and let the sediment flow into a pail. Let

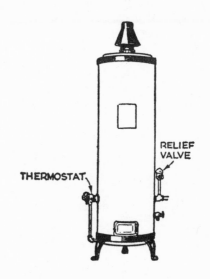

RELIEF VALVE

THERMOSTAT

201

the water run until it is clear. If this process is repeated every month or so, it will eliminate dirty hot water.

**Banging in Hot Water Lines.** If this occurs when a faucet is opened, it means that the water is too hot. For most domestic purposes, the temperature of hot water should be around 140°F. If, for one reason or another, it is allowed to become too hot, steam may form in the pipes when the pressure is released by the opening of a faucet, and this is the reason for the pounding. Adjust the thermostat on the heater so that the water temperature is kept at around 140°F.

## LEAKY FAUCETS

Next to a stopped-up drain, this is probably the most common household plumbing problem. Most faucets in the home are the compression type, which controls the flow of water by compressing a composition washer down onto a valve seat when a threaded spindle is turned. The most common reason for a compression faucet's dripping after it has been tightly closed is that the washer inside the faucet has become worn, and no longer fits tightly on top of the valve seat. Keep a package of assorted washers handy for just such repairs.

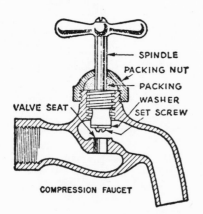

COMPRESSION FAUCET

To replace the washer, close the nearest shutoff valve to the fixture. Using an adjustable wrench, remove the large packing nut on top of the faucet body under the handle. In today's houses, there will usually be a housing on the faucet that conceals the packing nut, and this must be removed first. The housing is held in place by a nut which will differ in size and shape, depending on the brand of the faucet. Sometimes the housing is held in place by a setscrew. In any event, you've got to find a way to remove the housing before you can reach the packing nut. Once the nut has been loosened, remove the entire spindle and valve stem from the faucet by turning the handle counterclockwise; the valve stem will unscrew from the faucet body. You'll find the washer on the end, usually held in place with a setscrew. Remove the screw, select a washer of the same size and shape, and put it in place. If the screw is badly rusted or corroded, replace it with a new one that usually comes with the package of washers. Put the valve stem back into place in the body of the faucet and turn the handle counterclockwise, as if to close the faucet. Tighten the packing nut enough to keep water from coming up through it after the water supply has been turned on, but not so much that the handle will not turn easily.

**Worn Valve Seat.** Sometimes replacing a washer won't stop a faucet from dripping because the valve seat in the body of the faucet is worn or has become nicked in one way or another. The valve seat can be smoothed down with a device

VALVE SEAT
DRESSING TOOL

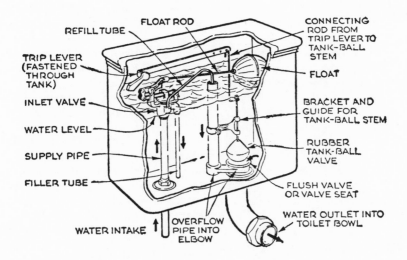

FLOAT ROD
REFILL TUBE
TRIP LEVER (FASTENED THROUGH TANK)
INLET VALVE
WATER LEVEL
SUPPLY PIPE
FILLER TUBE
WATER INTAKE
OVERFLOW PIPE INTO ELBOW
CONNECTING ROD FROM TRIP LEVER TO TANK-BALL STEM
FLOAT
BRACKET AND GUIDE FOR TANK-BALL STEM
RUBBER TANK-BALL VALVE
FLUSH VALVE OR VALVE SEAT
WATER OUTLET INTO TOILET BOWL

called a valve seat dressing tool, available at hardware stores. This tool is inserted in the body of the faucet after the valve stem has been removed and is rotated so that the cutting end smooths out the metal valve seat.

**Leaky Packing Nut.** Another point of leakage is around the stem, when the faucet is open. Such leakage will occur when the packing nut is not tight enough or when the packing or packing washer inside the cap is worn. Tighten the nut first, giving it a slight turn and checking to see whether or not the faucet handle still turns easily. If this fails to do any good, the packing washer should be replaced. Unscrew the setscrew that holds the handle in place and slip the handle off. The packing nut can then be taken off the stem and repacked, or string-type packing can be wound around the stem.

# LEAKY FLUSH TANK

Before attempting to repair a toilet tank which leaks, it is necessary to understand how the water enters the tank and how it is regulated so that the tank will not overflow.

**Operation.** Water enters the tank through an opening fitted with a valve. This valve has a washer, so that it will completely stop the flow of water when the valve is closed. The opening and closing of this inlet valve is governed by the copper or glass float which is connected to the valve by means of a rod. The float is airtight and rests on the surface of the water inside the tank. As the water rises in the tank, the float rises with it until, at a predetermined point, the inlet valve is closed by the action of the rod attached to the float. The flow of water into the tank is thus stopped.

The handle on the outside of the tank is connected by wire rods to a rubber flush valve which fits over the opening at the bottom of the tank. This opening is connected to the toilet bowl by a section of pipe. When the flush valve is lifted from the valve seat by turning the handle, water rushes out of the tank into the toilet bowl. As the water level in the tank drops, the float drops with it, and this action opens the inlet valve so that water can flow back into the tank. As soon as the handle on the outside of the tank is returned to its normal position, the flush valve drops over the valve seat to prevent any more water from flowing from the tank into the bowl. The tank then fills with water until the inlet valve is closed by the float's reaching a set height.

An overflow pipe inside the tank allows water to flow into the bowl, should the inlet valve fail to close at the proper time.

Keep in mind that all the mechanism inside the tank is delicate and can be thrown out of adjustment rather easily. Make sure that all the rods are working correctly before you begin replacing valves and washers.

There are several places inside the tank where a leak is likely to occur. It is possible to locate the cause of a leaky tank by removing the top and looking at the water level. If the water level is low and water is flowing out of the tank into the toilet bowl, the flush valve is not closing. If the level of the water inside the tank is high and water is flowing out of the tank by way of the overflow pipe, the inlet valve is not closing.

**Leak at Flush Valve.** A leak at this point can be caused by three conditions. A flush ball which becomes worn, rotten, or distorted in shape will no longer fit tightly over the valve seat. Rust or dirt on the valve seat will also prevent the ball from fitting evenly. The third condition occurs when the thin metal rods which connect the flush ball with the tank handle become bent or bind, and the ball cannot drop back over the valve seat.

To find which part of the system is at fault and to make the necessary repairs, you will have to shut off the water supply. Most tanks have a small valve located on the pipe running from the bottom of the tank through the floor. This is the supply line to the tank, and when this valve is closed no water will be able to enter the tank. If the tank does not have this valve, shut off the water by closing the right branch valve in the house plumbing system or by lifting the copper float inside the tank, and propping it to hold the inlet valve in a closed position.

Once the water has been shut off, you

can remove the flush ball and examine it for wear. This ball is fitted with threads at the top and screwed to the rod linking it to the tank handle. If the ball is worn or out of shape, it should be replaced.

Check the flush valve seat for dirt or rust after the ball is removed. If it appears to be rough, smooth it by rubbing the rim with emery cloth. Remove any sizable pieces of scale or rust with an old knife. After smoothing the valve seat, screw the new flush ball to the connecting rod.

Test the operation of the linkage between the handle and flush ball by turning the handle to the open position and then to the close. The ball should drop on the valve seat when the handle swings closed. If it fails to do this, examine the rods to see if they are bent. The lower rod attached to the flush ball is held in place by a metal guide arm connected to the overflow pipe. This guide arm is adjustable and should be positioned so that it is directly over the valve seat. If it is out of adjustment, the flush ball will not line up properly on the valve seat. If any metal rod is badly rusted, it should be replaced because a corroded rod will not long maintain its shape.

**Leak at Inlet Valve.** A leak due to failure of the inlet valve to close can also be caused by several factors. It may be due to a worn valve washer or a rough valve seat. If the rod connecting the float to the inlet valve is bent out of shape, it will cause the valve to remain open, as will a leak in the copper float.

To replace a worn inlet washer, shut off the water from the tank before disassembling the inlet valve. In some tanks this valve is located near the top of the tank, and in others it will be found at the bottom. If the latter is the case, you will have to flush all the water out of the tank to get at the valve. The plunger of the valve is held in place by thumbscrews which will probably have to be started with the aid of pliers. The washer is held in place by a nut and a brass ring cap.

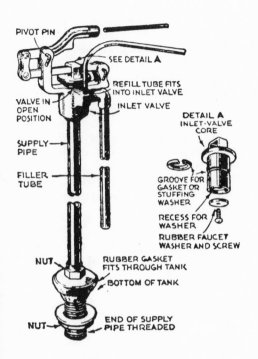

PIVOT PIN

SEE DETAIL **A**

REFILL TUBE FITS INTO INLET VALVE

VALVE IN OPEN POSITION

INLET VALVE

DETAIL **A** INLET-VALVE CORE

SUPPLY PIPE

FILLER TUBE

GROOVE FOR GASKET OR STUFFING WASHER

RECESS FOR WASHER

RUBBER FAUCET WASHER AND SCREW

NUT

RUBBER GASKET FITS THROUGH TANK

BOTTOM OF TANK

NUT

END OF SUPPLY PIPE THREADED

The ring cap may be so rusted that it will break while it is being removed. If this occurs, you will need a new cap as well as a new washer. While the valve is disassembled, check the valve seat to be sure that it is not rough or nicked.

A copper float which contains water will not rise high enough to shut off the inlet valve. You can solder a small leak in the float after draining the water out of it, but you should replace a float which has a bad leak.

The rod connecting the float to the valve has a great deal to do with how much water flows into the tank before the valve is closed. If the rod is bent upward, the level of water in the tank will be higher. If the rod is bent down, the water level will be lower. When a tank that is otherwise working correctly fails to deliver enough water to the toilet bowl, it is likely that the rod is bent out of shape.

This takes only a moment to repair. The water level in the tank should be almost to the top of the overflow pipe. If it is too far under this point, the toilet bowl will not be flushed properly.

In time the various parts of the flush mechanism will become so worn that it is more practical to replace them than to attempt repairs. Complete units are available at hardware stores, and these will fit almost any standard flush tank. An improved type of flush mechanism eliminates many of the moving parts, and therefore is less likely to get out of order. These are available under various brand names at hardware stores.

**Condensation on Tank.** A source of constant annoyance is moisture dripping off the sides of the toilet flush tank and onto the bathroom floor. This condition is most common in warm humid weather, but can occur at any time of the year when the air in the bathroom contains a lot of moisture and the water in the tank is cold. Often the trouble is that the tank mechanism is not working properly and water is constantly flowing into it and then into the bowl. The constant flow of cold water keeps the sides of the tank so cold that condensation occurs. But often condensation occurs when the temperature of the water normally flowing into the tank is far below that of the air around it in the bathroom.

One way to correct this situation is to insulate the inside of the tank so that the water inside it will not chill the outside walls of the tank. Rigid insulation designed for this purpose is available at hardware and plumbing stores. Another way to solve the problem is to bring a hot water line into the tank so that the temperature of the water inside the tank is around 70°F—just high enough to keep the tank from becoming chilled. Another solution of the problem is to install a little enameled pan which fits under the tank, catches the dripping water, and pipes it into the toilet bowl. Hardware and plumbing stores sell such pans.

# CARE AND REPAIR OF PLUMBING FIXTURES

Fixtures such as the kitchen sink, washbowls, and bathtubs are usually made of steel or cast iron with a baked enamel finish; more costly washbowls will sometimes be made of porcelain. In spite of their weight and rugged construction, the finish on steel and cast iron fixtures can be easily damaged and the smooth finish on porcelain can be scarred by improper use. Never use a harsh abrasive such as sandpaper or coarse scouring powder to clean plumbing fixtures. Use a mild scratchless type of cleaning powder. When you are making repairs on fixtures, cover them with paper or a cloth so that you won't damage the finish if you drop a heavy wrench on them. By the same token, protect the finish on faucets and other fittings from damage by a wrench or pliers when you work on them, by covering them with rags. It is a good habit to put a rubber kitchen sink mat in the sink when you are washing heavy pots and pans to prevent them from chipping the finish on the sink.

If some of the baked enamel finish does become chipped, it can be repaired with a special porcelain patching compound sold at paint and hardware stores. The area must be dry and the exposed metal should be washed with benzine to remove all traces of grease. Apply the liquid porcelain patching material as directed and follow the manufacturer's directions as to the amount of time required for drying.

Flush tanks and toilet bowls are made of porcelain, and if a heavy object is dropped on them, or they are improperly handled, they may crack or break. A crack in a flush tank can often be repaired by draining out the water, getting the inside of the tank dry, and then sealing the crack with an epoxy adhesive. In the case of a cracked toilet bowl, it is best to replace the unit rather than try to patch it, but if you can't afford to replace it at this particular time, use an epoxy adhesive for sealing the crack.

When bathtubs, sinks, and washbasins are badly scratched, chipped, or discolored they can sometimes be given a new lease on life by painting them with an epoxy paint. If this is properly applied, it will hold even when exposed to standing hot or cold water, but the surface must be carefully prepared. First, wash the surface with a detergent and water. Rinse and then scrub with fresh water and powdered pumice stone. Rinse again and allow to dry; then apply the epoxy paint according to the directions on the container. (See chapter 6, page 148.)

# NOISES IN PLUMBING SYSTEM

The most common plumbing noise is a banging or hammering in the pipes when a faucet is turned off. This is called "water hammer" and is due to the water under pressure being brought to a sudden stop. It is not only annoying, but also if allowed to continue, it can open up joints in the plumbing system and cause leaks. In the case of plumbing fixtures such as sinks, basins, and bathtubs, water hammer can often be eliminated just by turning the faucet off slowly so that the flow of water in the pipes is brought to a gradual, rather than a sudden, stop. But this can't be done in the case of automatic washing machines, dishwashers, and similar appliances, because here the valves that control the flow of water to the appliance are power-driven and close and open almost instantaneously.

The most common reason for water hammer is that the pipes are not properly supported and easily vibrate. If you can reach the pipes, secure them with pipe brackets, hangers, or other means, so that they can't be moved by hand. Use blocks of wood to brace 90-degree elbows. If the

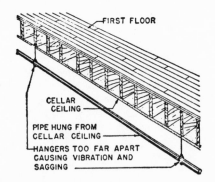

to operate until permanent repairs can be made. There are several ways to repair leaks in fresh-water lines. If it is just a matter of a pinpoint hole in the pipe, plastic tape will often do the trick. It's best if you first turn off the water supply so that you can dry the area on the pipe around the leak; then wrap the tape spirally with an ample overlap of the tape. Use about 3 layers and allow the tape to extend 2″ or 3″ on each side of the hole.

pipes are securely held, the hammering will be greatly reduced.

Another way to reduce water hammer is to install lengths of pipe in the system at various points—as close to fixtures as possible—to act as shock absorbers. The vertical length of pipe is capped at the end and contains air which cushions the water when the faucet is turned off. In

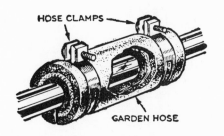

Another good temporary repair is made by taking a 3″ or 4″ length of garden hose, splitting it, slipping it over the pipe, and then securing it in place with hose clamps such as those used for automobile radiator connections, or the type used for plastic pipe. Hardware and plumbing stores often sell commercial pipe clamps consisting of metal plates and a gasket which can be tightened around the pipe, and these are excellent for the purpose.

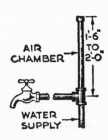

some cases, the best way to handle the problem is to reduce the pressure of the water flowing through the pipes. This is done by having a plumber install a pressure-reducing valve.

Chattering in a faucet usually means a loose or worn washer.

## LEAKY PIPES

The best way to deal with a leaky pipe is to replace it with a new section, but it is often necessary to make temporary repairs so that the plumbing system will continue

Leaks can also be repaired with a special epoxy compound designed for repairing metals such as iron and copper. For this compound to be effective, however, the area of the pipe must be dry and perfectly clean. Such a compound does very well for leaks in the drainage system where the size of the pipe is so great that friction tape and clamps cannot be used.

Leaks often occur at the joints in pipes. If it is a threaded joint, unmake the joint and then coat the external threads with pipe rope or the plastic-tape type of joint sealer. Then remake the joint. In the case of a sweated copper joint, first drain the line and then use a torch to heat the joint so that it can be taken apart. Remove all traces of the old solder and then clean the metal surfaces with steel wool. Be sure that the pieces that make the joint are dry. Coat the fitting with flux and then put the pieces together. Heat with a torch until the fitting is so hot that when solder is applied along the edge it will be drawn into the joint. (See chapter 15, page 377.)

## WATER PUMP

Other than an occasional oiling—if specified by the manufacturer—this equipment does not require much, if any, maintenance. It sometimes happens, however, that the pump will begin to run very frequently, but for very short periods. This usually means that the water storage tank has become waterlogged and there is not enough air inside it to allow for proper operation. If this situation is allowed to continue, it can burn out the pump motor. To correct this situation, turn off the pump, open a faucet in the house, and then drain the water out of the tank by opening the drain valve at the bottom. Allow all the water to drain out of the tank and keep the faucet open so that air can flow into the tank. When the tank is completely empty, close the faucet and the drain valve on the tank and start up the pump. The tank should now contain sufficient air to allow for normal operation.

## DRAINING PLUMBING

One of the most important steps in closing a house during the winter, if only for a short period, is draining the plumbing system. The entire system must be drained and prepared to preclude any possibility of a pipe's freezing and breaking, with consequent damage to decorations and furniture. Many owners of summer homes have returned after the winter months to find extensive damage caused by water from a cracked pipe. Plumbing should also be drained immediately if there is any breakdown of the home heating system during freezing weather.

Drain the plumbing system thoroughly. If one pipe is left undrained, it can cause great damage; consequently, it is recommended that a check list be used when draining the system. This list should include each branch line and plumbing fixture of the system. By checking off each portion of the system as it is drained, the home mechanic can be sure that he has completely emptied the system. Use the list, as well, for reference when putting the system back into service.

**Closing Water Supply.** The first step in draining the system is to shut off the water supply to the house. If this supply is furnished by a city water main, there is a valve located on the service line between the house and the water main. This valve is underground, below the frost line. A concrete curb box, fitted with a removable top, covers the valve. Remove the top of the curb box and use a long rod with a key at the end to turn off the valve. This key can be obtained from a plumber or from the local water authorities. After the curb valve has been closed, close the main shutoff valve inside the house. This valve should be fitted with a small drain cock to drain the valve and connecting pipe. Do not open this drain cock until the rest of the system has been emptied, or all the water remaining in the system will flow through the opening.

**Hot Water System.** Open all faucets after you have shut off the water supply at the curb valve and the main shutoff valve. This will drain the water out of the pipes to the level of the lowest fixture. With the faucets open, drain the hot water tank. Be sure that the hot water heater is turned off. Faucets must be kept open when draining the tank, or a partial vacuum will form inside the tank and prevent complete drainage. Drain the hot water tank by means of the valve located at the bottom of the tank. You will have to dispose of the water issuing from the tank, and you can do so by connecting a length of garden hose to the valve so that the water flows out of the basement, or by having a few pails on hand. Remove all the water from the coils of the water heater. It may be necessary to remove a section of pipe and use air pressure to blow the water completely out of the coils.

**Cold Water System.** With the hot water system completely drained, move on to the cold water supply. If the shutoff valve inside the house is provided with a drain cock, the system is easily drained. With all faucets opened, open the drain cock and allow the water to flow into buckets. If there is no drain cock, it will be necessary to disconnect a section of pipe at the lowest point in the system. You will need a stillson wrench for this. Have the faucets on the line closed while the pipes are being disconnected, to pre-

vent a minor flood. After the pipes are apart, place a bucket under the break and open the faucets.

Make a careful check of any horizontal sections of pipe to be sure that there is sufficient pitch to the pipe for drainage. If water remains in a horizontal section, you will have to disconnect a section of pipe and force the water out of the line with air pressure.

It is not necessary to drain the plumbing system when closing a house for the summer, but the main shutoff valve should be closed to prevent any loss of water through leaky faucets.

**Pumping System.** If the house is supplied with water by means of a pump and pressure tank, great care should be taken to remove all the water from pump, tank, and connecting lines. There is a special valve at the end of the pipe running from the pump to the well or spring. This valve prevents water from draining out of the pipe into the well and must be forced open to empty this section of pipe.

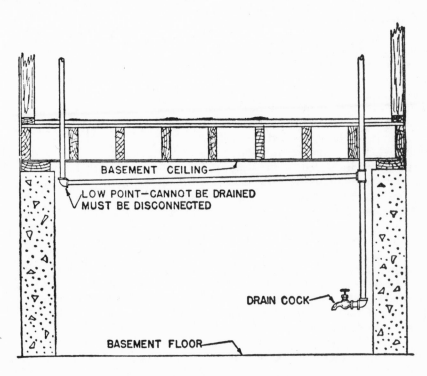

**Traps.** The traps for all fixtures should be drained and filled with some nonfreezing and nonevaporating liquid, such as kerosine. The traps under kitchen sinks and washbasins can be easily drained by removing the clean-out plug at the bottom of the trap and allowing the water to flow into a bucket. Replace the plug and pour several pints of kerosine slowly down the drain. Do not pour too rapidly, or the momentum of the liquid may force some of it out of the trap. After the trap has been filled, see that there is no leak around the clean-out plug.

Toilet traps can be partially cleared of water by flushing the toilet after the water supply has been turned off. The water that remains at the bottom of the bowl can be bailed out with a small container and a sponge. The trap should then be filled with kerosine.

Bathtub traps are difficult to get at unless there is an opening at the floor level. A good way to fill any bathtub trap is to slowly pour kerosine a few inches from the drain in the tub; the kerosine will flow into the trap and replace any water there. The main trap in the basement can be filled with kerosine by pouring a considerable quantity down a fixture located near the main trap. The kerosine will flow into the trap and replace the water as it did in the bathtub trap.

It is very important to fill a trap with kerosine after it has been drained. If this is not done, sewer gas can enter the house.

Water meters are sealed by the water company to prevent tampering with them. If there is no provision made for draining the meter without breaking this seal, contact the water company and have them send someone to do the necessary work on the meter.

**Heating System.** Steam and hot-water heating systems must be drained if the house is to be closed during the winter, or if, for any reason, the heating system must be shut down during freezing weather.

The fire in the furnace must be out before the system is drained. Close the main shutoff valve and open the drain valve located at the bottom of the boiler. If possible, connect a length of hose to the drain to carry the water to a floor drain or out of doors. If this cannot be done, have buckets on hand. Open the water supply valve to drain this line to the boiler. Open all the valves on the radiators in order to drain them and their connecting lines. This must also be done on a steam system, as there will be some moisture in the radiators from the condensed steam.

## Turning On Water

When the time comes to turn on the water, refer to the check list made when draining the system. Check the entire plumbing carefully to be sure that everything has been connected and that all the pipes are sound. Close all the branch valves and open the main valve and curb valve. If the system appears to be in good condition, open one branch valve at a time. Make certain that each branch line is in good working order before opening another valve. Do this carefully and there should be no difficulty. Do not open valves until you are sure that the system is performing satisfactorily.

# FROZEN PIPES

No attempt should be made to thaw frozen pipes until they have been thoroughly inspected for cracks or splits. A pipe will crack when the water inside freezes—not during the thawing process. If there are any cracks, they should be repaired or a section of pipe replaced before thawing begins. Until the necessary repairs have been made on a cracked pipe, keep it shut off from the water supply and no great amount of damage will be done if it thaws unaided.

The fact that the water inside a pipe is frozen does not necessarily mean that the pipe has split, but it is best to assume that the pipe is defective until proven otherwise by a close inspection.

If the pipe appears to be sound, open all faucets connected to it. This is done to decrease the pressure in the line, should there be an undetected opening. Thawing should begin at the point nearest a faucet, to allow the water to run out.

**Thawing.** There are various ways of applying heat to the frozen pipe. Bath towels, dipped in hot water and applied to the pipe, are an efficient and safe means of thawing, if there are no decorations or painted woodwork that might be damaged.

A blowtorch can also be used, provided there are no inflammable objects about. Play the blowtorch back and forth along the length of pipe, and avoid concentrating too much heat at one point. A heat lamp is also excellent for thawing the pipe.

Frozen drainpipes can be thawed by pouring hot water down the drain or by using chemicals which generate heat inside the pipe. Pour the chemicals down a drain in the same manner as that used for chemical drain cleaners. A very good method of thawing drain lines is to insert a length of small-diameter rubber tubing in the pipe until the end comes in contact with the ice. Attach the other end of the tubing to the spout of a teakettle containing boiling water. The steam from the kettle will flow through the tubing and soon melt the ice.

**Preventing Pipes from Freezing.** When it is impractical to set a pipe far enough below ground or otherwise protect it from freezing in cold weather, the best way to keep it open is to use an electric heating cable. These come in various lengths and are simply wrapped around the pipe. They have a built-in thermostat which will regulate the flow of electricity into the cable so that it will be warm only when required. These units are not expensive, and they can also be used to prevent ice from forming in gutters or along the eaves of the roof.

## Plastic Pipe

This is a relatively new material and is ideally suited for amateur plumbing projects such as running a line to a garden pool, outside hydrant, and so forth. Plastic pipe comes in several sizes and in rolls up to 100′ in length. It is not damaged by freezing, and therefore an outdoor line does not have to be set below frost line or drained, unless it must be kept open during cold weather. Plastic pipe is suitable for all types of cold water installations, but only special types can be used for hot water lines.

It requires practically no skill and no special tools to work with plastic pipe. It can be cut to the required length with a saw—even a hacksaw will do. Sections of the plastic pipe are joined together with special plastic fittings secured to the pipe with stainless-steel hose clamps that are tightened with a screwdriver. There are also special fittings, designed so that the plastic pipe can be connected into the existing plumbing system, whether it be copper tubing or galvanized iron. Plastic pipe, along with fittings, is available at most plumbing supply stores and at many hardware stores, as well as from mail-order houses.

# 9

# ELECTRICITY

In order to insure that all electrical household appliances operate efficiently, to avoid costly repairs of these appliances, and to be able to make minor repairs and additions to the electrical system, it is essential that every homeowner have some basic understanding of electricity and electric wiring in the home.

There are three key words to the understanding of electricity: volt, amp, and watt.

"Volt" is used to indicate electrical pressure in the line. This is similar in some respects to measuring the pressure of water in a pipe as so many pounds per-square inch. The fact that there is pressure in the pipe does not mean that the water is flowing—and the same holds true for electrical pressure. Most of the electrical equipment in the house operates on 120 volts, but some of the larger units, such as a kitchen range, hot water heater, electric heating equipment, or certain air conditioners, require 240 volts. Equipment designed for 240 volts won't operate on 120 volts; and 240 volts will burn out equipment designed for only 120 volts.

"Amp" is the unit used to measure the rate of flow of electrical current. It can be compared with the term "gallon per second," used for measuring the flow of water through a pipe. It takes voltage

(pressure) and amperage (rate of flow) to produce electric power.

"Watt" is the unit used to measure the amount of work that a given amount of electrical energy can do in a given amount of time. The number of watts is determined by multiplying the volts by the amps. On every appliance there will be a plate that specifies the number of watts required for that particular item. If there is an insufficient number of watts, the device will not operate properly.

In every house there are just so many watts available for use; if you try to use more than there are, you'll have trouble. The number of watts available depends on the capacity of the *service entrance*. This is the line from the utility company that comes into the house. In some older houses the service entrance may have a total capacity of only 30 amps with 120 volts. This means that the total number of watts available in the house is only 3,600 (30 $\times$ 120). In other cases there will be a 100-amp service entrance. Houses built in recent years usually have a service entrance of 150 or 200 amps and with a third wire can provide either 120 volts or 240 volts, depending on the needs of a particular appliance. A point to remember, of course, is that if your house has only 120 volts, you cannot use equipment that operates on

240 volts until you have had the size of the service entrance increased and had a third wire brought in from the utility pole.

The service entrance consists of a main switch, meter, and distribution panel which contains either fuses or circuit breakers. The main switch, usually a knife-type switch, controls all flow of electricity through the house. When this

switch is pulled, such as might be required in case of fire or when major repairs to the wiring system are to be made, there won't be any current flowing into the house system.

From the main switch the current flows through wires into the meter, which measures the flow so that you can be billed, and from there to the distribution panel. Here the power is distributed into individual circuits that go to various parts of the house. The capacity of each of these circuits depends on the size of the wire used for it. The heavier the wire, the more watts the circuit can handle.

Each of these circuits is protected by a fuse or, in newer systems, by a circuit breaker. If there is any trouble on a circuit due to an overload or a short, the fuse or circuit breaker will blow and cut off the current to that particular circuit without affecting the other circuits in the system.

There are several types of circuits.

**General-Purpose Circuits.** These are intended for lighting and for small appliances such as radios, TV sets, clocks, and other equipment that does not take many watts. They are designed to handle 15 or 20 amps, and this will be the capacity of the fuse or circuit breaker that protects the circuit. If you were to plug in too many appliances on one of these circuits or plug in a heavy piece of equipment such as an air conditioner, the fuse or circuit breaker would blow and cut off the flow of current.

**Appliance Circuits.** These are usually run to the kitchen, laundry, and other areas where heavy appliances such as toasters, coffeemakers, irons, and so forth, are used. Any heating appliance requires a good many watts, and therefore these circuits must be designed to handle more current than the general-purpose circuits.

**Individual Circuits.** These are used for heavy-duty equipment such as a kitchen range, hot water heater, water pump, or oil burner. Each circuit serves only one piece of equipment.

## Fuses

It's a good idea to familiarize yourself with the fuse box or circuit breaker panel, so that if and when there is any trouble you will be able to deal with it easily.

The most common type of fuse is the screw-in type. These have a little strip of

metal in back of a transparent window on the top of the fuse. If there is a short circuit or overload on the line, the heat generated will melt this strip of metal, and the fuse is then blown. You can easily spot a blown fuse of this type because the metal is visible.

The capacity of a fuse is measured in amps. Each fuse has its capacity stamped on the end or on the face. It's very important never to use a fuse larger than the capacity of the circuit. If you do, it is like tying down the safety valve on a steam engine; if there is trouble in the wiring, the fuse will not blow in time and you may end up with a fire. If you have any doubt as to what capacity of fuse to use on a particular circuit, consult your local power company or a local electrician.

In many rental units, a tamperproof fuse is used. This is somewhat similar to a screw-in fuse, except that it is so designed that only a fuse of the same number of amps can be used as replacement. This prevents someone using a larger fuse than he should simply to allow use of heavier-duty equipment.

There are also multiple fuses which contain several elements. When one blows, the fuse can be turned to a new element and the bother of replacing the fuse is avoided. And there are delayed-action fuses which are handy under certain circumstances. For example, when a motor-driven appliance starts, it requires a good deal more current than when it is already operating. Sometimes this quick demand for current will blow the fuse. The delayed-action fuse is designed to allow this overload for a few seconds.

It's a good idea to make a chart show-ing the location of each fuse in the fuse box, and the rooms and fixtures it controls. To do this, turn off one fuse at a time, with all the lights in the house on, and have someone call down to you when a particular area goes dark. Paste the chart on or near the fuse box for future reference.

One special type of fuse found in the house is the cartridge fuse used for the main power supply and for some of the heavy-duty equipment. These clip into place.

## Circuit Breakers

These have replaced the fuse box in new construction, except for the main fuses and some used for heavy-duty equipment. The circuit breaker works on the same general principle as a fuse; but instead of blowing, the little switch for each circuit goes from "on" to "off." As soon as the trouble has been corrected, the switch can be flicked to "on" and will remain there. If there is still trouble, it will jump back to the "off" position. You don't need any spares for a circuit breaker, but you should keep some of the cartridge fuses around for the main lines and special-equipment circuits.

## Why Fuses Blow

A fuse or a circuit breaker will blow for a couple of good reasons. One is that there is a short circuit on the line, due perhaps to a faulty cord or piece of equipment. When a short circuit occurs, there is a demand for more current, the wires start heating up, and the fuse or circuit breaker blows to protect them. Until the trouble has been located and corrected, the circuit will not function; and if a new fuse is installed, it too will blow. Another reason for a fuse blowing is overloading a circuit —plugging in more appliances that de-

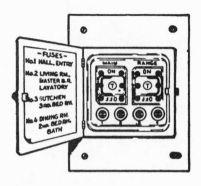

mand more watts than the circuit is designed to handle.

When a fuse does blow, the first thing to do is try and find the cause. If you have just plugged in a piece of equipment such as a toaster or iron, the trouble may be an overload. Or it may be a frayed lamp cord or a piece of faulty equipment. In any event, you must find the cause and either remove it or correct it. Only after that should you change the fuse.

**Overloaded Circuits.** Overloading a circuit means trying to get more current out of it than it is capable of producing. Often this results in a blown fuse—but sometimes it just means that the equipment won't operate properly and may eventually be damaged, requiring extensive repairs. This is particularly true of motor-driven appliances. However, a TV set may fail to operate properly just because it isn't getting enough juice.

The way to prevent overloading a circuit is to know its capacity and then never try to plug in more equipment than it can handle easily. For example, a circuit with a 15-amp fuse and 120 volts can produce 1,800 watts. This means that the combined wattage of all equipment plugged into that circuit that is in use at the same time should not total over 1,800. If it does, either the fuse will blow or the equipment will not operate properly. You'll find the wattage stamped on every piece of electrical equipment, so it is an easy matter to find out what the total on a particular circuit will be. And you'll be surprised at how many watts certain types of equipment require. For example, a TV set may only take about 250 watts, while a toaster will take over 1,000 and a portable electric heater possibly more than 1,500. If you must use all the equipment at one time and you find that it will overload a particular circuit, arrange to put some of it on another circuit that is not carrying its capacity. For example, if the circuit in the kitchen is close to being overloaded, plug the toaster or coffeemaker into a circuit in the living room or dining room.

## Safety with Electricity

There are some people who are terrified of household electricity and will remain for hours in a dark house rather than change a fuse. And there are others who treat it in a cavalier manner as if it could not harm a flea. The fact of the matter is that if you are careful and know what you are doing, you won't get hurt changing a fuse or doing other electrical repair jobs; on the other hand, if you handle electricity the wrong way, it can give you a nasty shock or even kill you. But so for that matter can a car, a boat, or a gun.

Rule number one in handling electrical equipment is: never handle it at all if there is current flowing through it. If you have to change a fuse, pull the main switch, so that if your hand should slip you won't get a shock. When you make simple repairs, pull the main switch, or unscrew the branch circuit fuse or flick the circuit breaker to "off."

Never handle electrical equipment with wet hands or when standing on a wet or damp floor. Be particularly careful not to place electrical equipment in the bathroom or kitchen close to any fixture such as sink, washbasin, or bathtub that might be touched at the same time you are in contact with the electrical device. The reason for this is that unless the device is grounded you might receive a shock, which under certain conditions could be fatal. To understand how this can occur, it's necessary to know a little about the house wiring.

In most houses there is a 2-wire 120-volt system serving most electrical outlets. One wire is covered with black insulation; this is the "hot" wire—the one that has current passing through it. The other wire is covered with white insulation; this is the "ground" wire. At some point in the system this wire is connected to a water pipe or metal rod driven into the earth to provide a good ground. The outlet boxes for electrical outlets, fixtures, and switches are also grounded, either by the metal covering on the wiring or, in the case of plastic house wiring, by a third wire in the cable. If all connections are firm and secure, any short circuit or failure in the wiring or equipment should produce a blown fuse. There are, however, many situations where a short circuit can occur and the fuse will not blow.

If some of the insulation on the interior wires of an appliance becomes frayed or if moisture gets inside, the outside of the device will become "hot"; and if some-

one touches it—especially if he is also touching a metal fixture or has wet hands —he will act as a ground and receive a shock.

This condition can be avoided by grounding the piece of equipment. If the equipment is independently grounded, any current that should flow into the portion that might be touched will either flow harmlessly to the ground or cause a short circuit sufficient to blow a fuse. In many newer houses you will notice that the outlet sockets contain 3 rather than 2 holes. The third hole is for a ground; if an appliance with a 3-prong plug is used, it will be automatically grounded. Most power tools, such as electric drills, saws, and hedge trimmers, have this 3-prong grounded plug. You can adapt this kind of plug to an ordinary 2-hole outlet with a special adapter which has a ground wire. The ground wire should be secured to the setscrew that holds the plate of the outlet socket to the outlet box. If this connection is secure, the appliance will be properly grounded.

Equipment such as a washing machine, portable dishwasher, clothes dryer, or similar item that is not permanently connected into the house plumbing system with metal pipe (copper or galvanized steel) should also be grounded. This can be done by fastening a length of No. 12 wire—it need not be covered with insulation—to the frame of the appliance and then securing it to a nearby pipe with a metal clamp made for this purpose. It's important to clean the surface where the wire and clamp are attached so that a good electrical contact will be made. Wipe away any grease or oil with a solvent and brighten the metal with steel wool or sandpaper to remove any rust or corrosion.

## Extension Cords

There are three basic types of extension cords used in the home. The most common and most familiar is the rubber- or plastic-coated lamp cord, sometimes called a rip cord. These are used for lamps, radios, clocks, and other light-duty appliances. They are made of No. 18 wire and have a total capacity of not much more than 7 amps with a maximum length of 25'. This means that they should never be used where the total wattage of equipment plugged into them is over 800.

For heavier-duty heating appliances such as toasters, waffle irons, and portable heaters, a special appliance cord is required. The most familiar has an outside covering of fabric with an inner layer of insulation, but the more modern type has a plastic outside coating. Never use a lamp cord in place of these appliance cords; it will not be able to handle the load, and either the appliance won't work properly or the wire will overheat and cause a short circuit or even a fire.

Heavy-duty cords have a plastic or rubber covering and are made of No. 14 wire. These are used as outside extension cords for portable electric grass trimmers, lawnmowers, power saws, and so forth. They have the 3-prong grounding plug. The exact size of cord required depends on its length and the number of amps required by the equipment to be used with it.

The life of any cord can be extended through proper use. When you want to remove a cord plug, pull the plug out rather than pull on the cord. Never place a cord where it will be subject to abrasion, such as under a rug or carpet or along the threshold of a door. Don't run cords around sharp edges or equipment, for this can break the insulation. Also, don't allow them to be overheated from pipes or radiators; this dries out the insulation and makes it brittle so that it cracks easily.

When the insulation on a cord is damaged, the cord should be replaced. Do not try to splice the cord.

## Replacing Cord Plugs

Much of today's electrical equipment, including lamps, small kitchen appliances, and radios, comes with a plug that is an intergral part of the cord. Such plugs are very sturdy and seldom give trouble; but when they do, they must be cut off and discarded, for there is no way they can be reconnected. For plastic and rubber rip cords, there are screwless plugs and other outlets available. These require no tools to install other than a knife so that the end of the cord can be cut clean. They should be used only on light-duty lines. When this type of plug cannot be used because of the size or type of cord, the screw-type plug is used.

To fasten a rip cord to a screw-type plug, slip the cord through the hole in the plug, then separate the 2 wires for a couple of inches. Tie them in an "underwriter's" knot. This will help prevent the wires from being pulled loose from the screws in the plug when and if someone pulls on the cord rather than on the plug. The knot must be tight enough so that it

UNDERWRITER'S KNOT

will fit in the recess provided for it inside the plug. Remove about 1/2" of the insulation for each of the 2 wires; try not to cut through the thin strands that make up the wire itself. For each wire, twist the strands together so that there are no loose strands, and then bring each of the wires around its screw. The wires should go around the screws in the same direction that the screws are turned to tighten them. Most plugs contain a little fiber cover which can be fitted over the prongs of the plug to cover the terminal screws, thereby pre-

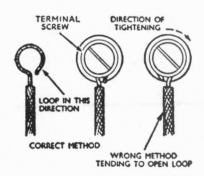
TERMINAL SCREW    DIRECTION OF TIGHTENING
LOOP IN THIS DIRECTION
CORRECT METHOD
WRONG METHOD TENDING TO OPEN LOOP

venting a short circuit should one of the wires come loose or should a stray strand of wire make contact with the outlet box.

Plugs used on appliance cords and heavy-duty cords should be the type with an extension so that they can be easily pulled out by hand.

Most kitchen appliances need a special type of female plug that is used to connect the cord to the appliance. There is a great variation in size and design of these plugs. When one breaks you should

ASBESTOS INSULATION
BROUGHT UP TO TERMINAL CLIPS

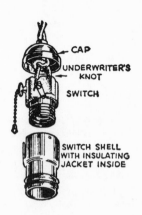

take it to a hardware or electrical supply store so you'll be sure to get one that is identical with the old one. The illustration shows the method used to attach wires to a new plug. When connecting cords with this type of plug to appliances, first insert the appliance into the plug and then fit the wall plug into the outlet. This procedure can save you work because if you do things the other way around, there may be some arcing when you insert the female plug into the appliance. This can pit or corrode the contact points so that in time there won't be a satisfactory electical connection between plug and appliance. The prongs of the plug will then have to be cleaned with sandpaper.

## Lamp Sockets

These often require removal, either to replace the lamp cord because it has become worn or a longer one is required or because the switch mechanism inside the socket has failed. The old-time lamp sockets were pretty durable, but the new ones are not; whether the switch inside is operated by a pull chain, push bar, or key, they all fail very quickly. If you have trouble of this sort, you can put a feedthrough switch in the cord so that the lamp can be turned off and on by this rather than by the switching mechanism inside.

When removing a lamp socket, the socket must be disassembled before the wires can be disconnected. The cap of the socket is usually secured to a threaded

metal bar in the lamp or, in the case of a ceiling or wall fixture, a bar secured to the outlet box. Sometimes you can make the necessary connections without removing the cap, but in other cases it will be necessary. The cap is held secure with a little setscrew. The shell of the socket is removed by pushing down on it where it fits into the cap. On most sockets this spot is indicated by the word "push." By pressing down at this point with your finger or a screwdriver, you can detach the shell and the fiber insulation jacket inside it from the cap. Remove the wires and replace them with a new cord—or replace the switch inside, if that is the cause of the problem.

## Feedthrough Switch

This is a handy little device to use on lightweight cords where the fixture has no switch in it or, as mentioned above, where you want to save wear and tear on a lamp socket switch. A feedthrough switch is designed to stop the flow of current through only one wire, the other wire bypassing the switching mechanism. Where plastic rip cord is used, feedthrough switches are available with screwless connectors. But in any event, the basic installation is the same regardless of type of switch used. Select a location for the switch that is con-

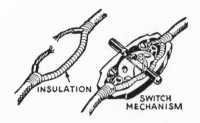

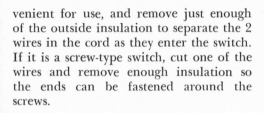

INSULATION  SWITCH MECHANISM

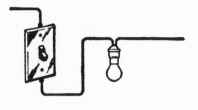

venient for use, and remove just enough of the outside insulation to separate the 2 wires in the cord as they enter the switch. If it is a screw-type switch, cut one of the wires and remove enough insulation so the ends can be fastened around the screws.

## Electric Wall Switches

There are two basic types of wall switches in the average house: the single-pole switch that controls lights from one point, and the 3-way switch used to control lights or outlets from two points. Occasionally a switch will fail and must be replaced. This is not a difficult job. Wall switches are available at most hardware and electrical goods stores. The best type are the silent mercury switches, but they are also more expensive than the ordinary type. In either case, you must be sure that the switch you get is right for the particular situation. A single-pole switch won't work as a replacement for a 3-way switch. And, needless to say, you can't make a 3-way hookup out of a single-switch circuit just by installing a 3-way switch; you also must have the third wire—and this requires a major rewiring job.

The first step in replacing a switch is to turn off the power. If you want to play safe, pull the main switch. First remove the 2 setscrews so you can take off the plate. The switch is secured to the outlet box by two screws; when these are removed, the switch can be pulled out to

the extent of the wires connected to it. Loosen the terminal screws on the switch so the wires can be disconnected, then connect them to the new switch. The black-covered wire should go to the brass screw on the switch, and the white wire to the silver screw. Make sure that the connections are secure, fit the switch back into place, and install the 2 screws that hold it to the outlet box. There are slotted adjustment holes in the switch so that it can be centered in the box. Finally, replace the cover plate.

With the 3-way switch, the same method applies as for a single-pole switch, except that there are 3 wires rather than just 2. The third wire may be green or it

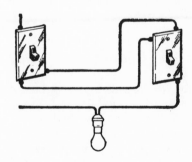

may be white with a black thread running through it. Before you disconnect the wires from the old switch, examine it carefully to see which wire goes to which terminal screw, to be sure that the wires are connected to the new switch in this same order.

## Replacing Wall Outlets

Sometimes a convenience wall outlet will fail. Like a switch, it is not difficult to replace. Turn off the power, remove the single setscrew that holds the plate in position, and then remove the outlet by unscrewing the 2 screws that hold it in the box. You will find 4 terminal screws on

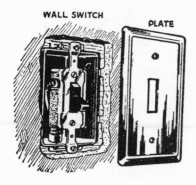

WALL SWITCH          PLATE

these outlets—2 brass and 2 silver. This is in order that certain outlets can be connected together. When installing the new outlet, just be sure that the white wire goes to the silver screw (it doesn't matter which one, if they are both free), and the black to the brass screw.

## Adding Outlets

Few houses have all the electrical outlets required, and usually they are not in the right location. While the ideal remedy for this situation is to have an electrician install additional outlets or move some to another location, this is usually a pretty expensive proposition. What most people do is to use extension cords with multiple-outlet plugs to provide more electrical outlets where required. While this is common practice, it also is somewhat dangerous. Lightweight extension lamp cords can carry only a small amount of current; if too much load is imposed on them they

may overheat. Don't use these extensions for anything other than lights or perhaps a radio, clock, or some other device that runs on very little current.

When the cord is secured to the baseboard or along the floor with nails or staples, there is always the chance of damage to the insulation, resulting in a shock if the exposed wire is touched. If you must use extension cords to increase the efficiency of your electrical system, be extremely careful to set them in such a way that they cannot be damaged. Don't splice wires.

A better way to get more outlets is with a surface extension strip. This is a plastic strip containing relatively heavy-duty wires and outlets which can be positioned along the strip where needed. The strip is plugged into a wall outlet. While it can't produce any more current than the outlet into which it is plugged, it is a lot safer than a lightweight extension cord.

## Replacing Ceiling and Wall Fixtures

How difficult this job will be depends on the type of fixture to be installed and the method that was used to install the old fixture. Some fixtures, such as the porcelain ceiling and wall fixtures often found in the bathroom and kitchen, are secured to the outlet box with 2 long screws. Remove the screws, and the fixture will drop down, exposing the wires. In other cases you will find that the fixture is attached to the outlet box by a strange and amazing assortment of metal fittings, some of which are held together by setscrews and some with threaded connections just like metal pipe. If you run into one of these situations, your best bet is to take the fittings from the box to a good hardware or electrical supply store and have them figure out what you will need to hang the new fixture. There is just no general rule that will cover even a frac-

**WESTERN UNION SPLICE**

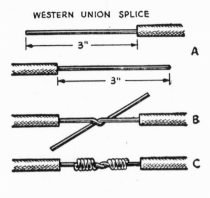

**TOP OR BRANCH SPLICE**

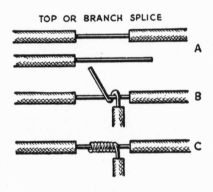

**PIGTAIL SPLICE**

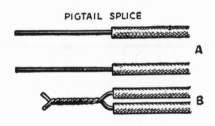

nected from the wires in the outlet box. When the new fixture is installed, the white wire from the fixture should go to the white wire in the outlet box, and the black wire to black wire. Connections should be carefully made so that they are mechanically and electrically sound. If the exposed portions of the wires in the outlet box are soiled from friction tape or discolored, clean them bright with sandpaper. (Never use steel wool when working around electricity.)

Splices in the wires should be carefully made. For fixtures, the pigtail splice is used. After it has been made, it should be soldered for a thorough job and then covered with either several layers of plastic electrical tape or plastic solderless connectors. The latter screw down over the pigtail splice and secure it, as well as insulating the connections.

## Reading a Meter

Electric power is sold by the electric company to the householder at so much for each kilowatt-hour. One kilowatt is equal to 1,000 watts. The amount of current consumed by the household is measured by an electric meter, located outside or in the basement along with the main switch and fuse box. A representative of the power company comes each month to make a reading of this meter, and the homeowner is billed accordingly.

It is sometimes very convenient to know in advance how much the month's electric bill is going to amount to. Anyone can figure this by knowing how to read the meter as well as the rate he is being charged. The way to find what rate you are being charged is to look over your old electric bill. In all probability this is a sliding-scale rate whereby the cost per kilowatt-hour is decreased in relation to the increase in current consumed.

The average home electric meter has 4 dials. As you face the meter, the dial at your right indicates 10 kwh when the nee-

tion of the different situations you can run into—even in the same house—with wall and ceiling fixtures.

The actual wiring of the fixture is not difficult. Naturally you want to turn off the electricity. Don't depend on the wall switch, because someone may turn it on by mistake when you are at work. Either pull the main switch or else unscrew the fuse or open the circuit breaker to the line that you are working on. The wires from the old fixture should be discon-

dle hand makes one complete revolution in a clockwise direction. The second dial registers 100 kwh; this rotates in a counter-clockwise direction. The third dial turns clockwise and registers up to 1,000 kwh. The fourth dial, on the extreme left, rotates counterclockwise and measures up to 10,000 kwh.

The meter is so constructed that the needle on the right-hand dial must make one complete revolution before the needle on the dial to the left of it moves one point. For example, the needle on the 10-kwh dial must go from 0 to 0 before the needle on the 100-kwh dial moves from 0 to 1. Because of this, when you read the meter and find the needle to be between two numbers, take the smaller of the numbers. When the needle is directly on a number, check the dial at the right. If the needle there has not passed 0, use the next lower number.

The correct reading on the meter shown in the illustration would be 1874.

To calculate the amount of electric power consumed since the last reading, subtract the reading taken previously from the present reading. The difference between these two figures is the amount of power for which you will be billed. When you multiply this figure by the rate you are being charged, the result will be the amount of your bill to the time of this reading.

## Motors

In the average home there are a number of electric motors of varying size used to operate the oil burner, refrigerator, freezer, forced-warm-air furnace, vacuum cleaner, and so forth. You can avoid costly repairs as well as inconvenience if you take the time to keep these motors in good working order.

Motors, and the vents in the housing (covering) around them, should be cleaned from time to time. A motor needs

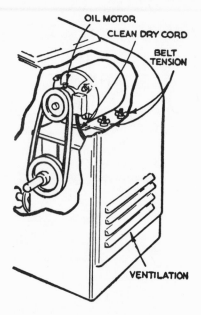

a supply of fresh air to keep from over-heating; if it is covered with a heavy accumulation of dust, it can burn out. Use a vacuum cleaner for this job where possible. The wand attachment is good for getting into louvers and other hard-to-reach spots.

Motors should also be wiped clean of grease and oil, for these can become a fire hazard. Use a nonflammable cleaning fluid for this job—never gasoline, benzine, naphtha, or similar flammable liquids.

Check the condition of the belt on belt-driven equipment to see that it is not worn, frayed, or out of alignment. This is particularly important in the case of a belt-driven blower on a forced-warm-air furnace; for a faulty belt can make for a noisy system, and if it fails you'll be out of heat. If the belt does not appear to be in first-class condition, replace it.

Some motors require oiling, and some have sealed bearings and don't need it. You can usually tell if a motor requires oil because there will be a little oil tube with a hinged cap on it at one or both bearings. It is best to follow the manufacturer's directions as to the grade of oil to be used and the frequency, but if these instructions are not available, use a No. 20 oil (on large motors such as for pumps or oil burners) and supply it once or at the most twice a year. Add the oil a few drops at a time to the cup; don't let it overflow, for it will get into the motor and cause trouble.

Some types of motors are equipped with carbon brushes, and these may become worn in time. These brushes are usually installed under spring tension in a housing covered with a plastic cap. Check the brushes from time to time and replace if they appear worn.

## Appliance Care, Repair, and Servicing

Most appliances today, both small and large, are made in such a fashion that when something goes wrong with them they require the services of an expert to repair. You can, however, save money by keeping the equipment in good condition and by making sure that it is the fault of the equipment and not something else before you call in a serviceman, keeping house calls to a minimum.

When small appliances such as toasters, coffeemakers, or irons do not work,

the fault may be that the switch is not on; that the circuit into which the appliance is plugged is dead because of a blown fuse or circuit breaker; or that the cord is faulty. Check all these possibilities before you decide that the appliance is out of order. If it is, take it to a service facility authorized by the manufacturer.

For large appliances such as dishwashers, washing machines, or refrigerators, first check to be sure that the plug is securely set in the outlet. Next check to be sure that the appliance has been switched to the "on" position. Some controls are very sensitive: while the switch may appear to be at the "on" position, it is just a fraction of a point away—in which case the appliance won't operate. Also check to see if the appliance itself is set to operate. Dishwashers, washing machines, dryers, and so forth, often will not work unless the door is securely latched. Next check the fuse or circuit breaker. Only after you have completed these checks should you call for service.

## Signaling System

The home signaling system provides the amateur electrician with an excellent proving ground to test his knowledge and skill in electrical work, without any of the hazards or restricting codes associated with the regular house electrical system. Doorbells, chimes, and buzzers are made to operate on a very low and harmless voltage. The size of wire used on low-voltage signaling systems is No. 18, known also as bell wire or annunciator wire.

The signaling system should, however, be treated with the same respect given to the regular electrical system. Do all installation work as neatly as possible; not only is this good training for future electrical jobs, but locating a short or open circuit in a signaling system is a lengthy and onerous task. Install the system correctly and spare yourself much difficulty.

**Sources of Power.** As doorbells and buzzers are made to operate on lower voltage than the 120 volts used for other electrical equipment, the power for these systems is furnished either by dry cell batteries or by the house current run through a transformer. The number of dry cells required depends upon the voltage required by each piece of equipment, with some allowance made for the voltage drop in the line. A simple doorbell may need only 1½ volts, while a set of door chimes may demand 3 volts or more. When more than 1½ volts are necessary, the batteries should be connected in series. In place of batteries, a transformer can be used.

**Transformer.** A transformer has a high-voltage side and a low-voltage side. Connect the high-voltage side to the house circuit, using wire of same size as that used throughout the 120-volt system.

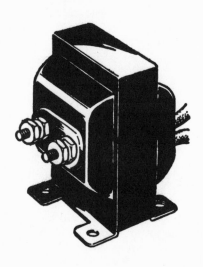

On the low-voltage side of the transformer are 2 or more terminal screws. If there are more than 2 terminals, each will have a different rating to supply power for several pieces of equipment requiring different voltages. The voltage rating at each terminal is clearly indicated by the maker. When connecting equipment to the transformer, be sure that the correct voltage is furnished each piece. If the voltage is too low, the equipment will not operate correctly; if it is too high, the equipment may burn out or the insulation on the wires may catch fire.

A transformer draws current from the house supply only when the circuit of the signaling system is closed. Pressing the button switch will close the circuit; but a short circuit in the wiring will also cause the transformer to draw current. If properly installed and maintained, a transformer will last indefinitely.

Once the transformer has been installed, there should be no reason to test the high-voltage side. All tests should be made on the low-voltage side.

**Vibrating Bells.** One of the most familiar pieces of home signaling equipment is the vibrating bell. It will ring as long as the circuit is closed.

The arrangement consists of a bell, an electromagnet, and an armature, at the end of which is a hammer. When the circuit is closed by pressing the pushbutton, the current flowing through the windings of the electromagnet actuates it, causing an attraction between the magnet and the armature. As the armature is drawn to the magnet, the hammer strikes the bell; at the same time, the armature breaks the circuit on contact with the electromagnet. This causes the armature, which is under slight spring tension, to return to its original position. As the armature returns, the circuit is restored; and the concatenation continues until the circuit is broken by releasing the pushbutton. A buzzer works on the same principle, except that there is no hammer and the sound is not as loud.

There are many kinds of bells, buzzers, and chimes. Choose signals with regard to intensity of sound and location. A single loud bell which can be heard throughout the house is, for example, sometimes more desirable than several soft-toned chimes placed at scattered points in the house.

**Bell Systems.** The wiring circuit for a simple one-bell system includes a source of power (dry cell batteries or a transformer), a pushbutton switch to control the flow of current, a bell or buzzer, and the necessary wiring to complete the circuit. A system of this type can be used at the front door or between the dining room and the kitchen. Install the pushbutton in a suitable location and attach 2 wires to it. One of these wires runs from the button to the source of power, the other runs to one terminal of the bell. Connect a wire between the other terminal of the bell and the second terminal of the battery or transformer. You may attach the wires to the woodwork by means of insulated staples. Avoid using the same staple for both wires. If you can keep the wires a fraction of an inch apart, there will be less chance of a short circuit occurring in the system.

Splices in bell wire do not have to be soldered, but you will make a better system by doing so. Tape splices with friction tape.

The diagram at the upper right shows a 2-bell system with one pushbutton. This arrangement permits multiple installation of signals. such as a buzzer or a set of

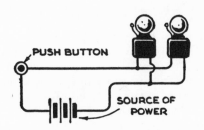

chimes at the front of the house and a bell in the kitchen.

**Annunciator.** An annunciator is a device to register the source of a call, using only one bell. It is so constructed that when the bell rings, a number or letter, indicating the source of the call, comes into view. Annunciators are made to register any number of calls. The wiring diagram shows a circuit in a 4-call system.

**Burglar Alarm.** A simple bell circuit may be installed as a burglar alarm. You can obtain special, concealed switches to fit to door frames and window sashes. If you can lay the wiring in such manner that it cannot be cut, use a simple arrangement like that shown in the accompanying illustration.

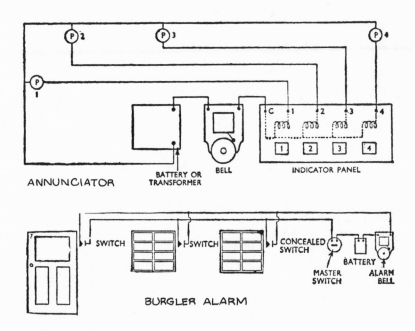

The master switch shown next to the battery is a single-pole switch like that used for ordinary electric lighting, and it puts the alarm system in or out of operation. The drawback of this switch is that, should someone forget to close it at night, the alarm system will not function. To avoid this, use a time switch, which can be set to turn on and off at predetermined times. (In shops or offices, a time switch with a seven-day dial, which makes allowances for different closing times on weekends, can be used.)

If the wire is placed so that any part of it can be cut, use the system shown in the diagram below. In this case the main circuit is normally energized, and the alarm bell is on a secondary circuit which operates only when a break occurs in the main circuit. All the points to be protected are provided with switches of the normally closed type, in contrast with the normally open type shown in the first system. These switches are connected in series with a magnetic relay. In principle, the relay is a switch actuated by an electromagnet. The current flowing in the electromagnet holds the switch contacts in the open position, and as soon as the current is cut off the contacts close under spring tension. These contacts are wired in the secondary circuit and operate the alarm bell.

The current consumption of the relay is very low, but since it must be continuously energized for long periods, it is advisable to use house current reduced by a transformer. Connect the bell with a battery and not with the house circuit, or the whole alarm system can be defeated by deliberate interference with the house current.

## Repair of Signaling System

A signaling system becomes out of order for a number of reasons, and there is a special procedure to be used in checking the equipment which saves much time.

**Power Supply.** When a signaling system fails, check first the source of supply. If the current is furnished by a dry cell battery or by several batteries, test the voltage with a voltmeter, or by means of a bell or buzzer with two short wires attached to the terminals. Place a wire on each of the battery terminals. If there is life in the battery, the bell will ring. Another method of testing dry cells is to connect one wire to a terminal, then touch the second wire lightly to the other terminal. If a slight spark can be seen between the wire and the terminal, the battery is good.

Some electricians test dry cells with the tongue. Place the tongue across both terminals. If the battery is alive, you will have a salty taste on the tip of your tongue. Never test a transformer by this method; use a voltmeter or a bell. Be sure that this equipment is placed on the low-

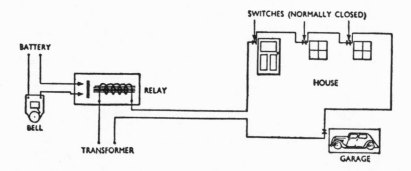

voltage terminals, not on the high-voltage side of the transformer.

**Bell.** If the source of current is satisfactory, check next the ringing mechanism. The best method of doing this is to connect a good dry cell directly to the bell or buzzer. It may be that the armature of the bell is stuck or the adjusting screw on the contact breaker has been moved. If this is unscrewed far enough to leave a gap between the contact points, no current can flow and the bell will not ring. If, on the other hand, it is screwed in too far, the contacts will not part when the armature is drawn to the magnet. Adjust the screw while the pushbutton is depressed, to give the most satisfactory ring. There is usually a locking screw to keep the contact screw in adjustment.

**Pushbutton.** If the bell works correctly when supplied with current from a dry cell, examine the pushbutton.

To test the pushbutton, it is usually necessary to remove it from the mounting and place a piece of metal between the two wires connected to the rear of the button. If the button is causing the system to fail, shorting out with the metal will make the bell ring. A pushbutton will not operate after long, hard use because the contact points become worn or bent.

**Wiring.** Assuming that the bell did not ring when the pushbutton was shorted out, check the wiring for a possible break which would cause an open circuit. In most cases, a break in the wires can be detected by a close visual inspection. If you cannot see the break, however, test out the circuit, by means of a bell with two wires attached to its terminals, at a point near the source of supply. Remove a small portion of the insulation from both circuit wires, and touch the testing bell wires to the exposed parts of the circuit wires. Work back over the entire circuit, testing at intervals. As long as the testing bell rings, the circuit is complete. By this process of elimination, you can narrow the possible locations of the break until you easily find it.

Short circuits occur in bell wiring circuits when two uninsulated wires come in contact with each other. A short circuit will cause a transformer to become overheated, and dry cell batteries to go dead. In some instances, it will cause the bell to ring continuously. Disconnect one of the wires from the source of power immediately and do not connect it again until the short circuit has been found and eliminated. Check the pushbutton as a possible cause of continuous ringing. Dirt inside the button assembly will often cause it to stick in a closed position.

# 10

# INTERIOR REPAIRS

## FLOORS

The floors in most homes are composed of two separate layers. The bottom layer is called the subflooring and is made of rough, tongued and grooved lumber nailed directly to the floor joists. In some cases the subflooring will run diagonally to the joists, and in others it will run at right angles to them. A layer of building paper covers the subfloor to keep out dust and dirt, and the finish, or hardwood, floor is laid over this. The finish floor runs at right angles to the subfloor and is nailed to it. The finish floor can be either of planks or of hardwood.

### Creaking Floors

In most cases, a creaking floor is caused by a loosening of the nails holding the subfloor to the joists. These may either pull loose or be loosened by shrinkage in the wood. Creaking is usually in the subfloor but it will sometimes occur in the finish floor, particularly if the floor was put down before the wood was completely seasoned. If the creak is in the subflooring and the underside is exposed, as when the flooring functions as the ceiling for an unfinished basement, drive a small wedge between the joist and the loose board. This

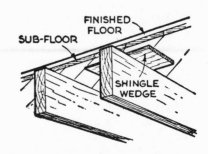

will take up the play in the board and the noise will stop.

If several boards are loose, nail a piece of wood to the joist, high enough to prevent these boards from moving down. The nail heads in the flooring will keep the boards from moving up, effectively ending the noise.

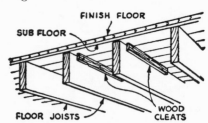

In many cases, it is impossible to reach the subflooring without tearing up the finish floor or moving a ceiling. As neither of these is feasible, the only alternative is to try to locate the floor joist by tapping on the floor. If a floor joist near the creak can be located, then 2″ or 3″ finishing nails can be driven through the finish floor and subfloor into the joist.

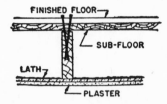

Drive the nail at an angle and when it is near the surface of the floor, use a nail set to drive it below the surface of the wood. This will prevent hitting the finish floor with the hammer and marring the finish. Make the nail inconspicuous by filling the hole with putty and applying a little paint or stain to match the rest of the floor.

Occasionally a creaking floor will be caused by a loose board in the finish floor. The board can be located by its movement when weight is placed upon it. Use 2″ finishing nails for this and drive them in at an angle, using the nail set in the manner described above. It is often possible to take the creak out of a finish floor by putting a little wood glue on a putty knife and running the blade between the boards.

When boards in the finish floor warp to such an extent that they pull away from the subfloor and bulge, they can sometimes be driven back into place by putting a piece of heavy paper and a block of wood over them, and tapping the wood sharply with a hammer. The piece of wood prevents the hammer from damaging the flooring. Take care in doing this, however, as the thin edges of tongued and grooved boards can easily be split.

## Sagging Floors

When this condition is found in a very old house, it is generally because the floor joists and girders have been weakened by rot or by insects. In a new house, a weak floor can, in most cases, be blamed directly on the builder. A flooring built of undersized materials and tacked together will be neither substantial nor capable of bearing much weight.

In dealing with a weak and sagging floor, you will first have to raise it to its proper level. If it is the first floor, with a basement underneath, the work is in the range of the home mechanic. Use heavy lumber and a screw jack to accomplish the work. The size of the lumber should be

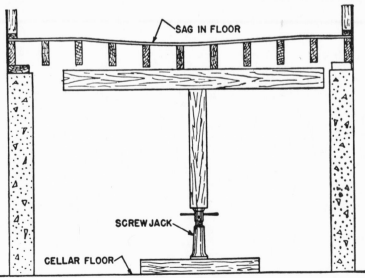

about 4″ × 4″. Place one of these timbers on the basement floor directly under the sag and put the screw jack on top of it. This beam will distribute the weight of the flooring over a relatively large portion of the basement flooring. (If the basement flooring is of heavy concrete, this step will not be required.) Nail a piece of 4″ × 4″ timber along the sagging joists. Use a third piece of timber as a vertical beam from the top of the jack to the under portion of the 4″ × 4″ timber nailed to the joists. Turn up the jack until the floor is level. Do not attempt to bring the floor to a level position all at once. If this is done, you are almost sure to crack the plaster walls and ceiling in the room above. Raise the jack only a fraction each week, and you will avoid doing extensive damage to the rooms above. Check the position of the floor with a level and when it is correct, measure the distance from the bottom of the horizontal 4 × 4 to the floor of the basement. Cut a piece of 4 × 4 to this length. Turn the jack up enough to allow this beam to stand on end under the horizontal timber. Make sure that it is perfectly vertical and that it rests firmly on the floor. Remove the jack, along with the other timbers, leaving only one vertical and one horizontal timber. If one entire floor is sagging, it will probably be necessary to use more than one vertical support. In this case, place a vertical timber under each end of the horizontal beam.

Another means of raising a floor is to use metal posts with screw jacks built into them. The post is provided with 2 plates, one of which rests on the basement floor and the other fits between the top of the post and the joist or girder to be raised. These posts are made so that they can be adjusted to different heights. Once the floor has been brought to the right level, the post can be left as a permanent support. As before, turn the jack only a small amount each week, so that the floor will be raised slowly.

**Footing.** When part of the total weight of a floor and the objects on it are

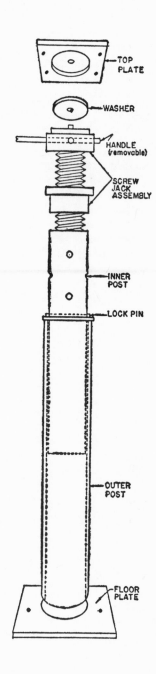

supported by posts, it is important that each post have the proper footing. Most concrete floors in the basement are rather thin and it is often necessary to prepare the floor before installing the posts.

To make a substantial footing for the posts in the basement floor, break up about 2 square feet of the concrete floor at the point where the post is to stand. Do this work with a heavy hammer (don't ruin a good claw hammer on it), or with a piece of pipe. Once the surface is broken, dig a hole about 12″ deep and fill it with concrete made with 1 part cement, 2 parts sand, and 3 parts coarse aggregate. Level this with the floor, making a smooth surface, and allow about a week for the footing to dry before placing the posts upon it. Cover the concrete during this period and keep it moist.

Fortunately, most defects are associated with the first floor, and the basement underneath allows one to put in posts and other kinds of reinforcements. Sagging floors above the first floor level cannot practicably be remedied, short of taking up the flooring and making extensive repairs. The services of a good carpenter are recommended for this job.

## Cracks in Floors

If the wood in a matched hardwood floor is properly seasoned, very few cracks should appear between the boards. Many houses, however, are equipped with plank floors in which cracks of varying size are almost sure to appear between the boards. In very old houses these cracks can be quite large. There are several kinds of plastic fillers, but many of these tend to shrink and crack as they dry. A good filler can be made of sawdust and wood glue mixed into a paste. If possible, the sawdust should be of the same wood as the flooring.

Before attempting to fill a crack, clean it out, for any dirt in it will prevent the filler from adhering to the wood. Pack

the filler in tightly, so that it stands slightly higher than the surface of the floor. After it is dry, sand the top to the floor level and apply a little stain to match the finish on the rest of the floor.

For very wide cracks glue a thin strip of wood into the crack and sand or plane it to match the floor surface.

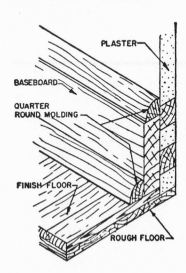

Cracks where the baseboard meets the floor or the wall may be repaired using quarter round molding.

## Other Defects and Repairs

Wooden floors become uneven through much wear, and leave high places, particularly where knots and heads of nails occur, since these possess a greater resistance to wear. Unevenness from another cause occasionally takes place along the edges of the floorboards, which become raised due to the boards curling up as they warp. If the underlying joists warp and twist, or if there is some settlement of the foundation walls on which these joists rest, the level of the floor may be disturbed.

**Replacing Worn Boards.** First study the accompanying diagram of a single wooden plank floor. The joists are usually 2" wide. The boards, which cross the

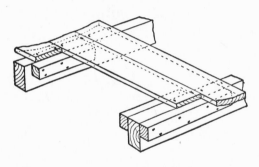

joists at right angles, are nailed at the center line of the joist. If the ends of 2 boards meet in the form of a heading joint on one joist, both boards must be nailed to the joist. To remove the boards without damage is not easy; but on the assumption that one board is to be discarded, in any case, we can bore a round hole as near as convenient to the side of the joist, and use a keyhole saw and compass saw to cut one board close up to the joists. If the other end of the board runs to a heading joint on another joist, work back along the board, prying it up at the intervening joists and taking it off the joist where it ends.

Perhaps only part of the lifted board is defective, in which event we can cut it across to end on a suitable joist, ready for replacement later. In prying up the board, the nails will most likely be pulled up out of the joist; rest the board, bottom side up, on a stool or sawhorse, and tap the nails back sufficiently for the heads to be gripped by pincers, or by the claws of the hammer. Obstinate boards may have to have the nails punched fully down into the joist to free the board. If a heading joint is not conveniently near, the board may have to be cut through at 2 places to remove the defective boards. Electricians and carpenters often use a special floorboard saw, with a curved cutting edge; it is possible to saw straight across one board without damaging the boards at either side. The handyman, however, will generally bore a ½" hole and cut across the board using a keyhole saw.

Find the run of the joists. The position of the nailheads will indicate this, and on the assumption that they mark approximately the middle line of the joist, measure an inch to either side of the nail, and square a line across with a square. Mark a penciled line. Put a fine brad awl through the board about a quarter of an inch away from the pencil line, on the free side, then bore a hole with a brace and bit or with a twist drill. If these dimensions have been correctly established, the joist will be visible and the saw can be put through to cut alongside the joist, across the board.

As soon as the cut is long enough, take out the keyhole saw and enter a compass saw, or a small crosscut saw, and complete the cut.

Beware of water pipes, gas lines, and electric cables when cutting the boards; they run usually in the space between joists. When there is a room below the floor where you are working, some guide to pipes, cables, and so on, can be secured from the position of lighting and plumbing fixtures in the room below.

Having cut the board, the ends of the fixed parts can be trimmed with a sharp chisel to a square edge. If several boards have to be cut away, take them back to joists one or two away to right or left from the one originally selected for the patch. In other words, break the joints, so that a board extending over a given joist is next to one at which a board ends, and

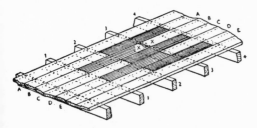

so on. Thus we shall not get a weak line of joints running along the same joist. A typical job is shown in the diagram; the joists are numbered and the floorboards lettered. A heading joint is shown at X,X, on board B. It is not always practical to make heading joints when replacing the boards, and the best thing to do is to support the ends of the replacement boards by nailing or screwing a strong cleat to the side of the joist where the end of the new board will rest. The cleat should be at least 1½″ thick and about 3″ wide; take it halfway along and under the boards adjoining the one that it will support. This arrangement is illustrated on page 232.

Two boards can be cut through obliquely, when they have to be joined over a single joist. In this instance it is assumed that both boards can be taken to the bench and cut by a tenon saw to a suitable angle. This makes a neat and sound job, the nails being driven through the oblique portion. The angle can be marked across the edges of the board with an adjustable bevel.

**Leveling a Worn Floor.** Sweep the floor, and brush out the cracks with a stiff brush. (A wire brush is excellent for the purpose.) Scrub down the floor and let it dry well before beginning operations. Then go along the boards with a hammer

and nail punch, driving down the nails well below the surface so that they will not damage the sharp cutting edge of the plane. Set the smoothing plane to make a medium cut and work over the high places. Follow the grain, and if the wood tears, change the direction of the planing. In bad cases a broad chisel may be convenient for removing the worst part. Next, reset the plane to make a finer cut; trim the edges of the boards and take off irregularities.

After new flooring has been laid, it may be found that the ends stand higher than the old floor; punch down the nails, and taper off the end part of the new board so as to make a gradual change. Of course, in order to make a really good job, the replacement boards ought to be reduced in thickness to match the older flooring, though often this may not be practicable.

**Parquet and Wood Block Floors.** Loose blocks in a floor, if there are not many, should be removed. It will then be possible to scrape off the old mastic underneath. Put in fresh mastic, which you can get at hardware stores, and bed in the block. If the defect is extensive, the repairs may be more than an amateur can successfully undertake.

Parquet floors are glued and, invariably, pinned; dampness may cause the parts of the design to come loose, and in such cases the cause of the dampness should be found before attempting a remedy. Wood glue can be used to hold the different parts of a pattern together if a whole unit is defective. These diamond shapes and so forth are bedded upon a piece of low-quality material with an open weave, which helps to hold them together. It will probably be best to unite the various parts of an element first, and let the glue harden, before re-laying, so as to ensure that all joints are firmly set and safe to handle.

**Opening a Floor.** Quite often the home mechanic is faced with the task of opening a floor to repair a water line or heating main running under the floor. If the floor is made of planks, this job can be done with the same directions as those given for replacing worn floorboards. If the flooring is made with tongued-and-grooved boards, the job is somewhat more complicated because the tongue of one board is fitted into the groove of the next, and any attempt to pry up a board would result in damage to either the tongue or the groove. It is quite true that in some cases the boards are so badly shrunk that there are large spaces between boards, allowing one to be lifted out without damage to the others, but this is the exception more than the general rule. The most practical way to lift one or more boards and not damage any of the flooring is as follows.

The first thing to do is to make a hole through the board at the tongue side so that a sharp-pointed compass or keyhole saw can be inserted to saw away the

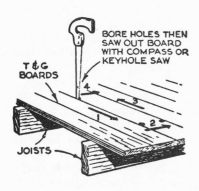

BORE HOLES THEN SAW OUT BOARD WITH COMPASS OR KEYHOLE SAW

T & G BOARDS

JOISTS

tongue. This hole can be made with a brace and bit or with a sharp chisel. Make the hole as close to one of the floor joists as possible, as you will need some method of nailing the board back in place. This can be done by spiking a cleat to the side of the joist, as when replacing a worn floorboard. Once the hole has been made, take the saw and start cutting up the length of the board. Be sure to saw straight and remove only the tongue of the board. When you have sawed from

one joist to another, cut across the board at each end as close to the joist as you can. Slip a chisel into any one of the cuts, and the board can be lifted out.

When one board has been removed, as many as needed can be lifted out by cutting them along the joists. When you are ready to put the flooring back, nail wood cleats to the side of each joist and use these to support the ends of the boards and as a base on which to nail the boards. Use finishing nails for this work and punch the heads below the wood surface, filling the resulting hole with plastic wood and staining to match the finish on the floor.

## Resilient Floors

These can be asphalt, vinyl-asbestos, vinyl, rubber, cork, or linoleum. Some are laid as tile; others, such as linoleum and vinyl, may be tile or large sheets. They are cemented to the subfloor with a special mastic.

The first rule in maintaining a resilient type of floor is never to flood it with water, because if some of the water gets down through the seams it may loosen the mastic and the material will come loose. Also, never use any harsh cleaners, as they can damage the flooring. Use only mild household detergents and warm water in limited amounts for cleaning.

The best type of cleaner to use on these floors is one recommended by the manufacturer of the floor materials.

The appearance of these floors can be maintained by coating them with wax. A thin, hard coating of wax not only prevents dirt being ground into the flooring but also makes a surface that is easy to wipe clean with a damp mop. There are two types of popular floor wax—the self-polishing wax and polishing wax. The self-polishing wax comes in liquid form and is the easiest to apply. But is does not stand up as long as the polishing wax, which must be buffed after it is applied.

Polishing wax contains solvents and is not suitable for certain flooring such as asphalt and rubber tile; use only water-thinned self-polishing wax for these.

Either type of wax must be applied in a thin even coat. If too much wax is applied, it will never dry hard and will readily absorb dirt and be difficult to wipe clean.

From time to time certain so-called "miracle" products are offered that are claimed to put an end to floor polishing and floor care. Don't fall for these products because they not only don't do any good but may ruin the floor. Flooring experts all agree that the way to keep a floor in good shape is to clean and wax it properly.

**Asphalt and Rubber Tile.** These can be cleaned with warm water and a household detergent, or with a special cleaner for asphalt tile floors. Stains that don't respond to the cleaning agent can be removed by rubbing with fine steel wool. Take the time to get the floor perfectly clean and after it is dry, apply a self-polishing floor wax. Do not use a polishing wax or a wax containing a solvent, because it will ruin the tile.

**Cork Tile.** This should not be cleaned with water, which is harmful to the tile. Instead, use a prepared cleaning agent recommended for cork floors. If dirt has been ground into the tile, it may be necessary to buff with fine steel wool to get the color back. The best way to do this is with an electric floor waxer with steel-wool buffing pads. Once the floor is clean, coat it with a polishing wax—do not use a water-base self-polishing wax on cork.

**Linoleum, Vinyl, and Vinyl-Asbestos.** Clean with water and a detergent or a prepared cleaning agent recommended for the material. Use either a polishing or self-polishing wax.

If linoleum or vinyl sheet flooring comes loose at the seams, take a knife with a flexible blade and scrape out as much of the hard mastic from under the loose area as you can. Apply fresh mastic or lino-leum cement to the underside of the material and force it back into place. Wipe off any excess cement that comes out around the seam and put a weight on the material to hold it down until the cement or mastic is hard.

This same method can be used with individual tiles that become loose. Take the tile up, scrape off the old mastic from the underside of the tile and the base, and recement.

If a piece of tile becomes damaged or badly stained, it can be removed and replaced with a fresh tile. Several methods are used to remove the damaged tile without harming the adjoining ones. Asphalt and vinyl-asbestos tile can be softened with heat so that they can be removed. Use a heat lamp for this purpose rather than a torch. A hot steam iron with a piece of damp cloth under it to protect the tile can also be used. As the tile becomes soft it will often curl up at the edges so that it can be lifted out or eased out with the aid of a putty knife.

On other kinds of tile, dry ice will sometimes do the job. Place the ice on the tile and let it remain until the tile is thoroughly chilled. Then drive a chisel into the center of the tile and pry up. If this fails, break the tile into small sections with the chisel.

Once the tile has been removed, scrape away the old mastic from the subflooring, apply fresh mastic and set the new tile in place. Immediately remove any of the mastic that may appear around the seams.

## Carpets

Every carpet should have an underlay, not only to give the carpet a softer tread but also to improve its wearing qualities and prolong its life.

Regular cleaning is also essential. If small hard grains of dirt are allowed to become embedded in the fabric, they will eventually cut the fabric apart. Carpets should be vacuumed once a day unless they get little if any use. A carpet sweeper may also be used but it's not as effective as a vacuum cleaner, especially if a vibrating brush attachment is used on the vacuum. It is also a good idea to give the carpet a very complete vacuuming about once each week, working over the carpet half a dozen times or so. Never beat or shake a rug or carpet, as this can damage the binding.

When a rug or carpet becomes soiled, it should be cleaned. If it is not too large and is of the washable variety, this can be done in the large washing machines at automatic laundry centers or by a firm specializing in rug cleaning. For large carpets or wall-to-wall carpeting, use one of the carpet-cleaning shampoos available at hardware stores and supermarkets.

# WINDOWS AND DOORS

Windows are classified as double-hung and casement. The double-hung window is made up of two parts, an upper and a lower sash, which slide vertically past one another. On a casement window the sash is attached to the frame by hinges and, depending on the style of the unit, will swing out or swing up or down.

The frames of the majority of windows in the home are made of wood or aluminum. In a few houses and especially in apartments, steel window frames are sometimes used.

## Wood Double-Hung Windows

Most window problems occur with the old-fashioned double-hung window. One of the most common is that the sash sticks so that it can't be moved to open the window. This condition frequently occurs during very humid weather because the sash absorbs moisture and the wood swells. But it can also be due to accumulations of paint getting into the joint where the sash fits into the window frame. When a sash sticks, don't try to force it open by pushing or by pulling hard on the horizontal rails of the sash because you might pull them loose. Also do not try to pry the

DOUBLE-HUNG

CASEMENT

window up from the inside by inserting a screwdriver or chisel under the bottom rail of the sash because you will scar the paint on the sash as well as the window-sill. Your first attempt at freeing the sash should be to take a putty knife and insert it into the seam between the edge of the sash and the inner guide and run it down the entire length of the sash. This will cut through any accumulation of paint that may be holding the sash so that it can't be moved. As you run the knife down the seam, pull the handle out slightly so that the blade will pry the outer guide away from the sash. A paint seal can also sometimes be broken by taking a piece of scrap wood, holding it on the side of the sash close to the guide, and tapping it with a hammer. Move the block of wood up and down the height of the sash.

You may also sometimes get a sash to move by prying it up from the outside. A good tool for this purpose is a hatchet. Insert the blade between the bottom rail of the sash and the sill and drive the hatchet in with a hammer.

If you can get the sash to move, take a piece of sandpaper and remove as much of the excess paint as you can from the groove in the frame where the sash runs up and down. It also helps make the sash move more easily if you lubricate this surface. Ordinary candle wax will do, but one of the silicone lubricants available in spray cans is superior and easier to apply.

When the above methods fail to help, you can find out what is causing the trouble and correct it by taking the sash out of the frame. This is done by removing one or perhaps both of the inner guide strips that hold the sash in the frame. These thin strips of wood are fastened to the frame with either wood screws or finishing nails. If nails are used, pry the strip off very gently by inserting a wood chisel under it and forcing the strip away from the frame. Once one or both strips have been removed, the sash can be pulled out of the frame, but first see if it moves. If it doesn't the trouble may be that paint has accumulated between the strips and the sash or that the strips were set too close to the sash. Pull the sash out and inspect the sides. Use sandpaper to remove any accumulations of paint from the edges of the sash and the groove in the frame. Test the sash by putting it back in the frame. If it still doesn't move easily, chances are that the sash has absorbed moisture and the wood has expanded slightly. In this case, sand down the edges slightly. Don't use a wood plane for this job because you may take off too much wood so that when the sash dries out, it will fit too loosely in the frame.

The edges of the sash should never be painted, since this will make them extremely hard to move. But the wood should be sealed so that it won't absorb moisture. A wood preservative is good for this purpose as is a light coating of linseed oil.

**Replacing Broken Sash Cords.** The newer type of double-hung wood windows use springs and friction devices to hold the sash in the desired open position, but in the older window units sash cord or sash chains and weights are used to hold the sash in place. Often one of the cords or chains will break and must be replaced if the window unit is to function properly. This procedure is not a difficult one and it is wise, while you're at it, to replace all the old weight cords with new ones, preferably of the chain type, as the chances are that if one cord has broken, the others are more than likely to break in the near future. And it is almost as easy to replace all the cords in a window unit as it is to replace one.

This work is done from the room side of the sash. First, remove the inner guide strip from one side of the frame. Once this is out of the way you can remove the lower sash from the frame. Next, remove the parting strip that separates the lower sash from the upper sash. This, like the guide strip, is held in place either with finishing nails or with wood screws. With this out of the way, the upper sash may be

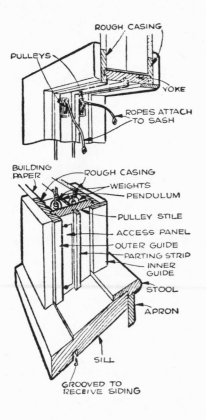

ROUGH CASING
PULLEYS
YOKE
ROPES ATTACH TO SASH

BUILDING PAPER
ROUGH CASING
WEIGHTS
PENDULUM
PULLEY STILE
ACCESS PANEL
OUTER GUIDE
PARTING STRIP
INNER GUIDE
STOOL
APRON
SILL
GROOVED TO RECEIVE SIDING

clips provided for this purpose. Set the sash in the frame and check its movement by watching the weight through the access. When the upper sash is up, the bottom of the weight should not be touching the bottom of the frame, and when the lower sash is down, the weight should not hit the pulley. Make the necessary adjustments and then replace the units.

**Rattling Windows.** This occurs when a sash fits too loosely in the frame. A simple remedy is to apply weatherstripping around the sash to hold it firmly in place. A more satisfactory remedy is to remove both the inner guides and move them a little closer to the sash, but this has to be done with care in order not to get them so close that the sash can't be moved.

## Metal Double-Hung Windows

When the sash units on these windows don't move easily, it usually means that there is dirt in the groove where the sash moves or that lubricating is in order. Wipe the groove out with a cloth and then spray with a silicone lubricant.

## Casement Windows

Most of these units, whether they are of aluminum, wood, or steel, are opened and closed by means of a geared mechanism with a crank that fits on the inside of the window. Attached to the gear mechanism is an arm that is fastened to the sash. All these exposed moving parts should be kept free of paint and dirt if the sash is to be opened and closed easily. Points where moving metal parts come together require lubricating. The gears inside the crank unit also require lubricating for ease of operating. Use one of the silicone spray lubricants on exposed moving metal parts. For the gears, clean out the old grease and dirt with kerosine and then coat the gears with a nonstaining grease. Other points on these units that need to be lubricated

removed from the frame. At the bottom of each side of the frame you'll find a little panel; when this is removed you can reach in and remove the weights. The access panel is held in place with wood screws. You may need to use a putty knife to pry the cover off after taking out the screws. Take out the weights and disconnect the old cord from them. Feed the new cord or chain over the pulley and down into the pocket and connect it to the weight. Be careful not to let the cord or chain run through the pulley for its entire length and fall into the pocket.

Put the weights back into the pocket and then attach the other end of the cord or chain to the sash. Hold the sash in its closed position in the frame so that you can determine the approximate length of the cord or chain. Cut it to this length and fasten it to the sash with a knot or

to keep the sash working freely are the hinges. A graphite lubricant is good for this purpose.

Wood casement windows must be sealed to prevent the wood from absorbing moisture and swelling, as this will make them stick. Either paint or a clear wood sealer can be used. Steel casement windows give the most trouble of all, because if they are not protected by paint, they will rust.

## Screens

To be completely effective, window and door screens must fit tightly in the frame so that there is no crack around the edges that might allow insects to get into the house. If there are such cracks, seal them with masking tape or caulking compound.

If holes are punched through the screening, they should be repaired or, better still, new screening installed. Screening used today is made of either fiber glass or aluminum. Fiber-glass screening can be patched by cutting a piece of screening somewhat larger than the opening and cementing it in place with a waterproof household cement. For aluminum and other types of metal screening, prepare a patch of the same metal as the screen is made of (or purchase it at your hardware or variety store). Take a piece of screening 2″ larger than the hole and strip off

some of the cross wires. Bend down the projecting wires to 90 degrees and put the patch in place so that the projecting wires go right through the screening. Then bend them over on the opposite side to hold the patch in place.

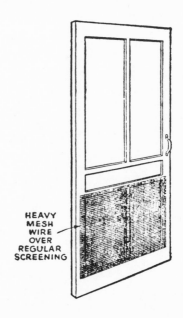

HEAVY
MESH
WIRE
OVER
REGULAR
SCREENING

The illustration shows how the lower section of a screen door, which is particularly subject to damage, may be protected.

**Replacing Screening.** On metal window-screen frames of the type used for combination screens and storm windows, the screening is held into a groove of the frame with a metal or plastic spline. This can be removed by prying it up with a screwdriver. Once the old screening is out of the way, it's a simple matter to set the new screening in place. Set one end and secure it by replacing the spline. Now pull the screening so that it is tight and put in the spline at the bottom of the frame. Now do the sides. After all four sides are secure, trim off the excess screening with a utility knife. This knife will cut aluminum as well as the fiber-glass type of screening. The same method can be used on metal screen doors.

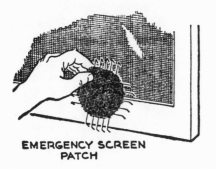

EMERGENCY SCREEN
PATCH

On older houses, wood-frame screens are often found. These are somewhat more difficult to repair because they are generally larger than the metal-frame screens and the screening must be fastened in place with tacks or staples.

To remove the old screening, take off the strip of molding nailed around the edges of the screen which cover the tacks or staples holding the screen in place. Pry these strips off with a wood chisel, being careful not to break them. When you have removed them, pull out the nails or staples. If the screen frame is well built, you can save time on this operation by removing a few of the fasteners from one corner and then giving the screening a good hard pull. With luck it will come off, pulling most of the tacks or staples along with it.

When attaching the screening, start at one end and tack or staple it, holding the material tightly as you nail. Then, hand-stretch the screening along the side, working toward the other end, and attach it, making sure that the weave is parallel to the ends and sides. Finally, fasten the sides and apply the molding. Another method which works well, if there's any doubt in your mind that you won't be able to stretch the screening evenly, is to place the sash on two sawhorses, attach the screening at one end, and then place weights of even value on the sash at the center. This will bow the sash a trifle. Now lightly stretch the screening and attach it at the other end. Remove the weights, which brings the sash back to normal, and attach the screening to the sides. Be careful not to bend the sash too much, otherwise it may stretch the screening too tightly, causing it to tear away or hold the sash in a bowed position.

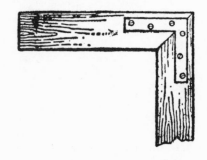

If the corner joint of a window-screen frame is not tight, it may be held together by a mending plate.

Before aluminum and fiber-glass screening became available, it was common practice to take screens down at the end of the season and store them so that the iron screening would not be exposed to the weather any longer than necessary. But as aluminum and fiber-glass screening do not corrode, the screens can be left up the year around. In fact, there is less danger of harming the screens by leaving them up than taking them down and storing them someplace where they may be damaged.

**Sagging Screen Doors.** A screen door that sags and binds at the bottom may have loose hinges. Tighten the hinge screws, or if this is impossible owing to the condition of the wood, move the hinges to other locations on the door and frame where they can be secured tightly. When the entire frame of the door sags because of poor construction, you can bring it true by using a turnbuckle. It is best to remove the door and place it on some flat surface for this repair. Insert a screw-eye in the flat side of the frame at the upper corner near the top hinge and another screw-eye at the corner diagonally

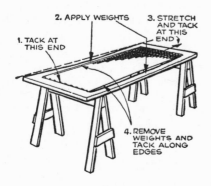

2. APPLY WEIGHTS  3. STRETCH AND TACK AT THIS END
1. TACK AT THIS END
4. REMOVE WEIGHTS AND TACK ALONG EDGES

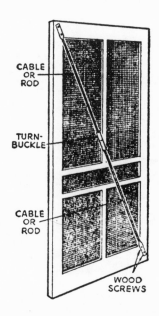

CABLE
OR
ROD

TURN-
BUCKLE

CABLE
OR
ROD

WOOD
SCREWS

opposite. Attach a piece of cable or rod to each screw-eye, and the turnbuckle to the other ends of these rods, so that it is located about halfway between the two screw-eyes. Tighten the turnbuckle, and check the frame by placing a square along the lower corner where the screw-eye is located. Tighten the turnbuckle until the corner of the door is an exact right angle. Replace the door in the frame and make additional adjustments with the turnbuckle so that the door works easily.

Most screen doors are equipped with some sort of device to keep them closed. This may be either a long spring attached to the wall and to the door or a spring-loaded hinge. To prevent a door from slamming, and eventually tearing itself loose, install some kind of door check.

## Weatherstripping

This is used to seal the small cracks around windows and doors. Unless these cracks are sealed, there will be a considerable amount of heat loss in the winter as well as annoying drafts in the house. Weatherstripping is also important if the house is air conditioned in summer, since these same cracks allow hot air from the outside to enter. They also allow dirt and soot to get into the house.

In newer and high-quality homes, doors and windows come with weatherstripping either applied by the builder at the time the house is put up or as part of the window and door unit provided by the manufacturer. In other houses, however, weatherstripping must be added.

There are many types of weatherstripping and all will be effective if applied according to the manufacturer's directions. Some are less expensive than others, some are more attractive, some easier to install, and some last longer. Which one to use depends on how much you want to pay and how much time you want to put into the job.

The least expensive type of weatherstripping is felt, which is tacked into place. It is not very attractive-looking and may last for only a few years, but it does the job. Somewhat more expensive but easier to apply is the foam rubber with an adhesive backing. This can be used on either wood or metal units. The metal-backed felt stripping and the various types of vinyl stripping are good and will give many years of service. There are also various types of metal stripping, some flexible and some rigid. The best type is the metal stripping which can be installed without having to take the window unit or door out of the frame and which will be hardly visible when in place. Metal weatherstripping should last for the life of the house.

## Replacing Broken Glass

This is a common household chore and whether it is a window sash, storm sash, or outside door, the same basic method of work will apply. You will find that it is a good deal easier to replace a pane of glass if you can take the unit out and put it on a bench or table to work on.

**Wood Units.** The first job is to remove the pieces of broken glass. Wear gloves for this and try to remove the pieces in as large sections as possible. Use about the same method as you did as a child with a loose tooth—wiggle the pieces back and forth and they'll eventually pull loose.

Next, the old putty and glazier's points must be removed. Sometimes you can get rid of the putty with a chisel, but often it will be so hard that trying to do the job with a chisel will damage the wood parts of the unit. Hard putty can be

GLAZIER'S POINT

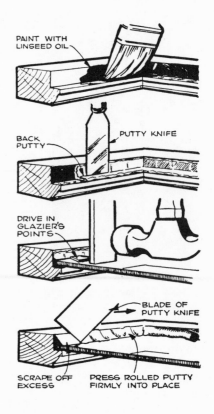

PAINT WITH LINSEED OIL

BACK PUTTY

PUTTY KNIFE

DRIVE IN GLAZIER'S POINTS

BLADE OF PUTTY KNIFE

SCRAPE OFF EXCESS

PRESS ROLLED PUTTY FIRMLY INTO PLACE

softened by holding a hot soldering iron on it. Coating it with a paint remover will also soften it, but naturally this method will damage the surrounding painted surfaces unless you use extreme care in applying the remover. The glazier's points can be pulled out with a pair of pliers or eased out with a screwdriver. Clean out the recess in the frame so that it is completely free of old putty and then coat the exposed wood with linseed oil, or a thin coat of paint. This is important to prevent the wood from absorbing the oils out of the putty or glazing compound.

Glass should always be about 1/8" smaller than the sash opening, to allow for any distortion in the sash which might break the glass (see page 243). Before inserting the glass, apply a thin layer of putty along the faces of the rabbet to form a bed for the glass. This is known as back-puttying and is essential to form a seal between glass and wood, which glass alone won't do. Set in the glass and drive glazier's points into the sash, allowing a projection of about 3/16" to hold the glass securely. For the average-size window glass you should use 2 points on each of the 4

sides. If the wood is relatively soft, the points can be pushed in with the blade of a screwdriver or, if this doesn't work, tap the end of the screwdriver with a hammer. Some points are especially made with a little flange on them so that they can be easily driven with a screwdriver. Turn the unit over after driving in a few of the points to make sure that the glass is in contact with the bed of putty along all edges.

The final step is to apply putty around the edge of the glass over the points. Most people find that the easiest way to do this is to roll the putty into a long string, set it in place and then smooth it out into a triangular shape with a putty knife. It takes a bit of practice before you can produce a smooth job. Allow the putty or glazing compound to dry for a week or so and then paint it. This is important, since unpainted putty will dry out and crack more readily than if it is painted.

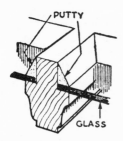

On wood windows you can use either putty or glazing compound to reset a pane of glass. Some prefer putty because they find it easier to work with and others use glazing compound because it works better for them. Take your choice—both do a good job.

After a period of time, some of the putty or compound around window glass will fail. Sometimes it just cracks, but often large sections will fall out. When this occurs, the damaged putty or compound should be removed and fresh applied. To do a first-class job, you should really do an entire glazing job—taking the glass out, removing the old putty, and starting off fresh. But as this can take so much time, most people just replace the putty or compound

**Metal Units.** For these you should not use putty but rather a special glazing compound recommended for metal windows. A special compound is required here to prevent the glass from cracking because of a difference in expansion and contraction between the glass and the metal frame. And although single-strength glass is suitable for wood windows, it's best to use double-strength glass for metal windows.

On some metal sash the glass is held in place with metal clips; on others there are metal strips, held in place with machine screws. The essential point in replacing glass in a metal window is to be

sure that the glass does not come into direct contact with the metal but is protected from it by a layer of the glazing compound.

Many windows today are made with insulating glass. Often it is not practical to have this replaced should it become broken, as the cost of the glass is frequently more than the cost of a new sash unit.

**Cutting Glass.** You can order window glass cut to size at most hardware stores, but sometimes you may find it convenient to cut the glass yourself. This is not difficult to do with an ordinary glass cutter. The same methods used for cutting window glass can also be used for mirrors.

The piece of glass to be cut should be placed on a clean, flat surface and the glass should be wiped with turpentine or kerosine. A glass cutter will not work well on a dirty surface. Place a straightedge on the glass where the cut is to be made and hold it securely with one hand. Dip the wheel of the cutter in turpentine or kero-

sine and then draw it along the line so that the small steel wheel makes a slight scratch in the glass. Do not try to go over the line again or turn the glass over and cut the other side. Only one cut should be necessary and additional cuts will only impair the result. Once the glass has been scored, there are several ways of breaking it along the line. One method is to place the handle of the cutter under the scored line and press down gently on each side.

If the glass has been cut properly, it will break along the line. Another method is to tap on the underside of the line with the handle of the cutter, then break the glass by placing it on the edge of the table and pressing down on the overhanging edge.

### Shades

When a shade will not roll up properly, pull the shade down about two thirds of the way and then take it off the brackets and roll it up by hand. Keep it rolled tightly and replace it in the brackets. If it still fails to roll up properly, repeat this process. If the shade does just the opposite and snaps up to the top when it is raised, raise it to the top and then remove it from the brackets. Now unroll it by hand for about half the length and replace it in the brackets.

Another common shade problem is that the shade doesn't stay put when it is pulled down. This is often because of dirt or the need for a drop of oil in the ratchet mechanism of the shade. Take the shade down and remove the end cap in back of the flat rotating pin. Clean out any dirt and apply some nonstaining lubricant.

Sometimes a shade will not work properly because the brackets that hold it in place are not set far enough apart and are binding the shade roller. Usually you can just bend one or both outward a fraction of an inch to correct the situation. If the brackets are too far apart, the shade

roller will have a tendency to fall out at times. Try bending the brackets in. If this does not solve the problem, remove one bracket and set it a fraction of an inch closer to the opposite bracket.

Window-shade brackets are often secured with small nails, which have a tendency to work loose after a time so that the bracket moves and allows the shade roller to fall out. Replace these nails with wood screws so that the bracket will be held securely.

## WALLS AND CEILINGS

The walls and ceilings of houses built since World War II are usually of gypsum wallboard, whereas those built prior to that time are covered with lath and plaster.

### Gypsum Wallboard

This material is often called by the trade name Sheet Rock or simply wallboard. It is made of a core of gypsum plaster covered with heavy kraft paper. The standard-size sheet is $4' \times 8'$ and the sheets are nailed directly to the wall studding. The joints between sheets are concealed by covering them with paper tape and then smoothing out the joint with several applications of joint cement made for this purpose. The heads of nails are set just a fraction of an inch below the surface and then joint cement is applied over the heads so that they are concealed.

Small holes in gypsum wallboard left by such things as picture-hook nails can be filled with Spackle in the same way as suggested for plaster walls. For large holes, pack some crumpled newspaper into the hole to serve as a base and then apply patching plaster as directed for patching plaster surfaces.

If a large area of the wallboard has been damaged, the best method of repair is to cut it out and put in a patch. To do this you need to cut back the damaged wallboard on each side to the studding. Use a saw and a utility knife for this purpose. Remove the nails on each side that hold the piece to the studding. Take a piece of gypsum board the same size as the opening, put it into place, and nail it to the exposed portions of the studding. Drive the nails so that they dent but do not break the paper covering. To conceal the joints, apply joint cement over them and then take strips of wallboard joint tape and bed them into the cement. Apply a thin coat of cement over the tape, smooth it out, and allow it to dry. When dry, sand lightly and apply two or more coats of cement until you have a perfectly smooth joint. Use the same cement to fill in over the nailheads.

Although gypsum wallboard is not subject to cracking as is plaster, improper application can create special problems. One of these is nail-popping in which the nails will come loose and the heads will appear above the surface of the material. It does not pay to drive the old nail back because it will just pop out again. Remove the nail carefully so as not to dent the surface or mar the paint and then drive in a new nail close to the hole left by the old one. Use a screw-type wallboard nail, since this has greater holding power than an ordinary smooth nail. As you drive the nail into place, push against the board so that it is forced tightly against the wall studding. Fill in over the nailhead with joint cement. When it is dry, sand lightly and touch up with paint.

Another problem that occurs with wallboard is that one or more joints will open up owing to improper application or serious shrinkage or movement of the wall framework. Sometimes a thin coat of joint cement forced into the seams will do the job, but often it's necessary to remove the old tape and cement and start off fresh. Use a broad putty knife to pry off the old tape and be as careful as you can not to damage the wallboard any more than necessary. Clean out the seam between the

two sections of board and then apply a coat of joint cement followed by a strip of tape in the same way as was suggested for applying a large patch. Follow up with enough coats of joint cement over the tape to make a smooth job.

## Plaster

Plaster is applied over lath. In older houses wood lath was used but in newer houses and apartments metal or gypsum board lath serves as a base for the plaster. Plaster is rather easy to repair, fortunately, since even the best jobs will occasionally crack for one reason or another.

Small holes and hairline cracks in plaster can be easily fixed by filling with Spackle—either the prepared type or the dry powder mixed with water before using. The Spackle can be applied with a small putty knife or the finger. When dry, sand lightly and then touch up with paint.

For large cracks and holes up to 2″ in diameter, use a prepared patching plaster rather than Spackle. Patching plaster is sold at paint and hardware stores and is mixed with water for use. Before applying the patch, cut out the crack to remove any loose plaster. A metal beer-can opener is good for this purpose. For a hole, it's best to undercut the edges of the surrounding plaster so that the opening is wider at the bottom than it is at the top. This produces a key which helps hold the patch in place. Remove the loose plaster from the exposed metal or wood lath so that some of the patch can get into the openings to provide additional strength. Wet down the edges of the plaster so that the moisture in the patch won't be absorbed and the patching compound dry too quickly to produce maximum strength. A toy water pistol is good for this job. Mix up the patching plaster according to the directions on the package and apply it with a broad putty knife. Force it into the opening with considerable pressure so that some of it will penetrate through the holes or opening in the lath.

You will find it easier to do a good job on a sizable hole if you apply the patch in two coats. The first coat should come to within about 1/4" of the surface. When this is hard, apply the finish coat and smooth this off level with the surrounding surface.

This same approach can be used on very large holes, but you will find that you can save time as well as patching plaster if you nail a piece of gypsum wallboard into the lath or the wall framework before you apply the patch. The wallboard not only fills up some of the cavity but also makes a good bond with the patching plaster.

Bulging plaster is a condition that occurs in older homes where the plaster has broken loose from the wood lath. If it occurs only in a limited area, the old plaster can be removed so that the lath is exposed and the hole can then be patched with patching plaster. If a large area of the plaster has bulged, as often occurs in very old houses or where there has been a leak so that the plaster has failed from being constantly damp, the best solution is to rip it all off and install gypsum wallboard.

Cracks often occur at the corners of a room where the two plaster wall surfaces join. A good way to fill these and also reinforce the joint so that the crack will not appear again is with a combination of gypsum-board joint cement and gypsum-board tape. Apply the cement to the area so that the crack is filled and the cement extends for 2" or 3" on each of the wall surfaces. Take a strip of gypsum-board tape long enough to run from baseboard to the top of the wall and fold it sharply in half lengthwise. Place the tape into the joint cement and bed it into place with a broad putty knife. Apply another coat of cement over the tape, taking care to produce a good, sharp corner. Let the cement dry, sand lightly, and apply additional coats of cement until the tape is completely concealed.

The use of tape and joint cement is also effective in patching cracks which keep appearing even after they have been covered with patching plaster.

Rough plaster can be made smooth by repeated thin applications of joint cement. Use a wide rectangular trowel and spread the joint cement over the surface in thin coats. Allow a day for each coat to dry before proceeding with the following coat. When the roughness in the plaster has been filled in, sand the final coat of joint cement lightly, and it is then ready for paint or paper.

## Prefinished Plywood

This type of paneling is very durable, and about the only repairs required are filling holes left by picture hooks when pictures are removed, and scratches. Both of these problems can be handled by means of special crayons sold at furniture and hardware stores for repairing minor flaws in furniture finishes. They come in a wide range of wood colors. If the hole in the plywood is large, say 1/4" or more, fill it first with plastic wood and then color the surface of the patch with the crayon.

## Tile

The most common kind of tile used for walls in bathrooms and kitchens is ceramic tile, although in some houses plastic or metal tile is used. The most common problem with all kinds of tile is that now and then one will come loose. Setting the tile back into place is a simple matter. A special tile cement is used for this purpose and is available at hardware stores. Scrape off as much as you can of the old cement from the back of the tile and from the area in the wall where it fits, and then apply the cement to the back of the tile. Only a thin coat is required. Press the tile into place and wipe off any of the excess cement that comes out along the edges.

Do not try to use ordinary cement mortar for resetting tile, even though ceramic tile is often originally set in place with cement mortar. If you do try, the thickness of the mortar will be so great that the tile cannot be pressed flush with the adjoining tile.

The joints between ceramic tile are filled with a white substance called grout. Sometimes some of the grout between the tile will fail. This is especially true of the tile around recessed bathtubs and showers, and this condition can be serious because moisture can get behind the tile and cause damage. Before renewing failing grout, remove all the loose material with a sharp-pointed tool such as an awl. Grout is available from paint, hardware, and masonry supply stores and comes in two forms. One is a cement powder which you mix with water to form a paste. The other type comes in a tube with a nozzle; it is more expensive but takes less time to install.

You will find that the best tool for applying either kind of grout is the finger. Use it to force the grout into the joint and then wipe off the excess from the surface of the tile with a damp cloth.

A cracked or otherwise damaged ceramic tile is not difficult to replace. To remove the tile, first scrape away the grout and then use a cold chisel and a hammer to break off one of the corners. Once a section of the wall in back of the tile is exposed, use an old screwdriver or chisel to pry off the tile, being careful not to damage the adjoining tile. To be sure of getting an exact color match, take a sample of the broken tile with you when you go for a replacement. There is a considerable range of shades in tile—even in the white tile.

The grout between tile on floors often becomes gray from dirt being ground into it. Often the appearance can be improved by bleaching with a household liquid bleach. If this fails, you can scrape out the old grout and replace it with fresh.

Tile surfaces should be cleaned by washing with a detergent and water. Do not use soap on tile, as it leaves a thin film that dulls the appearance.

## HINGES

Of all types of hinges, the butt hinge, used for room doors, cabinets, and furniture, is perhaps the best known. Butt hinges used for room doors have to support much weight, plus the leverage exerted when the door is opened and closed. This type of hinge consists of two plates held together by means of a pin. In most cases, this pin can be removed, so that the 2 plates will come apart; some pins are threaded and must be unscrewed before they can be removed. The plates are sunk

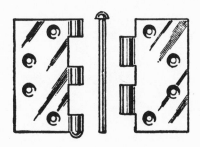

in the edge of the door and into the frame of the door so as to be flush with the surface, or slightly below, with the knuckle of the hinge, through which the pin passes, centered on the crevice between the door and the frame. Examine a door which has been correctly hung and verify these points. It will be seen that the door does not fit closely to the frame, but that there is a regular clearance of about $\frac{1}{16}''$ at the top and the sides. Hinges on room doors are commonly placed about 6″ below the top and 12″ above the bottom of the door, unless there are joints to be cleared.

**Fitting Hinges.** Two hinges are customary for light doors, with 3 for heavier

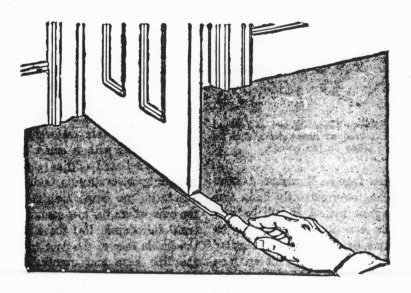

ones such as the front door of a house. In fitting a new door, the worker will need 2 marking gauges and 2 thin wedges. Prop the door against a bench or table with the hinge side up. Mark the top edge of the first hinge 6″ below the top of the door. Lay the hinge in position and carefully scribe around the hinge with a sharp knife, keeping the point close to the edge of the hinge. Gauge for both hinges in this manner. Set the marking gauge to the thickness of the hinge plate. This gives the depth of the recess to be cut, and this depth should be scribed by the gauge along the inside face of the door, for both hinges. With a square, connect the depth line and the end lines.

Using a fine-toothed tenon saw, cut down along the squared lines until the depth line is reached. Use the point of the saw. It will not be possible to go full depth the entire length of the line. Make 2 other similar cuts in between, to facilitate removal of the surplus wood with a chisel. Use a sharp chisel and outline the back margin by accurate cuts, taking care not to go too deep; also, complete the cuts where the saw cannot penetrate full

depth. Use the chisel on the inside face of the door to incise the line here and eventually cut out the waste wood and form the recess. Be very careful at this point not to take out too much wood. When the recess is correctly cut, fit the hinge and, using a brad awl, bore the holes for the screws. Insert the screws and turn them until they are tight and the hinge is secure.

With the first marking gauge, outline the width of the hinge on the inside edge of the door frame at the approximate position (top of hinge 6″ from top of frame plus top clearance, $\frac{1}{16}$″). You will need someone to hold the door in position against the frame, with the hinges opened out and the plates close against the door jamb. Use a wedge under the bottom outer edge of the door to raise it for accurate top clearance. The butts must align with the scribed lines made by the first marking gauge. Use a fine awl or a steel scribe to mark the position for the top and bottom of each wing, or flange, and to confirm the marks scribed by the first gauge.

Remove the door and, with the second marking gauge, scribe the line for the depth of the recess. Cut out the recess, replace the door with wedges beneath, and bore a hole for one screw in one hinge. Insert the screw and repeat the process for the second hinge. Slip out the wedge and test the door gently. It will probably be satisfactory, and the wedges can be replaced until the rest of the screws are inserted and turned down tightly. A mistake can then easily be corrected. A misplaced hole can be plugged with a small piece of hardwood driven in tightly and cut off level with a chisel.

**Sticking Door.** When a door fails to open and close easily, look first at the hinges. It very often happens that some of the screws holding the hinge become loose, causing the entire door to sag and stick against the frame. Try to tighten the screws with a screwdriver. If this fails because the screws will not hold properly in the wood, it may be possible to use longer screws. Another method is to remove all the loose screws and insert wood plugs, which should be glued into the wood frame. These plugs will provide a firm anchorage for the old screws. As a last resort, the position of the hinges can be changed so that the screws will go into sound wood.

The position of the door in the frame can be altered considerably by placing small wedges of cardboard or wood behind the hinge plate attached to the frame.

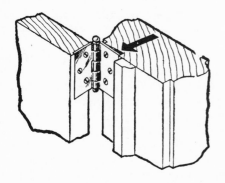

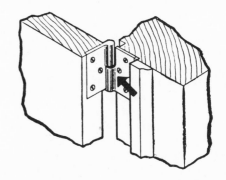

If a door sticks at the bottom, it may be possible to correct this by inserting a washer between the hinge plates.

Cutting out the hinge recess in the door frame so that the front is slightly deeper than the rear will tend to pull the entire door toward the frame jamb.

Not all sticking can be corrected by repositioning the hinges. Sometimes, it is necessary to plane off a portion of the door.

Whether or not it is necessary to remove the door from the frame to do this work will depend on how much wood is to be removed and whence it is to come. If the bottom or outer edge is the cause, the door should be taken down. If the top is to be cut down a little, this can often be done with the door in the frame.

The plates that make up the hinges on most doors are held together by means of a pin, and this can be taken out and the door removed without having to remove the hinges entirely. Free the bottom hinge first, and then the top. When removing the hinges, raise the door with a block or have someone hold it so that the entire weight of the door is not thrown on one hinge.

Before you remove the door, mark carefully the place from which wood is to be removed and plane off only enough to make the door fit easily. When it is necessary to plane an entire side, it is easier to do this on the hinge side rather than remove the lock and latch and then reset them again after the wood has been removed.

Be sure to set the blade of the plane to take off only a small shaving at a time and be very careful not to split the end grain of the door.

**Sagging Garage Doors.** One of the most frequent troubles encountered in the garage is sagging doors. If not given proper attention, a heavy garage door will sag so much that the bottom edge will strike the ground and the door can be opened and closed only with great effort.

The condition can be due to several factors, but the first step in repairing it is to take a block of wood or a wood wedge of some sort and drive it under the edge of the door until the door hangs properly. Now take a large screwdriver and check the screws in the hinges to see if they are loose. Use a heavy-duty screwdriver for this because you will not be able to get sufficient leverage with a small tool to do much good. If the screws can be tightened and appear to be holding, then the chances are that the trouble is over. Should the screws go into place too easily they will not get a tight hold and will soon pull loose again. Either replace them with longer screws or move the hinges so that the screws can be set in solid wood.

If the screws and the hinges appear to be holding well, then the sag is probably in the door itself. This can be fixed without the need of taking the door down. Jack the door up with a wood wedge until it is hanging plumb. Then attach a diagonal brace or a rod and turnbuckle between the upper inside corner and the lower outside corner.

# LOCKS AND LATCHES

There are many different lock designs, but the type most commonly found on interior doors is the mortice lock, recessed into the front edge of the door.

**Adjusting Latch.** When a door is first installed, the latch and the striking plate on the frame are aligned so that the spring latch will slip into the hole in the striking plate when the door is closed. Any subsequent movement of the door will throw the latch out of line with the striking plate and it will strike the metal instead of entering the hole.

In most cases, the latch will leave a mark on the striking plate, and this can be used as a guide in determining how much to move the striking plate so that the latch will slip easily into the hole. If there is only a slight variation between the latch and the plate, it may be possible to move the plate enough by placing a screwdriver against it and tapping it with a hammer. If there is a greater discrepancy between the location of the striking plate and the latch, remove the striking plate and enlarge the hole enough for the latch to fit. This can be done with a metal file. Replace the plate on the frame

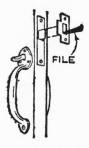

to see whether any wood will have to be removed from under the enlarged striking-plate hole. In some cases, it may be necessary to reposition the striking plate before the latch will catch properly. Remove the striking plate and, using a wood chisel, enlarge the mortice in the frame so that the striking place can be positioned properly. Fill old screw holes with plastic wood or wood pegs to provide a firm base for the new screws.

**Removing Lock.** Occasionally, mortice locks require oiling, or a key will break off inside the lock. It is necessary to remove the lock from the door before any oil can be applied or the broken half of the key removed.

Unscrew the setscrew holding one of the door knobs to the shaft. The shaft and knob may be threaded. If so, you will have to unscrew the knob from the shaft after the setscrew has been removed. Pull the shaft out of the lock by means of the other knob and remove the 2 screws at the face of the lock. With these removed, you can easily pry the lock out of the door with a screwdriver. A setscrew on the side

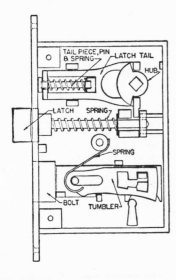

of the lock will have to be taken out to remove the plate. The working parts of the lock are now exposed. If some of the parts inside the lock fall out of position, they can easily be put back in their proper place. Remove the broken portion of the key or apply the oil. Replace the plate and check the operation of the lock to be sure that it works correctly.

**Padlocks.** Padlocks used on doors of garages and other outbuildings should be regularly oiled inside, as they are exposed to rain and damp weather. The moisture inside a lock during the winter will freeze, and this may make the lock impossible to open. Thaw the lock with a small flame

rather than hot water, as the water which leaks inside the lock will soon freeze again.

## BRASS HARDWARE

The brass hardware and other fittings of this nature about the house are usually brought to a high polish during the process of manufacturing and then coated with a clear lacquer to keep them from tarnishing. In time this coat of lacquer will wear off and subsequently the brass will tarnish and become unsightly.

Before the metal can be polished, all the remaining lacquer must be removed from the metal surface. This can be done with a clean cloth and some lacquer thinner—nail polish remover can be used as well as a regular thinner. Go over the metal several times to be sure that all the old lacquer has been removed. After this has been done, the metal should be polished with a cloth and a good brand of metal polish. The next step is to wipe off any oil or grease that may have been left by the polish or from soiled hands. This job should be done with a clean cloth dampened in benzine. Once the article has been wiped down, take great care not to touch it, since this will leave grease spots and will spoil the finish. Be careful also that dust is not allowed to collect on the surface, as this too will spoil the finish. Immediately after wiping, apply a coat of clear lacquer and be sure to cover all the metal surface. Brass hardware such as that used on front doors receives considerable wear, hence it should be given at least 2 coats of lacquer.

Copper articles about the house can be given the same treatment as that used for brass to prevent the need of constant polishing.

**Brass-Plated Hardware.** Many homes are furnished with brass-plated hardware instead of the more expensive solid-brass kind. When the brass plating wears off, the metal underneath may rust unless given a coat of paint. There is no home method of replating the metal with brass. The remaining brass plate should be removed with emery cloth and steel wool. After this, the surface should be treated and painted like any other metal surface. (See chapter 6, page 144.)

## FIRE PREVENTION

Each year many lives are lost and homes destroyed by fires. The home mechanic should take all steps to make his home as fireproof as possible and to see that the proper equipment is on hand for fighting a fire. There is nothing about the house more important than fire prevention.

**Precautions.** Frequent inspection trips should be made throughout the house, from attic to basement, looking for anything that could cause a fire or provide fuel for one that has started. Be on the lookout for faulty electrical equipment, such as appliance cords and heating devices, placed near flammable material.

Do not allow combustible trash to collect in the attic, basement, or closets. Flammable cleaning fluids should never be used indoors. Paint, paint removers, kerosine, and gasoline should never be stored in the house, and never use kerosine or gasoline to start a fire. Burn or throw out oily rags and keep oil mops in the open and away from an open flame. The fire hazards found in the average home number in the hundreds, and every one should be eliminated.

When a fire breaks out in a home, the first thing to do is to get everyone out of the house. If any rooms in the house are isolated from the stairways or other exits, these should be equipped with some type of rope ladder or even a rope tied to a radiator or some other object in the room. Turn in an alarm after everyone is out of the house. You can then turn your attention to bringing the fire under control. It

is true that the first few minutes of a fire are the most important, but it is even more important to clear the house of all persons.

Each member of the household should be warned never to open a door when there is a fire in the house without first checking around the bottom of the door for heat or smoke. Any indication of

overheated air on the other side of a door should be sufficient warning not to open the door.

**Extinguishers.** The type of fire-fighting equipment used depends entirely on the cause of the fire and what materials are burning. Water can be used effectively on burning wood and trash. A large quantity of water will be needed, and needed in a hurry, so it is wise to keep a garden hose connected in the basement or at a nearby outside faucet. A garden hose can deliver enough water to deal with most small fires.

Water should never be used on burning gasoline, cleaning fluid, or kerosine, as it will cause the fire to spread. The best way to combat a fire of this sort is with sand, a heavy cloth, or by using a foam-type fire extinguisher. Any of these will cut off the supply of oxygen to the fire and so kill it.

An electrical fire resulting from failure of a cord or appliance must be treated only with a nonconductor type of extinguisher, such as one containing carbon dioxide or carbon tetrachloride. Water is an excellent conductor of electricity and, if used on an electrical fire, may cause the individual applying water to receive a fatal shock.

Fire extinguishers should be placed where they can be reached quickly, and each member of the household should know their location and how they operate. Inspect or refill extinguishers according to the type and the manufacturer's specifications.

**Fireproofing.** Most homes are far from fireproof, but there are certain steps that the home mechanic can take to prevent a fire from spreading and getting out of control too quickly.

The average frame house is well suited to provide a fire with its prime necessity—a good draft. A fire which starts in the basement draws air from the outside and rushes up through the basement door and between the walls into the upper portion of the house, as though it were a giant fireplace.

The first step in fireproofing a house is to line the ceiling of the basement with some type of fireproof composition board. This can be done easily and at no great expense. Once the woodwork in the basement has been covered, the source of fuel for a fire has been removed.

The second step is to provide a heavy, tight-fitting door between the first floor and the basement. This will not only act as a fire stop and delay the fire's progress to the first floor but will also prevent the draft necessary for the fire to burn vigorously.

The door from the basement to the outside should also be made tight fitting, as this will reduce the amount of air reaching the fire. Remember that a fire must have plenty of fresh air if it is to burn at all.

After you have taken these steps, do not neglect to remove all combustible materials, or place them in fireproof containers.

# STAIRS

## Fixing Creaks

A noise in the staircase usually occurs when the tread, or board on which one steps, pulls loose from the riser, the upright board on which the tread rests. There are two ways of attaching the tread to the riser, nailing them together or fitting them together by means of a tongue and groove.

To eliminate the noise in a flight of stairs where the tread and riser are nailed together, force the tread down until it fits tightly on the riser. Fasten it securely with finishing nails driven through the tread and into the riser. These nails should be about 2″ long and driven down in pairs and at an angle, in such a way that if they were long enough the points would even-

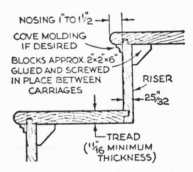

NOSING 1″ TO 1½″
COVE MOLDING IF DESIRED
BLOCKS APPROX. 2″×2″×6″ GLUED AND SCREWED IN PLACE BETWEEN CARRIAGES
RISER
25/32
TREAD (1¹⁄₁₆″ MINIMUM THICKNESS)

tually meet. This will provide greater strength than if they were driven straight down. Be sure that the nails are placed far enough from the edge of the tread for them to enter the riser and not pass in front or behind it. Set the head of the nail below the wood with a nail set and fill the hole with plastic wood.

On stairs where the tongue and groove method of construction is used, the procedure is somewhat different. There is a tongue on the top edge of the riser that fits into a groove along the bottom of the tread. To tighten this joint, it is necessary to remove the molding at the point where the tread and riser meet and drive thin wedges between the tongue and groove to take up any play.

## Basement Stairs

Rickety or poorly proportioned basement stairs constitute one of the chief danger spots in the home so far as bad falls go. In some cases it is possible to repair the stairs satisfactorily with a few well-placed braces, but more often than not the entire structure is in such poor condition that it is easier and better to tear it down and start off fresh, using new and sound lumber.

Unless you possess considerable skill at carpentry, it will pay you in the long run to make the stairs along as simple designs as possible. A flight of basement stairs does not have to be beautiful, but it must be rugged and safe to use.

The illustration shows a flight of stairs which is not only good and solid but also requires only a medium amount of skill to build. The stringers or sides are made of 2″ × 8″ or, better still, 2″ × 10″ lumber. The treads, the part you step on, are made of the same size materials. In the

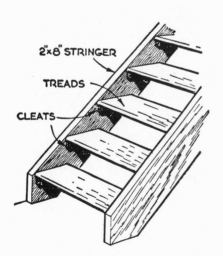

2″x8″ STRINGER

TREADS

CLEATS

interest of simplicity, risers are not used. The treads are attached to the stringers by means of wood cleats made out of 2″ × 2″ lumber. These cleats allow the treads to be nailed at two points. Nails are driven down through the edge of the treads into the cleats and other nails are driven through the stringer into the end of the tread.

The distance between treads should be 7″ or so, as this makes an easy step for the average person. Measure up from the floor 7″ and mark the spot on the stringer. Now measure up another 7″ from this point. Do not measure along the side of the stringer but measure the vertical distance from the location marked for the first tread. Continue to measure and mark the approximate location of each tread until you reach the top of the stringer. In all probability you will find that the distance between the top tread and the first floor of the house will not come out an even 7″ by any means. A slight discrepancy at this top step can be overlooked, but if you are off several inches, work back down, changing the location of each tread just enough until they all are spaced the same distance apart. This may seem like a great deal of trouble just to get the distance to the top tread to equal that between the others, but there is nothing more annoying, or in fact dangerous, than to put out your foot for the top step and not find it where you expected it to be. So take the time to get equal distance between all the treads. Once you have these points marked on one stringer, use it as a guide to mark off the other stringer. Put them together and square the lines across both.

The stringers can be nailed at the top or you can attach them by means of a metal hanger. An easy way to figure out the angle to cut the stringers at the floor is to set them in place and then lay a thin board on the floor alongside them. Draw a pencil line across the width of the stringers where they meet the board, and by cutting along this line the stringer will fit properly at the floor. Some basement stairs are not attached to the floor, but to be on the safe side, cut a piece of lumber, the same size as that used for the treads, so that it just fits between the stringers. Bolt this to the floor between the bottom ends of the stringers and spike the stringers to the board from each side.

Once the stringers are in place, take a level and draw a horizontal line across each stringer where the cleat is to be nailed. Spike on the cleats and then set and nail the treads.

Be sure you put up some sort of handrail when the stairs have been completed. This can be made out of 2″ × 4″ boards, one at top and one at bottom, to serve as posts and a long one running between them for the rail. The top edges of the rail should be planed off so that the surface is rounded and easily gripped by the hand. Give the wood a good sanding so that there will be no chance of splinters.

## HARDWOOD FLOORS

It is not difficult to put down a hardwood floor, provided necessary preparations are made, the new flooring is well seasoned, and the worker does not hurry and plans the work carefully before beginning.

Hardwood floorboards have a tongue on one edge and a groove on the other and are laid so that the tongue fits into the groove. They present a much neater appearance than do ordinary planks, and if the flooring is put down properly and the wood has been seasoned, there will be no cracks between the boards to collect dust and dirt.

Before laying the hardwood flooring, punch all nailheads below the surface of the subflooring. The subflooring should be nailed tightly to the floor joists because when the finish floor is put over it, any squeaks caused by loose subfloorboards will be difficult to eliminate. If there are

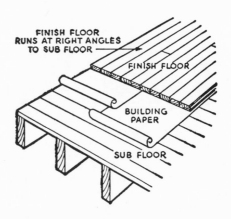

any rough edges on the subflooring, these should be planed. It is not essential that the floor be perfectly smooth, but it should be level.

Remove the baseboard around the walls, as well as the threshold of the doorway. You will probably have to take down the door also, and remove some wood from the bottom to allow for the added height of the new flooring.

Put a layer of heavy building paper over the subfloor and nail the finish floor at right angles to the old floor, rather than in the same direction. Lay the first board about ¼″ from the wall to prevent any possibility of the floor's buckling, which might happen if the boards were nailed flush against the wall. Be sure that the first board is parallel to the wall. This can best be done by means of a cord running from wall to wall. Check the work with this cord from time to time to be sure that all the boards are put down parallel with the walls of the room.

The first row of the new floorboards may be held in place, making certain that ¼″ is left for expansion, by first driving in finishing nails and then using floor nails. Put down the first row with the tongue toward the center of the room and the groove facing the wall. Drive the flooring nails in at a 45-degree angle and begin nailing at the top of the tongue. In this way, the nails are covered by the upper

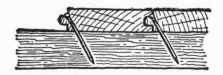

lip of the groove of the following board. Do not attempt to drive the nail all the way in with the hammer, as you are almost sure to strike the tongue and damage it. Use a nail set to finish driving the nails and force the heads down to the surface of the tongue so that the groove of the next board will slip over it easily. Nails should not be more than 9″ apart, and all end joints between boards should be staggered and more than 1′ apart.

To obtain a tight fit between boards and yet not damage the wood, keep a small piece of flooring to use as a buffer between the hammer and the floor. Put the groove of this short piece over the tongue of the board about to be nailed. Drive this board tight against the one already nailed by striking the small piece of wood with a hammer. While nailing each piece of flooring, apply pressure to it by kneeling or standing on it.

## GAS RANGES

The enamel portion of a gas range should not be washed with cold water when the surface is hot. Clean the enamel daily with a cloth and soapy water (do not use a gritty cleaning powder). If this is done, there should not be any thick accumulation of grease requiring scraping or other harsh treatment. Stains that will not respond to soap and water can generally be removed with kerosine. The pilot light should be cleaned from time to time by running a thin piece of wire through the opening.

Burners must be clean if they are to function satisfactorily. The burner can be lifted out of the stove and given a brushing with a stiff brush. It should then be boiled in a solution of 1 tablespoon of sal soda to 2 quarts of water. After boiling, the burner should be washed with clean water and placed in a warm oven to dry. If the burner is put back in the stove with moisture inside, it will not function properly.

**Adjusting Burner.** The operating efficiency of a gas range depends on the proper mixture of air and gas. The amount of gas reaching a burner is controlled by a 6-sided nut located on the gas cock. The volume of air is controlled by

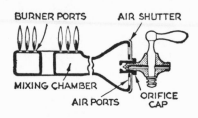

the air shutter on the gas cock. This shutter is held secure with a setscrew. The burner should be lighted when adjustments are being made.

The best flame from a standpoint of heat and gas economy is one with a green cone and darker blue edges. It should be 1½″ high. If the flame is too short, the size can be increased by turning the 6-sided nut. If the flame has a yellow tip, the air shutter should be moved to allow more air to mix with the gas. A flame that sputters and jumps indicates too much air. This is corrected by closing the air shutter enough to make the flame burn steadily with proper height and color.

As soon as the proper flame has been obtained, the setscrew on the air shutter should be tightened to prevent the shutter from being thrown out of adjustment.

# WALL FASTENERS

There are a wide variety of methods as well as devices for fastening objects to walls. The choice depends on the weight of the object to be fastened or hung and on the wall material.

An ordinary picture hook is adequate for hanging lightweight pictures,

PLASTER

mirrors, and other accessories on plaster, gypsum wallboard, plywood, and hardboard wall materials. The best type of picture hook is one that contains 2 or 3 nails rather than a single nail. This type provides more strength than the single-nail hook; moreover, since the nails are smaller in diameter, they leave only a very small hole in the wall material. If an object weighs more than about 35 pounds, it is better to use something more secure than a picture hook.

## Hollow Walls

To hang heavy fixtures on hollow walls, which are the kind usually found inside the house, use either a plastic expansion anchor, a Molly, or a toggle bolt. All of these come in a wide range of sizes and all require a hole to be drilled through the wall. All are so designed that when properly installed, a portion of them that is in back of the wall surface in

the hollow area expands and grips the rear side of the wall material so that they can be pulled out only by taking a section of the wall with them.

Plastic expansion anchors are the least expensive type of fastener and are good for all but very heavy objects. You must first drill a hole into the wall to accommodate the anchor. Slip the anchor into the hole and then insert the screw through the object to be attached. Then insert the screw into the anchor and tighten it with the screwdriver.

The Molly is a patented device which can be used to hang rather heavy objects on hollow walls. The entire unit is slipped into the hole until the flange at the top comes up against the wall surface. The screw in the unit is then tightened; as it is tightened, it pulls the rear of the unit up against the rear of the wall surface. The screw is then removed, put through the object to be fastened, and then put back into the Molly unit and tightened. The great advantage of the Molly over other hollow-wall fasteners is that as the unit remains in place in the wall, the object can be removed whenever necessary for cleaning or other reasons and easily replaced.

Both the plastic expansion anchor and the Molly come with special attachments for hanging pictures and mirrors.

The strongest type of hollow-wall fastener is the toggle bolt. This consists of a long bolt with a winged nut on the end. To fasten an object with a toggle bolt, first drill a hole in the wall. Remove the bolt from the wing assembly and insert it through the proper hole in the object to be hung. Now screw the wing assembly back onto the bolt, fold back the wings, and insert it into the hole in the wall. Tighten the bolt until the object to be secured is pulled tightly against the wall.

Expansion anchors and Mollys require that you drill a hole the exact diameter of the unit or they will not work. With a toggle bolt the hole can be any size so long as it is large enough to accommodate the wings when they are folded back.

How much a toggle bolt or any other kind of hollow-wall fastener will hold depends not only on the size of the unit but also on the strength of the wall; if you hang a very heavy object on a thin gypsum wallboard wall or on plaster that is not in good condition, a whole section of the wall may come loose. If you have a very heavy object to hang, such as a kitchen cabinet, it is best to secure it to the wall studding in back of the wall covering rather than just to the wall covering. The position of the wall studding can often be located by tapping on the wall with your fist. When you tap between studs you will get a hollow sound, but when you tap over a stud there will be a solid sound. There are also little magnet devices that you can buy to locate studding. The magnet is attracted by the nails used to secure the wallboard or lath to the studding. Once you find one stud, you can get the location of the others by measuring, as most studding is set 16″ from center to center.

If the location of the studding is such that it is impractical to fasten the cabinet or other item to one or more studs, install a horizontal length of 1″ × 3″ wood furring between the studs and then secure the fixture to it.

## Solid Masonry Walls

When it is necessary to fasten objects to a solid brick or concrete wall, other types of fasteners are required. For lightweight items such as light fixtures and fireplace accessories, the plastic expansion anchor is suitable. For heavier objects a lead plug or expansion shield is used. These all require a hole to be drilled. The best way to do this is with a masonry carbide-tipped drill in a portable electric drill. The hole can also be made by hand with a tool called a star drill. The tip of this drill is placed where the hole is to be made and then the head of the drill is struck with a hammer. After each blow the drill should be rotated one-quarter turn.

Holes for anchors in solid masonry should be small enough to require a light tap with a hammer to drive the anchor in place. Once it is in place, the screw is inserted into the object and then tightened into the anchor.

The type of anchor to use on concrete and cinder block depends on where the hole is made. If it goes into a solid part of the block, use an anchor for solid masonry; but if the hole hits one of the hollow voids in the block, use a toggle bolt.

**Securing Furring.** When a basement is to be finished off, it is common practice to first install vertical or horizontal lengths of 1″ × 2″ wood furring over the masonry walls to serve as a nailing base for the wall covering. It would be an endless job to drill holes in the masonry so that these wood strips could be secured with standard wall fasteners. If the concrete is not too dense, it may be possible to fasten the furring with special nails which are very tough and can often be driven in without having them bend. When this approach doesn't work, a stud driver can be used which drives a special stud through the wood and into the masonry. One type of driver is hand operated and requires only a heavy hammer to operate it. It costs around $6.00. The other type gets its power from a blank cartridge and will drive a stud into metal as well as masonry. It rents for around $15.00 a day but must be used with great caution because, even though it has many built-in safety features, it is by no means a toy and should be used only by someone experienced with it.

There are also special mastics which can be used to install wood furring and these are effective unless the wall has been painted. They don't work too well on painted walls because, unless the paint film is very secure, it will pull loose along with the mastic.

# FIREPLACE

A fireplace may smoke or fail to burn wood readily for a number of reasons. The fire must be hot enough to produce a good draft up the chimney to ensure against smoking. Wet wood or green wood may just smolder, rather than burn briskly, and this will produce a smoky condition. If the fireplace is used as an incinerator for trash, it is likely to smoke, and smoking will often occur if the fire is laid too close to the fireplace opening. The fire should be laid as far back as possible—the rear log just an inch or so away from the rear of the fireplace.

Many fires smoke just because there isn't enough air in the room to supply adequate oxygen. If the doors and windows in the room where the fireplace is located are kept tightly shut, there just won't be enough air to feed a good fire and it will begin to smolder and smoke.

Smoking is also caused by the damper not being all the way open; it may have become loose so that it can't be opened all the way.

Smoking can also be caused by downdrafts through the chimney. A chimney should extend at least 3′ above the highest point on a flat roof and 2′ above the highest point on a pitched roof. Branches of trees too close to the top of the chimney or even a TV antenna mounted to the chimney can create downdrafts and cause smoking at times.

In some cases the problem is with the fireplace itself. If the proportions of the fireplace opening are not correct, smoking can occur. Often this problem can be corrected by installing a metal hood across the top of the fireplace opening to reduce the height. In other cases it is necessary to install additional firebrick on the sides to reduce the width of the opening. It is best to call in a mason who understands fireplaces to correct the condition, but you can do it yourself by first experimenting to determine what needs to be done. Use some pieces of sheet metal to change the dimensions of the fireplace opening. Build a small fire and move the metal sheets about until you get a good draft and then replace the metal with firebrick set in fireclay.

**Fuels.** The best woods to use in a fireplace are hardwoods such as maple, oak, hickory, and ash. Softwoods such as pine do not produce a very hot fire and this may cause smoking. They also burn quickly and produce a creosote which may form in the chimney and in time cause a chimney fire.

Hard coal makes an excellent fuel for a fireplace. It is less expensive than good hardwood unless you have wood on your property that you can cut yourself. The fire will burn many hours without the need of any attention, and a coal fire produces a lot of heat. You need a coal-burning grate to burn hard coal or cannel coal, which is also good.

You will get a better fire and more heat from either coal or wood if you keep a bed of ashes on the fireplace hearth rather than keep it free of ashes. Do not, however, let the ash bed build up until the andirons are covered because there should be space between them and the ashes to allow circulation of air. If air can't flow under the andirons, they may become overheated and burn out.

**Cleaning the Chimney.** Under ordinary conditions a fireplace chimney does not have to be cleaned unless it becomes thickly coated on the inside with soot. Chemical soot removers are not recommended, as they cause the soot inside the chimney to burn and this can be a fire hazard. In some areas there are professionals who clean chimneys with vacuum equipment. The job can also be done by hand. Seal the fireplace opening with heavy plastic secured to the fireplace around the edges with masking tape. Put a few stones or heavy objects into a burlap bag, fill the bag with straw or excelsior, and lower it down the chimney flue. Bring it up and repeat this process a few times. This will dislodge most of the loose material and soot so that it falls into the fireplace, from which it can be removed.

# CLOSING THE HOUSE

Whenever a house is to be vacated for any length of time, at any season of the year, precautions should be taken so as to be sure that it will be in good condition when the family returns. Many a summer camp or cottage has been seriously damaged during the winter months because windows were left unlocked, thus inviting housebreakers, or chimneys were uncovered, inviting squirrels and other rodents inside the premises. The same holds equally true of winter homes when the family has gone away, leaving the plumbing or heating systems undrained or a back door unlocked. Taking the necessary time to close a house properly will save both grief and money.

Any home that is to be closed during the winter months, for any time whatsoever, should have the plumbing system drained and prepared for freezing weather. (See chapter 8, page 208.) If the house has a water or steam heating system, this too must be drained of all water. These may seem like very obvious precautions, but many homeowners neglect to follow them and find the results of their neglect upon their return.

The house should be given a good cleaning before it is closed. All rubbish and refuse should be removed from the premises, especially oily rags, mops, and the like, that might be a possible cause of spontaneous combustion. Matches should not be left around and highly combustible liquids such as paint, gasoline, or kerosine should be disposed of.

Bottles filled with liquids which will freeze must be removed because the bottle will probably break when the liquid freezes.

Articles of clothing, linen, blankets, and other materials that are to be left in the house should be cleaned or washed, allowed time to dry completely, and then packed away in trunks or closets with mothballs or some equally effective moth preventive.

Naturally, all foodstuff should be either taken away or thrown out, and the kitchen, pantry, and refrigerator given a good scrubbing to rid them of any small particles of food matter that might attract rats and mice.

Inspect the outside of the house to see if there are any loose shingles on the roof, cracks in the siding, or other such flaws in the exterior walls. Reputty any loose windowpanes and replace any that might be cracked. Cover the top of the chimney and any other such opening with fine-mesh wire netting to keep birds and squirrels out of the house.

A few days before you leave the house, call up the telephone company and arrange to have the telephone disconnected. It is a wise idea to have the gas turned off too, and if you do not know how to do this yourself, call the gas company; give a few days notice so that a serviceman can be sent after you have cooked your last meal. Turn off the electricity by pulling the main switch. This will prevent the possibility of a fire caused by a short circuit in the house wiring.

It is a good idea to inform the local officials or state police that you are going to be away. If they know the house is empty, they can make a point of keeping an eye on it.

The last thing before you leave, close and lock all windows. If there are shutters, these should be closed and locked too. Make sure that all outside doors are locked and that you have the keys. Do not make the usual mistake of forgetting the outside basement door or the garage.

# REGULAR INSPECTION

Most of the trouble caused in the average house by faulty and worn locks, hinges, electric lamp fittings, and so on, is due to lack of regular inspection and proper lubrication. It is a good plan to go through the house every 6 months with a screwdriver and oil can and inspect and repair every fitting, from the padlock on the garage door to hinges on the skylight.

In general, inspect screws to see that they are secure. All moving parts, such as hinges and window catches, should be lightly oiled or greased and any metal parts, in places where corrosion is likely to occur, should be regularly examined for rust. This is particularly important with chromium fittings, and an occasional drop of oil rubbed into angle corners of the fitting will prevent the deterioration of the chromium plating.

Tighten the hinges on the doors and check the locks and latches to be sure they operate easily.

Window-shade and curtain-rod fixtures are too often attached to the woodwork by means of small brads, which will not hold for very long. It is worthwhile to replace these brads with wood screws, for a neater and a more permanent fixture.

Check each window to see that both sashes operate easily but are not loose in the frame. Inspect the cords for signs of wear and put a drop of oil on each pulley.

See that all doors are equipped with some kind of doorstop to prevent damage to the door and adjoining wall. Doorstops are available to fit into the baseboard or the floor. They should have rubber pads at the point where contact is made with the door.

Check all the electric light fixtures to be sure that they work properly and do not flicker when turned on. See that each fixture is attached securely to the wall or ceiling, and that the electric cord is not carrying the entire weight of the fixture.

Examine the attic and basement stairs to be sure that they are solid. Many accidents occur each year when people fall down poorly built basement stairs. It is wise to have some kind of banister or, if there is none, a strong rope will help. It is

better to build a banister out of wood smoothed down until there are no splinters. It can be attached to the wall by means of brackets, or supported by 2″ × 4″ studding based on the floor if there is no wall near the stairs.

Slippery treads are another cause of accidents, and these can be corrected easily by nailing rubber mats to the treads. Mats are obtainable in different widths and provide sure footing.

There should be a light near attic and basement stairs, and the stairs should be kept clear of any trash or other objects over which someone might trip.

Look for signs of rot, not only in woodwork near the ground but also wherever the air is damp. Inspect the wood flooring under each plumbing fixture. This is particularly important in the case of a cabinet-type kitchen sink, where a leak at the trap can go undetected for a long time. While checking the floor, look for rat holes in corners and around the baseboard. These should be covered with metal.

# REDUCING NOISES IN THE HOUSE

There are many things that you can do to make a quieter house.

## Outside Sounds

These are the most difficult to deal with because you cannot do much to eliminate the source of the sound. Weatherstripping helps prevent sound from coming into the house through cracks; leaving storm windows in place or equipping windows with them can also help considerably.

A solid fence between the house and the street will deflect sound waves away from the house, but it must be rather high —8′ or so—and set as far away from the house and as close to the street as possible.

Low, thick hedges are not effective, but a hedge of evergreens 8′ high or higher will do some good.

## Inside Sounds

There are several ways to handle these. One is to prevent noises made in one part of the house being transferred to other areas. Most interior doors, for example, are not very effective sound barriers because of the cracks around them. Applying a gasket type of weatherstripping around doors of rooms that you wish to keep as quiet as possible—the children's room, for example—or on doors of rooms from which you don't want sounds to escape, such as the bathroom, will help. Use a type of threshold which will make a tight seal at the bottom of the door.

Sound will travel from one area in the house to another through the walls if there are openings in the walls that allow the sound to enter. Seal the joint around water and heating pipes with fibrous insulation or caulking compound. It may also be advisable to remove wall electric outlets and switches and pack the hollow space in back of them with fibrous insulation.

Warm-air heating systems frequently make a lot of noise which is sent throughout the house by means of the metal ducts. The best solution for this is to have a canvas or fiber-glass collar inserted into the duct system near the furnace so that there is no metal-to-metal connection between furnace and room registers. Heating noises can also be reduced by inserting a plastic gasket between the room register and the wall or floor surface.

One of the most difficult spots to stop noise transmission is from an upstairs room to the rooms below. Applying acoustical tile to the ceiling of the room below does no good. One good remedy is to cover the floors of the rooms above with carpeting. A more effective but costly method is to install a false ceiling over the existing one. The false ceiling should be suspended on metal hangers so that there is as little direct contact between the two ceilings as possible. The false ceiling can then be covered with gypsum wallboard.

The best way to prevent sound passing through an interior wall is to increase the thickness of the wall. Again, applying acoustical tile to one or both sides of the wall will not help. An easy way to increase the thickness of a wall is to apply ½-thick gypsum board to one or both sides.

Acoustical tile is effective in reducing the sound made in a particular room. As mentioned above, it will not prevent the sound being transferred to other areas, but it will make that particular room more quiet. It is especially good in the kitchen, where a great deal of noise is created. Carpet is also a good sound absorber and so are heavy draperies, upholstered furniture, and even books.

# PROTECTING AGAINST INTRUDERS

There are many things you can do to protect your home from burglars and other unwelcome intruders.

First of all, be sure that you have the proper kind of locks on all outside doors and windows and that these are locked when you leave the house for any length of time. The best type of lock for doors is the dead-bolt lock which cannot be opened without a key. Ordinary locks are easy to open with a piece of plastic. A variety of maximum-security locks are available today, but most law enforcement officials feel that a good quality dead-bolt lock is perfectly adequate.

Sliding glass doors that do not come with a keyed lock—one that can be opened only with a key—can be equipped with a special keyed wedge lock to secure them. These locks can be installed easily on either wood or aluminum units. Another way to prevent sliding glass doors from being opened is to cut a length of

¾″ wood dowel to the right size so that when it is placed inside the channel in which the door slides, the door can't be moved.

The latch on most double-hung windows is not much help in the way of protection, but it is better than nothing, provided it is latched. There are, however, several types of keyed window locks which can be installed on existing units so that the window can't be opened if the intruder breaks a pane of glass.

Leaving storm windows up the year around on windows not required for ventilation is helpful, as it means that before the intruder reaches the main window he must first break or remove the storm window—either making much noise or taking a lot of time.

Basement windows should be protected either with a metal bar set across them and fastened to the masonry foundation or with heavy screening over them, secured to the window frame with heavy staples.

One of the most effective ways to protect your house is always to give the appearance that someone is at home—even if they are not.

When you leave the house for the evening, don't turn on the light over the front door and leave the rest of the house dark. Pull down the shades and turn on all the lights that would normally be on when the family is at home. Leave the radio or TV playing.

If you are going to be away for several days or longer, be sure to stop all deliveries of papers, milk, and so on. Buy an electric timer—they cost under $10.00—and use it to regulate the lights. Set the timer so that it will turn on several inside house lights when it gets dark and then turn most of them off when the family would normally retire for the night. Do not pull the shades down because anyone passing the house during the day and seeing this would immediately know that the house was not occupied.

Many families use several timers to regulate the lights inside and outside the house when they are away, just as they would be turned on if the family was at home. For example, in early evening the lights in the kitchen and living area go on. Later on the upstairs lights go on and some of the downstairs or kitchen-living area lights go off. Finally, all the lights are out except in the hall and the bathroom.

When you leave the house during the day, if only for a few minutes, be sure that all doors and windows are locked. It takes an experienced burglar a matter of moments to open an unlocked door or window, get inside the house and take what he wants, and escape. When you leave the house, be sure to close the garage door, since an open empty garage is a good sign that no one is about. Many women, when home alone during the day, will take the car out of the garage and leave it in the driveway—a good sign that someone is at home.

Be careful not to advertise your activities. If you are planning a vacation trip, don't let the local paper publish your plans. Let them publish your activities after you return.

It is much better to have your street address rather than your name outside the house. If you have your name on a sign or a mailbox, it's easy for a potential housebreaker to get your telephone number and begin to keep track of your activities. All he has to do to find out if anyone is at home or not is to call the number. In this connection, many families have instructed their children, baby sitters, or cleaning women to say, when a stranger calls and asks for the man or woman of the house, "He [or she] can't come to the phone right now. Let me have your name and number and he'll call you right back." This is far better than saying, "They aren't home and I don't expect them back till late tonight or tomorrow."

Burglar alarms can be effective in protecting the house, but the degree of protection depends on the alarm. The simplest type is the local alarm which just gives off a loud noise when someone enters the house. If there are neighbors nearby who can hear the sound, this system is effective, but if there are no houses nearby, the intruder will know it and won't be too disturbed by the racket. Some of these local alarms are designed to be attached to doors and windows and operate by battery. The more expensive types are ultrasonic and send invisible beams across a room. When someone walks across one of these beams, the alarm goes off. Many of these systems are designed to be installed by the homeowner.

The most effective alarm system is one that is connected to a central office or directly to the local police station. These must be installed by firms specializing in alarm systems and may cost $500 or more, depending on the location of the house.

# 11

# EXTERIOR REPAIRS

The materials used for the construction of the outer walls and roof of a house are selected on the basis of how well they stand up under weather and temperature changes. Some types of materials are considerably better than others, but each requires some maintenance and repair if it is to give the best service. Do not put off doing exterior repair jobs any longer than is necessary. A small leak in the roof can damage the plaster in an entire room, as will a leak in the wall. Keep the exterior of your house in good repair, even if it means neglecting the interior. Do not paint the interior walls until you are sure that the exterior walls are well protected. Be less concerned with cracks in the inside plaster than with cracks in the exterior stucco or masonry. The exterior walls and roof keep out the weather and if they fail, the entire house may fail with them.

## CRACKS IN FOUNDATION

Cracks appear in foundations when there is any settling, or if the foundations are not well constructed. Small cracks can be filled by the home mechanic, but large, structural cracks which run the entire height of the foundation and continue to increase in size should be examined by an expert, for they may indicate serious trouble.

Small cracks should be filled as soon as possible. They will become larger if frost strikes them and they constitute a possible entrance for water into the basement.

To fill a crack in concrete, cut out the crack with a cold chisel to form a wedge with the inside wider than the outside. This will prevent the patch from falling out after it dries. Use a stiff wire brush to remove any dirt or loose concrete from inside the crack. Wet down the sides of the crack and mix mortar of 1 part cement and 3 parts fine sand, adding enough water so that the mortar can be worked into the opening. Force the mortar in, making certain that it completely fills the opening, and smooth off the outside surface. Keep the patch moist and covered until it sets.

CRACK

CUT OUT WITH A
COLD CHISEL

## WOOD SIDING

One of the most common materials used for exterior walls is wood siding. Wood siding is rather thin, and while it is usually backed with waterproof paper and sheathing, any flaw in the siding is bound to develop into a leak sooner or later.

There are several kinds of siding to be had. Some are thin, flat boards nailed so that they overlap; others have edges machined to fit and lock together. To keep wood siding waterproof, keep it properly painted. No other portion of the house needs good paint as much as the siding.

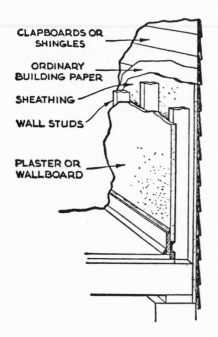

CLAPBOARDS OR SHINGLES

ORDINARY BUILDING PAPER

SHEATHING

WALL STUDS

PLASTER OR WALLBOARD

When a piece of siding cracks, pulls loose, or is broken, make repairs at once. If the board is damaged, it should be removed or replaced. Take care, when removing a piece of siding, not to split the edge of the board above. It may be possible to remove the nails from the broken board by prying up gently the board above, thus providing enough room to pull out the nails on the top portion of the lower board.

Notice the size of the nails and use this size when adding a new piece. Large nails will easily split thin siding.

### Wood Shingles

Wood shingles are another kind of wood siding commonly used. To remove a cracked or rotting shingle, split it lengthwise with a knife or wood chisel and remove the pieces. If the nails under the upper shingles cannot be pulled out, use a hacksaw blade to cut off the top portion of the nails so that the new shingle can be slipped into place. Select a shingle of the same width as the one removed, put it into place, and nail with shingle nails.

## STUCCO WALLS

Stucco exterior walls are usually made with several coats of portland cement stucco, built up from wood or metal laths. Small hairline cracks may appear on the surface and these should be examined to determine their depth. If just the surface coat has cracked, they can be disregarded. Deep cracks or large openings that run the full depth of the stucco should be filled, particularly around window and

door frames, as they will allow moisture to get behind the stucco and cause much damage, not only to the laths but to the interior walls as well. If large sections of stucco drop out, and large cracks appear, you may be sure that something is radically wrong with the stucco, the laths, or the construction of the house as a whole.

Cracks in stucco can be repaired with a mortar made of 1 part cement and 3 parts sand, or with a special stucco patching mixture, sold at hardware stores, which requires only the addition of water. These patching powders can be had in various colors, so that one can fill the crack with the same color stucco as the rest of the wall and avoid having an obtrusive patch.

Cut back the edges of the crack in the same manner as that employed in filling a crack in concrete. Wet down the sides of the crack and force in the patching mortar. Keep the patch damp and protected from the sun until it is dry. Small hairline cracks can be filled by brushing in a mixture of cement and water. After this is dry, the surface can be painted. (See chapter 6, page 142.)

## BRICK WALLS

Brick walls come in for their share of leakage, as do walls of wood or stucco. A brick wall, if properly built, should be waterproof under all normal conditions. Leaks that do occur are usually due to the fact that the joints between the bricks were not properly filled with mortar or the low-grade mortar used has shrunk, leaving a space between the bricks. All mortar joints between bricks must be packed tightly, and the mortar brought out flush with the surface of the brick. On horizontal joints, the mortar is brought out at the bottom, so that the joint slopes and resembles a shingle in its ability to shed water. If there are any depressions in the joints, water can collect in them and penetrate

the smallest crack in the wall. Once moisture has made its way into a brick wall, more cracks are sure to occur when the moisture freezes during the winter and expands.

Examine the brick wall carefully and mark any bricks around which the mortar is cracked or falling out. Remove all loose and cracked mortar before filling the joint. Use a cold chisel or small pick to

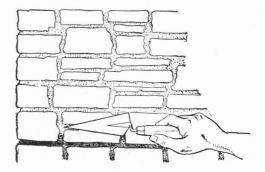

clean out the loose mortar, but be careful not to damage any of the sound mortar or the bricks. After cleaning the mortar, brush out the cavity and wet it down. Mix some cement mortar, 1 part cement to 3 parts fine sand, and pack this into the joint. Use a trowel to make it smooth and build out the lower portion slightly.

If all mortar joints appear to be sound, but water continues to seep through the wall, coat the entire wall surface with a waterproofing composition designed for use on bricks.

Occasionally, an entire brick will become loose or break. Remove all the mortar around the brick with a cold chisel or pick, taking care not to damage the other joints or bricks. Clean out the cavity in the wall and wet down the sides. Select a brick of the proper size and soak it in water for a short time. Spread cement mortar generously around the sides of the opening and over the brick. Force the brick into place and pack the joints tightly with mortar.

## Transparent Dampproofers

Where the surface of the masonry wall is giving trouble and it is desired to retain the texture and natural appearance of the wall, whether it be brick or stucco, the dampness can be stopped and the trouble overcome very often by the application of a commercial transparent dampproofer to the outside surface. This coats the surface and soaks into the porous material without hiding what is underneath. These transparent dampproofers are all water repellents. They have no filling property. As a result, it is necessary to fill or point up any cracks and holes in the stucco or mortar joints before applying a dampproofer.

Transparent dampproofers are of various compositions, but the most common contain silicones. They can be applied by brush or with a spray gun.

# EFFLORESCENCE

Sometimes a white, powdery, salty substance appears on the surface of masonry walls. This indicates that moisture is present within the wall itself. If this moisture is permitted to collect, it may lead eventually to the deterioration of the masonry. This condition is known as efflorescence.

On brick or tile masonry walls, efflorescence appears as a light, white powder, or crystallization. It may also take on the color of salts or impurities present in mortar, stucco, and other masonry. It is most noticeable, of course, when it occurs on material such as red brick, and it is sometimes overlooked when it takes place on white-colored materials.

Efflorescence actually takes place when moisture comes in contact with certain soluble salts in masonry. When the water evaporates, these salts are deposited on the surface of the masonry. Salts usually found in efflorescence are calcium sulfate (gypsum), magnesium sulfate (epsom salts), sodium chloride (table salt), sodium sulfate, and potassium sulfate. Efflorescence is produced when soluble salts are present in sufficient quantities in materials used to construct the wall and enough moisture is present to bring these salts to the surface.

Soluble salts may be present in masonry units, or in mortar or plaster. Most newly produced structural clay products do not contain enough soluble salts to cause efflorescence. Second-hand brick, however, may often be a source of efflorescence when used in new construction. This is because it usually has had previous contact with mortar or plaster which contained soluble salts. Portland cements contain soluble salts, as do some limes, sands, and even mixing water. Other masonry units, apart from brick, usually contain soluble salts too. When efflorescence appears only at the edges of the masonry unit, it is likely the mortar, rather than the masonry unit, contains soluble salts. Should efflorescence cover the entire unit, both the masonry and the mortar are responsible. If it appears only in the center of the unit, soluble salts are in the unit and not in the mortar.

Moisture must be present in sufficient quantities to effect efflorescence. It is important, therefore, to trace the source of the water. Usually, the presence of moisture is caused by some fault in construction. However, when a uniform coating of efflorescence appears on a newly constructed building, such may not be the case. An excessive amount of water may have been used during building operations. While this moisture is in the process of gradual evaporation, soluble salts present may be brought out to the wall surface. If the building is well designed and constructed, this condition is easily overcome. A final cleaning, or perhaps a few rains, will wash away the efflorescence and it may never reappear.

Should the efflorescence persist, however, moisture still penetrates the wall. Steps must be taken to determine the source of the water and eliminate it. Defective flashings (or the lack of flashings at vulnerable spots), clogged gutters and downspouts, faulty copings, or improperly filled mortar joints may, either singly or in combination, be responsible for the moisture and, indirectly, the efflorescence.

The location of the white powdery substance on the wall, however, does not always indicate the place where the water is coming from. The moisture could be penetrating at some other spot and leaving at the point where the efflorescence appears. The location of the efflorescence does nevertheless serve as a starting point in tracing the origin of the water. Efflorescence streaking down from the top of a wall, or patches some distance from the top, would indicate defective copings, gutters, or roof flashings. If efflorescence is spotted under windows, investigate the sills and caulking around the window frame. A defective mortar joint, or a projecting course of masonry forming a water table, may also be the cause of a single patch of efflorescence if masonry openings, copings, and gutters are not responsible. Sometimes efflorescence shows up on the foundation wall close to the ground. If especially porous units were used in the construction, this condition could be the result of ground water drawn up by capillary suction.

## Correcting Construction Faults

The permanent solution to an efflorescence problem is to remove the excessive moisture. This should be done before any attempt is made to remove the powdery substance itself, otherwise it is likely to reappear again.

Repair faulty flashings, gutters, and downspouts if they are the cause of the trouble. Where copings are at fault, take them up and relay them with thin, but well-filled mortar joints with rodded tooling. Place a noncorrosive metal or bituminous flashing directly under copings, cornices, chimney caps, sills, and any projecting courses of masonry.

Rake out improperly filled mortar joints in exposed walls and repoint them with a plastic mortar of approximately the same mix as that used in the original work. To eliminate as much of the original shrinkage as possible, the tuck-pointing mortar should be prehydrated by mixing with only a portion of the mixing water one or two hours before using. Then it may be remixed with sufficient added water to produce satisfactory workability. Avoid using cement, lime, sand, or water which might tend to cause efflorescence. If no caulking was used around window frames and door frames in the original construction, this should be undertaken. Fill all cracks with a good elastic caulking compound applied with a pressure gun. Remove the original caulking if it has become dried out, cracked, peeled or separated. Replace it with a new compound. Raking and repointing the mortar joints in the sills may also be necessary.

Efflorescence found on the lower parts of walls above grade may be due to a lack of drainage, improper dampproofing, or capillarity. Footing drains may be installed and a dampproofer applied to the outside surface of the wall.

## Removing Efflorescence

In new construction, as previously stated, efflorescence may disappear after a few rains. If it does not, the application of water with a stiff scrubbing brush will usually do the job. If this does not work, another method may be used.

First wet the wall. Then scrub it with water containing not more than 1 part of muriatic (hydrochloric) acid to 9 parts of water. Pour the acid very slowly into the water when mixing the solution so that it will not splash up into the eyes and face. Immediately thereafter, rinse the wall thoroughly with plain water. It is very important to rinse the wall with water both before and after washing with the acid. Protect all frames, trim, sills, and other installations adjacent to the masonry against contact with the acid solution. Wear rubber gloves and take precautions to protect eyes and exposed skin from contact with the acid solution.

The blotches may reappear again from time to time, and require additional washings. They will disappear completely, however, as soon as the supply of soluble salts in the materials has been exhausted. Colorless waterproofing compounds, applied to the surface of the wall to check absorption, will also tend to eliminate the formation of efflorescence.

On colored concrete, efflorescence, sometimes also called blooming, is particularly noticeable and objectionable. In addition to using the solution of muriatic acid, noted above, for removing efflorescence, it can be removed with a solution of equal parts of paraffin oil and benzine

rubbed vigorously into the surface when the concrete is dry. This treatment also improves the wearing qualities of the surface by filling the pores and bringing out the color more uniformly. Thus it is frequently applied to concrete surfaces for these reasons alone.

# ROOF

Even a small leak in the roof can cause considerable damage, and it should be repaired at once. Tracing the source of a leak in a shingled roof is sometimes difficult because the source quite frequently is not where the leakage shows. Defective flashing around chimneys and elsewhere oftener than not are contributing causes. However, damaged and badly warped wood shingles can also be the reason. Holes in a shingled roof, large enough for rain to leak through, can usually be discovered by the daylight which shows through them. An old stunt is to push a wire through this hole from the attic side to locate the hole for you when you're scrambling around on the roof.

There's a curious phenomenon, difficult to explain, concerning holes in a wood-shingled roof. There are some eighteenth century houses whose original roofs of hand-split shingles are so badly damaged in spots that you can see through them. Yet, when a severe rainstorm occurs, not a drop of water leaks through. Patching such a roof inevitably makes it leak like a sieve. Don't depend on this phenomenon—it doesn't happen too often. An old, badly damaged roof of any area larger than a few shingles here and there, must be recovered with new material.

Take necessary precautions. Don't work on a wet roof, as it may be slippery. Wear tennis shoes or shoes with rubber heels and soles rather than leather shoes. Walk on the roof as little as possible, since you can open up additional places or do serious damage, especially to asphalt

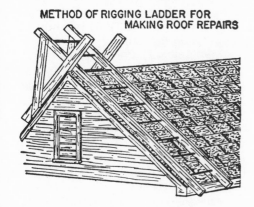

METHOD OF RIGGING LADDER FOR MAKING ROOF REPAIRS

gle has split. If a shingle is loose, simply drive it back into place, fasten it with roofing nails, and coat their heads with roofing cement.

To replace a damaged shingle that can't be repaired, the old shingle must be removed carefully so as not to damage the adjoining shingles. The way to do this is to lift the end of the shingle a little so that you can rock it sideways and break it away from the hidden nails—it will usually split away easily. Replace it with a

shingles in hot weather when they are soft, or to brittle asbestos cement and slate shingles. If considerable work must be done, rig a ladder.

## Shingles

**Wood Shingles.** Leaks usually occur here because a shingle has warped and curled up at the edges, has split, or has come loose. If the shingle has curled up, split it down the length with a chisel and then slip a piece of heavy roofing paper or aluminum under it. If the shingle won't lie flat, tack it down with one or two roofing nails and dab the heads with roofing cement. The use of building paper or a sheet of aluminum is also good if the shin-

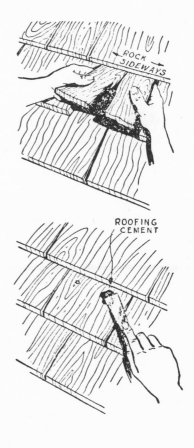

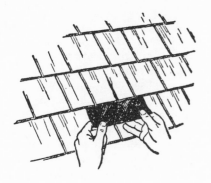

new shingle, which, of course, can't be blind-nailed like the original one. Nail into the exposed portion and then coat the nails with roofing cement.

A good-quality wood-shingle roof will last for 15 years or more, depending on the climate and other factors. When it begins to fail, a new roof is required. Under most conditions, the old shingles can remain in place and new wood shingles or asphalt shingles can be applied directly over them.

**Asphalt Shingles.** Repairing an asphalt-shingled roof is easy. First remove the nails holding the damaged shingle by lifting up the flap of the shingle covering it. Do not try this, however, when the shingles are very cold because they may be brittle and will crack. Wait until the sun

LIFT FLAP COVERING SHINGLE

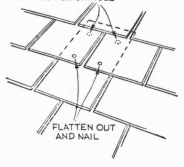

FIRST NAIL NEW SHINGLE

FLATTEN OUT AND NAIL

has had a chance to warm them so that they are pliable but not soft. Remove the damaged shingle and replace it with a new one. First nail the new shingle to hold the shingle under it, then flatten out the shingle above it and nail, securing the two layers.

The exposed portions of lightweight asphalt shingles will sometimes be lifted up by a strong wind. This not only can produce a leak in the roof but can also tear the shingles. To prevent this from occurring, lift the tab of each shingle and put a spot of roofing cement on the shingle under it. Press the tab into the cement, which will hold the tab so that it cannot be blown up by the wind.

Small holes in asphalt shingles left by nails used to secure Christmas decorations, TV antennas, and so forth, to the roof can be sealed with roofing cement.

**Asbestos Cement Shingles and Slate Shingles.** Repairing a broken asbestos or slate shingle requires a slater's shingle ripper—a long-bladed tool having a hook

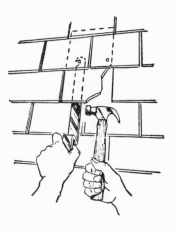

with a sharpened edge at one end and an offset handle at the other. The hook is slipped under the broken shingle, and concealed nailheads are cut off by striking the handle offset with a hammer. A hacksaw blade fixed into a handle, in place of a ripper, can be used to saw off the nailheads. Remove the shingle and replace it with a new one. Drill a hole for a nail through the side joint of the two shingles above the new one and drive a nail flush with the new shingle. Then slip a narrow

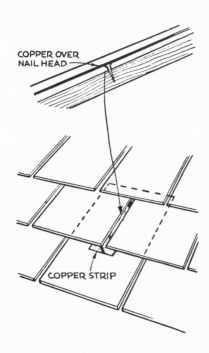

COPPER OVER NAIL HEAD

COPPER STRIP

piece of copper or aluminum under these shingles and over the nailhead of the new one. Another method of attaching the shingle is to nail a copper strip in the side joint of the two shingles above. Slip in the

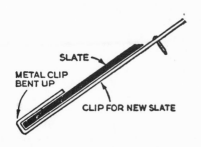

SLATE

METAL CLIP BENT UP

CLIP FOR NEW SLATE

new shingle, and bend the copper strip over the butt edge. The copper strip holds the shingle in place.

## Reroofing

Putting on the original roof is a job usually left to professional roofers, but re-

roofing is not too difficult a task for the home mechanic, since the old roof can be left to serve as a base for the new. The old roofing also provides a limited degree of protection until the new one is completed. After the new roof is on, the old will afford additional protection against any leakage, as well as provide an appreciable amount of insulation.

It is not suggested, however, that the home mechanic attempt to reroof the main dwelling, for he is likely to encounter varying roof angles which will necessitate valleys and flashings. Work of this type requires knowledge and experience and is best done by professionals. But the home mechanic should not have very much difficulty in reroofing a simple structure like a garage or workshop.

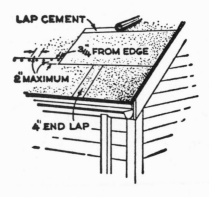

LAP CEMENT
¾" FROM EDGE
2" MAXIMUM
4" END LAP

Nearly any type of roofing material can be used over wood shingles. Cost is a primary factor in determining what materials to use, but remember, if you plan to do the work yourself, that the saving in labor should allow you to use the very best grade of materials.

Under normal conditions, the roof rafters will support the added weight of a new roof, but if the structure is very old or poorly constructed, it is wise to check the condition of the rafters and shingle laths.

Recondition the old roof before adding the new. Nail down any loose shingles, replace any that are missing or rotten, and be sure that there are no protruding nail-heads.

## Leaks at Flashing

One of the most common points for leaks to occur in a wall or roof is around the flashing. The flashings are strips of metal used to make watertight joints where two different structures, such as the chimney and roof, come together, or where two roof angles join to form a roof valley.

Because flashing is exposed to the weather it must be made of a noncorrosive metal like copper. Galvanized steel is sometimes used as flashing, but this and other metals which are not fully rustproof should be kept coated with some type of waterproofing.

Put on flashing so that it presents no opening which water can penetrate. When two sheets of flashing are used, the top will overlap the bottom in the same fashion as shingles that are properly laid.

Leaks will occur around the valley flashing when the width of the flashing is insufficient or the flashing has corroded. If the flashing is not wide enough, water will penetrate between flashing and roofing and into the house.

When a roof begins to leak around the valley flashings, the best thing to do is to call a roofing expert. This situation indicates that the flashing was not properly installed, and repairing it calls for considerable skill in order not to damage the rest of the roof. As a temporary measure, slip triangular pieces of metal under the shingles on each side of the flashing. Start this work at the bottom of the valley, and make each piece of metal overlap the one below it. As an added precaution, coat the underside of each sheet of metal with roofing cement.

The flashing around the chimney is usually in two layers for additional protection, since the point where the chimney and roof join is vulnerable. Flashing is laid along the side of the chimney and turned into the masonry. The cement mortar in the masonry holds the flashing in place and prevents water from getting under it. The bottom of the flashing is turned under the roofing, precluding the penetration of water under the roofing. A leak in the flashing at the chimney or the roof can easily be stopped. If the flashing has pulled out of the masonry because of high winds or poor mortar, secure it again by cleaning out the joint, reinserting the edge of the flashing, and filling the joint with cement mortar. For other leaks where the flashing enters the roof, apply roofing compound wherever necessary.

DETAIL OF CHIMNEY FLASHING

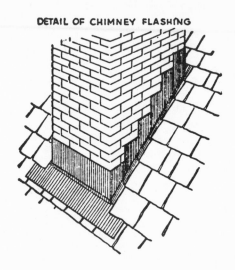

**Frames.** Place the flashing around window and door frames under the siding and then over the frame, so that water cannot enter this joint. Never nail down the exposed portions of the flashing, because this will provide a possible entrance for water. Pay particular attention to the flashing around window and door frames of brick and stucco houses; it is possible to make a tight fit between the siding and the frame when both are of wood, but almost impossible to do so when the

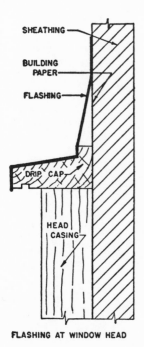

FLASHING AT WINDOW HEAD

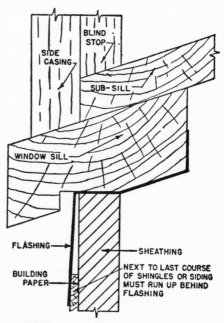

FLASHING AT WINDOW SILL

siding is of one material and the frame another. The frames should be flashed, not only at the top and sides, but also at the bottom, to prevent water from flowing along the underside of the sill and into the masonry. If there is no flashing at the bottom, a groove, cut along the underside of the sill, helps in keeping water from flowing into the masonry.

**Caulking.** Caulking compound is sold in many forms. Where large amounts are required you can buy it by the gallon and load it into a caulking gun. A more convenient type of caulking but somewhat more expensive comes in a cartridge that fits into a special type of gun; it is also available in large tubes similar to the type used for toothpaste.

Caulking does not stick well if the surface is dirty, damp, or greasy, so clean out the seam with a wire brush or sharp-pointed tool and see that it is dry. Caulking compound does not flow freely when cold, so if you have to use it in cold weather, allow it to warm to room temperature before using.

It takes a bit of practice to be able to apply an even and continuous bead of compound. Whether you use a gun or squeeze-tube applicator, you have to apply even pressure to get the right degree of flow.

CAULKING GUN

# GUTTERS AND DOWNSPOUTS

Gutters are designed to carry off the rainwater shed by the roof and to channel it into downspouts or leaders, and thence to sewers or dry wells. Unless these units are properly installed and maintained, they can cause a lot of trouble—sometimes serious trouble such as allowing water to flood the basement or causing exterior paint to blister and peel.

Gutters are usually made of aluminum, copper, galvanized steel, or wood. Downspouts or leaders are made of aluminum, copper, or galvanized steel. Aluminum downspouts and leaders do not require any protective coating, but they may be painted with trim enamel for decorative purposes. Copper units also do not require a protective finish, but often they

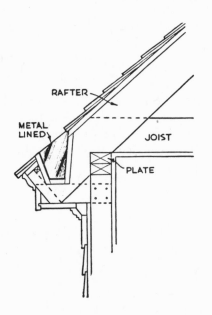

are coated with an exterior clear lacquer, spar varnish, or trim enamel so that water washing over the metal does not leave hard-to-remove copper stains on adjoining painted woodwork.

Galvanized steel gutters do require a protective coating because when the zinc coating wears away after a few years the metal will rust. For the inside of the gutter, apply a thin coat of asphalt roofing cement. This will last for a good many years. For the outside, use a trim enamel after applying a metal primer designed for galvanized steel.

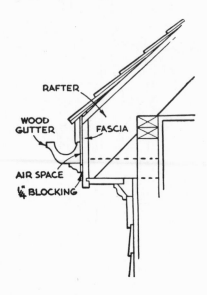

Wood gutters also need protection. Apply a special gutter paint or asphalt cement to the inside and paint the outside with latex house paint.

If rust holes should appear in galvanized gutters, clean the area and then patch them with a strip of heavy roofing paper or canvas imbedded in roofing cement. Hardware stores also sell excellent fiberglass patching materials for gutters.

Galvanized downspouts need to be painted on the outside. Usually they are not coated on the inside; but if you wish to give them maximum life, run a strong cord down the length of the downspout and fasten it to a wad of rags at the bottom. Pour some asphalt roofing cement down into the downspout and then pull the cord up so that the rag comes through the length of the pipe, coating the sides as it comes along. Add more of the asphalt roofing cement as required. The cement should be thinned somewhat with kerosine so that it flows like thick cream.

A gutter must have a slope toward the downspout or leader of not less than $\frac{1}{16}''$ per foot. If it doesn't have sufficient pitch, water flowing into it will not drain readily into the downspout and may flow over the sides of the gutter. This can damage planting near the house and also even cause the siding paint to blister and peel. You can check the pitch of a gutter either with a long level or by pouring water at the far end to see if it flows quickly to the opening at the other end that is connected to the downspout. If the pitch is not correct, it can usually be adjusted by tightening or loosening the brackets that hold the gutter to the roof, or installing additional brackets at sag points. In the case of a built-in gutter that is part of the roof and has no brackets, about all you can do is to fill in the low spot with several sheets of building paper and asphalt cement.

Gutters must be hung far enough below the roofing to prevent water from backing up under the roofing if the gutter becomes too full, causing a leaky roof. The only remedy here is to rehang the gutters. The outside edge of the gutter should always be lower than the lowest point of the roof. If it is not, snow sliding off the roof will catch in the gutter and create a snow dam. When the snow dam begins to melt, water can back up under

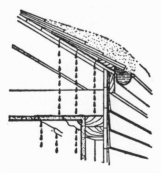

the shingles. It is often possible to correct a gutter in this condition by adjusting the brackets.

In spite of correct installation of gutters, ice and snow will collect in them in some situations, especially if the roof has a wide overhang. The best solution here is to lay a heating cable inside the gutter or along the edge of the roof. These thermostatically controlled heating cables will keep ice and snow from accumulating.

## Clogged Gutters

Gutters should be kept as free of leaves and other debris as possible. If the gutter is made of wood or galvanized steel, a collection of damp leaves will encourage rust or decay. But all gutters should be kept clear because leaves are like sponges and can absorb a good deal of water, the weight of which is often sufficient to pull

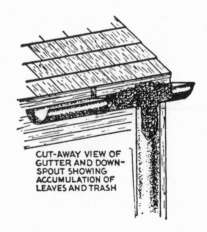

CUT-AWAY VIEW OF GUTTER AND DOWN-SPOUT SHOWING ACCUMULATION OF LEAVES AND TRASH

the gutter loose from the roof. Also, they will get down into the downspout and clog it.

The best way to keep leaves out of the gutters is to cover them with a wire metal guard. Guards made specifically for this purpose can be bought at hardware stores. A wire cage over the downspout

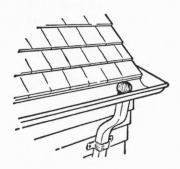

opening helps keep leaves out of this unit, but doesn't keep them away from the gutter.

If you don't use gutter guards, clean the gutters thoroughly in the fall after the leaves are off the trees, and again in the spring.

It's important to have a satisfactory way to handle the discharge from the downspouts. A concrete or plastic apron will help break the force of the water as it comes from the spout and spread it over a wider area, but still allows a good deal of water to sink into the soil close to the house. This may create a basement water problem or encourage termites, which prefer damp soil for their nests.

An inexpensive solution is to purchase one of the several plastic devices that are available and secure it to the end of the downspout; this will carry the water away from the house. One of these devices is spring-loaded so that under normal conditions it is tight up against the end of the downspout. When it rains and the plastic tube fills with water, it rolls out for 8' or more and transfers the water away from the house. A dry well is also most effective but more costly. (See chapter 12, page 287.)

## TERMITES

These insects obtain their food from the cellulose in wood and can, over a period of years, do extensive damage to the house structure. Termites are found in many sections of the country. You should know something about these insects and how you can protect your house from them because, aside from the damage they may do, many homeowners have spent money needlessly on ineffective protective devices and have even paid money to have termites exterminated when there were none about.

There are several different types of termites, but the type that does the most damage to the house structure is the subterranean termite. These insects make their nests in the ground—not in the house. They go from their nest to the house only in search of food. There are several members of the termite family, but the one you are most likely to see is the reproductive termite. It has wings and at certain times of the year—usually in the spring—will fly around. The reproductive termite looks something like a flying ant. The primary difference is that the ter-

REPRODUCTIVE
(NOTE WINGS)

WORKER

mite has a straight waist, whereas the ant has a constricted, or "wasp," waist. Also, the ant has one pair of wings shorter than the other, but the two pairs of termite wings are of the same length.

The termite that does damage to the house is the worker. He provides food for the other members of the nest. The worker is white, about 1/4" long, has no wings, and is blind. He must remain in the dark, and the only way you can see him is to break in on him. Because he cannot stand the light, he eats wood from the inside, leaving only the outer shell.

Not only is the termite worker unable to endure exposure to light, but he must return to the nest and the moist ground daily if he is to survive; further, unless he brings food back to the nest, the colony also will die of starvation.

In order to remain in the dark and still have access to the woodwork, the termite workers build earthen passageways

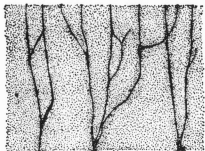

over masonry and metal surfaces to reach the woodwork from the earth.

The best way to be absolutely sure whether or not your house is infested with termites is to call in a reliable local exterminator. Select an established firm that has done business in your area for a number of years. Ask for references. Do not deal with the door-to-door type of operator who often will come around saying that he has been working in the neighborhood, has noticed termites around your house, and will give you a special price on an extermination project.

You can, of course, check your own property to see if it is infested with termites. One of the most common signs are those little earthen tunnels on the inside and outside of the foundation walls running from ground to woodwork. If you

find these, it's a definite sign of termites. In the spring and early summer you may also find the wings that have been discarded by the reproductive termites about the property. Finding these does not necessarily mean that termites are in your house, but they do mean that termites are close at hand.

Another way to check is to prod woodwork close to the ground with a sharp-pointed tool such as an awl, icepick, or penknife. If the point goes in easily, it may mean termites or decay.

The best way to deal with termites is not to allow them to get to the house—or near it, for that matter. Don't leave any scrap lumber or wood on or in the ground near the house. Remove tree stumps and keep fences and other wood structures several feet away from the house.

Keep foundation walls in good repair because if there are cracks in them, termites will use them to gain entrance into the house.

In some homes there is a copper plate between the top of the foundation wall

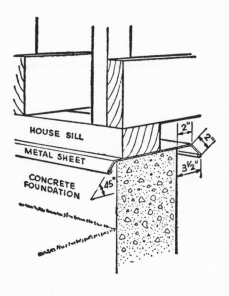

and the house woodwork. This is called a termite shield and is more or less effective in dealing with termites at that point; however, it should not be considered total protection.

Keep soil and debris clear of the house. It often happens that soil is allowed to build up so that it comes in contact with the lower part of the house siding; or soil, old leaves, and debris will collect around basement windows having wooden frames.

If you find that your house is infested with termites, there are several ways to deal with the problem. Breaking up the earthen tunnels will destroy those termites using them, but there may be other termites using other means of reaching the house.

The standard way to get rid of termites is to poison the soil around the house so that the termites in the ground are killed and those inside the house die because they can't get back to the moist soil. Spraying the woodwork of the house with poison is not effective because it does not reach the termites. There are several poisons used on termites. One of the most effective is chlordane, which is diluted in water for application. These substances should of course be handled with care.

To be effective, all the soil surrounding the house must be treated with the poison in sufficient amounts to kill off all the termites. This will involve digging a trench about 3' deep, or holes 30" or so apart, around the house and then pouring in the right quantity of the poison. This job can be done by the homeowner, but is best left to a reliable termite exterminator.

If you wish to do the job yourself, the poisons for termites are sold at hardware and garden supply stores as well as building supply stores. Be sure to get a complete set of directions and follow the manufacturer's directions to the letter. Remember, if you don't do a thorough job, the termites will find a safe route to your house and use it.

# PREVENTING WOOD DECAY

All woodwork that is in direct contact with the ground, such as fence posts, wood piers, and even outdoor wood furniture, as well as woodwork that is exposed to dampness, such as window frames and garage doors, are subject to attack by decay. Paint alone is not effective in protecting the wood from decay because a slight crack in the paint film allows moisture to reach the wood; once inside and trapped by the paint film, the moisture remains there. This is the reason that wood ladders should never be painted—it's too easy for moisture to get into the wood at the point where the rungs join the uprights.

All woodwork that is subject to decay should be treated with a preservative designed to protect the wood from decay. For years the common preservative was creosote; this does a good job, but it is not as effective as some of the newer materials, has a strong, unpleasant odor, and does not make a satisfactory base for paint.

The newer wood preservatives are designed not only to protect the wood from decay but also to stabilize it so that expansion and contraction due to a gain or loss of moisture content is reduced to a minimum. One of the most common of these preservatives is one containing pentachlorophenol. These are available in either an oil or a water base. A preservative must be applied directly to the wood—it does no good to apply it over a painted surface.

The most effective way to treat wood with a preservative is the pressure method of application. Lumberyards stock certain wood items that have had this treatment. The next most effective treatment is to soak the wood in a container of perservative; this can often be done in the case of fence posts and so on at the home site. For wood that does not lend itself to this method of application or wood that is in place, the preservative can be applied by brush or by spraying.

Especially critical parts of most wood items are at the joints between two pieces, because here is where moisture is most likely to get to the wood. If it is at all possible, disassemble the units so that the ends of each piece can be thoroughly coated with the preservative. If this is not possible, clean out the joint to remove any dirt or dust and then flood it with the preservative.

Many wood preservatives are very corrosive to the skin, so wear rubber gloves; and if some of the preservative gets on the skin, wash it off immediately.

Although wood preservatives are effective in preventing decay, they cannot, of course, restore wood that has already been damaged. But they will prevent further damage.

# CLEANING EXTERIOR SURFACES

Prefinished aluminum siding and vinyl siding don't require painting, but when the surface becomes dull or soiled by dirt, it should be washed. Painted wood siding should also be washed when it becomes soiled. A good paint job should last for 5 to 6 years, but in many areas it will become badly soiled before this amount of time has elapsed. It is better to wash a house if the paint is still in good condition rather than to put on another coat of paint. Aside from the cost involved in painting, applying paint too frequently will build up such a thick coating that there is danger of the paint film checking or cracking. And in spite of the fact that many house paints are self-cleaning, this process is not too effective where there is a considerable amount of dirt or dust in the air. Houses by the seashore should always be washed before they are painted to remove salt that has been deposited on the surface.

A good washing solution for any kind of wood, aluminum, or vinyl siding is a household detergent and water. You should first hose down the entire surface and then scrub with the detergent solution and a brush. Start at the bottom of the wall and work up. Never begin at the top and work down because this will allow dirty water to flow down over the unwashed portion and create dirt streaks which are difficult to remove. After scrubbing with the washing solution, rinse with clear water.

The best tool to use for washing a house is a special hose brush designed for this purpose and for washing cars. These brushes have a detergent dispenser attachment and an extension handle. But the job can also be done with an ordinary hose brush or with an ordinary hand brush. Clean a relatively small area at a time. As soon as the dirt has been scrubbed loose, flush it off with fresh water and proceed to the next area. When an entire section has been cleaned in this fashion, rinse it thoroughly with fresh water.

Pay particular attention to windowsills, cornices, and other spots where dirt is likely to accumulate.

Stains that won't respond to cleaning with the detergent solution may require something stronger. Trisodium phosphate, sold under such trade names as Spic and Span, is effective in most cases. Trisodium phosphate is also effective in removing mildew stains from painted surfaces if the mildew has not yet had a chance to damage the paint itself.

Unpainted concrete is very difficult to clean because the material is porous and once dirt gets into the surface pores, removing it completely is virtually impossible. Scrubbing with trisodium phosphate is about the most effective method of cleaning it. Brick, on the other hand, will respond well to a scrubbing with a mild solution of muriatic acid and water. Use a 20% solution.

Asbestos cement siding should be cleaned with a special siding cleaner made and sold for this purpose.

# INSTALLING A
# TV ANTENNA

Whenever anything is installed on a roof there is danger that the nails may cause holes which will lead to leakage. Considerable damage can be done to a roof, for example, if a TV antenna is not carefully installed. The antenna should not be attached to a chimney that has loose bricks or cracks in the mortar. Masonry must be in good condition before the added weight and strain of an antenna is put on it. It is important to select the proper size and style of bracket to fit your particular

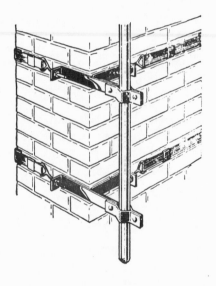

roof. If chimney straps are used, the brick and mortar can be protected by corner guards. Those with pipe clamps can be used, but the straps should be chosen and put on carefully.

A strap that is too narrow may cut into the mortar, damage the chimney, and result in a wobbly antenna. On the other hand, a strap that is too thin should not be trusted, since it might snap in a high wind and drop the mast. Do not use improvised straps, as they are not reliable.

Aluminum or galvanized steel straps about 1″ wide are usually satisfactory.

When attaching an antenna, such as one with a few arms on a short mast, to brick walls or roof parapets, screw a U-clamp or stand-off brackets into the brick. Make the holes with a star drill or masonry drill and insert lead anchors or expansion shields to fasten the screws. If the mast extends down the wall for about 3′, at least 2 of these brackets are needed; if it extends down the wall farther than this, the rule is to use a bracket every 3′.

A small antenna can be attached to the face of the gable end of a wood-sheathed house. Be sure the brackets are placed close to the peak and attached firmly to the wood. You can use lag screws or ordinary wood screws, although toggle bolts are recommended.

# LIGHTNING
# PROTECTION

Lightning is no particular problem in the city where there are many tall steel buildings, but it can be a problem in the country—especially in certain sections where there are frequent and violent thunder and lightning storms. Lightning can set a house on fire and also shatter valuable trees.

A house and valuable high trees can be protected from lightning by means of a lightning protection system. This should be installed by a qualified firm licensed to do this type of job—it is not a do-it-yourself project because unless the system is properly installed and grounded, it may do more harm than good.

Before going to the expense of this kind of installation, you should check around with some disinterested individuals to see whether or not you really need it. Your insurance agent can be of help in this matter and so can your local fire chief and county agent. None of them can guarantee that your house or trees will never be struck, but they can tell you if lightning is a problem in your area or if it is not—at least so far.

# DRIVEWAYS, FLOORS, AND WALKS

**Concrete.** Cracks and holes in concrete driveways, walks, and floors are not difficult to repair. It is a good idea to cut back the edges of the concrete around the crack or hole with a cold chisel to form a key. Dust the loose matter off the edges of the surrounding concrete and then wet them down. Mix some patching concrete or prepare a mixture of 1 part portland cement to 3 parts sand with enough water to make a workable plastic and force it into the opening. For large holes, the same general method applies except that you should use a concrete mix rather than a mortar mix.

**Blacktop.** The best way to maintain blacktop surfaces is to coat them from time to time with a special blacktop sealer made for this purpose. This sealer can be easily applied with a long-handled broom or brush. It will provide a protective coating that will keep oil and grease away from the asphalt and also prevent the blacktop from absorbing moisture which can cause damage, especially in cold weather when water in and under the paving will freeze.

Sealers should be applied whenever the surface of the driveway or walk appears porous, so that grease, oil, or water is absorbed by it rather than running off or remaining on the surface.

Holes can be repaired with a cold-mix patching compound that is sold by the bag, ready for use. Cut the sides of the paving around the hole so that they are straight. Pack down the subbase and add gravel if necessary to bring the level of the subbase up even with the underside of the paving. Apply the patching compound as directed, packing it down with a thick piece of lumber such as a $4 \times 4$.

# 12

# DAMP AND LEAKY BASEMENTS

A basement is a tremendous asset to a home if it is dry. It will then be completely satisfactory for storage purposes and for housing heating equipment and other appliances. In addition, it may also be used to provide space for a workshop, playroom, and even extra living quarters. It has an important bearing on the life and value of the home.

Water in the basement will cause woodwork to rot and metallic surfaces to rust. This weakens the framework of the house and deteriorates furniture and

woodwork upstairs. Walls are discolored and wallpaper may peel or buckle. Increased maintenance and repair costs result and the life of the home is shortened.

## CAUSES OF DAMPNESS

Rainwater which collects outside the foundation walls and exercises pressure against the masonry and basement floor may cause dampness or leakage in the cel-

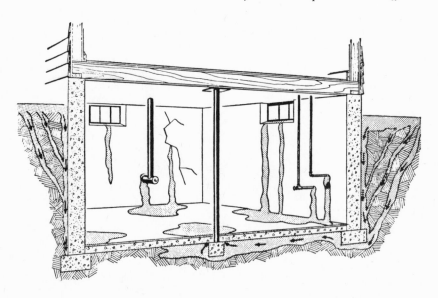

lar. This water may come from the roof when there is improper means of draining it away from the foundation. Then, too, when the ground beneath the surface of the earth is extremely wet because of underground streams, moisture may rise from the soil and penetrate into the basement by means of capillarity.

Humidity in the air will cause condensation on basement walls and floors when there is a temperature change. This usually occurs in warm weather when a kind of "sweating" takes place on concrete and metallic surfaces. It is especially noticeable on cold water pipes or cold basement walls when the water vapor in the warm air condenses on the cold surfaces. This may cause drops of water on the wall or pipes to drip onto the floor and create dampness and other water problems. Leaks from plumbing are also a factor in the basement, although they are usually easy to identify and repair. Dense masses of vines, shrubbery, and trees surrounding the outside of a house may collect water and direct it against the foundation wall. This water will then penetrate through the pores in the masonry by means of capillary action. Occasionally, a water problem may occur when an inside drain in the basement floor gets clogged and the water backs up and floods the floor. The means of preventing leakage and other water conditions brought on in these various ways will be dealt with in detail in this chapter.

**Points of Penetration.** Poor materials and faulty workmanship in construction are frequently responsible for excessive porosity of walls and floors which makes it possible for water to seep through them. Cracks in the masonry walls or floor are another source of openings through which water can enter. These are usually due to building settlement, or pressure of groundwater around the foundation. At all seams or joints of juncture between walls and floors and footings, and where iron or Lally columns penetrate through the floor, the possibility of tiny openings is great because the construction is not continuous. The same applies to openings where pipes, conduits, windows, steps, and door frames go through walls and floors. New conditions or developments, such as a converted heater, a fireplace, or new windows may also offer opportunities for water to break through the outside of the basement.

# REMEDYING DAMPNESS AND LEAKAGE

Leakage, seepage, moisture due to capillarity, and condensation occur individually or there may be a combination of two or all four, as sources of trouble. It is extremely important, however, to determine the form involved before attempting any remedy. Measures taken to prevent leakage will generally help stop seepage and capillarity as well, but condensation requires a completely different approach.

## Leakage

This is the easiest form of water and dampness to identify. It is simply the flow of water through visible openings that may occur in the basement floor or walls. Usually it takes place during, or after, a heavy rain. Water gathers on the surface next to the foundation wall. It runs down between the wall and the ground and finds openings or weak spots where it manages to get through. Such places are often present at points where the continuity of construction has been broken; where conduits or pipes enter the building, or at joints where the floor and wall come together. Also, when the foundation settles, it frequently causes a crack which acts as an opening for leakage.

It is important to understand that this rainwater does not strike the walls of the basement directly, since they are submerged. It is collected in the ground alongside the walls, or it may run down and gather beneath the floor. The body of water formed is capable of exerting great pressure. It is this pressure which forces the water against the walls and through existing openings. If a large quantity of water collects alongside foundation walls or beneath the floor, the pressure is tremendous. Consequently, even if there are no openings or holes through which this water can pass into the basement, the force it exerts may be so strong that it will be able to crack the concrete floor.

Leakage will frequently result in standing water in the cellar. It renders the entire basement damp and often causes dampness and water conditions in the floors above. It may flood the basement and rise high enough to put the fire out in a furnace or heater. The only way it can then be removed is to pump it out.

The logical approach to preventing leakage would appear to be simply to seal up the openings and plug up the holes where the water comes through. This is often effective if the pressure is not very great. But if it is, new openings will be discovered or created in different places.

Consequently, the source of the leakage must be traced. If the water can be kept away from the foundation walls and floor, the leakage may be eliminated. This calls for an examination of the drainage system. Oftentimes a clogged downspout which has caused roof water to overflow the gutter and run down over the outside of the house wall will collect around the foundation wall and seep in through openings. In such a case, removing the debris and cleaning out the downspout will be all that is necessary to direct the water away from the foundation. The purpose of proper drainage, therefore, is to permit the water to run off before it can collect around the foundation.

If the basement floor is below the level of the groundwater, however, drainage alone may not solve the problem. In such cases the foundation walls and floors must be waterproofed. In new construc-

tion this can be done by literally wrapping the entire foundation in a membrane waterproofing paper so that the water will be unable to find any openings. In old homes, or newly completed ones with a water problem, the walls and floors must be treated in such a way as to make them completely watertight. Both these methods, however, are almost always used in combination with drainage.

## Draining Roof Water

Homes with cellars should be provided with eaves, troughs (gutters), and downspouts (conductors or leaders). Otherwise the rainwater or snow will run off the roof and fall on the surface outside the foundation wall. It then collects in the ground next to the foundation and looks for weak points in the masonry, or openings between floors and walls. The eaves, troughs, and downspouts provide a means of controlling this water and draining it away from the foundation wall. If the ground has a natural slope, roof water drained down in this manner will be inclined to run away from the side of the building However, if the land is flat, some means of preventing the water from collecting outside the foundation wall must be provided. The downspouts should be connected to a drain emptying into a storm sewer, dry well, open water course, or other suitable outlet. Many communities, however, prohibit the draining of surface water into sanitary sewers. Where downspouts are not connected to an outlet, therefore, it is advisable to place a spatter board or splash block, or a gutter of good size, at the outlet to divert the roof water away from the wall.

This can be accomplished by means of an elbow or shoe. Place it at the bottom of each conductor pipe so that roof water may be drained into the concrete splash gutter. This should be constructed so that it will lead the water at least 10' or 15' away from the building wall. The de-

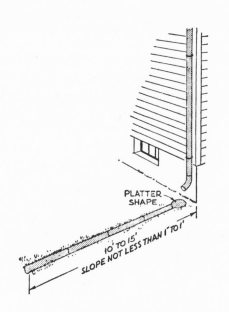

PLATTER SHAPE

10 TO 15'
SLOPE NOT LESS THAN 1" TO 1'

a Y-cleanout in the cast-iron riser. A branch with a removable plug just above the ground surface can also be used. This plug should be removed about once a year to make sure that no obstruction is forming. To clean it, merely insert a flexible metal snake. This is a long, flexible rod with a conical metal end which is used to push out dirt and debris. It's a good idea to have this rod as part of your maintenance equipment.

In some cities rainwater may be discharged into the same sewer that carries sewage. In still others, it may be discharged into a separate storm sewer; but in many cities, especially in suburban areas, some other means of disposing of water must be used. The usual method is to run water into structures called dry wells.

pression or gutter should be of the same width and depth as the corresponding eaves gutter, or an equivalent cross section which may be shallower and wider. The edges of the splash gutter are made level with the surrounding ground. The slope, away from the building, should be at least 1″ per foot of length. Splash gutters may be of brickwork, but a V-shaped wooden trough will do. Some are U-shaped and made of wood, brick, or stone. A few lengths of half-round vitrified gutter pipe may also be used. To catch all the discharge from a downspout, the upper end of the gutter should be widened and shaped like a platter.

Roof water can often be piped underground to a suitable drain, abandoned well, dry well, or surface outlet. The latter should be situated 15′ or more away from the building. Cement the downspout into a piece of cast-iron pipe about 2′ above the ground. Then extend it to a quarter-turn elbow set below frost depth. Complete the line to the well outlet using ordinary drain tile or sewer pipe with cemented joints. An easy way of removing obstructions in the elbow or drain is to set

## Dry Wells

The dry well should be made large enough to handle the number of downspouts connected to it. Its effectiveness, however, will depend upon the natural drainage of the ground at the location where the well is dug. Otherwise, the dry well will be only a temporary measure. The hole will fill up, overflow, and cause water to back up in the drain pipes.

Locate a dry well at least 8′ or 12′ away from the house. Line it with brick or cesspool block, laid up without cement to make it possible for water to seep in through the sides as well as at the bottom. The well should be covered with a slab of concrete or a cesspool cover. Dig the hole to a depth a little below the house footing. Make it deep enough to allow for at least 12″ of soil above the well cover. The well should be deeper and wider if the soil is of fine sand, sandy loam, clay, or loam. If the downspout measures 3″ in diameter, the well should be 3′ in diameter and 3½′ in depth if situated in coarse sand or gravel soil. In fine sand or sandy loam, where the size of the downspout is

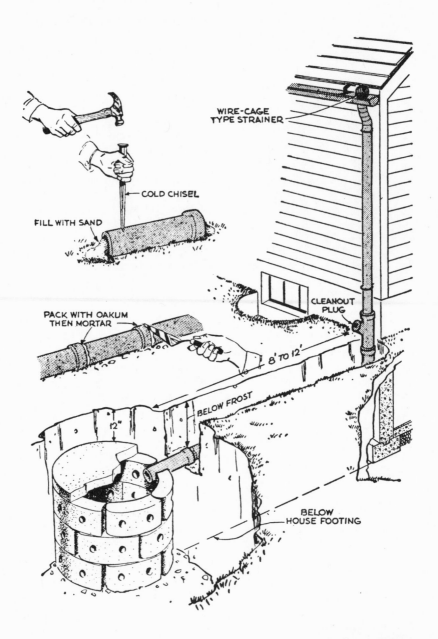

still only 3″ in diameter, the well should then have a width of 6′ and a depth of 5′. As the diameter of the downspout increases, the depth of the well should be increased.

Lay up the concrete blocks in tongue-and-groove style to give the well a cylindrical shape. Fill the space outside the well with sand. Use 4″-diameter terra cotta drain tile or tar-impregnated fiber pipe to carry water from the downspout. Lay the line at an angle of about 1″ to each foot so that the water will flow smoothly to the dry well.

If terra cotta tile is used and it is necessary to cut the tile, fill it with sand and cut with a cold chisel. The sand will keep the tile from cracking. Cement the tile joints, using mortar of 1 part cement to 3 parts fine sand. Pack oakum into the bell, or flared end of the tile, before working in the mortar.

Fiber pipe comes in 10′ lengths, and the sections are connected with fiber connector fittings supplied with the pipe. The fiber pipe can be cut easily with a handsaw, but a coarse rasp will be needed to taper the end after cutting so that the connector will fit.

Before filling in the earth above the drain, test the dry well by letting water run through it. Low spots are easily corrected. Simply raise the tiles or pipe by wedging small stones under both sides. The wire-cage type of strainer should be installed at the top of the downspout to catch leaves and prevent them from clogging the drainage system. If there is a great deal of snow and ice, be sure that it does not interfere with the flow of water into the well. Dry wells should be inspected once a year at least, and more often if there have been unusually severe snowstorms.

A temporary dry well can be made from an ordinary barrel or drum. Remove the top and bottom and sink the barrel into the ground about 6′. Fill it with gravel and coat it with asphalt. Then connect the drain. Put on a wire mesh or other cover and shovel back the topsoil. This kind of well, however, will give satisfactory performance for only a limited time. After a while it inevitably becomes clogged with leaves and other debris and is difficult to maintain. It is sometimes just as easy to make a brand-new well as to clean an old one.

## Surface Drainage

Dampness and leakage in the basement are often due to the fact that the ground around the house is flat, or slopes in the direction of the building. This causes water to flow down the sides of the building between the space where the ground and the foundation walls meet. If the rainfall has been particularly severe, this water may even penetrate below the foundation floor. It will exert a pressure and leak through any openings or passageways it can find.

Since water moves downward much more quickly than it moves laterally, proper surface drainage is often all that is needed to prevent leakage from occurring in this manner. The idea is to regrade the ground so that as soon as the water strikes it, it will tend to run off away from the building. Simply add soil and build a smooth, sharp, downward slope. Extend it so that it runs at least 10′ away from the building. When the grading has been completed it should be seeded with a good lawn grass, raked, and rolled. When regrading soil around a home that is set very low in the ground, care must be taken with windows. The new grading may run above the bottom of basement

REMOVE TOP AND BOTTOM, FILL WITH GRAVEL

WIRE MESH

6′

COAT WITH ASPHALT

windows. In order to maintain the same grade all the way around the house, therefore, it is necessary to build a small concrete parapet or wall around the outside of the window. This may be either curved or rectangular and can be made of concrete, brick, or tile. Sometimes a piece of steel or other metallic sheeting is used to shape the concrete wall and also to provide additional protection for the window.

The wells that are formed by these small dams in front of the windows should receive special treatment. Some way of draining the water which may collect in them must be devised. A 4′ to 6′ trench can be dug and a few lengths of tile installed so that the water will be led away from the window well and drained to some outside point, or the window-well drainage can be connected with the sub-surface drainage system. When severe rainstorms or snowstorms occur it is also a good idea to provide a temporary cover for these window wells. Covers should be large enough to prevent water from collecting in the well.

It is also possible to achieve surface drainage by building a sloping concrete strip around the outside of the house at the juncture of the wall and ground. The pavement may be made of portland-cement concrete or bituminous concrete and is usually 1′ to 3′ wide. It sheds water more quickly, but is often objected to because of its appearance. The strips should be rounded up where they join the wall. The water will tend to run off the strip and sink into the ground. If the ground does not slope away from the strip, therefore, it may be desirable to place a trough or gutter about 5″ along the outside edge of the strip. This gutter is usually made about 6″ wide and 4″ deep, and is sloped its entire length so that it will carry water to some low point where it can be discharged.

## Filling

After a house has been built, the open space between cellar walls and excavation is refilled. This should be done with the earth that was originally removed. It is common practice, however, for workers to fill the space with the leftovers they may have lying around so that they will not have to cart them away. They fill this area with pieces of stone, broken bricks, cement bags, bits of wood and mortar, and any other material they could not use in the construction.

When leakage or dampness appears in a basement of a relatively new home, it is always a good idea to check this fill. The porous nature of such materials will offer no resistance to water in the ground. Consequently, the water will easily pass through it and seek points at which it may penetrate through to the basement. Dig down a few feet and examine the material. If porous material has been used, it should be cleaned out. Then refill the area, using a layer of gravel at the bottom, a layer of sand above this, and finally, fill to the top with earth, packing it as tightly as possible. One or two rainstorms will tend to pack this earth fill more solidly. Then topsoil may

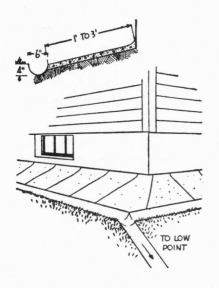

be added to complete the job. If the space is not too wide, concrete may be used.

## Subsurface Drainage

Sometimes adequate surface drainage is not possible. Shrubbery or trees close to the house may make it undesirable to re-grade or build a concrete strip. Then, too, standing water may appear regularly in the basement, indicating that the cellar floor is below the level of the groundwater for long periods. If so, subsurface drainage is necessary. In addition, where roof water cannot be properly drained away from the foundation walls by means of ground drainage, a connection can be made be-tween the downspouts and the subsurface drainage system.

Footing drains may be installed on ei-ther the outside or the inside of the foot-ing. In either case, however, a trench and drain are necessary to carry the water away after it has been collected. In order to install an outside footing drain, you must excavate down to the footing all around the house. To install an inside footing drain, it is necessary to cut through the basement floor around the cellar wall. Whether it is preferable to construct the drain on the outside or on the inside of the footing depends on many things.

If the cellar has a lot of equipment, a finished tile floor, or some expensive car-pentry which would have to be removed or destroyed in order to cut through the floor, it would probably be more practical and economical to dig a trench around the outside of the foundation. On the other hand, it is a costly and difficult job to excavate a trench all around the foun-dation walls. Moreover, it is extremely dif-ficult to work in such narrow confines. Generally, therefore, the inside footing drain is more convenient and satisfactory.

If the house is on a hillside, it may be necessary to install the drain only along the high side, but generally it is better to surround the basement with the drain. The idea is to capture the large quantity of water which is below the ground sur-face and run it away from the foundation.

To build an outside footing drain, use drain tile measuring about 4″ in di-ameter. Lay it along the bottom of the wall or footing course, taking care not to undermine the footing. Good fiber pipe, well-burned drain tile, or ordinary sewer pipe may be used. A very slight slope should be provided, about 1″ to every foot. This requires considerable care to make sure that all tile tilts in the direc-tion of the flow of the water. A simple method of maintaining the slope is to make a 6′ board $\frac{3}{20}$″ narrower at one end than at the other. Place this board edge-wise on the tile and mount a level on top of it. The narrower end of the board is, of course, upstream. When the top of the board is level, the bottom edge will be sloping down at the rate of 1′ in every 400′.

Another method is to grade pairs of stakes on each side of the trench. Then stretch a cord across so that it touches the tops of each pair in turn. The exact depth of the inside of each pipe is measured from the string by a stick having a right-angle foot at the bottom.

In very porous soils the tile can be placed directly on the bottom of the trench. In moderately porous soils, how-ever, it is better to make the trench wide enough for the tile to be surrounded with sand. The sand not only helps to collect water, but also hinders the flow of silt from the soil to the tile line. In clay soils the tile should be surrounded with coarse gravel instead of sand.

The joints should be kept open about the thickness of a knife's blade. Measures must also be taken to keep out loose dirt. Burlap, linen, or some other porous fabric 6″ wide and about 17″ long should be tied or wired around each joint.

Test the system by introducing water at various points. If the pitch is correct, the water will drain away from the house.

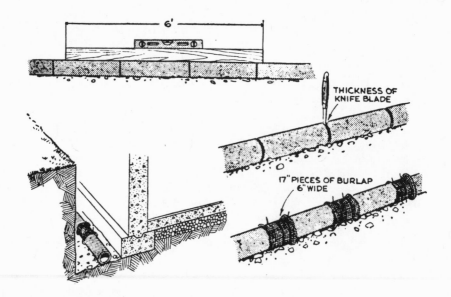

THICKNESS OF
KNIFE BLADE

17" PIECES OF BURLAP
6" WIDE

If it is not, it may settle at some low point in the system. Then the slope can be adjusted by wedging stones beneath the tile. An inexpensive subsurface drainage method is to fill the bottom of the trench with gravel or broken stone to a depth of about a foot. Then cover this gravel with a strip of roofing paper to prevent dirt and silt from filling up the spaces between the gravel. If the trench has been properly dug and graded, this will provide good drainage without the installation of drain tile. Backfill should then be added on top of the paper.

An extensive drainage system will contain two kinds of lines: those which collect the water and are called laterals, and those which carry away the water poured into them by the laterals. The lines into which laterals drain are made of bell-and-spigot tile. Joints are made by placing a spigot in a bell with the bell end downgrade. The spigot end is then wrapped with a piece of small rope so as to keep it centered in the bell.

The lines must be placed so that they will carry off the water, but otherwise it is not necessary to bury them more than 12"

or 15" even in regions with cold winters. Soil of this depth will give enough protection to the tile against damage by vehicles which might pass over the lines. Possible frost damage can also be ignored, because if the lines are laid so that their slope is uniform and the outlet is open, they will never be full of water when frost strikes them. A steep slope does no harm, but a slope as gradual as 1" to 50' is sufficient.

The excavation should be refilled very carefully. Sometimes two operations produce better results. In the first, the trench is filled approximately half full with soil from which all large stones and roots have been picked out. This fill is, of course, placed on top of the sand or gravel, which should range from $\frac{1}{4}$" to 1" in size, the finer pieces being placed over and around the pipe to give good bedding and protection. To prevent loose dirt from washing down into the stone or cinders, the top should be covered with old bagging, burlap, hay, straw, cornstalks, sods with grass side down, or fine brush. This should be allowed to settle for a week or longer. Then the remainder of the trench should be filled up to the finished grade. Cover with a foot of topsoil. Then grade and seed the soil, tamping it lightly as it is being placed.

A drain and belt of coarse material thus placed around a basement floor will help intercept moisture coming from the soil in the form of capillarity.

The drain tile should be conducted away from the building to a storm sewer or to low ground where it can discharge. It should not be piped into a nearby stream or body of water unless the high point of the stream or body of water is well below the level of the outlet from the drain. Otherwise a heavy rainfall or snowstorm will cause the stream to overflow its banks and the water will back up in the drain tile. Where a suitable outlet is not readily available, it may be necessary to connect the drain tile to a sump pit or cistern inside the basement. The pump, automatically controlled, with then remove the water when it reaches a predetermined level, even though the flow from the drains may be intermittent and varied.

Usually when the house is already built, it is more convenient and economical to install the drain tile on the inside. To do this, cut out the basement floor along the footing. Be sure enough of an opening is made for the installation of a 4″ drainpipe. To determine the necessary width of the opening, take a section of the drainpipe and mark out on the surface of the floor, with chalk, a line to indicate how much of the floor is to be removed. This can then be cut out with a cold chisel and a sledge or heavy hammer. It

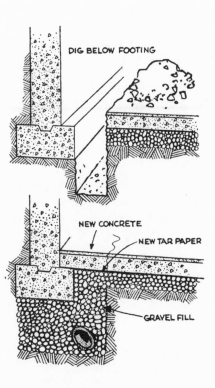

can even be cut with a pick. After the section has been removed, excavate the earth under the floor to a depth that will permit the pipe to rest below the bottom of the footing. It will also be necessary to remove enough earth under the footing to provide space for the connection between the drainpipe on the inside, and the pipes to be used to carry the water away. The drain should have open permeable joints and pass through, or under, the footing to an outlet that is open at all times. It should be laid in ⅜″ to ½″ gravel. If necessary to drain deeper than the foundation, the drain may be placed 4′ or 5′ away from the foundation, to avoid undermining it. It is sometimes desirable to lay one or two branch drains to tap springs within a cellar. Then fill up the drainage area with gravel to the level of the underside of the floor. Place a strip of roofing paper over the gravel so that the concrete will not be able to run into it. The floor should then be installed over the paper with a mixture of one part portland cement, two parts clean sand, and four parts broken stone or gravel. This concrete should be brought up to the level of the top of the floor. It should then be floated and troweled to the level of the old floor. The inside drain can then be connected with an outlet for disposing of the water collected by the drain.

## Sump Pump

If it is impractical to carry the water away from the footing drain to some low point outside the building, a sump pump should be installed in the basement. These pumps are constructed with electrical motors and float switches. When water reaches a predetermined height, the float automatically closes the switch and starts the motor and pump. The water in the pit is then pumped up to ground level where it may be run off. After the water has been pumped out of the pit to a predetermined lower level, the float opens

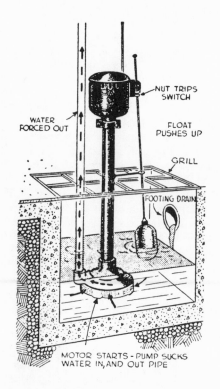

the switch and automatically stops the motor and pump.

The size and type of pump required is determined by the amount of water, measured in gallons, to be pumped per minute, and the height to which that water is to be raised before it is discharged. Where a great deal of leakage has occurred in the basement, it is a good idea to keep track of the number of pailfuls or shovelfuls removed. In this way, the amount of water that must be removed by a sump pump can be estimated.

**Sump Pit.** Since various types and sizes of sump pumps are available, pick out the type desired and obtain the dimension from the manufacturer so that you will know what size of pump pit is needed to accommodate that particular unit. The pit should be large enough to hold the body of water which will be removed by the pump in about half a minute. A pit that is too small will cause the automatic

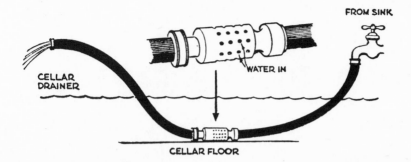

FROM SINK

CELLAR DRAINER

WATER IN

CELLAR FLOOR

switch to start and stop the motor more times each hour and will therefore create unnecessary wear and strain.

A pit of larger capacity will keep the pump operating for a longer period, so that it will start and stop less frequently each hour. The pit should be made of concrete, with openings for the footing drain to discharge its water. The top of the pit should be level with the basement floor. The bottom should be at the necessary depth to hold the amount of water predetermined as necessary for efficient and economical service of the pump and automatic switch. Drainage usually reaches the pit slowly and intermittently, depending on soil conditions and rainfall. Very effective sump pits may be constructed with a section of 36″ sewer pipe installed vertically through the floor. Holes will have to be drilled through the pipe, however, to permit the footing drain to empty into this sewer-pipe sump.

Another method that is sometimes effectively used for the construction of a sump pit is to place a large earthen crock through the basement floor so that the top of the crock is level with the floor. Holes are cut through the sides of the crock to permit the footing drain to empty into the sump.

### Cellar Drainer

If a large amount of water is discovered in the basement, the easiest way to remove it is to use some type of cellar drainer. This is a small, simple, compact appliance. It is about the size of an ordinary garden hose. The inlet and outlet ends are threaded, and perforations encircle the drainer about halfway from each end. It operates on the ejector principle. One end must be attached to a supply of water under pressure, and the other end to a pipe or hose, through which the water is discharged at ground level.

## WATERPROOFING

Once it has been decided how the basement is to be used, the necessity for waterproofing and dampproofing should be determined. Sometimes the cost of such operations will outweigh the value of using the basement for a particular purpose. If dampness interferes with healthy and comfortable living, however, remedial measures must be taken.

It is about one-tenth as expensive to properly waterproof a basement or foundation when the house is being built as it is to attempt to remedy dampness and leakage later on. A home buyer should therefore carefully check the condition of the cellar before making his purchase. Ask the builder what steps were taken to prevent water and dampness. In case trouble develops later on, this information may offer a clue as to why the waterproofing system failed. It will also provide a start-

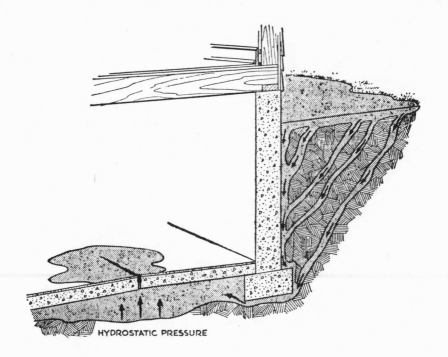

HYDROSTATIC PRESSURE

ing place from which you may proceed to correct the condition. If it is an old house, find out if the basement is usable throughout the year and inquire as to what waterproofing steps were taken in the original construction, or since the original construction was completed.

In a home where the basement has been habitually dry, anticipated changes or additions to the construction should not be undertaken without regard to their possible effect on the condition of the basement. New plumbing or fixtures, or even redecoration in the basement, may upset a watertight condition.

Basements are more vulnerable to water penetration than any other part of the house. Water which gets down around the sides of the foundation frequently forms pools under the basement floor. The resulting water pressure is often so powerful that it can lift and crack the floor and cause serious water problems in the cellar. Roofs are sometimes subject to

this hydrostatic pressure, but it is always an extremely serious threat to a basement.

Where the basement is constructed of concrete or some other type of masonry material, there is every reason to believe that it will be completely watertight. Nevertheless, the possibility of improper mixing of the concrete or the use of inferior materials, plus faulty workmanship, may create openings or cracks which will permit water to get through. This is particularly true today, when homes are being built very rapidly ,and the choice of materials and standard of workmanship are often of poor quality. When joints are improperly sealed, they provide space for water to get through. Moreover, if the concrete mixture is too porous, dampness due to capillarity occurs. As a result of these factors, water penetration is always a potent force to be reckoned with in the basement.

The location of a house in relation to the terrain is a factor to be considered, both when buying a home and in preventing dampness in an already occupied one. The surrounding soil offers a clue as to drainage possibilities. If the soil is open and porous so that air and water are easily admitted, the drainage problem will often take care of itself. This is true of sands, gravels, and loams. In less porous soils, however, the water will tend to collect and form pressure pools under the foundation.

Leakage is caused by water under pressure. This is important to bear in mind in order to properly understand waterproofing methods. To prevent leakage from occurring in a basement either the water must be diverted away from the foundation by some form of drainage, or the walls and floor of the foundation must be treated to withstand the pressure.

Satisfactory waterproofing involves treatment of all exposed surfaces. This is necessary because the water in the ground is always active. If you waterproof one side of a wall, for example, leakage may occur through the floor or through another side. In other words, one wall which has been waterproofed will simply force the water to seek some other place where it can enter the foundation. Unless the pressure is very small, therefore, partial waterproofing will never be completely satisfactory.

A membrane waterproofing system cannot be applied properly after construction has been completed. The idea of the membrane treatment involves wrapping the entire foundation in heavy waterproof paper. It is therefore virtually impossible to put in a membrane system once the building has been completed.

The usual method of waterproofing a foundation, which involves integrating a waterproofing compound with the concrete mixture, is also impossible to use once the building has been constructed. A new concrete floor can be waterproofed, but this should not be considered full protection for the entire basement against penetration by water under pressure. The water that has been coming through the basement floor may then merely be diverted against the walls. Concrete foundation walls, of course, cannot be easily replaced.

Forms of integral waterproofing may be used, however, to adequately waterproof the basement after construction has been completed. It should be emphasized again that the basement will be completely secure from the threat of leakage only if *all* walls and the floor are properly waterproofed. Merely plugging the holes or cracks in a wall where leakage has appeared will not assure dryness in the basement. At best, such methods will only temporarily alleviate the condition. Patching and repointing may have to be undertaken at regular intervals in order to prevent water under pressure from getting through at new points.

**Inside or Outside Waterproofing?** Once a house has been built, it is always easier and more effective to waterproof from the inside. Outside waterproofing requires an excavation all around the foundation and down to the footing. This is hard work if it is done by the homeowner himself, and expensive if it is not. In addition, it is extremely difficult to work properly in a narrow trench. It will be easier to apply the waterproofing at the top of the foundation walls than near the bottom. Yet it is at the bottom where the danger is greatest. The water pressure around footings is stronger and more likely to cause leakage than farther up the foundation wall.

A man cramped in a small trench cannot be expected to do as good a job on the lower portions. It is also natural that outside labor will be less concerned about workmanship on an exterior waterproofing job, because after they are through, the work is covered over and hidden. On the inside, however, the workmanship is always open for inspection, and poor craftsmanship is easy to detect.

Waterproofing from the inside is easier because there is plenty of room to move around and do an equally good job on both lower and upper portions of the walls. Be sure to use an integral waterproofing material, however, which will form a mixture that adheres properly to the surface of the wall. Some integral waterproofing compounds of the water-repellent type, for example, are difficult to handle and require expert manipulation in order to obtain a good bond, or make the mixture adhere properly to the surface of the wall.

Where brickwork is a part of the architectural design of the basement, outside waterproofing will be necessary, because any inside waterproofing would cover the brick.

If membrane waterproofing was used during construction of the building, outside repair work may be necessary. Leakage may be due to a tear in the membrane. The only way this can be corrected is to dig a trench around the outside foundation walls and down to the footings. Then the tear will have to be patched.

The following text concerns ways and means of preventing water under pressure from making cellars wet or damp. These are techniques which can be used if problems arise in old homes or in new ones shortly after construction. Planning ways and means of assuring a dry basement during initial construction, however, is a wise preventive measure.

## Inside Waterproofing

When leakage appears in a basement which was waterproofed during construction, several factors may be to blame. Faulty workmanship, poor materials, ineffective waterproofing, building settlement, and new conditions, such as remodeling and new plumbing, may be responsible. If the hydrostatic pressure is not too great, the leaks may be stopped by merely patching or plugging the spots where they appear. A more serious situation, however,

may require laying a new floor or applying fresh waterproofing to a wall. Where there are definite indications that proper waterproofing was included in the original construction, these corrective measures may be undertaken. However, where no waterproofing system was used, or evidence of it has completely disappeared, a complete waterproofing job for the entire basement is necessary. In any case, all of this work is easier and more effective when it is performed from the inside.

**Plugging Leaks.** When a small portion of a wall becomes sievelike or honeycombed, the entire piece should be removed. Using a cold chisel and hammer, cut the section away to the boundaries of the dense, solid concrete. Then clean the spot that has been cut out and wet it thoroughly. While the surface is still wet, scrub it with a grout composed of one part portland cement, one part fine sand, and water. Mix until it has the consistency of thick cream. Apply it with a stiff fiber brush, using a rotary motion. While the grout is still wet, patch the wall opening with new concrete.

Cracks are repaired as follows: Cut away the concrete on each side of the crack to a depth and total width of 1″ or 2″. Use hammer and chisel for this purpose also. First clean the cut surfaces, wet them, and seal the crack at the base of the opening by scrubbing in a cement grout. This should be done before the opening is filled. While the grout is still wet, fill the opening with a cement mortar containing one part portland cement to two parts of sand mixed with a waterproofing compound.

The method and materials used to plug leaks depend on the size and shape of the crack. Cracks at construction joints, such as those between the basement walls and floor, may be relatively wide and straight in direction. They are effectively sealed with oakum. The oakum must be rammed in so that its surface is slightly below the base of the cut in the concrete. The cut surface is then scrubbed, while still damp, with a cement grout. Cement mortar is used to fill the opening.

A fillet of the mortar may be placed at cracks situated at the junction of the wall and floor. It may be formed by finishing its surface with a round bottle. Rub

COLD CHISEL

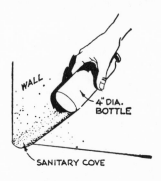

WALL

4" DIA. BOTTLE

SANITARY COVE

WET SURFACE

the bottle back and forth into the soft mortar and along the line of the joint between the wall and floor. This leaves a uniform quarter-round fillet or cove, and is easier to keep clean than a sharp intersection between wall and floor.

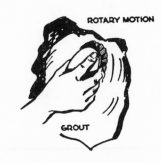

ROTARY MOTION

GROUT

To stop an actual flow of water, a mixture consisting of one part portland cement, one part sand, and water, having the consistency of putty, can be pressed into the opening and held there by means of a form or a small board until it is sufficiently hardened to stay in place.

**Bleeding the Wall.** If water is seeping rapidly through a sizable area of a basement wall, it may be difficult to repair the leaks as described above. This occurs when the water has a number of places it can get through. As soon as one hole is plugged, the water leaks through another one. Steps must be taken to localize the flow so that the water will be drawn through only one hole. Then the rest of the leaky section can be sealed with cement mortar. Sometimes this pressure can be relieved by pumping the water away from the outside of the foundation wall; but when this is not possible, a pipe inserted through a hole on the inside wall will do the job. The hole is sometimes referred to as a "weep hole."

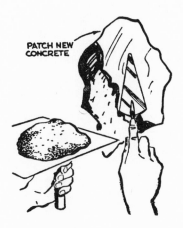

PATCH NEW CONCRETE

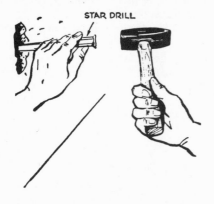

STAR DRILL

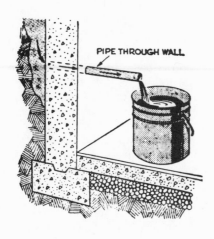

PIPE THROUGH WALL

To construct a weep hole, use a hammer and a star drill. Cut a hole through the wall near the floor, or below the porous section giving trouble. The water will then seek the point of least resistance in the wall; it will run through the hole and into the basement. Take an ordinary piece of pipe and insert it into the hole. Make sure that it is long enough to reach the exterior side of the wall. It should also extend far enough inside the cellar for the water running through it to be collected in buckets for removal, or it may be attached to a piece of hosing which will carry the water away to some drainage point. If large quantities of water come through the pipe, a sump pump or cellar

drainer should be used to remove the water from the basement floor.

If the water cannot be satisfactorily localized through one pipe, others should be inserted in the same manner. Once the water flow has been relegated to the pipes, the entire section should be treated with cement mortar. The water pressure must be kept away from the wall long enough to permit the mortar to harden and set. This may be a matter of 2 or 3 days.

After the porous section has been made watertight, the pipe should be removed and the hole plugged with cement mortar. If you wish to leave the pipe in the wall, the room end should be threaded so that a cap can be screwed on when it's time to shut off the water. Be sure that the place where the pipe enters the wall is tightly sealed.

**Openings in Floor.** Concrete floors that are badly cracked can be repaired with a 1″ topping of cement mortar comprised of 1 part portland cement to 2 parts sand. (See chapter 5, page 100.)

Sometimes a new floor can be laid. The thickness will depend on the amount of hydrostatic pressure pushing up against it and the availability of subsurface drainage. If subsurface drainage is not provided and hydrostatic pressure is great, a concrete floor of considerable thickness is necessary. Ordinary concrete will withstand pressure equal to a head of water $2\frac{1}{4}$ times the thickness of the concrete. A 6″ floor, for example, will hold against the pressure created by water that would stand 9″ above the floor line, or 15″ above the bottom of the floor.

When a floor cannot be underdrained and is subjected to strong hydrostatic pressure, it may be necessary to lay a basement floor of reinforced concrete. This requires a design of steel and concrete to be worked out by a structural engineer.

If the hydrostatic pressure is not too strong, and subsurface drainage is installed, a new basement floor between 2″ and 4″ thick will usually be satisfactory.

Before laying a new concrete floor, be

sure that it will not interfere with some piece of equipment or device installed in the basement. A new floor will reduce the height of the room. If this is not advisable, it will be necessary to repair the old concrete floor. Where subsurface drainage cannot be installed and hydrostatic pressure is powerful, it may be best to employ an engineer to determine the kind of floor needed to assure protection against leakage.

**Preparing Surfaces.** Before any application is put on a wall, whether it be mortar, paint, or a wash of some sort, be sure that the surface upon which the application is to be made is thoroughly clean and free of oils, grease, paint, or whitewash. Any sharp tool such as a scraper or a wire brush can be used to remove dry foreign matter on the surface. If, however, the foreign matter has penetrated into the surface as oil stains or grease, use a detergent to remove it. The surface should then be thoroughly hosed down with clean water so that none of the detergent, acid, or other material will be left in the masonry wall.

If the surface which is to be treated consists of any type of masonry mortar previously applied on the wall, such as a cement rendering or stucco, be sure that the existing coating is tight on the wall. This can be determined by gently tapping the surface with a hammer. Hollow sections will sound entirely different from the solid masonry. All hollow or loose parts should be cut out or cut away and replaced before any surface application of waterproofing or dampproofing material is applied.

**Cement Mortar Coatings.** When a complete waterproofing job is needed in the basement of an old house, coating the floor and walls, on the inside, with cement mortar is most effective. A cement mortar coating can also be used on a single wall, or on the floor, if other basement surfaces were properly waterproofed when the cellar was built. Otherwise, application of a cement mortar coating to a single surface

will merely divert the leakage to another part of the basement.

The best time of year to apply a cement mortar coating is during a dry spell when the basement walls or floor show little free water. First, remove everything from the basement walls and floor so that every inch of wall space may be covered with mortar. This includes not only loose furniture or garden equipment, but also water or hot air pipes, gas or electric meters, the boiler and the furnace—in fact, anything that might interfere with complete accessibility of walls and floor. This is essential. If any area is left uncovered, it will be the weak link through which water will enter the basement.

Proper preparation of all surfaces is also essential to the success of the cement mortar waterproofing. Remove any whitewash or paint with a cold chisel and hammer. Get right down to virgin masonry, be it brick, tile, cement, or cinder block. Use a wire brush to roughen the surface of the floor or wall slightly so that the mortar will stick. It should be kept wet by drenching with clean water for several hours prior to the application of the plaster. A dry surface will absorb moisture from the plaster and prevent proper setting and bonding.

Just before applying the plaster, give the moist surface a brush coat of neat portland-cement grout. Then, while this slush coat is still wet, apply a cement mortar made of 1 part portland cement and 2 parts clean sand mixed with a liquid, powder, or paste waterproofing compound, according to the instructions of the manufacturer. Each plaster coat should then be applied before the coat beneath it sets. This makes it easier to form a good bond. Scratch each undercoat lightly or score it with a sawtooth paddle, a piece of metal lath, or a sharp stick, in checkerboard-like fashion, to improve the mechanical bond with the next coat. All coats, except the final one, should be well worked with a wooden float to make the surface slightly granular. The last coat should, however, be floated carefully to leave a straight surface. A smooth, troweled surface is more likely to sweat than a rough, floated one.

Apply at least 2 coats of cement mortar to the walls to give a total thickness of not less than $5/8''$. The floor topping should be not less than $1''$ thick. Lay each coat in one operation on walls and floor. Cover all corners. Since joints, angles, and corners are the weak places, try for a minimum of these. Joints should be made on the wall, or on the floor, a foot or more from an angle or corner.

If the floor is to be plastered first and the walls must wait, the plastering should be carried up the walls about a foot, leaving a rough beveled edge. This is later wetted, brush-coated with grout, and bonded with the wall plaster. Wall plastering should be started by making a rough vertical beveled edge on the flat surface, as it is difficult to make a tight closure at a corner. The plastering should be completed with as few vertical joints as possible.

If the walls are done first, the plastering should be carried out onto the floor about a foot, leaving a rough beveled edge to be grouted and bonded with the floor plaster.

The latter method (walls first) is usually more convenient, but the first method (floor first) is more likely to give a watertight job because the jointwork is at a higher level. If the walls must be done first, a good procedure is to place boards along the bottom of the wall and apply the plaster down to the edge of the boards. When the plaster sets, remove the boards and install the floor with fillets which can be joined to the bottom of the wall plaster.

Plaster dries quickly and may crack. Just as soon as it is sufficiently hard so that the cement will not be washed away, it should be drenched, and kept continuously wet or flooded for at least a week. Properly applied, the cement mortar coating will be most effective in preventing

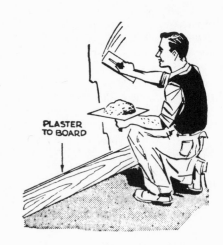

PLASTER TO BOARD

leakage. When a building settles, however, cracks may appear and disrupt the mortar waterproofing. These may be repaired in the manner described on page 298.

**Cement Grout Coatings.** Where leaks in masonry walls are relatively small, the entire wall can be coated with a cement grout, made and applied as described on page 298. A liquid waterproofing compound added to the grout will, however, increase its ability to resist leakage. The grout should have the consistency of thick cream.

**Cement Coatings Containing Powdered Iron.** Coatings containing powdered iron may also be used to waterproof the basement from the inside. They usually consist of powdered iron and an oxidizing agent mixed, either with or without the addition of portland cement. Use a brush or chipping hammer to roughen surfaces to a depth of $1/8''$ to $1/4''$ before applying an iron compound. Hack or chip the wall to remove the entire face. Chemical washes are usually not sufficient to roughen the surface for application of the iron mixture. From 3 to 5 coats should be used, depending on leakage conditions. Use a stiff bristle brush for the first coat and a soft brush for subsequent coats. A surface treated by the iron oxidation method should be finished with a neat brush coat of cement. To accelerate oxidation, dampen the wall with a water spray. An insecticide spray gun can be used. In confined spaces, air circulation may be secured by means of a fan. Windows should also be kept open during all applications. Iron oxidation mixtures applied to the floor require a protective coating. A 1″ topping, made of 1 part portland cement and 2 parts sand, properly bonded, may be used.

## Outside Waterproofing

Waterproofing treatments applied to the outside surfaces of basements are sometimes necessary. The chief objection to this approach is that a trench must be dug down to the foot of the foundation wall in order to apply the waterproofing. The excavation must be wide enough to work in, and should be extended all the way around the foundation walls.

**Repairing Membrane.** If a membrane waterproofing system was used to prevent leakage when the cellar was built, subsequent leakage may be due to a tear or hole in the membrane. Dig a trench around the entire foundation and to the footings. Locate the hole or tear and cover it with a piece of tar paper or felt. Then coat it with hot tar or asphalt.

Leakage sometimes occurs because the membrane was not carried high enough when it was originally laid. The water may pass over the top of the membrane and come down on the inside. It will then seek weak spots in foundation surfaces and leak through to the interior of the basement. The membrane should be extended so that it goes up to 6″ above the ground all around the foundation. Then seal it at the top with tar.

**Bituminous Coatings.** When water conditions are not so severe and walls are not subjected to water under pressure, a relatively inexpensive method of waterproofing the exterior walls is applying a coating of bituminous material without fabric. These coatings are both cold-applied and hot-applied. The latter are superior, however, because they provide more bitumen per unit area than the cold-applied coatings, even though the latter are easier to handle.

Bituminous coatings are sometimes used when it is necessary to install drain tile around the outside of the footings, or when some other work being done to the basement requires an excavation.

The exterior walls must first be coated with a cement mortar. Rough walls should be given a grout coat of cement mortar and allowed to dry before bituminous coatings are applied. Bituminous coatings are used only on the outside of either masonry-unit or monolithic walls. Such coatings on inside walls cause blistering and peeling.

Cold-applied coatings are of heavy-brushing or troweling consistency. Asphalt or coal-tar pitch is used as the base. They are easier to apply because no heating is necessary. When an asphalt coating is used, the wall should first be primed with an asphalt primer. Use a coal-tar or creo-

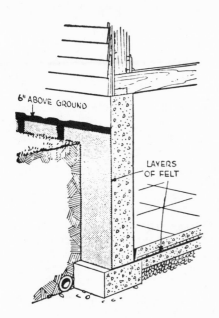

6″ ABOVE GROUND

LAYERS OF FELT

NEXT COAT AT RIGHT ANGLE TO FIRST

sote primer with coal-tar coatings. Bituminous coatings may also be applied to cement mortar coats.

Before applying hot coatings make walls smooth and dry. An asphalt primer should be used for hot coal-tar pitch. Use a roofer's mop to spread hot-applied coatings. Spread the coating to a thickness of at least $\frac{1}{8}''$ in one or more applications. Bituminous coatings, hot or cold, should extend from 6" above the ground line down over the top of the footing. The second coat should be applied with brush strokes at right angles to the strokes of the first coat.

Commercial bituminous mortars are also available. These plastic cements are applied with a plasterer's trowel. They are usually comprised of asphalt or some other bituminous material combined with asbestos fiber, mineral filler, and suitable volatile solvents. The cement, ready for use, comes in containers holding from 30 to 500 or more pounds. It should be spread smoothly and evenly without drawing or pulling. A $\frac{1}{8}''$ coating, requiring approximately 80 pounds for 100 square feet, is usually applied to the outside of cellar walls, and a $\frac{1}{4}''$ coat is laid on cellar floors. The trench around the foundation may be refilled after the plaster has been allowed to dry at least 24 to 48 hours. Care must be taken not to injure it.

Floor plaster should be given a heavy protective covering of portland-cement mortar or concrete.

**Repairing Cement Mortar Coatings.** If the basement was waterproofed by means of a cement mortar coating on outside foundation walls when the house was constructed, repairs to the waterproofing will also have to be made on the outside. Cracks in the walls are frequently caused when a building settles. The movement also severs the cement mortar waterproofing.

Cracks in outside monolithic concrete walls may be sealed by cutting a groove about 1" deep and 1" wide. The edges of the cut should first be scrubbed into the groove. Then pack a cement mortar of stiff consistency into the opening. Because the expense and inconvenience associated with digging a trench are often considerable, when an outside cement mortar coating is found to be faulty, outside repairs are frequently disregarded in favor of a new cement mortar coating applied to inside surfaces.

## SEEPAGE AND CAPILLARITY

Seepage is frequently confused and used interchangeably for leakage or capillarity. Actually, it may be used with both leakage and capillarity. When applied to leakage, it implies the movement of water through a surface by means of pressure. This pressure may be hydrostatic, or it may be direct pressure from rain or pipes. It is usually not very great.

Seepage due to hydrostatic pressure may be prevented by dampproofing as well as waterproofing methods. Seepage in the basement may occur when water overflows a tub or basin in the bathroom or kitchen above, finds its way through an opening, and drips down into the cellar. It also takes place when water seeps in through tiny holes or cracks in windows, doors, or even basement masonry above the surface of the ground. Sometimes seepage produced by hydrostatic pressure will gather around the outside of foundation surfaces and will be drawn into the interior by means of capillarity.

Dampness, as opposed to actual leakage or seepage, may be transmitted through basement surfaces by means of capillary action. This is particularly true when the soil surrounding the walls and floor is especially damp. Often, the amount of this moisture is so small that it is evaporated by the air, and the walls and floor appear to be dry. When there is a great deal of humidity or water vapor in the air in the basement, however, evaporation will not be possible and this moisture will then be deposited on the floor or walls. It is often very difficult to tell the difference between condensation and capillarity. When this moisture appears, therefore, it is suggested that a test for condensation be conducted. (See chapter 7, page 187.)

Capillarity, or "wick action," seldom results in any appreciable amount of moisture when it occurs alone. If the basement is being used for living quarters, or the floor and walls are covered with materials impervious to air, such as oil paint or linoleum, the moisture brought on by capillarity will be unpleasant and damaging.

A complication may arise when part of the moisture is the result of condensation. In such cases, additional examination of the damp area is necessary. Cover the damp area with a rubber mat, preferably 3′ × 3′. Let it stand for several days and then lift it. If the surface covered is dry, condensation and not capillary transmission is one of the causes of dampness. If the area under the mat remains damp after surrounding areas have dried, capillarity contributes to the dampness.

Moisture due to capillary action enters the basement through tiny holes or pores in the construction. A drainage which minimizes the dampness in the soil surrounding the foundation will reduce the possibility of capillarity. Treatments applied to basement surfaces which seal up the pores will prevent the moisture from reaching the interior of the basement. Methods used to prevent seepage will also provide good protection against capillary transmission of moisture.

## Sealing the Pores

Seepage or capillarity involves a penetration of water moisture through tiny holes in the walls and floor. The best and most logical means of preventing seepage, therefore, is to seal up the pores, using a dampproofer which integrates with the surface and thereby prevents water from seeping through. Most of the commercially available products are cement-base preparations that you simply mix with water. If you pick a kind that comes in a variety of pastel colors, you can decorate your cellar walls at the same time.

Simply mix portland cement into a solution of water and any liquid waterproofing material which reacts chemically with portland cement. The usual proportion is 1 part of the waterproofing with 3 parts of water. Then stir enough portland cement into the solution to form the consistency of heavy paint.

Regardless of what dampproofer you choose, the preparation of the wall surfaces is very important. Any sort of finish on them—such as calcimine or oil paint —must be removed, with wire brush, paint remover, solvent (made by dissolving 1 pound of trisodium phosphate in 1 quart of warm water), or a wash composed of 1 part muriatic acid and 5 to 10 parts water. Let the wash stand for about a half-hour. Then flush with a hose, or scrub with a wire or stiff bristle brush to wash off the acid, dirt, and loose particles.

Clean out and enlarge holes and cracks with a cold chisel and hammer. Undercut sides to form a dovetail that will hold the patch firmly in place. Then fill with mortar comprised of 1 part cement, 2

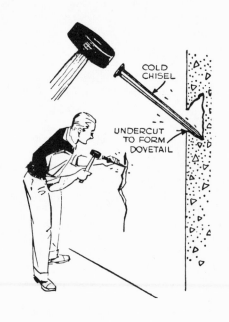

COLD CHISEL

UNDERCUT TO FORM DOVETAIL

and allowed to dry, you see moist spots here and there, some of the larger pores in the wall surface have not been completely filled. They should be enlarged with a cold chisel, filled with patching cement or a 1-to-2 mortar mixture, and treated again with the dampproofing solution.

Since all cement-base dampproofers are quick-setting preparations, be sure to wash off any drippings and spatters that might mar your basement floor or other surfaces. If you let them stand too long and they harden, you'll have trouble removing them.

The most widely used effective water-repellent admixtures for concrete contain calcium stearate or ammonium stearate as the water-repellent substance. The "water-proofed" portland cements, which are readily available from building supply dealers, contain a uniformly dispersed water repellent such as calcium stearate and may be used conveniently instead of an admixture and an ordinary cement.

parts sand, and water. If a leak is actually visible, a quick-setting patching cement must be used. After patches set, wet the wall with fine spray from a hose. Finally, mix the dampproofer according to the manufacturer's instructions, and scrub it into the wall with a stiff-bristled brush.

In applying the dampproofer, brush the material into the wall so that it fills every pore. Start at the bottom and gradually work up. Since this is a messy process, it's best to wear an old hat and goggles or glasses. Two coats of most dampproofers are generally required. The walls should be thoroughly wetted after the first coat has dried and before the second one is applied. Use the spray from a garden hose again. The drying time, in most cases, varies from about 2 to 4 hours. Don't rush it. After the second coat has dried, see if it will brush off. If not, the wall should be wetted again, and then again, every 12 hours for the next 3 days. This continual wetting and drying helps to cure the mixture slowly and makes it an integral part of the wall. If, after the second coat has been thoroughly cured

## Bituminous Dampproofers

Outside foundation walls may be effectively treated to prevent capillarity and given some protection from leakage by various applications of bituminous materials. These are similar in composition and application to those described on page 303. They include hot applications of coal-tar pitch or asphalt, and cold applications of prepared bituminous paints, water-gas tar, and coal tar. The latter are obtainable at city gasworks or from manufacturers of roofing materials.

Four very thin coats of water-gas tar are brushed or sprayed on the wall. Each 100 square feet of masonry require $2\frac{1}{2}$ gallons. Sufficient time must be allowed between coats for each to be properly absorbed by the masonry. After the last coat is dry, refined coal tar should be applied at the rate of $\frac{1}{2}$ to 1 gallon per 100 square feet. Then it is thoroughly brushed in and left to dry for 24 to 48 hours.

Bituminous paints are used strictly for dampproofing purposes. They are applied cold, with an ordinary paintbrush. At least 2 coats are required. The primer should be very thin and should be thoroughly brushed into all pores and minute cracks. The paint is usually applied at the rate of 1 to 1½ gallons per 100 square feet, but the quantity will vary with porosity and roughness of the surface. Apply the second coat within 24 hours after the first, and at the rate of 1 gallon per 100 square feet. Provide a film approximately ¹⁄₆₄″ thick. Earth backfilling may be done 24 hours after the application of the last coat, care being taken not to bruise or scar the paint.

# CONDENSATION

Since most of the basement is submerged in the ground, the temperature of the walls and floor is therefore greatly influenced by the ground temperature. This remains approximately constant throughout the year. As a matter of fact, even points only 2′ or 3′ below ground surface vary only a few degrees from the annual mean temperature of the locality.

As a result, the basement walls and floor are likely to be cooler than the outdoor air during summer months, the season when condensation usually occurs in the basement. The warm, humid air coming down from the rest of the house or entering through windows strikes the cold walls and floor of the basement and condenses. Water will also appear when this warm air comes in contact with equipment or furnishings in a basement with cold surfaces. (See chapter 7, page 185.) Condensation caused in this manner will usually be visible. When the water condition is not readily identified as condensation, however, tests may be performed. (See chapter 7, page 187.) Condensation may also occur within the masonry, behind inner surfaces, and this will sometimes not show up in tests. This moisture may later reach the inner surface of the wall by capillarity. If there is little ventilation and no chance for the moisture to evaporate, it will cause dampness on the walls. This latter condition occurs often in corners and behind large objects situated close to the masonry surfaces.

If the basement walls have been made glossy and impervious by an application of paint, the condensation, or "sweating," may be very great. It is quite possible that the lower parts of the walls may drip, and shallow pools of water may form on the floor. This condition may also be caused by water seeping in from the outside. It is, therefore, very important to identify the nature of the condition before undertaking costly waterproofing measures.

The amount of water vapor is increased when clothes are hung up to dry in a basement. This will not be so bad during the winter if proper ventilation is used, but during rainy summer weather when indoor drying is necessary it will greatly increase the possibility of condensation. The water-vapor content in the basement is also affected by the combustion of fuels containing hydrogen, such as gas, kerosine, or other fuel oil. Their fumes may, however, be carried outside the house by means of a suitable chimney or vent.

## Remedies

Condensation in the basement is a problem not only because of its damaging effect on surfaces and furnishings below the ground, but also because the dampness may be drawn up into other parts of the house where it will cause additional discomfort and destruction. It is also possible that a water condition in the upper floors of the home may be mistakenly attributed to some type of leakage. Dealing with condensation at its source in the basement, therefore, will often do away with dampness in other parts of the house.

The following are suggested ways and means of preventing condensation in the basement. (See also chapter 7, page 188.)

**Ventilation.** Merely opening windows and doors in order to introduce outside air which will raise the temperature of the surfaces is difficult to do in the basement. In the summertime this warm air may add to the water vapor and humidity in the cellar and increase condensation. It is sometimes better during warm periods to keep as much of the hot outside air as possible from getting into the basement. This will reduce the possibility of condensation.

When condensation takes place on basement walls or windows during the

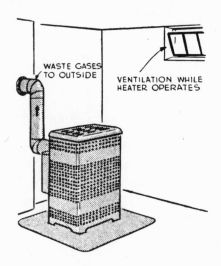

WASTE GASES TO OUTSIDE

VENTILATION WHILE HEATER OPERATES

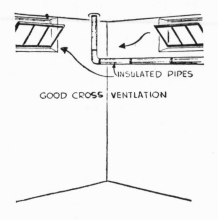

INSULATED PIPES

GOOD CROSS VENTILATION

winter, however, proper ventilation, by means of opening and closing doors and windows, will generally correct the situation.

**Heating.** Condensation during the summer is caused by hot outside air striking cold surfaces in the basement. The problem then is to increase the temperature of basement surfaces as much as possible so that it will come close to the temperature of the outside air. Heat from domestic hot water heaters, operating continuously during the summer, frequently solves condensation problems in basements. In addition, heating devices that are not insulated too effectively are

often valuable in reducing condensation in the cellar. A space heater may also be used to raise the temperature of masonry surfaces above the dew point, but ventilation must be provided while the heater is in operation. Waste gases from such heaters should be vented to the outside.

Although heating may be effective for most of the basement area, it often does not reach remote places such as wall closets, foot lockers, and areas behind drapes. Condensation will consequently still occur in these areas.

**Insulation.** If the temperature of the inside surfaces of the basement is raised so that it will be close to the temperature of the air, condensation may be prevented. Insulating surfaces with paint, varnish, paper, or other thin material, however, is not sufficient. The insulating material should be cellular glass, or another material which is a vapor barrier, is not absorptive, and is not damaged by moisture. Floor insulation may consist of a thin layer of lightweight aggregate concrete, structural clay tile, hollow concrete units, or cellular glass. It should be covered with a wearing surface of cement mortar, quarry tile, or asphalt tile of suitable thickness.

A layer of cellular glass set in and covered with cement mortar, or a tier of structural clay tile or hollow concrete units with or without a finished coating, may be used for insulating basement walls. Wood should not be used between the insulation and the old wall or floor because it may be damaged by moisture in this position.

Condensation is prevented by a vapor barrier placed behind a wood surface. It should run parallel to the furring strips and lap only over solid supports. The idea is to prevent accumulation of free water behind ornamental panels. The top and bottom furring strips, and those around windows and other openings, should be continuous in order to form a good seal. (See chapter 7, page 190.)

**Dehumidification.** Condensation in the basement can be prevented by removing some of the moisture from the air. Air conditioning will bring on an even temperature. This, however, is a costly way of preventing condensation and, unless the basement is used extensively, it is not recommended.

Chemical and mechanical dehumidifiers may also be used. The chemical type involves the use of calcium chloride, or some other substance, which has the capacity to absorb moisture from the air. Lithium chloride, silica gel, and activated alumina are also suitable materials. Supplies of calcium chloride, trays, and directions for use can be obtained from building supply dealers. The chemical is relatively inexpensive; however, it can be used only once, and must be disposed of when liquid. As it absorbs moisture from the air, it dissolves. This solution must be emptied into drains which must be flushed well, as the solution is highly corrosive to metal and somewhat injurious to concrete. It also has a harmful effect on

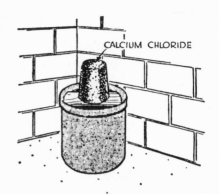

plants and vegetation in its concentrated form, and causes steel to corrode. Consequently, it is used in galvanized, enameled, or otherwise protected pans, screens, or trays.

Silica gel and lithium chloride have not attained as wide a usage in basements as has calcium chloride, presumably because their power of absorption is not as great. Silica gel, however, may be reused if the gel is reheated. A few mechanical dehumidifiers operate on a continuous cycle using silica gel. The heated moisture is vented to the outside.

Mechanical refrigeration dehumidifiers operate on the principle of condensing the moisture on a cooled coil called an evaporator. The temperature of the evaporator is maintained just above freezing. The basement is not cooled by this process, however, since the heat lost by the air is restored by blowing the same air through the condenser. This is an essential step in the refrigeration cycle. The condensed moisture, as water, runs down the coil into a container or drain. A pump may be needed for use with a drain. If a container is used, it must be emptied frequently.

# 13

# HOME AND PROPERTY IMPROVEMENTS

## FIRESTOPPING

Most houses in urban districts built during the past 40 years were constructed with adequate firestopping throughout their construction. But many older houses were not so constructed, depending on their locality and the building restrictions in force when they were built.

There is not much you can do in the way of installing firestops between floors of these houses unless you remove part of the wall covering near the juncture of the wall or partition, subfloor, and joists. If the wall covering is in first-class condition and you are happy with it, it is best left alone, particularly if you are not sure whether or not there is firestopping at these points. Firestopping means only fire retarding, that is, closing up the natural flues created by conventional stud-wall construction.

Houses with cellars, the ceilings of which are quite often unfinished, can be fire-retarded easily at the point of the joists and foundation wall, and since many fires start in the cellar, it is good insurance to install fireproof material if none exists. A finished ceiling of portland cement and expanded metal lath is excellent fire-retarding material, and one of the wallboards, preferably one with a gypsum core, works equally well and is much more

easily installed. Mineral wool, or vermiculite (a form of mica expanded under heat into millions of imprisoned air cells) which comes in "pebble" form, is excellent material for firestopping, besides being a first-class insulating material.

There are two methods of firestopping at the sill and foundation wall of a cellar. One method is to fill in the space between sill and subfloor with fireproof material and nail ¾" boards between the joists to hold the material in place. The other method, if the sill is deep enough, is to fill a space about 2" thick from the top of the foundation to the subfloor, and hold it in place with 2" lumber between the joists.

Partitions over a cellar girder can be similarly filled by removing 6" of wall about 12" from the subfloor, and filling the space between the studs with vermiculite. The same procedure can be used for partitions on other floors and outside walls, if desired.

Attics can be sealed off by nailing a 2" × 8" or 10" board to the underside of the roof rafters at the plate and filling the space with vermiculite. An unfinished attic with exposed joists can be thoroughly insulated with this material by pouring it evenly to a depth of about 3" between the joists. An easy way to level the vermiculite is to make a scraper, by

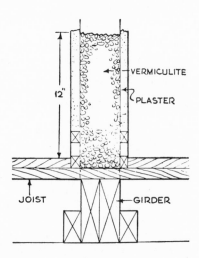

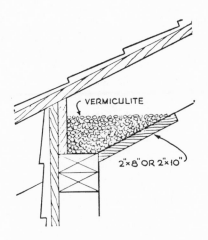

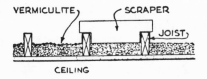

# INSULATION

There are numerous forms of insulating material designed for various methods of application. There are basically four types: loose fill; blankets and batts; insulating wallboards; and bright aluminum foil. Except for the last, these materials act on the principle of an accumulation of quiet or dead air which is the poorest of heat conductors. The bright aluminum foil works on the principle of heat reflection, being in itself an excellent conductor of heat.

Loose-fill insulation is one of the oldest types, exemplified by the old icehouses with their double walls filled with sawdust.

cutting out the ends of a board which spans the joists to a depth 3″ less than the depth of the joists. The cutout ends act as guides on the joists as the board scrapes the insulation evenly. An attic so insulated, in a small one-story house, can save up to 22% in fuel.

## Blankets and Batts

Blankets and batts are made up of vegetable or mineral-fiber material, and are different from insulating wallboards only in the degree of their compactness or compression. The wallboards have poorer insulating quality because of their compression. Solid wood has good insulating properties because of its cellular structure, but thickness for thickness, fiber insulating boards have better qualities because their cellular structure is less compact.

More heat is lost through a roof than through the walls of a house, particularly if the attic is unfinished and unheated, the warm air rising through the walls into the cold attic and out through the roof. That is why blocking off air circulation at the juncture of the attic joists and the plate, and at the cornice, with loose fill contributes a great deal toward preventing heat loss at these points. Insulating the attic joists and the space between the roof rafters, further reduces to a considerable extent the amount of heat loss.

Outside-wall insulating materials must have a vapor barrier to prevent the

**311**

interior warm air from striking the exterior cold air and condensing into trapped water. This holds true also for roof insulation, for the same reason. Blanket and batt insulation come with and without integral vapor barriers of glazed asphalt-saturated felt or kraft paper. The vapor barrier is always placed facing the interior, and should be as close to the wall or ceiling covering as possible.

Blankets are attached in several ways. One method is to bend over the ends of the blankets and attach them to the studs with wood lath, the blanket being placed midway between the thickness of the wall. This provides an extra dead-air space, which is added insulation. Another method is to nail the flaps of the vapor seal which extend beyond the blanket to the sides of the studs.

Batt insulation is applied in much the same manner, but fills practically the entire thickness of the walls, the vapor-seal flaps being nailed to the stud edges.

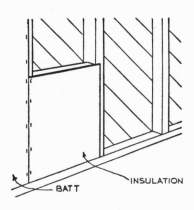

BATT      INSULATION

Both blanket and batt insulation come in standard widths to fit conventional stud spacing. The advantage of blanket or batt over loose fill in walls is that the insulating material is contained and kept compact, whereas loose fill may pack in time, leaving an uninsulated space at the top while it has packed too tightly at the bottom—losing some of its insulating properties.

Existing house walls lacking insulation are usually insulated with loose fill blown into openings cut through the exterior sheathing. This must be done by contractors having the necessary equipment. Since this method of insulating provides no vapor barrier, there is the possibility of condensation occurring, although many houses have been so insulated without any apparent signs of condensation.

Insulating boards are also structural in their purpose, and houses today are more often than not sheathed with fiberboard for the double purpose of insulation and structural rigidity. These fiberboards differ from interior wallboards only in that they are either saturated or surfaced with asphalt for weather resistance. Their structural strength is about the same as that of wood sheathing, but they have greater insulating properties. Moreover, they are more easily, quickly, and economically applied. They come in $1/2''$ and $25/32''$ thicknesses, and in a number of panel widths and lengths. Interior wallboards of fiber composition are particularly effective for remodeling attics, where they serve the dual purpose of supplying a finished wall plus insulation. Even without additional insulation, an attic thus surfaced will show an appreciable reduction in fuel bills.

## Aluminum Foil

Bright aluminum foil which comes in flat and crinkled form is more often used between first-floor joists, where there is no cellar, to prevent the cold air from the ground from being transmitted through the floor. Also used to some extent between studs in walls, the foil must form a tight seal where it is attached to the framing members in a similar manner as blanket insulation. This material has about two-thirds the insulating value of blanket, batt, or loose fill.

# INTERIOR WALL COVERINGS

Modern wall-covering materials of the "dry-wall" type—meaning walls put up without the use of water—are made in a variety of trade-name products, but can be classified roughly in four groups. They are pulpboards; fiberboards of either wood or cane fibers; gypsum-core wallboards; and plywood. Besides these, there are also cork tiles, linoleum, and wood-veneer on fabric.

The four groups come in panels of varying widths and lengths in tile form, and in plank or board form. Some are square-edged; others, beveled square-edged, tongued-and-grooved, or ship-lapped; others have recessed edges for the special application of tape and cement to achieve an unbroken wall surface which is then painted.

Wallboards in general were at one time considered only for cheap wall coverings with the conventional wood battens covering the joints in all directions. Today this is not true of these materials. They are still in most cases very economical to install, but they are not condemned to the category of cheapness or makeshift. Many owners of very expensive modern houses prefer such walls to plaster. The problem of joints still exists, with all but the boards that are tape-cemented, but more thought is now given to the handling of wallboard panels and joints so that they enhance a decorative scheme.

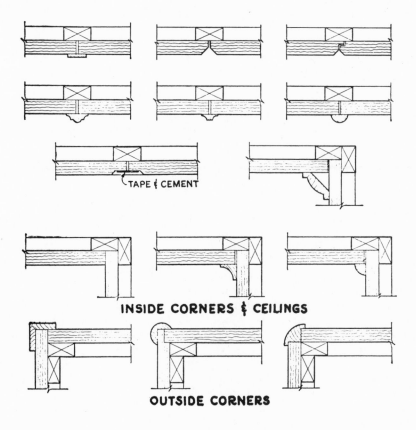

TAPE & CEMENT

**INSIDE CORNERS & CEILINGS**

**OUTSIDE CORNERS**

Basically, all wallboards of whatever material are nailed to 1″ × 2″ or 1″ × 3″ wood strips which are nailed to the existing plaster wall. Furring strips are also used on masonry walls in the cellar and on existing ceilings of plaster. The use of furring is for the purpose of obtaining a level flat surface for the wallboard, and to permit the arrangement of wallboard panels for a planned decorative effect. This is not always possible if the panels are nailed to the existing studding. Wallboards should also be nailed at intermediate points which, between normal stud spacing, would be the blocking between the studs. As this blocking was framed without regard to standard wallboard-panel sizes, it is all the more important to use furring to accommodate wallboard-panel sizes.

**Pulpboards.** Pulpboards are usually $\frac{3}{16}$″ thick and come in panels 4′ × 8′ in size. They need more bracing than the fiberboards, being more flexible, and the insulating properties are less. Some of these boards are manufactured with a pre-painted pebbled surface which takes paint readily, should you prefer another color. They are structurally quite strong and can easily be bent around curves of large radii.

**Fiberboards.** Fiberboards are usually $\frac{1}{2}$″ thick and come in panels 4′ × 6′ and longer; in tile form from 12″ × 12″ to 16″ × 32″; and in plank form from 8″ to 16″ wide and from 8′ to 12′ long. The tiles and planks have a special type of tongued-and-grooved edge with a beveled front which permits blind nailing. These fiberboards have excellent insulating qualities, having been designed for the purpose of efficient insulation combined with a finished wall surface. They have, however, relatively soft surfaces which mar easily if furniture or other hard objects strike them.

**Hardboards.** Hardboards are made "regular" and "tempered," the latter having a "skin" which is extremely hard and smooth. Hardboards range in thickness from $\frac{1}{8}$″ to $\frac{1}{4}$″, and are sold in panel form 4′ × 8′ and longer. Most of these boards are smooth-surfaced, but some brands can be had with a "leather-grain" texture. All are dark-brown in color. The tempered variety also comes in panels grooved in a 4″-square tile pattern, ready to be enameled in whatever color you choose and then varnished with a waterproof varnish, for bathrooms and kitchens. Hardboards make extremely rigid and hard wall coverings, but have little insulating value.

**Tileboards.** Tileboards are made from $\frac{1}{8}$″ tempered hardboard in tile patterns, usually 4′ × 4′, in a variety of colors which have been baked on, or hot-paint sprayed. These colors are extremely durable and waterproof, and the tileboard is an economical method of wainscoting a kitchen or bathroom. Tileboard is also sold in panel form with horizontal grooves and plain-surfaced for the modern effect of wall surfaces above a regular tile-pattern wainscoat, or as wainscoat material.

**Gypsum-Core Wallboards.** Gypsum-core wallboards run from $\frac{1}{4}$″ to $\frac{1}{2}$″ in thickness and come in panels 4′ × 6′ and longer. They are made square-edged and with recessed edges for tape-and-cement application. Their insulating properties are a bit less than that of the insulation fiberboards, but they are one of the few wallboards that can be treated so as to hide their joints when painted.

## Application

**Plywood.** Plywood paneling comes in a wide selection of beautiful woods. Most lumberyards have sample pieces on hand so that the home mechanic can examine the entire selection before he makes a final choice. Paneling can be stained, waxed, or varnished. If a painted surface is desired, then a wallboard or cheap grade of plywood should be used.

Plywood is sold in thicknesses from ¼″ to ¾″, and in panels 4′ × 8′ and longer. It is also obtainable in a special board form with grooved edges which produce a slightly lapped joint. This product is applied with metal clips and requires no finishing. The planks are ¼″ thick, 16¼″ wide, and from 6′ to 8′ long. Surfaces are birch, knotty pine, sliced oak, and Philippine mahogany. This type of wall can be put up easily, quickly, and permanently. Plywood is also obtainable with a striated surface and with the fir grain etched out, the latter producing a novel grain-relief effect.

The first step in paneling is to plan how the panels may be arranged for both balance and economy. It might be a good idea to make a scale drawing of each wall that is to be covered so that the panel arrangements can be worked out easily and accurately. In making up such drawings, the openings for windows and doors should be indicated, and you should also put in all dimensions. Do not just figure on the large areas and forget the small ones around doors or below windows.

Probably the easiest way to install the paneling is to have all seams run vertically. This will probably give a better appearance as well. As it is seldom found that the width of a wall will be divisible by an even number of panels, some of the panels will have to be cut down in width. Suppose your wall is 15′ wide and your panels are 4′ wide. It would not look well to have 3 full-width panels and then one 3′ wide. It would be better to take 6″ off each of the 2 end panels so that the final result will be well balanced. Or if the wall is 11′ wide, put a 3′ panel in the center and a full-width one at either end.

There are several ways to take care of the seams between sections of paneling. A simple V-joint is easily obtained and will give good results. If a butt joint is used, then the sections should be spaced a fraction of an inch apart and the seam covered with a strip of molding in the same manner as that used for wallboard.

Another point that must be considered and decided is how the corners are to be treated. Possibly the least complex method would be to bring the 2 sections forming the corner to within about ½″ of each other and then cover the opening or seam with a strip of molding. Another method would be to make a butt joint without using any additional molding. That calls for very careful cutting because the 2 pieces must fit together along the entire length of the seam. Special corner molding can be used; if so, this is put in place first and the panels brought up tight against it.

If the trim around windows and doors is not yet on or can be removed without too much difficulty, then the paneling can be brought in close to them so that the edges will be covered when the trim is replaced. But if the trim cannot be removed without danger of marring the wood, then the paneling should be brought up as close to the edge of the trim as possible. The ensuing joint or seam can be covered later with molding if you wish.

To ensure getting tight joints at all points, measure and saw with care and accuracy. Mistakes earlier in this work can be covered up, but when you get to the paneling there isn't anything to go over that.

To eliminate the possibility of any moisture from the masonry wall damaging the paneling, the furring should be covered with waterproof paper or the back side of the plywood should be painted with asphalt paint.

The ceiling should be installed first; when that work has been completed, the walls can go on. To provide additional support for the paneling, glue should be used as well as nails to attach it to the furring. The glue used for this work should be the kind recommended by the maker of the material, and the size and spacing of nails should be done in accordance with the manufacturer's directions. This information can be obtained from the lumberyard. Special molding is available to cover the joint between wall and ceiling.

Joints in wall covering can be finished in a variety of ways, depending on your personal preference and the effect you wish to achieve. There is a special type of plane made, with a form of razor-blade iron, with which you can bevel, groove, and shiplap insulation fiberboard cleanly and accurately.

Methods of applying various wallboards depend on the type, but most are nailed to whatever surface is used. Others, such as ceiling tile, are nailed and cemented; tileboards applied over flat surfaces are cemented, and nailed if applied to furring or framing, the nails set flush in the "joints" and then covered with matching-color "touch-up" paint.

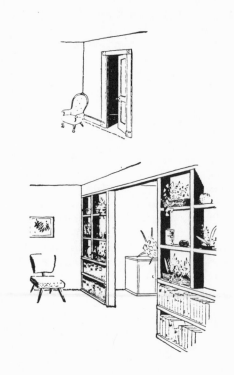

## REMODELING WITH A LOAD-BEARING PARTITION

If you have two small rooms separated by a load-bearing partition, and you would like to combine them in some way to achieve added spaciousness, light, and ventilation, you can do it by changing the old, solid partition into an open one. Moreover, if there is a narrow doorway in the partition, you can convert it to a wide opening. If no door exists, you can construct a wide opening in the partition.

Load-bearing partitions, as mentioned previously, are partitions that carry the joists of the ceiling or floor overhead. These cannot be completely removed unless a girder of equal load-bearing properties replaces the partition and spans the room from wall to wall, or from another partition to wall or partition. Such a girder would necessarily have to be of unusual depth and thickness.

Calculating the dimensions of such a girder to sustain a given load is a structural engineer's job and beyond the ability of the average amateur carpenter. The stud spacing necessary can, however, be utilized as an open decorative effect which will give you airiness, light, and ventilation, and the openings between the studs can be utilized to display potted plants and books by introducing spaced horizontal boards between the studs.

First, make sure that no water or sewage pipes are hidden in the existing partition. If such exist, the part of the partition containing them must be left as is, since it is a major operation to attempt to remove these pipes and place them elsewhere. Electrical conduits or BX cables and outlets can be removed and provision made for them in other partitions, or in a part of the existing one near the juncture of another partition or wall. Moreover, if BX cable is being used for baseboard receptacles, the cable can be run along the studs at the new location of the baseboard, which will cover the cable.

Remove the existing wall covering from ceiling to floor on both sides of the partition, exposing the old studding and plates. Old studs must be replaced with new, clear-finish lumber of the same dimensions, since the new studs will be exposed. Removing and replacing the old studs must be done one at a time so as not to weaken the structure. If the old studs are nailed to a plate under the floor joists, saw them off at the rough-floor line and nail the new studs to the rough floor with

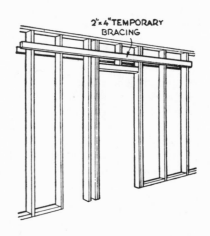

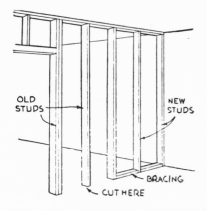

$2'' \times 4''$ blocking between them, also nailed to the rough floor and studs. Toenail the studs with 16d ($3\frac{1}{2}''$) common nails.

Studs that are nailed to a sole located on the rough floor can be removed by pulling out the nails and nailing new studs on the existing sole.

## Enlarging Doorway

An old narrow doorway can be enlarged, or a new large opening installed according to the general method of framing new openings in construction. (See chapter 3, page 66.) Before enlarging a doorway, however, temporary bracing is required to support the studs which are to be cut out for the larger opening. Nail a $2 \times 4$ or $2 \times 6$ with 20d ($4''$) nails across the studs on both sides of the partition, slightly higher than the top of the open-

ing-to-be, and extending at least 2 studs beyond those to be removed. These temporary braces act as temporary headers until the studs have been cut and headers have been framed in place. Now cut out the studs that are in the way of the new opening, and remove the trimmers and headers of the old doorway. Replace the headers with doubled headers ($2 \times 4$s for openings up to 6' wide, and $2 \times 6$s for openings 8' wide), supported by trimmers spiked with 20d spikes to the studs framing the new opening. Truss this new opening with diagonal braces at each corner and intermediate cripples (short studs) spaced evenly between the opening studs. Nail the cripples first (16d nails),

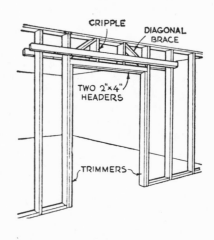

and frame 2″ × 4″ blocking between them, spiked (20d) to the plate. After this new framing has been well spiked together, remove the temporary braces. An 8′ opening is the widest you can make; use a 6′ opening if it will do.

The double studs forming the opening should be covered with ¼″ plywood or ¾″ solid stock to hide the stud joints, and the underside of the headers must be covered in a similar manner. Blocking between the studs is necessary for bracing

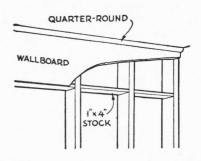

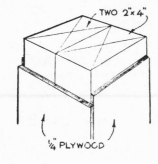

ished underside of the headers of the opening. A wallboard of your choice is best for this and is easily applied. Frame 1″ × 4″ stock between the studs, on a line with the bottom edge of the wallboard, closing off the space between the plate and bottom edge of the wallboard. Nail a quarter-round molding at the juncture of the ceiling and the wallboard for a finish at that point.

As a finish at the base of the open partition, nail 1″ stock between the studs at the height of the new baseboard, forming a closed box in which BX cable can be laid for baseboard outlets, if desired.

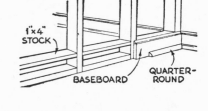

and can be 1″ × 4″ stock arranged in a symmetrical pattern, or 1″ × 6″ or 1″ × 8″ stock can be framed between the studs as shelves for potted plants, books, and so forth.

## Wall Covering

A new wall covering must be used below the ceiling, on a line with the fin-

Then nail the new baseboard to this and to the studs with finishing nails set and filled. Nail a quarter-round molding, as a base shoe, at the juncture of the floor and baseboard.

Variations in treatment of the open-partition idea are numerous, depending on the architectural arrangement of your rooms, but the preliminary steps are the same, whatever form the finished partition will take. Just make sure that each step is performed carefully, keeping in mind that when you remove a structural member, replace it before removing another. And *always* adequately brace an old opening before removing structural members to enlarge the opening.

Window openings can be enlarged in the same manner as door openings, but when doing this, temporary bracing must be nailed across the top and below the sill line before cutting studs, removing headers and trimmers, and replacing them.

## BUILDING A PARTITION

If you need an additional room and have a large one that can be partitioned, it is easy to do. The partition can have a door or not. Use 2″ × 4″ lumber for the plate, studs, and sole. No. 1 common dimension fir is good.

First, accurately mark out the line of the partition on the existing ceiling and on the floor. This is most easily done with a carpenter's line and blue chalk. The line is chalked, stretched between the walls of the room at the location of the proposed partition—about ½″ from the ceiling—and snapped. This leaves a chalk line on the ceiling. Do the same at the floor line. Then nail a plate to the existing ceiling joists through the plaster, using 20d spikes. Nail the sole to the finished floor in the same manner. Now mark out the locations of the studs on 16″ centers on the sole, and cut the studs to fit tightly between the plate and the sole. There may be variations in the floor or ceiling level, so each stud must be custom-fitted. Toenail the studs to the sole with 16d nails. Use a carpenter's level vertically to keep the studs plumb, and toenail them to the plate.

If you plan to have a doorway, frame trimmers on each side of the studs forming the opening, making allowance for the finished jambs and blocking—roughly about 1½″ on each side. Frame 2″ × 4″

headers between the studs and spike them securely. Frame one or two cripples between the headers and the plate, depending on the width of the opening. Since the partition is nonbearing, the opening for the door need not be trussed.

The wall covering easiest to apply is one of the wallboards. If you wish to have an unbroken wall surface which can be painted and not show panel joints, use gypsum-core wallboard with recessed edges. Blocking between the studs should

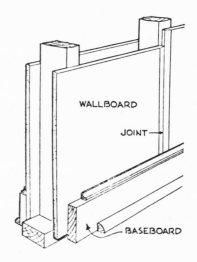

occur about midway between ceiling and floor for stud bracing, if this type of board is used, since the board is nailed to the studs horizontally.

To prepare the joints of gypsum-core wallboard for painting over them, first fill the recessed edges with the water-mix cement which is furnished with the wallboard. Then press the perforated fiber tape (also furnished) into the cement. The nubs of cement coming through the perforations are then smoothed out. After the cement has dried thoroughly, apply another thin coat and feather this out 3″ or 4″ on each side of the channel. When this coat has dried, apply another coat and feather this out 8″ to 10″ on each

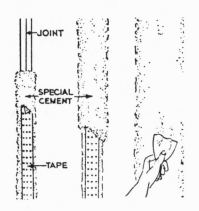

side of the channel. After 24 hours, sandpaper the cement smooth and level with the wallboard. Then coat the entire wallboard surface with a varnish size recommended by the manufacturer. Apply any type of paint, and you will have a wall with an unbroken surface similar to plaster in effect.

Should you prefer other types of wallboard or plywood, blocking between the studs is advisable for a rigid job. The blocking should be spaced about 24″ to 30″ horizontally between the studs, and the wallboard should be nailed to the studs and blocking. Forms of wallboard other than gypsum-core are usually applied vertically with the joints centering on the studs. These joints can then be battened or otherwise treated.

Wallboard, whatever the type, should be run about ¼″ to ½″ from the ceiling and floor, and covered at the ceiling with a molding, either quarter-round or crown, and at the floor line, covered with a baseboard and base-shoe molding. If BX electrical cable is to be installed in the new partition for baseboard receptacles, stop the bottom of the wallboard about 4″ from the floor, with blocking between the studs at this point as a nailing surface for the wallboard. Run the BX cable along the bottom edge across the studs. Wherever there are receptacles, blocking must be nailed between the studs to sup-

port the receptacles. If the wallboard is ½″ thick, the BX need not be notched into the studs, as it is about the same thickness. The baseboard will cover the cable, saving considerable work of notching out the stud edges. Framing the door jambs and casing is discussed in chapter 3 (page 67).

## MODERNIZING THE BATHROOM

Old-fashioned bathrooms need not stay that way for long if a bit of imagination is used to modernize them. The worst offender in an old-time bathroom is usually the bathtub with its four feet. Many bathrooms, in suburban and rural districts, have tongued-and-grooved wainscoats with layer upon layer of dark-brown varnish over them, and perhaps a wood floor. Not much thought was given in the old days to storage space in the bathroom, and the washbasin, tub, and toilet were disorganized, with considerable waste space between them.

The illustration shows how a typical old-fashioned bathroom can be modernized at a fraction of the cost of installing modern equipment. Obviously, the illustration can only offer suggestions, since, if you have an old-fashioned bathroom, it is more likely than not that the arrangement differs from that in the drawing. Some bathroom layouts lend themselves even more to modernization than the one illustrated, particularly if the bathtub is set in a corner next to two walls.

A toilet can quite frequently be completely isolated from the other fixtures by a wall around it with a door, if space permits. The main idea in the modern design of a bathroom is to make each fixture as private as possible, affording several members of a family the simultaneous use of the room.

Many bathrooms of yesterday were spacious for no particular purpose. This

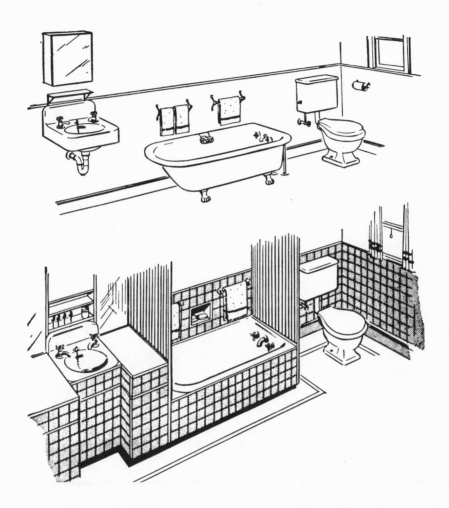

spaciousness can be used to good advantage when modernizing. Where space permits, a dressing-table alcove can be constructed; floor-to-ceiling closets and drawer units can be installed; a bathtub can be part of a curtained or glass-door enclosure; and many other efficient innovations can be added to make this room attractive and more useful.

## Converting the Bathtub

A bathtub off the floor and with feet can be converted into a modern type easily with a wood frame around three sides

of the tub, covered with tileboard. Tileboard can be had in a number of bright colors in square-scored tile, horizontally scored, and plain. Use 1″ × 2″ pine strips for the frame, and 2″ × 2″ for the corner posts. Most bathtubs with feet are made from ⅜″ formed steel with heavy porcelain enamel fused to the inner and curve-lip surfaces. One end is usually a half-circle and the other, or faucet, end has curved corners. The lip is curved with a square under edge.

Build the frame very much as you would build a stud partition, that is, frame a plate and sole with uprights spaced about 12″ on centers. Since the bathtub is curved at both ends, the frame, including the tileboard facing, must extend to the longest dimension of the tub and have square corners. The frame must be a little more than ⅛″ shorter at both ends than the length of the tub, so that the ⅛″-thick tileboard face will be a little less than flush with the bottom edge of the lip of the tub. Likewise, the height of the frame must be ⅛″ short of the under edge of the lip to permit a strip of tileboard to be inserted under the lip and to the edge of the tub.

Nail the sole to the floor, half-lapping the corners. Then frame all the uprights and posts to the plate which you also half-lap at the corners. Nail diagonal

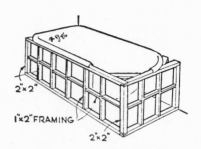

2″×2″

1″×2″ FRAMING

2″×2″

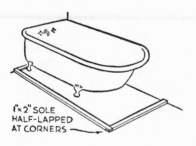

1″×2″ SOLE
HALF-LAPPED
AT CORNERS

pieces across the corners flush with the top of the plate to support the top pieces of tileboard. The uprights may have to be blocked at their back edges near the top of the tub to fit snugly against it. Frame horizontal pieces between the uprights, alternately staggering them so that you can nail them from the upright face side.

The assembled frame is then put in place on the soles and toe-nailed to them. Nail the corner posts at the open end of the frame against the wall or, if it is tiled, cement the posts to the tile. If your bathroom floor is already tiled, the soles can be cemented to the tile with a rubber-base cement made for cementing tile to wood and other surfaces, or holes can be drilled in the tile floor with a star drill, and expansion-screw anchors inserted. The sole is then screwed to the floor. The latter

method entails more work, but is perhaps the best way to attach the sole to a tile floor, although using the special cement and letting it dry for about 48 hours will hold the sole in place permanently.

Tileboard is easily sawed with a fine-tooth carpenter's saw, sawing from the face or finish side. Saw the board along a "tile joint," rather than through part of a tile face. Finishing nails are used when nailing tileboard, and should be driven flush—not set. When nailing tileboard, do not drive the nail flush with a hammer because you will probably mar the surface. Drive the nail almost flush and then use a nail set. The nailheads are hidden with touch-up paint to match the color of the board; the paint is sold by the manufacturer of the board and is also used to touch up any marred surfaces, edges, and so on.

To apply the board, nail and cement the end pieces first, the top edges flush with the top of the frame. The height of

TUB LIP PROJECTS SLIGHTLY

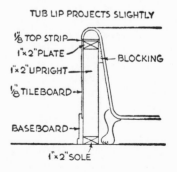

⅛ TOP STRIP

1″×2″ PLATE

1″×2″ UPRIGHT

⅛ TILEBOARD

BASEBOARD

BLOCKING

1″×2″ SOLE

the board should be such that a special tileboard base can be nailed or cemented in place, lapping the bottom edge of the end and front pieces. The width of these bases varies with the manufacturer's product, but is usually 3¾″ or 4″ wide with a rabbet ½″ deep to receive the tileboard proper. The front edges of the end pieces should be flush with the frame and sanded smooth. Now cut 2 pieces of tileboard for the front so that when they are butt-joined at the center of the tub, the ends will be flush with the faces of the end pieces. Before applying the front, sand the edges smooth and square, as any sanding done after they are in place will mar the finish of the adjoining piece. Use cement for the butted edges and, after the board is in place, immediately wipe off excess cement. The exposed edges can then be painted with touch-up paint matching the color of the surface.

After the end and front pieces are in place, cut top strips to slide under the curved lip of the bathtub, after you have sanded the outer edges of the strips. The front top strip is held in place with cement applied to the top surface of the plate which supports the strip. At the ends of the bathtub, top pieces are cut in a rough curve to loosely fit the contour of the tub, the outer edges forming a square

corner, flush with the vertical faces of the front and end pieces. These top end pieces are cemented to the diagonal braces across the corners and to the plate surface. The edges that are butt-joined are cemented. Butt-join the top end pieces to the top front strips at a point where the lip of the tub will hide them, that is, a little beyond the point where the lip begins its arc at both ends.

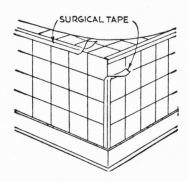

Another method of covering the exposed butt joints of the tileboard is to use ½″- or ¾″-wide *waterproof* surgical zinc oxide tape. Carefully lap the corners evenly with the tape and press it firmly in contact with the board. Zinc oxide tape will stick indefinitely if it is fresh and is not deliberately peeled off. This method of covering the joints leaves no exposed edges and makes a waterproof joint. Paint the tape with touch-up paint that matches the color of the tileboard.

## Washbasins

Treatment of washbasins is similar to that of bathtubs, if you desire a cabinet-type washbasin. Provision must be made at the front of the basin for the removal of the panel of tileboard, so that the plumbing may be reached. This panel should be screwed in place with chromium-plated or plain round-head wood screws. These can be painted with touch-up paint to match the color of the panel. Cabinet doors can be made up of 1″ × 2″ frames to which the tileboard is cemented, the doors being hinged in the usual manner. As tileboard comes in plain as well as scored colored sheets, door and drawer faces can be plain-surfaced tileboard of a contrasting color. Very attractive effects can be achieved by this method, and a wide variety of treatments is possible.

If your bathroom does not have a tiled wainscot, tileboard of the same color or another harmonizing color can be used to make a "decorator's" bathroom. Above the wainscoat the same material can be used with the tile pattern, horizontally grooved pattern, or plain, also in the same or harmonizing color. Tileboard manufacturers make stainless-steel inside and outside corner moldings and caps into which the board slips. Hardboard bases, caps, and insertions where 2 panels meet, are also available.

Tileboard can be applied with cement directly to a wall surface if the surface is level and even. Slight unevenness can be leveled out with patching plaster, but if the wall bulges badly, furring strips should first be nailed to the tileboard. Ceilings, too, can be covered with a ceiling tile with tongued-and-grooved interlocking edges which are blind-nailed. This tile comes $5/8'' \times 12'' \times 12''$ in a variety of rainbow colors hot-sprayed similarly to tileboard.

### Glass Partition

The use of ribbed glass as a partition which is translucent, yet affords privacy, can be installed to separate the various fixtures. This material requires a wood frame. Medicine cabinets which extend beyond the face of the wall can be recessed flush between the studs before the wallboard is applied. This can also be done with soap-holders, handholds for the bathtub, tissue-holders, and the like, replacing the old hanging types. Frameless mirrors and other fixtures can be installed to suit your taste and budget.

A shallow cabinet from floor to ceiling can be installed between the studs, or one stud can be removed to give added width. If you do this, be sure to put double $2'' \times 4''$ headers across the span, supported by trimmers if the partition bears a load. If you need more depth for a cabinet and want to equip it with drawers, extend it beyond the face of the wall besides recessing it between the studs. In this way

the floor space taken up by the cabinet is reduced.

Old wood floors can be covered with ceramic tile cemented with a rubber-base cement to a $1/4''$ fir plywood surface which has been nailed to the floor, without appreciably raising the bathroom floor level.

## BUILDING A STORAGE WALL

There never seems to be enough closet space in a home, no matter how numerous the closets. This is probably due to our instinctive urge to store all our possessions until they may become useful again. A storage wall is the answer to the problem of providing extra closet space. An existing partition between 2 rooms can be used as one wall face of the storage wall, and a new wall built across the room to contain the closet or storage space. A 24'' inside depth for the new storage space is about minimum for practical purposes, particularly if the closet is to contain clothes on hangers. A 30'' to 40'' depth is better if the room from which the space must be taken will warrant shortening by that much.

The wall coverings of the existing partition must be removed and one or 2 studs removed; removing one stud will give you a space of approximately 32'' between stud centers. Removing 2 studs will approximate 48'' between stud centers. The new wall which you build must correspond in stud spacing to the existing one. The procedure is the same as for putting up a regular partition: a plate at the ceiling and a sole at the floor, with studs nailed to both.

If the existing partition bears a load, care must be taken not to weaken the span between removed studs, and doubled $2'' \times 4''$ headers set on edge must be nailed to the existing plate, supported by trimmers spiked to the studs which remain. The new partition, being nonbear-

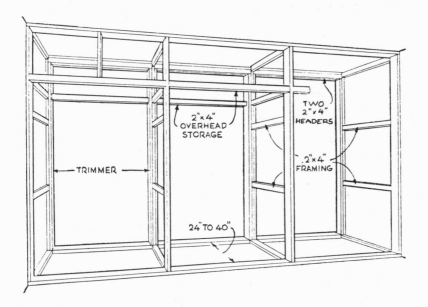

ing, does not require headers or trimmers. The best way to shore up the spans before removing any studs in the existing partition—if it bears a load—is to temporarily support each overhead joist with a $2 \times 4$ from the floor to the ceiling on *both sides* of the plate. These supports should be placed as close as possible to the plate, with just enough space between them to allow you room to work. The most efficient way to do this is to cut the studs shorter than the ceiling height, and drive wedges between the ceiling and studs for a tight fit.

Then cut out the studs not to be used, spike trimmers to those that remain, and frame headers to support the plate. The headers must be toenailed to the plate, and the trimmers toenailed to the doubled headers. The temporary stud bracing can then be removed.

## Utilization

There are many ways of utilizing a storage wall, depending on your particular storage problem. Usually these closets

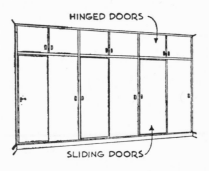

are designed for clothes, with storage space overhead, given access to by hinged or sliding cabinet doors of $\frac{3}{8}''$ or $\frac{1}{2}''$ plywood. Frequently the storage wall is divided so that one half, more or less, supplies storage space for each room. Another variation is to have a dressing-table alcove on one or both sides of the wall—separated by a wallboard thickness—for adjoining bedrooms. These alcoves can be flanked by storage space for both rooms, or one room.

The wall faces of storage walls are usually plywood doors, $\frac{3}{8}''$ or $\frac{1}{2}''$ thick, preferably of the sliding variety for closets, so that no additional space is lost to the rooms by hinged doors. Hardware can be purchased for sliding doors which run on overhead tracks, requiring no floor track, groove, or other obstructing device. However, since a sole is necessary in any event, the doors can be run on rollers of the showcase variety. These come in metal strips with the rollers attached. Matching 1/4"-thick plywood panels are used to surface that portion of the wall not giving access to closet space, and the studs are also faced with matching 1/4" plywood as a finish.

Drawers to supply the needs of both rooms can be made for storage walls if there is sufficient depth, or, if the space is shallow, for one room, replacing the conventional "his" and "her" dressers in bedrooms. Whatever the arrangement, the studs, which are the main framework of the storage wall, must be bridged horizontally at the top, bottom, and between these points for added rigidity, and to afford nailing surfaces for wallboards separating the closet space. This framing is also necessary for attaching clothes poles and the like. Additional framing is also necessary—if storage space above the closet doors is intended—to support a floor of 1/2" or 3/4" plywood.

It is amazing what additional storage space is afforded by a 24" storage wall, and the variety of arrangements possible with such a wall will not only solve an annoying storage problem, but also will result in a modern architectural treatment introducing charm to an otherwise uninteresting room. The storage-wall idea can be used in any part of the house where such a wall is feasible, making possible all sorts of built-in appliances, such as TV-radio-phono combinations, bookshelves, kitchen equipment, and dining services.

## MAKING A KITCHEN-SERVICE OPENING

One of the most efficient time and step savers is the service hatch, or opening between the kitchen and dining area. Most modern homes designed today are provided with a service opening, its architectural treatment as varied as modern house design. Some openings have sliding doors to close off the kitchen from the dining area when the opening is not in use; others open on a lunch counter used for breakfast and luncheon, and serve the dining area for dinner; still others have a

Venetian blind which disguises the opening, making it appear as a window until it is needed.

The last idea fits in more readily with an existing room arrangement, although any number of treatments are possible, more or less governed by the architectural features of both kitchen and dining area. The bottom of the opening should be about level with a kitchen counter top and, if possible, situated near the kitchen range and sink for easy service of cooked food and removal of used dishes. If only one choice of location is practical, near the sink is best. It is not at all difficult to construct one of these openings in an existing wall between the kitchen and dining area, and it need not interfere with overhead kitchen cabinets, as the service height need be only enough to serve food through it conveniently. Or the opening can be quite high, with the back of the kitchen wall cabinet exposed but actually hidden by a Venetian blind. The larger opening, of room-window height, will look better from the dining-area side and can be treated architecturally in the same manner as the windows of the room, that is, casings and an apron can be framed around the opening to match the windows.

To make an opening, first mark out on the wall the dimensions, taking into consideration the removal of one stud for an opening approximately 32" on stud centers. If a larger opening is desired, figure on removing two studs, which will give you a width of approximately 48" on stud centers. Then carefully remove enough of the wall on both sides of the partition to allow you to work comfortably when framing the opening—about 2" on each side of the studs, and enough at the top and bottom to enable you to frame the headers. If you remove the wall cleanly and more or less on a straight line all around, patching will not be necessary, as the casing or frame of the finished opening will cover the plaster edges.

If it is a bearing partition, first brace

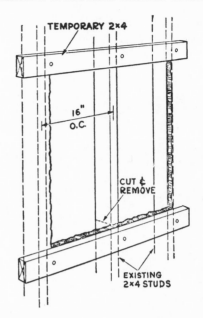

the proposed opening top and bottom by nailing a 2 × 4 across the studs in the same manner as for enlarging a window or door.

Then saw off the studs and frame the headers and trimmers. For the bottom or sill of the opening, use ¾" stock, plywood or solid, wide enough to butt the back edge of the work counter and overlap the apron on the dining-area side.

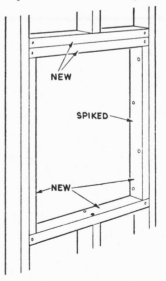

**TRIM TO MATCH
OTHER WINDOWS**

The lap should be about the same as that of the window stool. Use ¼" plywood or ¾" solid stock for the jambs at the top and sides, and frame a casing to match the other windows on the dining-area side. Matching the window casings is not necessary, of course, as a number of decorative treatments are possible to finish the opening, such as scalloped edges or decorative contour edges, cut out of ½" or ¾" stock.

On the kitchen side, a frame is also necessary; this depends on whether or not there is a wall cabinet overhead. If there is not, a decorative frame in harmony with the kitchen trim will look good, and if a cabinet is over the opening, run the frame to butt against the bottom edge of the cabinet. The frame can be plain or have decorative edges.

## HANGING WALL SHELVES

Wall shelves for kitchens and other rooms can easily be made without taking up the usual floor space. They can be extremely decorative and hung in a variety of patterns to add to the general decor of a room. There is a simple method of hanging shelves for books, objects-of-art, and so on, without the hangers showing when objects are placed on the shelf.

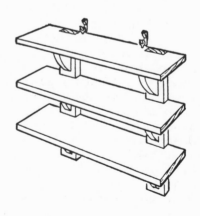

To make a hanging shelf, be it single or multiple, brackets are necessary as a fulcrum against the wall. These brackets can be as decorative as you desire, and should have a bearing surface against the wall of about 6″ for single shelves. For multiple shelves, the back pieces to which a number of shelves are attached, act in the same manner as a bracket for a single shelf.

The hanging device is 2 or more screw-eyes—depending on the length of the shelf—screwed about ¼″ from the

weight with practically no outward strain. Shelves made in this manner should have their brackets screwed to the shelf with flathead wood screws countersunk slightly deeper than flush and filled with water-mix wood putty or plastic wood. For both shelf and brackets ¾″ plywood or solid stock should be used.

To attach the shelf, tilt the front upward and engage the screw-eyes on the hooks. Corner shelves can be made in the same way, but with these the hooks of the hangers must be cut off enough to permit

PICTURE HOOK

SCREW EYES

FLAT HEAD WOOD SCREWS

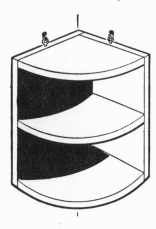

the screw-eyes to be slipped straight over the hooks without tilting the shelf—otherwise the shelf could not be hung in a corner.

back of the shelf and down into the brackets. Picture hangers of the type with needle-pointed nails, driven at an angle into the wall, support the shelf or shelves. The hook of the hanger is bent out a bit to engage the screw-eyes. Since this type of picture hanger is made in a variety of sizes, each hanger capable of sustaining weights up to 100 pounds, 2 of these hangers are more than sufficient for any weight a shelf would normally be expected to hold. Use the smallest hanger practical for whatever weight the shelf is to support. Since the weight exerts a downward pressure against the wall, the shelf brackets are merely braces, and the picture hangers sustain the

## DUTCH DOOR

A Dutch door is simply one divided horizontally, each section being separately hinged. Either section can be opened or closed, or the two sections can be bolted as one unit, making it a regular door. The advantage of a Dutch door is that it affords ventilation through the upper half, plus a barrier for small children and animals, and offers almost as much privacy as the conventional closed door. Dutch doors should swing inward.

If you would like to have a Dutch door, you can easily make one out of your existing front or back door, or you can make a new one. The door most easily converted is one with a series of horizontal panels, usually 5 in number, or any door with a horizontal rail whose center line is about 37″ from the bottom. The doorknob and lock are set about 3″ below this center line on most doors, and when converting, the knobs and lock are left in place, saving considerable work in remortising a new location and filling in the old mortise. If the horizontal rail which is to divide your door is more than 44″ from the bottom, or below the 36″ point, it is best to buy a new, inexpensive but well-made door with a horizontal rail somewhere between these dimensions.

Converting an existing hanging door into a Dutch door is much easier than making a new one, because the door is already hinged at 2 points and is fitted to the opening. If your door has a third hinge at the center, so much the better, as you will then have to add only one hinge for the lower section of the door. If the door has only 2 hinges, 2 additional hinges will be necessary: a total of 2 for the upper and 2 for the lower section.

Before removing the door, locate the places for the additional hinges on the door and jamb. These points should be equally spaced from the center line of the rail—3″ to the edge of the leaves, which should be the same size as those on the existing hinges. Then remove the door and attach the hinge leaves to it and the jamb, mortising them into the jamb and door edge. Hang the door again to check if the new hinges are working properly. Again remove it and divide the rail between what are to be the upper and lower sections exactly in half, making certain that the sawing line is square with the sides of the door.

Now saw along this line squarely across the door. The 2 halves should be weatherstripped where the edges come together. Get inswinging-casement-type metal stripping and measure the clearance between the edges of the door necessary to apply this weatherstripping. Then plane one edge enough to permit the application of the weatherstrip.

Next, cut horizontal rabbets in both

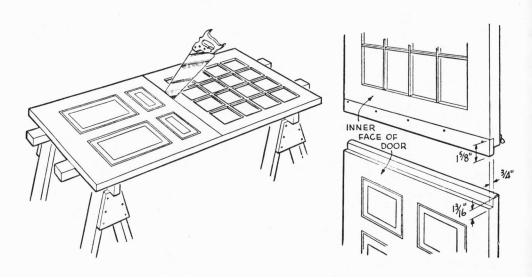

INNER FACE OF DOOR

1⅝″

¾″

1³⁄₁₆″

inner faces of the 2 sections, $\frac{3}{4}'' \times 1\frac{3}{16}''$. These rabbets are for a $\frac{3}{4}'' \times 1\frac{5}{8}''$ hardwood strip which acts as the horizontal stop for the sections. Glue (resorcinol resin glue) and screw this stop into the rabbet of the upper section.

Attach the weatherstrips to both sections and then screw a drip molding to

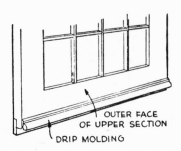

OUTER FACE OF UPPER SECTION

DRIP MOLDING

the outer face of the upper section so that the lip just clears the weatherstrip of the lower section.

Now hang the 2 sections, and you have a Dutch door that is weathertight and hangs perfectly. All that is needed to complete the job is to attach a snap catch or sliding bolt on the inner stile face near the doorknob, to hold the 2 sections together. Another snap catch or sliding bolt should be attached to the upper section to engage a strike in the doorjamb, to hold the upper section closed if the lower one is open. A knob should also be attached to the upper section for easy opening. Your existing lock in the door functions for both sections when together, or for the lower section when the upper one is open.

## Batten Type

If you prefer to make a Dutch door from scratch, the batten type is the easiest, with the battens on the inside. A door of this type requires separate stiles and rails for each section, the body or panels thus formed being of $\frac{3}{4}''$ tongued-and-grooved lumber. The stiles and rails should be

$1\frac{1}{8}''$ thick with a diagonal brace of the same thickness framed into both sections. Run one brace in one direction for the upper section, and the brace for the lower section in the opposite direction. Although $1\frac{1}{8}''$-thick stock will give you just enough thickness to mortise a lock, $1\frac{3}{8}''$ or $1\frac{5}{8}''$ stock is better. Be certain to leave that portion of the door where the lock is to be mortised, free of nails or screws when attaching the tongued-and-grooved lumber.

## LOUVER-TYPE RIGID AWNINGS

The only way to prevent the sun from radiating heat through windows is to prevent the rays from reaching the glass. Ei-

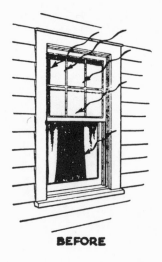

**BEFORE**                    **AFTER**

ther a large roof overhang or awnings to block the sun's rays is the answer. Conventional-type fabric awnings do the trick, but they also block off most of the air which would come through an open window. The modern method of having both air and protection from the sun and rain is to install louver-type awnings. You can buy these at considerable expense, or make them yourself at a fraction of the retail price. Not only is this type of awning more efficient than the conventional fabric type, but it also adds a decorative note to the house exterior, particularly if it is painted in gay colors harmonizing with the body color and trim.

The louver-type awning is also less obvious than the conventional type, giving just the right amount of decorative touch to the house. Basically, the idea is to make a frame with slats attached to the frame at an angle, the slats so angled that air and light can freely pass through the awning and yet block out direct sun's rays and rain. The frame is supported by 2 wood brackets which may be adjustable for various frame angles, if desired.

Use ¾″ × 2⅝″ white-pine stock for the frame and ¼″ × 4½″ exterior grade fir plywood, *sound on both sides,* for the slats. The exterior grade plywood is weatherproof and the veneer will not peel. Make the frames long enough for their bottom edges to be at about the horizontal center line of the window when the frames are at a 45-degree angle from

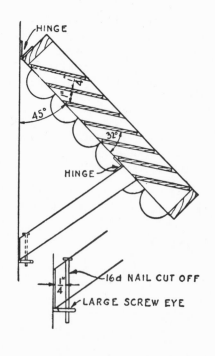

the face of the house. Moreover, make the frames wide enough to extend beyond the inner edge of the casing about 1″ to 2″ on both sides. The inside face of the 2 side pieces of the frame should be dadoed ¼″ × ¼″ to receive the slats, glued in with resorcinol resin glue, which is waterproof and heatproof.

When cutting the slats, cut them with the veneer grain running the long way. The dadoes for the slats should have an angle of 32 degrees upward from the bottom edge of the frame. No matter at what angle the frame is then positioned, air and light will pass almost straight through the slats, but the sun's rays and rain cannot— and rainwater will drain down and outward. The slats must be 1″ apart, that is, 1″ between the top of one slat and the bottom of the one above it, or 1⅛″ on centers. Butt-join the frame with resorcinol resin glue and 2 flathead wood screws for each corner. For inswinging casement and double-hung-sash windows, the frame can be hinged at the head casing, about 3″ to 4″ above the window opening. For outswinging casements, a supplementary frame with angled slats will have to be made to extend far enough out to permit the casement to clear the awning.

To arrive at this dimension accurately, open the casement as much as it is normally opened, and measure the clearance necessary. The awning, in this case, is hinged to the extension. Two wood brackets, ¾″ × 1⅝″, are hinged about ¼ the length of the awning from the bottom, with tight-pin narrow butt hinges. These and the frame hinges must be chromium-plated to resist rust. Cut the other ends of the brackets at an angle to fit flush against the casings. Then bore a hole about ¼″ from the ends through the width of the brackets for a drive fit of a 16d nail. Cut the nail off so that it extends about 1″ below the bracket. Use large and heavy screw-eyes of a diameter to allow enough play for the nail to permit you to remove it to another position if desired. Screw-eyes at different positions on the casings allow the awning to be angled to suit. Actually, no angle adjustment should be necessary if the general dimensions and angles suggested have been followed.

An added decorative note can be achieved by facing the outside of the frame on 3 sides with ¼″ exterior grade plywood with the bottom edges scalloped or contour-cut. This would require pieces 4¾″ wide, the scallops or contours cut out with a fine-tooth keyhole or coping saw. These facings can be either glued with resorcinol resin glue, or nailed on with brads—the glue being the more permanent method of attaching them.

# PICTURE-TYPE WINDOW

You can make a picture-type window out of your present window opening by enlarging it if it is less than 48″ wide. While it is impossible for you to make the double-pane, clean-dry-air-sealed type, you can approximate these factory-assembled windows. It requires, of course, the removal of the existing window frame and structural members framing the opening, and

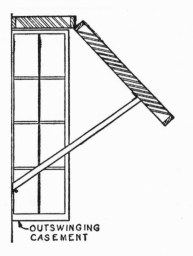

OUTSWINGING
CASEMENT

enlarging the opening to accommodate the larger panes of glass and sash. It will also require framing new trimmers and headers, top and bottom, the top headers being trussed to take care of the additional span.

If your windows are of the multiple type of 2, 3, or 4 sashes separated by mul-lions, the span was taken care of when the house was originally built, since the mullions of these windows rarely support loads, and are usually there for sash-framing purposes only. This can be readily determined when you remove the window frames. If the mullion is an integral part of the window frame and does not extend from a header to the sill, it is not load-bearing, and the window opening has been trussed to take care of the span. All that is necessary then, is to change the frame to one enclosing a pair of large panes of glass.

A 48″ pane of glass is about as wide and high as is practical for double-strength (DS) window glass. Wider and higher dimensions call for demiplate glass. This is considerably cheaper than regular plate, being about the same thickness but not free from slight waviness. This waviness is practically unnoticeable and for general use demiplate will serve for the more expensive plate glass.

If you plan to use double-strength window glass, which costs less than demiplate, you can use up to and including a 48″ width and height. Since window glass is sold in multiples of 2″ both ways, and always comes absolutely square on all sides, plan your window sizes accordingly so that no glass-cutting will be necessary. If you want a larger window than 48″ glass will permit, use 2 panes 48″ or less wide, separated by a 2″ × 4″ mullion—if the opening has been originally trussed.

If the opening is not trussed, it will have to be. If you double the 2″ × 4″ mullion, or use a 4″ × 4″ steel pipe and frame it from a doubled header to sill or sole, it will support the wide span of the window opening. The proposed opening must first be temporarily but well braced with 2″ × 6″ timbers nailed across the

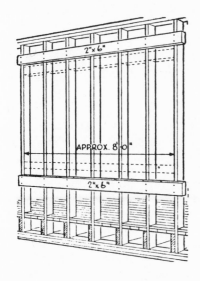

studs at the top and bottom before removing any studs. Since nonbearing mullions are framed into the sill as part of the window frame, a load-bearing one offers a slight complication, as the windowsill would have to be cut around the supporting mullion. However, blocking nailed to the stud or post, to support the sill, with the juncture of sill and post well caulked with caulking compound, will make the joint watertight.

## Double-Glass Type

To achieve the double glass of the commercial type, a secondary sash containing the inside pane must be made which, in effect, is similar to a regular storm-window installation—with one difference: the secondary sash is part of the picture window and need not be removed in warm weather. It must be so framed, however, that it can be removed, or (preferably) hinged so that it can be opened to permit cleaning of both panes of glass, and to remove any condensation which may occur. This is necessary because it is impossible for you to make the space between the glass absolutely airtight and to introduce clean, dry air just before sealing the air space.

The reason for 2 panes of glass is that a large glass surface will be extremely cold in winter, and the 2 panes separated by an air space offer good insulation. They offer much better insulation than the commercial type of double-glass window, since the air space in your homemade one is greater.

If you plan to use doubled 2″ × 4″ pieces to support the center of a wide span of 6′ to 8′, No. 1 common dimension fir is good enough because you will have

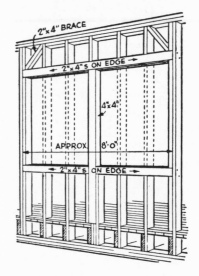

to face these supports with ¾″ finish lumber—actually, jambs and casings. Should you prefer the solid 4″ × 4″ post, it should be surfaced on all 4 sides (S4S) and be clear ponderosa white pine. Then you will not need to face it, and the sash could be permanently framed to it, reducing the overall thickness and increasing the illusion of one large window opening.

Another method of supporting a large span is to use a small-diameter steel column with a cap and base, and boxing it in on all sides with ¾″ stock as a framing device for the sash. A stock 2″-inside-diameter, galvanized steel pipe threaded at both ends, with stock floor flanges screwed on, makes a good column with cap and base.

## Height of Window

The height of your existing windows determines the glass size vertically, unless you drop the sill lower than the existing sill. New headers must be framed in either case. Ceiling heights also determine how high you can make your picture-type window. You can, of course, run the window

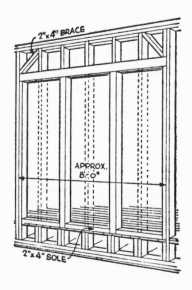

from the floor to its present height, bearing in mind that for DS window glass, 48″ is the limit per pane of glass. A finished 2″ × 4″ piece must then be framed horizontally between the sides of the opening and mullion to support the additional glass. If your window goes to the floor level, nail a 2″ × 4″ sole on the subfloor. The sill is then framed on the sole with ¾″ stock as a facing from the floor to the sill.

Sills should have a slight downward bevel to shed water quickly. They need not have the pitch of a sill for windows that open, as the window sash is permanently framed in with caulking compound sealing all joints between the sash, sill, and stops. The sill can be set flat on blocking on the header after you have planed a slight bevel outward from the point of sash contact. The sill should be 1⅛″ stock, wide enough to project about 1″ beyond the face of the siding on the outside.

## Sash

For 48″ glass, the sash should be 1⅝″ × 2⅝″ (nominally 2″ × 3″) stock. For glass 40″ or less, the sash material can be 1⅝″ × 1⅝″ (nominally 2″ × 2″). A good wood for the sash is ponderosa white pine, S4S and clear.

To make the sash, cut the standard rabbet for window glass in the outside edges of the frame—¼″ × ½″. Add ⅛″ to the glass size for the inside dimensions of the rabbet edge of the sash when assembled. You do this to prevent any shrinkage of the sash frame from breaking the glass. Do not forget to deduct the ¼″ rabbet on both sides and top and bottom of the sash when calculating the overall dimensions of the sash. These dimensions are also the dimensions of the finished opening. If you planned, for instance, to use glass 38″ × 38″, and sash material 1⅝″ × 1⅝″, the outside dimensions of the sash would be 40⅞″ × 40⅞″, which

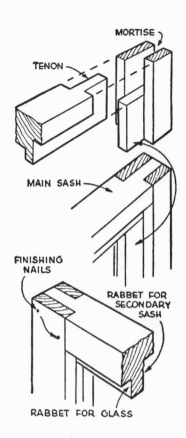

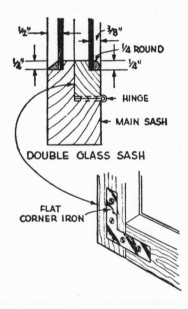

ondary one flush. Cut a $\frac{1}{4}'' \times \frac{3}{8}''$ rabbet in the edge of the secondary sash for the glass.

The main sash should be put together with open mortises and tenons at the corners, the horizontal rails being tenoned to fit into the mortises of the vertical stiles. The tenon and mortise shoulders are cut so that the rabbets form a continuous recess around the sash. The secondary sash can be butt-joined with resorcinol

would also be the dimensions of the *finished* opening to which the sash is framed:

> Glass: 38″ × 38″ plus ⅛″ equals 38⅛″ × 38⅛″.
>
> Sash (1⅝″ × 1⅝″), inside dimension: ¼″ less on 4 sides—or ½″ less than 38⅛″ × 38⅛″ equals 37⅝″ × 37⅝″.
>
> Sash, outside dimensions: 1⅝″ added on 4 sides—or 3¼″ plus 37⅝″ × 37⅝″ = 40⅞″ × 40⅞″.

To frame the second or inner pane of glass, a secondary sash is needed. For 48″ glass the sash should be ¾″ × 1⅝″ stock (nominally 1″ × 2″). If the main sash is 1⅝″ × 1⅝″ for glass 40″ or less, the secondary sash can be ¾″ × ¾″ (nominally 1″ × 1″). Cut a rabbet in the inner face of the main sash to receive the sec-

resin glue, and the corners reinforced with small flat corner irons recessed flush on the inner face to the rails and stiles.

The secondary sash should be either removable or hinged. If you prefer to make it removable, screw the sash to the main one with flathead wood screws near the corners and one screw in the center of each rail and stile. For cleaning purposes and removal of condensation, when necessary, the job would be easier to perform if you hinged the secondary sash at the bottom to the main sash with narrow, tight-pin butt hinges. The sash would be held in place with screws near the corners and one in the center of each stile, and top rail. By doing it this way the sash could be swung in and downward, yet held in place by the hinges.

The glass for the main sash is glazed in the regular manner, using glazier's points and putty. The secondary glass is held with ¼″ quarter-round molding, bradded.

To install the main sash, first coat all surfaces (edges of the sash, stop and jamb faces which contact the sash) with linseed oil, or white lead in linseed oil. Then liberally "butter" these surfaces with caulking compound and screw the sash to the stops with flathead wood screws countersunk slightly deeper than flush and filled with putty. Use plenty of screws evenly spaced—about 4″ on centers—so that the sash bears evenly. Then remove the excess caulking compound which has squeezed out.

The secondary sash can then be attached from the inside by one of the two methods suggested. A picture window should be framed like an outswinging casement, that is, about ¼″ back from the outer edge of the frame.

When deciding on a picture window, do not forget to provide ventilation for your room, as the picture window is sealed. If there are other conventional types of windows in the room they will provide the ventilation. Should your proposed picture window be the only one, you will have to provide movable windows at the sides or over the top of the window. The outswinging casement, hinged at the top, provides ideal ventilation over a picture window or, for that matter, at the sides, as it can be left open in average rainy weather—something you cannot do with other types of windows.

## MODERN CASEMENT WINDOW

There is not much to converting the regular outswinging wood casement window to one that is hinged at the top. All that is

necessary is to remove the hinges from the sides and place them at the top. With the inswinging type, nothing is gained by changing the hinges. The top-hinged casement does not afford the same amount of air passage as the conventional type, but it does permit ventilation in rainy weather. Brackets are necessary to keep the window open at several points. These can be made of hardwood with a notch cut in the bottom edge to engage metal pins in the jamb, and hinged to the sash.

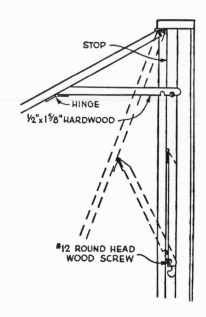

STOP

HINGE

½"x1⅝"HARDWOOD

#12 ROUND HEAD WOOD SCREW

When the window is closed and latched, these brackets, one on each side of the sash, fold against the sash and out of the way. The brackets must be hinged about midway between the top and bottom rail, to clear the sill when the window is closed. Hardwood stock, ½″ × 1⅛″, preferably maple or oak, is about right for the brackets, which should be hinged to the sash with ½″ tight-pin, chromium-plated butt hinges. Use chromium-plated round-head wood screws for the pins.

To make the casement, use standard 1⅜″ × 1¾″ sash stock which is rabbeted and molded, and cut open mortises and tenons for the corners, cutting the shoulders on the tenons and mortises to form a continuous recess around the sash. Glaze in the usual manner.

## COVERING AN OLD ROOF

If you have a shingled roof which is in poor condition, that is, with the shingles badly warped and split, it is only a matter of time when leaks will occur and cause serious damage to the interior of your home. Individual shingles can be easily removed and replaced when there are just a few scattered offenders, but when the entire roof requires repair, it is much cheaper to re-cover it. This is particularly true of a wood-shingled roof. Attempts to patch large areas, or many scattered areas, often cause additional and serious leaks by disturbing the old shingles.

Roofing materials for re-covering purposes, other than wood shingles and slate, are asbestos shingles and asphalt shingles. Asphalt roll-roofing does not work too well when re-covering over old roofing unless it, too, is of the roll variety, as this material requires a perfectly flat surface for best results.

To re-cover an old wood-shingled roof, it is best to first cut back the shingles at the eaves and the rakes 3″ so that when the new roof has been laid, all evidence of the old one is hidden. Cutting back the shingles at the eaves can best be done with a flooring saw, which has a point with a curved back with teeth. However, a back-

saw also works well, and if you temporarily nail a straight-edge strip as a guide for the saw, cutting the shingles will not be difficult. On the rake sides of the roof, a

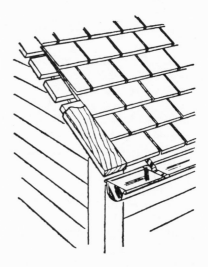

straightedge will also help to cut the shingles on an even straight line. This can best be done with a chisel, which will split them easily.

Next, remove the existing shingles or boards which form the old ridge or hip, and nail a furring strip—4″-wide beveled siding, thin edge facing down the roof, is fine—on each side of the ridge or hip.

Nail down all loose shingles and, if they are warped or cupped, split them and nail down the corners. Rotted shingles must be replaced by new wood ones. The idea in back of all this preparatory work is to afford as flat and smooth a surface as possible for the new asbestos or asphalt shingles. Where you have cut back the shingles at the eaves and rakes, nail ¾″ × 3″ boards, extending them beyond the rakes and eaves the same amount as did the old wood shingles.

Valleys of the roof should be filled in with boards of a thickness to be flush with the existing shingles as a base for the new flashing. If the existing wood shingles are the thick-butt type, it is best to nail wedge-shaped wood strips (horsefeathers)

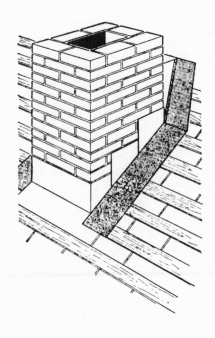

⅜″ × 4″ along the butts of the shingles, the thick edge against the butts, to level out the roof surface. Then surface the roof with 15-pound asphalt-saturated felt.

New base flashing around chimneys should be attached for the new shingles. To do this for asphalt shingles, cut 8″ strips of heavy roll-roofing and butt them against the old base flashing on the chimney sides, extending the strips a few inches over the apron of the front metal base flashing. Nail the outer edge of the strips to the existing shingles.

When the new shingle courses have been laid near these strips, coat the strips with asphalt plastic cement and lay the shingles against the chimney faces, firmly embedded in the cement. Lift the apron of the front base flashing enough to slip the shingles at this point under the flashing, and press the flashing back in place embedded in plastic cement.

Now cut strips of mineral-coated roll-roofing about 8″ wide. Coat about 3″ of the strips with plastic cement and carefully lift the existing metal cap flashing where it laps the old metal base flashing. Slip the cemented strips under the cap flashing, bending the corners around the metal flashing front and back. Then press the cap flashing back into place and into the cement. Now coat about 4″ of the tops of the shingles nearest the chimney with plastic cement and firmly embed the new flashing in the cement-coated shingles. The same general procedure applies to the "cricket" in back of the chimney.

If the existing metal flashing around vent pipes in the roof is in good condi-

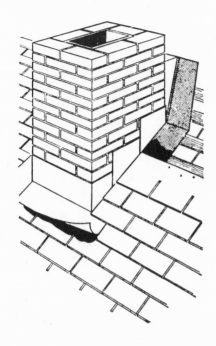

located 4″ from the bottom edge. Draw a freehand oval within the marked rectangle and cut it out. This oval will then fit snugly around the pipe when the flashing is fitted over the pipe and cemented down.

Form a flange by troweling plastic cement around the pipe and juncture of the flashing. It must be applied vigorously and thoroughly to make the cement adhere and to expel all air pockets in the cement. After the flashing is applied, the shingles are continued around the pipe. They are cut to fit snugly, and cemented where they lap over the flange. Nails should not be used too near the pipe.

Valleys are reflashed with heavy roll-roofing by first nailing down the outer edges of a strip about 9″ wide and then, over this, a strip about 18″ wide is cemented to the first. If these strips cannot be laid as one continuous piece, they must be lapped in cement about 9″.

tion, lift up the lower part of the flange and apply the shingles underneath it up to the pipe, cutting the shingles to fit around it. Replace the flange, bedding it in plastic cement. Apply generous quantities of plastic cement at the juncture of the metal sleeve and flange of the flashing. Then continue laying shingles around the pipe and up the roof.

Should the existing metal flashing be in poor condition, remove it and apply new roll-roofing flashing. First, the shingle courses are laid up to and just around the pipe, the shingles being fitted around it. Then make the flashing by cutting a rectangle of heavy roll-roofing large enough to extend 4″ below the pipe, 8″ above it, and 6″ on both sides. To locate the hole to be cut in this rectangle, first center it below the pipe and project the diameter by 2 lines marked on the roofing material. Then place the rectangle, in relation to its location, at the side of the pipe and project the diameter. This gives you a lined rectangle centered between the sides, and

## Sloping Roof

Where a sloping roof abuts a vertical wall, cut a strip of roll-roofing 8″ wide, butt one edge against the wall, and nail it along all edges to the existing shingles. Then as the new shingles are laid, coat this strip with plastic cement and bed the shingles in the cement, butting them tightly against the wall. Nail the shingles only beyond the flashing strip. Now caulk the juncture of the shingles and the wall with plastic cement, forcing it well down into the joint.

Flashing around chimneys should be of noncorrodible metal if asbestos shingles are used. The new base flashing is made up of bent pieces of the same length as the wather exposure of the shingle plus 3″. The base flashing is slipped under the existing cap flashing, each piece lapping the other 3″. The asbestos shingles are then laid over the flange on the roof, and nailed beyond the flange edges. (Methods of laying asbestos and asphalt shingles are described in chapter 11, page 272.)

## COVERING OLD SIDING

As a general rule, old siding materials may remain in place when you plan to apply new siding. Not only will considerable labor be saved in not removing the old material, but leaving it in place helps to further insulate the walls of your house. However, wood-shingled walls, if in very bad condition, are best removed if only for the reason that it is debatable which entails the most work—carefully going over the entire surface and nailing down cupped shingles, or removing them entirely. Moreover, if a wood-shingled wall is in bad shape, practically every shingle is also badly warped.

As in the case of roofing, the old siding must be well nailed down and decayed pieces must be removed and replaced with new, as both asbestos and asphalt siding are relatively thin, and any uneven or loose surface will either spoil the appearance of the new siding or damage it. From an appearance standpoint only, it is important to have a firm, reasonably level surface on which to apply new siding material.

Old beveled siding, if it is the thick-butt type, will have to be leveled off with wedge-shaped strips (horsefeathers), the thick end facing up and the strip placed along the siding at a point where it will level the slope. Wood lath is almost as good as the beveled strips for leveling pur-

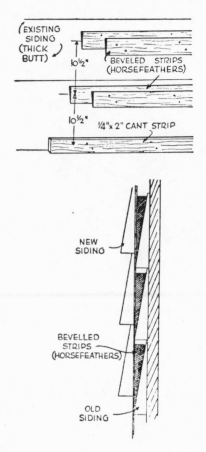

poses. In the case of thick-butt wide siding, it may be necessary to nail 2 strips to achieve a level surface. This is particularly necessary if asbestos shingles are used.

# 14

# FINISHING THE ATTIC

It is common practice these days for the builder of a house to leave the attic unfinished; but the necessary provisions are often arranged so that the attic can, at some later date, and at the convenience of the homeowner, be made into one or more rooms. These "expansion attics," as they are sometimes called, offer a great many possibilities to the home mechanic who is willing to spend a little time, effort, and money to add one or more attractive yet low-cost rooms to his house. For example, as the family grows in size, an extra bedroom is a great convenience; or this same space can be used for a quiet study, private sittingroom, playroom, or library. And finally, if the attic is large enough, a complete and self-contained small apartment can be made out of it. It is worth mentioning at this point that small attractive apartments are always in demand. The rent from such apartments will soon pay for the materials used in construction, and the homeowner can look forward, after this expense has been paid off, to a steady income which will help bolster the family budget.

Before the work of finishing the attic begins, however, it is wise to make a complete survey of the space at hand so that every detail may be used to the greatest advantage for the purpose in mind. Local building authorities should be consulted, for if the space is to be used for living quarters, certain regulations as to materials and construction methods must be complied with. For example, some communities demand that there be two methods of exit from a dwelling. If the attic has but one stairway, and this is usually the case, then it may be necessary to build another entrance and exit to the attic.

Some building codes demand that certain types of materials be used for the construction and finishing of the attic and if they are not used, then the apartment will not pass the local building inspection and hence cannot be put up for rental. Also you had better be sure there is no local zoning ordinance against two-family houses, as it would be a shame for you to go to the labor and expense of fixing up a small apartment and then find you could not legally rent it. However, difficulties of that nature will not prevent you from using the space yourself, which is what a homeowner would probably want to do anyway in a majority of cases.

There are quite a number of items of this general nature which must be given careful consideration before work begins. But regardless of the minimum requirements of local building codes and regulations, it is to the homeowner's own advantage to use only first-class materials for the job, no matter how the space is to be used.

As a general rule, better-grade materials will pay off in longer and better service.

The entire attic need not be utilized at one time. It may be more convenient to construct one room now, a bedroom perhaps, and then add other rooms such as a bath and kitchen at some later date. But if this is to be done, plans should be made now as to the exact location of these other rooms. It might even be wise to bring up the necessary pipes for the kitchen and bath fixtures and cap them. In that way work in the room finished first would not have to be ripped up later to permit fixtures to be put in.

In case you find it hard to visualize just what might be done about building a small but complete attic apartment, the illustration shows a plan view of such an apartment, with an attic space of about $17' \times 37'$. Remember that you can figure on using only that part of the attic far enough from the eaves to permit your side walls to be 3' or 4' high. Measure your attic and make your plans accordingly. In the illustration, five small dormer windows and an outside staircase are shown.

Once the plans for the attic space have been completed, then comes the question as to who is to do the work. Naturally, the cheapest method would be for the home mechanic to do the entire job in his spare time, but there are several reasons why this may not be possible. In the first place, many local codes insist that work such as plumbing and wiring be done only by experienced workmen; second, a job such as adding an extra bathroom requires many special tools, as well as special knowledge and experience.

It is very possible that by the time the home mechanic has purchased the necessary equipment, completed his work, and corrected his mistakes made by "trial and error," he will discover that it would have been cheaper to have had the work done by a professional. Barring any restrictions by building codes, the smart plan would

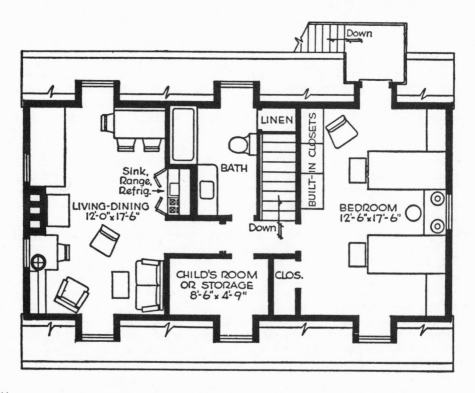

seem to be for the home mechanic to do all the work which he feels confident that he can do well, and to leave the more unfamiliar and specialized tasks to the trained workman.

Many homeowners have worked out excellent arrangements with skilled workers of one trade or another, whereby the home mechanic does most of the unskilled part of the jobs, while the skilled craftsman comes only to do the tricky work and to give advice. This is a great saving in time and labor, for during an evening the home mechanic can do the necessary preliminaries, so that on the following day the skilled professional need not waste his time on unskilled tasks but can devote his time to the complicated jobs.

## HEATING

A good deal of thought must be given to the matter of how the attic rooms are to be heated during the winter months. If no heating arrangement is made, then the rooms or apartment will be livable for perhaps only half the year—considerable loss in any case.

If the house is heated with warm air, it may be possible as well as practical to install registers in the attic floor or walls, so that warm air from the rooms below will flow up. Another possibility is to install additional hot-air ducts with electric fans to force the heated air from the furnace into the attic. For homes heated with steam or hot water, additional radiators and pipes will be required.

But heating the attic by means of the house heating plant depends on whether or not the plant can take on this extra load and still keep all the rooms on the lower floors comfortable. To answer this question, it would be wise to call in a heating engineer or contractor and let him check the capacity of the heating plant. If the furnace is too small to take on the extra load of the attic, then some other method must be used to heat it, or a larger heating plant must be installed. Electric or gas space-heaters can be used for heating the attic rooms, and they are convenient as well as clean. However, if electric heaters are to be used, remember that heavy-duty circuit wiring will be necessary to handle a heavy electric load. In any case, be sure that the necessary provisions are made to heat the attic so that it will be comfortable either for members of the family or for tenants.

## PLUMBING

If the attic is to be finished off as additional rooms for the house, then an attic bathroom is not necessary, although it may prove a great convenience. However, if a separate apartment is to be created, at least a small bathroom is essential.

Probably the best location for the attic bathroom will be directly above one on the floor below. It will be cheaper to run pipes up the shortest distance, naturally, but sometimes there are other considerations. The stairs to the attic may make such a location undesirable or the bathroom below may be too near the eaves. However, a large dormer window might solve the latter problem.

Also, if the house sewage system is taken care of by either a septic tank or cesspool, this equipment may not be large enough to carry the load of another bathroom and kitchen. To handle that problem, either a larger tank would have to be installed or an additional sewer system put in for the attic. In any event it would be most advisable to consult a plumber on plumbing problems before the location of the bathroom and kitchen are definitely decided on.

Another point to be considered is whether the size of the pipes used in the house is large enough to provide the attic with a proper flow of water. Then there is the question of hot water: is the house heater and tank large enough to supply the additional demands of attic rooms? If not, it may be necessary to install a larger heater or a larger tank or both in order to supply the attic rooms with adequate hot water.

The attic bathroom does not have to take up a great deal of floor space, but it should be complete. Attractive bathrooms can be constructed in a space of less than 6' square. Installing a shower bath instead

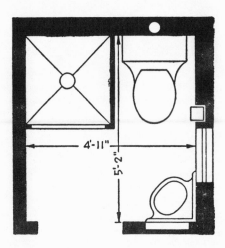

of a tub will save space if there is plenty of headroom for it, but on the other hand less headroom is needed over a tub, since people seldom stand in one unless there is a shower attached. Also, it is now possible to get tubs considerably smaller than the old-fashioned styles. Your local plumber or plumbing supply house can give you good advice for a modern, compact, and attractive bathroom.

A kitchen of some kind will be needed for an attic apartment. A kitchen sink involves plumbing, so the chances are that the best location for the kitchen would be next to the bathroom, as that would simplify the piping. When consulting a plumber about the bathroom, do not forget to mention a kitchen.

Another factor in connection with the kitchen is the cooking range. If a gas range is to be used, pipes will have to be

run up from the basement or ground floor. If an electric range is to be installed, a 3-wire 230-volt electric system will have to be brought up from the entrance of the service lines to the house. So neither possibility is likely to have any distinct advantage due to installation costs.

## FLOORING

In many cases, when the house is built, no flooring is laid in the attic, so the first job will be to put down a rough flooring over the joists. Care should be taken during this operation not to step between the joists or drop heavy objects onto the laths and plaster of the ceiling below. To avoid this and still be able to work in comfort, it is wise to have some wide planks available to lay over the joists and form a base on which to move about and work.

Next comes the question of getting building materials up to the attic. It may be possible to carry them up the stairs. Or that may be difficult to do without marring the finish in the hall or stairs below. An alternative method is to hoist the materials up outside and bring them in through an attic window. However, that may be difficult if the windows are small. So another possibility is to measure carefully and cut pieces to smaller size outside or in the cellar and carry the lengths ready to use upstairs.

The rough flooring can be made of tongued-and-grooved stock intended for this purpose. This will serve as a subflooring, and the finish flooring can be put down later when the heavy construction has been completed. Insulation is added before laying of the floor is begun (see page 353). It would be a waste of time and money to lay the finish flooring at this time, because it is almost sure to become damaged during the work on the rooms.

Start laying the flooring down the length of one side of the attic. The tongue side of the board should face toward the

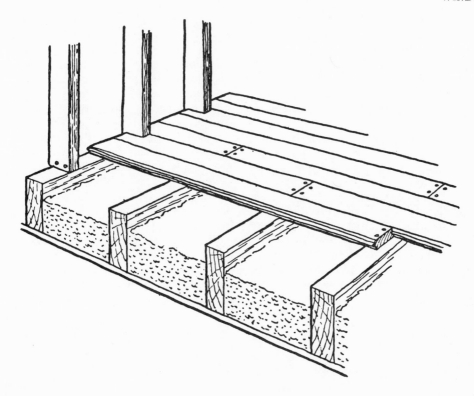

center of the room. When putting down the boards be sure that the end joints between pieces of flooring come over a floor joist. If the joints are not supported by a joist, the flooring at that point may sag or even break when stepped on. The chances are that all the ceiling joists are spaced an equal distance apart, and this spacing should be kept in mind when cutting the flooring boards. Make all joints in the rough flooring as tight as possible, and see that the tongue of each board fits well into the groove of the one beside it. Before a board is cut for length, sight along one edge to see if it is badly warped. If this is the case, you had better set it aside and use it for short lengths, using only the straight pieces of stock for the longer lengths.

Some difficulty will be experienced in nailing down the first few boards, as the pitch of the roof won't allow much room in which to work. As the floor progresses, however, and you move out toward the center of the attic, the work will become easier. It may be necessary to rip the last board in order to make it the proper width to fit. When the flooring is all laid, inspect it to make sure that all boards have been properly nailed and that all nails have been driven down. An insufficient number of nails, or nails not driven as far as they will go, will probably cause the floor to squeak later when walked on.

Once the rough flooring has been completed, other materials may be stored in the attic where they will be on hand when needed.

## WINDOWS

The chances are that the attic has only two windows, one at each gable, and they are probably rather small ones, hardly satisfactory if the attic is to be used for living quarters. You will likely decide to enlarge these openings, or cut more of them, in order to admit more light. There are many types of windows that can be selected for this purpose, but it will probably be best to pick some of the same general type used throughout the rest of the house, though perhaps smaller in size.

If the windows already located in the attic are large enough to provide sufficient ventilation and it is merely a question of desiring more light, this could be secured by installing solid-set windows on either side of the windows already in place. Solid-set windows, such as are used for storm windows, should be the same size as the windows you have, and the openings should be cut immediately adjoining the windows you have so that you can reach out to clean the solid-set windows. If more air is desirable, plan on two windows that open with one in between which does not. The foregoing suggestions apply only if your original attic windows are 2′ × 3′ in size or larger. If they are smaller than this you had better plan on replacing them with larger windows.

Windows of many types and sizes can be purchased, ready-cut and fitted, from lumberyards and mills. These are complete windows, consisting of sashes, frames, and trim, and should present no great problem in installation.

The opening cut in the inside wall should be somewhat larger than the size of the window frame so that the frame can be adjusted in the opening and placed absolutely straight.

A portion of the outside wall will have to be cut out, and this should be done with care and accuracy. If there are already small windows in the walls, these should be taken out along with the frames and saved for some other purpose. The opening is then enlarged until it is right for the new window.

If there is no opening in the outside walls, drill holes at the four corners of the section to be removed, and then use a keyhole or compass saw to start the cut. When the cut is large enough, a handsaw may be used to finish the job. Do this part of the cutting from the outside.

It will also be necessary to cut out and remove some of the house studding, and the opening should then be framed with double studding and double headers to provide the necessary support. The window frame can then be inserted into the opening, plumbed level and true with wood wedges, and nailed into place. A groove should be cut on the underside of the windowsill so that the house siding or shingles can be brought up into the sill. A strip of wood called an apron is then tacked over the joint. The purpose of this arrangement is to prevent rainwater blowing along under the sill and getting into the walls.

Next, flashing must be put on between window frame and outside wall. How to do this is explained in chapter 11 (see page 274).

## Dormer Windows

In remodeling an attic it may be found that even large windows at the gabled ends do not give the amount of light and ventilation that is required when more than two rooms are to be built. That brings up the possibility of installing one or more dormer windows.

In the accompanying series of drawings, the first figure shows the framework of a pitched-roof dormer; the second figure shows the finished job. The third figure shows the framework of the same narrow dormer as viewed from the inside, with part of the roof cut away to clarify the details. The last two figures show the framework and finished view of a flat-roof dormer. Two windows, side by side, could be put in instead of the one as shown.

There is no doubt that dormer windows along the sides of the roof will make any room in the attic more attractive, but it should also be borne in mind that win-

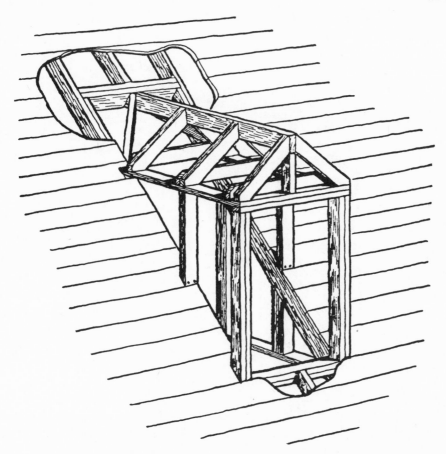

dows of this type will have a decided effect on the outside appearance, even to the point of throwing the general design of the house out of balance. Just how this change will affect the overall appearance of the house is sometimes difficult for the layman to visualize, and therefore it might be wise to consult an architect on this matter before a final decision is reached.

However, symmetry is a cardinal point to consider, particularly for dormers on the front of the house. The wide dormer shown would serve well for a bathroom, and would look best in the center of that side of the roof. If you put in a narrow dormer, it might be better to have two of them, equidistant from the ends of the roof.

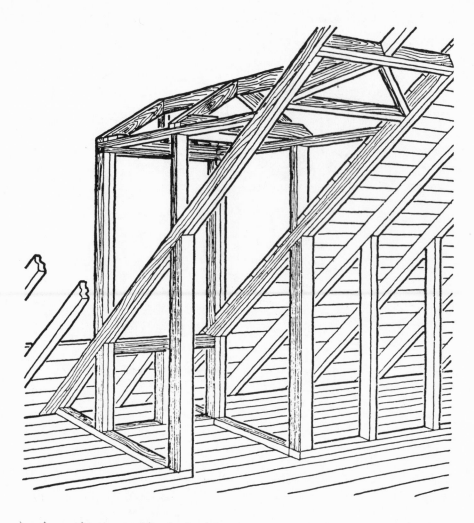

Another point to consider is that the proper construction of a dormer window is a rather sizable undertaking, as it requires the removal of a portion of the roof as well as cutting out some of the roof rafters. It might be safer to have this particular job done by a skilled carpenter. However, if the home mechanic decides to do the job himself, then he should take pains to plan and execute the job in a neat manner.

First of all, remember that most of this work will have to be done while on the roof; proper scaffolding should be set up so that you can work in comfort and safety. And as it will be necessary for the roof to be open for a considerable period of time, the job should be done in warm weather, during a dry spell if possible. In any event, a large sheet of canvas should be on hand for use in covering the opening in case of rain.

A dormer can be built entirely on a house roof, as shown in these pictures, or it can be a continuation of an outside wall. As mentioned, a dormer with a flat, sloped roof can be made large enough to serve a bathroom or a small kitchen. Aside from the outside appearance, the size and shape of the dormer will depend on the

purpose for which it is intended and the size of the window or windows to be installed.

On examination of the illustration showing the dormer with the pitched roof, it will be noted that the opening in the roof is framed with double rafters. In this respect, when deciding on the width and exact location of the dormer, arrange matters so that the roof rafters will form the two sides. Then double these by spiking rafters of the same size to them. The headers of the opening are also double. The top header is placed at a slight angle that corresponds with the roof pitch, and the lower header, which will act as the sill of the dormer, is placed upright, the end rafters being cut at an angle, so that this may be accomplished. The two corner posts at the front of the dormer are double, as is the top plate. Studding forming the sides of the dormer is supported by the double roof rafters on each side. Additional studding runs up from the attic floor to the bottom of these rafters, to form the interior wall of the dormer. The studding broken by the rafters should be in the same line. It will be seen, after studying the interior view of the dormer on page 350, that it will be necessary to determine in advance where the walls of the attic rooms are to be placed, before these interior studs can be set in position. The studding is not nailed directly to the attic floor but is attached to a 2″ × 4″ sole

plate which is nailed to the flooring. The sole (or sole plate) is the horizontal member which bears the studs of the partition.

The dormer with the flat, sloped roof presents something less of a construction problem than the pitched-roof type. Here again the opening for the dormer should be framed with double rafters and headers. Studding forming the sides of the dormer can be set on top of the rafters, as was the case with the pitched-roof dormer, or can be extended unbroken from the attic floor, running on the inside of the roof rafters.

After the dormer has been framed it can be covered with either tongue-and-groove sheathing, or a type of composition board used for this same purpose.

Because of the construction and location of a dormer window, it is very important that it be properly flashed to prevent water leaking through the seams. The second figure on page 349 shows the method of flashing this type of work. Use copper flashing or some other type that will not rust. When the flashing has been installed, the roofing and siding can be applied.

## LOUVERS

One last major change must be made in the outside walls of the attic before work on the attic rooms can begin. This is

the installation of louvers at the gable ends to prevent condensation of water vapor on the attic roof and to make the rooms more comfortable during hot weather. The louver should be installed at each gable end of the attic as near the roof peak as possible. Louvers can be purchased, or made so that they will not allow rain or snow to enter but will allow the free passage of air. The louver should also be provided with screening to keep insects out of the attic.

The size of the opening required will depend upon the number of square feet of insulated area in the attic, and also on the temperature that can be expected during the average winter. This information can be obtained from the concern where the insulation for the attic is purchased.

## INSULATION

If the attic rooms are to be comfortable in both summer and winter, they must be properly insulated. Blanket-type insulation is shown in the illustration, but other types of insulation can be applied in much the same manner. Notice that the insulation does not run from the eaves to the peak of the roof but instead is brought across just above the ceiling. This is done so that there will be a dead-air space between the insulation and the top of the roof. The attic space being finished off should be insulated on all sides. It does no good to insulate an attic room on the top and three sides and put no insulation between that room and an unfinished part of the attic.

If the attic has been provided with collar beams or ceiling joists running between opposite roof rafters, then these can be used as a base on which to attach the insulation, and they will also serve as a base for the room ceiling material. If there are no such beams they will have to be installed at this point, and they should be placed at the height that the room ceiling is to be. However, they must be placed at least 2' below the highest point of the roof to provide the necessary dead-air space.

As the only load which these collar beams or ceiling joists will have to carry will be the weight of the insulation and the ceiling material, they can be made of 2" × 4" stock unless the span happens to be very great, in which case it would be best to use 2" × 6" lumber, so that there will be no chance of the ceiling sagging. The ceiling rafters should run between each set of opposite roof rafters, and should be set on edge to provide the maximum amount of support. The ceiling joists can be attached to the rafters with an oblique butt joint, but as this joint depends upon nails alone for its strength, it would be wise to reinforce it by nailing short lengths of 2" × 4" stock on the sides.

To get the proper angle for cutting the ends of the joists so that they will fit tightly against the rafters, first mark on the rafters the exact location where the joist is to be fastened. Then cut a joist so that it can be placed between opposite rafters and let the ends of the joist extend an inch or so beyond the inner edge of the rafters. Put the joist up into position and attach it to the rafter with nails driven in only part of the way. Mark each end of the joist along the angle formed where it meets the rafter. Take down the joist and cut along those lines. Put the rafter up in place again to check the measurement. The two surfaces should come together in a tight fit. If this is the case, try the joist

between other rafters, and if it fits properly in all cases, use it as a pattern to cut the other joists.

All the ceiling joists can be put up in this manner, except those which occupy a spot intended for a wall partition. The top plate of the wall partition must run between rafters; and as a joist will be needed on each side of the partition to fasten the ceiling, some other arrangement must be made for nailing up the joists. What can be done is to spike odd lengths of 2" × 4" stock to the side of the rafters, so that the joists can be attached on each side, leaving a surface in the middle wide enough to attach the top plate—about 3⅝". By moving the joists in this manner there will be a slight difference in the distance between them, but as this difference will be smaller, rather than greater, than before, it will not cause trouble as far as the insulation and ceiling material are concerned.

Once all the ceiling joists are in place, little difficulty should be encountered in applying the insulation. This material can be purchased in standard widths to fit between the rafters and joists, or, in the event that the distance between these members is not standard, extra wide insulation can be purchased and cut to size. As the joists have been placed the same distance apart as the rafters (except in the

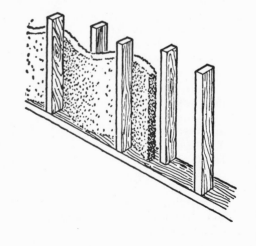

case of the partition), it is possible to use one long strip of insulation, from one eave to the other.

The insulation is held in place by nails or other fasteners driven through a flat on each side of the insulation and into the sides of the rafters and joists. Follow the manufacturer's directions as to what size fastener should be used and how far apart they should be spaced. The insulation at the gable ends of the attic will run down between the vertical house studding, from ceiling joists to floor. The dormer window must be insulated also. If only one side of the insulation has been covered with waterproof paper, make sure that in each instance this faces toward the inside of the room and is not placed against, or facing, the wall or roofing.

## WALL CONSTRUCTION

The next step is to put up the necessary studding to form the walls of the attic rooms. As a base for this studding, a 2″ × 4″ sole should be laid down along each side of the attic. The distance the sole is from the roof eaves will determine the height of the vertical walls of the rooms. It would be unwise to make these walls too short, as this space would be difficult to utilize in a room. Walls of 4′ are about right in many cases. This is not only a useful height for the room, but if small doors are placed in the wall at regular intervals, the space between the wall and the roof eaves can be used as a general storage bin.

When the distance of this wall from the eaves has been decided, the sole should be set down so that it is an equal distance from the roof eaves along its entire length. Nail the sole in place, spacing the nails so that they will go through the rough flooring and into the attic floor joists. Studding is now required between the sole and the rafters. Take a plumb line and drop it from the side of one raf-

ter to the sole. Mark on the sole where the line comes, and then stand a piece of studding on this line and let it come up a little beyond the lower edge of the rafter. Check the position of the studding with a level or square to be sure that it is upright, and then, holding the piece steady, mark with a pencil the angle formed on the studding where it crosses the lower edge of the rafter. Cut the piece of studding along this line and put it into position between the rafter and the sole. If it fits correctly it can be nailed in place at both ends, toeing the nails in. Before this is done, however, it would be a good idea to try this piece of studding between other rafters and the sole. If it should fit correctly at all points, then use it as a pattern to cut the remaining studs.

One point that should be borne in mind while doing any framing is the conservation of materials. Wallboard, plywood, and insulating material are usually made to fit a standard size of framing. This may be either 16″ or 24″ on center. If studding, for example, were placed 26″ on center, it would mean that a piece of wallboard of the standard width of 4′ (48″) would require additional studding at the seam, because the regular studding was spaced too far apart. The same holds true for insulating material which is made to fit snugly between members of standard framing, but which will have to be cut down if the studs are too close together.

Another point that is worth remembering is to try to take advantage of standardization wherever possible. Wallboard and plywood generally come 4′ in width and 8′ in length, or 12′ in some cases. With a little planning beforehand, it is often possible to arrange the framing of a room and its size so that you can use many complete sections of material, instead of wasting time cutting them down to size and having a lot of small pieces left over. If the vertical wall of the attic room is 4′ high, it will be possible to use one entire section of wallboard with no cutting whatsoever. Naturally, a room cannot be completely planned and built to meet all standards of building materials, but often if enough thought is given to all points of the problem in advance, details can be worked out to reduce effort and waste to a minimum.

On the other hand, it may be difficult, or impossible, to get large pieces of material, 4' × 8' or 12', up to the attic by small windows or around turns of the stairways. In that case your material will have to be cut before bring it upstairs, but remember to measure and cut it so that it can be nailed to the studs properly.

Now, if the studding and the ceiling joists have been correctly installed to the rafters so that all are in the same line, we should find, when it comes to installing the wallboard on the ceiling and walls, that the joints between sections of wallboard will line up in a regular pattern and not be staggered.

Before nailing the wallboard permanently in place it will be wise to have the electric wiring attended to (see page 357). That will save pulling down walls or cutting into them.

## Partitions

The next step is to divide the attic space into the required number of rooms by means of partitions.

At this stage it is a good idea to recheck your floor plan to be sure it is the most convenient and efficient arrangement possible. The addition of a dormer window may be the deciding factor in changing the location of a room.

Check to make sure that the stairs will lead up to a living room or kitchen, avoiding a bedroom if possible. Of course, if the apartment consists of only one room plus kitchen and bath, you may not have much choice.

Before taking up the actual framing of the wall partitions, it would be well to consider ways and means of preventing sound transmission, either between rooms

in the attic, or between attic and house proper.

Sound waves in the air can be absorbed by the use of special insulation which is applied and finished in much the same fashion as wallboard. On the other hand, the actual wall partitions will act as sound conductors, and that calls for special construction. The usual method is to build two separate walls with a heavy building felt placed between them. The thickness of such a wall can be reduced by staggering the wall studding. The effectiveness of this arrangement depends upon the fact that the two walls are completely independent of each other. Of course, this method of construction doubles the amount of material required for single walls.

If there are to be any doors in the partition walls, then it is a good idea to have them on hand so that the frames in the partition can be built to fit the door, instead of constructing the frame, only to find that a door of that particular size is not available, or that you must purchase an oversize door and spend considerable time cutting it down to the correct size.

The actual framing of the partition should not be difficult. The wall will be made up of 2" × 4" studding, running between the sole that is attached to the floor and the plate that runs between the roof rafters. The necessary steps were taken when the ceiling joists were put up, so that the partition plate can be nailed to the rafters. All that needs to be done now is to cut this plate to size, mitering each end at an angle, so that it will fit against the edges of the rafters. The plate is attached with the broad surfaces facing up and down. The bottom of the plate should be flush with the bottom of the ceiling joists on either side.

Set the sole of the partition in place and measure the distance from it to the bottom of the ceiling joists. Use this measurement for cutting the studding that will run between the sole and the plate. The plate of the partition will run only the same distance as that of the ceiling joists, but the sole will run the entire distance of the partition. The studding at each end of the wall will run up from the sole and be nailed to the rafters. The plate can be put into position and secured by nailing it at the ends to the rafters, and then driving nails through the joists into it. The full-length wall studding can then be attached to the sole by driving nails up through the bottom of the sole, into the bottom of the studding. The studding should be placed 16″ on center. Brace the vertical studding so that it is upright and then lift the assembly up and move it into position so that the top of the studding will be directly under the plate, which will make the entire framework plumb. The sole can then be nailed to the floor and the studding spiked to the plate. The short studding between the sole and the rafters is now measured, cut, and nailed in place. Openings for doors in the partition should be framed with double studding.

**Closet and Storage Space.** During framing, some provision should be made for closets and other storage areas. The space between the eaves of the roof and the sides of the attic rooms can be used for general storage space, or recessed cabinets may be built with shelves, or you can construct a built-in chest with drawers.

You make an attic bedroom larger, since you don't need so much movable furniture. But of course such storage space is close to the floor and will not serve too well for some articles, or for garments which you wish to hang up.

It would be well to construct at least one full-sized closet that runs to ceiling height. The top of it can be provided with shelves and used for storage. Closets should be framed in the same fashion as the walls and other partitions. Studding around the closet doors should be double.

**Ventilation for Bathroom and Kitchen.** It may not be possible, even by the addition of extra windows, to locate the bathroom and kitchen where there will be outside windows. In that case exhaust fans can be used to pull the air out of those rooms, allowing fresh air to be drawn in from other parts of the apartment. The exhaust fan is placed in an opening cut through the outside wall, and should be provided with a louver, which can be closed from the inside when the fan is not in operation, to prevent cold air from coming in.

The wiring for the fan should be permanent, and current to the fan should be governed by a conveniently located wall switch. If it is impossible to locate the fan in the room so that it is in an outside wall, then it can be located elsewhere and ducts used to connect it.

# ELECTRICAL SYSTEM

When the job of framing the attic has been completed, thought should be given to an adequate electrical system. Just how much of a task this will turn out to be will depend upon what provisions, if any, were made for attic wiring when the house was built. A considerate builder, who realizes that sooner or later the attic space will be converted into rooms, will see to it that adequate wiring and circuits are installed at the same time that the house is wired.

It should go without saying that this calls for little added expense or effort when the house is being built.

But if no provisions were made for attic wiring then, it will be necessary for the home mechanic to have wires run up from the main fuse box, through the wall spaces and perhaps under the flooring.

If there is no wiring whatever in the attic, then it would be best to call in an electrician and have the required number of additional circuits brought up from the point where the service lines enter the house. The job of installing additional circuits may require a larger or additional fuse box and major changes in wiring. When this work is being done the electrician should be given a full understanding of the electrical needs of the attic, in both the immediate and distant future, so that he can connect up a system that will be adequate, containing enough circuits and outlets. As mentioned earlier, if the attic is to be heated with electric space-heaters, or if an electric kitchen range is to be installed, special wiring will be required.

Assuming that the attic has been wired to some extent, it may be possible for the home mechanic to make the few minor changes necessary to cover present needs. But before such work is begun, the home mechanic should check with his local building authorities to see if there is any ordinance which forbids his doing this work. In many localities electrical work of this kind can be done legally only by a licensed electrician. In other places, the work must be checked over by an inspector before it can be put into operation.

The job of remodeling the attic wiring may consist only of removing an outlet box for a fixture, freeing some of the cable, and moving the box to some other location. However, it may be necessary to use longer cables in connection with this work, and because cables cannot be spliced except at light, switch, and junction boxes, either a longer cable must be substituted for the short one, or additional outlets of some type installed. Then again, it may be necessary as well as possible to install additional outlets, such as fixtures, to the existing attic circuits, provided, of course, these additional outlets will not overload the circuits.

(Refer to chapter 9 for additional information.)

## Types of Wire

Many different types of wire are used for interior electrical work. Two kinds which meet the approval of many codes for exposed or concealed interior wiring in dry locations, are nonmetallic sheathed cable and armored cable. Nonmetallic sheathed cable consists of two or more wires, each independently insulated, and then covered with a tough heavy outer fabric on plastic. These are inexpensive materials and easy to work with because of their flexibility and the fact that no special tools are required other than those found in the average home tool kit.

The other type of wiring often found in residential work is armored cable. This is sometimes called by the trade name BX Cable. It consists of 2 or more insulated

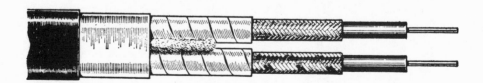

wires, covered with heavy paper and incased in a flexible steel jacket. The steel jacket provides considerable protection for the wires from possible injury to their insulation, but as the metal covering is not waterproof it should be used only in dry locations. Special cable, with an interior covering of lead, is used for wiring in damp locations.

The 2 wires inside either the nonmetallic sheathed cable or the armored cable, will have different colored insulation. The wire with the black insulation will be the live, or hot, wire, and the one with the white insulation, or insulation with a white tracer running through it, will be the ground wire. When making connections to wires, be sure that the black wire is attached to the black, and the white to the white. This will hold true in almost every case—except when a 2-wire cable is run to a switch from a fixture. In that case, the white wire of the cable running to the switch is spliced to the black wire from the source of current, and the black wire on the cable from the switch is connected to the black wire of the fixture. The wiring must always be arranged so that the switch breaks the flow of current through the black or hot wire, while the white or ground wire goes directly to the fixture and is never interrupted. Fixtures are provided with different colored terminal screws. The white or silver-colored screw is for the white wire, and the brass or gold-colored is for the black.

If the black and white wires were hooked up at random throughout the electrical system, it would mean that there would be current flowing to a fixture in spite of the fact that the switch was in the

"off" position. Such a situation could cause serious trouble if there were a short circuit.

Outlet boxes and switch boxes for use with nonmetallic sheathed cable or armored cable are made to standard design, so that not only can the cable be attached to them easily and securely but also the fixture or switch cover plate can be attached.

An outlet box must be used at each point where there is an electrical connection. Wires cannot be spliced at any point except inside an outlet box. These boxes, made of metal, are insurance against a short circuit in the connections; short circuits are the cause of many fires. The boxes must be mounted securely to the framework of the walls. Where an outlet box comes between studding, special hangers can be used to hold the box in place. Boxes are provided with metal cover plates which are to be screwed on tight after the wiring has been completed.

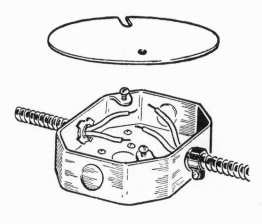

Before any actual wiring is begun, it would be well for the home mechanic to consult a catalog of electrical fittings and equipment at his local electrical shop so that he can select the size and type of fittings best suited to his needs.

Outlet boxes and other boxes for switches and the like are provided with "knockouts" so that wires and cables can be brought into the box. These knockouts are incomplete circular cuts made in the sides and bottom of the box. A sharp rap with a screwdriver or other tool will force out the round piece of metal, leaving the proper size hole. Mount the box solidly with screws through holes provided for that purpose in the bottom of the box. Mount it on a $2'' \times 4''$ or $1'' \times 4''$ piece of scrap lumber which you have nailed between two pieces of studding. Then remove only the number of knockouts necessary for the wires or cables that are brought into the box.

Nonmetallic sheathed cable or armored cable can be attached to the box so that they will be mechanically secure, by means of special clamps. These clamps are fitted over the ends of the cable and are secured to it by tightening a screw. The

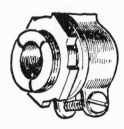

other end of the clamp is threaded and this is pushed through the hole in the box. A bushing is then slipped over the threads, and after this a nut is run on and tightened. The sides of this nut are notched so that it can be tightened with a screwdriver.

When connecting wires to terminal screws on fixtures and switches, remove only enough insulation from the wire ends to allow it to go around the terminal screw once. Be sure that the wire goes around the screw in the same direction that the screw rotates when it is tightened. Only one wire should be used on each terminal screw. If it is necessary to have another wire at this same point, use fixtures made for this purpose, which have two terminal screws on the same side. Wire ends used for connection to terminal screws or splicing must be completely clean of insulation, and the connection must be mechanically secure. In case of splices, the splice should be soldered.

The size of wire to be used for the attic wiring will be governed by the size used elsewhere in the house. A No. 14 wire is considered the minimum size allowed for interior wiring, but with the increased use of electrical appliances, many homes are wired with the heavier No. 12 to carry the additional load. Needless to say, a No. 14 should not be spliced onto a heavier size of wire.

**Cutting Armored Cable.** Armored cable can be cut satisfactorily with a hacksaw, but some practice may be necessary, as it is very important not to let the saw teeth damage the insulation around the wires. The cut should be made about 8″ from the end of the cable so that enough uncovered wire will be exposed for splicing and making connections. To make the cut with a saw, do not cut directly across the cable, but rather, hold the saw at an angle of about 60 degrees to the cable. Work slowly and cut through the metal jacket only—not through the paper. When the blade has cut through the metal, the free end of the cable can be twisted and pulled off. The cutting will leave a ragged edge on the end of the cable and this might damage the wire insulation. So a small fiber bushing known as an antishort bushing is slipped over the end of the cable to insulate the wires from the outside steel jacket.

The outer insulation on nonmetallic sheathed cable can be removed with a knife, but care must be taken not to let the knife blade damage the inner insulation around the wire.

Cable can be run through holes bored in the studding and joists, or it can follow the wall and ceiling structure. If there is any possibility that the cable could be mechanically damaged, it should be provided with a running board—a strip of wood secured in place and serving as a base for the cable.

Nonmetallic sheathed cable can be secured to the walls and other framing by means of special straps or clamps. Straps should be placed at least every $4\frac{1}{4}'$ and within at least 12" of outlet boxes. Ar-

mored cable can be attached with a similar strap or with large staples designed for this work. Staples can be installed faster than straps but they cannot be used on nonmetallic sheathed cable as there is danger that the sharp points of the staples might damage the wire insulation. The steel jacket protects armored cable from that danger.

In working with any type of wire or cable, sharp bends should be avoided as they can damage the insulation around the wires.

## Extending or Adding Outlets

Before starting to add an additional outlet, recheck to make sure that this will not overload that circuit. (See chapter 9, page 220.) Be sure that the current is off in that circuit before handling wires.

The first step in the job will be to locate the approximate position for the new fixture. After that, work back along the

attic wiring to find out where the extension can be tapped into the source. A tap can be made at a junction box, switch box, or outlet box, provided the box does not already contain the maximum number of wires set forth in the National Electrical Code. Under no circumstances should a splice be made directly into the wires unless a junction box is first installed so that the splice can be made inside the box.

Usually a light fixture or a wall outlet provides a convenient place to tap into, but there are a few considerations that must be understood before this can be done. There are several ways that light or wall fixtures can be wired. The accompanying figure shows one method, where the white wire from the supply (the

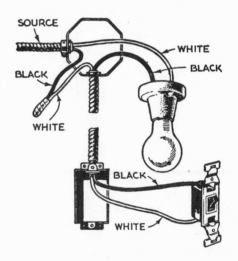

ground or neutral wire) is connected to the white wire on the fixture. The black wire from the supply is interrupted by a wall switch, so that when the switch is open no current will flow to the fixture. If the cable for the new outlet were to be spliced in, at the fixture, to the white wire, the outlet on this line would be controlled by the switch provided for the first fixture. This might not be a very convenient arrangement.

In a case of this kind it will be necessary to go back to the switch and take the supply of current for the new fixture off the hot side of the switch, tapping onto the black-to-white spliced wire shown at the left of the picture. Connect the white line of the new fixture to the white line in the junction box. If this is done we shall have an uninterrupted supply of current to the new fixture, regardless of the position of the wall switch.

If there is no wall switch—the light fixture being controlled by a pull chain or other device built into the fixture—then a tap can be made onto the black or power

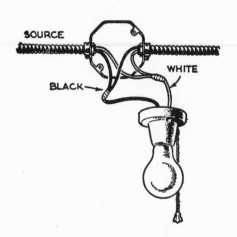

line. Connect the black wire to the black, and the white to the white; solder; and tape.

In certain hookups used in wiring, a tap can be made from a fixture controlled by a wall switch located at some distance from the fixture, and still have current going to the new outlet regardless of the position of the switch. In this hookup the cable coming from the power supply is brought to the fixture outlet box. The white wire of the supply cable is spliced to the white wire of the fixture. The black wire of the supply cable is spliced to the white wire in the cable that runs to the switch. The black wire in this switch cable

is connected to the black wire of the fixture. Now, if the cable to the new fixture were to be connected so that its white wire was spliced in with the other two white wires already spliced, and the black wire were connected to the splice between the supply black wire and the switch cable white wire, then current to the new fixture would not be interrupted by the switch.

After the wires have been spliced, the cable can be run to the desired location for either a light fixture or a wall outlet. If a wall outlet is to be installed, no switch may be required, but if a fixture is to be used, then a switch should be installed at some convenient point on the wall.

There are several ways of connecting the switch with the cable to the light fixture. It may be possible to work the switch into the lines as shown in the diagram.

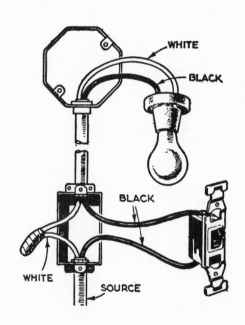

Notice that the black wires are connected to the switch, and the white wires are spliced together. The black, or hot wires, are always the ones to be broken by the

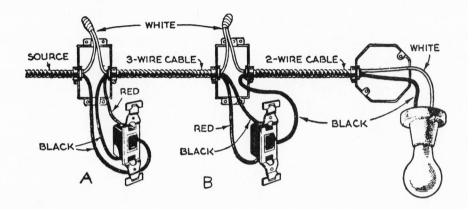

switch. An arrangement of this type can be used only when the switch can easily be located somewhere along the run of the cable.

It may be more convenient as well as more practical to place the switch at some distance from the cable running to the fixture, and in that case a hookup such as that shown on page 361 can be used. This is the same as the connection that was used on the fixture which was tapped for supply. It will be noted that in this hookup the rule about always connecting black to black and white to white, has apparently been disregarded; for the black wire from supply has been connected to the white wire to the switch. This is permissible under the code, provided the black return wire from the switch is connected to the black fixture wire.

## 3-Way Switches

It is often very convenient to be able to control a light fixture from switches located at either of two different points. For example, the light fixture at the head of the attic stairs should be wired so that it can be turned on and off by means of a switch located at the top of the stairs or a switch at the bottom.

For this particular hookup, 3-way switches as well as cable containing 3 in-

stead of the usual 2 wires must be used. The third wire in the cable is colored red.

There are several combinations for wiring the switches and fixture, and these will depend upon where the source of power comes in, as well as upon the location of the switches with respect to the fixture. The diagram shows a hookup in which the supply comes into one of the switches. The white wire from the supply is connected to the white wire in the 3-wire cable. The black wire of supply is connected to the common terminal on switch A. The black and red wires of the 3-wire cable are attached to the other 2 switch terminals, and at the corresponding terminals on switch B. The black wire in the cable to the fixture is then attached to the common terminal on switch B, and the white wire of the fixture cable is spliced to the white wire of the 3-wire cable.

## Testing the System

Before the system is completed or put into operation, it should be given a complete test so as to be sure that there are no short circuits or loose connections. The job of testing can be done with 2 dry cells and a bell or buzzer, or you can buy a ready-made testing device. Switches should be at the "on" position. There should be

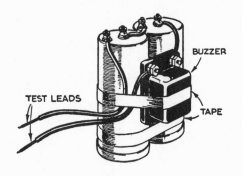

no current in the system during these tests. Remove all bulbs and outlet plugs. Take the 2 leads from the testing bell and battery and touch one to the black wire of the system and the other to the white wire. If the bell rings, then there is a short circuit somewhere in the line. This must be located and fixed at once. The next step is to attach one wire of the testing equipment to the black wire of the system, and the second wire of the testing equipment to the other end, or terminal point, of the black wire of the system, either at the fixture or the wall outlet. If the wire has been properly installed, the bell will ring. Do the same with the white wire.

The actual installation of fixtures should not be done at this time as they will be in the way when the wall and ceiling materials are put up.

## FINISHING THE WALLS AND CEILING

Once the basic electrical wiring is completed, the work of finishing off the walls and ceilings of the rooms can be undertaken. Again we assume that if plumbing is to be installed, the pipes have been run up from the floor below so that it will not be necessary to tear out sections of wall to bring in pipes. The actual plumbing fixtures cannot, of course, be put in place until the walls are up, but some provision

should be made for the washbowl if it is to be the type that is hung on the wall. The bathroom fixtures—washbowl, toilet, and tub or shower—should be purchased and on hand, even though not yet to be connected, so that you can measure them and make sure that you will not put your walls where the fixtures will not fit.

Several materials can be used for the walls and ceiling, such as plasterboard or plywood, which can be handled with saw and hammer and, if properly applied, will give good results.

There are many brands and grades of wallboard on the market. By all means get one of the better kind, as it will be easier to put on and will not be so liable to break.

When purchasing wallboard, secure all the necessary information from your dealer as to the recommended method for filling the seams between sections, and also find out whether or not sizing is necessary before painting. The usual method of dealing with seams is to either cover them over with strips of wood lath, or fill them with a special cement and reinforce the cement with a perforated or wire-mesh tape. A seam treated in this manner can be painted or papered over with good results.

But this requires that a space of about 1/8″ or so be left between sections, so that there will be room for the cement. If the seams are to be covered with wood laths, then it is important to have the wall and ceiling seams line up wherever possible. A room filled with irregularly spaced seams on wall and ceiling is difficult to decorate.

An inexpensive grade of plywood can be used for the walls and ceiling, and this can be painted or papered. But plywood with an attractive grain can be used as paneling, requiring no finish other than staining or waxing. If a room is to be paneled in plywood, it may be found that covering both walls and ceiling in this manner is not to your liking; in that case the ceiling can be covered with some other material and painted, or the lower half of the walls can be paneled and the upper portions painted or papered. (See chapter 13, page 313.) Because of wall studding and ceiling joists, it will not be necessary to provide furring.

If a room is to be finished in wallboard, then the ceiling should be covered first. This may be difficult for one person to accomplish alone, as it requires getting the large sheet into position, and then holding it in place while nails are driven in. If no helper is available, the task can be done by one person by constructing a large "T." Make it out of 1″ × 4″ stock, with the crossarm, or top of the T, the same width as the wallboard, and the upright an inch or two higher than the ceiling of the room. This T can be used to lift and support one end of the wallboard, while the other end is held, moved into the correct position, and nailed. The size and spacing of the nails used should be in accordance with the directions provided with the wallboard or learned from the dealer. Be sure to use enough nails to keep the ceiling from sagging.

The sections going up along the sidewalls do not present so much difficulty. The main point there is to be sure that the sections are properly supported and that they are plumb. Drive in nails close to the edge of the wallboard, so that they can all be covered with the wood lath which is only 2″ or so in width.

Bring the wallboard as close as possible to openings such as doors and windows. By doing so you reduce the size of the trim necessary around those areas to cover up the joint. Obviously, if the wallboard is brought only to within 3″ or 4″ of the opening, wide pieces of trim will be required.

In some cases it will be possible to cut a hole in the wallboard, where a light or other fixture is to be placed, before the wallboard is nailed into position. If this is done, check the distance carefully so that the hole will correspond exactly with the outlet box in the studding. If the hole is too far to one side, or is cut too large, the finish plate of the fixture will not completely cover the opening.

In the bathroom and kitchen it is desirable that the walls and ceilings have a smooth surface which can be cleaned easily. There are several materials which can be used for this purpose and which can be applied directly over the wallboard. Tileboard, linoleum, metal tiles, or vinyl fabric will do, and any of these can be easily installed. As they will require a base, walls of wallboard should be put up first. Then cover the entire walls with the selected material, or cover only the lower half of the walls and paint the top half and the ceiling with enamel. Do not use a water-soluble paint in either the bathroom or kitchen.

Once the walls and ceilings have been completed, the electric fixtures and switch panels can be installed. Holes are cut through the wallboard, if this was not done before the boards were nailed in place, and the electric wires are connected to the fixtures. Remember to have the electric current shut off, at least from the attic, before working around any of these wires. Each fixture is then connected by screws to the outlet box. In the case of switches, panels should be attached to the box so as to give a neat and finished appearance.

The next step is to put down some kind of finished flooring. It is a poor policy to leave the subflooring uncovered, because it will be hard to keep clean and is unattractive. A wide variety of materials can be used. A hardwood floor can be laid, or plain linoleum, tile designs, or other coverings can be used. If the subfloor is quite rough and not especially tight, it would be wise to cover it with building paper and lay sheets of plywood on it, so as to secure an even and tight base on which to lay the flooring material. Floors for the kitchen and bathroom should be of a kind that will stand hard usage and can be easily cleaned.

When the flooring is down, the

plumbing fixtures and kitchen equipment of the permanent type (stove, sink, cupboards, and so forth) should be installed. It is assumed that the necessary pipes have been put in, so that it should not be necessary to do any additional cutting into the walls or flooring.

## FINAL CARPENTRY

The rooms are now ready for the finished woodwork and trim. Doors are hung in the frames as explained in chapter 3 (see page 65). It will also be necessary to place wood trim around windows, doors, and baseboards, covering the joints between the walls and floor. If there is to be any built-in furniture in the attic, this should be constructed before the trim goes on. Built-in furniture, such as bookcases and shelves, kitchen cabinets, window

seats, and even beds, can be made with no great amount of extra effort or expense, and doing this will save just that much when it comes to furnishing the attic. An attic apartment is small, and having certain pieces of furniture permanently located will give more room for other things. Keep this built-in furniture along simple lines and it will blend well with almost any style of extra pieces that may be used.

Wood trim in stock designs can be purchased at most lumberyards, or if you want something a little different from what they have, it can be milled out to order at a slight additional cost. It is recommended that the trim used be of a moderately simple design, and, unless the home mechanic possesses special tools as well as special skill, the joints for fitting the trim together should be made as simple as possible. The miter joint can be used for most of such work, and miter

joints are easy to cut in a homemade miter box. (See chapter 3, page 74.) The width of the trim required will depend, to a large extent, on how close the wallboard has been fitted to the openings in the wall.

Trim should be cut carefully with a fine-toothed saw, and tacked loosely in place so that the other members of the assembly can be likewise installed, and the entire job checked for accuracy of measurements and cuts before it is finally nailed secure.

We all like to think that studding and other framing we have put up is all plumb and level, but it often proves to be otherwise; so be sure to use a level to check the position of a piece of trim before it is nailed in place. Your eye is not always infallible. Sometimes you can correct previous slight errors before you nail the trim. Nailing should be done with finishing nails, placed in inconspicuous places on the wood when possible, and countersunk slightly with a nail set, so that their heads will be below the wood surface. After the first coat of paint those holes can be filled with putty.

The baseboard covering the joint between the walls and floor should be about 6″ high and can be nailed to the wall studding. A strip of quarter-round molding can then be nailed along the bottom of the baseboard, making a rounded joint that will be easy to clean and will not collect dust and dirt.

If the floor is covered with linoleum or some other material of this type, which may need replacing in the future, let the linoleum come right up to the baseboards, and then cover the seam with the quarter-round. This will make a tight joint and when the linoleum is removed for replacement, only the quarter-round will have to be taken up, and this can be replaced when the new flooring is laid.

## PAINTING AND DECORATING

Before any painting is done, the attic rooms should be given a thorough cleaning. It will be difficult, if not impossible, to do a good painting job in rooms filled with dust and dirt. A vacuum cleaner is best for doing the cleaning.

The walls can be papered or painted. If paint is selected, there is a

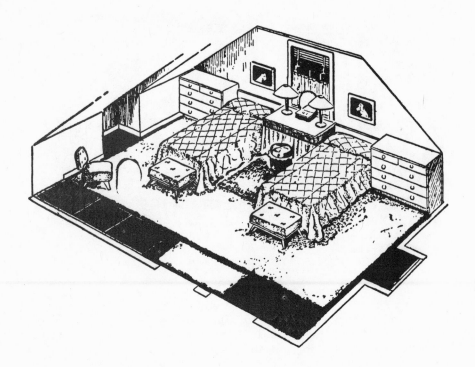

choice between water-thinned paints and oil paints. As was recommended previously, the bath and kitchen should be painted with enamel, a type of oil paint which dries with a smooth surface and therefore is easy to clean.

The woodwork in the rooms can be painted or stained. In any case the wood should be given a good sandpapering so that it is smooth, and the holes caused by nailheads filled with putty, if the wood is to be painted, or neutral plastic filler, if stained and varnished.

The floors, if they are of wood, can be either painted, varnished, or shellacked.

The outside work around a dormer window, or any other openings, should be given three coats of exterior paint of the same color as that used for the outside trim of the house.

(Refer to chapter 6 for additional information.)

The illustrations on page 367 and above give a conception of how the living room and bedroom of an attic apartment might look when fully finished and filled with suitable furnishings. (The plan view of these two rooms is shown on page 344.) Bear in mind that the side walls are not much more than 3′ high, and although space with such low ceilings can be made useful, it has definite limitations and cannot be used for every purpose.

# 15

# REMODELING
# THE BASEMENT

The basement in many homes is pretty much wasted space. It usually contains a few items of household equipment such as the furnace and hot-water heater, and perhaps serves as a general storage place for various odds and ends, but generally only a fraction of the total basement area is fully utilized. So in many cases it would be quite possible for the home mechanic to turn a good portion of this space into useful and attractive rooms.

The usual manner of finishing a basement is to make it into a game or recreation room, but it is just as feasible to use some of the space for a second living room, study, library, or hobby room. So it might be well to consider turning part of the basement into quarters which some of the family can use and enjoy frequently instead of merely fixing up a room to be used when parties are given. However, a game room may be the sort of room most wanted, where a little extra noise would not be so likely to disturb children or other members of the family who have gone to bed early.

In approaching the job of remodeling there is also the utilitarian angle. For example, unless there is a tool shed or an oversize garage, a portion of the basement should be set aside for garden tools and similar equipment. A wheelbarrow, lawn mower, garden hose and reel, lawn furniture, and things of this sort require ample storage space which should be located, when possible, near the outside basement door. Some of these things merely need dry storage space during a portion of the year, chiefly during the winter, and can be confined to a relatively small space if hooks and shelves are provided. Screens and storm windows need space but seldom at the same time. Sleds, skis, bicycles, and other recreational equipment must have a place where they can be stored conveniently, and that place generally turns out to be the basement. Many housewives put up their own preserves, jellies, and canned goods, and these should have a cabinet with adequate shelf space. More and more homes have deep-freeze units, and these often cannot be placed in the kitchen; they naturally go in the basement as the next best place. In some cases space is needed in the basement for the washer-dryer. If any member of the family is an amateur photographer, naturally he or she will want a room in the basement for a darkroom. And last, but not least, the home mechanic will want a place for his workbench, tools, and some space in which to store wood or other building materials. The illustration indicates how to build a lumber storage rack which will not take up very much room but which will conveniently take care of considerable

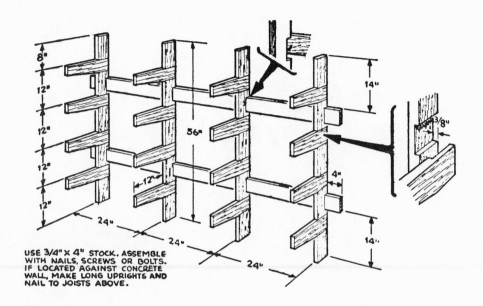

USE 3/4" x 4" STOCK. ASSEMBLE WITH NAILS, SCREWS OR BOLTS. IF LOCATED AGAINST CONCRETE WALL, MAKE LONG UPRIGHTS AND NAIL TO JOISTS ABOVE.

lumber. When remodeling a cellar or refinishing an attic it is much better and more economical to figure carefully what will be needed and to buy a substantial amount of lumber at one time rather than to keep trotting to the lumberyard every other day for another stick of wood.

Through careful planning and the efficient use of ceiling-height shelves, overhead racks, and hooks, it is possible to utilize almost every square inch of basement storage space and thus provide a greater area for a recreation room or other purpose. In fact, without such planning and some remodeling—the articles usually found in cellars just being dumped there helter-skelter—one might think the basement was filled too full to put in anything else.

The cost of remodeling a basement can run anywhere from a few dollars to several thousands. And so the first step is to decide exactly how much money can be spent at this time. Do not make the mistake of trying to stretch an inadequate

budget by using inferior-grade materials. It is much better to finish off merely half of the available space with good materials and let the rest of the area stand as it is until some later date. For example, a lavatory of some sort in the basement is a great convenience, but it is a rather expensive addition. If to complete the installation of the plumbing fixtures would mean running way over the budget, there is no harm in setting aside sufficient space for it and letting it wait. Later on bring in the pipes and have the fixtures connected.

Before any choice of materials for the basement is made, the home mechanic should consult the men of his local lumberyard, explain his plans, state the amount of money he has available, and let them help him in deciding what type and grade of materials he can best use.

(The most important requirement for a remodeled basement is that it be absolutely waterproof. Refer to chapter 12 for information.)

## PREPARATION

Often there are beams or posts in the basement running from the floor to the ceiling to help support the first-floor joists. These posts may make it difficult to plan and utilize the basement area to best advantage, and so they should be removed and some other method used to provide the necessary support for the first floor. This can sometimes be done by installing larger and heavier first-floor joists and by reinforcing those you have. In the illustration, 2 × 4's have been bolted in place on

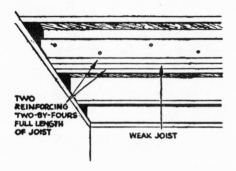

either side of the original 2″ × 6″ or 2″ × 8″ joist. Use good-sized bolts and put them in every 2′ or less.

Another method of providing additional support is to install a steel beam or girder that rests on top of the basement wall and provides support for all the

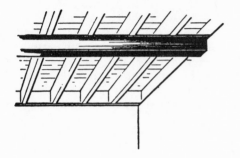

joists. However, the installation of such a beam is a task better left to a contractor.

Or you may have a beam supporting the joists which is in turn supported by a post in the center of the basement. That post may be directly in the way of your plans for remodeling. Perhaps you could replace it with two posts nearer the walls where they would not be so much in the way. A combination jack and steel post provide a good way to obtain adequate support. (See chapter 10, page 230.)

Any cracks or holes in the masonry of the basement walls should be filled and the inside surface washed or brushed clean. A complete inspection should be made of all the woodwork in the basement to make sure that none of it has been attacked and damaged by rot or termites. If there are any squeaks in the first floor, these should be taken care of now before the basement ceiling material goes up and covers the floor joists.

## STAIRS

The steps from the first floor to the basement are often rough and unfinished, but what is worse is that they are sometimes too steep and open risers make them dan-

gerous. And very frequently the stairs are rather poorly lighted. In many cases the stairs are not structurally sound. If the steps are not too steep, or not in too bad condition, it may be possible to fix them up so that they will be at least safe if not attractive. The first task is to inspect them carefully to see that they are anchored securely at the top and that the bottom of the stringers (or sides) sit level on the basement floor. They should have risers and a handrail.

Boards can be nailed across from one stringer to the other to close the risers. Nail a cleat to the underside of the stair tread and then nail the riser to that

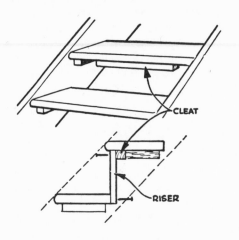

CLEAT

RISER

and to the back of the stair tread below. That is better than merely nailing through the stringers.

A good solid handrail can be made out of $2'' \times 4''$ stock, planed and sanded smooth so that there will be no danger from splinters. If the old stairs are in generally poor condition and too steep, then it would be better to install a new set. Directions for building a rough flight of stairs are given in chapter 10 (page 254); but such stairs may not fit in very well with the future plans for the basement. It is one thing to get along with rough stairs when they are used mostly by someone going down to tend the furnace, and it is

something entirely different when they are to be used by guests going to and from a basement party or recreation room. It might be preferable to buy stairs from a lumberyard. They generally carry stairs in stock with treads, risers, and stringers all cut and fitted, so that it is merely a matter of assembling them. The experienced home mechanic should have no great difficulty in putting those units together. Basement stairs should be at least 3' wide.

The location of the stairs should be considered. Of course, the top of the flight is probably settled—the stairs have to start where they do—but the point where they end could be changed. The stairs may go straight down and end in the middle of the basement, thus handicapping the layout of basement rooms. But you might be able to change their course—start them down a few steps as before, have a landing, and then continue at a 90-degree angle from the direction of the top stairs.

## REARRANGING EQUIPMENT

To save space for other purposes, it is wise to concentrate household equipment usually found in the basement in one area. This includes the furnace, hot-water heater, water softener (if any), and, in rural areas, the water pump and storage tank. If it is possible to put all of this equipment in one area, then it can be partitioned off so as to be out of sight. A partition also helps keep ashes and coal dust out of the rest of the basement.

Moving the heating plant is usually either too expensive or an impractical undertaking because it must be connected into a chimney, but it is often quite possible to move the other pieces of equipment to the same area as that occupied by the furnace.

If the home mechanic decides to do this work of moving the plumbing equipment himself, then he should first do a lit-

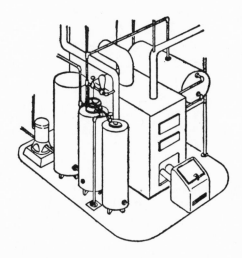

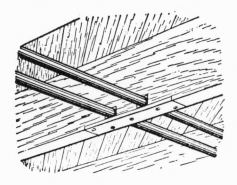

tle planning so that the house will be without water for the shortest possible time. Or he might pick a day when the other members of the family are going to be away most of the day. All the necessary pipe should be on hand as well as the tools which will be required for cutting and joining pipe, and any fittings that will be needed. If the hot-water heater is fired by gas or electricity, the proper concern should be notified so that they can send a man in the morning to disconnect the heater and then again in the afternoon to reconnect it.

## Basement Pipes

While work of rearranging the equipment is under way, the necessary pipes should be installed, when possible, so that they will not interfere with any future plans for finishing off the ceiling and walls. For example, if a pipe must run across the ceiling, it is often possible to cut notches in each joist, so that the pipe can be recessed up into the beam where it will not be in the way when the ceiling is put up.

However, you must remember that if notches are cut in the ceiling joists, they

will be weakened considerably and should be reinforced to prevent any possibility of their sagging. This job of reinforcing can be done with steel straps placed along the edge of the joists, or with 2″ × 2″ lumber running the length of the joists and spiked to each side.

Any valves, faucets, or other fittings in the plumbing and heating system that are to be accessible at one time or another should be located, when possible, in some spot outside the room to be finished off. If this cannot be done, it will be necessary, when it comes time to cover the ceiling and walls, to make openings so that these fittings can be reached without effort.

If it is not possible to recess pipes running across the ceiling into the joists so that they are covered by the ceiling material, then the ceiling material will have to go above the pipes. When it comes time to paint and decorate, paint the exposed pipe the same color as the surface in back of it, so that the pipe will not be too conspicuous. Do not make the usual mistake of painting exposed pipes gold or some other bright color, as this will only make them stand out.

When large pipes such as a heating main or sewer line run across the ceiling, it is possible to cover them with a wooden box. This can be made out of heavy plywood or 1″ stock wide enough to cover the pipe. It can be finished off to resemble an old hand-hewn beam by gouging the

surface with a wood chisel and then staining it. Additional false beams can be
made and spaced at regular intervals
along the ceiling or wall so that the finished work looks natural and in keeping.

If there are a great many pipes running along the ceiling and if there is
enough head room in the basement, a
false ceiling can be constructed under the
pipes. As this ceiling will not have to support any weight other than the ceiling material, $2'' \times 4''$ joists can be used and
then thin plywood.

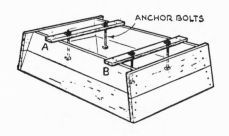

## Water Pump

In the case of a water pump, if you
have one, it is a good plan to mount it on
a solid concrete base when it is moved to
the new location. By providing a base to
which the pump can be anchored, vibration will be reduced and there is less
chance of pipe joints working loose. Another advantage is that the base will keep
the pump off the floor and perhaps prevent it from being damaged.

The area on the basement floor to be
occupied by the base should be roughened
up with a cold chisel so that the new concrete will bond to the old. Clean the area
and wet it down before pouring the fresh
concrete. A form for the concrete base can
be made out of odd scraps of lumber. The
best way to attach the pump to the base is
to sink machine bolts head first into the
fresh concrete, leaving enough of the
threaded end above the surface to fit
through the holes in the metal base of the
pump and motor and then take the nuts.
Accurate measuring is necessary.

The accompanying drawing shows a
method of placing the bolts so that they
will line up with the holes in the pump.
Nail boards together to form the sides of
the form as shown. Select two inch-thick
boards to go across the top. Set the water
pump on one board and drill down
through the holes in the base of the water
pump through the board underneath. Do

the same with the other board at the
other end of the pump. Nail template A
in place. Very carefully measure and place
template B the right distance from template A, so that the holes in the water-
pump base will line up, and nail template
B in place. Insert bolts and screw on nuts
as shown.

Mix concrete (1 part portland ce-
ment, $2\frac{3}{4}$ parts sand, 4 parts gravel) and
fill the form. After the concrete has set, remove nuts, knock off templates A and B,
and, if you have measured accurately, the
pump and motor can be put in place and
bolted down by putting on the nuts.

Before any of the fixtures are disconnected, their water supply should be
turned off and the fixture drained. In the
case of the hot-water tanks and water-sup-
ply tanks the water can be drained out by
opening the faucet at the bottom of the
tank. But before this is done, either open
faucets on the house fixtures or disconnect
one of the pipes running out of the top of
the tank. If this is not done, a partial vacuum will be built up inside the tank
when the water starts to drain out and
this will prevent a complete draining.

Be sure that the heating element is
off before draining the water out of a hot-
water tank.

Once all the fixtures have been
moved to their new location, the job of
connecting them back into the system can
be begun. The type of pipe selected for
extending existing lines should be the
same as that used in the house plumbing

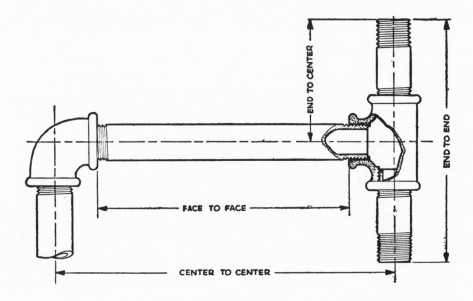

## Fitting Galvanized Iron Pipe

system, and it is important that any additions to existing pipes be the same size as the original lines.

If galvanized pipe is to be used, then some provision must be made for cutting and threading the various lengths of pipe required for the extension work. Pipes can be cut and threaded at plumbing and hardware stores for a slight additional charge per pipe, but this will require very accurate measuring on the part of the home mechanic if the threaded pipes are to fit perfectly when it comes to assembling. In the long run it would probably be better to rent a pipe cutter and the

proper size stock and die, and cut and thread the pipe right on the job. In that way, if you make an error in cutting one piece of pipe, you can compensate for it when you cut the next piece of pipe, whereas if your pieces are all cut beforehand, it may be impossible to fit them together.

Before a length of pipe is cut you should measure the distance between the two points it is to connect. Find the distance from the end or face of one fitting to the face of the other. However, each end of the pipe will be threaded and screwed into a fitting of one kind or another, and allowance must be made for that unexposed portion of the pipe. If, for example, the distance between the faces of two fittings is exactly 14″ and you are using ¾″ pipe, then it should be cut 15″ long to allow ½″ of thread at each end to screw into the fitting.

After measuring and marking the pipe, fasten it in a vise, and make the cut with a pipe cutter. The pipe is secured in a pipe vise, which grips the pipe on all sides equally. An ordinary vise with its two jaws might flatten the pipe slightly.

375

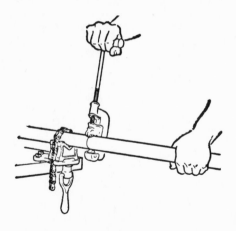

The pipe cutter has a handle which, when turned, either increases or decreases the distance between the cutting jaws. The cutting wheel of the cutter should be placed over the exact mark on the pipe where the cut is to be made. Tighten up on the cutter handle until the wheel bites into the pipe. Make one revolution around the pipe so that the cut is started straight. Turn the handle so that the cutter makes a deeper bite, and then apply oil over the cutting wheel. Make a half-turn around the pipe with the cutter in this position and then tighten up on the handle for the next half-revolution. Continue in this fashion until the pipe is cut through. A hacksaw is not a satisfactory tool to use in cutting galvanized pipe because it is difficult to get a perfectly straight cut with the saw, and unless the cut is straight, proper threading will be impossible.

**Threading.** Threads are cut with a special die that is held in a stock. Naturally the die must correspond in size to the pipe that is to be threaded. To be sure that the threads are started perfectly square, a guide bushing is used to center the die exactly on the pipe. During the cutting process, oil should be applied over the die. Press the die against the pipe and turn slowly in a clockwise direction. After the die begins to cut, turn it back a fraction of an inch after each half-turn to allow bits of metal to break off. After the pipe has been threaded, the inside should be reamed out to remove the metal burr left by cutting. This is taken off by means of a reamer that will fit in a hand brace. Be sure that this burr is removed because it will reduce the flow of water through the pipe if left on.

Be sure that the threads are clean and straight; if they are not, it will be impossible to get a leakproof joint. In any case, it is a good idea to coat the external threads of each connection with pipe compound or dope before fitting so that the joint will be absolutely watertight. Galvanized pipe is assembled or connected with a stillson or pipe wrench. Two wrenches will probably be required in most cases, one to hold the pipe and the other to hold the fitting.

## Fitting Copper Tubing

In most homes copper is used for the plumbing system. This kind of pipe can be assembled in two different ways. One method is with flared fittings and the other is with soldered fittings. The two kinds or grades of tubing in general use are K and L. L-tubing is used for interior work, and the somewhat heavier grade of K-tubing is used for outside work and heavy-duty jobs. Copper tubing can be bent, whereas galvanized pipe requires elbow fittings.

Of the two methods used in making up or connecting copper tubing, the flared method is probably the easier and requires the less amount of special equipment or skill. However, when correctly done, soldered connections are less likely to spring leaks.

Special fittings called flared fittings, the same size as the tubing, will be required for this method of assembly, as well as a flaring tool of the proper size. Copper tubing can be cut with a hacksaw, but care must be taken, if the tubing is held in a vise while cutting, not to tighten the jaws of the vise so much that you flat-

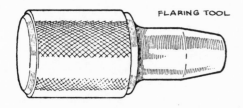

FLARING TOOL

ten the tubing. Make the cut straight and then ream out the burr on the inside of the tubing. Remove one of the slip nuts from the fitting and place it over the end of the tubing. The threaded opening of the nut should face the end of the tubing.

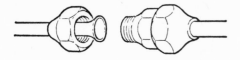

Be sure to do this before flaring the tubing. Then center the flaring tool at the end of the tubing and strike it with a hammer until the copper tubing spreads out flush with the outside edge of the flaring tool. The beveled edge of the fitting is then centered into the flared end of the tubing, and the slip nut brought up and screwed back to the fitting. Then the same thing is done to the other piece of tubing.

**Soldered Joints.** The other method of joining copper tubing and fittings is with a soldered joint. This assembly calls for fittings that have no internal or external threads but are made just large enough in diameter to be slipped over the tubing. After the tubing has been cut and reamed, the end should be cleaned with emery

STEEL WOOL

cloth or steel wool until it is bright. The same thing must be done to the inside of the fitting, because any dirt or grease on the metal parts to be joined will prevent the solder from taking hold.

Once the surfaces are clean, a light film of flux is applied to the inside of the fitting and to the outside of tubing, and the fitting is then slipped in place. Turn

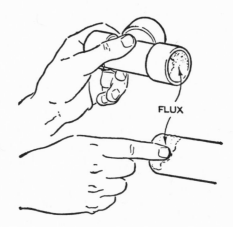

FLUX

the fitting back and forth a few times so that the flux will be well distributed over all the surfaces that are in contact with each other.

The fitting must next be heated with a blowtorch, until it is hot enough to melt

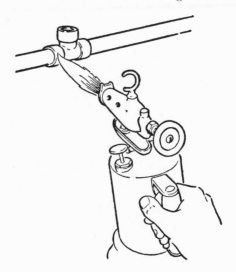

solder and cause it to flow up into the small seam between the tubing and the fitting.

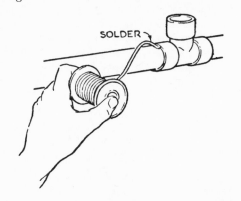

Wire solder is applied to the edge of the fitting, and is continued to be fed until it is no longer drawn into the seam.

It is often necessary to make two soldered joints at one fitting, and as it will be necessary to heat the fitting for each operation, the completed joint should be covered with wet cloth. This will prevent the solder from melting at this point while the other end of the fitting is being heated.

Certain types of fittings used for solder joints have a small hole at the ends, and the wire solder is fed into the hole instead of at the edge.

## Covering the Furnace

Sometimes it happens that the furnace is located in the approximate center of the basement and this presents a considerable problem. One method of solving it is to screen the furnace.

Be sure that there are enough open-ings to give the heating plant an adequate supply of fresh air. No heating plant will operate efficiently unless it has a proper amount of fresh air. For this same reason, if the furnace is to be partitioned off in a room with other mechanical equipment, either have an outside window opening into this space, or leave openings of some type in the partition wall for a supply of fresh air.

Of course another method of procedure, when the furnace is in the center of the basement, is to leave it there and arrange everything on one side of the basement, thus leaving the other half to be finished off.

However, some modern, automatic heating equipment is designed so that it can be left uncovered in a basement recreation room without detracting from the appearance of the room to any great degree. This equipment is covered with heat-resistant paint, and because of its compactness will not be particularly conspicuous.

## Fuel Storage

Another problem that must be worked out in connection with oil- or coal-burning heating equipment is where to store the fuel. No difficulty is presented in the case of a gas furnace, as here there is only a pipe running outside to the gas main. The fuel-supply tank for an oil burner can be inside or outside the basement. If the tank is inside, then it may be possible to move it to some other location in the basement, or to have it placed outside. In any event, the job of moving the tank and extending the oil pipes should be left to an oil-burner serviceman.

## Laundry and Bathroom Equipment

It may be necessary to leave a portion of the basement for the home-laundry

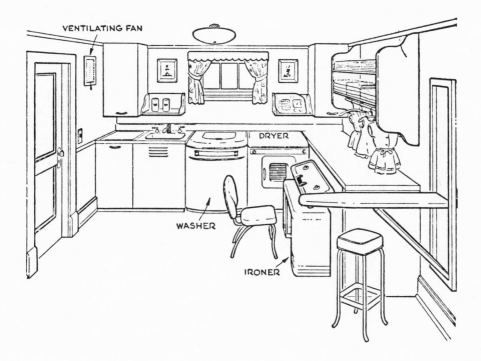

equipment. The laundry room does not have to be very large in this age of automatic washing machines, dryers, and ironers, but it should be well lighted, and ventilated by either natural or artificial means. If it is possible, the washing machine should have an outlet connected into the house sewer line, and hot and cold water pipes brought to it, so that the mess and bother of filling and draining the machine with lengths of rubber hose will be eliminated. If possible, you can try to locate the laundry so as to take advantage of the floor drain in the basement if there is one.

As mentioned earlier, in remodeling a basement it is a good plan to install toilet facilities if that is at all practical, or at least to allow space for such installation at a future date. Such fixtures will not only be a convenience in the basement, but may help to alleviate a possible shortage of plumbing facilities throughout the rest of the house. Generally speaking, it is not necessary here to plan a complete bathroom. The usual procedure is to install what is often called a half-bathroom or powder room, consisting of a toilet, wash basin, and perhaps a dressing table.

Because of the absence of bathtub or shower, a room of this sort can often be located under the basement stairs in space that is otherwise wasted or useful only for storage purposes. However, before any definite plans are made for such plumbing in the basement, a plumber should be consulted to determine whether or not the plan is feasible, and if so, where such a room had best be located in order to take advantage of the existing plumbing. It may be that the sewer line for the house runs along the basement ceiling or the walls, in which case it would be impossible to connect any basement fixtures to it because these fixtures would be lower than the sewer line. In such a case the only alternative would be to install an independent sewer system for the basement plumbing, and that might be too expensive to seem desirable.

# HEATING

If the basement rooms are to be comfortable throughout the year, then provision must be made so that they are properly heated during the winter months. A well-constructed and properly insulated furnace will not give off very much heat to its surroundings unless it happens to be of a design intended for that purpose. For the most part, it is best to discount heating the basement from the furnace proper, and turn to other methods for warmth. As far as hot-water or hot-air heating systems go, the radiators or registers can be hung from the basement ceiling so that they will be higher than the furnace, and thus operate properly. If this is not practical,

they can be installed elsewhere, and if lower than the heating plant, fans or pumps can be used to force the hot water or warm air into circulation. Steam radiators will have to be hung from the ceiling or not used at all. In making plans to heat the basement by the central heating plant, it is assumed that the plant is of sufficient size to take on this extra load without a loss of efficiency that might make the rest of the house uncomfortable or difficult to heat. If, for some reason, the central heating plant cannot be used, then electric or gas space-heaters can be used. These need not prove particularly expensive to operate, as basement rooms need not be heated except when in use.

When making changes in the heating system, try as far as possible to get the pipes out of the way in the same manner as was used for the plumbing pipes. If you

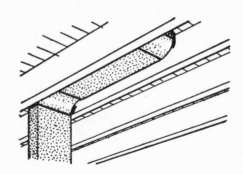

have a hot-air system, rectangular hot-air ducts can be fitted between the ceiling joists, and will require less depth than the round pipes usually found in old-fashioned hot-air heating systems.

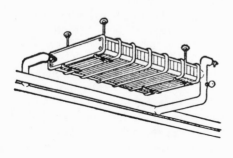

# WINDOWS

Most basements are not very well provided with windows. This is because the ground outside is usually at about the same level as the top of the basement walls, and also, until the last few decades,

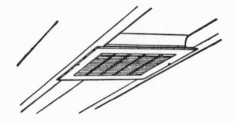

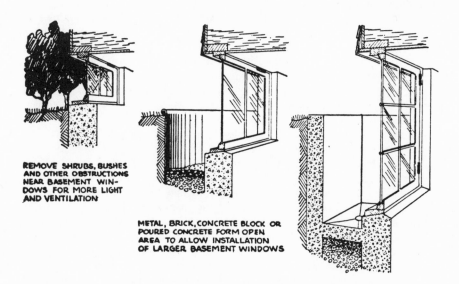

REMOVE SHRUBS, BUSHES AND OTHER OBSTRUCTIONS NEAR BASEMENT WINDOWS FOR MORE LIGHT AND VENTILATION

METAL, BRICK, CONCRETE BLOCK OR POURED CONCRETE FORM OPEN AREA TO ALLOW INSTALLATION OF LARGER BASEMENT WINDOWS

most basements were not used for much more than storage purposes and thus there was no need to provide them with many windows.

The first step in getting proper ventilation and natural lighting into the basement is to make the most of the few windows you already have. In many cases bushes and shrubs outside the house prevent very much sunlight or air from reaching the windows. Naturally such bushes and shrubs should be removed and any other obstructions around the window taken away.

Some types of basement windows are not designed to be opened and these should be replaced with windows that can be opened and closed if they face a part of the basement that is going to be finished off into a room. (If a solid window merely confronts an area that is going to be used for storage, there is no need to replace it.) The old window can be removed by chipping away the mortar around the frame with a cold chisel. Clean out the opening and secure the new frame in place with cement mortar. Some basement windows have to be kept sealed tight to prevent

water from entering around the seams. In a situation of that sort it is possible to install areaways or wells around the outside of the windows so that they can be opened without water coming in. Through the use of deep areaways it is often possible to install longer windows and thus provide many times more light and air than the usual shallow basement window will admit.

The first step in installing an areaway is to dig out the ground around the window to the necessary depth. If the bottom of the areaway is to be of concrete, the top of the concrete should be about 6″ below the bottom of the windowsill and should be given a slight pitch so that water will flow to and down a drain pipe that has its opening at the bottom of the areaway. If gravel and pebbles are to be used as the bottom of the areaway, then the pit should be dug deep enough to permit 18″ or more of these materials to be poured in.

The three sides of the areaway can be made out of poured concrete, bricks, or concrete blocks. Metal areaways can be purchased from building supply-houses;

these areaways are attached to the foundation wall with expansion bolts. The walls of a poured-concrete areaway should be about 8″ thick, and should be made with a mixture of 1 part portland cement, $2\frac{1}{2}$ parts clean fine sand, and $3\frac{1}{2}$ parts clean gravel.

Another interesting possibility, which can be put to good use when one side of the basement floor is level with the ground outside, is to remove a portion of the wall and replace it with either a large picture window or a wall made of glass blocks. As neither of these materials can support a load of more than its own weight, the opening in the wall will have to be reinforced in the same manner used for the fireplace opening.

Sometimes basement windows are so far above the floor that the average person cannot open or close them without standing on a bench or ladder. In that case some device should be installed so that they can be opened and closed easily. Various devices which do this are on sale at supply houses and can be attached without great difficulty.

It is important that the basement be properly ventilated, for not only will stale air make basement rooms uncomfortable but proper ventilation will help prevent condensation on walls and the floor.

If it is impossible to get the proper amount of air circulation by means of

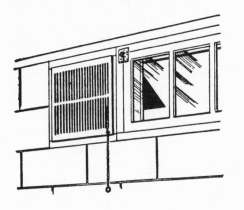

windows, then it will be necessary to install an exhaust fan. If there is a bathroom of any kind in the basement which does not have a window opening outside, it should be provided with an exhaust fan. The same holds true for a laundry room if there is one.

## FIREPLACE

Among the more radical improvements that can be made in the basement during the remodeling is the installation of a fireplace. Almost every homeowner would like to have such an addition to his game room or basement library, but certain factors must be taken into account before any definite plans for construction are decided.

If a fireplace is to operate properly, it must have its own flue and chimney. This chimney can run up inside the house so that the fireplace can be built up from the basement floor, but this calls for some major changes in the house construction because the chimney must be free of any and all structural members of the house. The chimney can also be on the outside of the house, and that presents fewer complications. Of course considerable excavation will have to be made along one portion of the foundation wall, so that a base for the fireplace can be set on about the same level as the basement floor. It will also be necessary to cut an opening in the foundation wall. If it so happens that the ground on which the house is built slopes to one side, so that the basement floor is on about the same level as the ground outside, then the job of building a fireplace at that side of the basement will be considerably easier. In such a case it would be necessary to remove only enough soil to set down a base for the fireplace.

Many home mechanics have built their own fireplaces and have had good results. For those who contemplate building one in the basement, it would be wise to consult with an architect first, and let him decide whether or not the planned fireplace is feasible. It is advisable to have a contractor cut through the foundation, as the job will require special tools, special knowledge, and the use of heavy reinforcing beams of some sort to compensate for that portion of the wall that has been removed.

## STAIRWAY CLOSET

A good place to build a large storage closet is under the basement stairs. This area is usually wasted, and while it may not be an ideal place to store articles used frequently, it does make an excellent place for long-term storage and thus frees

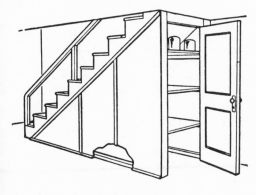

closet space throughout the rest of the house for daily needs. Naturally, if the basement is damp, no articles should be stored there until the cause of the dampness has been eliminated or the articles have been treated to prevent them from rusting or mildewing.

Assuming that the basement floor is made of concrete, the first job is to outline the base of the closet with 2 × 4s. These should be placed with the 4″ surface up, and secured to the concrete by means of expansion bolts. They should extend in length from the bottom of the stairs to a point directly below the top of the stairs.

To find this exact point, drop a plumb line from the top of the stairs down alongside one stringer and mark the location on the floor below. Make this same measurement on the floor on the opposite side. Use these two points to lay out the length of the closet, then attach a short length of lumber between them under the top of the stairs. Now uprights, made of 2 × 4s, should be dropped from the top of the stringer down to the floor. These will frame one end of the closet and should be cut at the top so that they can be nailed onto the bottom edge of the stringer. To find the correct angle at which to cut the uprights, place the lower end at the proper point and let the top end extend up a few inches along the side of the stringer. Take a pencil and mark along the upright where it meets the stringer. Cut along this line, and the upright should then fit snugly under the bottom edge of the stringer. Do this with the other upright, and nail them into place.

You will need a similar set of up- rights about half the total length of the closet. If the closet is to have a single door, the opening for it should be framed with additional uprights. If a double door is selected, there should be an upright where the two doors are to meet, in addition to one on each side, on which to hang the doors.

**Shelving.** When all the uprights are in place, you can put in the shelving, if any is to be used. Some method will be needed to hold the shelving in place; this can be done by nailing 2 × 4 cleats between the two rear uprights and also between the front uprights. One simple way to nail the shelving running to the stairs is to nail cleats to the bottoms of the risers. Each riser is about 7″ high, and if every other riser is used it will give a distance of 14″ between the shelves. If more space is required, skip another riser. Make sure that all cleats for one layer of shelving are the same distance from the floor.

The shelving should be made out of 1″ tongued-and-grooved stock. If short pieces are to be used, make sure that the joint occurs at the rear so that the end of each board can be nailed to the cleat. The first piece of shelving will have to be notched out to fit around the uprights.

The last piece of shelving will probably have to be cut down in length to make up the exact width of the closet.

The sides and back of the closet can be made of plywood or composition board. As a final point, it would be wise to have some sort of lighting facilities inside the closet. The best would be a light fixture hung to the underportion of the stairs and controlled by a switch near the closet door.

## MISCELLANEOUS BASEMENT REPAIRS

Before the actual work of building the basement rooms begins, a few small details should be checked. For instance, all pipes and fittings which will be covered by the walls or ceiling material should be inspected for signs of leaks or weak points that might cause leaks in the near future. Pipes and fittings that appear to be in poor condition should be replaced. All pipes should be properly supported so that they will not vibrate or sag. Pipes will vibrate from the momentum of the water flowing through and in time this movement will cause leaks around fittings. Sags in steam pipes will cause the system to pound when steam is coming up. Cold-water pipes should be insulated to prevent condensation of moisture that might damage the final room decorations. Hot-water and heating lines should be insulated to prevent heat loss.

## BUILDING PARTITIONS

The partitions can be made with a wood frame that is later covered with wallboard

or plywood. The frame for such a partition will have a 2″ × 4″ sole, to form the bottom of the wall. It should be anchored to the concrete basement floor with expansion bolts. A 2″ × 4″ plate is spiked to the basement ceiling joists to form the top of the partition. Vertical studding is run between sole and plate, and is spaced 16″ on center. All vertical studding should be plumb, and doubled around door and window openings.

When building a partition to ceiling height, it must be remembered that this will reduce the normal circulation of air throughout the basement. As basement rooms will require ample fresh air, if they are not to become damp and musty, some type of opening should be installed in each wall. These openings can be windows or louvers, anything to allow air to circulate.

If a partition wall is built for the purpose of concealing some object that is only a few feet high, such as a modern furnace, then it may be advisable to build only a half-wall. A wall of this sort, just high enough to hide the object back of it, will make the basement appear larger than it actually is. This arrangement is useful if the size of the recreation room has been reduced considerably to allow for necessary storage space. These considerations of a half-wall assume that the house is heated by oil or gas. If heated by coal, airtight partitions will be desirable or necessary between the heating unit and any finished-off rooms. However, there are certain conditions where a half-wall will be sufficient.

Such a wall does not have to be built in the conventional manner. It can be made of bricks, concrete blocks, or even glass blocks. By building the wall a little deeper than necessary, it will serve as a bookshelf or cabinet. Glass blocks can be laid with cement mortar, or by using wooden strips and wooden wedges. The advantage of the latter method of construction is that the wall can be taken down easily and all the materials used again under different circumstances. Blocks of this type are available at most building supply-houses and lumberyards, and come with the manufacturer's directions regarding installation.

Of course, individual circumstances sometimes make other materials or procedures satisfactory. For instance, a sturdy wooden bookshelf fastened to the basement floor would make a satisfactory section of wall. A basement library could be built with all the walls made of full length, ceiling-to-floor bookshelves, thus avoiding the necessity and cost of putting up any wall partitions.

## WALLS, CEILINGS, AND FLOORS

Concrete and masonry foundation walls can be finished in several ways. They can be painted, preferably with a portland-cement paint which will not be damaged by moisture or the action of the lime in the masonry. But merely painting the walls is not always satisfactory, owing to the possibility of condensation of moisture on their surface; furthermore, such walls do not always absorb sounds. It is probably better in the long run to cover the walls with wallboard or plywood. Regardless of which type of material is selected, it is necessary first to line the walls with furring strips, so that there will be a base to which the wall covering can be nailed, and also to prevent the wallboard or plywood coming into direct contact with the masonry. The small dead-air space between the wall covering and the masonry walls will act as insulation so that there will be no moisture collecting on the surface of the finished wall.

Furring strips may be $1'' \times 3''$, $2'' \times 2''$, or $2'' \times 4''$ lumber. If the furring can be placed against solid masonry at all points and still remain plumb and true, then the lighter stocks can be used. However, if there are any recessed portions of the wall, so that the furring will not be supported along its entire length by the wall, then it would be better to use the heavier $2'' \times 4''$ pieces. If there is any indication that the walls or the floor are damp at any time during the year, the furring, as well as the lumber used for the wall partitions, should be treated with a wood preservative to prevent rotting. Preservatives of this kind are available and many will also prevent damage by termites. These preservatives can be applied by brush by the home mechanic, but it is better to purchase wood which has already been treated with the preservative at the mill or lumberyard, because special equipment is used there to force the preservative into all the wood fibers and not just brush it over the surface.

One strip of furring should be put down at the base of the wall and another run along the top. Vertical strips are then placed between the top and bottom and attached to the masonry walls with special nails. These vertical strips should be spaced $16''$ on center. Furring must, of course, be used around all openings in the walls for doors and windows. It will also be needed around plumbing and heating valves, gas meters, and the like, which could not be moved to some other location but must remain in the part of the basement that is to be finished. What can be done about such things is to build cabinets with doors around them so that when it is necessary to read a meter or turn on or off a valve it can be done with the least inconvenience. But the doors should bear large signs painted in white so that strangers can locate them in a hurry if it is necessary to shut off gas or water or electricity in case of an accident or emergency.

With one exception, it will not be necessary to use any furring on the ceiling, as the joists will serve as a base for the ceiling material. The exception is in the case of a partition wall running directly under a joist. In such a case it will be necessary to nail a strip of $2'' \times 2''$ board along each side of the joist to serve as a base on which to nail the ceiling material.

## Wiring

After the partitions and furring are in place, any necessary changes in the basement wiring can be made. (Refer to chapters 9 and 14 for specific information.) One advantage in adding new circuits to the basement is that the main fuse box is usually located there. This will make it possible for an electrician to add whatever number of circuits may be needed for the proper lighting of the basement, without running wires up through the walls and under floors.

When improving the basement electrical system, be sure to provide a light halfway down the basement stairs and install a 3-way switch so that the light can be turned on or off from either the top or the bottom of the stairs. Most basements are provided with a minimum of lights by the builder, perhaps only one near the heating plant. Sometimes this is provided with a switch upstairs so that the light can be turned on before you go downstairs to the basement. As long as the basement was all open and free of partitions, that one light in the basement served to illuminate the stairs enough to use them safely, but once you begin putting up walls in the basement you need a light over the stairs, not only to see to use them safely but also to enable you to find your way to turn on other basement lights.

All exhaust fans used in basement rooms should be permanently wired and provided with wall switches. (And if ducts are required for any of the exhaust fans, such ducts should be installed at this time.) Special care should be given to see that the home laundry is provided with heavy-duty circuits, because equipment such as electric dryers and ironers require thousands of watts, too heavy a load for the average interior lighting circuit.

The home mechanic naturally will see to it that his workbench is provided with sufficient lighting and that enough outlets are located near his workbench to handle various power tools. (For information on building a workbench, see chapter 3, page 75.) A workshop room can be finished off as simply or elaborately as the home mechanic desires.

## Covering Walls and Ceiling

When it comes to covering the walls and ceiling, there are several possible choices of materials. The obvious one is wallboard, and this will make a durable and attractive finish. A somewhat more attractive and expensive finish may be had by using plywood paneling. An acoustic type of wallboard for the ceiling has much in its favor, especially if the room being finished is to later contain machinery which would make a noise that might be disturbing. If ordinary wallboard or plywood is used on the ceiling, it is best to put some sort of insulation between the ceiling joists so that sound originating in the basement will be absorbed and not pass to the rooms above. The insulation used for this purpose can be the same as that used to prevent the transmission of heat. This treatment should be used for basement rooms such as the workshop and laundry, where mechanical noise is likely to be made. It is well to have it also over a game or recreation room if there is a billiard table or other such equipment. On the other hand, if you plan a basement library, insulation may be desirable for the reverse reason, to muffle noise from above. (For wallboard and plywood installation, see chapter 13, page 313.)

## Floors

When it comes to finishing the floor of the recreation room, the home mechanic has a wide choice of materials. First, the floor can be painted with a floor enamel. However, that type of finish can be used only over an absolutely dry surface. To test the floor for possible dampness, cover it with a piece of linoleum or tar paper weighted down and leave it on the floor for 24 hours. If, at the end of that time when the linoleum is removed, there are no damp spots under it, the floor is safe for painting.

In the case of a new house, dampness in the floor is not necessarily a sign that the floor is not watertight. It takes some time for all the water in new concrete to evaporate, and the floor should therefore be left unfinished for additional drying and tests should be made for dampness at a later date.

Special paints that have been designed with a rubber or synthetic base are especially suitable for a concrete surface, as they will not be damaged by the lime or dampness in the material. You can very likely obtain these at your local paint or hardware store.

Linoleum, rubber tile, cork tile, and asphalt tile may also be used as a floor finish in the basement, provided the floor is free from dampness. Flooring materials such as these have to be attached to the concrete with a special mastic.

Another possibility for the floor is to use regular hardwood flooring. The first step in this job is to set down and attach strips of wood called sleepers to the concrete, to form a base to which the flooring can be nailed. These sleepers should be 2″ × 3″ or larger in size, and spaced 16″ on center or less. Before putting the sleepers down, they should be treated with a wood preservative. After they are in place and secured to the concrete, waterproof paper should be set over them to keep any dampness away from the wood flooring. The flooring is then nailed down, spacing the nails carefully so that they will go into the wooden sleepers. (Additional information on laying hardwood floors may be found in chapter 10, page 255.)

Parquet floors, which come in square sections, are fastened to the concrete with a mastic similar to that used for composition tiles and linoleum.

Because the concrete basement floor provides a good solid base, concrete or ceramic tile may be set down with little extra effort. The first task in this case is to mix a grout of cement and water, and apply it to the area that is to be covered. Before this grout is hard, a mixture of one part cement and 3 parts sand, with enough water added to make it a workable plastic, is applied to the floor. This coat should be at least ¾″ thick and of course should be of equal depth over the entire area.

Another point that it is quite important to observe carefully is to mix only as much mortar as you can cover with tile before the mortar sets, a period of about 30 minutes. Dust a light coating of dry cement over the mortar and place the tiles in position after dampening them. Be careful to make sure that each tile is level and on the same plane as the others. A small crack about ⅛″ wide is left between tiles. That crack is to be filled, after the mortar bed has set, with a mixture of one part cement to one part sand. Force this filler into the seams between the tiles, level off the surface, and then wipe the tiles clean before the filler hardens.

As soon as the basement floor has been completed, doors can be hung and the trim, including the baseboard, can go on. (To attach hinges and locks and to hang doors, see chapter 10, page 247.)

The treatment of walls, ceilings, and floors of the different basement rooms will vary considerably. So far as the room containing the furnace and other allied mechanical equipment is concerned, the masonry walls can be left uncovered unless there is considerable condensation on them, in which case they too should be covered. The ceiling and walls should be covered with a type of wallboard that has definite, fire-resistant qualities. The floor may be left unfinished unless it collects too much dust. If so, it should be painted so as to make sweeping easier.

## Darkroom

The main requirement for a basement darkroom is that it be lightproof. This can be accomplished by using trim over any exposed seams and by using felt weather stripping around the door if necessary. However, making it lightproof is likely to also make it airproof, and ventilation is necessary. Windows or louvers are entirely unsuitable, as they let in light. Perhaps the easiest method of supplying air would be to have some stovepipe painted black on the inside and curved so that light would not penetrate. Two such openings would be wanted, one as an inlet and the other as an outlet, and the latter might need a small fan attached to dispel fumes of photographic chemicals.

Another requirement of a darkroom is a water supply and drain, and of course electrical outlets will be needed. If the home mechanic is also the amateur photographer, he will know from his study of photographic handbooks and magazines just what he prefers in running water facilities, electric connections, shelves, and benches. If the photographer is another member of the household, let him or her describe what is needed.

The darkroom floor should be finished with tile or linoleum, something on which chemicals can be spilled and wiped up without damage to the floor. Cement or concrete is not very satisfactory.

Still another point that should have some consideration is dust, for dust has a bad effect on films and lenses. Be sure that a ventilation inlet does not open on a part of the basement that is near coal dust or ashes. Perhaps the air inlet should have a cover to shut it when the darkroom is not in use.

## Laundry

When finishing the floor of the basement laundry, tile will probably be found to be about the best material, for tile will not be damaged in any way by surface moisture and can be easily cleaned and dried. The walls and ceiling should be covered with wallboard, which should be painted with an enamel wall-paint so that the surface will not be damaged or stained by water, and will be easy to wipe clean. If pressing and ironing are to be done in this room, then ample shelf-space will be needed for the finished flatwork, and a rack of some kind will be very useful for hanging up freshly pressed garments.

The lumber used for the shelves need not be of high quality, but it should be planed and sanded down so that after it has been painted, the surface will be smooth, easily cleaned, and not likely to catch and hold dust.

A hanger for pressed clothes may easily be made by attaching short lengths of lumber on either side of the room, attaching hooks or screw-eyes to them, and stretching steel wire between them. Heavy cord may be used, but it will have a tendency to stretch and sag, and will require tightening from time to time. To save space in the laundry, it is a good plan to attach the ironing board to the wall, either with hinges or some other device, so that it can be folded up out of the way when not in use.

Aside from the wiring and outlets required for the washing machine, electric dryer, and presser, there should be a wall outlet near the ironing board so that the iron can be conveniently plugged in. To avoid the possibility of someone's leaving the laundry with the iron still connected, it is wise to have that wall outlet wired through the same switch as that which operates the laundry lighting fixtures. In that way, when the lights of the room are turned off, electric current to the iron will certainly be discontinued.

## Storage Room and Vegetable Bin

The main requirement for the room that is to serve as the storage place for canned goods and for other preserves, and possibly for a deep-freeze unit, is that it contain ample shelf-space and a light. It would be wise perhaps to enclose the shelves with either a cloth curtain or plywood doors so that the items on the shelves will not become dust-covered.

If the room is to be used as a cold cellar and vegetable bin, then it should be well insulated from the rest of the basement. This can be done by using insulating boards for the walls and ceiling of the room, or by using regular wallboard and filling the space between walls and above the ceiling with some kind of insu-

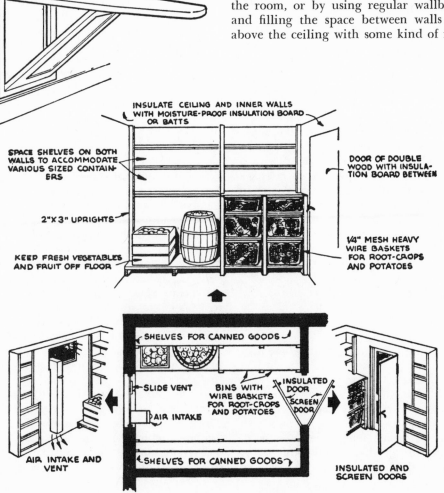

INSULATE CEILING AND INNER WALLS WITH MOISTURE-PROOF INSULATION BOARD OR BATTS

SPACE SHELVES ON BOTH WALLS TO ACCOMMODATE VARIOUS SIZED CONTAINERS

DOOR OF DOUBLE WOOD WITH INSULATION BOARD BETWEEN

2"X 3" UPRIGHTS

KEEP FRESH VEGETABLES AND FRUIT OFF FLOOR

1/4" MESH HEAVY WIRE BASKETS FOR ROOT-CROPS AND POTATOES

SHELVES FOR CANNED GOODS

SLIDE VENT

AIR INTAKE

BINS WITH WIRE BASKETS FOR ROOT-CROPS AND POTATOES

INSULATED DOOR

SCREEN DOOR

SHELVES FOR CANNED GOODS

AIR INTAKE AND VENT

INSULATED AND SCREEN DOORS

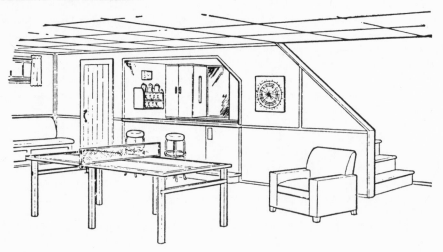

lation, either dry fill, batt, or blanket type.

To provide the necessary amount of cold, fresh air for the vegetable bin, some arrangement will be needed to bring in air from outdoors. This can be done by running stove-pipe through an opening such as a window (perhaps by removing one pane of glass) at the top of the outside wall. The pipe should extend to within a few inches of the bin floor. This pipe can be provided with a damper so that the amount of cold air entering the bin may be regulated to prevent the air inside from becoming so cold that the contents of the bin might freeze. An outlet will be necessary as well, and this should open near the top of the bin to allow the warm air inside to pass out.

### Bathroom

The walls and ceiling of a basement bathroom or lavatory should have a smooth surface that can be easily cleaned. There are several materials which would serve satisfactorily, but all need a base of some kind. So it is best to put up wallboard first. Then tileboard, linoleum, metal tiles, or oilcloth can be put on, either over the entire wall or

over only the bottom half, painting the top half in that case with oil enamel. The floor may be finished with any of the materials suggested for the main basement room, but wood is less desirable than most of the other alternatives mentioned.

## INSTALLING A BAR

When a basement room is finished for use as a game or recreation room, an attractive bar or lunch counter will be a pleasing addition. This may range from a simple, portable kind to a more elaborate type. It may not only serve as a bar but also be equipped to act as a lunch counter, so that simple meals or snacks can be cooked and served directly from it, thus eliminating the need of running back and forth to the upstairs kitchen. So if the home mechanic has a yen to sometimes play chef, he can build a place where he will be more or less free to do so.

A bar like the one in the illustration would not be too difficult to construct. The bar is built from a base of $2'' \times 4''$ lumber anchored to the basement floor. The framework is made from the same size of stock, or lighter materials may be used if they are properly braced. The front of the bar is covered with plywood, and a door can be installed to allow access to the back of the bar. The opening for such a door will require additional framing, and the door should be accurately fitted so that it will open and close easily but there will not be any wide seams or cracks to mar the appearance of the bar. You can use spring-loaded hinges for the door so that it will open either in or out and then return to a closed position of its own accord.

The top of the bar is covered with tongue-and-groove boards, but these serve merely as a base for a linoleum counter-top. The edges of the linoleum are covered with metal trim attached to the wood base with wood screws.

All wooden surfaces of the bar should be painted with enamel to provide a hard, durable surface and one that can be easily cleaned.

The serving counter of the bar has a wooden base and is covered with linoleum. Also run a strip of linoleum along the back wall and cover the corner where the two pieces of linoleum join the metal trim.

Shelves for glasses can be hung securely to the wall at the end of the bar as shown, or elsewhere. You can have a cupboard for dishes if desired. The space under the bar counter can be used for bottles, full or empty.

There is almost no limit to the amount of equipment that can be installed on the service counter of the bar. You can make it as simple or fancy as you choose. A hot plate for cooking hamburgers and other snacks should be wired in with BX Cable and there should be additional outlets for electric coffee pot, drink mixers, and other gadgets of that sort. An insulated container for ice can be installed, and a small sink with running water will be found to be a great convenience.

The home mechanic interested in building a really complete home bar would do well to visit a store dealing in new and used restaurant, bar, and soda-fountain equipment, and purchase such items as suit his fancy, available space, and pocketbook, and incorporate them into his basement bar.

The diagram here shows floor plans for a very elaborate basement and dem-

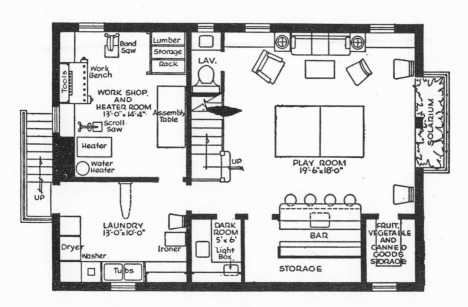

onstrates how many useful rooms could be fitted in. Note that the laundry is located next to the outside stairs to be convenient for hanging clothes outside to dry. Also note that the food storage room is located at the end of the basement opposite the heating unit. It is not expected that the average home mechanic will desire or be able to fix up quite as elaborate a layout as this, but he may want to finish off some useful rooms.

# 16

# BUYING A HOUSE

Buying a house is far more complex, not to mention more expensive, than buying a car, but even though most people have some knowledge of what to look for in a car, few have much idea of what to look for in a house other than the obvious—the number of rooms and the price. Whether you are going to buy a new house in a development or an older house in an established neighborhood, there are many areas you can check out yourself to determine the quality of construction and whether or not you are getting a good buy for the money.

One of the most important aspects in buying an existing house is to determine in advance just what is included in the house. There are, for example, certain items that are known in the real estate profession as "fixtures." These are items of personal property that may be part of the house but not permanently affixed to it. For example, a free-standing range is a fixture because it can be removed without damage to the house structure, but a built-in range is not a fixture because it cannot be removed without leaving a large hole in the wall. A window air conditioner is a fixture, but if the same unit was set in a hole in the wall under the window, it would not be a fixture. The point is that unless you

have a written agreement with the owner as to which fixtures are included in the deal, he can take them all with him and you have no grounds for legal action. The smart thing to do is to go over with the seller every item in the house which might be considered a fixture and have him put in writing those items that will go with the house. Among the items to look for are kitchen appliances, such as the range, refrigerator, freezer, washing machine, and dryer; built-in bookcases; drapery hardware; door mirrors; TV antenna; window air conditioners, storm windows, and screens; and above-ground swimming pools.

## THE NEW HOUSE

When you go shopping for a new house in a development, and this is where the vast majority of new houses are built today, you will naturally want to consider, if you have children, the quality of the local schools. You'll also want to look for convenient shopping areas and recreational areas, and to find out how long it will take you to get to work and how much it will cost. The wise home buyer will also take the time to talk to some of the people in the development, asking them how they like living there and also if they have any particular peeves.

If the development is just getting under way and there are few if any completed houses, and the streets are still unpaved, you will have to do a little more digging to find out what sort of development it will be when completed. The reputation of the developer is a very important item. If he has been responsible for other developments in the area, you can inspect them to see what sort of job he does. You should also look over the master plan in the sales office, since this will contain valuable information. Look for curved or winding streets, rather than a grid pattern. The grid pattern of straight streets is the most economical for the developer, but the curved streets produce a better-looking development and also slow down car traffic. Look for underground utilities such as electric and telephone lines. These usually indicate a quality development. Look for house lots of varying sizes and designs because this will produce a more interesting community than one where all the lots are the same size and shape. The developer should also be able to show you a commitment from the local township indicating that when the roads are completed they will be taken over by the town, so that you will not be assessed for their maintenance and repair.

## Inspecting the House

Most houses in a development are sold from a model. When you inspect a model, keep in mind that the builder or developer has done everything he can to make that model house just as attractive as he can. He will see that the land around it is well landscaped with trees, shrubs, flowers, and so on. The outside of the house will be bright and pleasing to the eye. This is called "curb appeal"—making the house just as attractive as possible from the street to attract potential home buyers.

When you go into the average model, you'll find it completely furnished and decorated. Very often the developer will use furniture that is smaller in scale than standard pieces, to make the rooms in the house look larger than they actually are. Again, this is fine as long as you know what's going on. He will also load the model with a good deal of optional features that are not included in the basic price of the house—air conditioning, a fireplace, a finished game room, and so forth.

Some developers will have a sign in each room indicating the optional features and what they will cost if you want them included in your house. In other cases you will have to ask one of the salesmen to point out all the optional features. In any event, find out exactly what you get in the basic house and what it will cost. And this information is what you want to use to evaluate the house. Forget about the landscaping, the furniture, the fancy decorating, and the optional features, and just concentrate on the basic house and its cost.

When you buy a house you are buying living space and, assuming the essential quality is there, the builder that gives you the most living space for the money is the one that is giving you the best buy. Living space is figured on the cost per square foot. You can easily figure out how much a square foot of living space costs by taking the floor plan of the house and adding up the total areas in square feet. When you have a total, divide it into the base price of the house and you'll get a cost per square foot. For example, if the house contains 1,200 square feet of living space and the total cost of the basic house is $24,000, then the square foot cost is $20.00. When you inspect other model houses, figure out the cost per square foot of each and then compare them. You can see right away which developer is giving you the most house for the money.

**Judging Quality.** Of course, the cost per square foot is not the only element that goes into judging a house. You are also interested in the quality of construction. Most houses you will inspect will have been approved by the FHA and/or VA. These agencies set forth minimum standards of design and construction which are of value in helping to determine quality, but you should not rely on them entirely.

There are many ways that you can judge the quality of construction of a house. One thing to look for is brand-name materials and equipment. These will usually cost the developer or builder more than off-brand products, but as they are often superior, the fact that he uses them indicates an interest in quality. Look for brand names in roofing materials, windows and doors, insulation, heating and air-conditioning equipment, plumbing fixtures, flooring, kitchen appliances, and so forth.

If the house has a basement, it is better if the basement walls are made of poured concrete rather than concrete blocks. If the walls are made of concrete block, find out if waterproofing is applied to the outside during construction. If this step is omitted, you may have trouble with water leaking through the block wall if there is not good natural or man-made drainage around the house. In a newly built house, you can expect to find that the basement will be somewhat damp, especially if the walls are made of poured concrete, because this contains a good deal of water when it is fresh, and some weeks or even months are required for the water to completely evaporate.

If the basement is designed to be converted into a game or recreation room, look for a type of construction having a minimum number of posts running from floor to ceiling, because these can interfere with the arrangement of the space for living purposes. In quality construction, you will find that a steel girder is used to provide support for the floor above, eliminating the need for the posts or at least reducing the number to a minimum.

Equipment normally found in the basement—heating and air-conditioning plant, hot-water heater, laundry equipment, and so forth—should all be grouped in one general area so as to leave the rest of the space free for other uses.

While inspecting the basement, you can take a look at the exposed floor framing, but in the case of a model house you can't learn very much about quality of materials or workmanship because obviously if the builder is trying to make the best impression, he isn't going to allow poor workmanship to show where it can be seen by everyone who visits the basement.

**Heating Systems.** Houses today are heated either by forced warm air, circulating hot water, or electric resistance heaters. All three of these systems are good when properly installed. Forced warm air is the type that lends itself most readily to the addition of air conditioning, which may be important if you wish to have or to add air conditioning at some future date. For forced warm air and circulating hot water, the energy is supplied by either gas or oil. Again, both of these fuels are excellent and the choice is really only what fuel is locally available at the lowest cost.

**The House Structure.** One important aspect of construction today is insulation. If a house is to be heated in winter or cooled in summer at the lowest cost, it must be adequately insulated. Good-quality construction will include 6″ of insulation at the roof or ceiling of the house, 4″ in the walls, and 3″ in the floor if the area below the floor is unheated.

Siding is another clue to quality, not so much because one kind of siding will give better protection than another, but with regard to maintenance. If the house has wood siding that is painted, you will have to figure on having to repaint every 5 or 6 years, and this is rather costly and time-consuming. If the wood siding has been stained or treated with a sealer, maintenance is reduced considerably, because no paint is required and it is a simple matter to renew the stain or sealer when required. Aluminum and vinyl siding have a good record as far as maintenance goes, as do some of the composition materials.

Interior walls and ceilings are usually made of gypsum wallboard. Only in relatively few areas will you find plaster. If the walls are of gypsum, look for quality in the thickness of the wallboard used. In low-quality construction the thickness may be only ⅜″. In better-quality work, ½″ or ⅝″ boards will be used. In top-quality construction, you will find walls covered with two layers of ⅜″ or ½″ material, which produces a superior job.

**Doors and Windows.** The best-quality doors are the solid-core flush type. These are used for exterior doors and in high-quality construction for interior doors as well. Panel and hollow-core flush doors are adequate for interior use but do not have much soundproofing quality. Probably the best-quality window available today is a wood type with a plastic coating which eliminates the need for painting and other maintenance. Ordinary wood windows are adequate if they have been pressure treated with a preservative. Bronze-coated aluminum windows are good. All windows, as well as sliding glass doors, should come with insect screening and storm sashes, which can be a help in reducing the cost of air conditioning in summer as well as heating the house in winter. The best-quality sliding glass doors as well as windows come with insulating glass that eliminates the need for storm windows in winter. In warm areas, the glass should be heat-absorbing to reduce heat gain.

**Roof.** Most roofs today are covered with asphalt shingles; these should be the 250-pound seal-down type rather than the lightweight 210-pound shingles. Wood shingles are considerably more expensive than the asphalt type and indicate, when

they are used, that the builder is not pinching pennies.

**Flooring.** The best-quality floors for the main living area will be of hardwood vinyl, or linoleum. Many houses are sold with wall-to-wall carpeting, and this is good if there is a finished floor underneath. If there is not, when and if carpeting is removed a new finished floor will have to be put down at the owner's expense. Tile, of course, is good in the bathrooms.

**Wiring.** Aside from seeing that there are a sufficient number of outlets in the various rooms, ask about the capacity of the service entrance. Good-quality construction will include a 200-amp service entrance. If it is only 100 or 150, you may have difficulty using all your electric appliances.

**Plumbing.** As far as sewage goes, the ideal is to have a house that is connected into a city sewer main or, in the case of many developments, into a centrally located sewage-treatment plant. If the house is to have its own septic treatment plant, ask to see a percolation test report for the site where your house is to be located. This report will state the capacity of the soil to absorb liquid waste.

Also find out about the quality of the water supply. In many areas the water contains such a high percentage of minerals that water-treatment equipment will be required to make the water fit to drink and use for household purposes.

## THE OLDER HOUSE

When you go out to buy an older or existing house, you must remember that you are very much on your own. Neither the owner nor his broker is required to point out the flaws in the property. If you ask them a direct question as to the condition of a particular item and if they know the answer, they are required to give you an honest reply, but if you don't ask them, they don't have to volunteer. So when you buy an old house, ask a lot of questions and be sure that they are the important questions.

One way you can save considerable time and effort in buying an old house is to hire an architect or an engineer to check it out for you. The charge for this may run to $100 or more, but the service can be well worth the price. If you don't wish to go to this expense, you must put forth the necessary time and effort to check the house thoroughly and ascertain its condition.

What you need to know is the general condition of the house and also what you may have to put into it in the immediate future for basic repairs and improvements. And the age of the house will have considerable bearing on what problems you can expect to run into. For example, a wood shingle roof may last for 20 years or so and one of asphalt for about 15 years. If the roof covering is 20 to 30 years old, you can expect to have to reroof almost immediately. If the outside of the house has not been painted in the past 6 or 7 years, you will have to do this shortly. The older the house, the more careful your inspection must be.

**Underside of the House.** Whether there is a basement or just crawl space, you should check its condition carefully. If there is a basement, look for signs of dampness or stains on the walls that indicate leaks at certain times of the year. Use a penknife to check any woodwork close to the ground or masonry for signs of decay or termites. If the wood is soft, decay may be present. Or there may be termites. Look for little earthen tunnels along foundation walls running to the woodwork, because these indicate termites.

Check the underside of the floor to see if any of the floor joists have cracked. A considerable number of posts running from the ground to the floor above usually means that the floor was not adequately framed and additional supports are re-

quired to keep it from sagging or vibrating when walked across.

While you are at the underside of the house, inspect the water lines. If they are copper or brass, that's good. If they are galvanized iron, it means that the system is rather old and in time you may have to replace the pipes because they have been blocked by mineral deposits or rust, or because they became so badly rusted that they leaked. You can get a good idea of the condition of the pipes by opening all the faucets in all the fixtures about the house at the same time. If you get a good flow of water out of the fixtures in the upper part of the house, it means that the lines are clear and the pressure is good. But if you get no water or just a trickle, it means that the pipes are either too small or have become clogged.

Take a look at the heating system. If it's an old cast-iron boiler or furnace, it will probably continue to function for years—not too efficiently, of course—but the burner may need to be replaced. If it's a sheet-steel piece of equipment badly rusted, it may have to be replaced almost at once.

**Exterior Siding.** Brick walls should be checked to see if the mortar between bricks is sound and if there are any structural cracks running through the bricks. If there are, it can mean that the house is sinking on its foundation and this is a serious matter. A few bad mortar joints are no problem, but if there are numerous poor joints, you are in for heavy repairs.

In the case of a house with painted wood siding, check the condition of the paint. Peeling paint may indicate a moist condition inside the walls—a leaky roof, perhaps—or the use of an inferior paint. In any event, if peeling occurs in all portions of the wall, the old paint will have to be removed, the cause of the peeling corrected, and then the wall repainted. Deep cracks in a painted surface are not very serious, but before you can get a good paint job the old paint will have to be removed. Also check the condition of the wood siding at the base of the walls for signs of decay.

**Roofs.** As we indicated earlier, any roof of wood or asphalt that is 15 years old or more should be considered a potential problem. If the roof is covered with asbestos shingles or slate and appears to be in good shape, you can usually figure that it will not present any problem, because these materials will last almost indefinitely. But wood and asphalt will not, and if the wood shingles are curled along the edges, if some have come loose, or if the mineral granules on the surface of asphalt shingles have worn away, be prepared to lay a new roof soon.

**Windows and Doors.** Check the condition of windows by visual inspection. Stains on the wall directly below the window indicate that there are open joints along the frame that allow water to get inside. Open and close the windows to test for ease of operation. If the windows don't work easily, it may be nothing more than some paint along the edges that has sealed them tight, but it can also be that the house has settled and thrown the frames out of alignment, so that the sashes cannot be moved without having to rebuild the window frame.

Find out if the windows are equipped with screens and storm sash. If they aren't, it will cost about $20 a window for a combination screen and storm sash.

Open and close all doors to test for ease of operation and whether or not the door will latch when closed. Unless you do the job yourself, it may cost you several dollars to get each door so that it locks and latches properly.

**Floors.** A good way to test a floor for strength is to jump up and down on it a few times. If it feels springy or if doors and windows rattle, it means either that the floor joists are undersize or that one or more have cracked or been cut away for one reason or another. In any event, it's going to cost you money to put them back in shape. Squeaks can be detected just by walking about the floor. An occasional

squeak is something you can expect in almost any house, but if almost every other board squeaks, it can mean improper nailing; and to correct the situation will involve much time or money. In the case of wood floors, also note the finish. If the finish is in poor condition, you can figure it will cost you about $50 to have the floor in an average-size room sanded and refinished. If the floor is covered with linoleum, inspect it to see if it has become worn, if some of the seams are opened, and so forth. If the floor covering is in poor shape, pull some up so that you can inspect the condition of the wood floor underneath.

**Walls and Ceilings.** In older homes these are usually covered with plaster. Small holes and a few hairline cracks are to be expected, and do not indicate any serious condition. But if sections of the plaster have bulged, if there are large holes where the lath is exposed, or if there are long, wide cracks, it can mean that the plaster or the base over which it is applied is in poor condition, and you may have to rip it all out and apply gypsum wallboard.

**Wiring.** In most older homes the electric wiring is not adequate for present-day needs. Ask the owner or his broker to tell you the capacity of the service entrance; this information will give you a key as to how much it will cost to bring the system up to date. If the house has a 30-amp service entrance, the wiring is probably totally inadequate and you'll have to spend a good deal of money on it—possibly $300 to $400. If there is a 100-amp service entrance, you are a little better off, and if it is 150 or 200 amp, you won't be in for additional costs.

You will, however, want to inspect each room to see the number and location of outlets and switches. If they are inadequate for your needs, it will cost about $7.50 to add an outlet, lighting fixture, or switch.

If a particular house is going to require extensive alterations to make it suitable for your needs, remember that remodeling is not only time-consuming but also far more expensive than new construction. There are two reasons for this: one is that more labor is involved in remodeling than in new construction, and the other is that you have to pay twice for everything—once to have it ripped out, and the second time to have it rebuilt. Before you buy a house that is going to require extensive alterations, get an estimate from a contractor on what it will cost to have the work done. You may find that by the time you have paid for the remodeling, you would have done better to look for another house, perhaps more expensive, that would not require as much work.

# INDEX